RESEARCH IN THE HISTORY OF ECONOMIC THOUGHT AND METHODOLOGY

A Research Annual

RESEARCH IN THE HISTORY OF ECONOMIC THOUGHT AND METHODOLOGY

Series Editors: Warren J. Samuels and Jeff E. Biddle

RESEARCH IN THE HISTORY OF ECONOMIC THOUGHT
AND METHODOLOGY   VOLUME 22-A

RESEARCH IN THE HISTORY OF ECONOMIC THOUGHT AND METHODOLOGY
A Research Annual

EDITED BY

WARREN J. SAMUELS

*Department of Economics, Michigan State University,
East Lansing, MI 48824, USA*

JEFF E. BIDDLE

*Department of Economics, Michigan State University,
East Lansing, MI 48824, USA*

2004

ELSEVIER
JAI

Amsterdam – Boston – Heidelberg – London – New York – Oxford – Paris
San Diego – San Francisco – Singapore – Sydney – Tokyo

ELSEVIER B.V.
Sara Burgerhartstraat 25
P.O. Box 211,
1000 AE Amsterdam
The Netherlands

ELSEVIER Inc.
525 B Street, Suite 1900
San Diego,
CA 92101-4495
USA

ELSEVIER Ltd
The Boulevard, Langford
Lane Kidlington,
Oxford OX5 1GB
UK

ELSEVIER Ltd
84 Theobalds Road
London
WC1X 8RR
UK

First edition 2004

Library of Congress Cataloging in Publication Data
A catalog record is available from the Library of Congress.

British Library Cataloguing in Publication Data
A catalogue record is available from the British Library.

ISBN: 07623-1089-8
ISSN: 0743-4154

⊗ The paper used in this publication meets the requirements of ANSI/NISO Z39.48-1992 (Permanence of Paper). Printed in The Netherlands.

CONTENTS

LIST OF CONTRIBUTORS   *ix*

EDITORIAL BOARD   *xi*

ACKNOWLEDGMENTS   *xiii*

DYNAMICS, TRADE AND MONEY IN THE
CORRESPONDENCE BETWEEN ROY HARROD AND
DENNIS ROBERTSON
  Daniele Besomi   *1*

KEYNES, UNCERTAINTY AND THE COMPETITIVE
PROCESS
  Stephen P. Dunn   *65*

THE PRUDENCE OF PROJECTORS: ADAM SMITH'S
PREMONITION OF FINANCIAL FRAGILITY AND THE
ORIGINS OF MONETARY POLICY
  Jan Toporowski   *93*

CATALYSING GROWTH?: MENDELEEV AND THE 1891
TARIFF
  Vincent Barnett   *123*

VEBLEN IN CHICAGO: THE WINDS OF CREATIVITY
  Geoffrey M. Hodgson   *145*

JOHN MAURICE CLARK AND THE MUTLIPLIER: A NOTE
  Luca Fiorito   *161*

ROUNDTABLE ON THE HISTORIOGRAPHY OF
INSTITUTIONAL ECONOMICS

INTRODUCTION AND SUMMARY
  J. Daniel Hammond and Warren J. Samuels   175

INSTITUTIONAL ECONOMICS: THE TERM AND ITS
MEANINGS
  Malcolm Rutherford   179

IS INSTITUTIONALISM STILL A USEFUL CATEGORY?
  Ross B. Emmett   185

INSTITUTIONAL ECONOMICS AS A CATEGORY FOR
HISTORICAL ANALYSIS
  Warren J. Samuels   189

WHY INSTITUTIONAL ECONOMICS MATTERS AS A
CATEGORY OF HISTORICAL ANALYSIS
  Bradley W. Bateman   193

J. DANIEL HAMMOND, NORMA JEANE MORTENSON, AND
AMERICAN INSTITUTIONALISM: A VIEW FROM THE TOP
ROW
  Steven G. Medema   203

REFLECTIONS ON INSTITUTIONAL AND CHICAGO
ECONOMICS
  J. Daniel Hammond   211

THE BUCHANAN COLLOQUIUM ON THE STATUS OF THE
STATUS QUO: REPORTS ON A CONFERENCE

THE STATUS OF THE STATUS QUO: THE BUCHANAN
COLLOQUIUM
  Warren J. Samuels   219

THE PROBLEM OF THE STATUS OF THE STATUS QUO:
SOME COMMENTS
Warren J. Samuels   235

REVIEW ESSAYS

Walker's EQUILIBRIUM
Glenn Hueckel   259

Burk's TROUBLEMAKER: THE LIFE AND HISTORY OF
A. J. P. TAYLOR AND HASLAM'S THE VICES OF
INTEGRITY: E. H. CARR, 1892–1982
Warren J. Samuels   291

SOCIALISM LOST?
Rod Cross   317

Cullenberg, Amariglio and Ruccio's POSTMODERNISM,
ECONOMICS AND KNOWLEDGE
W. D. Sockwell   329

Hands' REFLECTION WITHOUT RULES
Ana Maria Bianchi   341

Fligstein's THE ARCHITECTURE OF MARKETS
A. Allan Schmid   347

Resnick's and Wolff's CLASSS THEORY AND HISTORY
Simon Clarke   355

Churchman's DAVID RICARDO ON PUBLIC DEBT
Denis P. O'Brien   365

ECONOMICS, BIOLOGY, AND CULTURE: HODGSON ON
HISTORY
Alexander J. Field   373

THE GERMAN HISTORICAL APPROACH TO ECONOMICS
  Harald Hagemann   *399*

Carpenter's THE DISSEMINATION OF THE WEALTH OF
NATIONS IN FRENCH AND IN FRANCE, 1776–1843
  Robert F. Hebert   *413*

Strathern's A BRIEF HISTORY OF ECONOMIC GENIUS
  Edith Kuiper   *419*

Findlay, Jonung and Lundahl's BERTIL OHLIN:
A CENTENNIAL CELEBRATION
  Lars Magnusson   *429*

NEW BOOKS RECEIVED   *437*

LIST OF CONTRIBUTORS

Vincent Barnett	School of Social Science, University of Birmingham, UK
Bradley W. Bateman	Department of Economics, Grinnell College, Iowa, USA
Daniele Besomi	Gola di Lago, Switzerland
Ana Maria Bianchi	Department of Economics, Universidad de Sao Paulo, Brazil
Simon Clarke	Department of Sociology, University of Warwick, Coventry, UK
Rod Cross	Department of Economics, University of Strathclyde, Scotland, UK
Stephen P. Dunn	Department of Health, Whitehall, London, UK
Ross B. Emmett	James Madison College, Michigan State University, USA
Alexander J. Field	Department of Economics, Santa Clara University, USA
Luca Fiorito	Department of Economics, University of Siena, Italy
Harald Hagemann	Department of Economics, University of Hohenheim, Germany
J. Daniel Hammond	Department of Economics, Wake Forest University, USA
Robert F. Hebert	Department of Economics, University of Louisiana at Lafyette, USA
Geoffrey M. Hodgson	Business School, University of Hertfordshire, UK

Glenn Hueckel   Department of Economics, Pomona College,
                         USA

Edith Kuiper   Faculty of Economics and Econometrics,
                         University of Amsterdam, The Netherlands

Lars Magnusson   Department of Economic History, Uppsala
                         University, Sweden

Steven G. Medema   Department of Economics, University of
                         Colorado-Denver, USA

Denis O'Brien   Department of Economics, University of
                         Durham, UK

Malcolm Rutherford   Department of Economics, University of
                         Victoria, Canada

Warren J. Samuels   Department of Economics, Michigan State
                         University, USA

A. Allan Schmid   Department of Agricultural Economics,
                         Michigan State University, USA

W. D. Sockwell   Department of Economics, Berry College,
                         USA

Jan Toporowski   Business School, South Bank University,
                         London, UK

EDITORIAL BOARD

ACKNOWLEDGMENTS

The editors wish to express their gratitude for assistance in the review process and other consultation to the members of the Editorial Board and to the following persons:

Andy Denis
Robert Dimand
Jerry Evensky
Daniel Fusfeld
Richard Gonce
Geoff Harcourt
Lawrence Klein
Fred Lee
Donald Moggridge
Leon Montes

F. Taylor Ostrander
Spencer Park
Melvin Reder
Sylvia Samuels
Myron Sharpe
Rick Tilman
Anthony Waterman
Randall Wray
Jeffrey Young

The editors take pleasure in announcing that Ross Emmett will become co-editor of this annual, commencing Volume 23. Manuscripts may be submitted to either of the three co-editors.

DYNAMICS, TRADE AND MONEY IN THE CORRESPONDENCE BETWEEN ROY HARROD AND DENNIS ROBERTSON ☆

Daniele Besomi

> ... interchanges for the benefit (or confusion) of future research students (Robertson to Harrod, 9 August 1949).

The correspondence between Harrod and Robertson was second in size, for each of the two authors, only to their respective correspondence with Keynes.[1] It extends from 1926 to 1960, and is fairly continuous except during the war years. Robertson did not normally preserve the letters he received,[2] unless he deemed them of extraordinary importance.[3] However, he had the habit of sending a number of them back to his correspondent for reference; Harrod's "instinct for hoarding" (Harrod to Florence Ada Keynes, 7 November 1950) led him to preserve most of the letters received from Robertson, including Harrod's own returned letters. Of the 194 letters and notes extant, 129 were found among Harrod's papers[4] (of which 34 are Harrod's own communications to Robertson), while only 18 items were found among Robertson's papers;[5] and 47 letters and notes are preserved among the *Economic Journal* files in the Royal Economic Society Archives. A chronological list of the extant correspondence exchanged between Harrod and Robertson is given in the Appendix.

☆ In citations, square brackets indicate as usual editorial alterations, the symbol ⟨+⟩ indicates an illegible word, while a word in angled brackets indicates the best guess for a hardly legible word.

Research in the History of Economic Thought and Methodology A Research Annual
Research in the History of Economic Thought and Methodology, Volume 22-A, 1–64
ISSN: 0743-4154/doi:10.1016/S0743-4154(03)22001-0

This correspondence demonstrates that Harrod and Robertson often sought and relied on each other's judgement (Robertson asked for Harrod's advice more often than Harrod asked for Robertson's). They shared a number of theoretical interests, in particular trade cycle theory and international economics, and these issues re-emerged repeatedly in the light of the correspondents' theoretical advances and of other people's contributions being published. Keynes's position, in various stages of development, more or less explicitly was frequently in the background. The exchanges were not limited to letters: Robertson and Harrod from time to time, visited each other, giving themselves additional chances to discuss these themes; traces of these visits and discussions occasionally emerge from the correspondence. Moreover, they have occasionally been members of the same research groups and committees, for instance the Royal Institute of International Affairs's group on International Monetary Problems in 1933–1934 and a League of Nations committee discussing Tinbergen's statistical inquiry on business cycles (they met in Geneva in September 1937 and in Cambridge in July 1938).[6]

These exchanges are therefore rather tangled, with limited number of themes recurring at a distance of years and being debated in different perspectives. The presentation of this correspondence can therefore be offered either chronologically or thematically; the choice fell on the former strategy, in order to respect the development of the authors' thought in the evolving intellectual context of those "years of high theory" and not to lose sight of the intricacy of the exchanges and of the relationships between different topics, although this at times may make it less easy to keep track of the temporary disappearance and sudden re-emergence of a specific topic. Two exceptions to this procedure, however, are outstanding. One concerns the discussions on Harrod's *International Economics*: some issues related to this book re-emerged from time to time, and it seemed convenient to group them together (in Sections 2 and 11, corresponding to the first two editions of Harrod's book) in view of their occasionality. The second exception is due to the fact that as time went by, both Robertson and Harrod more and more frequently gave vent to their personal difficulties with Keynes's temperament (and, in the case of Robertson, with Keynes's younger disciples), as distinct from their appreciation of the theoretical developments taking place in Cambridge; these feelings, as emerging from the correspondence, will be illustrated in the last section.

1. ROBERTSON'S *BANKING POLICY AND THE PRICE LEVEL*

The scientific correspondence between Harrod and Robertson was initiated by Harrod's criticism of Robertson's *Banking Policy and the Price Level* (1926).[7]

Harrod first wrote on 18 May 1926 (letter 2) raising at once the following "salient point":

> Much of your argument depends on the view that justifiable expansions and contractions as defined by you are desirable. Why are they desirable? You give reasons on p. 22 why you think *some* instability in output desirable. But the reasons mentioned there (and I can't find any others) don't seem particularly directed to show that the special form of instability constituted by the so-called "justifiable" expansions and contractions is desirable. They seem to me to show that perhaps some instability, that, presumably, of less degree than we have been accustomed to in the past, is good, but by no means precisely how much is good. Thus, suppose the "hypothetical group member" or "the actual workman" of p. 19 were able to govern output according to their own self interest, there would still, according to the arguments of ch. 2, be *some* instability. Would not that be enough? Or if you want more, why stop at the "justifiable"? Why not have some of that due to "secondary" causes? It seems to me that you have been led away by purely aesthetic interests to identify that more moderate amount of instability which we really need (as shown on p. 22.) with that which we would get: (i) if secondary causes were removed; and (ii) if control of output stayed where it is now – in the hands of the entrepreneur. I don't see how you can say to the banks more than "damp down fluctuation a bit, but leave some fluctuation, as that is healthful for the body economic".

He added two notes to his letter, in the first of which he commented upon the four proposed courses of policy outlined by Robertson on pp. 25–26 of his book. In the second note Harrod suggested that Robertson's calculations in Appendix I to Ch. 5 of *Banking Policy* assumed the following behaviour of the public:

> (i) People do not allow for the effect of their withholding on the price level (this is reasonable). (ii) They are ignorant as the future course of inflation (or do nothing to meet it). (iii) On this basis they decide what withholding is necessary to restore H, decide that it would be too much effort to restore it at once, and . . . spread the restoration over K – 1 days. It so happens that by choosing K – 1 their 2 errors (or failures to take everything into account) cancel each other out, and they do effect the restoration in that time. If K or K – 2 had been chosen, this would not have been so.

Harrod further argued that Robertson's "so-called reasonable assumption of a restoration in K – 1 days is purely arbitrary," and that "all this reasoning is rendered of doubtful value by the fact that we must suppose an alteration in view as to 'the appropriate proportion between Real Hoarding and Real Income' during the process of inflation. Not only will people not replenish H at once, but they may well voluntarily reduce it."

Robertson immediately perceived that Harrod might "have successfully convicted [him] of serious error!" (letter 3 of 20 May 1926). A few days later (26 May, letter 4) he took up Harrod's points in turn. As to the variations of output, Robertson first proposed to agree on a few definitions:

> "Capitalistic" variations in output are those which enlightened self-interest of capitalists tends to bring about. "Ideal" variations in output are those which enlightened self-interest of "group

members" would tend to bring about. "Good" variations in output are those which in all the circumstances we ought to acquiesce in and promote.

He thus specified his thought as follows:

> Then all I am saying is that, "ideal" variations being ruled out owing to the impossibility of here & now establishing a guild system, "capitalistic" variations must be regarded as "good". They are, I suggest probably "better" than those variations which the *immediate* self-interest of workmen, if they could dictate the scale of output, would bring about, because there is a danger that workmen would neglect their *ultimate* self-interest. In any case, I am assuming for purposes of this book that you have got to have "capitalism", & therefore a regulation of output in accordance with the imagined self-interest of employers: the best we can hope for is that their imagined self-interest shall be in accord with their real self-interest.

As to the effects of various policies, Robertson explained the various hypotheses lying behind his proposal, agreed with Harrod on the various assumptions on which his argument in the Appendix to Ch. 5 was based, and conceded that the K − 1 hypothesis is arbitrary.

Harrod's reply on the variations of output pointed out that the appropriate degree of 'capitalistic' variation is not independent of banking policy, and cannot therefore be taken as a guide for banking policy itself. He represented the various kinds of fluctuation by means of a diagram:

> Therefore I dont see why you should identify "good" variations, (those "which in all circumstances we ought to acquiesce in and promote") with "justified capitalistic" variations. "Good" might be more or less. Thus:

> The most fluctuating line is the "capitalistic" fluctuation which would be produced by our banking system.
> [The dashed line] represents "justified capitalistic variation".
> [The dotted line] represents "justified guild-socialistic variation" = the capitalistic variation which would be produced by the banking policy which I propose.
> The straight line represents the elimination of variation in the cyclical period.
> You have still, I hold, to show which of the various possible positions intermediate between my two continuous lines we are to regard as "good." The arguments of p. 22 do not especially justify variation shown by [the dashed line] (letter 5, undated).

Robertson replied (letter 6, undated) by acknowledging that Harrod had "convicted [him] of a good deal of muddle with [his] very searching criticism": he admitted that "capitalistic variations are a function of the banking policy in force," and that therefore to say " 'that banking policy is good which brings about capitalistic variations' leaves the answer to the question 'what banking policy is good?'

indeterminate. There might be many 'good' policies." Robertson invited Harrod to criticise his book in print; the result was Harrod's first article in a learned Journal (1927),[8] on which no further correspondence is extant. Robertson, however, briefly commented on a rejoinder by Marjorie Tappan (1928), who he thought argued "fairly powerfully in some points [but] less powerfully in others" (Robertson to Harrod, 19 November 1927, letter 8; see also letter 11 of 13 March 1928). Robertson stressed, in particular, that in her answer to the charge of circularity Tappan had misunderstood Harrod's point (Robertson, "Mr. Robertson's views on Miss Tappan's views . . .," unpublished).

The importance of this exchange for the future development of Harrod's thoughts on cycles and dynamics can hardly be overemphasised. The diagram shows, in fact, that he understood Robertson's *Banking Policy* as describing fluctuations as taking place around growth trend. Harrod's own trade cycle theory takes in fact as its starting point an unstable moving equilibrium, out of which departures are amplified and give rise to fluctuations. The origin of this assumption is likely to be found in Robertson: it was, in fact, one of the shared presuppositions of the young economists in the New Fabian Research Bureau in which Harrod and Meade in Oxford followed a Keynesian approach in policy, and Durbin and Gaitskell in London took on a more Hayekian position.[9] These discussions gave rise to Harrod's first contribution on dynamics (Harrod, 1934a; see also Section 5 below). In this light, it is rather unfortunate that Robertson did not discuss in detail Tappan's argument that his 'appropriate fluctuations' can be expressed "in terms of the appropriate familiar physical analogy of a *moving equilibrium* in which long-run and short-run positions of equilibrium are distinguished" (1928, p. 98). Robertson only commented: "I expect 'moving equilibria' are also all right, though I'm not much at home among them!" (Robertson, "Mr. Robertson's views . . .," cited).

The topic of the moving equilibrium was to become one of the main recurrent themes in the correspondence between Harrod and Robertson. It is therefore only necessary to stress at this point that the obvious reason why Robertson was one of the very few people who understood that, in *The Trade Cycle*, Harrod was assuming a base of steady progress[10] lay in the fact that he originated the idea.

2. HARROD'S *INTERNATIONAL ECONOMICS* (FIRST EDITION)

In April 1932 Robertson was sent, in his capacity of assistant editor of the Cambridge Economics Handbook series, the first draft of Harrod's *International Economics* (1933). This gave rise to a prolonged correspondence before publication (12 letters are extant, dated from 6 April 1932 to 3 April 1933,[11] three quarters of which were written by Robertson[12]), and to a number of occasional exchanges at a subsequent time.

Robertson's comments on Harrod's draft were concerned in the first place with a number of matters of detail. Little of this remains in the correspondence, most of the annotations having been written directly on Harrod's draft, which is not extant. The second point regarded the intrinsic difficulty of Harrod's text: for some time there was a doubt that it was suitable for the series, but after the matter was discussed between Keynes (the editor of the series) and Robertson it was agreed that the book, after all, met the CEH purpose in spite of being "Packed full of meat" (Robertson to Harrod, 3 April 1933, letter 26, and 10 August 1934, letter 32).

The topic last touched on in this correspondence arose after Harrod received Keynes's criticism of Harrod's automatic balancing of the foreign balance (briefly discussed in Besomi, 2004). Robertson refrained from taking sides:

> Yes, I rather suspect there was a fundamental difference of opinion between you & JMK on that matter! I *think* I am on his side, but am not sure. But I also think that to water the difference down so as to leave the reader in a fog would be a mistake, and that if you do anything to the chapter at all, the best way would be to say "Another view of what happens is . . .". After all, if I remember the thing right at all, you have Ohlin, Angell, etc. on your side (it *is* really the same question as "the transfer problem", isn't it?). Anyhow the C. E. Handbooks have been full of "doubtful doctrine" from Hubert's onwards,[13] – what doctrine isn't doubtful nowadays? (Robertson to Harrod, 31 December 1932, letter 24).

It is important to remark that Harrod's argument on the foreign balance never seems to have got under Robertson's skin. On 3 April 1933 (letter 26), when Harrod's book was in proofs, Robertson confessed:

> I don't feel that ch. VI has really sunk into me yet at all. In particular I find myself jibbing at being asked to imagine people finding their incomes reduced and their money stocks intact, and then *afterwards* setting deliberately about reducing their money stocks (p. 115).

The subject was soon resumed by Robertson, who asked for Harrod's opinion on Keynes's " 'foreign balance' doctrine in the extreme arithmetical form now presented (today's *Times*, and the last chapter of Mult[iplier] pamphlet[14])," suggesting that "unless all sorts of unstated assumptions are fulfilled, the purchase of £1m worth of Jamaican securities imprisons as much purchasing power, which might otherwise be 'creating employment,' as the purchase of £1m worth of Jamaican bananas."[15] The reply to this letter does not seem to be extant. However, Harrod compared his foreign trade multiplier with Keynes's in a subsequent letter:

> My doctrine is that improvement in the foreign current credit account has the same potentiality of giving employment as public works. But if that potentiality becomes an actuality (i.e. is not countered by hoarding or some such process) the increased employment will wipe out the

balance. The extra credit will be offset by an extra debit. What JMK ought therefore to have looked at was not the decline of the balance but the decline of the credit account.

There is however one complication. If a balance is achieved by a tariff or a change of taste, that balance has the same effect as an increase of the credit account. Here again if the balance has its full natural effect in stimulating employment, it will be destroyed. So even in that case it isn't the achievement of a favorable balance, but its achievement + its utilization + its consequent annihilation that goes with improved employed.

Where I think Maynard has got muddled is in his attempt to include in one formula the stimulation that may be given: (i) by an improvement in the credit account; and (ii) by an improvement in the balance due to a tariff or change of taste.

In both cases the good thing takes the form in the first instance in an improved balance. But in so far as the improved balance does stimulate employment in full measure it disappears. And in fact its improvement and its annihilation may well go pari passu. So it is very deceptive to attempt to measure the gain to the country in a period of time by the net outstanding improvement in the balance at the end of the period (letter 30 of 29 April 1933).

The foreign trade multiplier was also discussed a few years later. In January 1937, Robertson submitted to Harrod a note which was later expanded as "Mr. Clark and the Foreign Trade Multiplier" (Robertson, 1939), where Harrod's and Keynes's formulas were compared. In the accompanying letter (which has not been found) Robertson must have pointed out some divergence of opinion with Keynes, as Harrod replied that he could not see what Keynes refused to accept, as the formulas were interchangeable (Harrod to Robertson, 2 February 1937, letter 66). This exchange is interesting, as it indicates that at this point Robertson had overcome his initial difficulties with Harrod's approach (Robertson to Harrod, 2 February 1937, letter 67), while Keynes was still struggling with it – he actually confessed to Robertson (undated letter [January or February 1937]) that he did not understand Harrod's equation, as re-expressed in *The Trade Cycle* (Harrod, 1936, pp. 145–156). Oddly enough, however, Harrod had to explain the point all over again to Robertson in 1945 (see Section 11).

Another topic occasionally discussed under the head of *International Economics* was Harrod's "rehabilitation of comparative costs" (Robertson to Harrod, 5 August 1934, letter 31. Reference is to Harrod, 1933, Ch. 2). At first Robertson was struck by the difference with the treatment of Marshall and Edgeworth, who huddled "comp[arative]. costs into the background in form of reciprocal demand," and was not sure how far he agreed with Harrod (letter 14 of 6 April 1932). After Ohlin's *Interregional and International Trade* (1933) was published, however, Robertson pleaded with Harrod to convince him:

I want to be convinced, for I hate the Ohlin method of approach, which throws overboard the great classical achievement of showing how the monetary epiphenomena – relative levels of incomes or rates of exchange – are the *result* of the underlying "real" situation (letter 31, 5 August 1934).

Robertson suggested that the difficulty lay in the different conceptions of "rent," Ohlin being concerned with " 'Pigouvian rent,' viz. the enhanced earnings in all uses of a (quite possibly homogeneous) factor of production which arise from the expansion of an industry, or set of industries, which make particularly large use of it," while Harrod was concerned with "Shovian rent, viz. the excess earnings derived by some bits of factors of production from being more useful then in their existing use than in any other." Harrod's reply was not found, but Robertson felt "consoled, and I think persuaded" by it (but added: "though I might be burnt at the stake if I admitted it: for one may not deal in Pigouvian rents here nowadays in connection with the cost curves of particular industries!") (letter 32 of 10 August 1934).

It is important to stress the emergence of another recurrent theme in Robertson's economics, namely, the relationship between real phenomena and monetary epiphenomena. Although the subject remained at the margin of the correspondence, on a few occasions Robertson referred to his preference for real as opposed to monetary analysis: an instance is cited in Section 6.1 below, and a further occasion was given by Harrod's *Trade Cycle* (1936), of which Robertson wrote: it "looks for real causes behind the monetary ones, – of that I heartily approve" (Robertson to Harrod, 22 July 1936, letter 58).

3. IMPERFECT COMPETITION

During summer 1932, Robertson tried to get to grips with the recent literature on imperfect competition. The resulting "A Note on the Supply Curve" was sent to Harrod, Shove, Kahn and Pigou for comments, on the grounds of which the paper remained unpublished: Robertson later recapitulated, in fact, that "Harrod, Shove and Kahn thought it wrong, and Pigou thought it uninteresting" (note written on the cover page, dated 1959).

Robertson's Note examined an issue raised by Harrod in "The Law of Decreasing Costs" (1931), namely, whether consideration of decreasing costs would affect the possibility to "draw up a long period supply curve which is a proper denizen of a two-dimensional surface, – a true hypothetical curve, really independent of the demand curve and fit to be yoked with it as co-blade of a pair of Marshallian scissors" ("A Note on the Supply Curve," p. 1). Harrod had argued that in conditions of imperfect competition decreasing costs (increasing returns) could be compatible with equilibrium, under either or both of these assumptions. First, a firm could incur marketing costs "to ward off competitors at the frontier of a sphere of influence"; these costs, to be computed on the supply side, depend not only on the quantity of output, but also – directly and indirectly – on demand.

> But if this is so, a complete reconstruction of the notion of supply schedule becomes necessary. In the usual analysis supply and demand schedules are regarded as independent of one another. On the new view every demand schedule has its own appropriate supply schedule. To determine equilibrium after a change in the former, the latter also must be changed. The customary graphical representation of supply is no longer possible. . . . To draw a single supply schedule to be valid for all states of demand, it is necessary to use three dimensions. Cost becomes a function of two independent variables quantity of output and state of demand. Thus, the traditional analysis breaks down.

In such a case, "it cannot be determined *a priori* from the upward slope of the old curve whether the point of intersection of the two new curves will be above or below the old point. If the new price is below the old one, then in the accepted sense of the term the firm is subjected to decreasing costs" (Harrod, 1931, pp. 567–568).

The second assumption making it possible that equilibrium is compatible with decreasing costs is that the demand curve is downward sloping: in such a case, marginal cost and marginal revenue ("the increment of aggregate demand curve," as Harrod originally named it) may intersect in correspondence of the decreasing part of the cost curve (Harrod, 1931, p. 570).

Robertson considered three cases:

> (1) The case of perfect competition. (2) A case in which the individual firm, working under conditions of decreasing cost in respect of its manufacturing expenses, is prevented from expanding its sales, at a price determined in the general market, by the heavy marketing expenses which it would have to incur to attract trade from its rivals: but in which an expansion in the whole industry will enable it to expand its market without incurring such expenses and thus to reap the advantages of decreasing manufacturing costs. (3) A case in which heavy initial outlay has to be incurred by a firm in order to produce any output at all, but the cost of additional output is small ("A Note on the Supply Curve", pp. 1–2).

Cases two and three reflect Harrod's assumptions (and for this reason Robertson was criticised by Kahn: "I cannot see that your case (2), in which the market is perfect, but marketing costs are rising, is a possible one. You seem to realise this, and this is really a criticism of Harrod": Kahn to Robertson, 5 October 1932). With reference to case 2, Robertson criticised Harrod's conclusion:

> The fact that price now depends on scale of total output for a new reason, viz. because an increase in the scale of output lowers competitive marketing as well as (or instead of) other sorts of costs, does not serve to differentiate this case, from the present standpoint, from the case of perfect competition. In both cases it is assumed that the industry is adapted to the scale of output, which is the same thing as saying that it is adapted to the state of demand: and in both cases there is a unique relation between scale of output and average cost of production. Mr Harrod, perhaps not having noticed the ghost of demand curves in the background of case

(1), is unduly alarmed at their appearance in case (2), and is led into asserting a functional dependence of supply price on demand curve which in this case does not – or at all events need not – exist (pp. 5–6).

Harrod's reply contributes to better specify his viewpoint.

> I was very interested in what you wrote about demand being in some sense implicit in the ordinary cost curve. But I still think that marketing expenses give rise to a special problem, not covered by the ordinary notion of the adaptation of an industry to its scale of output, and that in tackling this problem we may make an advance towards explaining how decreasing costs are consistent with the equilibrium of individual firms in competition (Harrod to Robertson, 3 September 1932, letter 21).

In Harrod's view, Robertson was confused "between the effect of a change in demand on costs *indirectly* thro' changing the optimum lay out of the plant and that on costs *directly* thro' changing marketing expenses. The first (indirect) effect is already taken account of in the Pigovian supply curve, but not the second (direct) effect" (ibid., emphasis added). Therefore "if we are convinced that in fact cost is a function of two *independent* variables, amount of output and 'state of demand,' we must require more than two dimensions. However, we play around with language we cannot get over this simple mathematical fact." He further specified, as a footnote to the word "independent":

> The use of the word independent here is vital, vital both to secure my conclusion mathematically and to interpret the economic facts correctly. It also differentiates between the case in which demand may be implicitly represented in the cost curve and where it may not. The amount of output no doubt depends on demand; productive costs depend on amount of output and ∴ indirectly on state of demand. Thus, making cost a function of amount of output makes it indirectly a function of state of demand. But marketing costs unlike productive costs depend on state of demand directly and this dependence is *not* mediated by the amount of output. Thus, the marketing cost of the *same* amount of output, x_0, will change if the state of demand changes. This proves that the influence of the state of demand on marketing cost is not mediated by amount of output ∴ we must take state of demand as an independent variable of which cost is a function directly. It may also be a function of state of demand indirectly via the other variable. Per contra a change in the state of demand will have no effect on productive cost, if there is no change in output. Consequently where there are no marketing costs (as in case one) the need for a second independent variable is eliminated, all variations in the state of demand necessarily acting through the variable you already have, viz. quantity of output. But this is not so in case 2 (*ibid.*).

Unfortunately we do not have the benefit of Robertson's viewpoint on this issue: "about your distinction between 'direct' and 'indirect' influence of the 'state of demand' on cost I must think again" (letter 22 of 9 September 1932); the discussion does not seem to have been resumed, probably also in the light of the reaction of the other readers of the note.[16]

It should be noted that this is the last occurrence in Harrod's published or unpublished writings of the notion of 'marketing costs' and of the suggestion that they cause traditional analysis to break down: as Shackle put it effectively, "[s]uddenly marketing costs are thrown overboard" (1967, p. 34).

4. SAVING AND INVESTMENT: FIRST DIATRIBE

The saving and investment relationship is, not surprisingly, one of the most frequently recurring topics in the correspondence between Robertson and Harrod. It first appears as an aftermath of a viva voce discussion between Shove, our two correspondents, and possibly other people. It would seem that the discussion regarded the apparatus of Keynes's *Treatise on Money* (1930, in 1971–1989, Vols V and VI) and the consequences of a divergence between saving and investment, on which Shove and Robertson disagreed. Harrod suggested that perhaps Shove was right in claiming that, if $S > I$, *output* must recede, while Robertson was right that *prices* may be stationary at a low level (letter 28 of 26 April 1933). Robertson, however, thought that even

> during a period in which $S > I$, output and employment may easily be *increasing*. For [...] in such a period prices may well be *rising*, and the consequent increase of prime profits will induce many entrepreneurs to increase output, – the effect of this outweighing the contraction of output which comes about through *some* entrepreneurs (who are in a position to 're-contract') closing down or cutting down the scale of production because profits are still below normal. This is, I should say, the typical position in the early phases of recovery from the bottom of a slump (Robertson to Harrod, 28 April 1933, letter 29).

Robertson continued by arguing that the difficulty could be "inherent in the paradoxical definition of S, but does not arise if S is defined in a common sense way, which it easily can be by anyone who is prepared to accept the "atomic" mechanism of my BP & the PL [Robertson, 1926], and is not determined, as JMK is, to apply over a period of time which is not internally homogeneous equations of a form which is only suitable for periods which are homogeneous." Finally, he announced that he had written an article on this subject.

The article was "Saving and Hoarding" (1933a), which was submitted to Keynes for publication in the *Economic Journal* in April 1933 and was accepted on 3 May, and subsequently further discussed by the author and the journal's editor (the related correspondence is published in Keynes, 1971–1989, Vol. XXIX, pp. 16–26 and Vol. XIII, pp. 306–309). As to the homogeneity of the periods of time, Robertson explained to Keynes that time is divided in "atomic" units ("days"), in such a way that "income may be different on one 'day' from what it was on the 'day' before, but it cannot change during the 'day' " (Robertson to Keynes,

19 May 1933, in Keynes, 1971–1989, Vol. XXIX, p. 26). This topic will recur frequently in the correspondence between Harrod and Robertson, and is discussed below in Section 6.

5. ON HARROD ON THE EXPANSION OF CREDIT

A second occasion for Robertson to criticise the Keynesian approach to saving, investment and their dynamics presented itself when Harrod criticised the Hayekian view that credit injections would cause disproportions between production and consumption goods sectors of the economy (Harrod, 1934a). Harrod argued that in a progressive economy,[17] money needs are growing, if only for transaction purposes, so that some credit injection is necessary to keep the system going.[18]

Robertson found the second part of the article – where Harrod laid out the conditions regarding the rate of money injection necessary to satisfy the business community's demand for money in conditions of expansion – "so misguided" that he felt compelled to write a "brief assault": "I *had* to do this, for if your line of reasoning is right, it makes nonsense of everything which I (as well as Hayek & Co[19]) have been trying to say for the last 8 years!" (letter 33 of 27 September 1934). The result was a brief article in *Economica* (Robertson, 1934a), to which Harrod immediately rejoined (Harrod, 1934d). The debate took place in print as well as in correspondence, but again all of Harrod's five letters to Robertson are missing, while Robertson's letters are rather brief and do not offer us many informative comments.[20] A passage, however, is worth citing. Robertson considered Harrod's approach as being on the same lines as Keynes's:

> It appears to me that your new scheme resembles Maynard's Treatise one (now, I gather, abandoned) in that, setting out to be an analysis of *causes*, it ends by being a repetition of *results*. You are really both of you (& this applies to what I have been able to gather about his more recent work as well) dealing with a succession of static positions, and not, as you set out to be, with the *process* of change (letter 35 of 6 October 1934).

This interpretation was strengthened and made more precise in Robertson's correspondence with Haberler regarding Harrod's article and some subsequent writings (Harrod, 1934b, c): Robertson grouped Harrod with Keynes and Kahn in having developed a "Grand Tautology," namely, the equality between saving and investment (Robertson to Haberler, 1 November 1934; the passage is cited in Besomi, 2000, p. 359). Such a statement is rather surprising in the light of Harrod's being, at the time, completely unaware of the developments taking place in Keynes's thought.[21] Perhaps Robertson inferred that Harrod should have taken such a step from his previous statements on the foreign trade multiplier (the relevant passages of the correspondence on the topic are cited in Section 2 above). At any rate, Robertson's interpretation is symptomatic of his mounting disagreement with Keynes's approach – now including the investment multiplier.

6. MORE ON CREDIT, INTEREST, SAVING AND INVESTMENT, AND LAGS

At the end of September 1935, Robertson sent Harrod a paper he had previously read before an unidentified economic society in Oxford. "Money Flows" is a survey of the very recent developments in monetary theory in Cambridge (some of which, including Keynes's *The General Theory*, 1936, was still in the pipeline). Robertson focused again on the "Great Truism" saving = investment, discussing how this equality is maintained in different analytical settings. The paper remained unpublished, but gave rise to a prolonged and intricate exchange with Harrod, where several distinct but related issues were discussed at once: 12 long letters are extant, forming an almost complete set (only one letter seems to be missing), dated from 30 September to 18 November 1935.

In his paper, Robertson took up a number of points regarding methodology and analysis, and – with specific reference to Harrod – resumed the controversy in the columns of *Economica* of the previous year (see Section 5 above). It is now clear that Harrod's rejoinder (1934d) had failed to convince Robertson:

> [Harrod] assumes that all money incomes are scaled up, presumably by decree, in exact proportion to the increase in productivity per head: so that the new money created by the bank is all required for payment of the enhanced incomes of existing factors, and none of it is available for promoting the formation of new material capital. No danger of disequilibrium therefore arises. Real additional savings = real additional investment = zero, if we like to put it so. All Harrod has proved is what we already know, – that in a world in which every money payment or contract could be altered instantaneously to match, alterations in the absolute quantity of money would not matter a whit. But he has not proved that, in a world where such things are not possible, a banking system set the task of increasing money in proportion to the increase of productivity per head, would not inevitably proceed by methods which do involve the formation of new material capital, unbalanced by contemporary acts of spontaneous abstinence (Robertson, "Money Flows", pp. 13–14).

6.1. Saving, Investment and Inflation

Harrod answered (3 October 1935, letter 38) by sending his review of Evan Durbin's *The Problem of Credit Policy* (1935), where he discussed the problem of rises in monetary wages and salaries and their "stickiness" (Harrod, 1935, pp. 725–726). Harrod also pointed out that in general he liked "to think of saving as equal to investment" and that he had not been able to use Robertson's (legitimate) definition of saving by reference to the previous period's income,[22] and eventually addressed a different point, related to the relationship between "inflation" and Robertson's and the "simple-minded" definitions of "saving." Harrod explained that he thought of inflation by reference to the behaviour of prices relatively to money costs, while he interpreted Robertson's notion of inflation to depend on $I > S$, and asked how these two notions are related.

Robertson was not inclined to accept Harrod's "crucial question." He explained that his analysis of inflation in *Banking Policy and the Price Level* implied "the assumption of a small-independent-trader-and-producer economy, in which 'profit' & 'loss' in the *Treatise* sense were impossible," and that, even granted a "profit economy," he was "reluctant to be pinned down to statements about the relation between inflation and '$I > S$'" as he thought the meaning of I not to be clear enough. He insisted that in Harrod's "world of instantly reacting factor-incomes, the increase in I does not involve any increase in real investment at all, – only a scaling-up of factor-rewards. As I have said in my paper, real additional Saving = real additional investment = zero: so there is no maladjustment." Finally, he stressed, once again and not for the last time,[23] his predilection for real vs. monetary analysis, by expressing a grievance about people liking "to talk endlessly about the relation between (money) Savings and (money) Investment," while his "own thoughts run . . . in terms of acts of real abstinence and increments of real capital" (Robertson to Harrod, 5 October 1935, letter 39).

This part of the debate did not come to a definite conclusion, as Robertson insisted that Harrod's attempt to better specify the terms of the problem (Harrod to Robertson, 9 October 1935, letter 42) did not permit an unequivocal answer (Robertson to Harrod, 12 October 1935, letter 43). Harrod concluded as follows:

> I am sorry that you did not find my crucial question as pointed as I thought it. I had hoped that you would agree that to avoid cumulative processes, prices should behave in the same way as sticky costs, viz. quantity of factors required per unit of output [times] prices, where these prices were sticky, and that you would agree to give this criterion priority over S must be equal to I on your definition of S. But apparently you do not agree. I confess that I am in a complete fog as to the practical deductions which would follow acceptance of the criterion of $S = I$ of your def[inition]. of S, and still seek enlightenment on that point. (Harrod to Robertson, 11 November 1935, letter 44).

6.2. Credit Creation

Meanwhile, a passage in Harrod's review of Durbin, where Harrod for the first time in print referred to the acceleration principle (Harrod, 1935, p. 728), induced

Robertson to raise another related issue: "The motive to 'unmaintainable' investment may come partly from an expansion in the consumption trades, but the means comes from abundant producers' credit" (Robertson to Harrod, 5 October 1935, letter 39). The issue was discussed at length in the remainder of the exchange. Harrod objected that banks, by means of their credit operation, may create additional means of payment, but cannot create additional lending: "it is perfectly clear that the banks can *only* lend what is lent to them" (Harrod to Robertson, 8 October 1935, letter 41). Robertson's reply is unfortunately missing, but it must have related credit and interest. Harrod thus continued:

> Banks cant supply the means for additional investment, since they can lend out no more than is lent to them and their action produces no effect on the total of loanable funds available for enterprise. How then can they affect the rate of interest? Why, they can cause the community other than themselves to have less interest bearing and more non-interest bearing assets (here you see the sinister influence of JMK![24]) thus sending up the value of the interest-bearing. A lower rate of interest stimulates investment and the funds for the extra investment are – not provided by the banks – but found out of the higher savings from the higher income which the extra investment necessarily entails. And if you say – ah, but there may be a time lag before the higher income materializes, the answer is that there will be within the lag *you* are thinking of, either some dis-investment (drawing on stocks) so that *net* investment isnt as high as it looks or some abnormally large savings in the interval in which income receivers receive but do not spend their income (letter 42 to Robertson, 9 October 1935).[25]

After warning Harrod that "these pseudo-names ending in -ing [. . .] are terrible verbal traps,"[26] Robertson answered: "this is accountancy, not economics: it tells me nothing which as an economist I want to know," and explained:

> What I want to know is: (i) what effect the above process has on the distribution of real income between (e.g.) creditors & debtors, property-owners & workers, beneficiaries-of-Gov[ernmen]t.-expenditures and others; (ii) whether the stimulus given to production by the process will be durable, or carry in itself the seeds of its own reversal (whether because of distributional changes wrought under (i) or for other reasons). If your (this is a collective adjective) apparatus helps you to throw light on these problems, I must try not to mind you using it. But surely the apparatus can't be *in itself* a great achievement of thought, even if I am misguided in thinking it actually muddling and retrograde?
>
> For instance, if you like your complicated way of explaining why the rate of interest falls, you must use it: but does it give any result which is not yielded by my (i.e. Wicksell's) simple way of regarding the rate of interest as the market price of loanable funds, the supply of which is increased by the "additional lending" put on the market by the bank? For once more let me insist you *haven't* shown that the bank doesn't create "additional lending", but only at the most that when it creates one dollop of "additional lending" which comes on the market it inevitably creates another dollop of "additional lending" which doesn't (letter 43 to Harrod, 12 October 1935).

The correspondence broke off for about a month, and was resumed by Harrod on 11 November (letter 44). He insisted:

you seem to suggest that since one piece of additional lending is 'on the market' and the other is not, there is a *net* addition to lending and that the fall in the rate of interest can be explained in that way. This is surely wrong. So far as direct creation is concerned, what the banks do is to create one bit of additional lending (i.e. they lend that much extra) and one bit of additional *borrowing* (i.e. this extra dep[osit]. liabilities = *their* borrowing from the public) (*this you leave out*). Then, for indirect creation – they may be said to create the lending by the public to them – constituted by the additional holding of deposits, since if they did not themselves lend and so make the additional deposits, this could not occur. They also indirectly in this sense create another bit of additional *borrowing*, since if they were unwilling to lend so much to the public the public could not have borrowed that amount from them. The net result is no change in the *balance* of lending and borrowing.

He also resumed his reference to Keynes's liquidity preference theory, explaining that the fall in the rate of interest is explained by the shift towards non-interest-bearing assets. Robertson replied by reminding Harrod of having warned him "about these dreadful names in -ing – gerunds or whatever they are," and explained that he "never said that the bank creates 'lending in excess of borrowing,'" but that "it creates 'additional lending,' i.e. lending in excess of what would have existed had the bank not done what it *has* done" (letter 45, undated). At this point the discussion became a bit confused. Robertson charged Harrod with having "discovered a new Tautology, – 'amount lent = amount borrowed,'" and resorted to an analogy with a coffee dealer who created additional selling and additional buying. Harrod answered that the charge did not disturb him, as

A valid generalization, in my view, is either a tautology or based on empirical evidence. Unhappily the number of generalizations in economics based on empirical evidence is extremely small. And if you decry tautology, you are decrying almost the whole of economic theory (letter 46 to Robertson, 15 November 1935).[27]

He also contested Robertson's analogy and offered a different one, but "committed a grammatical ambiguity" (letter 48 of 18 November 1935), leaving the whole matter in the fog. At any rate, Robertson was not convinced:

I'm afraid it seems to me indisputable that the bank can, in any unit of time, put on the market additional loanable funds created *ad hoc*. If it thinks that as a result some people will, instead of holding its I.O.Us, repay their old debts to it, and if it wants to counteract this, it must press further loanable funds on the market per unit of time, then lowering the price still further. We agree, I think, that if it is sufficiently resolute and sufficiently catholic about its assets, the last word about the volume of money lies with it ("the banks – subject to reservations about gold – determine the quantity of i.o.u.'s outstanding"). We also agree that if it falters or flags in the face of a kick-back by the public, it surrenders this power of determination to the public ("the net effect of the lending is not an addition to bank loans" – nor to bank deposits). All this comes quite easily out of a supply-and-demand-of-loanable-funds analysis (letter 47 of 16 November 1935).

Harrod concluded the exchange in similar terms, trying to convince Robertson that there are some merits in the liquidity preference approach, but also giving some way to the loanable funds alternative:

> I hope that you do feel that this method of approach is at least not incorrect – does get the right result. I should regard your method as a short cut – for some purposes the holding of bank i.o.u.'s need not be regarded as loans and can ∴ be left out of the picture – so long as it used with proper reservations. [. . .] The new treatment of the holding of bank money as loans to banks may seem a trifle pedantic. But I fear that this pedantry is necessary in view of the gross abuse of the short hand treatment (Harrod to Robertson, 18 November 1935, letter 48; the concluding polemical remark is addressed to Hayek's 'flagrant misuse' of the shortcut).

So far, the exchange seems to conclude in a draw. Both Harrod and Robertson, however, soon became less generous towards the liquidity preference approach, as will be seen in Section 9 below. Harrod's position was revised while writing *The Trade Cycle* (1936) and "Mr. Keynes and Traditional Theory."[28]

6.3. Time-Lags

Harrod also took up – but did not yet discuss at length – the point in Robertson's paper on "Money Flows" which turned out to become one of the recurring themes of their correspondence as well as one of Robertson's main grievances against the "neo-Cambridge method":

> What makes me doubtful of your appreciation of it is the stress you attach to his [Keynes's] neglect of lags, which, as I see it, is a comparatively unimportant point about it. Grant his system and begin to work upon it and the lags all come into their own again. Not but what you *may* have a damaging and final criticism of the system itself, but that cannot be developed by reference to the quite irrelevant question of lags (7 October 1935, letter 40).

In the light of the exchanges which followed, it is important to detail and compare Harrod's and Robertson's respective positions on this topic. Robertson had already raised the issue on a previous occasion, discussed in Section 4 above, and eventually developed his viewpoint in "Saving and Hoarding" (Robertson, 1933a) and in a more critical vein in "Money Flows." In the former of these pieces Robertson simply "suspected" that "discontinuity is the essence of the story" (1933, p. 413), and in "Industrial Fluctuation and the Natural Rate of Interest" he added that "*some* conception of lag still seems to me necessary to protect us against the peril of confounding causes with results, and *processes* of change with *states* of abnormality" (Robertson, 1934b, p. 650). He also explained that the notion of a lag is necessary to make possible a "divergence between the rate of industrial borrowings and the rate of available new savings per atom of time" (*ibid.*, p. 656), on which "the *movement* of the price-level (not, as in Mr. Keynes's scheme, the *state* of the price-level as compared with some normal state) depends" (Robertson, 1933a, p. 411).

In these writings several facets of the same problem show at once. We have the *methodological* aspects of the causal interpretation of the relationships between variables, and of the charge to those who ignore lags of illicitly mixing up periods which are not internally homogeneous (*ibid.*, p. 411); there is the *theoretical* aspect of how to explain movements in the price level (as opposed to the Keynesian emphasis on output, clearly recognised in "Money Flows," p. 19). The *analytical* aspects regard how a step-by-step approach enables one to explain the system's dynamics, and whether or not the results are affected by the choice of the length of the period (Keynes, 1933c, pp. 699–700; Robertson, 1933b, p. 710); finally, there is the *ontological* aspect of which of the "simple minded," the Robertsonian and the Keynesian (in the *Treatise*) definitions of 'saving' is the one which better corresponds to "the usage of ordinary life" (Robertson, 1933a, pp. 410–411).

In "Money Flows" these issues are taken up at length. Robertson wrote:

> From a methodological point of view the main difference seems to be between those writers who find themselves unable to think without a more or less explicit parcelling of time into discrete period, and those in whose analysis the temporal element is blurred, its place being sometimes (although not always) taken by that agreeable instrument, the infinite convergent series. My own position in this respect is so well expressed in a hitherto unpublished paper by one of my colleagues that I cannot forbear to quote. Speaking of the concept of the latter group, he says 'It might seem at first sight that such a conception makes things simple. But in truth it renders continuity and process unintelligible, and brings the enquiry to a full stop. The timeless world with which it confronts us is a fiction, not merely worthless for the study of reality but seriously misleading. . . . It is the existence of these time gaps which enables the money income of one period, with or without increment or decrement, to generate the money income of a later interval. This process of successive generations, income generating later expenditure . . . and expenditure . . . generating later income, is fundamental. Unless it is clearly grasped the whole of monetary analysis must remain in confusion' (pp. 3–4).

As to the length of the period, he commented:

> That there must be *some* delay [between receipt of income and its expenditure] was, and is, fundamental to my way of thought. My Cambridge critics, among whom I rank Harrod, seeing my day so short, have girded me for not being willing to abolish it altogether and to join them in that timeless world where anything may happen, – that nightmare world, as I think it, of the widow's cruse and the Danaides' sieve: 'de minimis' they urge sternly 'non curat lex', and when I reply with St. James, 'Behold how great a matter a little fire kindleth' they are moved not a whit (p. 7).

Robertson maintained that the saving-investment identity is a direct consequence of the neglect of time:

> By leaving the essential time-element out of one's analysis it is possible to define the word saving as to include any increment to one's balance which has occurred, even a minute and a

half ago, owing to the determination of somebody or other to fire money into one's pocket. The great truism ["the money which has been injected into the income-stream must, at the end of a period of time however short, be in possession of somebody"] can then be re-expressed in the words 'Savings must always equal Investments' (p. 11).

In Robertson's view, however, the banking system has the power to create money "to promote acts of capital-formation which are not balanced by contemporary acts of spontaneous abstinence on the part of the public," and private individuals may decide to divert into the income-expenditure circuit parts of the balances they used to keep outside it. This situation – Robertson recalled – was described by some people as "investment exceeding savings," and a step-by-step analysis has no problem of validating this use of words by appropriately defining "savings," while the $S = I$ form of the great truism tries to strangle these fears at birth. Robertson, however, insists that "it *is* within the power of the banking system or of private individuals to commit a disequilibrating act of the kind described" (pp. 11–12).

As to Harrod, when the issue was first raised in correspondence by Robertson in April 1933 his views were at a much less elaborated stage than Robertson's. Harrod had not yet developed his methodological views on instantaneous analysis, which made its first appearance in his *Economica* rejoinder to Robertson:

> The difference between the two sets of problems is analogous to the difference between the dynamics of getting a train to move and the dynamics of a train in motion at a constant velocity. I was concerned to investigate the latter problem, and for that purpose *it is proper to take a cross-sectional view*, assuming that the immediately preceding and succeeding periods yield similar developments, and to find out what assumptions with regard to the increase and mutual relations of the factors concerned are self-consistent and consistent with normal economic motives (Harrod, 1934d, p. 478).[29]

When writing these lines Harrod also had no idea of how to develop a trade cycle mechanism. He was, however, gathering the first elements: he already had the idea, although this was quite a recent achievement, that an endogenous destabilising factor is necessary in order to provide an appropriate explanation of the trade cycle, based on the argument that a stable state of equilibrium would not permit fluctuations unless caused by exogenous factors, upon which the burden of an explanation would fall.[30] He had recently become acquainted with the acceleration principle: from a preliminary draft of Haberler's *Prosperity and Depression* he learned of the possibility of applying it to the trade cycle.[31] He had not yet, however, understood the implications of the multiplier, which he only grasped after reading *The General Theory* in proofs during summer 1935. By October 1935, however, he had further thought about continuity of change and instantaneous analysis, as apparent from the above-mentioned review of Durbin (Harrod, 1935, p. 727), and was about to interlace these elements to form his trade cycle theory: he started writing *The Trade Cycle* at the end of 1935, and the main bones were ready by

January 1936. There, his criticism of the 'time-lag theories of the cycle' was fully developed in the terms which we see adumbrated in the correspondence; Robertson's period analysis was one of the exponents of this approach, probably the one Harrod had in mind as a critical target.

We have here two quite distinct views of dynamics clashing for the first time, although not yet as clearly as they did in the later exchanges. In Harrod's view, dynamics must take as its starting point the study of a system growing in equilibrium at a regular pace. In these conditions, the most appropriate method is that of taking a cross-section and analysing the relationships between variables at a single point of time. This, of course, does not exhaust the dynamic problems: cycles are considered as well, as departures from the moving equilibrium made necessary by the intrinsic instability of equilibrium growth. This stage of analysis, however, where it is appropriate to consider time-lags, is logically subsequent to the determination of the equilibrium relationships.

Robertson is also concerned with systems with accumulation of capital. But, as there is no reason why the supply of savings should exactly match the demand for them, the disequilibrium saving-investment relationship – with all its implications for the price level and further motives for accumulation on the one hand, and for the "kinds of saving" (including hoarding and forced savings) on the other hand – is the real engine of his trade cycle mechanism. In this perspective, it is therefore necessary to adopt a definition of "savings" permitting deviations from "investment," and therefore to reject the timeless notion defining them as identically equal to each other.[32]

7. HARROD'S *TRADE CYCLE*

On 18 May 1936, Harrod asked Robertson's opinion on a passage in *The Trade Cycle* where Robertson's definition of "savings" as related to the income of the past period was mentioned (Harrod, 1936, p. 128).[33] The resulting correspondence amounts to seven letters, dated from 18 May to 5 June 1936, the first three of which resume the debate on savings and investment while the four remaining ones only concern Harrod's rephrasing of the passages where Robertson was mentioned.

Harrod's original wording, referring to "a view advanced by Mr. D. H. Robertson, that in any period the amount that people spend is related not to what they earn in that period, but to what they earn in the preceding period" (Harrod to Robertson, 18 May 1936, letter 50), raised Robertson's protest that he had not been advancing a different *view* about how people behave, but felt it "necessary to employ a different law of thought, so to speak, in order to analyse their behaviour" in order to escape the *impasse* described by Hawtrey in his comment on Robertson's "Saving and Hoarding" (Hawtrey, 1933, p. 703). In other words, Robertson claimed not to "have made an important psychological discovery," but only

> to have made (fairly!) explicit a mode of thought which is in fact implicit in these previous discussions of the subject which deal in terms of 'forced levies and anti-levies' and similar concepts, – concepts which still seem to me to express an important truth which is wholly obscured by what I have ventured to call the Grand Tautology (Robertson to Harrod, 19 May 1936, letter 51).

Robertson repeated in a subsequent letter, dated 21 May, that he was not propounding a 'view' but an "apparatus of thought."

Robertson's problem, as described by Hawtrey, consisted in the necessity of keeping consumer's incomes and consumer's outlay in distinct slices of time, otherwise – on the assumption that a decrease in consumption due to an act of saving is met not by a decrease in supply but by a proportionate fall in prices – one could not account for savings taking place. In such a case, in fact, the receipts from the sale of consumption goods would fall by the amount saved, as well as would the consumers' income including savings. Hawtrey suggested that if Robertson had accounted for the accumulation of unsold output, the impasse would not have reasons to exist (Hawtrey, 1933, pp. 703–704). Robertson asked Harrod what his own solution would be. Harrod answered as follows:

> My view is that in a depression and in the absence of sufficient 'hoarding' in your sense, the money automatically gets trapped into the capital accounts of firms. They cannot redistribute it as dividends, because it is not part of profit; they may buy securities, but I, like Maynard, treat the relation between the quantity of money held on capital account to the price of securities in a sort of pt II, pt I being concerned with the relation between the money flowing into and out of the income stream and the flow of goods. I believe that my notion of the trapping of money in this way is new (letter 52 to Robertson, 21 May 1936).

Harrod's answer, however, does not really deal with Robertson's problem.[34] This notion of trapped money, as expressed in detail in *The Trade Cycle* (Harrod, 1936, pp. 125–145), was elaborated to answer the problem of how changes in the level of output in the whole system, as caused by the action of the "dynamic determinants" (i.e. the combined effect of the multiplier and the acceleration principle), are transmitted – via changes in the velocity of circulation of money and its repercussions on the price level – to the individual entrepreneur.[35] Robertson's problem, however, is the methodological counterpart of the ontological problem of the "important truth" summarized by the concept of forced savings.

So far, Harrod seems to have failed to understand the methodological nature of Robertson's problem. The topic, however, called for further discussion.

8. KEYNESIAN THEMES, AND DYNAMICS

Two exchanges concerned Harrod's and Robertson's respective assessments of the *General Theory*. A first, short exchange of which only Robertson's two letters to Harrod are extant concerned Harrod's "Mr. Keynes and Traditional Theory" (1937), as read before the Oxford meeting of the Econometric Society.[36] Robertson agreed with Harrod that

> the G. T. (i) doesn't introduce any new 'pieces', but only rearranges the old ones in a way which you find to be illuminating and I find to be muddling, (ii) isn't really doing 'dynamics' at all, – *I* should add, is doing an exceedingly uncomfortable compromise between 'comparative statics' and 'dynamics', which may be very misleading to practice (letter 59, 28 October 1936).

On the other hand, Robertson was surprised by Harrod's "claims made for illuminating changes in respect of"

  (i)   the importance of expectations (pp. 6, 22);
  (ii) the precision of the concept of liquidity preference (proper) and its relation with the marginal principle and with the rate of interest (pp. 19, 20);
  (iii) the manner in which changes in the quantity of money operate through the rate of interest (pp. 20–21);
  (iv) the influence of rigidity of wage-rates in terms of money (p. 12).[37]

He supplied a number of references to writings by himself, Marshall, Pigou and Lavington proving that these topics had long since been discussed in the literature[38] (letter 60 of 9 November 1936).

The second brief but intense exchange (five very long letters) was initiated by Harrod on 9 December 1936 (letter 61) upon reading Robertson's review of the *General Theory* in the *Quarterly Journal of Economics* (Robertson, 1936). With two of Harrod's quibbles we are not concerned here; the third is, instead, of extreme interest, as it led him and Robertson to discuss of thrift, interest and dynamics.

Taking exception of Robertson's point that "if there exists for the community as a whole a negatively inclined curve of "liquidity preference proper" [. . .], some part of the additional savings devoted by individuals to the purchase of securities will come to rest in the banking accounts of those who, at the higher price of securities, desire to hold an increased quantity of money" (1936, p. 188), Harrod suggested that "that there is unlikely to be any net rise in securities generally":

> in the first place if the increase of thrift is correctly foreseen by producers, the increased demand for securities will not occur because there will be no increase of saving (operation of multiplier). The common sense view of thrifty savers wanting to buy securities presupposes an error of judgement on the part of entrepreneurs (which ought to be mentioned) in not anticipating the increase of thrift (letter 61 of 9 December 1936).

Secondly,

> so far as equities are concerned, surely the decreased value of real assets due to decreased consumption will have some effect on the price of securities. All holders of securities are potential sellers if they think the prices too high. If at a moment when the prospective yield of assets fell, there was any tendency for the prices of the titles to them to rise, a large flock of existing holders would become sellers and there would be no *net* increase of demand. If you confine yourself to gilt edged securities, you should say so. A large fall of industrials accompanied by some rise in gilt-edged securities might well have an adverse effect on investment.

Harrod added that the classical argument requires not only that the price of securities rises, but also that this stimulates investment: the classical theory "requires a sufficient rise to make methods of production so much more roundabout as fully to replace the demand for capital goods knocked off by the fall in consumption by capital goods required to make the productive process more roundabout" (*ibid.*)

To the first argument, Robertson replied that it "seems to me to imply *partial* but not complete pre-adaptation to changes in demand, and also that *instantaneous* operation of the 'multiplier' at its full normal strength which I dispute." The answer to the second argument runs as follows:

> I conceive of the extra supply of saving as coming up against two demand curves, one representing the productivity use, one the liquidity. For there to be *no* increase in investment, either PP′ must be completely inelastic or LL′ completely elastic or both [Robertson drew two curves, PP′ representing productivity and LL′ representing liquidity preference, the former ascending and the latter decreasing]. It can be plausibly argued that both are likely to be the case in face of a large sudden increase of saving, occurring in a depression, and/or expected to be reversed. It does not seem to me plausible to suppose that this is a correct account of the operation of a gradual increase in the propensity to save in a normally prosperous community with a well organised capital market. That the elaboration of the capital market should actually operate *against* the effective utilisation of desire-to-save seems to me a paradox too great to be acceptable (Robertson to Harrod, 23 December 1936, letter 62).

Harrod's reply is interesting, as it makes clear that saving and investments are maintained equal to each other instant after instant by unwanted changes in the volume of stocks[39] – i.e. Hawtrey's solution to Robertson's *impasse*: see Section 7 – *and* as it refers to the Swedish distinction between ex post and ex ante investment:

> You speak of the instantaneous operation of the multiplier which you dispute. You are right in disputing it if you mean what the Swedes call investment ex ante. But I think Maynard's argument for the instantaneous operation is irrefutable if you mean investment ex post (which includes the *un*intended accumulation of stocks). While the temporary maintenance of income in the face of thrift is a force making for the rise of securities due to the demand of savers, the un-intended accumulation of stocks, which by hypothesis must be present if income does not shrink as a result of thrift in accordance with the normal multiplier, is a manifest token of the redundancy of capital goods and could be a strong force making for the writing down of the values of securities (letter 63 of 25 December 1936).

Robertson's final observation left the matter in suspense – to be resumed a few months later (see Section 9):

> I don't accept the difference between intended and unintended *investment* as a sufficient way out of the difficulties of the s[tatic]. t[heory]. The Swedish difference between i[ntended]. and u[nintended]. *savings* is much more to the point. The 'normal multiplier' is a snare and a delusion as soon as we begin to analyse change! (But this, I realise, raises large issues, which it's no use trying to carry further by correspondence. I cannot breathe in your claustrophobic world!) (letter 64 of 3 January 1937).

Besides introducing a new element in the saving-investments debate, the discussion gave Harrod the opportunity of expressing rather extemporaneous reflections on the necessity of having a dynamic theory of interest – reflections which he does not seem to have developed elsewhere in his writings, either published or unpublished. Harrod maintained that "any analysis of the rate of interest is nonsense in which the rate of acceleration of income does not appear as a term in the equations by which the rate of interest is determined" (25 December 1936, letter 63). He found the "fundamental flaw" in the classical theory of interest to consist in analysing rates of interest rather than their rates of increase or decrease – namely, to analyse their dynamics:

> Now in certain circumstances full employment requires a steady fall in the rate of interest. But the long-term rate is of such a nature that we cannot contemplate a steadily falling rate as a normal feature in the equilibrium of a steady advance. One requirement of equilibrium is that anticipations should be justified. If the fall in the rate is *not* foreseen the position will not be an equilibrium one. If it *is* foreseen, it will be anticipated in present values and ∴ it will not occur.

Harrod continued by stressing the point already raised in "Mr. Keynes and Traditional Theory" (then forthcoming as Harrod, 1937) that Keynes had thrown out some hints on dynamics but that his "work does *not* imply an overthrow of the static system"; on the contrary, Harrod stressed that "the classical theory breaks down in not analysing growth," and as saving implies growth "the doctrine of what governs the volume of saving and the rate of interest must be thrown out bag and baggage." Nevertheless, when there are no savings and investment "[t]he static system retains its place as a foundation."

This same letter also contains Harrod's interpretation of the "time-lag theories of the cycle," of which Robertson's period analysis was – in Harrod's view – an eminent member:

> What I feel about people broadly in your position is that you cling a little too tenaciously to the view that the classical analysis shows that the system must be self-adjusting in the end. You are inclined therefore to emphasize time-lags and miscalculations.

To Robertson such a statement must have appeared rather cryptic. Its meaning, however, can be clearly understood by comparing Harrod's similar statements referring to other authors. In Harrod's view, the 'very causa' of the cycle lies in the instability of equilibrium, while the time-lag theories pin down fluctuations to the errors in judgement on the part of entrepreneurs. He therefore interpreted Robertson's approach as a consequence of the implicit assumption that the system tends to a stable state of equilibrium, for escaping which some kind of exogenous cause or systematic friction has to be called in (Besomi, 1998b).

Although, generally speaking, Harrod had a point, he seems to have failed once again to understand the nature of Robertson's methodological choice, as expressed in the writings and correspondence cited in Section 6.3. Robertson himself denied the charge by stressing that

> in point of fact most of my published writings have been directed to pointing out deep-seated lacks of harmony in the system. But I expect I have rather a large element of cussedness in me, which makes me always react against the case which I feel to be overstated at the moment (letter 64 of 3 January 1937).

9. MORE ON SAVING, INVESTMENT, INTEREST, AND EQUILIBRIUM

After a brief interlude, during which Harrod and Robertson discussed Harrod's and Keynes's approaches to foreign trade (see Section 2 above), the correspondence on the various issues relating to saving and investment resumed, the occasion being Robertson's review of Harrod's *Trade Cycle* (Harrod, 1936; Robertson, 1937a)[40] and a visit by Harrod to Cambridge – during which, presumably, the discussion was continued viva voce. The exchanges took place in distinct batches: in February (one letter from Robertson), April (three letters, two of which from Robertson), October and November 1937 (three letters, one of which from Robertson) and finally January 1938 (one letter each).

Robertson's letter 68 of 10 February 1937 replies to a letter not found in which Harrod seems to have complained that in his review Robertson failed to stress the nature of Harrod's dynamic problem. Robertson's reply confirms the kinship between their respective views on the process of accumulation of capital, stressed in Section 1:

> I wish I *had* put in a sentence expressing more explicit welcome of your way of looking at the whole problem – "What will preserve a *moving* equilibrium?" – as being valuable in itself whether or not the pessimism of your own solution is justified. It's probably because I've always – or for long – been so much under the influence of Cassel's "Th. of Soc. Ec." in this respect that I rather took this approach for granted: but I quite agree that it isn't prominent enough in even the best English work (A. C. P. as well as JMK) and deserved more explicit welcome in your own. Well, well, – please try to forgive me.

Robertson returned to the heart of the saving-investment debate in his next letter, again with reference to *The Trade Cycle*. Robertson was then convinced that Harrod's solution (Harrod, 1936, pp. 67–68) to the *impasse* which, in Robertson's view, made it necessary to adopt period analysis (see Section 7) belonged to the same family as Hawtrey's:

> I believe that even now it might be argued that you do not stick *consistently* to your amendment of JMK's sterile truism, & that both you & Hawtrey need to be more explicit (like the Swedes) about the unplanned saving which takes place at each phase of the expansory process (not only the unplanned disinvestment) if you are to provide a satisfactory alternative to the definitions employed by those who have preferred the so-called 'guilty fallacy'[41] (letter 70, 1 April 1937).

Harrod answered by producing a brief history of the course of events, according to which after Keynes introduced the idea that Investment needs not be equal to Saving, the concept was taken up in the literature but, instead of referring to Keynes's definition of saving, the divergence between saving and investment was interpreted as depending on expansion of credit by the banks. As to unplanned savings, Harrod asked for references, and inquired on the notion and forced savings:

> What precisely is the level of income of the entrepreneurs at which you say that there is neither forced saving nor forced dis-saving. You may say – that level of entrepreneurial income which is consistent with steady advance. All right. But then I say that the whole conception of forced saving is otiose. All we have to ask is – what level of entrepreneurial income is consistent with steady advance? The further question – at what level of entrepreneurial income will there neither be forced saving nor forced dis-savings *adds* nothing and engenders confusion through the use of forced in a Pickwickian sense (letter 71 of 3 April 1937).

As to unplanned savings, Robertson gave references to Lindahl (1934) (sent to Harrod as a mimeograph) and Myrdal (1933); on the other issue, he maintained that Harrod's comments and queries got "down to the root of our differences so far as they are methodological":

> *I* think the propensity of the natural intelligent man to suppose that saving and investment (in the sense of capital outlay) frequently differ is thoroughly sound.[42] [. . .] I think that JMK created a great deal of unnecessary fog, first in 1931 by implying that this use of language required a much more paradoxical use of the word saving than it does, and secondly in 1936 by tying himself up with a definition which forced him to abandon this use of language without giving us anything to put in its place.
>
> That we need something to put in its place I feel most strongly. You, I think, are closer to me than to the complete Keynesians in that you do not dismiss the whole concept of 'money equilibrium under progress' as nonsense. But you regard attempts to express the conditions for it in terms of thrift and its utilisation as otiose. That might perhaps be so in a world in which all operations on the money-stream were made by the use of the taxing and dole-giving powers of the Govt. But in fact we live in a world where they are still made by the use of the lending and loan-recalling powers of the banks, – institutions which started as, & believe themselves to be, instruments for the effective utilisation of the public's thrift. What more natural than to attempt to demonstrate a connection between the success with which they fulfil that function and the

preservation of monetary equilibrium? What more barren than to say, as you do, that they are inevitably fulfilling that function perfectly, whether they preserve equilibrium or create violent disequilibrium in either direction? [emphasis added]

He added an historical and bibliographical note:[43]

> As regards dogmengeschichte, I do not know who first used the formula of difference between saving & investment *in the sense of capital outlay*. I seem to remember seeing it in "Nation" articles in the years just before 1931, – whether by JMK or HDH I do not know. I am inclined to think JMK invented it, & this use of the word investment (a most important invention, I think); but I find it also on p. 24 of the 1st edt of Hayek's Prices & Production, – for the temporal relation of this work to the Treatise on Money, see p. xiv of the preface to the former. The importance of divergence between saving and investment *in the ordinary sense* is clearly set out by Lavington, The Capital Market, pp. 70–72, the connection of the latter with capital outlay being separately discussed. Wicksell's discussion is in terms of the divergence between 'the demand for loan capital and the supply of savings' (Lectures, II, 193). In the introductory chapter of the same work (pp. 6–14) he explains very clearly how saving may fail to eventuate in the accumulation of real capital, without actually using the phrase of a divergence between them (Robertson to Harrod, 28 April 1937, letter 72).

Harrod replied in two long letters a few months later, and brought together all the strains of thought touched upon in the previous exchanges. First, he focused on the notion of long-period equilibrium, and its relationship to forced savings and the Swedish approach. The passage italicised in the first of the excerpts from Robertson's letter of 28 April cited above stimulated the following comment:

> The notion of equilibrium is necessary to the definition of forced saving, I gather from your letter. This gives us forced saving throughout the revival and boom. This seems to me a little unhelpful and not at all in accord with common notions. I don't want to condemn forced saving out and out. The concept is quite attractive. But I do feel that the definition wants refurbishing and that it is going to be extremely difficult to do so (letter 73 of 4 October 1937).

This statement is doubly puzzling. In the first place, it is based on an inference which does not seem to be based on Harrod's own theory, neither as expressed in *The Trade Cycle* nor on the revised version that appeared later as the "Essay in Dynamic Theory" (Harrod, 1939a): "You may refer to a rate of advance that can be maintained. To which I add as a corollary that this means keeping things perpetually as they are at the bottom of the depression. As soon as you allow any revival (e.g. drop in percentage unemployed), you have an advance exceeding the long period trend." Secondly, Harrod does not seem to have appreciated that Robertson's method, and in particular his emphasis on forced savings, is based on the recognition that the trade cycle involves a disequilibrium process. A few paragraphs below, Harrod himself stressed the importance of equilibrium processes in his dynamic setting; in fact, after having inquired about the precise relationship between the Swedes' notion of unplanned saving and Robertson's approach, he commented:

I suppose Lindahl's definition is serviceable, but it conceals a distinction of the first importance. Saving exceeds planned saving because income exceeds expected income. But does the saving exceed the saving you would have planned had you correctly foreseen your income?[44] It is easier to fit an unexpected increase of income with saving, albeit not in anticipation, adjusted thereto, into a model of a steadily advancing economy than unplanned saving in the sense that if you had foreseen your income you would not have allowed it or so much of it to occur (*ibid.*).

In the postscript to the same letter which was stimulated by Robertson's contribution to the debate on the "Alternative Theories of the Rate of Interest" (1937b), and in the following letter, Harrod resumed his argument that "to treat saving as on a par with the other factors of production is logically fallacious because saving involves growth which contradicts the static assumptions" (4 October 1937, letter 73). He thus commented on the state of interest theory, with special regard to Keynes's liquidity preference approach:

If you could accept Maynard's liquidity preference as a rather rough and tumble working account, good enough to go on with, you could put it in Pt I [statics]. If you wont accept it, all you can say in Pt I *is* that there *is* a rate of interest, we shant tell you till later what fixes it, and this is important in determining the degree of round-aboutness of production and the relative prices of goods.

There is no theory orthodox or other about what determines the rate of interest. Supply and demand for loanable funds forsooth! Apart from Maynard's point that the supply depends on the total volume of income, which itself *depends* on the rate of interest, there is the still more important one that you have nothing to say about the demand. This depends on the rate of growth; but about this you have nothing to say in Pt I. With tastes and technique remaining the same – the assumption you always have to make in any Pt I analysis –, there is *no* demand for loanable funds. But there is some supply ∴ the rate of interest must always be zero. Very instructive for the young! (*ibid.*).

In his next letter, Harrod insisted –and by doing so, he expounded three fundamental components of his notion of dynamics, namely continuity of change, emphasis on growth rates, and stress on the systemic properties of dynamics (see, for a discussion, Besomi, 1999):

You may now be tempted to say – well, then the rate of interest will fall to stimulate demand sufficiently to absorb the supply. Quite so; but again this stimulus will only – tastes and technique being the same – *provoke a once over demand*. When that is exhausted the rate will have to fall again. In fact we come to this. Given tastes and technique and the supply schedule, there is no sense in the question what rate of interest will allow demand to absorb the supply. We have to ask what rate of fall in the rate of interest will allow demand to absorb the supply. But this is not at all on all fours with our treatment of the other factors. We do not say what rise or fall in wages or rents is required to get labour and land used (assuming constant supply schedule) but what level of wages or rents. This is what I mean by saying that the orthodox theory of interest is one dimension out.

[...] Put it another way. You may perceive that to bring interest theory into line with the others, one must consider the whole quantum of capital including all past savings, however this may be measured. You have your demand for the use of so and so much capital as a whole per week which is on all fours with your demand for so much labour per week. There will be a demand schedule corresponding to various rates of interest. This gives you a particular rate related to each quantum of capital. It does *not* give give you a particular rate related to a given amount of addition to the capital. Which comes back to the same point. Given your tastes, technique, time-preference and all the rest of it, what comes out of the hat isn't a rate of interest at all, but a rate of fall in the rate of interest.

Why not, you may say? But I say that you cannot admit the concept of a rate of fall in the rate of interest in your Pt I and not talk about any other rates of increase and decrease. You have now to *consider the economy as a whole*, with the tendency to increase or decrease in all its parts. In fact *you are in the dynamic system* (Harrod to Robertson, 8 October 1937, letter 74, emphasis added).

Unfortunately Robertson did not feel like commenting on Harrod's considerations on the Swedes; he thought, however, that in the passages cited above Harrod had "struck a mare's nest":

Of course if you insist on confining your vol I to the discussion of stationary states you must frame your theory of interest accordingly, and not talk about it being the price of net saving or about its being influenced by the progress of invention, etc. But neither roundaboutness nor time preference ceases to be relevant in a stationary state. The condition for full static equilibrium, with no growth of capital, is not that interest should be zero but that it should be equal to the rate of time preference. See Pigou, Economics of Stationary States, chs X and XXXII; Ramsey, A Mathematical Theory of Saving, Ec. Journal 1928.[45]

Personally, having been brought up in the Marshallian tradition, tempered by Cassel, I am not shocked at introducing progress into vol I, & framing my discussion of interest accordingly. But the mere fact that so deep and subtle a thinker as you can fall into this Schumpeterian pit does seem to indicate that it will be better for us each to write *three* volumes in future, – Stationariness, Progress and Fluctuation (letter 75 of 23 November 1937).

Harrod, meanwhile having married, did not reply until January 1938. He concluded the exchange declaring that he was "un-repentant about the rate of interest in a stationary state":

Current new investment involves an increase in the means of production but this contradicts the static assumptions. If you are prepared to waive this and allow growth of capital in an otherwise stationary state, then the laws of supply & demand give you not a rate of interest but a rate of fall in the rate of interest with nothing said as to the absolute level of the rate of interest. The ordinary analysis does not provide any account of what determines the absolute level (letter 78 of 22 January 1938).

10. FINANCE, AND "NORMAL" GROWTH

The correspondence on kindred topics was resumed in July 1938. Harrod's comments on Robertson's "A Survey of Modern Monetary Controversy" (1938) gave rise to a short exchange (4 letters only) focusing on the new subject of "finance."

Harrod's criticism of Robertson's survey is based on an old bone of contention:

> If the new money supplied by the banks is not wholly saved, but partly expended on consumption
> – as of course it will be – the real capital in another part of the community will not be left intact.
> Stocks in the shops will be pro tanto diminished. The expansion (which *you* say is financed by
> the supply of new money) I say is financed by contraction in another place. If now the shops
> take pains to replenish stocks, they will only succeed in doing so to the extent to which the
> newly employed as a result of the shops' extra orders *save*. Thus, the increased demand for
> funds is met in full: (a) by a release of funds by those who have let their stocks run down (or,
> putting it another way, the new net expansion = that financed by the new money *minus* the
> contraction elsewhere); and (b) by the saving of those receiving additional incomes (Harrod to
> Robertson, 5 July 1938, letter 79).

Robertson answered by asking Harrod to re-read a note on p. 126 of Robertson's
review of *The Trade Cycle* (Robertson, 1937a) and p. 430 of his contribution
to the debate on the "Alternative Theories of the Rate of Interest" (1937b), and
commented:

> It seems to me quite misleading to say that the borrower's demand for funds is "met by" the ex
> post savings of those into whose hands the money passes when the loan is spent: it is "met by"
> the lender & by no one else!
>   Keynes appears to me, by his rediscovery of what he is pleased to call "finance", to have
> surrendered, without realising it, the untenable position which you have all taken up in this
> matter (letter 80 of 23 July 1938).

Harrod took up the issue on finance by denying

> that the requirement for finance in advance constitutes a demand for saving. (Perhaps you dont
> contend it does). I put it this way. If the demand is a demand for saving, and if the demand is
> met, and presumably it is met, since the entrepreneur gets his funds, saving must have occurred.
> But until the entrepreneur's enterprise goes into bricks and mortar, no saving does occur. *In
> advance*, no additional capital comes into existence, or, to put it in another way, no additional
> gap between income and consumption occurs. To suppose that it did would appear to me to be
> embracing the old Wages Fund theory in one of its fallacious forms. Therefore if his demand
> is met, and no saving has occurred, his demand cannot have been a demand for saving. I plead
> for agreement so far.
>   When the bricks and mortar come into being, then undoubtedly saving occurs. This saving
> is fully covered in the way I describe in my letter [the passage is cited above]. Might a quarrel
> arise here on the question of forced lacking? I dont think it need. I dont wish to deny the truth
> of a number of propositions in the Banking Policy [Robertson, 1926]. I would only plead that
> it is only a part of the truth, each part having its importance in relation to the line of approach
> we find it convenient to adopt at the moment. The other part of the truth is that the new *net*
> investment is wholly covered by the voluntary saving of the new income receivers. I dont think
> this can be said to be misleading simpliciter, since it is undoubtedly true. Can you find any fault
> in the argument? (Harrod to Robertson, 3 August 1938, letter 81).

Robertson answered by stressing that the loanable funds and the liquidity preference approaches provide alternative explanations of interest:

Let us remember what the question at issue is. It is not whether the acts of individual money saving (defined in a certain way) performed during a certain slice of time add up to the same total as the acts of "investment" performed during the same slice of time, – defined in a certain way. They do. It is what are the forces tending in a certain slice of time to raise or lower the rate of interest. I have not denied (see later in my paper [Robertson, 1938, pp. 14–15]) that these forces can be expressed in terms of a demand for a stock of money to hold for various purposes and of a supply of money in the sense of the stock of money permitted by the banks to be in existence. I have merely asserted that it can *also* (and to the plain City man and schoolboy more intelligibly) be expressed in terms of a demand for and supply of loans. The two routes are *alternative*, not mutually exclusive. If we adopt the latter, it is the loan made by the bank which tends to lower the rate of interest, not the act of money saving (in your sense) which eventuated from the fact that, so soon as the loan is spent, somebody's money income is increased. That fact in itself does nothing whatever to ease the pressure on the capital market (what may happen later, owing to the increase and redistribution of real income, is another matter): the easing has already been effected by the willingness of the bank to lend (Robertson to Harrod, 11 August 1938, letter 82).

In parallel to this discussion on "finance," another topic in Robertson's "Survey of Modern Monetary Controversy" caught Harrod's attention. Robertson's discussion of the different attitudes towards the process of economic expansion that one can detect in the literature "unduly excited" Harrod, as he was about to compose his "Essay in Dynamic Theory"[46] and had in mind "a satisfactory formulation of the problem of a 'normal' increase in terms of a law of growth – a fundamental equation governing the normal rate of growth" (letter 79 of 5 July 1938). Robertson assured his sympathy for such a project, and pointed out that his

two fundamental objections to the neo-Keynesian analysis have always been:

(1) its substitution of comparative statics for true dynamics in the treatment of short period situations, which I regard as *reactionary*;
(2) Its complete and unnecessary throwing overboard of the whole notion of long-period or normal, which I regard as *unduly revolutionary* (letter 80 of 23 July 1938).

Harrod agreed with Robertson as to the static character of the *General Theory*, and reiterated his attack on the time-lag theories of the cycle:

orthodox static theory [. . .] does not give us all we want in the way of a framework of explanation of phenomena *before* we begin to play about with lags. In the end we have got to face the questions of lags. But we can only do so profitably if we are sure that we are using lag hypotheses in a framework of concepts which does justice to the forces determining normal equilibrium or normal trend. I dont think we are yet in that position. I think J. M. K. is right to suppose that we need a further clearing up of the general theory, but he has not gone far enough.

This passage shows, again, that Harrod failed to understand Robertson's methodological reasons for the adoption of a period analysis, and opposed to this his own – methodological – objection to the identification of lags as the primary cause of the cycle.

As to the long-period normal, Harrod expressed the concern that Robertson was still thinking in terms of "successive adjustments to a long period static equilibrium" and that he meant the Marshallian long-period (letter 81 to Robertson, 3 August 1938). Robertson closed the exchange by specifying that he did not profess to be clear what Marshall's 'normal' was, although he disagreed that it was static ("I think he conceived of capital growth and population growth as 'normal' "), and by launching a further attack on the neo-Keynesian approach:

> I do not wish to decry the study of short-period equilibrium situations, which I agree are a necessary half-way house to dynamics, – only to deprecate the tendency to mistake them for the study of dynamics (Robertson to Harrod, 11 August 1938, letter 82).

11. *INTERNATIONAL ECONOMICS*, SECOND EDITION

In September 1938, Harrod began revising *International Economics* (1939c), and submitted to Robertson his preliminary ideas. The brief exchange (three letters, from Harrod on 5 September and from Robertson on 25 September and 4 October) is not particularly interesting, except for Robertson's appreciation of Harrod's "gallant rehabilitation of comp[arative] cost" (letter 84 of 25 September).

Robertson took up Harrod's book again in February 1945. The discussion which followed (14 letters, numbers 87 to 100, eight being written by Harrod, two of which are commented upon by Robertson on the same sheet, dated from 1 February to 14 June 1945) soon focused on one of the issues raised by Robertson, concerning the working of the foreign trade multiplier:

> Accepting the multiplier mechanism, I do not think your attempted distinction between the effect of a change in exports and a change in the foreign balance is valid. As I showed in E. J. 1939, p. 354, provided the propensity to consume is taken as constant, it makes no difference whether you put the import factor into the multiplier or into the 'base' (letter 87 of 1 February 1945; reference is to Robertson, 1939).

This is the same bone of contention which divided Harrod and Keynes in 1937 (as discussed by Robertson himself in a note sent to Harrod in February 1937 and later elaborated into the article referred to in a passage cited in Section 2). In correspondence with Keynes, Robertson described the point "on which Harrod has always insisted" as follows: accepting, "for the sake of argument," the multiplier method and its implication, "the level of income does not depend on what happens to the balance of payments on economic account, but on what happens to: (a) the credit side of that balance ("exports"); (b) the proportion of income spent on home-produced goods" (Robertson to Keynes, 28 January 1937). In his reply (letter 88 of 8 February 1945), Harrod blamed Keynes for having lumped "the favorable balance into investment,"[47] and explained that "the causal factor (on activity) is the change in the volume of exports and the favorable balance is the effect. An increase of exports is always good for employment; an increase in the favorable balance may or may not be," for in a country with a high propensity to import an increase of exports would generate employment but also an increase of imports, and turn a favourable balance into an unfavourable one. This argument made Harrod's point clear to Robertson, but failed to convince him:

> I doubt if your argument can stand. For, *on the assumption of a fixed propensity to consume,*[48] so that, e.g. if we cannot get foreign bananas we spend the money on buying tomatoes from one another, I do not see why the stimulus given to home industries by a curtailment of imports should not generate as much secondary investment as the stimulus given by an expansion of exports. Are you not implicitly slipping into your argument the proposition (for which I personally think there is a good deal to be said) that the propensity to consume must *not* be taken as fixed, but is liable to be reduced if customary avenues of consumption are closed? (letter 89 of 11 February 1945).

The correspondence continued on other points; Harrod, however, took up the matter again on 3 April (letter 94), probably answering to a letter from Robertson no longer extant, and elaborated his case in much detail, considering in turn the cases of the marginal propensity to save out of the new income generated, directly and indirectly, by the exports being positive or non-positive. If the latter, extra exports would give new employment and cause the external balance to be less positive, or more negative, or unchanged if the marginal propensity to save was zero. If the marginal propensity to save was most likely positive:

> all depends on whether extra exports call for extra capital outlay. It is surely not improbable that they will. If they do, there may be extra employment without the balance becoming more positive. If they do not, then I grant you that the balance will become more pos.
> But it is logically incorrect to say that the extra employment is due to the pos. balance. The extra employment is due to the extra exports and will occur (the measure of it depending on the marg. prop. to save, as well as of course on the marg. prop. to import) whether the balance becomes more pos. or not.

Thus:

> According to the multiplier method, what gives employment is earning income by producing goods which do not come into the market as consumer goods. On the one hand the production of home capital goods does this. On the other the production of exports does it. It is exports as a whole (not the balance) which is the true analogue of home investment.
> [...] What is more, the greater the pos. balance caused by the exports, the less the extra employment due to the exports, so that the positive balance way of stating the matter definitely contains suggestio falsi.

Harrod kept pressing on this point in another letter (95) also dated 3 April. In view of "the un-symmetrical nature of home investment & foreign balance as generator of employment," he tackled the opposite case where employment depends on the total volume of exports plus the balance of home investment over saving by a *reductio ad absurdum*.

Robertson, to whom the whole method seemed "full of pitfalls," suggested that Harrod's argument should be debated publicly with someone more multiplier-minded than himself, and summed up as follows:

> there are two elements in your position. (1) is the old point to which I drew attention on p. 354 of E. J. 1939, – on your method the marginal propensity to import is explicitly revealed as a determinant, on Keynes's it is wrapped up in the balance of payments. I think I would agree that, logically and aesthetically, your method is the superior. (2) is your point that an increase in exports may be expected to lead to an increase in home investment. True, but so may all sorts of other things that occur during the sequence of events set in motion by any initial change. The difficulty is to reduce these various forces acting (positively or negatively) on investment to any kind of equational system; that, presumably, is what your forthcoming work on Dynamic Theory is going to achieve (letter 96 of 22 April 1945).

Nothing seems to have come out of the suggestion of a public debate: Harrod toyed for a while with the idea (letter 97 of 25 April), Robertson suggested *Economica* or the *Review of Economic Studies* as a possible outlet (letter 98 of 28 April) and eventually returned to Harrod all the correspondence, in case he decided to write about this. Harrod's bibliography, however, does not report any such debate.

12. HARROD'S DELUSION ON DYNAMICS

Robertson's reference to Harrod's forthcoming Dynamic Theory concludes a small exchange, carried out in parallel with the topic referred to in the previous section, in which Harrod gave vent to his feeling regarding the reception of his dynamics. There had already been a hint of his disappointment after publication of *The Trade Cycle*:

> I may say that in spite of a number of fingerposts in my book pointing at these dynamic determinants, no review that I have seen has paid any attention to them. I have no doubt it is my fault for being too cryptic (Harrod to Robertson, 8 October 1937, letter 74).

The publication of the "Essay in Dynamic Theory" in March 1939 did not raise much dust. It is interesting to note that Harrod's disappointment at this point did not regard any of his particular propositions, but his very *notion* of dynamics:

> I have been burbling for some time here and there in various things I have published for the need of dynamic economics. Yet no one takes the slightest notice of it. I see that this is going to become a grievance and I a nuisance. People seem to think that dynamics should be concerned with the transition from one static equilibrium to another[49] or with expectations or uncertainties. There is much written about this. That is all that Hicks deals with in his big book.[50] *I say that*

this isn't dynamics at all. And no one ever mentions what I call dynamics. We say this and that determines that a million tons of wheat or two hundred million tons of coal are produced p.a. at such and such equilibrium price. I want a system (and I believe it would be quite easy to get it) in which one determined that wheat production would increase steadily by 1%. That would be a genuine parallel to the velocities and accelerations that are the subject of dynamics in any school primer on mechanics, while statics deals with the forces acting on a particle at rest (+ constant price, constant output p.a.). We cannot get a proper theory of investment until the whole business of production, distribution and foreign trade is dealt with in terms of dynamic laws (letter 90 to Robertson, 11 March 1945).

Robertson agreed that Harrod's "sense of the word 'dynamic' is the most natural one to start with," but suggested that Marshall and Cassel were doing dynamics in Harrod's sense and concluded somewhat pessimistically:

But how far, once one departs from the simple assumptions of 'steady progress', there is a hope of discovering the laws of such a system I do not know. The 'multiplier' seems to me wobbly enough as a sheet-anchor, but the 'principle of acceleration' is worse. I am not optimistic about the claims of economics to be a real science (Robertson to Harrod, 15 March 1945, letter 92).

Harrod specified that he did not regard the multiplier as dynamic anyway, as it does not involve rates of growth; as to Cassel and Marshall, he expressed the belief that "both only touch the problem," while instead "the classics were full of dynamics," with reference to Ricardo's tendency of rent to rise and profits to fall.[51] He concluded:

I am afraid my dynamics wouldnt be very scientific in the proper sense. I am still thinking rather in terms of a geometry, of a system of relations which can be defined by pure thought. I am not altogether pessimistic about the Tinbergen type of empiricism, but that is beyond me. What I have in mind is something much simpler. I shall evidently have to try to get it down on paper and I shall trouble you – burden you – with my questions (Harrod to Robertson, 20 March 1945, letter 93).

These passages are important for the reconstruction of the history of Harrod's reaction to the interpretations of his dynamics. They are, in fact, the first expression of his disappointment. This was mellowed after the publication of *Towards a Dynamic Economics* (1948, composed in autumn 1946) and the consequent popularity of Harrod's growth rates equations.

After a few years of debates on these topics, however, he realised that the scholarly interpretation of his writings focused on the multiplier-acceleration mechanism and on the stability of the growth rate depicted by his "fundamental equation," which was reconstructed in terms of functional equations and interpreted as describing a *path* rather than an instantaneous equilibrium state. Again, he complained about the neglect of his proposed notion of dynamics as opposed to the "time-lag theories of the cycle," namely, the notion propounded by Ragnar Frisch in 1933 and widely adopted by the mainstream approach to dynamics.

Harrod's grievances are thus much older than it would seem at first glance, indicating that he was consistent in caring more for the conceptual apparatus than for the specific propositions which, needless to say, enjoyed wide recognition.[52]

The decade-long debate between Harrod and Robertson on the appropriate method of dynamic analysis thus ended with an ironic twist: both insisted less on their analytical propositions than on the methodological aspect of their research, but they reached neither agreement nor, probably, mutual understanding on this point: Robertson's method implied the parcelling of time into discrete periods while Harrod's method brought him to consider a time-section and thus to confine himself to a single instant.

13. HARROD EDITOR OF THE *ECONOMIC JOURNAL*, AND ROBERTSON'S CONTRIBUTIONS

Harrod succeeded Keynes as Editor of the *Economic Journal* in 1945 and remained in charge until 1961. He therefore dealt with papers submitted for publication, on which he often commented. The related correspondence is held in the Royal Economic Society archives, where 37 letters and notes from Robertson to Harrod and 10 letters from Harrod to Robertson are preserved. Most of these letters regard purely editorial or organizational matters (i.e. proof corrections, revisions of articles, publication or submission dates, and the sending, or failure to send, offprints).

Some letters, however, reveal the amount of trouble behind the writing or the revising of some pieces. For instance, Robertson felt rather uneasy about writing the obituary of Hubert Henderson[53] (Robertson, 1953) after the special issue of *Oxford Economic Papers* pulished earlier in the same year, and proposed that a critical appraisal of Henderson's work would be more suitable on the occasion of the imminent publication of his papers (Henderson, 1955; Robertson to Harrod, 13 August 1953, letter 146). Harrod managed to convince Robertson that not many of the *Jounal*'s subscribers would have read the *OEP* Henderson issue (Harrod to Robertson, letter 147 of 17 August 1953), and eventually Robertson produced an "admirable [. . .], well-balanced and beautifully expressed" notice (Harrod to Robertson, letter 150, 5 October 1953).

Robertson's article on "Utility and All What?" was also somehow troubled. Originally read as a paper before the Sheffield University Economic Society on 27 February 1954, Robertson submitted it to the *Economic Journal* on 8 March (letter 153) explaining that he wanted to retain the form of oral presentation and expounding some problems relating to permission to cite from unpublished writings. The latter were eventually solved, but Harrod brought to Robertson's attention two other writings on the subject, Tyskynski (1955) and Ellsberg (1954). Robertson felt that the former had nothing to say except that, as Robertson himself had already pointed out, "a cardinal measurement of utility requires an arbitrary starting-point for the scale as well as an arbitrary unit of measurement." But Ellsberg's

> formidable article [...] does say something, viz. that Morg[enstern]. and Neu[mann] aren't saying what they seem to be saying, and ⟨even⟩ sometimes say that they aren't saying what they seem to be saying. But they still seem to me to be saying something very like what they seem to be saying, and I may add a note to say this![54] (Robertson to Harrod, 18 April 1954, letter 155).

The article was published in December (Robertson, 1954b), but gave rise to a debate with Friedman the public outcome of which were a reply by Friedman (1955) and a rejoinder by Robertson (1955a) but was preceded by a number of letters to the Editor (letters 165, 167, 168, 169 and 170 of 22 April, 7 May, 25 May, and 6 June 1955).

Another contribution by Robertson that gave rise to prolonged exchanges was a note (Robertson, 1955b) on de Jong's (1954) and Hawtrey's (1954) articles on supply functions in Keynesian economics, extending the comment to Dillard and Hansen's expositions of the *General Theory*. The note, interpreting the role of the supply function in Keynes's scheme and rejecting its reduction to a tautology by means of its representation as a 45° line, was submitted on 31 December 1954 (letter 161). Harrod accepted it on 22 February 1955 (letter 162), as "the Editors always welcome any contribution from you,"[55] but confessed he had not learned much from it, neither on Keynes or on economics in general, or on what the problem was. He asked Robertson to add a footnote on his regarding the notion of 'involuntary employment' as serviceable and important, and commented – citing p. 43 of the *General Theory* – that Keynes did not intend to deal in real aggregates. Robertson obligingly inserted the footnote (Robertson, 1955b, p. 477n), but insisted that in the passages under examination (*General Theory*, pp. 25–30) Keynes had, as a matter of fact, dealt in terms of aggregate real output: "*D* and *Z* are quite clearly the aggregate demand price and aggregate supply price of aggregate real output" (Robertson to Harrod, 14 March 1955, letter 164). He found Harrod's criticism "disturbing" as it implied, in spite of the kind phraseology, that Robertson's "Rabbinics"[56] was "valueless." Yet, in view of his "connection with it from the start," Robertson felt "specially qualified" for the task, which is an important one for

> in these pages of the General Theory, is what purports to be a summary in a nutshell of the argument of what has turned out to be a most important and influential book. Yet the early expositors ignored it completely; later expositors – Hansen, Dillard, de Jong himself – have all, if I am right, slipped up on one point or another: and Hawtrey's prolix contribution in the Dec. Journal has, if I may venture to say so, only added to the confusion. I do think there is a good deal more to be said, and, with all respect, that I have said some of it (Robertson to Harrod, letter 163, 6 March 1955).[57]

Robertson's note induced de Jong to rejoin (de Jong, 1955), but his reply "leaves a good deal to say." He therefore wrote a second note which was sent round to Dillard, Hansen and some others including Harrod for comments. Robertson insisted that Harrod should give his opinion on this issue:

> I know you think all this quite uninteresting and valueless, but I venture to suggest you have no right to do so! As one of the people who claim to know what Keynes meant, you *ought* to mind if these popolarisers are getting the thing wrong with their $45°$ lines: you ought to tell us what you make of the ⟨mysterious⟩ passage marked in pencil on p. 476 of my first instalment; and, in view of n. 1 inserted at your request on p. 477 you *ought* to tell us what you think of the subject-matter of my note 2 on same page! (Robertson to Harrod, letter 173, 25 October 1955).

Harrod replied explaining that he had a note from Hawtrey saying that Robertson's note on de Jong "cries out for an answer," explained that Robertson would be sent the galleys of Hawtrey's reply (Hawtrey, 1956) in order to compose a cumulative rejoinder (Robertson, 1956), and that de Jong would have the final word (de Jong, 1956). Harrod declined to enter the debate: "How can you expect me during the course of this battle of giants to give a verdict on your particular proposition?" (Harrod to Robertson, 9 November 1955, letter 174). After a few more letters, galley proofs and revisions,[58] Robertson unsuccessfully tried again to extort Harrod's judgement on this affair:

> You will not think me, I hope, too malicious if I say that I hope to see in the September Journal an authoritative pronouncement on the question at issue from the person who claims to have understood this apparatus (*Life* [Harrod, 1951a], p. 453 top) when others showed that they had failed to do so (*ibid*. p. 452)! (letter 179 to Harrod, 8 February 1956).

14. THE LAST EXCHANGE: BLISS

The last documented exchange between Harrod and Robertson[59] took place in July and August 1960. It was occasioned by Harrod's "Second Essay in Dynamic Theory" (Harrod, 1960a), about which Robertson wrote some notes "to clear my thoughts, and [. . .] not, for the moment at least, submitted as a candidate for publication" (Robertson to Harrod, letter 188, 28 July 1960). Robertson's paper is not extant, but his comments to Harrod reveal where his problem lay:

> I just can't see how the different bits of your system – whether we suppress *?* forcibly or whether we don't – tie up together. It seems to me there must be some general theory of production and distribution in the background which hasn't been discolsed (*ibid*.).[60]

The resulting exchange, in spite of the missing documents, remains nonetheless interesting, as Robertson raised two problems which do not seem to have been taken up in the secondary literature.

One concerned the nature of the natural rate of growth of which, in Robertson's view, an unequivocal definition was not given in Harrod's article. Harrod, in fact, takes the natural rate as a welfare optimum. But, due to the diminishing utility of consumption, the welfare optimum rate could, on occasions (Robertson refers to Harrod's § 30, p. 287), be lower than the maximum rate of growth of output physically maintainable. Robertson therefore wonders whether the corresponding optimum rate should be re-defined as "the maximum rate which is compatible both with the rate of technical progress and with the physical requirements of enlightened [. . .] Harrodian man" (letter 191 to Harrod, 15 August 1960). Harrod seems to have answered this question (Robertson to Harrod, 20 August 1960, letter 193), but the letter is no longer extant. We are more fortunate with Robertson's other query, the answer to which survives as Robertson sent Harrod's letter back to the sender (Robertson to Harrod, 1 September 1960, letter 194).

Harrod's reply to Robertson's note focused on one of the formulas, which Harrod could not accept as it was inconsistent with his own assumptions. He concluded that Robertson had let his "mind stray right away from the content of my article" (Harrod to Robertson, letter 189, 6 August 1960). Robertson recognised this: "Naturally I did – I let it stray to Ramsey," for Harrod himself acknowledged the influence of Ramsey (1928) on his equation of the rate of interest appropriate to a welfare optimum rate of growth (Harrod, 1960a, p. 281). Robertson thus asked himself "How then does Harrod reach such a very different result from Ramsey about the proportion of income saved?"

> One explanation that suggests itself is that Ramsey is ignoring 'the probability that future inventions and improvements in organization are likely to make income obtainable with less sacrifice than at present' (op. cit. [Ramsey, 1928] p. 549); whereas you are definitely dealing with technical advance. This raises the whole question of the nature of this 'rate of technical advance' whose assumed constancy is solely responsible (in the case of stationary population) for the assumed constant natural rate of growth of output. By some people, e.g. by Reddaway in his statistical study in the March 1960 Journal, this 'rate of technical advance' is treated as a residual, remaining after all the influence of all capital-growth on output has been sweated out. But in your treatment technical advance is completely non-operative on output unless it is "moulded" or "supported" by appropriate capital-growth. Harrodian man, unlike Ramseyan man, won't get his technical progress unless he saves for it; prima facie therefore one would expect him to save an even greater proportion of his income than Ramseyan man! So there must be some other explanation (letter 190 to Harrod, 13 August 1960).

Harrod agreed that Robertson interpreted the problem correctly. In Harrod's view, Ramsey "is thinking of a bliss obtainable from the mere accumulation of capital," ignoring technological progress. In such conditions, in order to maximise utility it is sensible to spread savings over a number of years. Accordingly, Ramsey's problem was: "What is the optimal number of years over which to spread the saving? When one approaches the problem in this way, such questions as one's attitude to one's heirs and the value one puts on future pleasures, comes into the forefront of the picture." Harrod tackled instead the problem under a different assumption:

> bliss certainly cannot be obtained by saving alone, and [. . .] the speed with which bliss is obtained can only be accelerated in some degree by a willingness to save. Far more important, in my judgment, are the progress of science, technology and the general level of education, and the incidence of incentives to work and enterprise. If we suppose that there is no progress in science etc., and only a weak incentive to enterprise, then I suggest that more saving, put it as high as you like, will only take us on the road to bliss at a very slow pace indeed, and may eventually fail to advance us at all.
>
> If one supposes that bliss is obtainable by saving only, and then proceeds to eliminate all time preference [. . .], then one may find that utility is maximised by a very high rate of saving.[61] But if one regards the path to bliss as determined mainly by the progress of science, etc., then the problem is entirely transformed. One wants as much saving as will finance the new equipment that is suggested by the progress of technology and to support such labour as is released by this new equipment with other equipment. But, given that we cannot expect an increase of output per caput, of more than 5% [. . .] the amount of saving that can be fruitfully employed is strictly limited. I am not denying that in this country we might do well with more saving than we are currently making.
>
> It is because one is thinking of a maximum rate of progress achievable through advancing technology, that the whole question of our attitude to our heirs or remote descendants becomes irrelevant. To my mind the Ramsey analysis of bliss is in terms of the longest of Marshall's long periods. Whereas I would claim without in any way derogating from the importance of the Marshallian concept, that we get a new approach to the problem of thinking in "dynamic" terms, that is in terms of rates of progress currently achieved or achievable (Harrod to Robertson, letter 192 of 17 August 1960).

15. PERSONAL RELATIONSHIPS WITH KEYNES, AND HARROD'S BIOGRAPHY

It is well known that Robertson's relationship with Keynes and his pupils in Cambridge deteriorated after the publication of the *Treatise* and even more after *The General Theory*. Of this, there are numerous signs in the correspondence with Harrod, who was also not satisfied with Keynes's attitude towards the "classics." Robertson therefore found in Harrod a sympathetic listener.

The first signs of uneasiness on Robertson's part emerged early in 1933: "I also, to say truth, find JMK pretty consumptive nowadays to anything that isn't in his own Gedankengang" (Robertson to Harrod, 14 January 1933, letter 25). At first, Robertson seemed to attribute his difficulties with Keynes's economics to his own dislike of Keynes's attitude towards the "classics":

> I am quite conscious that my regret at his snooks at the "classics" (which seem to include everyone from Say to Pigou) and at the very high claims he is making (I just don't believe economic truth is like that!) constitute psychological obstacles to my judging it on its merits:

> I *try* to discount that, and remain unconvinced that anything "path-breaking" has happened. It is all, entre nous, very painful to me, personally as well as professionally (Robertson to Harrod, letter 39, 5 October 1935).

Harrod replied that, although he was a "convert," he shared Robertson's feelings about the violence of Keynes's criticism: "I have attacked him for them,[62] but have only succeeded in getting the most offending chapter printed in smaller type as an appendix. I regret them, I feel they will raise un-necessary dust – but there it is, that is his way" (Harrod to Robertson, letter 49 of 7 October 1935).

As Harrod was planning to write "a posh article on J. M. K.'s book"[63] with the ambition "to trace the development of his thought from certain origins in [Robertson]" and to show how Keynes's pieces were nothing but a re-arrangement of ingredients already to be found in traditional economics (Harrod to Robertson, 11 November 1935, letter 44), Robertson summarised the whole position:

> I am most anxious that in your dogmengeschichte when it appears you should not overstress JMK's obligations to me. He has always been most generous in his acknowledgments (see preface to Treatise): & I in return avow that a good deal of the central point of BP & PL was his, – including the "induced lacking" which was the germ of what seems to me sound in his later developments. It is the most painful part of this whole position that my attempts to show that the new doctrines are largely a re-statement of old truths are apt to seem like assertions of my own priority. And one is tempted at times to self-assertiveness, – not so much against JMK himself as against his enthusiastic young disciples, who have never thought of these things till the last 2 years, and to whom the whole thing seems a brand-new revelation straight from heaven! But the real point is not a personal one to me, – it is the spiritual necessity which JMK seems to be under to disparage all previous work in these fields and to resent any attempt to show the affinity between some of his concepts and conclusions and those of previous writers, – it is a greater crime to reach agreement with him by other lines of thought than to differ from him!
>
> So please go carefully, & in such wise as not to make a difficult situation worse! (Robertson to Harrod, undated November 1935, letter 45).

Later Robertson explained that a "widespread campaign of proselytisation" was taking place in Cambridge, and that he found "the whole situation very saddening and completely inhibiting" (Robertson to Harrod, 22 July 1936, letter 58):

> Meanwhile, I hope you will feel as charitably as you can towards our "irritation". It *is* irritating to be misrepresented as Pigou was misrepresented, or to be regarded (as I am) as a victim of premature arterio-sclerosis. But I think you must credit us also with some deeper feelings of more or less disinterested regret and anxiety about the effect of all this (at all events temporarily) on economic education, on the reputation of economics with the outside world, on public policy. No doubt you will say all this is worth while if a real advance has been achieved in theory, and the ground laid for a real advance in practice. You are fortunate enough to believe it has, and I unlucky enough to be sceptical! (Robertson to Harrod, 28 October 1936, letter 59).

It is interesting to note that Harrod eventually changed his evaluation of Keynes's criticism of the classics: having found a deep-seated flaw in Robertson's argument,[64] he expressed the feeling "that Maynard's pother is to some extent justified – tho' as I think I have repeatedly said I sympathize with you in deploring his manner of emphasizing that and his needless polemics"[65] (Harrod to Robertson, letter 63 of 25 December 1936).

Robertson's uneasy feelings regarding his personal and intellectual relationship with Keynes emerged with more strength after Maynard's death. In a letter reacting to a draft of Austin Robinson's obituary of Keynes (Robinson, 1947), Robertson gave vent to his puzzlement that, after the publication of the *Treatise on Money*, Keynes had to be reminded by the Cambridge Circus of the relationship between the theory of money and the analysis of output, and gave detailed reference to his own writings where the analysis was conducted in terms of output, employment, consumption and investment (Robertson, 1915, 1922, 1923, 1926). Robertson's letter to Robinson (dated 2 January 1947) was later forwarded to Harrod, who had by then been appointed official biographer of Keynes, "so that RFH does not fall into the same pitfalls as I" (note to Robertson by E. A. G. Robinson, undated; Robertson to Harrod, 12 and 15 October 1947, letters 112 and 113).

After this preliminary exchange, Harrod's correspondence with Robertson on *The Life of Keynes* resumes in 1949. The first exchange (letters 117 to 120, between 1 and 10 June 1949) is rather innocuous, as it regards the "expurgated" citation of a passage from one of Robertson's letters to Keynes. On 30 June (letter 121), however, Robertson gave a first answer to Harrod's request of help (in letter 117 of 1 June 1949) for briefly stating the grounds of Robertson's doctrinal differences with Keynes, which consisted in a list of his relevant writings (those marked with * and °) in the subject:

On the Treatise on Money
"Mr. Keynes's Theory of money", E. J. Sept. 1931. (I have also an important reply to Keynes' Rejoinder).

"A note on the Theory of Money", *Economica* Aug. 1933. Reprinted as No. VI of Essays in Monetary Theory.

Further comments are contained in "Saving and Hoarding", E. J. Sept. 1933, reprinted as No. IV of EMT, see esp. pp. 79–81.

On the General Theory and Keynes's supplementary articles
"Some notes on Mr. Keynes's General Theory of Employment", QJE Nov. 1936.

"Alternative theories of the rate of Interest", E. J. Sept. 1937

"Mr. Keynes and Finance", E. J. June 1938

[Here again there is an unpublished reply to Keynes' Rejoinder, – suppressed for lack of space in favour of a short note; E. J. Sept. 1938]

*"Mr. Keynes and the Rate of Interest", No. I of Essays in Monetary Theory, 1940.

*"Effective demand and the Multiplier", No. IX of the same book.

Further comments are contained in Money, 1948 edition, Ch. X and in °New preface to 1948 reprint of A Study of Industrial Fluctuations pp. xii–xvii.[66]

Robertson commented that Keynes was so immersed in his train of thought that he could not appreciate that other people – Ohlin, Haberler and himself – were reaching similar conclusions regarding interest rates using different apparatuses of thought, and was psychologically driven to suppose that they were making muddles of which they were not guilty (Robertson to Harrod, 30 June 1949, letter 121).

A few weeks later Robertson raised a similar charge, but with respect to the claim that Keynes made a revolutionary discovery in emphasizing the relationship of money and output, both in print and in correspondence with Harrod. In August 1949, Robertson was writing a new preface to *Banking Policy and the Price Level* for the Staples and Kelly reprint (Robertson, 1949). He sent Harrod a draft on 5 September 1949 (letter 125), commenting that he was dragged into this "posthumous controversy" by "the Faithful," that is, the Robinsons, especially Joan, and Kahn.

Harrod's comment are not extant, but led Robertson to revise some passages (in particular the last paragraph of the footnote to p. xii) and to comment as follows (with reference to p. xiii):

> What was claimed as being the great change from the Treatise was the connexion of Money Theory with a Theory of Output. I must try you to re-read J.V.R[obinson]'s article on "The Theory of Money and the Analysis of Output" in Review of Economic Studies, 1933–1934, pp. 22 ff. Stanley Dennison confirms having heard her lecture on the same lines, and of being a good deal puzzled, since he had always supposed that all trade cycle theory had been a theory of changes in output! And I have heard her talk on the same lines at a gathering of research students since the war.
>
> You may say that all this is JVR not JMK, and of course that is always the difficulty. But surely he must have known and approved, and surely his own preface to GTE is much on the same lines. And of course there is this truth in it, that in the formal system of the GTE, O (or something like it) appears as the determinand and P (as fixed by the Trade Unions and operating through liquidity-preference-in-the-hard-sense) as one of the determinants. I am much more sceptical, probably, than you as to whether this was really an advance; but granted that it was, it was quite ridiculous to represent this technical fact as a revolutionary change of outlook, and if I'm going to write this preface at all (as I now must) I do feel entitled to strike a blow for myself and Pigou (I have put in a reference to Ind. Fluc., which appeared in 1927) and all the other people who for years had been trying to apply monetary theory to the behaviour of output. So I can't compromise further than to substitute "or at least" for "and" at the point in question,[67] on the ground that JMK's own article, in spite of his preface, may have been in this respect less extravagant than that of the disciples. But I don't think it was, – really I don't.
>
> Do look up the reference to Marget on all this when you have time (Robertson to Harrod, letter 126 of 19 September 1949).

Reference is to Marget's *Theory of Prices* (1942), Vol. 2, pp. 82–83 and 522–524. Robertson had already referred Harrod to Marget's interpretation of the relationship of Robertson's writings with Keynes and his Cambridge followers. In a letter accompanying a review of his *Essays in Monetary Theory*, Robertson wrote:

"Prosy old bore as the author is, I am naturally grateful to him for having said, at the top of p. 148 col. 2 and again in the footnote on 149, just what I should like some future historian of ideas to say about the relation of my work to JMK's" (Robertson to Harrod, letter 109 of 23 July 1946). The piece seems to be Marget (1941); the corresponding passages run as follows: "in the end more will have been done to establish Mr. Keynes's claim to a position of eminence in the history of economics by writers like Mr. Robertson, who have refused to accept uncritically every latest utterance of Mr. Keynes at the same time that they avow with the utmost frankess their intellectual indebtness to him [. . .] than will have been done by those who preach the Keynesian gospel with greater intolerance and fewer qualifications than Keynes himself" (p. 148). "[I]n a review published in the *Economic Journal* for 1925, Mr. Robertson provided a further example of the way in which a refusal to accept all of Mr. Keynes's own dicta as to the relation of his later to his earlier analysis can result in the establishment of greater claims of gratitude to Mr. Keynes on the part of monetary theorists than have been established by the fulminations of the more extreme Keynesians, with their undiscriminating rejection of everything that appeared in monetary literature prior to the General Theory, including the earlier writings of Mr. Keynes himself" (p. 149n).

Robertson was given a further occasion to express his grievances when Harrod asked Robertson[68] to comment about Abbati's complaints that Keynes failed to acknowledge his contributions. Having specified that he was really

the worst person in the world to assess fairly the grievances of Abbati or of anyone else (such as L. A. Hahn, whose remarks in the *American Economic Review*, March 1945, p. 29, are probably familiar to you[69]) who thinks (as I do) that in the world's eyes, too much credit has gathered round the name of one man for a set of ideas which was evolving simultaneously in many heads. And still more to assess how far the One Man is to be accounted blameworthy for that situation

Robertson offered some comments on the value of Abbati's books (*The Unclaimed Wealth*, 1924, and *The Final Buyer*, 1928) and the following remark on Keynes's rethoric:

But in my heart I do think (though I don't expect you to agree) that Ch. 23 of the General Theory is rather an outrage. If K. was going in for Dogmengeschichte at all at this stage, he had no business to stop short at Mummery and Gesell, thereby giving the impression that apart from a handful of dead cranks he was the first person to question the alleged "classical" hypothesis of an automatically and instantaneously self-righting economy. He ought to have gone on to say something serious and appreciative of the work of his contemporaries, – the Swedes, Haberler, myself; and a repetition of the pat on the back for Abbati would then have been in place. K. found it easier to be generous to cranks than to professional economists, but I think it is not unfair to say that he preferred even his cranks to be dead (Robertson to Harrod, letter 130, 4 April 1950).[70]

When the *Life of Keynes* was finished, Harrod wrote to Robertson anticipating the points of probable disagreement in the evaluation of Keynes's work. The first regarded Harrod's appreciation of Keynes's "welding of monetary theory with the theory of value." The second regarded the evaluation of Keynes's interpretation of the disagreements with his contemporaries. While Robertson had attributed the reasons for the lack of communication in some psychological obstacle which prevented Keynes from recognizing the similitudes with other lines of thought, Harrod thought instead that the difficulty lay in Keynes's contemporaries being unable to grasp the core of Keynes's message, Harrod himself excepted:[71]

> The other point which will displease is one that I bring out very strongly – viz. M's sense from about the time of publication of the Treatise that his old colleagues simply did not understand what he was trying to say. This was a most important element governing his behaviour and the biographer is bound to underline. It was main cause of his truculence in the General Theory which has been so much criticized.
>
> Perhaps if you had had my task you might have concluded that M was wrong in this. I have been through vast bundles of correspondence, including yours & Hawtrey's and mine, prior to the appearance of the G. T., and the result is that my own sense of it going back over the old ground, comparing my letters which were in some respect extremely bullying (but which did show comprehension) with the others, is that the others did not follow the main points M was trying to make. I am sure that if I had had these letters I should have felt the same (Harrod to Robertson, letter 137 of 11 May 1950).

These passages of private, and occasionally intimate, correspondence between the two friends throws some additional light on Robertson's problematic relationship with Keynes, which has sometimes been exaggerated in the literature. It has been suggested, for instance, that Robertson's difficulties with Keynes's economics were "emotional rather than intellectual" (Fletcher, 2000, p. 364 and passim). It should be noted, however, that – at least in the inter-war years – Robertson's and Harrod's grievances with Keynes's manners were not a systematic topic of discussion, but were only mentioned in passing when evoked by the other issues under discussion. After Keynes's death Robertson did indeed express his disappointment, but his double reference to Marget's passages quoted above suggests that his complaints were directed more against Kahn and Joan Robinson than Keynes himself.[72]

Although in the months immediately following the publication of *The General Theory* Robertson seems to have been rather depressed by the situation, his correspondence with Harrod taken as a whole shows that the Robertsonian rejection of Keynes's economics was deeply rooted in a different conception of the movement of economic variables and of the appropriate method for accounting for it. The latter aspect seems to have been overlooked both by contemporaries – including those, such as Harrod, who had the benefit of receiving hundred of pages of correspondence and unpublished papers in Robertson's hand – and by most of later commentators, who either admired or disparaged him for his "rearguard actions"[73] in defence of orthodoxy. But, as Robertson himself wished to stress,[74] his moods were sometimes far from orthodox; and the correspondence with Harrod shows that Robertson's points – whether correct or not – were at any rate very far from vulgar.

NOTES

1. As to Robertson, see the (now out of date) tables published by Mizen, Moggridge and Presley (1997). As to Harrod, the statement is correct so far as economists are concerned; some of his non-economic correspondence, however, is very bulky; for instance, the correspondence with Harold Macmillan (as preserved in the Harrod papers) includes over a hundred items.

2. Robertson described himself as "a great destroyer in the 1920s – more so than in the 1930s and 1940s" (letter 125 to Harrod, 5 September 1949). Professor Moggridge informs me that Robertson's literary executor seems to have played a part in the dispersal of Robertson's papers.

3. See for instance the following comments: "The concluding portions of your letter are full of justice, wisdom and humanity, and I will do my best to let them sink in. For this reason I retain the letter in a safe place, in order to read it again after an interval: and therefore copy out below the paragraph on which I am commenting in (ii) above" (Robertson to Harrod, 16 November 1935, letter 47). And: "I return all of your letters for reference, and in case you ever think the original worth while criticising in print anywhere. If not, I hope you'll keep them or let me have them back sometime, as I should like to refer to them again if ever it comes to a re-writing" (Robertson to Harrod, undated – but May or June 1926, letter 6).

4. The main corpus is kept with the correspondence held at Chiba University of Commerce, Japan; a few items are at the British Library, some in the "Keynes and Harrod – Letters and Memoranda" collection at the University of Tokyo, and a paper by Robertson in the Harrod collection at the Nagoya University of Commerce and Business Administration.

5. Robertson's papers are housed at the Wren Library, Trinity College, Cambridge.
Most of the Harrod-Robertson interwar correspondence is published in full or summarised in *The Collected Interwar Papers and Correspondence of Roy Harrod* (2003), edited by D. Besomi, while as much as possible of the whole run will be included in the forthcoming edition of Robertson's correspondence, edited by D. E. Moggridge (forthcoming). Several excerpts are cited in Young (1989) (with, however, a large number of silent emendations to the original text).

6. Robertson had been appointed by Arthur Loveday, the Director of the Financial Section and Economic Intelligence Service of the League of Nations, as adviser to Tinbergen. Harrod was invited to these meetings on Robertson's suggestion.

7. The first extant letter was Harrod's invitation to Robertson to Oxford, which he could not accept (12 February 1926, letter 1).

8. Abstracting from reviews, of which the 27-year old Oxford economist had already published more than a dozen.

9. Harrod and Meade were surely inspired by Robertson (Meade, having worked for a year in Cambridge under Robertson's guidance, acknowldged his debt to him in the preface of *The Rate of Interest in a Progressive State* and Robertson stressed, in his review

of Meade's book, the importance of Meade's focus on the conditions of equilibrium in a progressive society: Meade, 1933, p. vii, and Robertson, 1933d), Durbin probably was too (Durbin, 1985, pp. 154–155).

10. See, for a survey, Besomi (1998a, pp. 46–48).

11. Robertson's letters are dated 6 April, undated (mid-April 1932), 14 April, 26 April, 24 August, 9 September (mostly concerned with the topic discussed in Section 3), 31 December 1932, and 14 January and 3 April 1933 (letters 14, 16, 17, 19, 20, 22, 24, 25 and 26). Of Harrod's letters, one is undated (approximately mid-April 1932), the others are dated 3 September (mostly concerned, however, with the topic discussed in Section 3) and 13 October 1932 (letters 15, 21 and 23).

12. Unfortunately most of Harrod's correspondence on *International Economics* is one-sided: Keynes did not preserve any of the letters he received from Harrod, nor did Kahn (at the preliminary stage of Harrod's writing).

13. Reference is to Henderson (1922).

14. Refers to Keynes (1933a, b).

15. Robertson to Harrod, 5 April 1933, letter 27. On 1 April, Robertson had expressed the same doubts in a letter to Keynes, reproduced in Keynes, 1971–1989, Vol. XXIX, p. 17.

16. The topic of imperfect competition was briefly discussed again after the publication of Harrod's "important new article" (letter 145 to Harrod, 11 August 1953, with reference to Harrod's "Theory of Imperfect Competition Revised," 1952). Having obtained the requested explanations on some obscure points, Robertson commented: "I wonder whether the protagonists accept your account of their theories. I had always supposed they were both intended to be theories of *long-term* equilibrium using *long-run demand curves*. I've also always supposed that for the generality of cases they tended to greatly to over-estimate the slope of these curves (Austin in E. J. Dec. 1950, p. 773, admits as much and says rather naively it had to be done for printing convenience!) So I think I feel quite sympathetic to your general conclusions. I also like the final pages on ⟨+⟩ or time-requiring increasing returns which are very Marshallian (and very non-Pigovian!); but I should have thought such i. r. *could* be said to be compatible with perfect competition" (letter 149 of 20 September 1953; reference is to Harrod, 1952, pp. 184–186).

17. It should be emphasised that at this point the "progress" considered by Harrod was brought about by an (exogenous) increase in the productivity per head, not yet by the (endogenous) combined action of the multiplier and the acceleration principle. This was only developed towards the end of 1935 (see, for a chronology, Besomi, 1999, Ch. 3).

18. Harrod's critical target was not only Hayek, but the London Hayekians in the New Fabian Research Bureau, namely Durbin and Gaitskell. See Section 2 and, for full context, Besomi (1999, pp. 38–42).

19. This is not to say that Robertson identified his views with Hayek's: in the following letter of the exchange, he stressed that he had "never felt that *on this part of the story* [i.e. the forced savings process] there has been much difference except of language between [his] analysis and H[ayek]'s" (Robertson to Harrod, 4 October 1934, letter 34). The role played by this process in their respective trade cycle theories is a rather different part of the story.

20. Four letters from Harrod are acknowledged in Robertson's replies 34 and 35 of 4 and 6 October 1934, a fifth one gave rise to Robertson's last letter in the exchange dated 19 October (letter 36 which is, however, more concerned with a subject discussed in parallel, namely, an addendum written by Harrod as a complement to the Royal Institute of International Affairs' report on *The Future of Monetary Policy* (1935), in which both Harrod

and Robertson took part. Although this piece was also discussed with Keynes (Harrod to Keynes, 26 October 1934, and Keynes to Harrod, 28 October 1934), the extant evidence is too scant to enable one to make sense of the discussion). Excerpts from Robertson's letters are commented upon, in particular with reference to Harrod and Robertson exchanging their respective pieces before publication in order to tone down their respective languages and set "an example to our elders and betters" – with obvious reference to the Keynes-Sraffa-Hayek debate on the *Treatise* and *Prices and Production* by Warren Young (1989, pp. 76–78). The theoretical implications of the exchange, concerning Harrod's emphasis on the *continuity* of the process of change, are discussed in Besomi (1999, pp. 42–45).

21. Harrod's difficulties in understanding what was going on in the Keynesian field are discussed in detail in Besomi (2000, pp. 358–367).

22. Robertson (1933a). Harrod's difficulties remained: on 11 November 1935 he confessed: "I have been worried by the definition of Saving, which has currency under your name, which makes it the difference between spending in the present period and income in the last. I feel that is a very awkward definition" (letter 44 to Robertson).

23. See the concluding paragraph of Section 2.

24. Harrod had read *The General Theory* in proof during summer 1935: the correspondence with Keynes in published in Keynes, 1971–1989, Vol. XIII, pp. 525–565.

25. This explanation of how the *ex post* equality of saving and investment is maintained, instant after instant, when investment changes via unwanted variations in stocks was not new, but was already expressed by Harrod on 29 February 1935 in correspondence with Haberler.

26. Robertson later discussed this difficulty in "Mr. Keynes and the Rate of Interest" (1940, pp. 5–6).

27. On Harrod's appreciation of the logical positivist tenet and its significance for his dynamic thought see Besomi (1999, pp. 117–126).

28. For a chronology regarding this article see Note 36.

29. Harrod expressed the same view to Haberler, with reference to the same example. Harrod expounded in fact his criticism to Hayek explaining that "He implicitly assumes that we have a stationary society and considers the effect of injecting new credit after a period of stationariness. Whereas I am considering a regularly advancing society. It is the difference between the dynamics of starting a train that has been stationary and the dynamics of the train when in motion at uniform velocity. The two problems are really quite different. I am concerned with the second" (letter to Haberler, 8 September 1934).

30. On the significance and origin of this principle see respectively Besomi, 1999 and 2002.

31. Haberler, *Systematic Analysis of Business Cycle Theories*, mimeograph.

32. While this discussion between Harrod and Robertson on the role of lags in dynamics unfolded, a rather different approach to this issue was taken by the "econometricians," who developed formal models of fluctuating systems in which time-lags played a fundamental part in explaining oscillations. Tinbergen later pointed out that Harrod's lagless multiplier accelerator mechanism is incapable of generating oscillations but only steady advance (Tinbergen, 1937). Tinbergen, however, had couched Harrod's non-formal discussion in terms of a linear equation, while Harrod's approach was intrinsically non-linear due to the systematic changes in his 'dynamic determinants' (see Besomi, 1998b for a discussion). Samuelson later pointed out that oscillations could be produced without having recourse to nonlinearities, provided lags were introduced and appropriate values of the parameters were

assumed (Samuelson, 1939; for a discussion see Besomi, 2003, in particular pp. 317–318). Harrod and Robertson do not seem to have discussed this branch of literature. It is however interesting to remark that Harrod considered Robertson's period analysis as essentially similar to Tinbergen's method, as he wrote to Keynes: "The introduction of a lag into an otherwise smoothly working system may set up an oscillation. Tinbergen reviews a number of theories of this sort in *Econometrica* (1935). Kalecki, Lundberg and others have been working on them. I think it is really only doing systematically and with the help of a sine curve what Dennis does laboriously with his day by day analysis. I take it that the more mathematical part enables one to detect the quantitative implications of one's own theory more easily and with an exactitude that it would be superhumanly laborious to get by the sort of methods Dennis uses" (Harrod to Keynes, 18 September 1938, in Keynes, 1971–1989, Vol. XIV, pp. 304–305).

33. Harrod's book was almost ready for press.

34. A more pertinent comment by Harrod came a few month later: see the passage from letter 63 of 25 December 1936 cited in Section 8.

35. Here lies a fundamental difference between Harrod's and Robertson's understanding of the relationships between individuals and the whole economic system in the trade cycle. In Harrod's view, the main determinants of the cycle (i.e. the influences determining the multiplier and the accelerator during the cycle, together with the instability principle) affect the system as a whole; individual entrepreneurs are compelled to oblige by the effect of these forces on the price level, which transmit the signals inducing them to adjust the level of production (Besomi, 1999, Ch. 4). In Robertson's theory, entrepreneurs are affected in their individual investment decisions by the forces of productivity and thrift, which fluctuate in their own right (i.e. the "justified fluctuations" of *Banking Policy and the Price Level*: 1926, Ch. 2) and are subject to occasional boosts due, e.g. to inventions, increase of population or opening of new markets. The system as a whole is called into play when the banking system forces savings to catch up with investment by supplying credit to entrepreneurs, which induce price changes thereby extorting lacking from consumers and encouraging the public to dishoard (Robertson, 1926, Ch. 5).

36. This article had a long gestation. Harrod announced the intention of writing on the relation of Keynes and orthodox theory shortly after reading the *General Theory* in proofs, and accordingly inquired on the Robertsonian origins of some of Keynes's ideas. This exchange took place in November 1935, and is further discussed in Section 15. A preliminary draft was read before the Oxford Political Economy Club in February 1936, and a revised version was read at the Oxford meeting of the Econometric Society in October 1936. The final version was published in *Econometrica* in February 1937.

37. References are to the following pages in the printed version (Harrod, 1937): pp. 77 top and 86 top; pp. 84–85; p. 85; and p. 80 middle.

38. Robertson later took further exception of such claims of originality: see Section 15.

39. This solution was also propounded in *The Trade Cycle* (Harrod, 1936, pp. 73–74).

40. The correspondence on *The Trade Cycle* confirms that Harrod's book was instrumental in changing Robertson's mind as regards the acceleration principle, about which he was skeptical in his previous writings (Presley, 1978, p. 60). In the first passage about *The Trade Cycle* to be found in the correspondence, Robertson wrote: "Apropos of this whole topic, and of your book, I feel that there is probably an important distinction to be drawn between forms of investment which are closely 'geared' by the 'principle of acceleration' to the demand prices of particular kinds of consumption goods, & those – especially power

and transport in all their numerous forms – which are highly susceptible to invention on the one hand, and dependent on rather vague estimates of ultimate consumers' prosperity on the other. In general I sympathise with your restoration of the principle of acceleration to its proper place in the theory of fluctuation (but if you were handing out bouquets, why not one to Pigou for his extremely clear statement of the case in Ind. Fluc. 1929 ed. Part I, ch. IX): but to elevate it into the position of a dragon which devours all long period thrift seems to me to do it too much honour" (Robertson to Harrod, 23 December 1936, letter 63). This "general sympathy," however, does not imply enthusiastic acceptance of the principle: see the passage from Robertson's letter 92 to Harrod of 15 March 1945 cited in Section 12, and Robertson's later thought on meeting this "important person" (1954a, pp. 181–182).

41. The expression, indicating violations of the truism savings = investment not supported by special definitions of "savings," was used by Harrod in *The Trade Cycle* (1936, p. 68) and criticised by Robertson in his review of the book (Robertson, 1937a, p. 126n).

42. Robertson referred to Haberler (in connection with Lindahl, 1934, of which he enclosed a copy), and to Clark (1934) and Hansen (1936).

43. If I am allowed a personal note, such passages – in which Robertson's correspondence abounds – never fail to impress me with their erudition.

44. Harrod surely had this distinction in mind when he re-defined the term "ex ante" in the "Essay in Dynamic Theory" (Harrod, 1939a, p. 19). The topic was discussed in correspondence with Keynes (1971–1989, Vol. XIV, pp. 322 and 333–337); see, for a comment, Besomi (1996b, pp. 282–283).

45. This challenge of dynamizing the theory of interest was taken up by Harrod much later, in his "Second Essay in Dynamic Theory" (1960a), which indeed took as a point of departure Ramsey's essay. For an account of the corresponding discussion with Robertson see Section 14.

46. Harrod (1939a). Although Harrod announced to Robertson on 3 August 1938 (letter 81) that the "Essay" was in the hands of the typist and hoped Robertson would like it, there is no evidence of a discussion between them on the draft. For a chronology of the drafting and the revision stages see Besomi (1996a).

47. Harrod later interpreted as follows the origin of the problem: "The trouble all arose from the Treatise on Money. There JMK was all in hot on *S* and *I*. He knew that the foreign trade also had something to do with it, but he did not want to go into all that as his own brain was setting with new ideas as regards the home situation. He saw a way of saving himself bother, which was formally correct, by calling the foreign balance a part of *I*. That was all right as a temporary makeshift. But it really meant that he did not look into the causal relation between foreign trade and the home employment. He neglected it (as he may have been justified pro. tem. in doing). There is ample stylistic evidence of this neglect in the book (Harrod to Robertson, 3 April 1945, letter 94).

48. The assumption was clearly stated in Harrod's previous letter (88).

49. This passage is worth comparing with the excerpt, cited on p. 12, written by Robertson more than a decade earlier.

50. Hicks, *Value and Capital* (1939). Half of Harrod's review of Hicks's book is dedicated to the notion of "dynamics" (Harrod, 1939b, pp. 298–300). A later statement, concerning Hicks's *Trade Cycle* (1950) is worth quoting in this connection: "I may say that I like Hicks' book immensely. I have written part of an article (or note) for E. J. on it – not the official review – but there are one or two points where I feel I differ from him which still baffle me and to my irritation I have not succeeded in thinking the matter through in the time

I assigned to the task. Hicks with his mathematical expertise has succeeded in giving a much more polished rendering of the theory than I could ever have achieved" (Harrod to Robertson, 15 April 1950, letter 131. Harrod's piece on Hicks was published as "Notes on Trade Cycle Theory," 1951b).

51. These considerations found their way in *Towards a Dynamic Economics*: Harrod (1948, pp. 15–19).

52. This is not to say that Harrod did not care about the "rather boring question of priorities." His complaints about the marginal revenue curve are well known, for they were repeated on several occasions (see for instance the "egoistic footnote" to pp. 159–160 of Harrod, 1951a, 1967, p. 65n, 1972, p. 394). Harrod expressed similar grievances in correspondence with Robertson: "I am not sure that I havent at least as much ground for grievance – not in connexion with M[aynard] at all, but generally. We had better form a society of anti-refiners! On the marginal revenue curve, the foreign trade multiplier, the interaction of the multiplier and accelerator, which, like it or not, is now widely accepted, and on other points embodied by Hicks with acknowledgements, which while generous – I have no complaints – don't cover the whole ground, I seem to myself to have been in at the birth and get seldom to get mentioned (much less than you) in learned footnotes. I dare say it is my own fault. I have never worked up my stuff enough. In the earlier years I was oppressed by the ⟨cares⟩ of life and now lately I have let myself be distracted by other things, such as writing the Life of M, and also other less academic activities which are not altogether unconnected with being a family man! However that is no matter" (Harrod to Robertson, 15 April 1950). And again: "I have suffered myself in other ⟨fields⟩ from the non-comprehension of others in relation to a radically new idea" (Harrod to Robertson, letter 137 of 11 May 1950).

53. Henderson died in 1952. On 20 August 1951 (letter 142) Robertson asked Harrod's help for his pre-obituary for *The Times*, with respect to Henderson's Oxford career of which he knew practically nothing. Robertson thanked Harrod for his help on 28 August (letter 144).

54. The note on Ellsberg is on p. 675 of Robertson (1954b).

55. On another occasion Harrod wrote that "any article from [Robertson's] distinguished pen should be accepted for the *Economic Journal* without question or any reference to referees" adding, to safeguard his successors, that he thought "that this should apply to so distinguished person as [Robertson] up to the age of 80. After that everyone is liable to go off a little!" (Harrod to Robertson, 6 August 1960, letter 189). Robertson called this a "(. . . reasonable) Free-Entry-for-Ex-Presidents-under-80 rule" (letter 190 of 13 August 1960).

56. Robertson also used the same expression, which recurs three times in the letter under consideration, to characterize "Some Marshallian Concepts" (Robertson, 1959; letter 186 to Harrod of 10 February 1959).

57. As to the highly condensed, "pellety" form of his contribution, Robertson commented: "I am rather tired of being told that I write well, and more concerned to show that (within my own narrow range and subject to my mathematical incompetence) I can still think well!"

58. Letters 175, 176, 177, 178, 179 and 181 of 11 November, 3, 11 and 20 December 1955, 8 February and 26 April 1956.

59. A few occasional exchanges should be mentioned for completeness. On 10 January 1928 (letter 10), Harrod sent an appreciation and a few minor criticisms on Robertson's

"magnificient article on the Colwyn Report" (Robertson, 1927). In July 1936, Robertson asked for Harrod's comments on a criticism of Joan Robinson's "Disguised unemployment" (1936). Harrod's reply is not extant; Robertson, however, dropped his note as Sraffa showed him that "on her logic JR is correct" (letters 57 and 58 of 8 and 22 July 1936). On 4 June 1946 (letter 105) Robertson commented on Harrod's review of Lange's *Price Flexibility and Employment* (Harrod, 1946). On 24 October 1947 (letter 115), Robertson commented on a note by Harrod on "point prices," commenting that it would be worth publishing it (but it does not seem it was). On 31 October 1948 Robertson inquired on "the assumptions behind, and steps leading to [Harrod's], equations on p. 42 of [Towards a] Dynamic Economics" (letter 116); Harrod's answer is not extant.

On 18 October 1950, with reference to Harrod's review of Ohlin's *The Problem of Employment Stabilization*, Robertson disagrees that Keynes's doctrine of an optimum rate of interest meets "those critics who have complained that he divorced interest from the forces of productivity and thrift and left interest theory 'hanging by its own boot straps.' Keynes's optimum rate of interest is clearly governed by productivity and thrift" (Harrod, 1960b, p. 556): "I do think JMK would have conceded that his 'optimum rate' was governed by productivity and thrift. It is simply that rate, governed by liquidity preference and the supply of money, which would produce 'full employment' (whatever that is). But how, in the 'classical' situation, there is a rate of interest at all remains a mystery, since when L2 and M2 are zero (GTE, p. 204), the forces which we have then told determine the rate of interest have vanished" (Robertson to Harrod, letter 140).

60. Robertson also pointed out a couple of mistakes in Harrod's formulas. One concerned the omission of brackets, the second regarded the relationship between the *per caput* natural rate of growth of income, the natural rate of growth, and the rate of growth of the working population (Harrod, 1960a, p. 282); these were acknowledged in Harrod's letter 189 of 6 August 1960.

61. In his previous letter of 6 August, Harrod had already explained: "I can conceive no circumstance in the world which we know, in which so high a rate of saving would be desirable. If we suppose the maximum possible growth rate per caput, having regard to personnel and know-how, were 5% – a high figure – and if we suppose the rate of interest were zero and consequently a very high figure for the capital output ratio of 5, then we get the required saving as 25% of income. Any saving above that would be utter waste. It would have to be embodied in equipment that did not pay its own amortisation" (letter 189).

62. Refers to the correspondence with Keynes on the proofs of the *General Theory* during summer 1935: see Note 24 for references.

63. Harrod (1937) (see Note 36).

64. With reference to the passage on time-lags and equilibrium cited at the end of Section 8.

65. Such a change in Harrod's attitude is also evident in his correspondence with Henderson. Harrod admitted that Keynes's "manners, where his own theories are concerned, are impossible" (Harrod to Henderson, 28 March 1936). However, Harrod's disagreement with Henderson's ideas on Marshall led "to a considerable revulsion of feeling": "I am not sure that I feel that now. When I find someone like you supposing that there really is enshrined in Marshall a theory about the way things work themselves out in the long period, that will wash, that will do, that really works and holds together, then I feel that Maynard is amply justified. I begin to understand why he fusses so much about Marshall. He lives in Cambridge and probably comes in touch with other people like yourself who take him au grand serieux. Nothing is more dangerous than to lull oneself into believing

that one has stored up somewhere in the less-used brain-cells a theory that does explain the main working of the system when that is not the case. If we are naked, let us know it. Far be it from me to disparage Marshall. I have the highest regard for him. But do not let us suppose that he has provided a coherent theory of the long period working of economic forces that is in any sense complete" (Harrod to Henderson, 23 February 1936).

66. Robertson to Harrod, 30 June 1949, letter 121. The two unpublished papers cited by Robertson are preserved in Robertson's archives: "Mr. Keynes' Theory of Money. – Supplementary Note" and "Mr Keynes and 'Finance.' "

67. Refers to the following passage in the 1949 Preface to *Banking Policy*: "it is bound to remain to me a source of some bewilderment that at some time in the period following 1930 the idea that monetary analysis [. . .] is concerned with the behaviour of output as well as of prices should apparently have struck Keynes, or at any rate the able little group who were then advising him, with the force of a new discovery" (p. xiii). References are to E. A. G. Robinson (1947), and J. Robinson (1933).

68. The letter is not extant.

69. Hahn claimed that in his *Volkswirtschaftliche Theorie des Bankkredits* (1920) he had "advanced a 'credit expansion theory of employment' very similar to that of Keynes," which, however, he substantially modified in the 1930 edition.

70. The correspondence on the footnote on Abbati (Harrod, 1951a, p. 410) continued for a while, with interesting reflections on both sides on how "this business of 'influence' is a very elusive one" (letters and notes 130–136, exchanged between 14 and 28 April 1950).

71. See also Robertson's remark cited at the end of Section 13 (p. 38).

72. Commenting on Kahn, Robertson wrote: "Of course his personality, and the Lady's [Joan Robinson], were among the tragically complicating factors in the whole story" (Robertson to Harrod, 28 April 1950, letter 136). On the clash between Robertson and Joan Robinson, which seems to have culminated in Robertson "getting dangerously near to trying to prevent her from lecturing," see Moggridge (1992, pp. 599–601) and, for a different interpretation, Aslanbeigui and Oakes (2002, pp. 23–33) (both cite the passage from Keynes's letter to Lydia Keynes of 4 March 1936).

73. This expression was used by Robertson himself to describe, in 1959, his 1932 "Note on the Supply Curve," cited in Section 2 (the note is hand-written on the cover page of Robertson's own copy).

74. On 3 January 1937 (letter 64) Robertson sent Harrod "a 1933 product, which was so hurried that you may never have seen it, & which will show you that sometimes at least I have 'unorthodox' moods!" Reference is to Robertson (1933c).

ACKNOWLEDGMENTS

I am grateful to the curators of the collections of Harrod's and Robertson's papers for their invaluable assistance, and to Lilia Costabile, Geoff Harcourt, Donald Moggridge, John Presley and an anonymous referee for their helpful comments on earlier drafts of this paper; to Donald Moggridge I am also indebted beyond words for information regarding the location, content and context of a number of items of correspondence between Harrod and Robertson. I also wish to thank Cristina Marcuzzo for helpful bibliographic suggestions. I am obliged to the copyright holder for giving me permission to cite passages of hitherto unpublished writings: Chiba University of Commerce for Harrod's writings in their possession, Dominick and Lady Harrod for the remainder of Harrod's writings, and Judith M. R. Brown for Robertson's writings.

REFERENCES

Unpublished Documents and Correspondence

Haberler, G. (1934). Systematic analysis of business cycle theories. Mimeograph, Geneva: League of Nations, August (copy in LoN 10B/12653/12653).
Harrod to Florence Ada Keynes, 7 November 1950, in HP III-250/2.
Harrod to Haberler, 8 September 1934, in Haberler Papers, Hoover Institution, Box 66.
Harrod to Haberler, 29 February 1935, in Haberler Papers, Hoover Institutions, Box 66.
Harrod to Henderson, 23 February 1936, in Henderson Papers, Nuffield College, Oxford, Box 22A.
Harrod to Henderson, 28 March 1936, in Henderson Papers, Nuffield College, Oxford, Box 22A.
Kahn to Robertson, 5 October 1932, in DHR C18/10.
Keynes to Robertson, undated (January or February 1937), in Keynes Papers, King's College, Cambridge CO/3/46.
Robertson, D. H. (1928). Mr. Robertson's views on Miss Tappan's views on Mr. Harrod's views on Mr. Robertson's view on banking policy. Autograph document, six pages, initialled, in DHR C3/11.
Robertson, D. H. (1931). Mr. Keynes' theory of money – Supplementary note. Autograph, 10 pages, in DHR D2/14.
Robertson, D. H. (1932). A note on the supply curve. Ts, 10 pages and a cover page, in DHR C18/8(6–16).
Robertson, D. H. (1935). Money flows. Ts, in DHR D4/6; revised copy in HCN 11.28.1.
Robertson, D. H. (1938). Mr. Keynes and 'finance'. TS, eight pages, in DHR C5/2.
Robertson to Haberler, 1 November 1934, League of Nations Archives, Geneva, 10B/12563/12653.
Robertson to Keynes, 28 January 1937, in Keynes' Papers, King's College, Cambridge CO/3/44.
Robertson to E. A. G. Robinson, 2 January 1947, in HP III-789–820.
Robinson, E. A. G. to Robertson, undated note (1947), in HP III-789–820.

Published Documents

Abbati, A. H. (1924). *The unclaimed wealth: How money stops production*. London: Allen & Unwin.
Abbati, A. H. (1928). *The final buyer*. London: King.
Aslanbeigui, N., & Oakes, G. (2002). The theory arsenal: The Cambridge circus and the origin of the Keynesian revolution. *Journal of the History of Economic Thought, 24*(1), 5–37.
Besomi, D. (1996a). Introduction to 'an essay in dynamic theory': 1938 draft by Roy F. Harrod. *History of Political Economy, 28*(2), 245–251.
Besomi, D. (1996b). An additional note on the Harrod–Keynes correspondence. *History of Political Economy, 28*(2), 281–294.

Besomi, D. (1998a). Failing to win consent. Harrod's dynamics in the eyes of his readers. In: G. Rampa, L. Stella & A. Thirlwall (Eds), *Economic Dynamics, Trade and Growth: Essays on Harrodian Themes* (pp. 38–88). London: Macmillan.

Besomi, D. (1998b). Harrod and the econometricians: Instability, time-lags and the foundations of economic dynamics. In: G. Rampa, L. Stella & A. Thirlwall (Eds), *Economic Dynamics, Trade and Growth: Essays on Harrodian Themes* (pp. 107–148). London: Macmillan.

Besomi, D. (1999). *The making of Harrod's dynamics.* Basingstoke and New York: Macmillan and St. Martin's Press.

Besomi, D. (2000). On the spread of an idea: The strange case of Mr. Harrod and the multiplier. *History of Political Economy, 32*(2), 347–379.

Besomi, D. (2002). Löwe's and Hayek's influence on Harrod's trade cycle theory. *European Journal of the History of Economic Thought, 9*(1).

Besomi, D. (2003). Harrod, Hansen and Samuelson on the multiplier-acceleration model. A further note. *History of Political Economy, 35*(2), 307–324.

Besomi, D. (2004). Keynes and Harrod. In: M. C. Marcuzzo & A. Rosselli (Eds), *Economists in Cambridge. A Study of their Correspondence.* London: Routledge.

Clark, J. M. (1934). *Strategic factors in business cycles.* New York: National Bureau of Economic Research.

de Jong, F. J. (1954). Supply functions in Keynesian economics. *Economic Journal, LXIV*(March), 3–24.

de Jong, F. J. (1955). Keynes and supply functions: Second rejoinder with a note on the concept of monetary equilibrium. *Economic Journal, LXV*(September), 479–484.

de Jong, F. J. (1956). Keynes and supply functions: Third rejoinder and final observations. *Economic Journal, LXVI*(September), 488–492.

Durbin, E. F. M. (1935). *The problem of credit policy.* London: Chapman & Hall.

Durbin, E. F. (1985). *New Jerusalems. The Labour Party and the economics of democratic socialism.* London: Routledge & Kegan Paul.

Ellsberg, D. (1954). Classic and current notions of 'measurable utility'. *Economic Journal, LXIV*(September), 528–556.

Fletcher, G. (2000). *Understanding Dennis Robertson. The man and his work.* Cheltenham: Elgar.

Friedman, M. (1955). What all is utility? *Economic Journal, LXV*(September), 405–409.

Frisch, R. (1933). Propagation problems and impulse problems in dynamic economics. *Economic Essays in Honour of Gustav Cassel*, 171–205.

Hahn, L. A. (1920). *Volkswirtschaftliche Theorie des Bankkredits.* Tübingen: Mohr (2nd ed. 1924, 3rd ed. 1930).

Hahn, L. A. (1945). Compensating reactions to compensatory spending. *American Economic Review, 35*(1), 28–39.

Hansen, A. H. (1936). Mr. Keynes on underemployment equilibrium. *Journal of Political Economy, XLIV*(5), 667–686.

Harrod, R. F. (1927). Mr. Robertson's views on banking policy. *Economica, XXXVII*(June), 224–232.

Harrod, R. F. (1931). The law of decreasing costs. *Economic Journal, XLI*(December), 566–576.

Harrod, R. F. (1933). *International economics.* London and Cambridge: Nisbet and Cambridge University Press.

Harrod, R. F. (1934a). The expansion of credit in an advancing community. *Economica, NS*(1), 287–299.

Harrod, R. F. (1934b). Banking policy and stable prices. Letter to the Editor of *The Economist, CXIX* (Book Suppl., 6 October), 8.

Harrod, R. F. (1934c). Banking policy and stable prices. Letter to the Editor of *The Economist, CXIX* (Book Suppl., 10 November), 8.

Harrod, R. F. (1934d). Rejoinder to Mr. Robertson. *Economica, NS*(1), 476–478.

Harrod, R. F. (1935). *The problem of credit policy*, by E. F. M. Durbin. *Economic Journal*, *XLV*(December), 725–729.

Harrod, R. F. (1936). *The trade cycle. An essay*. Oxford: Clarendon Press.

Harrod, R. F. (1937). Mr. Keynes and traditional theory. *Econometrica*, *5*(January), 74–86.

Harrod, R. F. (1939a). An essay in dynamic theory. *Economic Journal*, *IL*(March), 14–33.

Harrod, R. F. (1939b). *Value and capital*, by J. R. Hicks. *Economic Journal*, *XLIX*, 294–300.

Harrod, R. F. (1939c). *International economics* (2nd ed.). London and Cambridge: Nisbet and Cambridge University Press.

Harrod, R. F. (1946). *Price flexibility and employment*, by Oscar Lange. *Economic Journal*, *LVI*(March), 102–107.

Harrod, R. F. (1951a). *The life of John Maynard Keynes*. London: Macmillan.

Harrod, R. F. (1951b). Notes on trade cycle theory. *Economic Journal*, *LXI*(June), 261–275.

Harrod, R. F. (1952). Theory of imperfect competition revised. In: *Economic Essays* (pp. 139–187). London: Macmillan.

Harrod, R. F. (1960a). Second essay in dynamic theory. *Economic Journal*, *LXX*(June), 277–293.

Harrod, R. F. (1960b). *The problem of employment stabilization*, by B. Ohlin. *Economic Journal*, *LXX*(September), 552–556.

Harrod, R. F. (1967). Increasing returns. In: R. E. Kuenne (Ed.), *Monopolistic Competition Theory: Studies in Impact. Essays in Honor of Edward H. Chamberlin* (pp. 63–76). New York: Wiley.

Harrod, R. F. (1972). Imperfect competition, aggregate demand and inflation. *Economic Journal*, *LXXXII*(March), 392–401.

Harrod, R. F. (2003). *The collected interwar papers and correspondence of Roy Harrod*. In: D. Besomi (Ed.). Cheltenham: Elgar.

Hawtrey, R. G. (1933). Mr. Robertson on 'saving and hoarding'. II. *Economic Journal*, *XLIII*(December), 701–708.

Henderson, H. D. (1922). *Supply and demand*. London and Cambridge: Nisbet and Cambridge University Press.

Henderson, H. D. (1955). *The inter-war years and other papers*. In: H. Clay (Ed.). Oxford: Clarendon Press.

Hicks, J. R. (1939). *Value and capital*. Oxford: Clarendon Press.

Keynes, J. M. (1933a). *The means to prosperity*. London: Macmillan. Reprinted in: *Collected Writings* (1971–1989) (Vol. IX, pp. 335–366).

Keynes, J. M. (1933b). The means to prosperity. Mr. Keynes's reply to criticism. Work and spending. *The Times* (5 April), 15–16. In: Keynes 1971–1989 (Vol. XXI, pp. 178–185).

Keynes, J. M. (1933c). Mr. Robertson on 'saving and hoarding'. I. *Economic Journal*, *LXIII*(December), 699–701.

Keynes, J. M. (1936). *The general theory of employment, interest and money*. In: Keynes, 1971–1989 (Vol. VII). London: Macmillan.

Keynes, J. M. (1971–1989). *The collected writings of John Maynard Keynes*. 30 vols. In: E. A. G. Robinson, E. Johnson & D. Moggridge (Eds). London: Macmillan.

Lindahl, E. (1934). A note on the dynamic pricing problem. Mimeo, later published in: O. Steiger (Ed.), *Studien zur Entstehung der Neuen Wirtschaftslehre in Schweden. Eine Anti-Kritik* (1971, pp. 204–211). Berlin: Duncker & Humblot.

Marget, A. W. (1941). *Essays in monetary theory*, by D. H. Robertson. *Review of Economics and Statistics*, *23*(3), 147–151.

Marget, A. W. (1942). *The theory of prices. A re-examination of the central problems of monetary theory* (Vol. 2). New York: Prentice-Hall.

Meade, J. E. (1933). *The rate of interest in a progressive state*. London: Macmillan.

Mizen, P., Moggridge, D. E., & Presley, J. (1997). The papers of Dennis Robertson: The discovery of unexpected riches. *History of Political Economy, 29*(4), 573–592.

Moggridge, D. E. (1992). *Maynard Keynes. An economist's biography.* London and New York: Routledge.

Myrdal, G. (1933). Der Gleichgewichtsbegriff als Instrument der geldtheoretischen Analyse. In: F. A. Hayek (Ed.), *Beiträge zur Geldtheorie.* Wien: Springer.

Ohlin, B. (1933). *Interregional and international trade.* Oxford and Cambridge, MA: Oxford University Press and Harvard University Press.

Presley, J. R. (1978). *Robertsonian economics. An examination of the work of Sir D. H. Robertson on industrial fluctuations.* London: Macmillan.

Ramsey, F. P. (1928). A mathematical theory of saving. *Economic Journal, XXXVIII*(December), 543–559.

Robertson, D. H. (1915). *A study of industrial fluctuations. An enquiry into the character and causes of the so-called cyclical movement of trade.* London: King.

Robertson, D. H. (1922). *Money.* Cambridge and London: Cambridge University Press and Nisbet.

Robertson, D. H. (1923). The ebb and flow of unemployment. London: *The Daily News.* Reprinted as "The Stabilization of Unemployment" in: *Economic Fragments,* London: King, 1931.

Robertson, D. H. (1926). *Banking policy and the price level. An essay in the theory of the trade cycle.* London: King.

Robertson, D. H. (1927). The Colwyn committee, the income tax and the price level. *Economic Journal, XXXVII*(December), 566–581.

Robertson, D. H. (1933a). Saving and hoarding. *Economic Journal, XLIII*(September), 399–413.

Robertson, D. H. (1933b). Mr. Robertson on 'saving and hoarding'. III. *Economic Journal, XLIII*(December), 709–712.

Robertson, D. H. (1933c). Untitled contribution to *Der Stand und die nächstre Zukunft der Konjuncturforschung. Festschrift für Arthur Spiethoff,* München: Duncker & Humblot, 1933, pp. 238–242 (reprinted as "The Future of Trade-Cycle Theory" in: Robertson (Ed.), *Essays in Monetary Theory.* London: Staples Press, 1940).

Robertson, D. H. (1933d). Equilibrium in the state. Review of *The Rate of Interest in a Progressive State,* by J. E. Meade. *The Spectator* (17 November).

Robertson, D. H. (1934a). Mr. Harrod and the expansion of credit. *Economica, NS*(1), 473–475.

Robertson, D. H. (1934b). Industrial fluctuation and the natural rate of interest. *Economic Journal, XLIV*(December), 650–656.

Robertson, D. H. (1936). Some notes on Mr. Keynes' general theory of employment. *Quarterly Journal of Economics, 51*(November), 168–191.

Robertson, D. H. (1937a). *The trade cycle,* by R. F. Harrod. *The Canadian Journal of Economics and Political Science, 3*(February), 124–127.

Robertson, D. H. (1937b). Alternative theories of the rate of interest. II. *Economic Journal, XLVII*(September), 428–436.

Robertson, D. H. (1938). A survey of modern monetary controversy. *The Manchester School of Economic and Social Studies, 9,* 1–19.

Robertson, D. H. (1939). Mr. Clark and the foreign trade multiplier. *Economic Journal, XLIX*(June), 354–356.

Robertson, D. H. (1940). Mr. Keynes and the rate of interest. In: *Essays in Monetary Theory.* London: King.

Robertson, D. H. (1949). Preface to 1949 edition (of Robertson 1926). London and New York: Staples and Kelly.

Robertson, D. H. (1953). Sir Hubert Henderson. *Economic Journal, LXIII*(December), 923–931.

Robertson, D. H. (1954a). Thoughts on meeting some important persons. *Quarterly Journal of Economics*, *68*(2), 181–190.

Robertson, D. H. (1954b). Utility and all what? *Economic Journal*, *LXIV*(December), 665–678.

Robertson, D. H. (1955a). What all is utility? A rejoinder. *Economic Journal*, *LXV*(September), 410.

Robertson, D. H. (1955b). Keynes and supply functions. *Economic Journal*, *LXIV*(September), 474–477.

Robertson, D. H. (1956). Keynes and supply functions. *Economic Journal*, *LXIV*(September), 485–487.

Robertson, D. H. (1959). Some Marshallian concepts. *Economic Journal*, *LXIX*(June), 382–384.

Robinson, E. A. G. (1947). John Maynard Keynes 1883–1946. *Economic Journal*, *LVII*(March), 1–68.

Robinson, J. V. (1933). The theory of money and the analysis of output. *Review of Economic Studies*, *I*(1), 22–38.

Robinson, J. V. (1936). Disguised unemployment. *Economic Journal*, *XLVI*(June), 225–237.

Royal Institute of International Affairs (1935). *The future of monetary policy. A report on international monetary problems by a group of the Royal Institute of Economic Affairs*. Oxford and London: Oxford University Press and Humphrey Milford.

Samuelson, P. A. (1939). Interactions between the multiplier analysis and the principle of acceleration. *Review of Economics and Statistics*, *21*, 75–78.

Shackle, G. L. S. (1967). *The years of high theory. Invention and tradition in economic thought 1926–1936*. Cambridge: Cambridge University Press.

Tappan, M. (1928). Mr. Robertson's views on banking policy: A reply to Mr. Harrod. *Economica*, *22*(March), 95–109.

Tinbergen, J. (1935). Annual survey: Suggestions on quantitative business cycle theory. *Econometrica*, *3*(July), 241–308.

Tinbergen, J. (1937). (Review of) Harrod, R.F., the Trade Cycle. An Essay. Weltwirtschaftliches Archiv 45.3, pp. 89*–91*.

Tyskynski, H. (1955). Economic theory as a guide to policy: Some suggestions for a re-appraisal. *Economic Journal*, *LXV*(June), 195–215.

Young, W. (1989). *Harrod and his trade cycle group. The origins and development of the growth research programme*. London: Macmillan.

APPENDIX: LIST OF LETTERS AND NOTES

Dates in square brackets are inferred from internal references or external sources, such as postmarks or other correspondence. Repositories are abbreviated as follows: DHR stands for Robertson Papers, Wren Library, Trinity College, Cambridge; HCN abbreviates the Harrod Collection, Nagoya University of Commerce and Business Administration, Nisshin-Shi, Japan; HP indicates the Harrod Papers, Chiba University of Commerce, Ichikawa, Japan; HPBL stands for the Harrod Papers, British Library, London; KHLN the Keynes and Harrod Letters and Memoranda, Tokyo University; LoN indicates the League of Nations Archives, Geneva; RES abbreviates the Royal Economic Society Archives, British Library of Political and Economic Science, London.

1	Robertson to Harrod, 12 February 1926 (KHLM 208–215).
2	Harrod to D. H. Robertson, 18 May 1926 (HP IV-990–1069d/3–4).
3	D. H. Robertson to Harrod, 20 May [1926] (KHLM 208–215).
4	D. H. Robertson to Harrod, 26 May [1926] (HP IV-990–1069d/5).
5	Harrod to D. H. Robertson, [May or June 1926] (HP IV-990–1069d/1–2).
6	D. H. Robertson to Harrod, [May or June 1926] (HP IV-990–1069d/6).
7	Harrod to D. H. Robertson, [May or June 1926] (DHR C3/71–74).
8	D. H. Robertson to Harrod, 19 November 1927 (KHLM 210).
9	D. H. Robertson to Harrod, 7 December 1927 (KHLM 211).
10	Harrod to D. H. Robertson, 10 January 1928 (HP IV-990–1069d/7).[a]
11	D. H. Robertson to Harrod, 13 March 1928 (KHLM 212).
12	Robertson to Harrod, 24 April 1929 (HPBL 71188/141).
13	Harrod to D. H. Robertson, [June 1931] (HP IV-586–668).
14	D. H. Robertson to Harrod, 6 April 1932 (HP IV-990–1069d/8).
15	Harrod to D. H. Robertson, [April 1932] (HP IV-990–1069d/9).
16	D. H. Robertson to Harrod, [April 1932] (HP IV-990–1069/9).
17	D. H. Robertson to Harrod, 14 April 1932 (HP IV-990–1069/9).
18	Robertson to Harrod, 22 April, 1932 (HP IV-990–1069d/10).
19	D. H. Robertson to Harrod, 26 April 1932 (HP IV-990–1069d/11).
20	D. H. Robertson to Harrod, 24 August 1932 (HP IV-990–1069d/12).
21	Harrod to D. H. Robertson, 3 September 1932 (DHR C18/71–75).
22	D. H. Robertson to Harrod, 9 September 1932 (HP IV-990–1069d/13).
23	Harrod to D. H. Robertson, 13 October 1932 (HP IV 990–1069d/14).
24	D. H. Robertson to Harrod, 31 December 1932 (HP IV-990–1069d/15).
25	D. H. Robertson to Harrod, 14 January 1933 (HP IV-990–1069d/16).
26	D. H. Robertson to Harrod, 3 April 1933 (HP IV-990–1069/17).
27	D. H. Robertson to Harrod, 5 April 1933 (KHLM 215).
28	Harrod to D. H. Robertson, 26 April 1933 (KHLM 213).
29	D. H. Robertson to Harrod, [28 April 1933] (KHLM 213).
30	Harrod to D. H. Robertson, 29 April 1933 (DHR C3/21–22; photocopy in HP (NC)).
31	D. H. Robertson to Harrod, 5 August 1934 (HP IV-990–1069d/18).
32	D. H. Robertson to Harrod, 10 August 1934 (HP IV-990–1069/19).
33	D. H. Robertson to Harrod, 27 September 1934 (HP IV-990–1069d/20).
34	D. H. Robertson to Harrod, 4 October 1934 (HP IV-990–1069d/21).
35	D. H. Robertson to Harrod, 6 October 1934 (HP IV-990–1069d/22).
36	D. H. Robertson to Harrod, 19 October 1934 (HP IV-990–1069d/23).
37	D. H. Robertson to Harrod, 30 September 1935 (HP IV-990–1069d/24).
38	Harrod to D. H. Robertson, 3 October 1935 (HP IV-990–1069d/25).

39   D. H. Robertson to Harrod, 5 October 1935 (HP IV-990–1069d/26).
40   Harrod to D. H. Robertson, 7 October 1935 (DHR C3/23).
41   Harrod to D. H. Robertson, 8 October 1935 (HP IV-990–1069d/27).
42   Harrod to D. H. Robertson, 9 October 1935 (HP IV-990–1069d-28).
43   D. H. Robertson to Harrod, 12 October 1935 (HP IV-990–1069d-29;
        draft in DHR 3/24).
44   Harrod to D. H. Robertson, 11 November 1935 (HP IV-990–1069d/30).
45   D. H. Robertson to Harrod, [November 1935] (HP IV-990–1069d/31).
46   Harrod to D. H. Robertson, 15 November 1935 (DHR 3/25–26).
47   D. H. Robertson to Harrod, 16 November 1935 (HP IV-990–1069d/32).
48   Harrod to D. H. Robertson, 18 November 1935 (DHR 3/27–28).
49   D. H. Robertson to Harrod, 17 May 1936 (HPBL Add. 71188/142).
50   Harrod to D. H. Robertson, 18 May 1936 (HP IV-990–1069d/33).
51   D. H. Robertson to Harrod, 19 May 1936 (HP IV-990–1069d/34).
52   Harrod to D. H. Robertson, 21 May 1936 (HP IV-990–1069d/35).
53   D. H. Robertson to Harrod, 21 May 1936 (HP IV-990–1069d/36).
54   Harrod to D. H. Robertson, 22 May 1936 (HP IV-990–1069d/37).
55   Harrod to D. H. Robertson, 4 June 1936 (HP IV-990–1069d/38).
56   D. H. Robertson to Harrod, 5 June 1936 (HP IV-990–1069d/39).
57   D. H. Robertson to Harrod, 8 July 1936 (HP IV-990–1069d/40).
58   D. H. Robertson to Harrod, 22 July 1936 (HP IV-990–1069d/41).
59   D. H. Robertson to Harrod, 28 October 1936 (HP IV-990–1069d/42).
60   D. H. Robertson to Harrod, 9 November 1936 (HP IV-990–1069d/43).
61   Harrod to D. H. Robertson, 9 December 1936 (HP IV-990–1069d/44).
62   D. H. Robertson to Harrod, 23 December 1936 (HP IV-990–1069d/45).
63   Harrod to D. H. Robertson, 25 December 1936 (HP IV-990–1069d/46).
64   D. H. Robertson to Harrod, 3 January [1937] (HP IV-990–1069d/47).
65   [D. H. Robertson's note on Foreign Trade Multiplier] (DHR 3/211 and
        Keynes Papers, King's College, Cambridge, CO/3/45).
66   Harrod to D. H. Robertson, 2 February 1937 (DHR C3/29).
67   D. H. Robertson to Harrod, 2 February 1937 (DHR C3/210).
68   D. H. Robertson to Harrod, 10 February 1937 (KHLM 215).
69   D. H. Robertson to Harrod, 15 February 1937 (KHLM 214).
70   D. H. Robertson to Harrod, 1 April 1937 (HP IV-990–1069d/49).
71   Harrod to D. H. Robertson, 3 April 1937 (HP IV-990–1069d/50).
72   D. H. Robertson to Harrod, 28 April 1937 (HP IV-990–1069d/51).
73   Harrod to D. H. Robertson, 4 October 1937 (HP IV-990–1069d/52).
74   Harrod to D. H. Robertson, 8 October 1937 (HP IV-990–1069d/53).
75   D. H. Robertson to Harrod, 23 November 1937 (HP IV-990–1069d/54).

76   D. H. Robertson to Harrod, 3 December 1937 (HP VI-117).
77   D. H. Robertson to Harrod, 21 January 1938 (HPBL Add. 72764/118).
78   Harrod to D. H. Robertson, 22 January 1938 (DHR C3/3; photocopy in HP (NC)).
79   Harrod to D. H. Robertson, 5 July 1938 (HP IV-990–1069d/55).
80   D. H. Robertson to Harrod, 23 July 1938 (HP IV-990–1069/56).
81   Harrod to D. H. Robertson, 3 August 1938 (HP IV-990–1069d/57).
82   D. H. Robertson to Harrod, 11 August 1938 (HP IV-990–1069d/58).
83   Harrod to D. H. Robertson, 5 September 1938 (HP IV-990–1069d/59).
84   D. H. Robertson to Harrod, 25 September 1938 (HP IV-990–1069d/60).
85   D. H. Robertson to Harrod, 4 October 1938 (HP IV-990–1069d/61).
86   Robertson to Harrod, 27 February 1944 (HPBL 71188/143).
87   Robertson to Harrod, 1 February 1945 (in DHR C3/42–43).
88   Harrod to Robertson, 8 February 1945 (in DHR C3/44–45).
89   Robertson to Harrod, 11 February 1945 (in DHR C3/46–47).
90   Harrod to Robertson, 11 March 1945 (in DHR C3/48–49).
91   Harrod to Robertson, 12 March 1945 (in DHR C3/410).
92   Robertson to Harrod, 15 March 1945 (HP IV-990–1069d/62).
93   Harrod to Robertson, 20 March 1945 (HP IV-990–1069d/63).
94   Harrod to Robertson, 3 April 1945 (HP IV-990–1069d/64).
95   Harrod to Robertson, 3 April 1945[b] (HP IV-990–1069d/65).
96   Robertson to Harrod, 22 April 1945 (HP IV-990–1069d/66).
97   Harrod to Robertson, 25 April 1945 (HP IV-990–1069d/67).
98   Robertson to Harrod, 28 April 1945 (HP IV-990–1069d/67).
99   Harrod to Robertson, 3 May 1945 (HP IV-990–1069d/68).
100   Robertson's comment, 14 June 1945 (HP IV-990–1069d/68).
101   Robertson to Harrod, 24 September 1945 (RES 6/1/407).
102   Robertson to Harrod, 17 October 1945 (HPBL 71188/144).
103   Robertson to Harrod, 13 February 1946 (HPBL 71188/145).
104   Robertson to Harrod, 6 May 1946 (HPBL 71188/146).
105   Robertson to Harrod, 4 June 1946 (HP IV-990–1069d/69).
106   Robertson to Harrod, 7 June 1946 (HPBL 71188/147).
107   Robertson to Harrod, 18 June 1946 (HPBL 71188/148).
108   Robertson to Harrod, 19 July 1946 (HP IV-990–1069d/70).
109   Robertson to Harrod, 23 July 1946 (HP IV-990–1069d/71).
110   Robertson to Harrod, 20 May 1947 (RES 6/1/407).
111   Harrod to Robertson, 23 May 1947 (RES 6/1/407).
112   Robertson to Harrod, from Trinity, 12 October 1947 (HP III-765–782/1).
113   Note by Robertson to Harrod, 15 October 1947 (HP III-765–782/1).

114   Note by Harrod (HP III-765–782/1).
115   Robertson to Harrod, 24 October 1947 (HP III-765–782–2).
116   Robertson to Harrod, 31 October 1948 (HP IV-990–1069d/72).
117   Harrod to Robertson, 1 June 1949 (HP III-765–782–3).
118   Robertson to Harrod, 3 June 1949 (HP III-765–782–4).
119   Harrod to Robertson, 8 June 1949 (HP III-765–782–5).
120   Robertson to Harrod, 10 June 1949 (HP III-765–782–6).
121   Robertson to Harrod, 30 June 1949 (HP III-765–782–7).
122   Robertson to Harrod, 9 August 1949 (HP III-765–782–9).
123   Robertson to Harrod, 13 August 1949 (HP III-765–782–10).
124   Robertson to Harrod, 19 August 1949 (HP III-765–782–11).
125   Robertson to Harrod, 5 September 1949 (HP III-765–782–12).
126   Robertson to Harrod, 19 September 1949 (HP III-765–782–13).
127   Robertson to Harrod, 12 October 1949 (HP IV-990–1069d/73).
128   Robertson to Harrod, 21 January 1950 (HP IV-/E/B-24).
129   Harrod to Robertson, 24 January 1950 (HP IV-/E/B-24).
130   Robertson to Harrod, 4 April 1950 (HP III-765–782–14).
131   Harrod to Robertson, 15 April 1950 (DHR, C3/63–4).
132   Harrod's proposed footnote for the life (HP III-765–782).
133   Robertson's Comment (HP III-765–782).
134   Robertson to Harrod, 17 April 1950 (HP III-765–782–15).
135   Harrod to Robertson, 28 April 1950 (DHR C3/65).
136   Robertson to Harrod, 28 April 1950 (HP III-765–782–16).
137   Robertson to Harrod, 11 May 1950 (DHR C3/66).
138   Robertson to Harrod, 12 May 1950 (HP III-765–782–17).
139   Robertson to Harrod, 7 October 1950 (HP III-765–782–18).
140   Robertson to Harrod, 18 October 1950 (HP IV-990–1069d/74).
141   Harrod to Robertson, 30 January 1951 (DHR C3/61–62).
142   Robertson to Harrod, 20 August 1951 (HP IV-990–1069d/75).
143   Robertson to Harrod, 20 August 1951 (RES 6/1/407).
144   Robertson to Harrod, 28 August 1951 (RES 6/1/407).
145   Robertson to Harrod, 11 August 1953 (HCN, harrmono).
146   Robertson to Harrod, 13 August 1953 (RES 6/1/407).
147   Harrod to Robertson, 17 August 1953 (RES 6/1/407).
148   Robertson to Harrod, 21 August 1953 (RES 6/1/407).
149   Robertson to Harrod, 20 September 1953 (HCN harrmono).
150   Harrod to Robertson, 5 October 1953 (RES 6/1/407).
151   Harrod to Robertson, 10 November 1953 (RES 6/1/407).
152   Robertson to Harrod, 12 November 1953 (RES 6/1/407).

153   Robertson to Harrod, 8 March 1954 (RES 6/1/407).
154   Robertson to Harrod, 12 March 1954 (RES 6/1/407).
155   Robertson to Harrod, Easter day [18 April] 1954 (RES 6/1/407).
156   Robertson to Harrod, 19 July 1954 (RES 6/1/407).
157   Robertson to Harrod, 28 September 1954 (RES 6/1/407).
158   Robertson to Harrod, 4 October 1954 (RES 6/1/407).
159   Robertson to Harrod, 7 October 1954 (RES 6/1/407).
160   Robertson to Harrod, 7 October 1954 (RES 6/1/407).
161   Robertson to Harrod, 31 December 1954 (RES 6/1/407).
162   Harrod to Robertson, 22 February 1955 (RES 6/1/407).
163   Robertson to Harrod, 6 March 1955 (RES 6/1/407).
164   Robertson to Harrod, 14 March 1955 (RES 6/1/407).
165   Robertson to Harrod, 22 April 1955 (RES 6/1/407).
166   Robertson to Harrod, 30 April 1955 (RES 6/1/407).
167   Robertson to Harrod, 7 May 1955 (RES 6/1/407).
168   Robertson to Harrod, 25 May 1955 (RES 6/1/66).
169   Heads to DHR's reply to MF's letter of May 18 (attached to 168) (RES
       6/1/407).
170   Robertson to Harrod, 6 June 1955 (RES 6/1/407).
171   Robertson to Harrod, 6 October 1955 (RES 6/1/407).
172   Robertson to Harrod, 10 October 1955 (RES 6/1/407).
173   Robertson to Harrod, 25 October 1955 (RES 6/1/407).
174   Harrod to Robertson, 9 November 1955 (RES 6/1/407).
175   Robertson to Harrod, 11 November 1955 (RES 6/1/407).
176   Robertson to Harrod, 3 December 1955 (RES 6/1/407).
177   Robertson to Harrod, 11 December 1955 (RES 6/1/407).
178   Harrod to Robertson, 20 December 1955 (RES 6/1/407).
179   Robertson to Harrod, 8 February 1956 (RES 6/1/407).
180   Robertson to Harrod, 2 April 1956 (RES 6/1/407).
181   Robertson to Harrod, 26 April 1956 (RES 6/1/407).
182   Robertson to Harrod, 7 November 1956 (RES 6/1/407).
183   Harrod to Robertson, 5 December 1956 (RES 6/1/407).
184   Robertson to Harrod, 7 December 1956 (RES 6/1/407).
185   Robertson to Harrod, 10 February 1959 (RES 6/1/407).
186   Robertson to Harrod, 10 February 1959 (RES 6/1/407).
187   Harrod to Robertson, 16 February 1959 (RES 6/1/407).
188   Robertson to Harrod, 28 July 1960 (RES 6/1/407).
189   Harrod to Robertson, 6 August 1960 (RES 6/1/407).
190   Robertson to Harrod, 13 August 1960 (HP IV-990–1069d/76).

191	Robertson to Harrod, 15 August 1960 (HP IV-990–1069d/77).
192	Harrod to Robertson, 17 August 1960 (HP IV-990–1069d/78).
193	Robertson to Harrod, 20 August 1960 (HP IV-990–1069d/79).
194	Robertson to Harrod, 1 September 1960 (HP IV-990–1069d/80).

[a] Robertson's answer, dated 13 January, consists in three remarks written in the margin of Harrod's letter.

[b] Probably misdated, should be 4 April: the letter begins, in fact: "In pursuance of yesterday's," referring to letter 94 of 3 April.

KEYNES, UNCERTAINTY AND THE COMPETITIVE PROCESS

Stephen P. Dunn

Keynes brought *time* back into economic theory . . . The descent into time has brought economic theory also into touch with history (Joan Robinson, 1962, pp. 73–74).

1. INTRODUCTION

Uncertainty was a lifetime preoccupation for J. M. Keynes. The notion of uncertainty features prominently in his economic writings and implicitly in his fellowship dissertation, *A Treatise on Probability*. A substantial interpretative literature has arisen on the nature of the conceptualisation of uncertainty and epistemic roots of Keynes's discussion of the importance of expectations in the *General Theory*. Much of this literature has approached Keynes's discussion from a variety of different perspectives exploring the nexus of Keynes's contribution to the history of economic thought, philosophy, the foundations of probability, economics, psychology and contemporary economic events and analysis. Substantial light has been shed on Keynes's discussion.

Keynes was clearly challenging the Benthamite calculus that underpins much of orthodoxy. The decision to invest suggests a decision which broaches an uncertain future. And as the future is uncertain it must presumably be imagined prior to decision and created through action. It is such chains of reasoning that have led some commentators to stress that Keynes's contribution endorsed the view that social reality was transmutable. However, many Keynes scholars have

Research in the History of Economic Thought and Methodology A Research Annual
Research in the History of Economic Thought and Methodology, Volume 22-A, 65–92
© **2004 Published by Elsevier Ltd.**
ISSN: 0743-4154/doi:10.1016/S0743-4154(03)22002-2

not reflected on the extent to which Keynes's conceptualisation of uncertainty is embedded in a vision of the competitive process as creative. Here we attempt to fill this lacuna.

This essay is a modest attempt to reflect on aspects of Keynes's philosophical, economic, social and literary contributions to evaluate the reasonableness of ascribing a conception of the economic process as transmutable to him. In so doing we consider whether Keynes espoused a view of uncertainty and action that is transmutable, and the extent to which it was embedded in a creative view of the competitive process. The assessment is provocative but the intention is to encourage further reflection and debate on the nature on the ontology underlying Keynes's vision. In so doing we will broach a series of substantive issues pertaining to how the nexus between uncertainty and the historical evolution of capitalism should be conceptualised in future research.

The outline of the essay is as follows. In the next section we briefly consider the philosophy of practice and action embedded in Keynes's *Treatise on Probability*. We then consider the link between Keynes's discussion of uncertainty and the notion of animal spirits and enterprise elaborated in the *General Theory* and after. We then proceed to assess Keynes's view of the competitive process. This discussion is then further illuminated with reference to his musings on the social system and the processes of capitalism suggested by the *General Theory*. We conclude by noting that aspects of Keynes's discussion of uncertainty are ahistorical and need to be further augmented by a philosophy of emergence and transmutability.

2. "A GUIDE TO CONDUCT": THE *TREATISE ON PROBABILITY*

The renewed interest in the *Treatise on Probability* raises three principal issues. Firstly, what is the ontological and epistemological nature of Keynes's theory of probability and action under uncertainty? What is the nature of the continuity, if any, between the discussion contained in the *Treatise* and in the *General Theory*? And what does this mean for a theory of behaviour under conditions of "fundamental" uncertainty? For present purposes we do not propose a detailed exegesis on such matters, as comprehensive discussions are to be found elsewhere (see Bateman, 1987, 1996; Carabelli, 1988; Davis, 1994; Dequech, 1999; Meeks, 1991; O'Donnell, 1989; Runde, 1990, 1994).[1] However, we will briefly encroach onto aspects of this debate as it pertains to our assessment of the nature of Keynes's discussion of the transmutability of the entrepreneurial process.

It is possible to view the *Treatise* as an attempt to extend the domain of rational judgement and action to the study of uncertainty.[2] Keynes (CW VIII, p. 9)[3] seeks to challenge and move beyond frequency theories of probability and "to emphasise the existence of a *logical relation between two sets of propositions* in cases where it is not possible to argue demonstratively from one to the other." That is to say Keynes considers the nature of acting in instances when one is unable to assign probability ratios to future events, namely under conditions of uncertainty.[4]

According to Keynes, any conclusion or proposition a is related to a given premiss or such available evidence h via a probability relation, which can be written as $a|h$. This probability relation can be thought of as the "objective" degree of belief that it is rational to hold in any judgement given current knowledge. Keynes then introduces the notion of the weight of argument which refers to the amount of available relevant evidence. The weight of argument relates to the confidence that one has in the evidence pertaining to any probability relation. Nevertheless as Runde (1990) notes, Keynes employs several different definitions of "weight" in the *Treatise* using it to refer either to the absolute amount, or the degree of completeness, of the relevant evidence, or to the balance between knowledge and ignorance. Thus, additional information that reveals either the incompleteness of the existing relevant evidence, or one's relative ignorance, may in fact reduce the probability; but new information always increases the evidential "weight" (Keynes CW VIII, p. 77). The discovery of additional evidence h_1 augments the weight of argument and gives rise to a new probability relation $a|hh_1$. However, there is no unique monotonic relationship between the weight of argument and the degree of belief held in any proposition. The accretion of new knowledge or evidence may or may not alter the probability relation. It does not entail that the previous argument is wrong; it merely yields a new judgement (see Gerrard, 1992; Lawson, 1985; Runde, 1990). As such, probability relations need not correspond to numerical values or be directly comparable, and thus extends the province of probability to the study of rational decision making under uncertainty.[5]

For Keynes, deciding on a course of action meant judging the means to deliver ends, where "[j]udgement of means took place in the 'twilight of Probability.' Rational action was constrained by two further principles, the 'weight of argument' and the doctrine of 'least risk' . . . [P]robability might be the 'guide of life'; but the guide had to make his way through the fog of uncertainty" (Skidelsky, 1992, p. 409). The central argument of the *Treatise* is that the perceptions of probability, "weight" and "moral risk," roughly, the magnitude of the expected loss (or "badness") that might eventuate under averse conditions, depend upon the exercise of judgement. *Ceteris paribus* "a high weight and the absence of risk increase *pro tanto* the desirability of the action to which they refer" (Keynes, CW VIII, p. 348).

What is clear from this discussion is that Keynes's concern with the nature of acting is ahistorical and primarily philosophical.[6] That is to say the *Treatise* does not provide many clues as to the nature of the social ontology within which the decision maker is embedded.[7] As O'Donnell (1989) makes plain, while Keynes's view of the physical world in the *Treatise* is deterministic, his treatment of the social realm is more ambiguous. Keynes does not tell us in the *Treatise*, "how stable he thought social, as opposed to natural structures were" (Skidelsky, 1992, p. 61). In the *Treatise* Keynes does not explicitly challenge the notion of immutability of the cosmos. "Keynes's theory is both optimistic about the power of human reason and pessimistic about its ability to penetrate the secrets of the universe. We have only limited insight into the 'nature of reality' " (Skidelsky, 1992, p. 61). Keynes leaves the conceptual door ajar: "[w]hether there is a map in heaven, there is none on earth" (Skidelsky, 1992, p. 61).[8]

Keynes's discussion primarily considers the rational grounds for acting in the absence of numerical probabilities rather than the psychological nature of acting or the emergent novelty, creativity or reproducibility associated with action and imagination.[9] But, "[h]aving opted for the supremacy of reason, [one] rejects what conflicts with reason . . . [one cuts oneself off] from the most ascendant and superb of human faculties. Imagination, the source of novelty, the basis of mens' claims, if they have one, to be makers and not mere executants of history, is exempted" (Shackle, 1979, p. 44). Keynes does not consider the emergent historical processes that shape and contextualise the decision to act.[10] Moreover, notions such as evidential completeness or relative ignorance appear to place clear bounds on knowledge. But if knowledge, especially economic knowledge, is embedded in an unending, emergent, creative process existing in historical time then in what sense does it have meaning to talk about the completeness of economic knowledge, or to make evaluations of the balance between knowledge and ignorance with respect to the evolution of rationality, especially as decisions constantly have to be made at discrete points in time?[11]

For the Keynes of the *Treatise*, the guidelines for action in an uncertain world can be deduced from logic on the basis of available evidence. The conceptualisation of action is epistemic and ahistorical. The *Treatise* displays little evidence that institutions, time and history are important for Keynes's philosophy of practise.[12] It is an appeal to reason, not observation.[13] For the Keynes of the *Treatise*, the question of how to act is approached from an ethical and philosophical perspective, and he does not consider the origins of action, nor does he offer considerations of how they may find conduits for expression in the realm of practical affairs. For this we must turn to his economic writings.

3. UNCERTAINTY AND ANIMAL SPIRITS

Many commentators have claimed that the revolutionary essence of the *General Theory* is the role accorded to uncertainty. This, though, is misleading. Coddington (1983, p. 53, emphasis added) has cogently summarised the role of uncertainty in the *General Theory*: "it is not the fact of uncertainty that is important for Keynes's argument, *but rather how individuals are supposed to respond to the fact of uncertainty*."[14] In developing this aspect of his argument Keynes begins by noting the salience of the passing of time:

> All production is for the purpose of ultimately satisfying a consumer. Time usually elapses, however – and sometimes much time – between the incurring of costs by the producer (with the consumer in view) and the purchase of the output by the ultimate consumer. Meanwhile the entrepreneur (including both the producer and the investor in this description) has to form the best expectations he can as to what the consumers will be prepared to pay when he is ready to supply them (directly or indirectly) after the elapse of what may be a lengthy period; and he has no choice but to be guided by these expectations, if he is to produce at all by processes which occupy time (Keynes, CW VII, p. 46).

Keynes divides these expectations, upon which business decisions depend, into two groups, long- and short-term expectations. Short-term expectations refer to the expected revenue associated with a production run against the current capital stock whereas long-term expectations refer to "what the entrepreneur can hope to earn in the shape of future returns if he purchases (or, perhaps, manufactures) 'finished' output as an addition to his capital equipment" (Keynes, CW VII, p. 47). Accordingly the volume of current and future investment depends upon the state of these forward-looking long-term expectations as they impinge on the psychological propensities to act:

> It would be foolish, in forming our expectations, to attach great weight to matters which are very uncertain.[15] It is reasonable, therefore, to be guided to a considerable degree by the facts about which we feel somewhat confident, even though they may be less decisively relevant to the issue than other facts about which our knowledge is vague and scanty. For this reason the facts of the existing situation enter, in a sense disproportionately, into the formation of our long-term expectations; our usual practice being to take the existing situation and to project it into the future, modified only to the extent that we have more or less definite reasons for expecting a change (Keynes, CW VII, p. 148).

Thus, the decision to invest depends up the "most probable forecast" that can be made and the "confidence" in the forecasts of the future. It is such business confidence that is pivotal to enterprise:

> The outstanding fact is the extreme precariousness of the basis of knowledge on which our estimates of prospective yield have to be made. Our knowledge of the factors which will govern the yield of an investment some years hence is usually very slight and often negligible. If we

speak frankly, we have to admit that our basis of knowledge for estimating the yield ten years hence of a railway, a copper mine, a textile factory, the goodwill of a patent medicine, an Atlantic liner, a building in the City of London amounts to little and sometimes to nothing; or even five years hence (Keynes, CW VII, pp. 149–150).[16]

Nevertheless a salient and oft-ignored aspect of this discussion is that Keynes embeds the state of long-term expectations within the evolution of the institutions of capitalism, such as the emergence of the joint-stock corporation and rise of the stock market:

> In former times, when enterprises were mainly owned by those who undertook them or by their friends and associates, investment depended on a sufficient supply of individuals of sanguine temperament and constructive impulses who embarked on business as a way of life, not really relying on a precise calculation of prospective profit. The affair was partly a lottery, though with the ultimate result largely governed by whether the abilities and character of the managers were above or below the average. Some would fail and some would succeed. But even after the event no one would know whether the average results in terms of the sums invested had exceeded, equalled or fallen short of the prevailing rate of interest; though, if we exclude the exploitation of natural resources and monopolies, it is probable that the actual average results of investments, even during periods of progress and prosperity, have disappointed the hopes which prompted them . . . If human nature felt no temptation to take a chance, no satisfaction (profit apart) in constructing a factory, a railway, a mine or a farm, there might not be much investment merely as a result of cold calculation. Decisions to invest in private business of the old fashioned type were, however, decisions largely irrevocable, not only for the community as a whole, but also for the individual. With the separation between ownership and management which prevails today and with the development of organised investment markets, a new factor of great importance has entered in, which sometimes facilitates investment but sometimes adds greatly to the instability of the system (Keynes, CW VII, pp. 150–151).

Such passages are instructive in several respects. Firstly the view of the entrepreneur, being based upon "sanguine temperament" and "constructive impulses," appears to emphasise the creative and transmutable potential embedded within the competitive process. Secondly the recognition of the emergence of the stock exchange appears to embed the discussion of uncertainty into a historical process. Thirdly such institutional developments fundamentally change the nature of the investment process so that "certain classes of investment are governed by the average expectation of those who deal on the Stock Exchange as revealed in the price of shares, rather than by the genuine expectations of the professional entrepreneur" (Keynes, CW VII, p. 151). Nevertheless the competitive processes within which they are engaged is "partly a lottery," a metaphor that is suggestive of situations of risk, and partly dependent on the genetic endowments of the entrepreneurs. Thus, one could quite plausibly interpret this passage as being implicitly underpinned by an immutable, ergodic conception of the competitive processes of capitalism.[17]

Moving on, Keynes argues that a uniquely correct market valuation (of future prospective yields) cannot be calculated because current knowledge does not provide a sufficient foundation for a precise mathematical expectation:

> We are assuming, in effect, that the existing market valuation, however arrived at, is uniquely *correct* in relation to our existing knowledge of the facts which will influence the yield of the investment, and that it will only change in proportion to changes in this knowledge; though, *philosophically speaking*, it cannot be uniquely correct, since our existing knowledge does not provide a sufficient basis for a calculated mathematical expectation (Keynes, CW VII, p. 152, emphasis added).

This passage seemingly suggests a strong conception of the economic process as transmutable. *Even if* agents had the ability to collect and successfully process all the information relating to past and current outcomes, such (market) information does not, and could not, provide the evidential basis for forecasting future outcomes. In such a world the past provides a limited guide as to the course of future events, economic agents are unable to discover the future and are truly uncertain, e.g. there presently *does not exist information* which will enable them to discover the uniquely correct market valuation. Nevertheless as we shall elaborate the subsequent passages at times appear to directly contradict such a strong view.

Keynes (CW VII, p. 153) proceeds to link the problems of uncertainty to the decision to invest, noting that it is the "precariousness [of this market valuation] which creates no small part of our contemporary problem of securing sufficient investment." He then goes on consider the factors that accentuate this precariousness, such as the "gradual increase in the proportion of the equity in the community's aggregate capital investment which is owned by persons who do not manage and have no special knowledge of the circumstances, either actual or prospective, of the business in question, [so that] the element of real knowledge in the valuation of investments by those who own them or contemplate purchasing them has seriously declined" which gives rise to a "conventional valuation which is established as the outcome of the mass psychology of a large number of ignorant individuals" (Keynes CW VII, pp. 153–154).[18,19]

Nevertheless there is "one feature in particular which deserves our attention" – the role of experts. Keynes (CW VII, p. 154) suggests that "[i]t might have been supposed that competition between expert professionals, possessing judgement and knowledge beyond that of the average private investor, would correct the vagaries of the ignorant individual left to himself." From a perspective that recognises the transmutably of the economic process we would expect to find the subsequent passages elaborating why this does not "correct the vagaries of the ignorant individual left to himself," to allude to notions of novelty, emergence, imagination or the nature of economic time, i.e. a consideration of the fact that while experts may be able to correctly discern and interpret the information contained in the past (and the present), they cannot mirror this into the future. That is to say, from a perspective which embraces transmutability, all individual agents, *including expert professionals*, are ignorant of the available courses of action or of the extent of future states of the world because of the irreversible and open-ended nature of time, because the future has yet to be created, and not merely because of limitations in the processing abilities of economic agents (see Dunn, 2001a). A conception of the economic process which a posteriori recognises its transmutability means that the future cannot be known prior to its *creation*, regardless of the processing powers we impute to agents – it is for this reason that a uniquely correct valuation cannot be arrived at.

According to Keynes, however, one of the reasons why a uniquely correct valuation cannot be made is not that the future cannot be known in advance of its creation, but that experts are forced to follow the short-termism of the herd – social convention dictates it:

> It is an inevitable result of an investment market organised along the lines described. For it is not sensible to pay 25 for an investment of which you believe the prospective yield to justify a value of 30, if you also believe that the market will value it at 20 three months hence. Thus, the professional investor is forced to concern himself with the anticipation of impending changes . . . Professional investment may be likened to those newspaper competitions in which the competitors have to pick out the six prettiest faces from a hundred photographs, the prize being awarded to the competitor whose choice most nearly corresponds to the average preferences of the competitors as a whole; so that each competitor has to pick, not those faces which he himself finds prettiest, but those which he thinks likeliest to catch the fancy of the other competitors, all of whom are looking at the problem from the same point of view. It is not a case of choosing those which, to the best of one's judgement, are really the prettiest, nor even those which average opinion genuinely thinks the prettiest. We have reached the third degree where we devote our intelligences to anticipating what average opinion expects the average opinion to be (Keynes, CW VII, pp. 155–156).[20]

The nature of the stock market decrees that the professional expert investor is forced to follow the general market valuation rather than anything based upon fundamentals or "intrinsic values" because the short-termism and ignorance of the stock market swamp reason.[21] To draw on Keynes's metaphor, it is not that is not possible to define beauty, rather the nature of the contest is such that beauty is defined by social conventions rather than by an objective assessment.[22] Indeed there is nothing in Keynes's discussion that precludes the professional investor from forming a correct judgement:

> If the reader interjects that there must surely be large profits to be gained from the other players in the long run by a skilled individual who, unperturbed by the prevailing pastime, continues to purchase investments on the best genuine long-term expectations he can frame, he must be answered, first of all, that there are, indeed, such serious-minded individuals and that it makes a vast difference to an investment market whether or not they predominate in their influence

over the game-players. But we must also add that there are several factors which jeopardise the predominance of such individuals in modern investment markets. Investment based on genuine long-term expectation is so difficult to-day as to be scarcely practicable (Keynes, CW VII, pp. 156–157).

For Keynes the process of investment is a "game" (see Skidelsky, 1992, p. 323).[23] The problem is that institutions and social conventions conspire against reason. If the professional investor is "successful, that will only confirm the general belief in his rashness; and if in the short-term he is unsuccessful, which is very likely, he will not receive much mercy. Worldly wisdom teaches that it is better for reputation to fail conventionally than to succeed unconventionally" (Keynes, CW VII, p. 158). It is precisely for such reasons that Keynes normatively notes that "[t]he social object of *skilled* investment *should* be to *defeat the dark forces of time and ignorance* which envelop our future" (Keynes, CW VII, p. 155, emphasis added). The fact that it is possible to defeat the "dark forces of time and ignorance" is suggestive that perhaps ultimately a correct valuation is possible, i.e. that an immutable conception of economic processes hides behind the distorting irrationality of stock market investment. From a genuinely transmutable perspective, however, it would be impossible to defeat the "dark forces of time and ignorance" – however much time the professional investor is faced with (cf. Davidson, 1998). And hence Keynes appears inconsistent on such matters.

Keynes's discussion clearly centres on the unintended consequences of the institutional shift being observed in capitalism.[24] The rise of the joint stock company and its associated institutions has given rise to a cadre of dilettante investors who are able to alter their investment portfolios quickly and without appreciable cost, nor consideration of the consequences of their actions upon the wider community. Consequently Keynes argues that if one were married to one's decisions, as in earlier times (see the quotation above), there would not be a market to follow, and one would be compelled to consider a longer time horizon for the prospective yield, rather than focusing on short-term yields and price movements:

> The spectacle of modern investment markets has sometimes moved me towards the conclusion that to make the purchase of an investment permanent and indissoluble, like marriage, except by reason of death or other grave cause, might be a useful remedy for our contemporary evils. For this would force the investor to direct his mind to the long-term prospects and to those only (Keynes, CW VII, p. 160).[25]

Nevertheless the answer, though, is not to return to earlier, more primitive times, which is somewhat prescient given this was before marriage came to resemble the stock market; rather Keynes (CW VII, p. 378) urged a "comprehensive socialisation of investment" which can usher in a more rational approach to investment.[26] However, as we shall elaborate further in the next section, Keynes's

(CW VII, pp. 376–379) advocacy of a socialisation of investment was aimed at offsetting the shrinking investment opportunities in an "old" economy, which runs counter to the view that the essence of entrepreneurship is the creation of new investment opportunities.

Notwithstanding the instabilities generated by the febrile atmosphere of the stock exchange, however, there are further instabilities to be recognised; the fact that it is a "characteristic of human nature that a large proportion of our positive activities depend on spontaneous optimism rather than on a mathematical expectation, whether moral or hedonistic or economic. Most, probably, of our decisions to do something positive, the full consequences of which will be drawn out over many days to come, can only be taken as a result of animal spirits – of a spontaneous urge to action rather than inaction, and not as the outcome of a weighted average of quantitative benefits multiplied by quantitative probabilities" (Keynes, CW VII, p. 161). That is to say given the uncertainties surrounding the future, investment is very much a matter of animal spirits (for a discussion see Koppl, 1991; Marchionatti, 1998). This again appears suggestive of a conception of the economic process which assumes transmutability, especially as this discussion seemingly encompasses the professional investor. Nevertheless, the causal sequence in Keynes is clear: it is because of the uncertain nature of the future that economic agents rely on their animal spirits, or fall back on convention. Moreover the emergence of the stock exchange accentuates the precarious nature of such investment decisions. This is quite distinct from a creative view of the economic process. That is to say, we might have expected Keynes to argue that because of the animal spirits and novelty inducing actions of agents (especially those concerned with investment), uncertainty for other agents emerges.

Fluctuations, in the *General Theory*, originate in business psychology and find their conduit in monetary circulation.[27] But although "[m]oney in its significant attributes is, above all, a subtle device for linking the present to the future; and we cannot even begin to discuss the effect of changing expectations on current activities except in monetary terms" (Keynes, CW VII, p. 294), the focus is on the *reaction* to unforeseen events, rather than how the process of accumulation generates uncertainty. Even though Keynes links the notion of animal spirits to the plunge into the abyss of the unknown, he does not make the link with the emergent process of origination and fecundity which are fuelled by the competitive process.[28]

What is more, while the notion of animal spirits is perhaps the closest that Keynes comes to a stress on the creative and emergent nature of the competitive process, as a metaphor it is misleading, at best unflattering, at worst contemptuous, reducing the propensity to invest to animalistic and basic impulses and seemingly eschewing creativity and imagination. Moreover the notion of animal spirits raises pertinent questions about the continuity with Keynes's discussion in the *Treatise on Probability*, which attempts to sketch out a theory of *rational* decision making under situations when non-numerical probabilities cannot be assigned. That is to say, the notion of animal spirits points to what we may call the "non-rational" interpretative thesis associated with Shackle (1967) and Winslow (1986a, b) among others.

In summary, the whole focus on expectations is as a *reaction* to new events, to new circumstances, to "shifting and unreliable evidence" (Keynes, CW VII, p. 315).[29] Keynes's whole emphasis is quite distinct from one which suggests that expectations provide the raw imagination to create a new future. Expectations in Keynes refer to the response to circumstance rather than the creation of circumstance.[30] Arguably both are important and should be part of the same general story (see Davidson, 1996). Moreover the precariousness of expectations is founded on the "uncontrollable and disobedient psychology of the business world" (Keynes, CW VII, p. 317). This results in the associated suggestion that if this psychology could be tamed, then the associated problems of a collapse in business confidence can be overcome. Indeed this is the more general argument of the *General Theory*, which deserves further consideration.

4. TRANSFORMATION AND THE *GENERAL THEORY*

Let us take stock of the argument thus far. It is clear from the discussion above that Keynes's discussion of uncertainty, as it impinges upon expectations, does not appear to find its origins in the creative dynamics of the economic process. That is to say uncertainty does not have its origins in the novelty-inducing actions of economic agents.[31] But it should not be inferred from this discussion that one is necessarily arguing that Keynes was a theorist who assumed the future was immutable. Throughout the *General Theory*, and elsewhere, Keynes makes many pregnant suggestions as to the transmutability of the economic realm.[32] Indeed, in the *General Theory* Keynes develops a structured and differentiated social ontology. One can identify three different levels of transformation in the *General Theory*, focusing on the actions and influence of individuals, institutions and governments. The *General Theory* is a treatise devoted to changing the philosophies of governments and hence the institutional structures of the economy, especially as it impinges on the "free" actions of individuals within the economy.

Keynes clearly rejects immutable, natural law philosophy and embraces a view that agents, and groups of agents, can alter the rules of the game. For instance Keynes warns us that although we oscillate around "an intermediate position" below full employment and above that which would "endanger life," we "must not conclude that the mean position thus determined by 'natural' tendencies, namely, by those tendencies which are likely to persist, failing measures expressly designed to correct them, is, therefore, established by laws of necessity . . . [It] is a fact of observation concerning the world at it is or has been, and *not a necessary principle which cannot be changed*" (Keynes, CW VII, p. 254, emphasis added).[33] This clearly provides for an open, transformative view of the economic system.[34]

Indeed, Keynes (CW VII, p. 65) recognises the power of the individual, noting that a "decision to consume or not to consume truly lies within the power of the individual; so does a decision to invest or not to invest. The amounts of aggregate income and of aggregate savings are the *results* of the free choice of individuals." This is suggestive of a transmutable conceptualisation of the economic system, and especially the decision to invest. What is more, the organic link between individual choices and collective outcomes is apparent. That is to say that free choices made by individuals over, say, consumption, are heavily constrained by the decisions of others which serve to determine that individual's income. Similarly, Keynes recognises the role of decentralised entrepreneurship:

> The advantages of efficiency of the decentralisation of decisions and of individual responsibility is even greater, perhaps, than the nineteenth century supposed; and the reaction against the appeal to self-interest may have gone too far. But, above all, individualism, if it can be purged of its defects and its abuses, is the best safeguard of personal liberty in the sense that, compared to any other system, it greatly widens the field for the exercise of personal choice. It is also the best safeguard of the variety of life, which emerges precisely from this extended field of personal choice, and the loss of which is the greatest of all the losses of the homogenous or totalitarian states. For this variety preserves the traditions which embody the most secure and successful choices of former generations; it colours the present with the diversification of its fancy; and, being the handmaid of experiment as well as of tradition and of fancy it is the most powerful instrument to better the future (Keynes, CW VII, p. 380).

Nevertheless while this points to a transformative conception of choice there is a failure to explore how the emergent novelty associated with enterprise might generate uncertainty for other investors. There is failure to link the transformative actions of agents to the emergence of uncertainty in the minds of other agents.

Equally when re-stating the *General Theory* Keynes (CW VII, p. 252) notes the psychological propensities which "limit the instability resulting from rapid changes in the prospective yields of capital assets due to sharp fluctuations in business psychology or to epoch-making inventions." This allusion to epoch-making inventions suggests that Keynes does espouse a view which embodies the transmutability of the economic process.[35] Moreover in his response to Tinbergen Keynes (CW XIV, pp. 285–289), questioning the method of econometrics, asked: "What place is left for expectation and the state of confidence relating to the future? What place is allowed for non-numerical factors, such as inventions, politics, labour troubles, wars, earthquakes, financial crises," saliently arguing that "the economic environment is not homogenous over time."[36] Nevertheless such creative acts are not linked up to a discussion and recognition of the nexus to the emergence and salience of uncertainty historically. There is a failure to link such allusions and insinuations to the creative and imaginative impulse associated with enterprise and the emergence of the salience of uncertainty throughout the *General Theory* and after.[37]

Moreover, such comments should be considered alongside Keynes's (CW VII, pp. 372–384) identification of the propensity of capitalism to stagnate due to the exhaustion of investment opportunities and a rising propensity to save (which embody the concomitant implication that there are notional limits to human demands). According to Keynes, in wealthy communities the propensity to invest is weaker reflecting a lower propensity to consume and a capital richness. Keynes's (CW VII, p. 31) logic leads him to a stagnationist *obiter dictum*: "not only is the marginal propensity to consume weaker in a wealthy community, but, owing to its accumulation of capital being already larger, the opportunities for further investment are less attractive unless the rate of interest falls at a sufficiently rapid rate." But this seemingly points to the satiation of wants and capital, and not the manufacture of wants and the pervasive and invasive thrust of creatively destructive capital accumulation and the uncertainties that this generates. For Keynes, the entrepreneurial function is linked to the stagnating vices of the accumulating elite.[38] He fails to link the explosive energy of capitalism to the long-run "pathological vices" of accumulation existing in historical time.

All in all Keynes's discussion in the *General Theory* (and subsequent defence) is a short-run snapshot of a dynamic long-run process. This is clear from Keynes's employment of the shifting equilibrium model outlined in the *General Theory* (see Kregel, 1976). Keynes appears to treat uncertainty as an epistemological and/or as a reactive, psychological phenomenon, rather than viewing it also as a product of the processes of accumulation. As Schumpeter (1954, p. 1175) observed of the *General Theory*, but has now been forgotten, "[t]hose who look for the essence of capitalism in the phenomena that attend the incessant recreation of this apparatus and the incessant revolution that goes on within it must therefore be excused if they hold that Keynes's theory abstracts from the essence of the capitalist process." But is it the case that elsewhere Keynes "abstracts from the essence of the capitalist process?"

5. UNCERTAINTY AND THE ECONOMIC PROCESS

Keynes was not ahistorical. He recognised several institutional shifts, in the *General Theory* and elsewhere, that had occurred since Victorian times, such as "the eclipse of the independent entrepreneur, maximising his profits, by the joint-stock company, mainly interested in the general stability of trade; the organisation of the labour market by trade unions; the increasingly dominant role of the banking system in determining monetary conditions; and growing state responsibility for investment through the rise of the public corporation" (Skidelsky, 1992, p. 229). Moreover in the 1925 lectures "Am I a Liberal?" and the "The Economic Transition in England," Keynes, drawing on Commons, attempted to develop a non-Marxist conceptualisation of the economic process circumscribed by three distinct epochs: the ages of scarcity, abundance and stabilisation.[39] The age of scarcity referred to pre-capitalist modes of governance and coercion, including communitarian, feudal and medieval power structures. The age of abundance was associated with the dawn of capitalism and the early success of an individualist liberal economic order. The third age of stabilisation is characterised by:

> a diminution of individual liberty, enforced in part by governmental sanctions, but mainly by economic sanctions through concerted action, whether secret, semi-open, or arbitrational, of associations, corporations, unions, and other collective movements of manufacturers, merchants, labourer, farmers, and bankers . . . The transition from economic anarchy to a regime which deliberately aims at controlling and directing economic forces in the interests of social justice and social stability, will present enormous difficulties both technical and political (Keynes, CW IX, pp. 303–305).

However, the Keynes/Commons framework fails to provide a historical appreciation of the fact that widespread acknowledgement of the importance of risk and uncertainty and its nexus to accumulation is a comparatively recent phenomenon. There is no recognition of the link between the forward-looking nature of monetary accumulation that characterises the emergence of capitalism, and the rise and increasingly widespread usage of future orientated concepts such as risk and uncertainty.[40] There is no attempt to link the emergence of uncertainty with the "age of stabilisation," e.g. to the fact that many of the institutions of the "age of stabilisation" may have emerged to mitigate the impact of an uncertain future.[41] But concepts such as risk and uncertainty are the product of social relations and are embedded in emergent structures and institutions.[42]

Moreover, Keynes contemplates an age when enormous technical and political difficulties are overcome such that the economic problem is largely solved. In his essay, "Economic Possibilities for Our Grandchildren," Keynes ponders a future where people will be freed from the pathologies of money making. Even Keynes's (mature) views on the relationship between saving and the macroeconomic position were embedded in a static (and even stagnating) conception of the nature of the economic process. Keynes "came to see [saving] as excessive in relation to the investment opportunity available in an 'old' economy like Britain's" (Skidelsky, 1992, p. 274). Keynes judged the economic problem to be largely solved with the near exhaustion of profitable ventures upon which enterprise could embark, i.e. a view of enterprise as decreasingly important and valuable. Arguably, this points to a view of enterprise in which lays stress on the discovery of profitable opportunities rather than the creation of them (cf. Dunn, 2002).

Keynes's historical vision succeeds in playing down the creative nature of the competitive process and diminishes the impact of the "new consumers' goods, the new methods of production or transportation, the new markets, the new forms of industrial organisation that capitalist enterprise creates" (Schumpeter, 1943, p. 83). As Plumptre (1983, p. 153) has commented, critically reflecting first-hand on Keynes's "Economic Possibilities for our Grandchildren": "society is not likely to run out of new wants as long as consumption is conspicuous and competitive." Or, to put it another way, Keynes does not consider how firms engage in the creation of new wants and desires and attempt to mitigate uncertainties so as to preserve accumulation and to enable themselves to reproduce (cf. Dunn, 2001b; Galbraith, 1967). The creative manner of the competitive process and its nexus to uncertainty lies dormant in Keynes, and is perhaps symptomatic of the fact that he "was less interested in processes than in outcomes" (Skidelsky, 1992, p. 274).

6. TRANSFORMATION AND THE ENTREPRENEUR

Keynes does on occasion, however, elsewhere allude to the creativity and change induced by the entrepreneur. In his essay "The End of Laissez Faire," Keynes (CW IX, p. 291) argues that "[m]any of the greatest economic evils of our time are the fruits of risk, uncertainty, and ignorance." Keynes's discussion is suggestive of a creative view of the economic process: "[i]t is because particular individuals, fortunate in situation or in abilities, are able to take advantage of uncertainty and ignorance, and also because for the same reason big business is often a lottery, that great inequalities of wealth come about; and these same factors are also the cause of unemployment of labour, or the disappointment of reasonable business expectations, and of the impairment of efficiency and production" (Keynes, CW IX, p. 291).

This discussion appears to link the discussion of uncertainty to capitalism's incessant drive to introduce product innovations and technological revolutions. Moreover, such an interpretation links well with Keynes's (CW IX, pp. 276, 282–283) rejection of simplistic market-based selection-of-the-fittest arguments. If the future cannot be known in advance of its creation, then the market (or governments for that matter) cannot select and learn the optimal rules and routines that characterise the environments because *they are not yet there to be discovered*. However, a moment's reflection reveals that such an interpretation is contentious. To describe the economic process as approximating a lottery is suggestive of a world of (ergodic) risk. Similarly, individuals "take advantage of uncertainty" rather than create it. In Keynes, uncertainty exists independently of the process of competition. Uncertainty is not transformed in its significance over time as new products, new methods of organisation, new governments and new institutional structures are originated within the process of competition and history.

Likewise, in his review of H. G. Wells's *The World of William Clissold*, Keynes (CW IX, pp. 315–320) recognised the "creative force and constructive will" of the elite, arguing that the force for change came from men of knowledge and power – the business tycoons and the scientists. For Keynes it is the "profiteer" who injects life into capitalism. Investment is an uncertain vocation: "It is enterprise which builds and improves the world's possessions . . . [and] the engine which drives enterprise is . . . profit" (Keynes CW VI, p. 132). Such creativity, however, was most important in the earlier individualistic "age of abundance." By the time of the "age of stabilisation" all the profitable opportunities were nearing exhaustion; the entrepreneurial class had become degenerative, not least due to the corrupting pursuit of avarice.

For instance in his essay "Am I a Liberal?," Keynes (CW IX, p. 327) argued that the transmission of wealth and power via the hereditary principle underscores the decadence and decay of individualistic capitalism. As Skidelsky (1992, p. 259) documents, Keynes, unlike Marshall, "had little respect for the business vocation . . . Keynes ranked business life so low partly because he considered that the material goods produced by entrepreneurs has less ethical value that the intellectual and aesthetic goods produced by dons and artists, [and] partly because he despised the 'love of money' as a motive for action." In sharp contrast to, say, Schumpeter, Shackle, Marshall, or even Marx, Keynes seems to regard the entrepreneur as a necessary evil and far from heroic: "What chiefly impressed Keynes about British businessmen was their stupidity and laziness. He was a firm believer in the three-generation cycle: the man of energy and imagination creates the business: the son coasts along; the grandson goes bankrupt" (Skidelsky, 1992, p. 259).[43] And while Keynes talks about the "spirit of enterprise," this is not equal to a recognition of the change – and uncertainty – inducing activities of enterprise.

Overall, Keynes's vision of the capitalist process is "one lurching forward by fits and starts, while opportunities for exceptional profit cause, briefly, the gambling spirit to swamp the counsels of prudence" (Skidelsky, 1992, p. 335). Indeed it is significant, although from our perspective unsurprising, that Keynes (quoted in Skidelsky, 1992, p. 267) argued that the "necessity of profit as a spur to effort . . . was greatly exaggerated." Keynes's theoretical discussion stands in sharp contrast to Knight (1921) who, while also identified with introducing the distinction between risk and uncertainty in economics, defended profit as a reward for risk-taking and uncertainty bearing, and linked it up to the historical process of accumulation.[44] What Keynes "underestimated was humanity's ingenuity in inventing ways to keep capital scarce" (Skidelsky, 1992, p. 609). Keynes seeks to play down a heroic conceptualisation of the entrepreneurial function. His elitist orientation led Keynes to regard entrepreneurs as a necessary evil who could contribute, not to civilisation, but to the possibility of civilisation.

7. CONCLUDING COMMENTS

We have considered Keynes's conception of uncertainty and its role in the process of accumulation. It is clear that for Keynes the exigency of emergent creativity does not give rise to the uncertainties that pertain to the process of competition. This should not be surprising, as his conception of uncertainty across his social, literary and economic writings is primarily philosophical and ahistorical.[45] The failure to link creativity and novelty to uncertainty results in a usurpation of the antecedence and origins of uncertainty and its nexus to the process of accumulation.[46]

Keynes's whole discussion, while suggestive of a transmutable conception of the economic process, does not seek to emphasise the emergent creativity associated with the process of accumulation that gives rise to uncertainty and reverberates through the state of long-term expectations. In the *General Theory* and after, uncertainty is an ahistorical *deus ex machina* that drives a stake into institutional stability. Such an approach, however, leaves the origins and emergence of the salience of uncertainty unaddressed. Why is the future uncertain? Is it just that we simply cannot know the future? Or are there reasons why our knowledge about the future is limited?

Shackle recognised the salience of such questions and responded by noting that the origins of uncertainty are to be found in the creative, emergent processes associated with competition and capital accumulation. This stands in stark distinction to Keynes's *deus ex machina* treatment of uncertainty. While Keynes recognises that avarice and accumulation are the driving force of capitalism, this is not the same as locating the origins of uncertainty in the process of competition. Nevertheless, as we have seen, Keynes leaves the theoretical door slightly ajar, paving the way for the development of a transmutable economics.[47] Clearly that is the next task ahead.

NOTES

1. While it is safe to argue that uncertainty is a continuous strand in Keynes's thinking, it is far from clear that its theoretical status and relationship with his economics is unchanging. Thus, for the purposes of exposition the discussions contained in the *Treatise*, the *General*

Theory, and beyond, will be considered on their own terms, and little explicit attempt to link them will be made. Treating the debates in this way strengthens the present argument and avoids entering an already overcrowded playing field.

2. Notwithstanding the fact that much of *Treatise* deals with abstract issues of probability theory rather than an elaboration of the nature of human action.

3. References to Keynes's *Collected Writings* (CW) take the form of the volume number in Roman numerals followed by the page numbers.

4. Although it is important to note, as Lawson (1985, p. 913) has lamented, that "[u]nfortunately Keynes nowhere explicitly defines uncertainty in the *Treatise on Probability*."

5. Lawson (1985, p. 911) notes that "[p]robability in this (inductive) framework is not, therefore, a property of the actual physical world but a property of the way in which we think about the world . . . If we interpret this probability relation as a degree of belief then clearly it is seen to be subjective in the sense that the information *h* may vary from person to person (and possibly also in the sense that individuals may differ in their reasoning powers). It is not, however, subjective in the sense that the probability bestowed upon a proposition *a* given the evidence *h* is subject to a human caprice. Rather the probability in a conclusion *a* given the evidence *h* is objective or fixed and corresponds to the degree of belief it is *rational* for a person to hold in the hypothesis given the information available."

6. Following Hodgson (2001, p. 50) "the term 'ahistorical' applies to any concept or theory that is claimed to pertain to *all* possible socio-economic systems." It is abundantly clear from Keynes's discussion in the *Treatise* that his framework is applicable to all possible socio-economic systems. Keynes's (CW VIII, pp. 272–275) distinction between the rational from the true is particularly illustrative in this regard.

7. Although Keynes's discussion, as with all decision theory, is philosophical in orientation, his approach need not preclude the processes of history. That is to the processes of history can provide the evidential basis upon which decisions are made. However Keynes in the *Treatise* does not tell us whether the passage of time and decisions of agents affects the laws governing processes, i.e. whether human history ultimately matters.

8. Cf. Knight (1921, p. 198) who has suggested that it "is *conceivable* that all changes might take place in accordance with known laws."

9. Cf. Shackle (1979, p. 48): "Beginning I use here as the term for a taking-place in which some element, aspect or character is *ex nihilo*. No knowledge of antecedents, however complete and exact, would make possible a foreknowledge of that aspect of character."

10. According to Keynes (CW VIII, p. 356), "[t]he importance of probability can only be derived from the judgement that it is *rational* to be guided by it in action; and a practical dependence on it can only be justified by a judgement that in action we *ought* to act to take some account of it. It is for this reason that probability is to use the 'guide of life,' since to us, as Locke says, 'in the greatest part of our concernment, God has afforded only the Twilight, as I may so say, of Probability, suitable, I presume, to that state of Mediocrity and Probationership He has been pleased to place us in here.'"

11. With respect to the theory of value, Shackle (1972, p. 446) argues that: "It shows men as acting rationally, whereas to be human is to be denied the necessary condition of rationality, complete relevant knowledge."

12. Cf. Knight's (1921) famous treatise on entrepreneurship, which exhibits many similarities with Keynes's more philosophical treatment:

The business man himself not merely forms the best estimate he can of the outcome of his actions, but he is likely also to estimate the probability that his estimate is correct. The 'degree' of certainty or of confidence felt in this conclusion after it is reached cannot be ignored, for it is of the greatest practical significance. The action which follows upon an opinion depends as much upon the amount of confidence in that opinion as it does the favourableness of the opinion itself (Knight, 1921, pp. 226–227).

13. Cf. Skidelsky (1992, p. 423) who argues that Keynes "accepted the conventions of economics, especially the convention of rationality." But as Shackle (1972, p. xviii) has pointed out "there is a fundamental conflict between the appeal to rationality and the consideration of the consequences of time as it imprisons us actuality, the theoretician is confronted with a stark choice. He can reject rationality or time." Moreover there is a sense in which Keynes (CW X, pp. 448–449) recognised this later in life, as exemplified by his remarks in his essay "My Early Beliefs" where he argued: "I still suffer incurably from attributing an unreal rationality to other people's feelings and behaviour (and doubtless to my own, too). There is one small but extraordinarily silly manifestation of this absurd idea of what is 'normal,' namely the impulse to *protest* – to write a letter to *The Times*, call a meeting in the Guildhall, subscribe to some fund when my presuppositions as to what is 'normal' are not fulfilled. I behave as if there really existed some authority or standard to which I can successfully appeal if I shout loud enough – perhaps it is some hereditary vestige of a belief in the efficacy of prayer... Our [early Bloomsbury's] comments on life and affairs were bright and amusing, but brittle... because there was no solid diagnosis of human nature underlying them." Such passages are suggestive of the adoption of a transmutable perspective of "life and affairs" as it appears to reject the notion of some invariant standard or authority against which action should be compared, and rationality adjudged. Nevertheless there is a failure to link such a view of human action to the emergence of uncertainty and the nexus with accumulation. For a variety of perspectives on Keynes's approach to rationality see Bateman (1996), Meeks (1991), O'Donnell (1989) and Winslow (1993).

14. Coddington's (1983, pp. 53–54) reasoning, is thus "if there is great uncertainty surrounding investment decisions, and producers respond to this by making, so far as is possible, the same investment decisions this period as last period (since, after all, the result of previous decisions are the one thing they do know something about), this would not result in private sector investment's being wayward and unruly; indeed, it might result in greater stability than would result from sophisticated calculations based on epistemologically privileged beliefs or an uncanny degree of foresight. Thus, the fact of uncertainty does not of itself establish the conclusion concerning the wayward and unruly behaviour of particular macroeconomics variables. Indeed, it is not evident that this argument helps to establish Keynes's conclusion rather than the opposite conclusion... For what is required within Keynes's scheme is not the uncertainty, as such, surrounding private sector investment decisions; it is the wayward and unruly behaviour of the aggregates resulting from the decisions taken in the face of this uncertainty. Indeed, Keynes's system requires private sector investment to display this unruliness in two quite distinct senses: first, when compared with private sector *consumer* expenditure (this is required in order for Keynes's model to work); and, second when compared with *public* sector investment expenditure (this is required in order for Keynes's policies to work)."

15. "By 'very uncertain' I do not mean the same thing as 'very improbable.' Cf. My Treatise on Probability, Chap. 6 on 'The Weight of Arguments' " (Keynes, CW VII, p. 148, n. 1).

16. But if the world is uncertain, then the world is uncertain, and it could be said that we have no basis for estimating the yield of a railway tomorrow: after all ten years hence is only the culmination of 3,650 tomorrows. Do we find it more difficult to forecast what will happen in ten years relative to what will happen tomorrow because of complexity – that is there are more things which could happen over 10 years than tomorrow – or because of change, and more things can change in 10 years? Indeed it is for such reasons that many have tried to link Keynes's discussion to change and creativity or complexity (cf. Dequech, 1999; Marchionatti, 1998).

17. Ergodicity refers to the property by which the time and space averages that originate and are computed from any data generating process, either coincide for a series of infinite observations, or converge as the number of observations increases (with a probability of one) for a finite number (Davidson, 1991). The ergodic assumption implies that the past reveals the future – that over time agents can predict the future with actuarial certainty-equivalence. On the ergodic hypothesis the passage of time does not affect the joint probability laws governing processes, history ultimately does not matter. The notion of immutability is broader and encompasses the ergodic axiom, embodying "the presumption of a programmed stable, conservative system where the past, present and future reality are predetermined whether the system is stochastic or not" (Davidson, 1996, pp. 480–481).

18. Keynes claims that "the vast majority of those who are concerned with the buying and selling of securities know almost nothing whatever about what they are doing. They do not possess even the rudiments of what is required for a valid judgement, and are the prey of hopes and fears easily aroused by transient events and as easily dispelled. This is one of the odd characteristics of the capitalist system under which we live, which, when we are dealing with the real world, is not to be overlooked . . . [Hence] it may often profit the wisest to anticipate mob psychology rather than the real trend of events, and to ape unreason proleptically" (Keynes, CW VI, p. 323).

19. What is interesting is that here Keynes seems to assume that stock market valuations matter for real investment decisions, which is far from uncontentious. Indeed Tobin's q, which reflects stock market valuation, has not been successful in investment equations.

20. A much overlooked aspect of this passage is the overlap and possible origins of the "beauty contest" metaphor in Keynes's (CW VIII, pp. 27–29) prior discussion in the *Treatise* of the salience of an actual competition run by the *Daily Express* for the logical theory of probability.

21. As Skidelsky (1992, p. 525) has highlighted: "In the 1920s Keynes saw himself as a scientific gambler. He speculated on currencies and commodities. His aim was to play the cycle. This was the height of his 'barometric' enthusiasm . . . when he believed it was possible, by forecasting short-term rhythms, to beat the market. The gambling instinct was never quite extinguished." Keynes's whole philosophy of investment was governed by the principle of purchasing stock which he reasoned was under-priced "relative to its intrinsic worth." Indeed is quite clear from the following exegetical passages that Keynes held an "intrinsic values" approach to investment at some point after 1924, which suggests that the discussion in the *General Theory* was an elaboration of Keynes own investment philosophy:

> One is doing a fundamentally sound thing, that is to say, backing intrinsic values, enormously in excess of the market price, which at some utterly unpredictable date will in due course bring the ship home (Keynes, CWXII, p. 77).

I preferred one investment about which I had sufficient information to form a judgement to ten securities about which I know little or nothing (Keynes, CWXII, p. 81).

There are very few investors, I should say, who eschew the attempt to snatch capital profits at an early date more than I do. I lay myself open to criticism because I am generally trying to look a long way ahead and am prepared to ignore immediate fluctuations, if I am satisfied that the assets and the earning power are there. My purpose is to buy securities where I am satisfied as to assets and ultimate earning power and where the market price seems cheap in relation to these. If I succeed in this, I shall simultaneously have achieved safety-first and capital profits. All stocks and shares go up and down so violently that a safety-first policy is practically certain, if it is successful, to result in capital profits. For when the safety, excellence and cheapness of a share is generally realised, its price is bound to go up . . .. I am quite incapable of having adequate knowledge of more than a very limited range of investments. Time and opportunity do not allow more. Therefore, as the investible sums increase, the size of the unit must increase. I am in favour of having as large a unit as market conditions will allow and, apart from a small group of securities, this generally means a smaller unit than would be made necessary by the size of the investible fund.

As good examples of speculative attempts at capital profits I should instance South American shares and oil companies within the area of hostilities. I should not deny for a moment that such investments may result in capital profits. My objection is that I have no information on which to reach a good judgement, and the risks are clearly enormous. To suppose that safety-first consists in having a small gamble in a large number of different directions of the above kind, as compared with a substantial stake in a company where's [sic] one information is adequate, strikes me as a travesty of investment policy" (Keynes, CW XII, p. 82).

It is vastly easier to find 130 satisfactory investments than to find 325; particularly if you are largely depending on the repertory of one man . . . I myself follow fairly closely, or think I have some knowledge, of upwards of perhaps 200 investments; and whilst, say, 50 others (at the outside) may be followed closely by other members of the Finance Committee, I should say that the Provincial holds 50 to 100 securities about which none of the Board know much. Now out of the 200 which one tries to follow more or less, there are probably less than 50 in all classes about which, at any given time, one feels really enthusiastic. I am convinced that the good results shown by King's are mainly due to the large proportion of its assets held in the less than 50 favourite securities. To carry one's eggs in a great number of baskets, without having time or opportunity to discover how many have holes in the bottom, is the surest way of increasing risk and loss (Keynes, CW XII, p. 99).

One can put the distinction like this: By credit cycling I mean buying and selling according as you think shares cheap in relation to money. By my alternative I mean acting according as you think them cheap in relation to other shares, with particular reference to the possibilities of large relative appreciation; – which means buying them on their intrinsic value when, for one reason or another, they are unfashionable or appear very vulnerable on a short view. One may be, and no doubt is, inclined to be too slow to sell one's pets after they have had most of their rise. But looking back I don't blame myself much on this score; – it would have been easy to lose a great deal more by selling them too soon (Keynes, CW XII, p. 101).

> As time goes on I get more and more convinced that the right method in investment is to put fairly large sums into enterprises which one thinks one knows something about and in the management of which one thoroughly believes. It is a mistake to think that one limits one's risks by spreading too much between enterprises about which one knows little and has no reason for special confidence. Obviously this principle ought not to be carried too far. The real limitation, however, on its application in practice is in my experience the small number of enterprises about which at any given time one feels in this way. One's knowledge and experience are definitely limited and there are seldom more than two or three enterprises at any given time in which I personally feel myself entitled to put *full* confidence (CW XII, p. 57).

Nevertheless the whole notions of fundamentals or intrinsic values is suggestive of an immutable conception of economic processes (see Davidson, 1998).

22.   For an extended reflection on Keynes's views on "beauty" see O'Donnell (1995).

23.   Indeed gambling and gaming metaphors pervade the *General Theory*. But such metaphors are clearly suggestive of situations of risk and not radical uncertainty. Arguably this points to the fact that it is institutions and convention that conspire against rationality and not imagination and creativity.

24.   Cf. Skidelsky (1992, p. 556) who has suggested that "Keynes contention, in Chap. 12, is that the uncertainty attaching to expectations of the future yield of investment have given birth to a particular institution through which most of investment is channelled in a capitalist society – the stock market."

25.   Keynes (CW VII, p. 161) continues noting that the "only radical cure for the crises of confidence which afflict the economic life of the modern world would be to allow the individual no choice between consuming his income and ordering the production of the specific capital-asset which, even though it be on precarious evidence, impresses him as the most promising investment available to him. It might be that, at times when he was more than usually assailed by doubts concerning the future, he would turn in his perplexity towards more consumption and less new investment. But that would avoid the disastrous, cumulative and far-reaching repercussions of its being open to him, when thus assailed by doubts, to spend his income neither on the one nor on the other."

26.   Many have interpreted this as an argument for nationalisation. Clearly this is not what Keynes had in mind. Rather it was that more rational institutions for allocating capital could, and should, be devised so as to reconcile public and private interest. But this need not entail public provision nor "exclude all manner of compromises and of devices by which public authority will co-operate with private initiative . . . it is not the ownership of the instruments of production which it is important for the State to assume. If the State is able to determine the aggregate amount of resources devoted to augmenting the instruments and the basic rate of reward to those who own them, it will have accomplished all that is necessary" (Keynes, CW VII, p. 378).

27.   Accordingly it is business psychology which should be the focus of investigation for the study of economic vacillations and this leads one to Keynes's study of Freud and the dismal disdain of money-making and enterprise (see Winslow, 1986a, b, 1989, 1990, 1992).

28.   Indeed Keynes tends to make scant reference to the creativity of the entrepreneur, preferring to reserve it for the more aesthetic, higher pursuits. In "My Early Beliefs" Keynes (CW X, pp. 436–437) argues as still "nearer the truth than any other that I know," his previous convictions that "nothing mattered except states of mind" and that "the appropriate subjects of passionate contemplation and communion were a beloved person, beauty and truth, and one's prime objects in life were love, the creation and enjoyment of aesthetic experience and

the pursuit of knowledge." Indeed this forms the foundation of the contrast in "Economic Possibilities for Our Grandchildren" between capitalism and the ideal republic. Here he anticipates a future when we shall be "free . . . to return to some of the most sure and certain principles of religion and traditional virtue – that avarice is a vice, that the exaction of usury is a misdemeanour, and the love of money is detestable, that those walk most truly in the paths of virtue and sane wisdom who take least thought for the morrow. We shall once more value ends above means and prefer the good to the useful. We shall honour those who can teach us how to pluck the hour and the day virtuously and well, the delightful people who are capable of taking direct enjoyment in things, the lilies of the field who toil not, neither do they spin" (Keynes, CW IX, pp. 330–331).

29. But as Schumpeter (1936, p. 793) pointed out, "[a]n expectation acquires explanatory value only if we are made to understand why people expect what they expect. Otherwise expectation is a mere *deus ex machina* that conceals problems instead of solving them" (Schumpeter, 1936, p. 793).

30. We may consider Keynes's correspondence with Townshend, his most intellectually radical interpreter according to Shackle (1967), on 7th December 1938. Keynes (CW XXIX, p. 294) noted that "[t]o avoid being in the position of Buridan's ass, we fall back, therefore, and necessarily do so, on motives of another kind, which are not 'rational' in the sense of being concerned with the evaluation of consequences, but are decided by habit, instinct, preference, desire, will, etc." But it should be remembered that Buridan's ass, relates to the problem of decision making such that when faced with deciding between two equidistant and equally desirable bales of hay the ass starved to death due to the absence of grounds for preferring to go to one bale of hay than another. However, from a transmutable perspective the bales of hay were *pre-existing* and the allusion is clearly one of scholastic philosophy rather than one of considering the consequences of imagination and of practical action.

31. Compare, for example, Cliffe Leslie who recognised that variety, disruption and uncertainty were themselves embedded in the corrupting pursuit of avarice:

> The desire for wealth, or of its representative – money – instead of enabling the economist to foretell values and prices, destroys the power of prediction that formerly existed, because it is the mainspring of industrial and commercial activity and progress, of infinite variety and incessant alteration in the structure and operations of the economic world (Leslie, 1888, p. 223).

32. There are also many other equally pregnant immutable metaphors in the *General Theory*. Keynes (see for example CW VII, pp. 9, 50), in several places, appears to characterise the economic system and process as "a machine." One should also consult Skidelsky (1992, p. 406) who argues that the zeitgeist was very much that "society was a machine whose working could be improved by deliberative action, with unintended side-effects being equally amenable to correction and control, much as a mechanic fine-tunes an engine." Equally, as noted above (see note 21), gambling metaphors pervade the *General Theory* (see for example CW VII, pp. 150–151, 155–156, 159, 381), and especially Chap. 12, which is illuminating in terms of the present discussion as they relate ostensibly to situations that approximate ergodic risk. Does it really matter what metaphor's Keynes uses to think about the economy? Clearly it does! Metaphors shape the way we frame problems, understand solutions and act. Changing the metaphors provide us with the freedom to act differently. Indeed the employment of such metaphors can be viewed as encouraging the hydraulic view of the economic process that came to exemplify the Keynesianism of the 1960s (cf. Coddington, 1983).

33. Cf. Keynes (CW XIV, p. 300; referred to by Skidelsky, 1992, p. 540) who in a letter to Harrod 16th July 1938 noted: "I also want to emphasise strongly the point about economics being a moral science. I mentioned before that it deals with introspection and with values. I might have added that it deals with motives, expectations, psychological uncertainties. One has to be constantly on guard against treating the material as constant and homogenous. It is as though the fall of the apple to the ground depended on the apple's motives, on whether it is worth falling to the ground, the whether the ground wanted the apple to fall, and on mistaken calculations on the part of the apple as to how far it was from the centre of the earth." While in one sense this captures the thinking, acting, transforming subject, the emphasis pertains to whether the apple wanted to do something and how it evaluated a course of action, rather than capturing the creativity associated with decision and agency.

34. The same can also be said of Keynes's (CW VII, p. 243) discussion against the natural rate of interest.

35. Skidelsky (1992, p. 326) holds that "Keynes followed both Schumpeter and Robertson in holding that innovations come in waves; but he had no real theory of profit."

36. This points to a clarification of a detail left ambiguous in the *Treatise on Probability*, that social structures are not immutable through time. See also note 33.

37. One should consider Keynes's (CW XIV, p. 113) *Quarterly Journal of Economics* article, which provides perhaps the most compelling evidence of a radical conceptualisation of uncertainty:

> By 'uncertain' knowledge, let me explain, I do not mean merely to distinguish what is known for certain from what is only probable. The game of roulette is not subject, in this sense, to uncertainty; nor is the prospect of a Victory bond being drawn. Or, again, the expectation of life is only slightly uncertain. Even the weather is only moderately uncertain. The sense in which I am using the term is that in which the prospect of a European war is uncertain, or the price of copper and the rate of interest twenty years hence, or the obsolescence of a new invention, or the position of private wealth owners in the social system in 1970. About these matters there is no scientific basis on which to form any calculable probability whatever. We simply do not know. Nevertheless, the necessity for action and for decision compels us as practical men to do our best to overlook this awkward fact and to behave exactly as we should if we had behind us a good Benthamite calculation of a series of prospective advantages and disadvantages, each multiplied by its appropriate probability, waiting to be summed.

But what is clear from such passages is that the whole tone of Keynes's QJE article is reactive and does not use concepts such as creativity, imagination and novelty. That is to say the emphasis does not allude to the creative and change inducing role of entrepreneurs and firms who "reform or revolutionize the pattern of production by exploiting an invention or, more generally, an untried technological possibility for producing a new commodity or producing an old one in a new way, by opening up a new source of supply of materials or a new outlet for products, by reorganizing an industry and so on" (Schumpeter, 1943, p. 132). Rather the QJE article is best interpreted as an attempt to establish reasonable grounds for belief under conditions of uncertainty such that in addition to ordinary logic and empirical analysis, knowledge is also composed of conventions and intuition (Davis, 1994).

38. And although the rentier would disappear the entrepreneur would still have a role, it would not be linked to the novelty inducing creativity of the entrepreneur, rather "enterprise and skill" is associated with the "estimation of prospective yields about which opinions could differ" (Keynes, CW VII, p. 221).

39. Commons (1934, pp. 773–788) in his *Institutional Economics*, outlined three "economic stages" namely:

> a period of Scarcity preceding the 'industrial revolution,' the latter beginning in the Eighteenth Century . . . a period of Abundance with its alternations of oversupply and undersupply for a hundred years or more . . . and a period of Stabilization, beginning with the concerted movements of capitalists and laborers in the Nineteenth Century (Commons, 1934, p. 773).

40. Notwithstanding Giddens' (1999) idiosyncratic conceptualisation of risk, his comments in his Reith lectures are apposite: "Risk is the mobilising dynamic of a society bent on change, that wants to determine its own future rather than leaving it to religion, tradition, or the vagaries of nature. Modern capitalism differs from all previous forms of economic system in terms of its attitudes towards the future . . . Modern capitalism embeds itself into the future by calculating future profit and loss, and therefore risk, as a continuous process. This wasn't possible until the invention of double entry bookkeeping in the 15th Century in Europe, which made it possible to track in a precise way how money can be invested to make more money."

41. At a superficial level Galbraith's (1977) *The Age of Uncertainty* appears to fill this void. However Galbraith's contention is that the great certainties of the Victorian age have been given way to social upheaval and the uncertainties associated with a delicate ideological stand off between Communism and Capitalism, rather than elaborating on the increasing preoccupation with the uncertainties of accumulation. Nevertheless Galbraith's (1967; see also Dunn, 2001b) *The New Industrial State* can be viewed as an attempt to theorise on the rise and emergence of the large corporate enterprise as a means to mitigate the uncertainties that pertain to investment and accumulation.

42. As Giddens (1999) notes "Apart from some marginal contexts, in the Middle Ages there was no concept of risk. Nor . . . was there in most other traditional cultures. The idea of risk appears to have taken hold in the 16th and 17th centuries, and was first coined by Western explorers as they set off on their voyages across the world. The word 'risk' seems to have come into English through Spanish or Portuguese, where it was used to refer to sailing into uncharted waters. Originally, in other words, it had an orientation to space. Later, it became transferred to time, as used in banking and investment – to mean calculation of the probable consequences of investment decisions for borrowers and lenders. It subsequently came to refer to a wide range of other situations of uncertainty."

43. This should be no surprise to students of Keynes. He was statist and elitist, embracing the ascendance to power of the new class of Platonic Guardians (Skidelsky, 1992, p. 224). Prior to the twentieth century, nineteenth century economists argued for a liberal political system to underwrite economic prosperity. Keynes in effect reversed this and sought to sustain economic prosperity and safeguard the liberal political system. Keynes "welcomed the 'aggregation of production' as tending to stabilise the economy; he accepted uncritically the view that captains of industry were constrained, by the size of their undertakings, to serve the public interest; and he assumed, without further argument, that an interconnected elite of business managers, bankers, civil servants, economists and scientists, all trained at Oxford and Cambridge and imbued with a public service ethic, would come to run these organs of state, whether private or public, and make them hum to the same tune. He wanted to decentralise and devolve only down to the level of Top People" (Skidelsky, 1992, p. 228).

44. For Keynes (CW V, p. 111), profit is defined as "the difference between the costs of production of the current output and its actual sales proceeds." This clearly does not preclude

a conceptualisation of profits as a reward for risk taking, or stepping into an uncertain future, but nevertheless the difference of emphasis is palpable.

45. In Keynes's (CW VI) "amateur" economic history in the *Treatise on Money* what is striking is the absence of "any explicit reference to uncertainty" (Skidelsky, 1992, p. 335).

46. As Hodgson (2001, p. 3) has pointed out, "[i]f history matters – at least in the sense of social development being path dependent – then our analyses must explore the particularities of the past. While we may retain general principles or guidelines, detailed analyses of particular events, structures and circumstances are required."

47. While it is not presented as such, Davidson's (1991, 1996) discussion of non-ergodicity offers the prospect of further augmenting Keynes's discussion. At a superficial level Davidson's elaboration of non-ergodicity parallels Keynes's *deus ex machina* treatment. However a much neglected aspect of Davidson's discussion is the role accorded to creative, crucial decision making. Crucial decisions represent a *sufficient* (but not a necessary) condition for the existence of non-ergodic processes and pave the way for developing a transmutable conception of the competitive process that integrates key insights from Shackle, Schumpeter and Keynes.

ACKNOWLEDGMENTS

Supported by The Commonwealth Fund, a New York City-based private independent foundation. The views presented here are those of the author and not necessarily those of The Commonwealth Fund, its director, officers, or staff. I would like to thank Vicky Chick, Geoff Harcourt, Geoff Hodgson, John King, Mike Oliver, Tony Lawson, Jochen Runde, Lord Robert Skidelsky, Malcolm Sawyer, Ted Winslow and the participants of the Workshop on Realism and Economics, Newnham College, Cambridge University, 25th February 2002 for their comments on earlier versions of this work. The usual disclaimer applies.

REFERENCES

Bateman, B. W. (1987). Keynes's changing conception of probability. *Economics and Philosophy, 3*, 97–119.
Bateman, B. W. (1996). *Keynes's uncertain revolution*. Ann Arbor: University of Michigan Press.
Carabelli, A. (1988). *On Keynes's method*. New York: St. Martin's Press.
Coddington, A. (1983). *Keynesian economics: The search for first principles*. London: Allen & Unwin.
Commons, J. R. (1934). *Institutional economics – its place in political economy*. New York: Macmillan.
Davidson, P. (1991). Is probability theory relevant for uncertainty? A post Keynesian perspective. *Journal of Economic Perspectives, 5*(1), 129–143.
Davidson, P. (1996). Reality and economic theory. *Journal of Post Keynesian Economics, 18*, 479–508. Reprinted in: L. Davidson (Ed.) (1999), *Uncertainty, International Money, Employment and Theory: The Collected Writings of Paul Davidson* (Vol. 3, pp. 3–29). London: Macmillan.
Davidson, P. (1998). Volatile financial markets and the speculator. *Economic Issues*.

Davis, J. B. (1994). *Keynes's philosophical development*. Cambridge: Cambridge University Press.

Dequech, D. (1999). Expectations and confidence under conditions of uncertainty. *Journal of Post Keynesian Economics, 21*, 415–430.

Dunn, S. P. (2001a). Bounded rationality is not fundamental uncertainty: A post Keynesian perspective. *Journal of Post Keynesian Economics, 23*, 567–587.

Dunn, S. P. (2001b). Galbraith, uncertainty and the modern corporation. In: M. Keaney (Ed.), *Economist with a Public Purpose: Essays in Honour of John Kenneth Galbraith*. London: Routledge.

Dunn, S. P. (2002). Towards a transmutable economics? A comment on Wynarczyk. *Economic Issues, 7*(1), 15–20.

Galbraith, J. K. (1967). *The new industrial state* (2nd ed., 1974). Harmondsworth: Penguin.

Galbraith, J. K. (1977). *The age of uncertainty*. London: BBC.

Gerrard, W. J. (1992). From *a treatise on probability* to the *general theory*: Continuity or change in Keynes's thought? In: W. J. Gerrard & J. V. Hillard (Eds), *The Philosophy and Economics of J. M. Keynes*. Aldershot: Edward Elgar.

Giddens, A. (1999). *Reith lectures – 'Runaway world': Lecture 2 – Risk*. BBC, London, http://news.bbc.co.uk/hi/english/static/events/reith_99/week2/week2.htm

Hodgson, G. M. (2001). *How economics forgot history: The problem of historical specificity in social science*. London: Routledge.

Keynes, J. M. (1972–1982). *The collected writings of John Maynard Keynes*. London: Macmillan.

Knight, F. H. (1921). *Risk, uncertainty and profit*. London: LSE, 1946.

Koppl, R. (1991). Animal spirits. *Journal of Economic Perspectives, 5*, 203–210.

Kregel, J. A. (1976). Economic methodology in the face of uncertainty: The modelling methods of Keynes and the post Keynesians. *Economic Journal, 86*, 209–225.

Lawson, T. (1985). Uncertainty and economic analysis. *Economic Journal, 95*, 909–927.

Leslie, T. E. C. (1888). *Essays in political economy* (2nd ed.). London: Longmans, Green.

Marchionatti, R. (1998). On Keynes's animal spirits. *Kyklos, 52*, 415–439.

Meeks, J. G. T. (1991). Keynes on the rationality of decision procedures under uncertainty: The investment decision. In: J. G. T. Meeks (Ed.), *Thoughtful Economic Man: Essays on Rationality, Moral Rules and Benevolence*. Cambridge: Cambridge University Press.

O'Donnell, R. (1989). *Keynes: Philosophy, economics and politics*. London: Macmillan.

O'Donnell, R. (1995). Keynes on aesthetics. In: A. F. Cottrell & M. S. Lawlor (Eds), *New Perspectives on Keynes: Annual Supplement to Volume 27 History of Political Economy*. Durham and London: Duke University Press.

Plumptre, A. F. W. (1983). Keynes in Cambridge. *Canadian Journal of Economics*, August 1947, 366–371. Reprinted in: J. C. Wood (Ed.), *John Maynard Keynes: Critical Assessments* (Vol. I). London: Croom Helm.

Robinson, J. (1962). *Economic philosophy*. Penguin: Harmondsworth.

Runde, J. H. (1990). Keynesian uncertainty and the weight of arguments. *Economics and Philosophy, 6*, 275–292.

Runde, J. H. (1994). Keynes after Ramsey: In defence of a treatise on probability. *Studies in History and Philosophy of Science, 25*, 97–121.

Schumpeter, J. A. (1936). Review of *The general theory of employment, interest and money* by John Maynard Keynes. *Journal of the American Statistical Association, 31*(196), 791–795.

Schumpeter, J. A. (1943). *Capitalism, socialism and democracy*. London: Allen & Unwin.

Schumpeter, J. A. (1954). *A history of economic analysis*. London: Routledge.

Shackle, G. L. S. (1967). *The years of high theory: Invention and tradition in economic thought 1926–1939*. Cambridge: Cambridge University Press.

Shackle, G. L. S. (1972). *Epistemics and economics*. Cambridge: Cambridge University Press.

Shackle, G. L. S. (1979). *Imagination and the nature of choice*. Edinburgh: Edinburgh University Press.
Skidelsky, R. (1992). *John Maynard Keynes: Volume II, The economist as saviour, 1920–1937*. London: Macmillan.
Winslow, E. G. (1986a). 'Human logic' and Keynes's economics. *Eastern Economic Journal, 12*, 413–430.
Winslow, E. G. (1986b). Keynes and freud: Psychoanalysis and Keynes's account of the 'animal spirits' of capitalism. *Social Research, 53*, 549–578.
Winslow, E. G. (1989). Organic interdependence, uncertainty and economic analysis. *Economic Journal, 99*, 1173–1182.
Winslow, E. G. (1990). Bloomsbury, Freud, and the vulgar passions. *Social Research, 57*, 785–819.
Winslow, E. G. (1992). Psychoanalysis and Keynes's account of the psychology of the trade cycle. In: W. J. Gerrard & J. V. Hillard (Eds), *The Philosophy and Economics of J. M. Keynes*. Cheltenham: Edward Elgar.
Winslow, E. G. (1993). Keynes on rationality. In: W. J. Gerrard (Ed.), *The Economics of Rationality*. London: Routledge.

THE PRUDENCE OF PROJECTORS: ADAM SMITH'S PREMONITION OF FINANCIAL FRAGILITY AND THE ORIGINS OF MONETARY POLICY

Jan Toporowski

The relationship of finance with the rest of the economy has been argued over since the emergence of money, and the concentration of trade in particular geographical locations and at times that did not coincide exactly with production and consumption. The trade in money that this required lies at the origin of finance. Social attitudes towards it were focused on the distribution of gains or losses arising out of that trade. In the past, those attitudes were obviously influenced by religious proscriptions against usury and, among the less religious, by Aristotle's argument that the mere trade in money is sterile. Aristotle's view reached the highest point of its sophistication in Marx's analysis of circuits of capital, showing how the application of money capital (or what Marx termed "fictitious capital") to production releases from labour the surplus that is the real basis of interest and gain from money. Modern finance is inextricably bound up with the emergence of capitalism and corporate requirements for money that exceed the pockets of entrepreneurs. The emergence of capitalism changed the terms in which that argument was conducted. This, however, has not been very well reflected in histories of economic thought about finance. These have tended to follow the view of John Stuart Mill, and the financial interest that influenced classical political economy. According to this view, arguments against usury follow from religious prejudice or, in the case of Aristotle, misunderstanding

Research in the History of Economic Thought and Methodology A Research Annual
Research in the History of Economic Thought and Methodology, Volume 22-A, 93–122
Copyright © 2004 Elsevier Ltd.
ISSN: 0743-4154/doi:10.1016/S0743-4154(03)22003-4

of the *functions* of money and finance (see, for example, the article on usury in the *New Palgrave: A Dictionary of Economic Theory and Doctrine*, Spiegel, 1987). Classical political economy is supposed to have brought enlightenment by removing religious considerations from economic questions and subjecting them to rational (logical and empirical) enquiry. Such enquiry reveals the fundamental harmony of finance with economic progress in general, and capital accumulation in particular, a conclusion which forms the basis still of modern finance theory.

However, closer examination of the arguments of classical political economy around usury show that the more favourable attitude towards finance that emerged was not the triumph over prejudice and misunderstanding that it now appears. The *economic* arguments of those who advocated restrictions on usury and finance are now widely overlooked, even where they raised issues that concern many citizens, politicians, businessmen and bankers today. The sections that follow show how those economic arguments were disputed and overtaken by events.

1. ADAM SMITH'S ECONOMIC CASE AGAINST USURY

For approximately a century and a half after their dramatic deflation, the South Sea and Mississippi Bubbles of 1710–1720 had discredited finance. With the exception of government bond markets and a few chartered companies, the rapid rise and fall of fortunes associated with the South Sea Company, in Britain, and the Mississippi Company in France, had made the joint stock system of corporate finance almost synonymous with fraud and financial debauchery. (The most authoritative account of these schemes is given in Murphy, 1997.) The joint stock system of finance was seen as seriously flawed, and an indictment of the theories on credit money of the schemes' instigator, John Law. During those one hundred and fifty years, classical political economy rose and flowered. Not surprisingly finance then came to be considered for its fiscal and monetary consequences. This pre-occupation left its mark on twentieth-century economics in an attitude that the fiscal and monetary implications of finance, eventually its influence on consumption, are more important than its balance sheet effects in the corporate sector. This attitude is apparent even in the work of perhaps the pre-eminent twentieth century critical finance theorist, John Maynard Keynes.

However, during this long slumber of finance, a premonition of its disturbing potential may be found in the work of the founder of classical political economy, Adam Smith. By and large, Smith shared his contemporaries' disapproving attitude towards the stock market system of corporate finance. In the last quarter of the eighteenth century, the theft and pillage by the East India Company, culminating in the scandalous trial, from 1788 to 1795, for corruption and cruelty, of the first Governor General of India, Warren Hastings, could only confirm the unfavourable views on finance of people whose opinions on the matter had been formed in the wake of the South Sea Bubble. (References to Adam Smith's condemnation of joint stock finance may be found in Toporowski, 2000, pp. 19–20, 139 and 144–145.)

The prospect of embezzlement, and deception with fraudulent intent, has always haunted financial markets. Such markets are based on the trust with which a depositor or financing partner places his money in the hands of a financial intermediary. Theft and deception are merely the obverse or denial of that trust. But they do not amount to an explanation of how the financial system can disturb an economy in a systematic way any more than, in the more contemporary example of the "New Keynesian Theory" of Joseph Stiglitz, the lack of information which a lender may have on a borrower's intent amounts to a complete account of financial disturbance (Stiglitz & Weiss, 1981). To explain how the financial system may destabilise an economy, it is necessary to provide a comprehensive view of how finance works in the real economy. In *An Inquiry into the Nature and Causes of The Wealth of Nations*, Adam Smith put forward the elements of a critical finance view of the economy (i.e. an explanation of how the monetary or financial system can disturb the economy), more as a possibility than a reality in his own time.

The first of these elements was an explanation of how entrepreneurs, or "projectors" as he called them, tend to exaggerate their business prospects. True to his method of reducing economic explanation to moral sentiment, Smith saw this tendency to view future business outcomes favourably as arising out of a natural self-regard affecting all men:

> The over-weening conceit which the greater part of men have of their own abilities, is an ancient evil remarked by philosophers and moralists of all ages. Their absurd presumption in their own good fortune has been less taken notice of. It is, however, if possible, still more universal. There is no man living, who, when in tolerable health and spirits, has not some share of it. The chance of gain is by every man more or less over-valued, and the chance of loss is by most men under-valued, and by scarce any man, who is in tolerable health and spirits, valued more than it is worth . . . The establishment of any manufacture, of any new branch of commerce, or of any new practice in agriculture, is always a speculation from which the projector promises himself extraordinary profits. These profits sometimes are very great, and sometimes, more frequently, perhaps, they are quite otherwise . . . (WN I, x, Part I, 26 and 44).

(In view of the large number of differently paginated editions of Adam Smith's *The Wealth of Nations*, references to this book [WN] indicate, in roman numerals, first the book, followed by the chapter, then the part, if any, then the article, if any, followed by the paragraph in Arabic numerals. The above reference is therefore to Book I, Chap. X, Part I, para. 26 and 44.)

Accordingly, in making business plans, there is a bias towards exaggerating future returns. Actual returns in business, i.e. the productivity of labour, are, according to Smith, determined by the location of the business, its technology, trade and competition in that line of business. Returns, he argued, were lower in manufacturing countries where there exists free trade and a high degree of competition in the various trades, and higher in industrially backward countries where trade was restricted (WN I, x, Part II, 32).

The second element of Smith's implied critical finance was played by banks. These were supposed to play an important part in financing trade. Indeed, Smith was an early and principal advocate of the Real Bills Doctrine: The view that banks could issue bills of exchange without inflationary consequences, providing those bills financed traders' stocks and were repaid from the sales proceeds of those stocks (WN II, ii, see also Perlman, 1989). It was vital, Smith argued, that banks should fulfil this trade-financing function efficiently and without over-charging for their credit or services. Otherwise, the benefits of trade and industrial progress would be lost. In contrast to his well-known views in support of free trade and laissez-faire in business, Smith advocated the regulation of banks in general and, in particular, limits on the rate of interest that could be charged by banks. The interest chargeable for loans had been regulated in England since the time of Henry VIII and by Smith's time was fixed at 5%. Smith was a firm supporter of the Usury Laws. In the course of justifying such government regulation, Smith outlined what he considered to be the likely consequences of allowing interest rates higher than the rate that is "somewhat above the lowest market price, or the price which is commonly paid for the use of money by those who can give the most undoubted security." (WN II, iv, 14):

> If the legal rate of interest in Great Britain, for example, were fixed so high as eight or ten percent. the greater part of the money which was to be lent, would be lent to prodigals and projectors, who alone would be willing to give this high interest. Sober people, who will give for the use of money no more than a part of what they are likely to make by use of it, would not venture into the competition. A great part of the capital of the country would thus be kept out of the hands that were most likely to make a profitable and advantageous use of it, and thrown into those which were most likely to waste and destroy it. Where the legal rate of interest, on the contrary, is fixed but a very little above the lowest market rate, sober people are universally preferred, as borrowers, to prodigals and projectors. The person who lends money gets nearly as much interest from the former as he dares to take from the latter, and his money is much safer in the hands of one set of people than in those of the other. A great part of the capital of the country is thus thrown into the hands in which it is most likely to be employed with advantage (*Ibid.*).

Smith's argument here is clearly over the limit that should be placed by the usury laws on the possible interest charged. But, given that the purpose of the usury laws was to prevent banks charging interest above the legal ceiling, it is an obvious implication that, without such a ceiling, banks would charge higher rates of interest.

As Smith pointed out, the composition of business would then change in favour of "prodigals and projectors" who are willing to pay higher interest and would waste finance on their schemes. (Mathieu Carlson gives a similar interpretation of Smith's views on usury in Carlson, 1999, as also did Bentham and Keynes.)

Smith distinguished this bank-induced instability in the economy from what he called "the over-trading of some bold projectors" whose speculations "was the original cause of . . . excessive circulation of money" (WN II, ii, 59). The term "over-trading" entered the business and economic lexicon. Essentially, it meant using bank credit to finance stocks of commodities and finished goods built up by traders in the expectation of higher prices. Smith believed that due adherence to the Real Bills Doctrine would avoid such speculative credit inflation.

Smith's argument may be visualised in the form of a graph in two dimensions. On the horizontal axis the users of credit may be lined up in order of their expected return on their borrowing, gross of the interest paid on their borrowing. On the extreme left of the axis will be the prudent borrowers operating established businesses in which competition holds down the gross return on their borrowing to the minimum. Moving right along the axis, the expected return rises because businesses are less well established, earning putative returns exaggerated by monopolies, the vanity of projectors, and the desperation of prodigals. The vertical axis represents the expected gross return on the capital borrowed. In its essentials, Smith's argument is that usury laws are necessary in order to hold down the rate of interest below the gross return that the most prudent businessmen can obtain. If the rate of interest is allowed to rise above this level, then the most prudent businessmen drop out of the market for credit. The population of borrowers in the market is then reduced to less prudent businessmen whose expected returns are (just) in excess of the new, higher, rate of interest. If the rate of interest rises still further, the less prudent borrowers drop out and are replaced by even less prudent borrowers.

Therefore, as the rate of interest rises, so the population of borrowers changes from the more cautious to the less prudent. This analysis amounts to a theory of financial fragility in the sense of providing a complete explanation of how an economy becomes more prone to financial collapse. The "quality" of borrowing is reduced when the prudent cannot afford to borrow and credit is advanced increasingly to those trading on their confidence, as the rate of interest rises in the absence of a legal ceiling.

2. A PREMONITION OF ASYMMETRIC INFORMATION?

It has been suggested by no less an authority than Mark Blaug that Adam Smith's exposition of the likely consequences of abolishing this legal ceiling on the rate of interest are an anticipation of late twentieth-century views on "imperfections" in financial markets: "Remarks such as this have been seized on in recent years as signs that Smith recognized the problem of asymmetric information and moral hazard in credit markets, which make capital rationing a normal, and even typical feature of such markets" (Blaug, 1996, p. 55). Samuel Hollander has also observed that "Smith's justification for a legal maximum interest rate in some respects resembles the rationalization of credit rationing by Stiglitz and Weiss" (Hollander, 1999). As will be apparent from the discussion below, Blaug's view is more appropriate to Bentham's critique of Smith, and Keynes's analysis of uncertainty, than to Smith himself. The theory of asymmetric information, associated with the U.S. economists Ben Bernanke, Frederic S. Mishkin and Joseph Stiglitz, emerged during the 1980s in response to the manifest absurdities of the "market efficiency" theory (manifest at least to anyone who has worked in the financial markets and experienced at first hand the large share in their daily diet of rumour and misinformation). The theory of market efficiency holds that financial markets are perfect information exchanges. It spawned a rash of econometric studies relating market "efficiency" to the variance of stock prices around their mean. But the main significance of the theory, outside the sphere of academic calculation, was to justify financial deregulation. By contrast, the theory of "asymmetric information" suggests the banks cannot be fully aware of the purposes to which their credit will be applied, and the true returns from those purposes. The banker offering a loan, in effect, loses control over the money once he has handed over the loan to the borrower, who has a financial interest in minimising the risks of the business that the loan will finance. In this situation, contracts cannot be "complete." Underlying it is a fundamental uncertainty, a lack of knowledge on the part of both the supplier of finance and the user of finance, about the future returns of business. Only over a period of time working with a client can a bank or financial institution acquire reliable information about that client's credit-worthiness. The possibility of raising finance at a rate of interest below that appropriate to the risks of the business being financed is supposed to give rise to "moral hazard." "Moral hazard" is a term drawn from the business of insurance, where it refers to the careless behaviour that may arise because those insured know that they can obtain monetary compensation in the event of loss. Any contraction of lending, or raising of interest rates, is supposed to lead to "adverse selection," as new lending is concentrated on entrepreneurs with risky projects, and expecting correspondingly higher rates of return. Credit rationing is supposed to arise when bank capital ratios fall, or when credit is extended to sectors in which it was previously constrained by credit ceilings. Banks are supposed then to make loan decisions in ignorance of true future returns on the loan. Rationing credit is banks' way of limiting their commitment of funds to activities whose true risk is unknown. Credit is frequently rationed using collateral values or the borrower's liquidity as proxies for the "riskiness" of the loan. The collateral may consist of assets, financial or otherwise, whose value decreases when the rate of interest rises, for example, if the market yield (rate of interest or dividend rate, divided by the market price of the security) of long-term securities rises with a rise in the short-term or bank rate of interest. In this way, when collateral values are reduced by higher interest rates the quality of loans in bank balance sheets deteriorates (Mishkin, 1991).

Ben Bernanke has suggested that the Great Depression was exacerbated by bank failures that destroyed the information which banks held on their borrowers. This was then supposed to have raised the real cost of intermediation, giving rise to credit rationing and driving businesses into insolvency (Bernanke, 1983). Joseph Stiglitz and Andrew Weiss put forward a celebrated formalisation of a system of lending under such asymmetric information in which credit rationing leads to an unemployment equilibrium in the economy (Stiglitz & Weiss). Stiglitz went on to use his position as Chief Economist at the World Bank during the 1990s to denounce premature financial liberalisation in developing countries. He argued that a rapid expansion of credit facilities, before the establishment of developed economic infrastructure in other sectors, can only lead to financial speculation and collapse (Stiglitz, 1998).

In arguing that the theories of perfect financial intermediation invoked in favour of financial liberalisation take no account of the limitations of human knowledge, Stiglitz, Mishkin and Bernanke area really echoing Fisher's ingenious explanation of credit cycles. They thus place themselves into a mainstream academic tradition established by Alfred Marshall (". . . the economist studies mental states," Marshall, 1938, p. 16). The tradition goes back ultimately to the moral philosophy of Adam Smith, and takes in Keynes and the majority of his followers, among whom Stiglitz, Mishkin and Bernanke count themselves. This tradition holds that adequate explanation has been advanced when economic phenomena have been reduced to universal aspects of the human perception, inclination and reasoning. In the case of Stiglitz, Mishkin and Bernanke, these universal features of human existence are uncertainty about the future, the borrower's preference for gain at the expense of the lender, and the lender's ignorance of the borrower's true intentions. Indeed, the theoretical foundation for their work can best be described as the microeconomics of imperfect information as an aspect of human perception. However, the problems of financial instability are far from universal human predicaments, but arise in the specific historical circumstances when the financial liabilities that are the counterparts of the assets of capitalist corporations, are inflated. The financial intermediation that takes place in such an economy is not between individuals, but between corporations. At the very least these may be expected to behave in a more rational and circumspect manner than individual human beings. This is one of the fundamental principles of corporate organisation.

Business management throughout rests on increasing precision, steadiness, and, above all, the speed of operations ... Bureaucratization offers above all the optimum possibility for carrying through the principle of specializing administrative functions according to purely objective considerations. Individual performances are allocated to functionaries who have specialized training and who by constant practice learn more and more. The "objective" discharge of business primarily means a discharge of business according to *calculable rules* and "without regard for persons." "Without regard for persons" is also the watchword of the "market" and, "in general, of all pursuits of naked economic interests" (Weber, 1948, p. 215).

Max Weber went on to write that "Every bureaucracy seeks to increase the superiority of the professionally informed by keeping their knowledge and intentions secret" (*ibid.*, p. 233), but this was more in connection with political and religious administration, than the business management referred to earlier. That, in principle, may be expected to operate along more rational lines than the individuals undertaking financial transactions who appear to be the agents experiencing "asymmetric information" in the theories of Stiglitz, Bernanke and Mishkin. The writings of the microeconomists of imperfect information are replete with references to "individual" borrowers or investors, so-called "principal/agent problems" of the individual landlord-tenant, or employer-employee type. (Gary Dymski points out that "New Keynesian models treat agents as simple entities and the risks they take as axiomatic and pre-social." He goes on to argue that "asymmetric information" cannot explain the United States savings and loans associations collapse of the early 1980s, the East Asian crisis in the 1990s, and the social problem of the "redlining" of poorer districts, that is the treatment by banks of loan requests from particular poor areas as inherently risky. Dymski, 1998.)

The confusion between individuals and corporations is crucial because, whereas the former are prone to individual failings, as Max Weber argued, corporations are organised in order to overcome individual limitations. This is most obvious in the case of Adam Smith's explanation of how the division of labour in the factory extends the productive capability of the individuals concerned. Indeed, while Adam Smith had few illusions about the distorted perceptions and frailties of individuals, his political economy was about organising human relations and institutions in such a way that improves the outcome of human actions (Harcourt, 1995). The capitalist corporation cannot get rid of the uncertainty concerning other corporations' activities and intentions, and their consequences in unpredictable business cycles. But it can protect itself from their adverse consequences through liquidity preference (maintaining stocks of liquid assets) securing lines of credit, insurance and so on. Asymmetric information undoubtedly exists, but affects corporations and financial institutions differently from the way in which it affects individuals. Among corporations and financial institutions, some are more badly affected by "asymmetric information" and "adverse selection" than others. For example, venture capitalists and individual speculators seem to experience greater losses than department stores and betting shops. The question is not whether "asymmetric information" exists, but how capitalist institutions accommodate it, and what rational rules they use to cope with uncertainty, lack of information and so on. To give him his due, this is essence of Stiglitz's criticism of the establishment of U.S.-style financial institutions in other countries (Stiglitz, 1998). He is at his strongest here precisely because this criticism recognises that financial instability and crisis are features of particular forms of capitalist financial organisation, rather than universal limitations of human perception and reasoning. Similarly, Bernanke, in his study of the consequences of bank failure in the 1930s depression, recognised that banks hold far more information on credit risks than an individual may possess (Bernanke, 1983). However, his was a study of bank lending to small companies. While such companies may be the closest modern equivalent to Smith's myopic and self-aggrandising merchants and "projectors," they were arguably marginal to the course of the Great Depression, which was precipitated and extended by the failure of large corporations and the decline in their capital spending.

In fact, there is a very easy way of overcoming the worst aspects of asymmetric information in the relationship between corporations and financial institutions. This is found in the German type of capitalism where banks hold shares, in some cases controlling shares, in the companies that borrow from them. This gets rid of differences between the bank and the borrower over the credit-worthiness of the borrower by making the bank a co-manager of the company borrowing from it. Paradoxically, this system was not the result of some "natural" evolution towards the most information-efficient form of corporate organisation. Nor was it as universal as Hilferding, Lenin and their followers believed. It was in fact the result of successive collapses of capital markets in continental Europe from 1873 onwards, and the great inflation of the 1920s that destroyed the bond markets which are the core, even today, of stock market activity. It is curious that this apparently more information-efficient variant of capitalism was the incidental outcome of financial crisis and an, initially frankly socialist, utopian ideology of Saint-Simon (Hu, 1979; Kindleberger, 1993, Chaps 6 and 7; Toporowski, 2002). Even more curiously, the inflation of international finance in the final decades of the twentieth century has put this seemingly more "information-efficient" variant at risk, in the face of an increasingly widespread adoption of the ostensibly less "information-efficient" financial systems based on capital markets. The recent emphasis on "asymmetric information" as a source of financial instability remains unclear not only about the relationship between individual and corporate forms of activity, but also how these are affected by changes in capitalist institutions and the political regulation of markets. Its advocates are at their best in criticising utopian financial reforms in developing and post-Communist economies. But basing themselves on one rather obvious aspect of financial transactions, their account is less systematic than that of authors who have more developed theories of capitalism and its evolution. Arguably it is also less systematic than the view put forward by Smith.

Hollander makes the important point that Stiglitz and Weiss put forward a system in which banks ration credit and set the rate of interest, because they do not know what the true returns to borrowers will be, whereas Smith argues that the State should set the maximum rate of interest (Hollander, 1999). Smith did not confuse human characteristics with those of institutions, although in his time, legal limitations on joint stock companies prevented the widespread use of corporate systems of industrial and commercial organisation and finance. Moreover, while Smith had no illusions about the limited understanding of bankers, credit rationing does not arise because of this. According to the microeconomists of imperfect information, credit is rationed to borrowers because bankers cannot distinguish between more prudent and less prudent borrowers. Smith's bankers "rationed" credit because they were limited by the amount of cash in their tills. (It is only with the arrival of the "pure credit" economy, in which lending may be advanced without ever running out of credit, that "rationing" arises from bankers' considerations of possible and unknown differences in the risks associated with their customers' activities. See Chick, 1986.) Those bankers lent to the best borrowers in the market on the terms available. However, they could not bring into the market the most prudent borrowers who have left it because they cannot afford to pay a high rate of interest. In discussing the appropriate sphere of joint stock corporate activity, Smith hinted at a much more rational form of "asymmetric information," in which the boundary between uncertainty and known risk or certainty, is drawn according to the nature of economic operations, rather than the limitations of human perception:

"The only trades which it seems possible for a joint-stock company to carry on successfully, without an exclusive privilege, are those, of which all the operations are capable of being reduced to what is called a routine, or to such a uniformity of method as admits of little or no variation." (WN V, i, Part III, art. 1, 50.) Smith suggested four "trades" as suitable for such endeavours: banking, insurance, canals and water supplies. In the case of manufactures (the prototype of the modern corporation, according to economics textbooks), Smith was sceptical, but uncertain:

The English copper company of London, the lead-smelting company, the glass-grinding company, have not even the pretext of any great or singular utility in the object which they pursue; nor does the pursuit of that object seem to require any expense unsuitable to the fortunes of many private men. Whether the trade which those companies carry on, is reducible to such strict rule and method as to render it fit for the management of a joint stock company, or whether they have any reason to boast of their extraordinary profit, I do not pretend to know . . . The joint stock companies, which are established for the public-spirited purpose of promoting some particular manufacture, over and above managing their own affairs ill, to the diminution of the general stock of the society, can, in other respects, scarce ever fail to do more harm than good. Notwithstanding the most upright intentions, the unavoidable partiality of their directors to particular branches of the manufacture, of which the undertakers mislead and impose upon them, is a real discouragement to the rest, and necessarily breaks, more or less, that natural proportion which would otherwise establish itself between judicious industry and profit . . . (WN V, I, Part III, art., 1, 58).

This is the closest that Adam Smith came to suggesting that manufacturing investment is best limited to that which can be undertaken by individuals out of their own wealth, and that undertakings that depart from known routines of production and distribution are vulnerable to waste and fraud. However, this is not due to "asymmetric information," leaving the fortunes of outside investors at the mercy of "inside" managers who really know what is happening. Rather it is due to the "partiality" of entrepreneurs, naturally inclined to exaggerate the success of their undertakings, a partiality that misleads them and everyone else.

3. THE VINDICATION OF FINANCE: JEREMY BENTHAM'S *DEFENCE OF USURY*

Within years of the publication of *The Wealth of Nations*, Jeremy Bentham took issue with Smith over his views on usury. Bentham was an ardent enthusiast for Adam Smith's laissez-faire political economy, which complemented his own liberal political and legislative ideas. He read *The Wealth of Nations* soon after it was published and re-read it. The editor of Bentham's economic writings, Werner Stark, wrote that "a most thorough study of Smith's illustrious treatise was the mainspring of all Bentham's economic knowledge" (Stark, 1952, p. 14). Bentham acknowledged that "as far as your track coincides with mine, . . . I owed you everything" (Bentham, 1787, p. 167). Precisely for this reason he was outraged by Smith's argument for regulating the rate of interest. Travelling in Russia, he heard a rumour that the administration of William Pitt the Younger was planning to cut the legal rate of interest down from 5% to 4%. This turned out to be a false rumour, but it proved to be the catalyst for Bentham to bring his thoughts together in a pamphlet entitled *The Defence of Usury*. The pamphlet was in the form of a set of rhetorical letters to Adam Smith, making clear that it was Smith rather than Pitt to whom Bentham's reproaches were addressed.

Bentham's *Defence of Usury* mounted a serious political case against the Usury Laws. In his view, banking is like any other business and it was no business of the government to regulate the "hire of money" any more than the hire of horses (Letter IX). The laws, he argued, did not discourage prodigality, since this could usually and equally be financed from savings or the sale of assets (Letter III). The laws were widely evaded, and this tended to discredit the law in general (Letters VII and VIII). Its roots lay in muddled thinking: the Aristotelian notion that money is unproductive; the prejudice of borrowers, as opposed to lenders; and anti-semitism (Letter X). (Bentham was much ahead of his time in condemning anti-semitism). Limiting interest reduces the "parsimony" that augments the "capital" that is the basis of trade (Letter XIII, p. 198).

But Bentham reserved his most furious economic arguments for a defence of "projectors." Their speculations, he argued, were the foundation of economic progress, and it was wrong to deny them finance on any terms that they were willing to pay. The Usury Laws themselves did not concentrate finance on good projects, but merely deprived all projects of finance (Letter XIII). A notable omission is the absence of any mention that the level of interest rates may itself discourage "projectors." Bentham argues as if only government limitations on interest rates can hold back projectors. In this way Bentham established finance as the partner of capitalist enterprise, rather than, according to mercantilist thought, a usurious parasite on that enterprise. In Marx's words, with Bentham "unrestricted usury is recognised as an element of capitalist production" (Marx, 1975, p. 534). This is not really surprising. Bentham himself was the author of a new model prison, the Panopticon, for whose construction he singularly failed to raise money or interest from the Government. But it made him identify with "projectors" to a personal degree.

Bentham's argument in favour of industrial speculation was to attract Keynes's attention. In the "Notes on Mercantilism, etc." in his *General Theory*, Keynes noted Smith's preference for "cheap money" and Bentham's defence of projectors. In a footnote, Keynes wrote:

> Having started to quote Bentham in this context, I must remind the reader of his finest passage: 'The career of art, the great road which receives the footsteps of projectors, may be considered as a vast, and perhaps unbounded, plain, bestrewed with gulphs, such as Curtius was swallowed up in. Each requires a human victim to fall into it ere it can close, but when it once closes, it closes to open no more, and so much of the path is safe to those who follow' (Keynes, 1936, p. 353).

The quotation clearly recommends itself to Keynes for Bentham's apparent recognition of the economic problem of uncertainty, whose analysis was to be such a distinctive part of Keynes's thought. If there was such a recognition on the part of Bentham, its scope was narrower than may appear from Keynes's citation, in a footnote to and semi-detached from the discussion of the financing of projectors. Bentham in fact continues:

> If the want of perfect information of former miscarriages renders the reality of human life less happy than this picture, still the similitude must be acknowledged still nearer and nearer to perfection; I mean the framing the history of the projects of time past, and (what may be executed in much greater perfection were but a finger held up by the hand of government) the making provision for recording, and collecting and as they are brought forth, the race of those with which the womb of futurity is still pregnant . . . (Bentham, 1787, p. 180).

Bentham therefore has in mind less the uncertainty of the human condition that was the cornerstone of Keynes's philosophy, and more the uncertainty over the outcome of industrial innovations. His view here is arguably much closer to that of Hayek's entrepreneur, carefully seeking to avoid the errors of others in his market, and trying to avoid ending up as the exemplar of error to others. (Cf. "Competition is essentially a process of the formation of opinion: by spreading information, it creates the unity and coherence of the economic system . . . It creates the views people have about what is best and cheapest, and it is because of it that people know about what is best and cheapest, and it is because of it that people know at least as much about possibilities and opportunities as they in fact do" Hayek, 1946, p. 106.)

Bentham and Keynes had in common an outstanding ability to throw off brilliant observations on the margins of their discussions. Bentham realised that he had drifted away from his defence of usury, to which he returned with renewed vigour, leaving his philosophical and political economic intuition, like so many of his other insights, dangling inconsequentially in his text.

Bentham's *Defence of Usury* is therefore essentially a plea for commercial freedom to be extended to banking; an argument that the Usury Laws were ineffective and that they constrained saving, and therefore investment; and an account of the economic benefits of projectors. He did not deal with the main burden of Adam Smith's argument in support of the Usury Laws, namely that a rise in the rate of interest would cause a decline in the quality of credit as sound competitive businesses with lower rates of profit reduce their demand for credit.

This context has to be borne in mind when considering the evidence that Adam Smith may have been won round by Bentham's arguments. On the 4 December 1788, George Wilson wrote to Bentham as follows:

> Did we ever tell you what Dr. Adam Smith said to Mr. Wm Adam the Counsel M.P. last Summer in Scotland? The Doctor's Expressions were "That the Defence of Usury was the Work of a very superior Man; and that tho' he had given Him some hard hard knocks, it was done in so handsome a way that he could not Complain" and seemed to admit that you were in the right (Milne, 1981, Letter 633, pp. 19–20).

In early July 1790, Bentham wrote to Adam Smith outlining his plans for a new edition of the *Defence of Usury*. "I have been flattered with the intelligence that, upon the whole, your sentiments with respect to the points of difference are at present the same as mine . . . If, then, you think proper to honour me with your allowance for that purpose, then and not otherwise, I will make it known to the public, in such words as you give me, that you no longer look upon the rate of interest as fit subject for restraint . . ." (op. cit. Letter 702, pp. 132–134, published in Stark, 1952, pp. 188–190).

Adam Smith was on his death-bed. He was to die on the 17 July. In acknowledgement he sent Bentham a dedication copy of *The Wealth of Nations*, "a present," Bentham was to write, "I had the melancholy consolation of receiving from Adam Smith at the same time with the news of the loss which, as a citizen of the world, I had sustained by his death . . . a token of that magnanimity which, it were to be wished, were always the accompaniment of the inevitable war of opinions, as carried on by writing and thinking men" (Stark, 1952, p. 27).

From this ambiguous evidence, Smith's biographer John Rae concluded that the *Defence of Usury* "had the very unusual controversial effect of converting the antagonist against whom it was written . . . It is reasonable to think that if Smith had lived to publish another edition of his work he would have modified his position on the rate of interest" (Rae, 1895, pp. 423–424, cited in Stark, 1952, p. 27). More recently, Pressman wrote that: "After reading Bentham's book, Adam Smith was persuaded that his support of usury laws was in error, and that there should be no government regulations on interest" (Pressman, 1999, p. 27).

However, the editor of Bentham's economic writings, Werner Stark, came to a more ambiguous conclusion that "It must be an open question whether Rae is on firm ground." Since Bentham did not deal with Smith's main argument in support of the Usury Laws, the exclusion from credit by higher interest rates of sound competitive businesses, it must be seriously doubted whether Smith was convinced by Bentham. Schumpeter, who was by no means convinced of the validity of Smith's theory of interest, dismissed "an entirely unjustified attack from Bentham" on Smith's "moderate and judicious argument about legal maxima" on interest (Schumpeter, 1954, p. 193). Pesciarelli has suggested that Smith had the opportunity to change his views in revising the *Wealth of Nations* for its second and third editions, in 1789 and 1791. He made substantial revisions of his *Theory of Moral Sentiments* at this time, and so would not have been deterred by the infirmities of his last years from correcting an earlier view which he might now have believed was wrong (Pesciarelli, 1989). Hollander also doubts that Bentham's pleading made Smith change his mind (Hollander, 1999).

4. THE BANKER'S VIEW OF HENRY THORNTON

Bentham's argument against Smith was essentially political, namely a criticism of restraint on commercial endeavour. Even his editor was obliged to admit that Bentham's economic argument was weak, his "most outstanding shortcoming" being "the complete absence of a theory of interest" (Stark, 1952, pp. 33–34). In the event, this did not matter. Within a few years, the economic and monetary circumstances that Smith and Bentham had described were transformed by the French Revolution and its wars, the wars against Napoleon Buonaparte, and his commercial blockade of Britain. In 1797, following a deflationary outflow of currency from the country in the wake of the *assignat* collapse in France, the convertibility of banknotes against gold was suspended, and was not resumed until 1819. The banknote issue was inflated to pay for the Wars, and the focus of monetary discussions shifted to questions of price stability and convertibility. Directly involved in these monetary and financial disturbances was the banker Henry Thornton (1760–1815). From 1782 to 1815 he was also a Member of Parliament, where he gave evidence to three committees of Parliament that, in 1797, investigated the suspension of the Bank of England's obligation to convert its notes into gold (the House of Commons Committee of Secrecy on the Outstanding Demands on the Bank of England, the Committee on the Restriction of Payments in Cash by the Bank, and the House of Lords Committee of Secrecy Appointed to Enquire into the Causes which produced the Order in Council of the 26th of February 1797). Thornton went on to write an extensive explanation and defence of paper money entitled *An Enquiry into the Nature and Effects of the Paper Credit of Great Britain* (Thornton, 1802). Together with two Speeches to the House of Commons on the Bullion Report of 1811 (which recommended the resumption of gold payments by the Bank of England) and some notes on Lord King's *Thoughts on the Effects of the Bank Restriction* in 1804, these works exhaust the published writings of a thoughtful and public-spirited banker. After many years of neglect his work was revived and republished in 1939, in a volume edited by Friedrich von Hayek that is, arguably, among this scholarly Austrian's greatest achievements. Later scholars of economic thought were to find in his works ideas on money (the difference between nominal and real interest rates, interest premiums for expected inflation, forced saving, and the precautionary demand for money) that had been attributed to Wicksell, von Mises, Fisher, Keynes and Lucas. Like Smith, he had no doubt that bankers have the measure of their clients. However, Thornton went further and argued that this gives bankers the most profound understanding of credit which, shared among themselves, could maintain the balanced expansion of such credit:

The banker also enjoys, from the nature of his situation, very superior means of distinguishing the careful trader from him who is improvident. The bill transactions of the neighbourhood pass under his view; the knowledge, thus obtained, aids his judgement; and confidence may therefore be measured out by him more nearly than by another person, in the proportion in which ground for it exists. Through the creation of banks, the appreciation of the credit of numberless persons engaged in commerce has become a science; and to the height which this science is now carried in Great Britain we are in no small degree indebted for the flourishing state of our internal commerce, for the general reputation of our merchants abroad, and for the preference which in that respect they enjoy over the traders of all other nations . . . (Thornton, p. 177).

The Revolutionary and Napoleonic Wars had brought a considerable prosperity to Britain, the result of its government's high expenditure on prosecuting hostilities, rather than the superlative intelligence of its bankers. This prosperity inspired the presumption of a "natural" equilibrium in economic activity that is found in Thornton's writings ("the natural state of things" he called it), and that has endeared him to those, like his editor Hayek, for example, who believe that the market capitalist economy is the Mecca of economic civilization. On one occasion he even argued that any reduction in the Bank of England's paper money issue would have virtually no impact on commercial activity, because businessmen and bankers would develop new forms of credit, trade credit in particular, to overcome any shortage of circulating medium: ". . . I cannot conceive that the mercantile world would suffer such a diminution to take place, without substituting a circulating medium of their own. . . " (Thornton, 1797, p. 282). In *Paper Credit*, he pointed to the variety of means of payment and credit instruments in commercial use, whose only prerequisite was "confidence" that an exchange could eventually be effected for Bank of England notes. This, together with his sceptical remarks about the efficacy of changes in the Bank of England's note issue, is entirely consistent with the view, championed by Post-Keynesian economists after Kaldor, that the money supply is "endogenous." This means that the supply of money is entirely determined by the demand for credit. Thornton criticised Smith's Real Bills Doctrine on the grounds that lending against collateral could itself be inflationary if the value of the collateral was rising or if the term of the bill were extended (Thornton, p. 251). Bankers themselves would naturally be aware of this, and would want to limit their lending:

It is certainly the interest, and, I believe, it is also the general practice, of banks to limit not only the loan which any one trader shall obtain from themselves, but the total amount also, as far as they are able, of the sum which the same person shall borrow in different places; at the same time, reciprocally to communicate intelligence for their mutual assistance; and above all to discourage bills of accommodation . . . Thus a system of check is established, which, though certainly very imperfect, answers many important purposes, and, in particular, opposes many impediments to wild speculation (Thornton, pp. 177–178).

In Thornton's view, an excessive note issue might stimulate a short-term increase in economic activity, but must inevitably lead to higher prices (Thornton, 1802, Chaps VIII and XI). Indeed, his *Paper Credit* can be understood as an extended argument that the Bank of England's note issue since 1797 had not been excessive, and the rise in prices experienced since 1797 was due to poor harvests, trade disturbances and the exigencies of the War, an interpretation of events that would appeal to the advocates of endogenous money. This defence of the Bank perhaps caused McCulloch later erroneously to describe Thornton as a Director of the Bank of England. (It was in fact Henry Thornton's brother Samuel, who was a Director of the Bank. See Hayek, 1939, p. 15.) In Thornton's view, reductions in the note issue bore most heavily and immediately on the banking system. With fewer Bank of England notes which they could get from deposits, discounting, or by exchanging other bankers' notes (the Bank of England's monopoly of issuing bank notes was restricted to the London area until 1844), banks would be vulnerable to withdrawals of deposits (runs) and would seek to conserve their gold coins and Bank of England notes by refusing to lend, or discount merchant's bills. This would precipitate "commercial distress" and stock market crisis as merchants and businessmen would find themselves unable to finance stocks or work in progress, and investors would be forced to sell stocks:

> ...the Suppression of the Bank of England's Paper, to any considerable extent, must, unless some other Paper is substituted, in my Opinion, pull down the Price of Exchequer Bills, of India Bonds, and other Government Securities, which will be sold by those who possess them, in order to secure a sufficient Quantity of Bank Notes to carry on their payments, and which a Variety of Bankers will be selling at the same Time, each endeavouring, though in vain, to possess himself of the notes held by the others. It must produce, therefore, Discredit to the Government, a consequent Distrust in the Minds of the Public, who will not understand the Cause of this Depreciation of the Stocks; it must produce, at the same Time, Commercial Failures, and an Appearance of Bankruptcy, even in Times when the Individuals in the Nation, and the Nation itself, might be rich and prosperous ... (Thornton, 1797, p. 305).

However, such disturbances are caused by deliberate manipulations of the note issue by the monetary authorities. In this respect, Thornton's may be classed with later thinkers, such as Hayek, Lucas, Wicksell, and Wojnilower who, even if they did not believe in general equilibrium, attributed financial disturbances to the implementation of inappropriate policies by the monetary authorities.

However, his reputation as a monetary economist has obscured what is arguably Thornton's most widely accepted idea, even though most individuals who have held it would be unable to identify his authorship of it. This is the idea that a low rate of interest gives rise to an excess demand for credit. The classical political economists rapidly took up this assertion to invert Adam Smith's argument that *high* rates of interest induce deteriorating credit, and to conclude that low rates of interest lead to "speculation."

Thornton put forward this argument by postulating that the rate of profit on mercantile activity varies according to the economic circumstances of a country. But it is not just the rate of profit that determines the demand for credit. That demand arises from a comparison of the rate of profit with the rate of interest that must be paid to borrow the (circulating) capital necessary to obtain that profit. The 5% rate of interest laid down by the Usury Laws, or 4 or 6%, may be appropriate in times of peace. But "the temptation to borrow, in time of war, too largely at the bank, rises . . . from the high rate of mercantile profit. Capital is then scarce, and the gain accruing from the employment of it is proportionately considerable." Curiously, Thornton himself was more concerned about the effect of an excess demand for credit on the liquidity of banks, rather than on prices, which worried later economists more: "It is, therefore, unreasonable to presume that there will always be a disposition in the borrowers at the bank to prescribe to themselves exactly those bounds which a regard to the safety of the bank would suggest" (Thornton, pp. 254–255). Thornton was also concerned that British merchants and foreign stockholders would find more remunerative employment for their capital abroad than in Britain. The outcome of this was to oblige the Bank of England to limit the loans it granted to merchants to a fixed weekly total, an early example of credit rationing (Thornton, p. 258). Thornton therefore argued for the removal of the ceiling on the rate of interest.

Thornton had one other argument against the Usury Laws that is notable as an example of how two economists may draw mutually contradictory conclusions from the same fact. In his evidence before the Lord's Committee of Secrecy Appointed to Enquire into the Causes which Produced the Order in Council of the 26th of February 1797 (this was the Order in Council under which the Bank of England ceased to pay gold in exchange for its banknotes), Thornton was asked:

> Has not the low Price of the Funds and other Government securities, by affording an higher interest than 5%, operated as an Hindrance to Mercantile Discounts?

Thornton answered, "It undoubtedly has operated in that Manner very effectually" (Thornton, 1797, p. 310).

His eventual conclusion was that the Usury Laws operated against credit stability by removing the possibility of raising interest rates to keep capital in the country and discourage the demand for credit. Jean-Baptiste Say was to conclude otherwise, that Usury Laws were necessary to prevent precisely such a diversion of credit from industry and agriculture (see below).

5. RICARDO AND THE ABOLITION OF THE USURY LAWS

When David Ricardo went to the House of Commons on the 30 April 1818 to give evidence to the Select Committee on the Usury Laws, which had been set up on the initiative of the Member of Parliament for Guildford, Serjeant Onslow, the economic and monetary circumstances of Britain were fundamentally different to the ones that had inspired Adam Smith. Although, like Bentham, Ricardo formed his views on political economy from his reading and re-reading of Smith's *The Wealth of Nations*, he owed his monetary thinking more to his practical experience as stockbroker during the War-time inflation. As is well known, he advocated a return to the gold standard, but on the basis of the convertibility of high value banknotes for gold bullion as a way of maintaining stable prices and trade equilibrium. In his *Principles of Political Economy*, Ricardo criticised Smith for believing that the market rate of interest followed the legal rate, whereas in fact the actual market rate of interest varies from the legal rate, sometimes quite substantially and the legal rate was widely evaded: "During the present war, Exchequer and Navy Bill have been frequently at so high a discount, as to afford the purchasers of them 7, 8%, or a greater rate of interest for their money. Loans have been raised by government at an interest exceeding 6%..." while the legal rate remained fixed at 5% (Ricardo, 1951, pp. 296–297). Hollander has pointed out that rates of interest on British government loans had exceeded the legal rate as early as the late 1770s, as a result of the large amount of loans required to prosecute the American War (Hollander, 1999). The market rate of interest, in its turn, was ultimately determined by the rate of profit that, in Ricardo's economics, would tend to fall with capital accumulation. By implication so too, eventually, would the market rate of interest. Indeed, the attempt to repeal the Usury Laws was introduced in 1818 precisely at a time when the market rate of interest was below the legal rate.

In his evidence to the House of Commons Select Committee on the Usury Laws, which he gave after the publication of his *Principles of Political Economy* in 1817, Ricardo reiterated his view that the Usury Laws were widely evaded, including by the Government. There would be no commercial disadvantage in their abolition. Indeed, by restricting the competition to lend, the Laws actually raise the rate of interest which borrowers are obliged to pay. There would be no injury to "mercantile interests" if the Laws were abolished, and it would help to discourage the export of capital (Ricardo, 1818). There is a curious coincidence between the views expressed by Ricardo and those of Jeremy Bentham. The two men were friends, with a correspondence dating back to 1811. There is ample evidence in the volumes of Ricardo's *Works and Correspondence* that he knew of

Bentham's papers and pamphlets on legislative reform. But Ricardo's comments on Bentham's economic writings are restricted by and large to Bentham's proposal for using circulating annuities as a currency and his papers on currency, arguing that the increase in paper money was the cause of rising prices (see Ricardo, 1811). In particular, there is no mention in Ricardo's writings or correspondence of Bentham's *Defence of Usury*. The connection was to be made after Ricardo's death by his disciple John Ramsay McCulloch.

Ricardo also attempted to deal with another argument for regulating the rate of interest, that of Jean-Baptiste Say. Say had put forward in his *Traité d'Économie politique* a version of Smith's view on usury using a "crowding-out" argument: Agriculture, manufacture and commerce would be driven out of the credit market if "a borrower may be found ready to pay" a higher rate of interest, especially the Government. The "profit on stock" would rise as merchants increased prices to pay higher interest, to the detriment of consumption and more productive activities (cited in Ricardo, 1951, p. 299. Hollander observes similarly that the government could "crowd out" private industrial and commercial borrowing by raising loans at a rate of interest higher than the legal maximum which private sector borrowers were obliged to observe. Hollander, 1999.). Ricardo's answer to this was:

> To the question: "who would lend money to farmers, manufacturers, and merchants, at 5%. per annum, when another borrower, having little credit, would give 7 or 8?" I reply, that every prudent and reasonable man would. Because the rate of interest is 7 or 8%. there, where the lender runs extraordinary risk, is this any reason why it should be equally high in those places where they are secured from such risks? M. Say allows, that the rate of interest depends on the rate of profit; but it does not therefore follow, that the rate of profits depends on the rate of interest. One is the cause, the other the effect, and it is impossible for any circumstances to make them change places (*Ibid.*, pp. 299–300).

Ricardo was not so much refuting Say as (unconsciously) reiterating Bentham's earlier argument that loans at higher rates of interest reflected objectively higher profit opportunities, with correspondingly higher business risk.

Henry Thornton and David Ricardo were crucial in putting forward the ideas that were to persuade legislators that, for the sake of sound banking and monetary policy, as well as in the interests of commercial freedom, the laws limiting the rate of interest should be abolished. However, in so doing they changed the elements that constituted Adam Smith's argument by narrowing the scope of the demand for credit and changing its nature. Adam Smith envisaged merchants and industrialists borrowing money, with the latter in particular prone to exaggerate the success of their enterprises. Smith also discussed the financing of enterprise through banks and joint stock issues. Thornton and Ricardo, London banker and stock-broker respectively, envisaged the demand for credit as essentially that of the individuals and institutions who did business with them in their professional lives, namely merchants and financial investors, the Treasury, the country banks who presented their bills to Thornton for re-discount against Bank of England notes, international bill brokers and bullion dealers. The demand for industrial credit appears from beyond the orbit of their practical work as a demand for finance to undertake works with an objectively known rate of profit in a world of certain prices and incomes (Harcourt, 1995). Adam Smith may have been more realistic in his treatment of business motives and prospects, but Thornton and Ricardo better represented the business optimism and social confidence of the emerging financial markets of London (Niebyl, 1946, p. 75). By contrast, the anti-bullionist spokesman of the Birmingham manufacturers, Thomas Attwood, was represented as "a provincial banker labouring under a financial monomania." (The description is attributed to Benjamin Disraeli, Corry, 1962, p. 83.)

6. THE EMERGENCE OF MONETARY POLICY

Say's point about higher interest, charged to consumers in higher prices, crowding out productive enterprise, was soon stripped of its regulatory implications by the bullionist critics of the Real Bills Doctrine. Thornton argued that speculative inflation was more likely if interest rates were kept low (Thornton, 1802, p. 253. See also Corry, 1962, pp. 52–55). Among the bullionists, John Ramsay McCulloch distinguished himself by bringing back into the discussion Smith's views on usury and the Ricardians' opposition to them. In 1828 he published an annotated edition of Adam Smith's *The Wealth of Nations*. In Volume II of this edition, after Smith's sentence "If the legal rate of interest in Great Britain, for example, were fixed so high as eight or ten percent. the greater part of the money which was to be lent, would be lent to prodigals and projectors, who alone would be willing to give this high interest." McCulloch added the following note:

> It is singular that Dr. Smith should have advanced so untenable a proposition. There is evidently no reason whatever for supposing that if the usury laws were repealed, and men allowed to bargain for the use of money as they are allowed to bargain for the use of land, houses, &c. they would be less careful and attentive to their interests in the former case than in the latter. The prudence and success of persons engaged in new and unusual undertakings are always considered doubtful; and they were never able to obtain loans on such easy terms as those who are engaged in ordinary and understood branches of industry. It is, however, unnecessary to enlarge on this subject, as it has been most ably discussed, and every objection to the unconditional repeal of the usury laws, on the grounds of its encouragement of projectors, satisfactorily answered by Mr. Bentham, in his letter to Dr. Smith, in his *Defence of Usury*. I shall give, in a note on the Usury Laws in the last volume, some account of their practical operation during the late War, and of the efforts that have been made to procure their repeal (McCulloch, 1828, Vol. II, p. 138).

McCulloch never wrote his note on the Usury Laws. By this time economic circumstances were evolving in a way that was to ensure the eventual abolition of the Usury Laws, irrespective of the merits of projectors. The resumption of convertibility in 1819, at the pre-War price of gold, was facilitated by a deflationary reduction of the note issue by the Bank of England and speculation that drove down the price of gold. Thereafter the Bank of England needed an instrument to facilitate the stabilisation of its gold reserves. This instrument was to be the Bank Rate, i.e. the rate at which the Bank of England discounted the best quality bills, which was supposed to discourage discounting in London for banknotes convertible into gold at the Bank. In 1811, Henry Thornton had suggested that raising the rate of interest would attract gold to London (Thornton, 1811, p. 331). Beginning in 1833, the scope of the Usury Acts was limited until their final repeal in 1854. But regulating gold deposits was not the only possible use of interest rates that was envisaged as the Usury Laws were being abolished. In 1839, an outflow of gold from the country to the Continent and America caused problems with reducing the quantity of paper money in circulation. The Bank of England raised its Bank Rate above the 5% maximum laid down in the Usury Laws, to 6%. This was as much to reduce the outflow of gold reserves as to check the expansion of credit, by reducing the number of bills presented to the Bank of England for discount, so that its note issue could be diminished without refusing to discount. (In the event, the inflow of gold failed to materialise, and the Bank of England was forced to borrow gold in Paris and Hamburg.) Avoiding a refusal to discount was important for maintaining the liquidity of banks. The Bank of England had on three occasions, in 1793, in 1799 and 1811 refused to discount, out of a desire to limit the amount of banknotes that were issued at discount. On all three occasions, the Government's Treasury forced accommodation by issuing Exchequer Bills, which the Bank of England could not refuse to discount, and which were therefore acceptable as means of payment among merchants and their banks. In 1825, the Bank of England refused again, but gave way and resumed discounting at the height of the crisis (Hawtrey, 1933, pp. 121–122). According to Keynes, in 1839 "the new-fangled notion was invented that bank rate had an independent influence through its effect on 'speculation'" (Keynes, 1930, p. 195). The resulting tendency of money market interest rates to fluctuate with the business cycle was noted by the banker Samuel Lloyd, Lord Overstone, in his 1837 pamphlet *Reflections . . . on the causes and consequences of the pressure on the Money Market* (Overstone, 1858). Overstone was to be very influential in the thinking underlying the 1844 Bank Charter Act, designed to limit the issue of paper currency. Using a loanable funds model, the classical political economists attributed changes in money market interest rates to changes in the demand for loans, relative to supply. "In speculative times," during a boom, interest rates rise while, "in the intervals between commercial crises, there is a tendency in the rate of interest to a progressive decline from the gradual process of accumulation," so that only in equilibrium is the rate of interest determined by the rate of profit (Mill, 1867, Book III, Chap. XXIII; see also Marx, 1959, pp. 512–514).

7. JOHN STUART MILL AND SPECULATION

"Speculation" played an important part in the explanation of "commercial crisis" that prevailed among the classical political economists of the nineteenth century. A separate category of financial disturbance, bank "runs" which Thornton had analysed, caused bank collapses but did not, apart from the loss of deposits, transmit such distress into the rest of the economy. The notion of speculation placed the starting point of commercial crises in speculative trade in the real economy, which they believed could be facilitated by easy finance of speculative stocks through credit or paper money. This view, echoing Smith's earlier explanation of "overtrading" was summed up by that great synthesiser of classical political economy, John Stuart Mill as follows:

> The inclination of the mercantile public to increase their demand for commodities by making use of all or much of their credit as a purchasing power, depends on their expectation of profit. When there is a general impression that the price of some commodity is likely to rise, from an extra demand, a short crop, obstructions to importation, or any other cause, there is a disposition among dealers to increase their stocks, in order to profit by the expected rise. This disposition tends in itself to produce the effect which it looks forward to, a rise in price: and if the rise is considerable and progressive, other speculators are attracted, who, so long as the price has not begun to fall, are willing to believe that it will rise. These, by further purchases, produce a further advance: and thus a rise in price for which there were originally some rational grounds is often heightened by mere speculative purchases, until it greatly exceeds what the original grounds will justify. After a time this begins to be perceived; the price ceases to rise, and the holders, thinking it time to realize their gains, are anxious to sell. Then the price begins to decline: the holders rush into the market to avoid a still greater loss, and, few being willing to buy in a falling market, the price falls much more suddenly than it rose. Those who have bought at a higher price than reasonable calculation justified, and who have been overtaken by the revulsion before they had realized, are losers in proportion to the greatness of the fall, and to the quantity of the commodity which they hold, or have bound themselves to pay for.
>   . . . If there were no such thing as credit, this could hardly happen with respect to commodities generally . . . But . . . when people go into the market and purchase with money which they hope to receive hereafter, they are drawing upon an unlimited, not a limited fund . . . This is . . . what is called a commercial crisis (Mill, 1867, Book III, Chap. XII, pp. 318–319).

John Stuart Mill was perhaps the last of the nineteenth-century political economists to take issue with Smith's argument against usury. Mill had no doubt that it was "next to the system of protection, among mischievous interferences with the spontaneous course of industrial transactions" (Mill, 1867, Book V, Chap. X, pp. 558–559). Predictably he commended "the triumphant onslaught made upon it by Bentham in his 'Letters on Usury,' which may still be referred to as the best extant writing on the subject" (*ibid.*, p. 559). Like his friend Bentham, Mill saw the origins of restrictions on usury as being in a "religious prejudice against receiving interest on money," and defended "projectors" as entrepreneurs engaged in industrial progress. However, Mill now put forward what came later to be known as a "loanable funds" theory of capital to criticise restrictions on usury. In his view the rate of interest was naturally determined "by the spontaneous play of supply and demand." Attempts to hold the rate of interest below this level would give rise to excessive demand for credit, which would be satisfied only at excessive rates outside the protection that the law provides for commercial contracts.

> If the competition of borrowers, left unrestrained, would raise the rate of interest to 6%, this proves that at five there would be a greater demand for loans than there is capital in the market to supply. If the law in these circumstances permits no interest beyond 5%, there will be some lenders, who not choosing to disobey the law, and not being in a condition to employ their capital otherwise, will content themselves with the legal rate: but others, finding that in a season of pressing demand, more may be made of their capital by other means than they are permitted to make by lending it, will not lend at all; and the loanable capital, already too small for the demand, will be still further diminished. Of the disappointed candidates there will be many at such periods who must have their necessities supplied at any price, and these will readily find a third section of lenders, who will not be averse to join in a violation of the law, either by circuitous transactions partaking of the nature of fraud, or by relying on the honour of the borrower. The extra expense of the roundabout mode of proceeding, and an equivalent for the risk of non-payment and of the legal penalties, must be paid by the borrower, over and above the extra interest that would have been required of him by the general state of the market. The laws which were intended to lower the price paid by him for pecuniary accommodation, end thus in greatly increasing it (Mill, 1867, p. 559).

On the supply side, Mill's argument depended on a presumption that "competition will limit the extra demand [for higher interest] to a fair equivalent for the risk" (*ibid.*, p. 560).

Mill further argued that the usury laws exacerbated commercial crises. Here he reinterpreted Smith somewhat:

> Adam Smith rather hastily expressed the opinion that only two kinds of persons, "prodigals and projectors," could require to borrow money at more than the market rate of interest. He should have included all persons who are in any pecuniary difficulties, however temporary their necessities may be. It may happen to any person in business, to be disappointed of the resources on which he has calculated for meeting some engagement, the non-fulfilment of which on a fixed day would be bankruptcy. In periods of commercial difficulty, this is the condition of many prosperous mercantile firms, who become competitors for the small amount of disposable capital which, at a time of general distrust, the owners are willing to part with. Under the English usury laws, now happily abolished, the limitations imposed by these laws were felt as a most

serious aggravation of every commercial crisis. Merchants who could have obtained the aid they required at an interest of seven or eight percent for short periods, were obliged to give 20 or 30%, or to resort to forced sales of goods at a still greater loss (loc. cit.).

In fact Smith put forward a policy of mercantile support that was even more favourable to merchants in distress. His Real Bills Doctrine, combined with the usury laws, offered the possibility of flexible credit against future sales at a rate of interest that would not rise because of additional demand for credit. Arguably this would relieve commercial distress much more effectively than Mill's loanable funds model in which, without an increase in saving, the rate of interest would rise at the first signs of "pecuniary difficulties."

Mill's association of paper money with speculation was a life-long conviction expressed in one of his first articles "Paper Currency – Commercial Distress" which he published in 1826. Here he echoed Smith to decry "the universal propensity of mankind to overestimate the chances in their own favour" and looked forward to a time when "sober calculation may gradually take the place of gambling" (Mill, 1826). However, the "speculation" of which Mill and the classical political economists wrote was a merchant's pursuit, whereas the "projectors" of Smith and Bentham, were industrial capitalists *in spe* if not in fact. Karl Niebyl has pointed out that in their considerations of credit, the classical political economists regarded enterprise as an essentially mercantile activity (Niebyl, 1946, pp. 74–75).

In this regard Marx was an exception. Anticipating Minsky's Ponzi finance analysis, he noted that, in times of crisis, "everyone borrows only for the purpose of paying, in order to settle previously contracted obligations. . . " and only subsequently, ". . . in time of renewed activity after a crisis, loan capital is demanded for the purpose of buying and for the purpose of transforming money-capital into productive and commercial capital" (Marx, 1959, p. 513).

The opponents of bullionism (the doctrine that prices would be stable if paper currency were limited to the amount of gold reserves) pressed the case of manufacturers keen to have more elastic credit facilities. They argued that the price level determined the quantity of currency, and not vice versa and attributed the industrial depression after 1815 to the return to the gold standard and its effects on credit. The preference of anti-bullionists, for example the Birmingham banker Thomas Attwood and his brother the Member of Parliament Matthias Attwood, was for a paper currency that they envisaged working much like the system Thornton examined in the early chapters of *Paper Credit* (Corry, 1962, pp. 85–95; Laidler, 1991, p. 23). But it was not until the twentieth century, in the work of Ralph Hawtrey, that these anti-bullionist ideas were developed into a systematic argument about disturbance of the economy by the credit system.

Mill's analysis of speculative crises was to be immortalised by Alfred Marshall. In *The Economics of Industry*, which he published with his wife Mary Paley Marshall, he put forward a credit cycle that, in its essentials was Mill's speculative cycle. The main innovation was that an over-supply of credit, rather than paper money, was now held to be responsible for inflationary, speculative booms and crises (Marshall & Marshall, 1879, Book III, Chap. 1). A faint echo of Smith found its way into *The Economics of Industry*, in a forecast that the rate of interest is destined to fall over time, in accordance with the Law of Diminishing Marginal Returns. Marshall's analysis of "credit fluctuations" then found its way into Marshall's *Money Credit and Commerce*, where he reiterated the classical doctrine that "prompt action by the Bank of England in regard to the rate of discount" may check speculative excess. However, he noted the difficulty of doing this if the Bank Rate is being used to regulate gold reserves, and was best done where currency is inconvertible (Marshall, 1924, pp. 258–259). Thus, through Marshall, the classical doctrine of raising the money rate of interest to check speculation, was transmitted into the twentieth-century work of Hawtrey and later monetarists.

8. CONCLUSION

The discussion around Adam Smith's views on usury, and the reaction of later classical political economists to those views, provides intriguing anticipations of current ideas of saving, uncertainty, risk-adjusted interest rates, loanable funds, capital rationing, asymmetric information, Ponzi finance and financial fragility. That in itself makes it worthwhile re-visiting this debate. But by far the most important element of the debate was Adam Smith's premonition of financial fragility, the decline in the "quality" of credit with higher interest rates. The prevailing currency school in classical political economy replaced the notion that high interest rates concentrate credit on the financing of speculative projectors with the notion that high interest rates discourage speculation.

Smith's argument on usury was never refuted in its own terms (of high interest rates excluding prudent borrowers and thereby shifting the demand for credit towards speculators, etc.). It simply got left behind, because the situation changed: the Revolutionary and Napoleonic Wars required the suspension of convertibility, with the result that the expansion of paper currency was associated with price inflation; and the terms of the discussion changed: Bentham and Ricardo emphasised that freedom to set the terms of loans was an essential element of normal commercial freedom. Even after that freedom proved to be elusive, with the Bank of England influencing money market rates through its discounting policy, cyclical movements in money market interest rates linked high interest rates with the bursting of speculative bubbles. This was not inconsistent with Smith's argument: The financial collapse following a speculative bubble was, as Marx implied, just as likely because of a decline in the quality of credit as interest rates rose. Smith's argument came to be replaced by the doctrine taught to students today that "those who find it easiest to borrow are those whose financial position is basically sound" (Hanson, 1967, p. 420). "Commercial distress" came to be regarded by classical political economy as being due to speculation that is naturally squeezed out by higher rates of interest. Monetary and credit problems came to be viewed as the consequences of inappropriate monetary policy on the part of the authorities. The banking and financial system, while vulnerable to runs and collapses, nevertheless makes exchange more efficient and raises finance for industry and commerce. But the responsibility for financial fragility in the economy was placed firmly with merchant speculators and the monetary authorities. Out of this comes the modern view that Smith's advocacy of legal regulation of interest was a reversal along an otherwise direct path to laissez-faire that must have occurred to him "in an incautious moment" (Robbins, 1968, p. 86), an "aberration . . . inconsistent with Smith's basic theory of sensible economic behaviour" (Stigler, 1975, p. 208). Smith's reluctance to recognise Bentham's superior wisdom is supposed to illustrate how "the able economist . . . seldom admits or corrects a mistake" (loc. cit.). Even his most recent biographer, Ian Simpson Ross, recognising that Bentham was unlikely to have convinced Smith, opines:

> It is an interesting speculation that, had Smith lived beyond 1790, he might have altered his stand on reducing interest and equating projectors with prodigals', especially since 'the message about the detrimental effects of most economic legislation intensified in the third edition' of 1791 (Ross, 1995, pp. 359–360).

But Smith's argument in favour of usury laws was not about the wisdom of unregulated markets, but was about the role of finance in the economy. The issues that he raised remain important today.

ACKNOWLEDGMENTS

I wish to thank Victoria Chick, David Cobham, Gary Dymski, Geoffrey Harcourt, Tracy Mott, and Alfredo Saad-Filho for helpful remarks on an earlier version of this paper, Mary French-Sokol for advice on the published work of Jeremy Bentham, and to Noemi Levy-Orlik and her colleagues and students at UNAM, Mexico City, with whom I was able to discuss some of the ideas in this paper. This paper has been greatly improved by suggestions from Warren Samuels and anonymous referees to whom he sent an earlier draft.

REFERENCES

Bentham, J. (1787). Defence of Usury. In: W. Stark (Ed.), *Jeremy Bentham's Economic Writings*. London: George Allen and Unwin for the Royal Economic Society, 1952.

Bernanke, B. S. (1983). Non-monetary effects of the financial crisis in the propogation of the great depression. *American Economic Review, 73*, 257–279.

Blaug, M. (1996). *Economic theory in retrospect*. Cambridge: Cambridge University Press.

Carlson, M. (1999). Adam Smith's support for money and banking regulation: A case of inconsistency? *History of Economics Review*, (29), 1–15.

Chick, V. (1986). The evolution of the banking system and the theory of saving, investment and interest. In: S. C. Dow & P. Arestis (Eds), *On Money, Method and Keynes Selected Essays*. London: Macmillan, 1992.

Corry, B. A. (1962). *Money saving and investment in English Economics 1800–1850*. New York: St. Martin's Press.

Dymski, G. A. (1998). Disembodied risk or the social construction of credit-worthiness? An enquiry into the new Keynesian microfoundations. In: R. Rotheim (Ed.), *New Keynesian Economics – Post Keynesian Alternatives*. London: Routledge.

Hanson, J. L. (1967). *A dictionary of economics and commerce*. London: MacDonald and Evans.

Harcourt, G. C. (1995). What Adam Smith really said. *Economic Review, 12*(2), 24–27. Reprinted in: *Capitalism, Socialism and Post-Keynesianism*. Aldershot: Edward Elgar, 1995.

Hawtrey, R. G. (1933). *The art of central banking*. London: Longmans, Green and Co.

Hayek, F. A. (1939). Introduction. In: F. A. Hayek (Ed.), *An Inquiry into the Nature and Effects of the Paper Credit of Great Britain by Henry Thornton Together with His Evidence Given Before the Committees of Secrecy of the Two Houses of Parliament in the Bank of england, March and April, 1797, Some Manuscript Notes and His Speeches on the Bullion Report, May 1811*. London: George Allen and Unwin, 1939.

Hayek, F. A. (1946). The meaning of competition. The Stafford Little Lecture delivered at Princeton University. In: *Individualism and Economic Order*. London: Routledge and Kegan Paul 1949.

Hollander, S. (1999). Jeremy Bentham and Adam Smith on the Usury laws: A "Smithian" reply to Bentham and a new problem. *European Journal of the History of Economic Thought, VI*(4), 523–552.

Hu, Y.-S. (1979). *National attitudes and the financing of industry*. London: Political and Economic Planning, Vol. XLI Broadsheet No. 559 (December).

Keynes, J. M. (1930). *A treatise on money in two volumes. 1: The pure theory of money. 2: The applied theory of money*. London: Macmillan.

Keynes, J. M. (1936). *The general theory of employment, interest and money*. London: Macmillan.

Kindleberger, C. P. (1993). *A financial history of Western Europe*. New York: Oxford University Press.

Laidler, D. (1991). *The golden age of the quantity theory*. Princeton, NJ: Princeton University Press.

Marshall, A. (1924). *Money, credit and commerce*. London: Macmillan.

Marshall, A. (1938). *Principles of economics*. London: Macmillan.

Marshall, A., & Marshall, M. P. (1879). *The economics of industry*. Bristol: Thoemmes Press, reprint 1994.

Marx, K. (1959). *Capital, a critique of political economy Volume III: The process of capitalist production as a whole*. F. Engels (Ed.). Moscow: Progress Publishers.

Marx, K. (1975). *Theories of surplus value, Volume IV of capital, Part III*. Moscow: Progress Publishers.

McCulloch, J. R. (1828). Supplemental notes and dissertations. In: A. Smith (Ed.), *An Inquiry into the Nature and Causes of the Wealth of Nations*. Edinburgh: Adam Black and William Tait, London: Longman, Rees, Orme, Brown and Green.

Mill, J. S. (1826). Paper currency – commercial distress. *The Parliamentary History and Review, II*, cited in Corry 1962, 104–105.

Mill, J. S. (1867). *Principles of political economy with some of their applications to social philosophy* (people's ed.). London: Longmans, Green, Reader and Dyer.

Milne, A. T. (1981). *The correspondence of Jeremy Bentham Volume 4. October 1788–December 1793*. London: Athlone Press.

Mishkin, F. S. (1991). Asymmetric information and financial crises: A historical perspective. In: R. G. Hubbard (Ed.), *Financial Markets and Financial Crises*. Chicago: University of Chicago Press.

Murphy, A. E. (1997). *John Law: Economic theorist and policy-maker*. Oxford: Clarendon Press.

Niebyl, K. H. (1946). *Studies in the classical theories of money*. New York: Columbia University Press.

Overstone, S. J. (1858). *Tracts and other publications on metallic and paper currencies*. London.

Perlman, M. (1989). Adam Smith and the paternity of the Real Bills Doctrine. *History of Political Economy, 21*(1), 77–90.

Pesciarelli, E. (1989). Smith, Bentham and the development of contrasting ideas on entrepreneurship. *History of Political Economy, 21*, 521–536.

Pressman, S. (1999). *Fifty major economists*. London: Routledge.

Rae, J. (1895). *Life of Adam Smith*. London: Macmillan.

Ricardo, D. (1811). Notes on Bentham. In: P. Sraffa (Ed.), with the collaboration of M. H. Dobb, *The Works and Correspondence of David Ricardo Volume III: Pamphlets and Papers*. Cambridge: Cambridge University Press for the Royal Economic Society, 1962.

Ricardo, D. (1818). Minutes of evidence taken before the select committee on the usury laws, 30 April 1818. In: P. Sraffa (Ed.), with the collaboration of M. H. Dobb, *The Works and Correspondence of David Ricardo Volume V. Speeches and Evidence*. Cambridge: Cambridge University Press for the Royal Economic Society, 1952.

Ricardo, D. (1951). *The works and correspondence of David Ricardo Volume I. On the principles of political economy and taxation*. P. Sraffa (Ed.) with the collaboration of M. H. Dobb. Cambridge: Cambridge University Press for the Royal Economic Society.

Robbins, L. (1968). *The theory of economic development in the history of economic thought*. London: Macmillan.

Ross, I. S. (1995). *The life of Adam Smith*. Oxford: Clarendon Press.

Schumpeter, J. A. (1954). *History of economic analysis*. London: Allen and Unwin.

Smith, A. (1904). *An inquiry into the nature and causes of the wealth of nations*. London: Oxford University Press.

Spiegel, H. W. (1987). Usury. In: J. Eatwell, M. Milgate & P. Newman (Eds), *The New Palgrave: A Dictionary of Economic Theory and Doctrine*. London: Macmillan.

Stark, W. (1952). Introduction. In: W. Stark (Ed.), *Jeremy Bentham's Economic Writings*. London: George Allen and Unwin for the Royal Economic Society.

Stigler, G. J. (1975). *The citizen and the state: Essays on regulation*. Chicago: University of Chicago Press.

Stiglitz, J. E. (1998). Preventing financial crises in developing countries. In: *Global Economic Prospects and the Developing Countries 1998–1999, Beyond Financial Crisis*. Washington, DC: World Bank.

Stiglitz, J. E., & Weiss, A. (1981). Credit rationing in markets with imperfect information. *American Economic Review, 71*, 393–410.

Thornton, H. (1797). The evidence given by Henry Thornton before the Committees of Secrecy of the two Houses of Parliament on the Bank of England March and April 1797. In: F. A. Hayek (Ed.), *An Inquiry into the Nature and Effects of the Paper Credit of Great Britain by Henry Thornton Together with His Evidence Given Before the Committees of Secrecy of the Two Houses of Parliament in the Bank of England, March and April, 1797, Some Manuscript Notes and His Speeches on the Bullion Report, May 1811*. London: George Allen and Unwin, 1939.

Thornton, H. (1802). An inquiry into the nature and effects of the paper credit of Great Britain. In: F. A. Hayek (Ed.), *An Inquiry into the Nature and Effects of the Paper Credit of Great Britain by Henry Thornton Together with His Evidence Given Before the Committees of Secrecy of the Two Houses of Parliament in the Bank of England, March and April, 1797, Some Manuscript Notes and His Speeches on the Bullion Report, May 1811*. London: George Allen and Unwin, 1939.

Thornton, H. (1811). Two speeches of Henry Thornton, Esq. on the bullion report. In: F. A. Hayek (Ed.), *An Inquiry into the Nature and Effects of the Paper Credit of Great Britain by Henry Thornton Together with His Evidence Given Before the Committees of Secrecy of the Two Houses of Parliament in the Bank of England, March and April, 1797, Some Manuscript Notes and His Speeches on the Bullion Report, May 1811*. London: George Allen and Unwin, 1939.

Toporowski, J. (2000). *The end of finance: The theory of capital market inflation, financial derivatives and pension fund capitalism*. London: Routledge.

Toporowski, J. (2002). La banque mutuelle: de l'Utopie au marché des capitaux Le case britannique. *Revue d'Économie financière, 67*, 45–56.

Weber, M. (1948). *From Max Weber: Essays in sociology*. Translated, Edited and with an Introduction by H. H. Gerth and C. Wright Mills, London: Routledge and Kegan Paul.

CATALYSING GROWTH?: MENDELEEV AND THE 1891 TARIFF

Vincent Barnett

> Nations judge one another by what they see of each other, and the first things they see of each other are their respective tariffs. The greater or less conformity of the tariff to the rules of science is a test of the *mathematical intelligence* of the government of the country.[1]
>
> Julius Faucher, 1872, p. 280

> In Russian literature the ideas of free traders predominate, but in Russian life the protectionist understanding dominates...
>
> D. I. Mendeleev, 1897a, p. 85.

Dmitrii Ivanovich Mendeleev (1834–1907), inventor of the periodic table of the elements and world-renowned father of modern chemistry, played a major role in supporting and designing the 1891 Russian tariff.[2] Indeed this tariff has been called "the Mendeleev tariff" in his honour, just as the 101st chemical element to be discovered was named Mendelevium (Gregory, 1982, p.140).[3] This article presents an analytical account of Mendeleev's role in supporting and designing the tariff, and connects this with an analysis of his theoretical arguments for protectionism and the free trade vs. protectionism debate in general. It does not claim to be a definitive and complete account of the factual history of these topics, aiming only to highlight some of the motivational issues involved (at least as Mendeleev perceived them at the time). The overall goal is to provoke further discussion of a neglected but still resonant theme in Russian history. A survey of evaluations of the effects of the 1891 tariff is also included in the second part of the article, although this should be acknowledged as only a preliminary account (by a historian of ideas), awaiting a more definitive empirical treatment.

Research in the History of Economic Thought and Methodology A Research Annual
Research in the History of Economic Thought and Methodology, Volume 22-A, 123–144
Copyright © 2004 by Elsevier Ltd.
All rights of reproduction in any form reserved
ISSN: 0743-4154/doi:10.1016/S0743-4154(03)22004-6

Protectionism is of course the intellectual *bete noire* of free trade liberalism, although periodically it makes a resurgence in some part of the world in response to perceived threats from economically more powerful states. The legitimacy of mainstream economics is perhaps never felt to be more unreasonably threatened than by intellectual support for nationalistic anti-liberal policies, although in Europe in the second half of the nineteenth century free trade ideas were not quite so all conquering. Friedrich List's *National System of Political Economy* was widely read and followed, although so of course was Adam Smith's *Wealth of Nations*.[4] List had written of the "beneficial effects of the Russian protective system," although many would vigorously dispute this claim (List, 1904, p. 74). Today many commentators (but by no means all) repeatedly emphasize the benefits of GATT and the WTO, and ongoing attempts at reducing tariff barriers are an accepted part of contemporary international economic relations. This was not always the case, in particular at the end of the nineteenth century, when protectionist sentiment surged across both Europe and America (Capie, 1994, p. 33). At this time "the American system" was a well-known euphemism for industrial development under tariff protection, at least in the Northern states of the union (Galbraith, 1987, p. 157). Mitchell evaluated the McKinley tariff for example, introduced in the USA in 1890, as providing "a bounty to American sugar interests" (Mitchell, 1970, p. 46). Was the Mendeleev tariff similarly sector interest-generated, or was it of purely doctrinal inspiration?

1. TARIFFS AND GROWTH

There has recently been a flurry of interest in analysing trade policy regimes and their particular historical expressions among economists. This has been provoked in part by new developments in trade theory such as those based on the concepts of increasing returns and market structure, and in part by more awareness among the general public on development issues. For example a significant empirical study of the late nineteenth century concluded that a previously identified positive correlation between tariffs and growth was surprisingly robust (O'Rourke, 2000, p. 473). The previous study had concluded that:

> The reintroduction of protective tariffs (around 1880–1890) in the 'less developed' countries coincided in each case with a total reversal of the economic trends: growth accelerated and the pace of innovation and investment speeded up (Bairoch, 1972, p. 211).

Hence protection was associated with high rates of economic growth at least for less developed states such as Germany and the USA in the period specified. This was in contrast to an identified negative correlation observed for much of the twentieth century, one predicted by the conventional neoclassical theory of free trade.

What has consequently been called the late nineteenth century tariff-growth paradox has been explained by positing that "world environment matters," or that the benefits of free trade depend on the existing state of the world with respect to tariff barriers (Clemens & Williamson, 2001, p. 23). Thus, raising tariffs may be a successful strategy for one country only in a context where many other countries are doing the same. Given that the international environment in the late nineteenth century showed a definite sympathy for protection, this article investigates how Mendeleev responded to this situation both theoretically and practically.

2. MENDELEEV'S INTEREST IN ECONOMIC AFFAIRS

In respect of indigenous intellectual capacity, Russia has never lacked natural scientific talent. Amann described Mendeleev as "the greatest of all Russian scientists," his importance being both theoretical and administrative (Amann, 1977, p. 288). Mendeleev's family had at one time owned a glass factory in Tobolsk, and he was directed to the study of economic matters by a profound concern for Russian natural resources and various attempts to develop them for the benefits of the Russian people (Leicester, 1961, p. 719). Mendeleev believed that the huge growth of industrial capacity in the nineteenth century could partly be explained by the fact that knowledge in the field of chemistry had achieved extraordinary successes in this period, and hence there was a direct connection between his natural and social scientific work (Mendeleev, 1900, pp. 116–117). Comparing the Russian economy in general to that of the USA, Mendeleev was particularly concerned that, while in the USA, 38% of the population were what he categorised as "feeders and supporters," the corresponding figure for Russia was only 24%. This was identified as a root cause of Russia's relative poverty, protracted industrial development being touted as part of the cure (Posin, 1948, p. 314).

Mendeleev eventually became an internationally renowned figure for his many scientific achievements. He had proudly represented Russia at the 1867 International Paris Exposition and he subsequently visited chemical plants in Germany, France and Belgium. One account of Mendeleev's life showed him being sent to the Caucasus for an inspection tour, with the aim of designing schemes for oil installations (Posin, 1948, p. 204); eventually he visited Baku on two separate occasions, in 1863 and 1880 (Tishchenko & Mladentsev, 1993, pp. 296–311). Another account suggested that Mendeleev's influence on the development of the petroleum industry in Baku was profound:

Fifteen years ago (i.e. in 1879 – VB) the production of petroleum in Russia was a monopoly, and was accompanied by all the evils which usually springs from monopolies . . . Thanks largely to his action, both on the platform and in the press, the opening up of the boundless supplies of the peninsula of Aspheron was thrown open to the world, with the result that petroleum threatens to effect an industrial revolution in Eastern Europe and in Asia (Thorpe, 1894, p. 364).

On a visit to America in 1876 Mendeleev was impressed by the ability of competition and specialisation to enable economic growth (Stackenwalt, 1976, p. 549), and on returning from the trip he presented "Notes on the Necessity of the Abolition of the Excise Duty on Lighting Oil" to the Ministry of Finance (Tishchenko & Mladentsev, 1993, p. 303). Perhaps unsurprisingly Mendeleev had close friends in high business circles and was even accused by some of selling out to business interests (Owen, 1991, p. 112). A personal friend of Sergei Witte, he published detailed studies of Russia's natural resource base and his knowledge of potential energy sources was extensive. He even proposed a theory of the carbide origin of petroleum, in which inorganic metallic carbides produced methane that was then transformed into petroleum (Graham, 1973, pp. 265–266). Mendeleev was not of course a professionally trained economist, although political economy as a subject in the 1890s was certainly not beyond the self-teaching capabilities of an acknowledged scientific genius. Some of what Mendeleev produced in this area is analysed in the following three sections of this article.

3. MENDELEEV'S GENERAL ANALYSIS OF INDUSTRY

As early as 1863 Mendeleev had began the study of various aspects of the industrial development of Russia. Initially his interest focused on specific branches of industry such as chemicals, petroleum, coal and metallurgy, these being branches where his natural scientific knowledge was obviously relevant. Out of this early interest Mendeleev published works such as "On the Contemporary Development of the Chemical Industry Applied to Russia" (1867) and "Petroleum Affairs in Pennsylvania and the Caucasus" (1877).[5] From the beginning of the 1880s Mendeleev's interests broadened and he began working on the more general topic of the origins of industry and on the economic development path best suited to Russia. As a result he published more wide-ranging works such as "On the Conditions of the Development of Factories in Russia" (1882) and "Foundations of Manufacturing Industry" (1897).

Mendeleev came to believe profoundly in the strategic significance of heavy industry. He argued that a few basic types of industry were connected to a multitude of other industries and that without securing these basic types within the country, the development of other secondary branches would be unthinkable. These strategic types of industry were specified as being coal, iron, steel, metallic tools and machinery (Kudryavtseva & Shekhter, 1952, p. 15). In 1888, Mendeleev even proposed three general goals for the Russian Ministry for Industry – creating the conditions for the extensive development of private industry, the establishment of Russian factories to supply domestically and to England, and supporting the trading network – and his published efforts were designed to contribute to achieving these aims (Mendeleev, 1888, pp. 28–29).

In order to fully comprehend Mendeleev's specific case for Russian protection, an understanding of his view of the foundations of industry is first required as background. A summary of Mendeleev's general conception of industrial development can be found in "Foundations of Manufacturing Industry" of 1897. Here he initially distinguished between various types of economic activity such as agriculture and hunting and various types of industry such as artisan industry (*remeslennaya*), mining industry (*gornaya promyshlennost*) and manufacturing industry (*fabrichno-zavodskaya promyshlennost*) (Mendeleev, 1897b, pp. 22–24). Analysing manufacturing industry in particular he concluded that:

(1) Factories were the natural result of the development of industrial activity, being determined both by complex heterogeneous needs and the growth of scientific understanding;

(2) The basic goal of manufacturing industry was to substitute animal products by vegetable, and vegetable products by mineral. This path for industry facilitated the liberation of people from the naturally existing inequalities that were created by various differences in the climate, soil and access to air, water and the oceans;

(3) The contemporary significance of manufacturing industry was that it increased national income and enlightened the nation-state generally;

(4) Manufacturing industry should capture ever wider fields of human activity;

(5) In order to strengthen manufacturing industry and for the influence of science on nature to prevail, all countries must aspire to participate in the progress of humanity (Mendeleev, 1897b, p. 36).

These five points marked out the position of manufacturing industry against all other types of industrial activity and suggested why for Mendeleev such industry needed to be vigorously fostered in Russia.

Overall Mendeleev strongly supported the necessity of the capitalistic industrialisation of Russia based on machine production, and he continually emphasised the benefits of this process in terms of the increased welfare of the general population and the growth of education and culture that would result. In order to assist this process Mendeleev advocated the establishment of special banks that could offer financial capital to industrialists at low rates of interest (Stackenwalt, 1976, p. 108). He believed that history taught that industrialisation had begun in the U.K. and the USA through state assistance, and in turn this general approach led Mendeleev to the idea of industrial protection.

4. MENDELEEV'S THEORETICAL JUSTIFICATION OF PROTECTION

The idea that protectionist policies were beneficial to Russian economic development permeated Mendeleev's voluminous writings on economic affairs, indeed it might be seen as the doctrinal bedrock on which they were based. Witte in his memoirs described Mendeleev as being "at times a fervent protectionist" as well as having an independent character (*Mendeleev v vospominaniyakh*, 1973, p. 139). Mendeleev simply did not countenance the notion that Russia at the end of the nineteenth century might have benefited from unfettered free trade, and the allegedly positive effects of protection were highlighted repeatedly in his works. The Ricardian concept of comparative advantage was not often mentioned.

A good general example of Mendeleev's doctrinal justification of protection, taken from a work entitled "Explaining the Tariff" published in 1892, went as follows:

> Since in the majority of cases Russian requirements for foreign goods can be compensated for by products of Russian production, customs duties on foreign goods increases the possibility of the domestic production of the taxed good, and all rises in productivity inside the country provide wages and increase the weight of internal free circulation within our borders (Mendeleev, 1892, p. 187).

Mendeleev clearly believed that indigenous Russian producers could and should match foreign producers in many cases. Another example of Mendeleev's justification of protection was from a work published in 1893, where its past success was highlighted:

> The great increase in the home production of cotton goods, cast iron, coal, sugar, and the products obtained from the treatment of petroleum . . . coinciding with the temporary introduction of protective duties, clearly demonstrates the expediency of the application of the principles of protection with the object of rousing the people to strengthen those forms of industry to which the natural resources and forces of the country correspond . . . (Mendeleeff, 1893, p. vi).

In this passage Mendeleev saw protection as being conducted in harmony with natural factor endowments rather than against them, or of being the spark that ignited a dormant existing potential. This might easily be interpreted as the infant industry argument for protection. Mendeleev also believed that protection should be intricately connected to the overall state management of industrial growth. In an article from 1897 entitled "The Justification of Protectionism" he wrote:

> ... the state has a duty to stimulate, promote and protect the industry and trade of its country by all possible means ... Protectionism encompasses not only customs tariffs but all the totality of state measures favouring industry and trade ... (Mendeleev, 1897a, p. 86).

A mercantalist overtone might be detected in this approach, although Mendeleev explicitly rejected the mercantile desire for a country to accumulate gold (Mendeleev, 1892, p. 187).[6] Mercantilism had been somewhat influential in Russia well before the 1890s (Lodyzhensky, 1886, p. 101).

Mendeleev's argument for protection was historically as well as theoretically grounded, relying partly on Lodyzhensky's *History of the Russian Customs Tariff* of 1886 for support. Regarding the history of tariff policy in Russia Mendeleev outlined:

> From 1822 right up to 1850 and especially in 1867 the general plan remained the same: protectionism was obvious but not extreme, now and then it was provocative; prohibition of some imports was repealed but permitted goods were taxed on a large scale; export duties were reduced and then abandoned; all industries that began production were protected ... (Mendeleev, 1892, p. 207).

Mendeleev explained that the customs duties adopted from 1857 to 1877 protected those branches of industry that transformed raw materials into finished goods, the tariff itself applying only to finished goods in this period. Consequently Russian mills and manufactures of the time had the character of finishing works only, turning foreign cast iron into iron rails, having received raw materials and semi-manufactured goods from overseas. The 1891 tariff however further extended protection to all kinds of minerals, for example to sulphur and pyrites, all sorts of ores, stones and coal. Forms of industry transforming indigenous raw materials, e.g. chemical manufacturing and metals, were also encouraged. Mendeleev explicated:

> The present industrial policy of Russia is directed precisely to the end that the productive forces of the country should be turned to the manufacture of the abundant supplies of agricultural and mineral raw materials in the Empire ... (Mendeleeff, 1893, p. x).

Thus, Mendeleev implied that since tariffs had succeeded before 1891, their application should certainly be expanded. The idea that there might be limits to the size of tariffs if they were to be effective was not emphasised at this point in the argument.

On other occasions Mendeleev's justification for protection involved comparison with the industrial development of other countries, for example the U.K. At a meeting of the Anglo-Russian Literary Society on 5 June 1894, Mendeleev gave a speech entitled "The Commercial Policy of Russia." Here he reasoned that the idea that protection would be for the interest of Russia was suggested by the fact that domestic agriculture did not suffice to maintain the increasing population. This was because the price of corn, instead of rising, was constantly falling, in consequence of the great production of this staple not only in Russia but also overseas. For this reason it was necessary to devise new means for increasing the scanty income of the agricultural classes, which were the great bulk of the Russian people:

> The Professor [i.e. Mendeleev – VB] pointed to the lessons of history, which show how other countries have been enriched. He considered that the laws which gave a monopoly to the English merchant-fleet, and other exclusive measures, had contributed two-and-a-half centuries ago (when English trade and industry were about as advanced as they are now in Russia) to strengthen the industrial and commercial power of this country (The Commercial Policy, 1894, p. 18).

Thus, Britain had used interventionist policies to achieve its developed status, and only then did it turn to promoting the ideology of free trade. This was a standard "free trade benefits only the wealthy" argument for protection, in association with the subtle overtones of a "declining terms of trade for primary commodities" argument.

On the occasion of the Anglo-Russian Literary Society meeting in 1894 Mendeleev's support for protection was found totally objectionable by the founder of *The Economist*, James Wilson, author of *Capital, Currency and Banking* and fervent campaigner against the Corn Laws. In response to Mendeleev, Wilson argued that protectionist policies were against the natural order of the distribution of the earth's physical products, imposed additional costs on those purchasing the goods and on those collecting the duties, and also encouraged smuggling (The Commercial Policy, 1894, p. 21).[7] In terms of locating protectionism within the appropriate strand of economic thinking Mendeleev was bold and clear. In the preface to "Explaining the Tariff" he wrote:

> The doctrine of free-traders may be logical, rational and beautiful. That does not mean it is true. 'Phlogiston' was very logical, rational and beautiful, but it did not pass the test of experiment and turned into something completely different, to the degree that all chemistry was at one time called 'anti-Phlogiston teaching'. It must be understood that the economic doctrines of the 'nationalists', 'sociologists' and the 'historical school' have long since broken free-tradism at the roots, and contemporary economic science should, for clarity, be called 'anti-free trade' (Mendeleev, 1892, pp. 35–36).[8]

Hence Mendeleev placed his own support for protection within an existing current of economic thinking, historical political economy, which flourished at the end of the nineteenth century. Having strong Germanic roots, the historical school had a powerful influence in late nineteenth century Russia, a Russian translation of List's *National System* appearing (not coincidentally) in 1891 (Henderson, 1983,

p. 214). However, only a minority of economists shared Mendeleev's belief that the historical school had "broken free-tradism at its roots."

Mendeleev also employed biological metaphors to justify state interference in economic affairs. After describing Russia as a "historical organism" in an article entitled "On the Stimulation of Russian Industrial Development" from 1884, he argued that "the maturing historical organism demands a conscious relation to its development if abnormalities, diseases and random factors are not desired" (Mendeleev, 1884, pp. 79, 81). Mendeleev's instinct for encouraging industrial development was evident in his functional approach to price determination. In 1889, he commented that a price of five kopeks per pud for crude oil in Baku was a "desirable and normal one," this being a price calculated to further develop the supply of oil (Mendeleeff, 1889, p. 755). Finally, Mendeleev offered a military self-reliance argument for protection in relation to arms supplies such as gunpowder and guns (Stackenwalt, 1976, p. 190). In general, Mendeleev's theoretical justification for protection was certainly wholehearted and apparently sincere, but might be criticized for lacking serious consideration of the overall rationality of the international division of labour and its theoretical foundations in comparative advantage. While Mendeleev knew his List, he did not know his Smith or Ricardo quite so well, or was doctrinally predisposed to reject free trade ideas.

5. MENDELEEV'S POLICY WORK ON THE 1891 TARIFF

Mendeleev's theoretical justification of protection found its empirical expression in the 1891 tariff. Work on revising the existing Russian tariff structure began in 1887 when various specialists were appointed to investigate foreign trade matters (Curtiss, 1912, p. 460). According to Stackenwalt it was Mendeleev who first proposed to the Russian Minister of Finance I. A. Vyshnegradsky that import duties on raw cotton should be increased in order to encourage indigenous cotton production. At first Vyshnegradsky was unconvinced, but later changed his mind (Stackenwalt, 1976, p. 147). As a consequence Vyshnegradsky initially assigned Mendeleev to prepare notes on the general principles of tariff reform, but Mendeleev went on to write extensive analyses of various articles of the tariff and even to prepare a detailed draft of the level of the proposed new rates. In these materials Mendeleev recognised the necessity of limiting protectionist policy to those branches of industry where it might be most successful, and admitted that the fiscal motive for creating tariffs might contradict the industry-establishing motive in some instances. Vyshnegradsky had declared that the aim of the protection was to create a situation where the price of a native product was less than or at least no more than the price (including duty) of an identical good from overseas (Sobolev, 1911, pp. 702–705).

In the event Mendeleev was intimately involved with preparing the materials for deciding the detail of the 1891 tariff, and these materials help to throw some light on the reasoning of those who designed it. For example in the "Materials for a Review of the General Customs Tariff of the Russian Empire Regarding European Trade," which Mendeleev prepared as a Member of the Council of Trade and Manufacture in October 1890, he presented proposals for revising the tariff structure with particular concern for possible future changes in the exchange rate. In this work Mendeleev argued that industrial capacity must be fostered in order to improve the balance of trade and hence stabilize the currency. The development of new types of industry would also strengthen agriculture. He wrote:

> Thus, only then, when Russia adds to its free grain allotment exports of products from mining and manufacturing industry, can we be confident that the trade balance will serve to support a stable exchange rate and establish normal relations between Russia and foreign states (Mendeleev, 1890, p. 522).

Mendeleev was thus implying that higher tariffs would help to improve the balance of trade by enabling manufacturing goods to be exported from Russia in greater quantity.[9]

Haberler dismissed this argument for protection as resting on a lack of understanding of the balance of payments equilibrium mechanism, since so long as the forces causing an excess of imports continued, a decline in imports would lead only to a corresponding decline in exports. If a tariff resulted in an import of capital then a worsening of the trade balance in the future was likely (Haberler, 1936, p. 249). Mendeleev was however banking on the creation of indigenous Russian capital, and might have disputed Haberler's assertion that declining imports would necessarily result in declining exports in the particular situation specified. As a general rule Mendeleev proposed as a main consideration for the imposition of a higher duty in the 1891 restructuring that the good must be capable of being produced and consumed in large quantities with increasing economies of scale, and be capable of competing effectively with foreign manufacturers (Stackenwalt, 1976, p. 154).

Mendeleev's most detailed and lengthy work on customs policy was entitled "Explaining the Tariff, or investigations in the development of Russian industry in connections with the general customs tariff of 1891" of 1892. The stated aim of this work was to lay bare the relation between industrial development and tariffs by employing export/import data together with information on conditions of production and domestic and overseas demand. The foundations on which Mendeleev based his support for the 1891 tariff were outlined in four points as follows. Firstly, there was no necessary connection between increased bilateral trade and the balancing of imports against exports. Secondly, a country could operate successfully without necessarily preserving the balance of trade, i.e. with the predominance of imports or exports. Thirdly, for Russia the international sale of grain, levied in exchange for other goods such as coal and iron to be imported from overseas, had for a long time been impossible, unprofitable and even dangerous. Fourthly, abstaining from selling Russian grain overseas, with the development of all types of domestic industry, would develop Russian prosperity equally, simply and profitably (Mendeleev, 1892, p. 251). These points were given as unquestionable fact.

As well as such general points, Mendeleev outlined eight more specific principles for tariff construction that had been applied by him to the 1891 reforms, the five most important of which were as follows:

(1) Fiscal duties which already existed on goods such as tea, chocolate and spirits were not possible to modify, as this might have led to declining revenue;[10]
(2) As Russia possessed the natural conditions for the mining of various types of raw materials, moderate duties on imported raw materials would facilitate the development of domestic raw materials production;
(3) Conceiving of any general tariff system was only a dream, rather tariffs would always be a temporary matter applicable only to the conditions and circumstances of the particular country to which they were applied;
(4) As a consequence of Russia's extensive and continental position, it must develop domestically such types of production as coal, iron and soda manufacture;
(5) Since the amount of free capital and intellectual capacity within Russia was limited, only a few new industries must be selected for development (Mendeleev, 1892, pp. 237–240).

These principles appeared at first sight to be quite rational, although Mendeleev did not specify exactly when such "temporary" tariffs would be rescinded. At one point Mendeleev indicated that ten years of protection would be sufficient to ensure viable Russian industry, but this was a rather catchall statement without concrete expression (Stackenwalt, 1976, p. 148).

Regarding the spatial particularities of designing a tariff for Russia, Mendeleev partitioned the Russian Empire into four geographical units. His four border regions for tariff purposes were the Baltic Sea ports, the Western land borders, the Black Sea ports and the Azov Sea ports, with different import duty schedules tailored to the requirements of each region. Mendeleev also distinguished between five basic types of industry: goods obtained by mining, from plants, from animals, factory goods made from chemical processes, and finished goods produced mechanically, which again required varying degrees of scheduled protection (Stackenwalt, 1976, pp. 154–157). In general the level of detail at which Mendeleev undertook to apply protection to the specificities of Russia was at least on the face of it rather impressive.

Mendeleev ended "Explaining the Tariff" by concluding that Russia must maintain relatively high customs duties for three reasons: in order to obtain government income, to preserve existing businesses from the threat of foreign competition, and to develop new industries which had not yet been established. He presented data showing the relation between the value of customs revenue and Russian state income over the period 1869 to 1889, shown in Table 1.

Mendeleev pointed out that such data indicated that until 1881, the value of total imports into Russia was very close to the value of state income, but after 1881 it fell to only a little more than half state income. In comparison the value of foreign imports exceeded the value of state income in many other countries such as the USA, Brazil, Germany and England at the end of the 1880s, with the

Table 1.   Customs Income in Russia, 1869–1989.

Year	Customs Income (In Millions of Credit Rubles)	Total Imports (In Millions of Credit Rubles)	Percentage Relation of Customs Income:	
			To All Income	To Value of Imported Goods
1869	41	339	9.5	12.1
1870	43	345	9.3	12.5
1871	49	380	10.0	12.9
1872	55	441	11.2	12.5
1873	56	446	11.0	12.6
1874	58	469	10.9	12.4
1875	64	544	11.5	11.8
1876	72	455	13.3	15.8
1877	78	347	14.8	22.5
1878	81	603	13.2	13.4
1879	93	591	14.2	15.7
1880	96	604	15.0	15.9
1881	88	540	13.8	16.3
1882	97	568	14.0	17.1
1883	98	562	14.3	17.4
1884	99	537	14.2	18.4
1885	97	434	13.5	22.4
1886	102	438	14.3	23.3
1887	107	393	14.5	27.2
1888	141	390	17.5	36.2
1889	138	437	16.6	31.6

Source: Mendeleev (1892, p. 920).

single exception of Italy. This was due according to Mendeleev to a greater need for foreign goods in these countries and to more liberal maritime relations (Mendeleev, 1892, pp. 921–925). By implication the observed trend of rising customs income should be seen as beneficial to Russia in the future as it had allegedly been in the past.

6. AN ANALYSIS OF THE 1891 TARIFF

In the event, the 1891 tariff raised duties on some goods by three or four times, the industries most affected being metallurgy, machine building and cotton (Lyashchenko, 1949, p. 558). Comparing the increases made by the 1891 tariff against its 1868 predecessor with the changes that had been made in 1857 and 1850, the increases made in 1891 were unquestionably of a much greater magnitude. Tariffs on 69.7% of the articles included in the protective scheme were increased (432 out of 620 items), against 6.3% of articles that had their tariff rates reduced (Sobolev, 1911, p. 789).

Existing accounts of the 1891 tariff explain its underlying motivation in different ways as follows. Tugan-Baranovsky believed simply that "the tariff of 1891 was a triumph for the protectionists" (Tugan-Baranovsky, 1970, p. 444). For others however it was "dominated by fiscal and monetary considerations although the protectionist aims also had their importance" (Crisp, 1976, p. 100). These fiscal and monetary considerations were to raise revenue for the state budget and to improve the foreign trade balance. Lyashchenko suggested that the tariffs introduced after 1877 were originally for fiscal purposes, but by 1890 the protectionist element had become dominant, implying an evolving doctrinal justification (Lyashchenko, 1949, p. 557). Some pointed out that the 1891 tariff remained in force long after the relevant industries had been established, this being interpreted as providing evidence that its real impetus was not simply infant-industry protectionism (Gatrell & Davies, 1990, p. 149). Others suggested that many foreign firms manoeuvered around the tariff by setting up company branches inside Russia with Russian-sounding names. Once established behind the tariff barrier the foreign firm could then benefit from it (White, 1994, p. 12). Supporters of protection, however, might have seen this as constituting a success, since domestic industry of some type was being boosted in this process, and one Russian economist of the time highlighted the attraction of foreign capital as an explicit goal of tariff policy (Ozerov, 1905, p. 58).

From the socialist camp, Luxemburg was convinced that those who opposed the tariff most strongly were the landowning gentry and agrarian interests in general. Producers of exported grain and consumers of foreign goods campaigned for a reduction in Russian customs duties and in favour of unrestricted commerce (Luxemburg, 1951, p. 449, fn. 1). Finn-Enotaevskii was scathing about the real significance of the tariff, the motive for its creation being characterised as overwhelmingly fiscal. This was (allegedly) obvious given that duties were raised on raw materials that were not even produced in Russia but which were required in order to develop Russian industry. Moreover duties were also raised not only on luxury consumer items but also on vital consumer goods not manufactured in Russia. Finn-Enotaevskii concluded that its real aim was to provide support for the 'decrepit bureaucratic regime' (Finn-Enotaevskii, 1925, p. 177). The assorted characterisations presented above suggest how difficult it is to lay bare the complicated web of motivations that generate protectionist sentiment.

In terms of its consequences the 1891 tariff led directly to German retaliation and eventually to an open tariff war, suggesting that its benefits were at best only temporary (Crisp, 1976, p. 104). This tariff war between Russia and Germany began in August 1893 and was precipitated by the failure of ongoing trade negotiations that had begun at the end of 1891 (Ashley, 1904, p. 92). The conflict lasted until February 1894 when a Russo-German Tariff Treaty was signed (Kohn, 1991, p. 287). Some have highlighted the penalising effects of this tariff war, which "scotched the German export trade to Russia and practically ruined large classes of affected traders" (Brooks, 1931, p. 93). It was certainly an acrimonious affair since in one Berlin newspaper, the Russians who had previously been involved in dumping corn were described as "perfect barbarians" (Johnston, 1894, p. 136).[11]

Although the 1891 tariff affected all nations equally, it discriminated against land-borne and in favour of sea-borne goods, something which hindered German competition with Britain. In October 1892, had Russia offered a "minimum tariff" level to German goods in return for Most Favoured Nation treatment, while in response Germany had asked in March 1893 for a considerable reduction on the minimum tariff that was offered to them. This proved unacceptable to the Russian side and so a tariff war duly began with the imposition of a "maximum tariff" level on German goods (Ashley, 1904, pp. 91–92). The blame for generating this tariff war cannot be pinned solely on Russia however as Germany had instituted its own tariffs in 1879 which were the outcome of a protracted debate between German free traders and protectionists, the latter led by Gustav Schmoller (Sheehan, 1966, p. 85).[12]

At the time that it was being developed the 1891 tariff was also subject to various criticisms from within Russia. For example the Imperial Free Economic Society published a detailed petition on the proposed changes to Russian customs duties in 1890. Here the cost of agricultural tools and machinery produced in Russia was compared to those imported from overseas at various exchange rates. Even at a rate of 60 kopeks per mark the imported goods were cheaper, an average of

12 pieces of imported equipment costing 6 rubles 29 kopeks per pud against 6 rubles 54 kopeks for the Russian equivalent. At an exchange rate of 40 kopeks per mark the imported equipment cost just 3 rubles 90 kopeks. According to the petition this difference was not only due to the duties on materials that were levied (*Khodataistva*, 1890, pp. 48–50). The Free Economic Society considered that:

> ... the duty free import into Russia of foreign tools and equipment not only does not hinder but on the contrary develops the dissemination in the country of machinery of internal procurement, which in the majority of representations is only a more or less successful copy of the foreign original ... (*Khodataistva*, 1890, p. 14).

It also blamed excessive tariffs for various crises that had beset Russian agriculture between 1822 and 1882, clearly suggesting that all interested parties did not share Mendeleev's enthusiasm for protection (*Khodataistva*, 1890, p. 148).

Luxemburg had characterized the Free Economic Society as "champions of agrarian interests" as against the interests of the manufacturing groups (Luxemburg, 1951, p. 449, fn. 1). As explained sometime later by Lewis, successfully generating economic growth may require the replacement of an existing ruling class by another, the Russian commercial classes for a long time having restricted freedom of manoeuvre compared to those in Britain (Lewis, 1955, p. 87). The debate over the 1891 tariff could thus be interpreted structurally, as an expression of shifting class fortunes within Tsarist society.

7. MENDELEEV'S PROTECTIONISM EVALUATED EMPIRICALLY

It is often very difficult to disentangle the effects of a tariff (or the lack of them) from all the other interacting factors in the surrounding situation (Kemp, 1978, p. 88). Schumpeter suggested that the positive effects of a tariff were always more visible than the negative effects (Schumpeter, 1939, Vol. 1, p. 259). Even given these acknowledged difficulties, a preliminary evaluation of the effects of the Mendeleev tariff is presented in the following section by analysing what various authorities have concluded on the topic. Mendeleev himself believed that the 1891 tariff had been successful in its aim of promoting indigenous Russian industry. In 1897 he pointed out that for the five years before 1891 Russian mining of cast iron did not exceed 32 million puds per year, but in the five years after 1891 it reached 97 million puds. Moreover he suggested that this increase was not at the expense of discouraging imports, which rose from 410 million rubles in 1888–1890 to 520 million in 1893–1895, due to increased payment of wages and hence the enlivening of turnover (Mendeleev, 1897a, pp. 91–92). Keep also suggested that in general, the Russian industrial expansion of the 1890s owed much to government tariff policy (Keep, 1962, p. 368).

Others have evaluated Mendeleev's efforts rather differently. On the consumption side of the equation, Lyashchenko concluded that the 1891 tariff had succeeded in raising domestic prices and providing dividends for Russian industrialists, but the added costs had been borne by the consumer, who purchased poorly made goods at higher prices than similar goods from overseas (Lyashchenko, 1949, p. 559). Kahan calculated that while the consumption cost of protection in the 1890s to Russian consumers of coal was negligible, on metals and cotton it was considerable. His figures also indicated that after 1890 the consumption costs of protection increased significantly, for example for pig iron from 10.2 million rubles in 1890, to 18.2 million in 1891 and 21 million in 1892 (Kahan, 1989, p. 101).[13] Kahan concluded that the losses borne by Russian consumers exceeded the benefits obtained by the Russian Treasury. This evaluation was in line with what supporters of the theory of free trade would predict.

On the production side of the equation Barkai outlined that the tariff altered indigenous relative prices considerably, slanting the industrial structure towards heavy engineering and some producer goods industries, resulting in a loss of productive potential due to a misallocation of resources (Barkai, 1973, p. 365–366). Kahan also suggested that the production cost of the tariff was considerable, quoting a figure of 22% of estimated net output of Russian manufactures for 1900 (Kahan, 1989, p. 102).[14] On this view the 1891 tariff only hindered the natural development of Russian industry by skewing production towards certain uneconomic sectors of the economy, although which particular sectors were unambiguously "economic" to actually develop were not always made explicit by critics.

Sobolev provided a general empirical evaluation of the effects of the tariff as follows. He compared the yearly percentage rate of growth of Russian industries in the third quarter of the nineteenth century with the same industries in the fourth quarter, the third quarter being a period of weakening tariffs, the fourth quarter one of heightened protection. His general conclusion was that growth rates had fallen dramatically from the third to the fourth quarter of the nineteenth century precisely in those branches of industry in which protection was increased the most. For example in sugar, rails and coal mining the yearly rate of growth of industry was 101, 57.9 and 48.7% respectively for the third quarter, falling to 9.3, 7.5 and 23.4% for the fourth quarter. In many other branches of industry growth rates were also less in the fourth quarter than the third, although in some branches such as paper and textiles, chemicals and paints they were higher.

Overall Sobolev concluded that the total value of production in branches of industry that witnessed more significant growth in the fourth quarter than the third was 486 million rubles, against a total value of branches with lower growth of 667.5 million rubles, suggesting an overall negative impact (Sobolev, 1911, p. 796). One factor not mentioned by Sobolev could be that a slackening in rates of growth between the third and fourth quarter might have been inevitable due to the very low starting levels at which growth was calculated to begin and the very high rates seen initially in the third quarter. Hence, not all the observed slackening should necessarily be attributed to increased protection, but rather in part to inevitable declining returns.

Perhaps the most profound analysis of the effects of the tariff undertaken at the time was provided by Tugan-Baranovsky. For Tugan-Baranovsky the rapid increase in the rate of growth of the Russian iron industry after 1887 was indeed explained in part by the rise in tariff rates. However, it would be wrong to conclude generally in favour of tariffs because of such concomitant rapid growth. Iron smelting had been protected in Russia before 1861, but instead of leading to increased development, the result was in fact stagnation. Protectionists who argued that the slow growth of iron smelting in Russia in the 1860s and 1870s was due to a lack of tariff protection had forgotten that the duty free import of rails and railway materials in this period had favoured railway network construction. In reality it was the subsequent expansion of the railway network that was a principal cause of the observed development of Russian industry in the 1890s, rather than simply increased protection (Tugan-Baranovsky, 1970, pp. 291–292). Hence, for Tugan-Baranovsky the 1891 tariff had been successful in part precisely because of the effects of the previous period of relatively low levels of protection, and any evaluation of the effect of tariffs must therefore be fully sensitive to historical specificity.

A more complex account of the effects of protection was also indicated by Kirchner. He suggested that the imposition of the tariff had a knock-on effect, increased domestic production of locomotives generating increased imports of associated parts such as brakes, wheels and pistons. In addition the impact of the tariff was modified by various complicating factors. For example, protected Russian firms sometimes made less desirable inferior goods, freight rates hindered domestic sales in some parts of Russia as against goods imported by sea, slow domestic delivery times were a factor favouring imports, as was the lack of Russian marketing capacity and advertising. Patents, while difficult to secure, ensured duties had little effect, and credit and currency factors also modified the results of protection (Kirchner, 1981, pp. 368–374). Kirchner concluded that the emphasis placed on the effects of the tariff in historical accounts was too great, as entrepreneurs often adjusted to them in various ways. Moreover for business people tariffs were just one amongst many factors influencing industrial production, and impediments other than customs duties often overshadowed the inhibiting effects of the tariff. This does not mean of course that the tariff did not have any hindering effects at all.

8. MENDELEEV'S PROTECTIONISM EVALUATED THEORETICALLY

How might those in the Heckscher-Ohlin-Samuelson tradition evaluate Mendeleev's theoretical case for protection? Quite poorly it would seem. The only strictly economic case for a tariff that is currently acknowledged by contemporary mainstream economists is the optimum tariff argument. This accepts that it might be possible to raise domestic welfare by trade restriction but only if monopoly power in international markets can be taken advantage of, and then only if no reciprocal tariffs are introduced.[15] Mainstream economists do not now allow the infant industry argument, as output subsidies are deemed superior to tariffs for engendering new industries (Findlay, 1987, Vol. 2, p. 421).

Haberler listed various non-economic arguments for protection such as national defence, the need to preserve the special ethos of the nation and/or certain classes of the population, but these were not Mendeleev's primary justification (Haberler, 1936, pp. 239–240). In his defence Mendeleev accepted in theory that protection was only a temporary imposition, to be employed only until Russia had drawn level with more advanced countries (Mendeleev, 1892, p. 926). Haberler suggested that, even if an infant-industry case was theoretically conceded, in practice this argument was nearly always used as a mere pretext, a criticism that could reasonably be made of some of the support for the 1891 tariff (Haberler, 1936, p. 284). As concluded by Corden, in the case of oligopoly-induced distortions there are various different ways of dealing with them which can be ranked according to their welfare benefits, but which might involve trade policies such as protection (Corden, 1991, p. 287). But such policies can have even a chance of success only if decisive retaliation can be ruled out, something that Russia was unsuccessful in avoiding after 1891.

The only commentator at the time who had the foresight to glimpse what the recent studies of the tariff-growth paradox would suggest vis-à-vis the importance of historical specificity to understanding the success of tariffs in the late nineteenth century was Tugan-Baranovsky. Mendeleev appeared far too emotionally attached to the doctrine of protection in its pure and abstract form to countenance that increased protection might be a successful strategy only in an environment of mutually high tariffs, at least for some regions of the world economy (Clemens & Williamson, 2001, p. 23). Even so this was indeed the environment that Mendeleev found Russia in, and on this view he would be evaluated as being right (for the time) but not for the right reasons. On the other hand it could reasonably be said that Mendeleev had himself contributed (in some small measure) to the creation of the environment in which tariffs were seen as a necessary strategy for Russia in the first place.

9. CONCLUSION

It might be remarked that trade wars come and go, but the perceived problems generating them remain. One of Russia's problems in the 1890s was how to engender economic development, particularly in those areas in which it possessed rich natural resources such as oil and coal. The tariff of 1891 was Mendeleev's attempt to solve this problem, although it had a mixed outcome, one that might have been less successful than purely laissez faire (at least as evaluated from a Ricardian point of view), and yet might have been partially successful only because of the previous period of relatively free trade and the historical context that engendered it.

While Mendeleev was an acknowledged genius in the field of chemistry, his understanding of economic theory was somewhat less impressive. His display of argument favouring protection, while very well written in a stylistic sense and presented with unquestionable depth of feeling, was not particularly original at the time of its first appearance and would be thought by mainstream economists as even less convincing today. A basic point against Mendeleev was that, while some Russian industry might have been stimulated by the tariff, a calculation of the price paid for this in terms of the loss of the alternative uses of the resources utilised was not seriously considered. Within this point of view Mendeleev can be seen as the mouthpiece of specific industrial interests, against the interests of the Russian nation as a whole. As Capie outlined, those who gained from protection were generally producers and governments, the losers usually being consumers (Capie, 1994, p. 19).

Even given the mixed success of the 1891 tariff with respect to catalysing Russian growth, the problem of how this should best be accomplished in economically "backward" countries remained at the beginning of the twentieth century, leading eventually to the Stalinist solution in Russia after 1929. One non-economic argument for partially ignoring the idea of natural factor endowment location not often heard is that it might be beneficial for all countries to forgo some purely economic rationality, for an increase in perceived fairness in terms of the international distribution of industrial production. If the perceived economic equality of nations were seen to be higher, then the damaging conflicts sometimes generated by the associated simmering jealousy and resentment might be diminished. This was not an argument made forcefully by Mendeleev, but it might be one relevant to today's post-9/11 world.

NOTES

1. Faucher encouraged the Russian government to demonstrate their own mathematical intelligence by lowering their tariff barriers.

2. This article is part of a larger project investigating "The Economic Mind in Russian Civilisation, 1880–1917," funded by the ESRC (grant number R000239937). I am grateful also to CREES, Birmingham University, for support and to Professor Philip Hanson for helpful comments on an earlier draft.

3. Mendelevium has a relative atomic mass of 258.0986 and is classified as an artificial radioactive element.

4. For an account of Smith's influence in Russia, see Barnett (2002).

5. In "Petroleum Affairs in Pennsylvania and the Caucasus" Mendeleev explained the observed differences in physical deposits of petroleum as resulting from the two regions being of different geological ages, together with the continued existence of mud volcanoes in one area as against the other. See Posin (1948, p. 217).

6. Roger Backhouse warned that the term "mercantalism" was sometimes applied too generally. See Backhouse (2002, p. 58).

7. M. I. Tugan-Baranovsky's analysis of the repeal of the Corn Laws in terms of trade policy regimes for structuring business cycles was similarly first presented to a Russian audience in 1894. See Barnett (2001, pp. 448–449).

8. Phlogiston was believed for a time to be a so-called "original element" that could be known only by the effects it produced when combustion occurred.

9. In a memorandum of September 1930 J. M. Keynes had also suggested that the U.K. trade balance could be improved by means of a tariff, although the situation facing the U.K. in 1930 was very different to that facing Russia in 1890. See Keynes (1973, p. 190).

10. Haberler suggested that the best way to distinguish revenue from protective duties was to examine whether there was any difference in the duty levied on domestic and foreign supply of the particular good bearing the tariff. See Haberler (1936, p. 238).

11. Johnston incorrectly identified the German differential tariff of February 1892 as the first step that led up to the tariff war. See Johnston (1894, pp. 137–139).

12. Schmoller was a key member of the "younger" German historical school of political economists.

13. The consumption cost of the tariff is a measure of the distortion in the allocation of consumer expenditure caused by raised prices.

14. The production cost of the tariff is a measure of the distortion caused in the allocation of productive resources due to the subsidies provided to domestic producers.

15. Bhagwati called this justification the "monopoly-power-in-trade" argument for protection, noting that it required non-negligible international market power, but admitting that an ultimate net gain was theoretically possible even given some types of retaliation. See Bhagwati (1988, p. 25 and pp. 32–33).

REFERENCES

Amann, R. (1977). The chemical industry. In: R. Amann, J. M. Cooper & R. W. Davies (Eds), *The Technological Level of Soviet Industry*. New Haven: Yale University Press.

Ashley, P. (1904). *Modern tariff history*. London: Murray.

Backhouse, R. (2002). *The penguin history of economics*. London: Penguin.

Bairoch, P. (1972). Free trade and European economic development in the 19th century. *European Economic Review, 3*.

Barkai, H. (1973). The macro-economics of Tsarist Russia in the industrialization era. *The Journal of Economic History, XXXIII* (2).

Barnett, V. (2001). Tugan-Baranovsky as a pioneer of trade cycle analysis. *Journal of the History of Economic Thought, 23*(4).

Barnett, V. (2002). Mr. Smith goes to Moscow: Russian editions of *The Wealth of Nations*. In: *Research in the History of Economic Thought and Methodology* (Vol. 20-A). Amsterdam: JAI Press.

Bhagwati, J. (1988). *Protectionism*. Cambridge, MA: MIT Press.

Brooks, C. (1931). *This tariff question*. London: Arnold.

Capie, F. (1994). *Tariffs and growth*. Manchester: Manchester University Press.

Clemens, M. A., & Williamson, J. G. (2001). A tariff-growth paradox? Protection's impact the world around 1875–1997. National Bureau of Economic Research Working Paper 8459. Cambridge, MA (September).

Corden, W. M. (1991). Strategic trade policy. In: D. Greenaway, M. Bleaney & I. Stewart (Eds), *Companion to Contemporary Economic Thought*. London: Routledge.

Crisp, O. (1976). Russian financial policy and the gold standard at the end of the nineteenth century. In: *Studies in the Russian Economy before 1914*. London: Macmillan.

Curtiss, G. B. (1912). *The industrial development of nations* (Vol. 1). Binghampton, NY: Curtiss.

Faucher, J. (1872). A new commercial treaty between Great Britain and Germany. In: *Cobden Club Essays*. London: Cassell, Second Series.

Findlay, R. (1987). Free trade and protection. In: J. Eatwell, M. Milgate & P. Newman (Eds), *The New Palgrave Dictionary of Economics*. London: Macmillan.

Finn-Enotaevskii, A. (1925). *Kapitalizm v Rossii, 1890–1917* (Vol. 1). Moscow: NKFin.

Galbraith, J. K. (1987). *A history of economics*. London: Hamish Hamilton.

Gatrell, P., & Davies, R. W. (1990). The industrial economy. In: R. W. Davies (Ed.), *From Tsarism to the New Economic Policy*. London: Macmillan.

Graham, L. (1973). *Science and philosophy in the Soviet Union*. London: Allen Lane.

Gregory, P. (1982). *Russian national income, 1885–1913*. Cambridge: CUP.

Haberler, G. (1936). *The theory of international trade*. London: Hodge and Co.

Henderson, W. O. (1983). *Friedrich list*. London: Cass.

Johnston, C. (1894). The Russo-German tariff war. *Economic Journal, IV*.

Kahan, A. (1989). *Russian economic history*. Chicago: Chicago University.

Keep, J. L. (1962). Russia. In: *The New Cambridge Modern History* (Vol. XI). Cambridge: CUP.

Kemp, T. (1978). *Historical patterns of industrialization*. London: Longman.

Keynes, J. M. (1973). *The collected writings of J. M. Keynes* (Vol. XIII, Part I). London: Macmillan.

Khodataistva Imperatorskago vol'nago ekonomicheskago obshchestva ob izmeneniyakh v Russkom tamozhennom tariff (1890). St. Petersburg: Demakova.

Kirchner, W. (1981). Russian tariffs and foreign industries before 1914. *Journal of Economic History, XLI*(2).

Kohn, G. C. (1991). *Dictionary of historic documents*. New York: Facts on File.

Kudryavtseva, T. S., & Shekhter, M. E. (1952). *D. I. Mendeleev i ugol'haya promyshlennost' Rossii*. Moscow: UgletekhIzdat.

Leicester, H. M. (1961). Mendeleev. In: E. Farber (Ed.), *Great Chemists*. New York: Interscience.

Lewis, W. A. (1955). *The theory of economic growth*. London: Allen & Unwin.

List, F. (1904). *The national system of political economy*. London: Longmans.

Lodyzhensky, K. (1886). *Istoriya Russkago tamozhennago tarifa*. St. Petersburg: Balasheva.

Luxemburg, R. (1951). *The accumulation of capital*. London: RKP.

Lyashchenko, P. I. (1949). *History of the national economy of Russia to the 1917 revolution*. New York: Macmillan.

Mendeleeff, D. (1889). The present position and prospects of the Caucasian petroleum industry. *The Journal of the Society of Chemical Industry, VIII*(10).

Mendeleeff, D. I. (1893). Introduction: Review of the manufactures and trade of Russia. In: J. M. Crawford (Ed.), *The Industries of Russia, Manufactures and Trade* (Vols I and II). St. Petersburg.

Mendeleev, D. I. (1884). O vozbuzhdenii promyshlennogo razvitiya v Rossii'. In: *Sochineniya* (Vol. XX). Moscow: AN SSSR (1950).

Mendeleev, D. I. (1888). Perveishaya nadobnost' Russkoi promyshlennosti. In: *Sochineniya* (Vol. XXI). Leningrad-Moscow: AN SSSR (1952).

Mendeleev, D. I. (1890). Materialy dlya peresmotra obshchago tamozhennago tarifa Rossiiskoi Imperii po Evropeiskoi torgovl. In: *Sochineniya* (Vol. XVII). Moscow: AN SSSR (1950).

Mendeleev, D. I. (1892). Tolkovyi tarif, ili issledovanie o razvitii promyshlennosti Rossii v svyazi c eya obshchim tamozhennym tarifom 1891 goda. In: *Sochineniya* (Vol. XIX). Moscow: AN SSSR (1950).

Mendeleev, D. I. (1897a). Opravdanie protektsionizma. In: *Problemy ekonomicheskogo razvitiya Rossii*. Moscow: Sots-Ekon (1960).

Mendeleev, D. I. (1897b). Osnovy fabrichno-zavodskoi promyshlennost. In: *C dumoyu o blage rossi-iskom*. Novosibirsk: Nauka (1991).

Mendeleev, D. I. (1900). Uchenie o promyshlennosti. In: *C dumoyu o blage rossiiskom*. Novosibirsk: Nauka (1991).

Mendeleev, D. I., v vospominaniyakh sovremennikov. (1973). Moscow: Atomizdat.

Mitchell, W. (1970). *Business cycles*. New York: Franklin.

O'Rourke, K. H. (2000). Tariffs and growth in the late 19th century. *Economic Journal, 110* (April).

Owen, T. (1991). *The corporation under Russian law, 1800–1917*. Cambridge: CUP.

Ozerov, I. Kh. (1905). *Ekonomicheskaya Rossiya eya finansovaya politika na iskhod XIX i v nachal XX veka*. Moscow: Gorshkov.

Posin, D. (1948). *Mendeleyev*. New York: McGraw-Hill.

Schumpeter, J. (1939). *Business cycles*. New York: McGraw-Hill.

Sheehan, J. J. (1966). *The career of Lujo Brentano*. Chicago: University of Chicago.

Sobolev, M. N. (1911). *Tamozhennaya politika Rossii vo vtoroi polovin XIX veka*. Tomsk: Sibirskago Tovarishchestva.

Stackenwalt, F. H. (1976). *The economic thought and work of D. I. Mendeleev*. Unpublished Ph.D. Thesis, University of Illinois at Urbana-Champaign.

The Commercial Policy of Russia (1894). In: *The Anglo-Russian Literary Society*. Proceedings (May–July), No. 7.

Thorpe, T. E. (1894). *Essays in historical chemistry*. London: Macmillan.

Tishchenko, V. E., & Mladentsev, M. I. (1993). *D. I. Mendeleev, ego zhizn' i deyatel'nost', 1861–1890*. Moscow: Nauka.

Tugan-Baranovsky, M. I. (1970). *The Russian factory in the nineteenth century*. Illinois: AEA.

White, J. D. (1994). *The Russian revolution, 1917–1921*. London: Arnold.

VEBLEN IN CHICAGO:
THE WINDS OF CREATIVITY

Geoffrey M. Hodgson

Thorstein Veblen is widely acknowledged as one of the most brilliant economists ever to emerge in the United States. For example, Allyn Young, in a letter of recommendation written in 1910 declared: "I feel no hesitation in saying that Veblen is the most gifted man whom I have ever known. His scholarship is extraordinary, both in range and thoroughness" (Dorfman, 1934, p. 299). Joan Robinson (1979, p. 95) concluded that Veblen was "the most original economist born and bred in the USA."

However, in a huge secondary literature on Veblen, few have dwelt sufficiently on the fact that his greatest achievements were published in twelve concentrated years from 1898 to 1909. In this period, two of Veblen's three most important books were published, and the third was largely complete in draft (Veblen, 1899, 1904, 1914). In addition, Veblen produced a number of path-breaking articles in leading journals of economics and sociology, mostly in the *Quarterly Journal of Economics*, the *American Journal of Sociology* and the *Journal of Political Economy*.[1] These include the seminal "Why economics is not an evolutionary science?" and his remarkable critiques of both orthodox economics and Marxism (Veblen, 1898, 1906, 1907, 1908a, b, c, 1909a, b). This extraordinary outburst of creativity followed a revolution in his thinking in 1896 and 1897. Similarly, the nature of, and stimuli behind, Veblen's intellectual breakthrough in 1896–1898 have been inadequately investigated (Hodgson, 1998).[2]

What were the causes of Veblen's creative success in those twelve years? This inquiry would have to take note of Veblen's personal, professional and institutional

Research in the History of Economic Thought and Methodology A Research Annual
Research in the History of Economic Thought and Methodology, Volume 22-A, 145–160
Copyright © 2004 by Elsevier Ltd.
ISSN: 0743-4154/doi:10.1016/S0743-4154(03)22005-8

circumstances. In particular, Veblen was employed at the University of Chicago from 1892 to 1906 and hence most of those twelve inspired years were at that institution. In addition, ongoing research into Veblen's personal life (Dorfman, 1934; Eby, 2001; Jorgensen & Jorgensen, 1999) provides further insight into the circumstances of his creativity.

The purpose of this essay is to address some of Veblen's many achievements in the 1896–1909 period, and to consider the professional and personal circumstances that stimulated one of the most remarkable creative explosions in the history of the social sciences. Veblen's creative episode of 1896–1909 is as worthy as a study of creative activity as that of Antoine Lavoisier in 1773–1792 (Holmes, 1985), Charles Darwin in 1837–1859 (Gruber, 1974), the young Albert Einstein (Pyenson, 1985) and of other great scientists. In their general study of scientific creativity, Paula Stephan and Sharon Levin (1992) emphasise the importance of being in the right place in the right time, the stimulation of the peer group and the intellectual environment, and the advantages of being trained in a period of intellectual upheaval and breakthrough, including periods of growth of university institutions and of their research activity. These general considerations would seem to apply to Veblen, along with particular circumstances concerning his personal life.

1. CHICAGO AND ITS FACULTY

The first American university to have a graduate programme was Johns Hopkins, founded in 1876. Between 1880 and 1914 a number of new universities such as Stanford and Chicago were established, and older institutions such as Yale and Harvard were modernised. The University of Chicago was founded in 1892, with the help of a large founding endowment from the oil tycoon, John D. Rockefeller.

In 1892 Thorstein Veblen – aged 35 – took up a low-paid junior post in the Department of Political Economy at Chicago. He remained there for fourteen years. It was the first time that Veblen had lived in a city. Veblen was there during the 1893 Chicago World Fair, with its conspicuous displays of wealth and waste. Veblen saw the sharp divisions between Chicago's gushing wealth and its grinding poverty, as well as some of its outbursts of industrial and civil unrest.

In the new university, most of the burden of editing the Chicago house *Journal of Political Economy* "fell upon Veblen's shoulders" (Dorfman, 1934, p. 95). "It was in Chicago that Veblen had the most sympathetic and stimulating colleagues and where most of his best work was done" (Riesman, 1963, p. 18). There he was influenced by many thinkers, including his friend and leading biologist Jacques Loeb. Loeb advocated a positivist and reductionist version of Darwinian theory, arguing that all living phenomena could and should be ultimately explained entirely in terms of their physical and chemical constituents. Although Veblen never embraced Loeb's reductionism or positivism, Loeb "appears to have helped give Veblen his life-long credo that only a social science shaped in the image of post-Darwinian biology could lay claim to being 'scientific' " (Riesman, 1963, p. 19).[3]

Chicago had the first university department of sociology in the world. The head of the sociology department at Chicago was Albion Small, a disciple of Lester Frank Ward. Another colleague at Chicago was the pragmatist philosopher George Herbert Mead. Mead had addressed Kant's argument that the conditions of objective knowledge had to be found in concepts held by the knowing subject prior to experience. He pointed out that Kant gave no explanation of the origin and development of those concepts (Joas, 1991). For Veblen, this provided a further entrée for an evolutionary analysis of categories and habits of thought (Fontana et al., 1992).

The philosopher John Dewey came to Chicago in 1894 and remained there until 1902. The academic careers of Veblen and Dewey thus overlapped, as they had done so briefly at Johns Hopkins University in the early 1880s and were later to do so again, after the First World War at the New School for Social Research in New York. However, despite the intellectual communalities later imputed by Clarence Ayres and others, there is no clear and definite evidence of a major influence of John Dewey's thought on Veblen (Tilman, 1996, 1998). Nevertheless, Dewey's work was beginning to have a wide impact. For instance, in his famous essay on the "the reflex arc concept," Dewey (1896) provided a critique of one of the assumptions that would later be central to behaviourist psychology. For Dewey, the stimulus-response mechanism was flawed because stimuli are not given data. For Dewey, the agent acting intentionally and cognitively is necessary to perceive the stimulus. Veblen (1900, pp. 246–247) replicated this argument with approval, but without mentioning Dewey by name.[4]

The American anthropologist Franz Boas was in Chicago in the 1890s. He promoted a radical transformation of anthropological presuppositions and approaches. Earlier anthropologists had used the word "culture" as virtually a synonym for "civilisation," and embraced a teleological and unilinear notion of its development (Sanderson, 1990, pp. 41–43). Boas criticised stage-by-stage schemes of "cultural evolution" and introduced the modern anthropological meaning of the word "culture" into the English language (Stocking, 1968). Boas saw culture and social environment as the major influence on human character and intelligence. His writings from the 1890s referred not to culture in a singular sense but in a plural manner, referring to several different cultures.

Veblen read widely in anthropology and broadly followed Boas's usage of the term culture. It is likely that Boas (1894) influenced Veblen with his insistence that the evolution of culture and civilisation did not simply track the biological evolution of the human mind and body. But Boas did not explain in sufficient detail how institutions or culture evolved. Like Boas, Veblen rejected universal schemes of social or cultural evolution, as developed by Spencer and others. However, although Boas and Veblen were both in Chicago there are sparse references to this influential anthropologist in Veblen's work, although later they did briefly correspond with one another.[5]

2. VEBLEN'S INTELLECTUAL DEVELOPMENT IN THE 1890s

Veblen's knowledge of French and German also opened him up to major Continental European influences and developments. While editing the *Journal of Political Economy*, Veblen frequently reviewed works on Marxism and socialism. Overall, Veblen published 21 items in the years 1893–1897 inclusive. No less than 17 of these were book reviews in that journal. In turn, 11 of these 17 were reviews of books, mostly in German or French, concerned primarily with socialism or Marxism.[6]

There is good reason to believe that, by 1895 or earlier, Veblen had developed his "post-Darwinian" position, and had rejected what we may now refer to as methodological individualism, methodological collectivism and cultural determinism. In January 1895, Veblen described *The Theory of the Leisure Class* as being at least "half written" in "first draft" (Dorfman, 1934, p. 174; Jorgensen & Jorgensen, 1999, p. 192). This work contains Veblen's key ideas in this area, including his application of Darwinism to the social sciences. In addition, the following letter gives some indication of his frame of mind. On 23 January 1896, Veblen wrote to Sarah Hardy, a former graduate student, that he had "a theory" which he wished to propound:

> My theory touches the immediate future of the development of economic science, and it is not so new or novel as I make it out to be . . . Economics is to be brought in line with modern evolutionary science, which it has not been hitherto. The point of departure of this rehabilitation, or rather the basis of it, will be the modern anthropological and psychological sciences . . . Starting from this preliminary study of usages, aptitudes, propensities and habits of thought (much of which is already worked out in a more or less available form) the science, taken generally, is to shape itself into a science of the evolution of economic institutions. (Quoted in Jorgensen & Jorgensen, 1999, p. 194.)

In this letter, Veblen hints at a sudden innovation in his thinking, inspired by others. He was certainly referring to some of the key ideas that were to appear later in *The Theory of the Leisure Class*. But Veblen did not go further into details. The phrase "evolution of economic institutions" in this letter does not necessarily imply a concept of evolutionary *selection* or "selective elimination" of institutions, which was to first appear in Veblen's (1897, p. 390) published writings in June 1897, and was also manifest in the *Leisure Class*.

Also in early 1896, Conwy Lloyd Morgan, a British philosopher of biology, visited Chicago. In early 1896, Morgan delivered a lecture at the University of Chicago, entitled "Habit and Custom: A Study in Heredity" (Dorfman, 1934, p. 139). Some key points of this talk were published in Morgan's (1896) book *Habit and Instinct*. Morgan was Professor of Geology and Zoology at the University College, Bristol (later the University of Bristol), in England. Dorfman does not tell us whether Veblen attended this lecture or was even availed of its content. And Morgan's visit to Chicago was probably a few days after Veblen's letter to Hardy. Nevertheless, Morgan's imminent visit to Chicago might have prompted Veblen's interest in the ideas of the visiting lecturer.[7]

The hypothesis considered here is that Morgan's presence in Chicago provided a key stimulus in the development of Veblen's theory of socio-economic evolution. Although it was some years later that Veblen (1914, p. 30 n.) first referred to Morgan, it was with definite approval, showing that Veblen was familiar with Morgan's (1896) book.

Rejecting Lamarckism in favour of the research of August Weismann (1893), Morgan contended that acquired habits are not inherited. Morgan then asked: if human beings had evolved only slightly in genetic terms, then *what* had evolved in the last millennium or so of human society? In this period, human achievements have been transformed beyond measure. Morgan's (1896, p. 340) answer to the puzzle was "that evolution *has been transferred from the organism to the environment.*" Each generation adapted itself to this evolving environment, consisting of "the written record, in social traditions, in the manifold inventions which make scientific and industrial progress possible, in the products of art, and the recorded examples of noble lives." Consequently, "this transference of evolution from the individual to the environment may leave the *faculty* of the race at a standstill, while the *achievements* of the race are progressing by leaps and bounds." Essentially, Morgan brought to America the idea of the social environment as a storehouse of knowledge.[8]

In the Lamarckian view, socio-economic evolution proceeded by the acquisition of new habits, which could then be passed on by human genetic inheritance, as well as by imitation or learning. Following Weismann, Morgan denied that the human genetic endowment was evolving so rapidly. We now know that on this point at least, Morgan was right.

Morgan's understanding of evolution hinted at an *emergent level* of socio-economic evolution that was not explicable exclusively in terms of the biological characteristics of the individuals involved. Evolution occurred at this emergent level as well, and without any necessary change in human biotic characteristics.

Accordingly, the crucial concepts of emergence and emergent properties were liberated by the Weismannian insistence of a barrier between acquired habit and biotic inheritance. Because of the Weismann barrier, Darwinians were driven to consider the biological and the social spheres as partially autonomous, but linked, levels of analysis. In later works, Morgan (1923) and others developed the philosophical concept of emergence (Blitz, 1992).

Morgan's early statements of 1896 concerning the "transference of evolution from the individual to the environment" clearly hinted at a social level of evolution that could not be explained simply in terms of the evolution of individuals alone. As this social environment itself evolved, the Darwinian process of natural selection brought about very slight changes in the human organism. These phylogenetic changes were too gradual to play any significant influence on social evolution itself. Nevertheless, the rapid changes in the social environment were a moving target for the *ontogenetic* development of each human individual. It is primarily the social system that would preserve or develop the capacity for change, not significantly the human genotype. As Veblen (1914, p. 18) himself later wrote, in terms redolent of Morgan:

> The typical human endowment of instincts, as well as the typical make-up of the race in the physical respect, has according to this current view been transmitted intact from the beginning of humanity . . . On the other hand the habitual elements of human life change unremittingly and cumulatively, resulting in a continued proliferous growth of institutions. Changes in the institutional structure are continually taking place in response to the altered discipline of life under changing cultural conditions, but [instinctive] human nature remains specifically the same.

The possible influence of Morgan may be detected in other passages in Veblen's (1899, pp. 188–192, 220; 1914, pp. 38–39) work. All these should be compared with Morgan (1896, p. 340) quoted above. However, without any explicit mention of Morgan by Veblen in the 1890s, this evidence is circumstantial rather than decisive. It is possible that both Morgan and Veblen were separately influenced by others who were thinking along similar lines. From the evidence available it is difficult to confirm or deny this. However, it is clear and significant that by 1897 Veblen was thinking of institutions as the objects of selection in socio-economic evolution. This dating is consistent with Morgan's visit to Chicago in 1896.[9]

In contrast to Morgan and Veblen, Spencer (1881, pp. 400–401) and Marshall (1923, p. 260) argued that economic institutions could change only as fast as the evolution of human nature. Veblen differed, by making use of Morgan's suggestion of multiple levels of evolution. However, Morgan did not make the objects and mechanisms of socio-economic evolution clear. He did not identify any social units of selection, their sources of variation or any selective process at the social level. He simply indicated the possibility of "storage in the social environment" through the written record, in social traditions, technology and art. This was, nevertheless, a highly significant point. Morgan's conception of "environmental" evolution implied that, despite change, some degree of inertia and continuity in environmental conditions was necessary, so that appropriate ontogenetic development could occur. In short, the means of preservation of information were necessary for learning. It was left to Veblen to make the crucial next step: institutions became objects of selection in socio-economic evolution. What was enormously significant was that Veblen did not accept that culture or institutions could be or had to be explained in biological terms. As Veblen (1909a, p. 300) wrote a few years later:

> If . . . men universally acted not on the conventional grounds and values afforded by the fabric of institutions, but solely and directly on the grounds and values afforded by the unconventionalised propensities and aptitudes of hereditary human nature, then there would be no institutions and no culture.

Veblen thus suggested that if socio-economic phenomena were determined exclusively by biological factors then the concepts of institution and culture would be redundant. Culture and institutions are irreducible to biological factors alone. Veblen broke decisively from biological reductionism. Accordingly, the concepts of cultural and institutional evolution were developed in *The Theory of the Leisure Class*.

With Morgan's intervention, the scene was set for Veblen's intellectual revolution: the concept of the evolution and selection of institutions, as emergent entities in the socio-economic sphere. It is thus perhaps no accident that about the time of Morgan's visit to Chicago the idea of an evolutionary process of selection of institutions began to develop in Veblen's work. This idea began to surface in two book reviews of Marxist texts, which appeared in the *Journal of Political Economy* in December 1896 and June 1897. The first of these two reviews considered a work by the Italian socialist and criminologist Enrico Ferri (1896, 1906), which attempted to show that Marxism was compatible with the evolutionary approaches of both Charles Darwin and Herbert Spencer. Ferri's eclectic and superficial attempt at an amalgam of Darwin, Spencer and Marx melded the "struggle for existence" with the "class struggle," by arguing that struggle between classes overshadowed rivalry between individuals or nations. Veblen (1896, p. 99) extended Ferri's argument by noting that the "struggle for existence, as applied within the field of social evolution, is a struggle between groups and institutions rather than a competition . . . between the individuals of the group."

Even more poignantly, in yet another book review, Veblen (1897, p. 390) saw in Antonio Labriola's (1897, 1908) Marxism the doctrine that the "economic exigencies" of the industrial process "afford the definitive test of fitness in the adaptation of all human institutions by a process of selective elimination of the economically unfit." But these were Veblen's words, not Labriola's. Labriola had no intention of applying Darwinism to social evolution. Veblen made the additional and substantial theoretical leap of applying the principle of selection to institutions, and not merely to individuals or groups. Veblen was giving his own pregnant interpretation to a work that he found sometimes "tedious" and uninspiring. Extrapolating Labriola's Marxism for his own purposes, Veblen (1897, p. 391) saw a "materialist ... conception of the evolution of social structure according to which the economic activities, and the habits bred by them, determine the activities and the habitual view of things in other directions than the economic one." To enhance this approach, Veblen briefly suggested the possibility of an amended version of Marxism that might be "affiliated with Darwinism," while providing his own meaningful theoretical hint of a process of selection of social institutions and of individual habits of thought. While these ideas were absent from Labriola's lacklustre volume, nevertheless it helped Veblen to make the intellectual leap of applying the principles of Darwinian selection to emergent social structures or institutions.

Veblen went further than Morgan, seeing the institutional structure of society was not merely "the environment," as Morgan had put it. Veblen indicated that "the environment" consisted of institutional elements that were themselves, like organisms, subject to evolutionary processes of selection. Veblen (1898, p. 393) wrote: "an evolutionary economics must be a theory of a process of cultural growth as determined by the economic interest, a theory of a cumulative sequence of economic institutions stated in terms of the process itself." This was essentially the core theoretical project of *The Theory of the Leisure Class*. Whenever it was put down in the draft manuscript, the appearance of the Darwinian phrase "natural selection" in the *Leisure Class* was extremely significant and played a crucial role in Veblen's argument. In a key passage, Veblen (1899, p. 188) declared:

> The life of man in society, just like the life of other species, is a struggle for existence, and therefore it is a process of selective adaptation. The evolution of social structure has been a process of natural selection of institutions. The progress which has been and is being made in human institutions and in human character may be set down, broadly, to a natural selection of the fittest habits of thought and to a process of enforced adaptation of individuals to an environment which has progressively changed with the growth of community and with the changing institutions under which men have lived. Institutions are not only themselves the result of a selective and adaptive process which shapes the prevailing or dominant types of spiritual attitude and aptitudes; they are at the same time special methods of life and human relations, and are therefore in their turn efficient factors of selection. So that the changing institutions in their turn make for a further selection of individuals endowed with the fittest temperament, and a further adaptation of individual temperament and habits to the changing environment through the formation of new institutions.

It was no accident that Darwin's phrases "natural selection" and "struggle for existence" appeared here. Veblen (1899, p. 207) wrote also of "the law of natural selection, as applied to human institutions." Veblen, however, was not the first person after Darwin to write explicitly of institutions as units of Darwinian selection. David Ritchie (1896, pp. 170–171) had done this a few months earlier. But Ritchie, as far as I am aware, is the only person to precede Veblen on this point. Furthermore, as quoted above, Veblen (1896, p. 99) had noted the "struggle for existence" between multiple "groups and institutions." Apparently without the influence of Ritchie, but with the probable inspiration of Morgan, Veblen became the second writer after the publication of the *Origin of Species* to apply with some rigour Darwin's principle of selection to the evolution of customs and institutions. Veblen was the second person to publish in English the concept of the "natural selection of institutions."[10]

The decisive implication here was to open up the possibility that Darwinism could be applied to human society without necessarily reducing explanations of social phenomena entirely to innate human proclivities. Once we consider the natural selection of *institutions*, and in turn treat institutions as emergent properties in the social realm, then that road is opened. Veblen did not fully map this route, but he did point the way.

3. FOURTEEN YEARS: 1896–1909

With one exception, Veblen's most important published works appeared in twelve crammed years from 1898 to 1909 inclusive. They include his *Theory of the Leisure Class* (1899) and *The Theory of Business Enterprise* (1904). Fifteen of the eighteen classic essays collected together in Veblen's *Place of Science in Modern Civilization* (1919a) appeared in these years. Ten of the eighteen appeared when Veblen was at Chicago. The foremost theoretical work that lies outside the 1898–1909 period is his *Instinct of Workmanship* (1914). Veblen himself regarded the *Instinct of Workmanship* as his most important work. It laid out more completely than any other the psychological foundations of his approach. However, this later volume was planned as early as 1900, and five of its seven long chapters were probably drafted by 1911 (Dorfman, 1934, p. 197; Jorgensen & Jorgensen, 1999, pp. 140, 207). In addition, Veblen (1919, p. v) himself pointed out that his *Higher Learning in America*, although published in 1918, was drafted by 1906. Other works after 1909, especially his *Imperial Germany* (1915), are also of importance, but they are less concerned with the further development of theoretical and conceptual foundations and more with applications of his ideas.

What happened to Veblen himself in the period up to 1909? Both his academic and his personal life are relevant to understand the conditions of his creativity. Employment at the Department of Political Economy at the University of Chicago was not secure. In the 1890s the university trustees sacked two people from the department for their leftist political views. Veblen's own position was always vulnerable. As for his personal life, his marriage was no longer a happy one. In 1896 he professed to one of his previous graduate students – Sarah Hardy – that he was in love with her, knowing that she was engaged to someone else. Five weeks later he confessed this declaration to his wife, pronouncing that their marriage had been an "awful mistake." Two months later he asked her for a divorce. But she resisted and they remained married in name until 1912.[11]

In 1900 – at an age of 43 – Veblen was appointed to the rank of assistant professor. But his position in Chicago remained untenured, insecure and relatively underpaid. In 1904 unproven rumours erupted of an affair between Veblen and the wife of a faculty member. Prompted by this alleged scandal, aided by what might seem as corroborative evidence of the affair from Veblen's wife, and enraged by Veblen's written disapproval of the ties between universities and big business, the university president made it clear that he wished Veblen to leave.

Veblen had been searching for another position for some time. He wrote to Ward, asking for his help in his application for the post of chief of the Division of Documents at the Library of Congress at Washington DC. Ward did his best for Veblen, describing the *Leisure Class* "as one of the most brilliant productions of the country." Ward also nominated Veblen to the prestigious *Institut International de Sociologie*, which was limited to 100 members, including at that time Alfred Marshall, Carl Menger, Eugen von Böhm-Bawerk, Adolph Wagner, Alchille Loria and Gustav Schmoller. But both the job application and the *Institut* nomination were unsuccessful (Dorfman, 1934, pp. 254–257; Jorgensen & Jorgensen, 1999, pp. 78–84).

To his relief, in 1906 Veblen secured a post at Stanford University. At least initially, he found its atmosphere and governance much more conducive than Chicago. He was given a higher salary and allowed "to teach as little as he wished and devote his time to writing" (Dorfman, 1934, p. 269). There Veblen continued to find intellectual stimulation, with colleagues such as Allyn Young in the Department. At Stanford he produced and published a number of highly significant articles.

He was briefly reconciled with his wife Ellen, who joined him in Palo Alto. But the marital repair was not permanent. Veblen had already started a discrete affair with another of his former Chicago students, Ann Bradley Bevans. Twenty years his junior, with children by a previous marriage, she was destined to become Veblen's second wife. She wrote repeatedly to Ellen Veblen urging her claim on Ellen's husband. Bevans claimed that she alone could make Veblen more productive as an economist and bring him world fame (Eby, 2001, p. 279). Thus, knowing of her husband's enduring relationship with Bevans, a vengeful Ellen Veblen sent a dossier of letters to the president of Stanford in 1909. They included information on Veblen's imagined or real extra-marital affairs with Hardy, Bevans and others. Eventually, the president asked for his resignation. Veblen obliged. Ellen Veblen also wrote to the authorities at Chicago and Columbia, alluding to her husband's extra-marital behaviour. For a while, Veblen believed that no university would ever hire him again. Nevertheless, in 1911, Veblen moved to the University of Missouri.[12]

Veblen's most creative and brilliant years, from 1896 to 1909, were also years of suffering in his personal life and of persecution in his career. 1896 was the year in which his marital relationship broke down, and 1909 was the year in which he returned to a stable and devoted sexual partnership. Similarly, his academic troubles began in the late 1890s and lasted until 1911. After 1909 – and contrary to the promise of Ann Bevans – domestic emotional stability and support would divert Veblen's surplus energies into his adopted family and away from his academic work. He wrote to Wesley Mitchell on 3 August 1910: "Domestic circumstances, interesting enough in their way, are all there is time for" (Jorgensen & Jorgensen, 1999, p. 135). Subsequently, he went through a divorce and a second marriage. Then the outbreak of war in 1914 diverted his scholarly attention from theoretical fundamentals to matters of imperialism and peace.[13]

Prior to 1909, his intense creativity in the face of adversity is explicable in terms of someone who retreated into the solitude of his study and threw himself into his writing. He then found solace and refuge from the emotional and institutional storms around him. His very own "instinct of workmanship" was energised in a context of personal pain and unfulfilment. The spurs to creativity are often mysterious. In this period of personal distress, Veblen produced a remarkable revolution in social and economic thought, even if in some crucial aspects it was flawed or incomplete.

A striking fact emerges from an analysis of Veblen's citations of other authors. After 1914 he cites relatively few new works. Veblen's citations show that his years of magnificent productivity – from 1896 to 1909 – drew largely on the great intellectual store that he had built up in the 1880s and 1890s. In those years, personal difficulties impelled him into writing, but after he brought out his ideas he did not fully replenish his intellectual warehouse. In the works that followed *The Instinct of Workmanship* (1914) he made fewer citations to the works of others, and he often repeated his earlier ideas. In the last sixteen years of his life, Veblen lost touch with the pulse of intellectual life and with the new ideas that were closest to his own specialisms and achievements. Perhaps this can be excused on the grounds of

Veblen's tragic personal circumstances and his poor health, but this omission was to have deleterious consequences not only for his own intellectual development but also for institutional economics as a whole. If Veblen had made more of the key developments, then he would have also have prepared the ground for his followers, of which fortunately, and with justification, there were to be many.

4. CONCLUSION

An analysis of Veblen's creativity in the fourteen years from 1896 to 1909 would have to point to the quality of the intellectual environment at Chicago and the stimulation of colleagues from several disciplines. Even a superficial review of the circumstances at the University of Chicago in the years immediately after its foundation in 1892 would recognise the extraordinary calibre of a group of diverse intellectuals from several disciplines, including economics, sociology, anthropology, psychology and biology, all of which were highly relevant to Veblen's evolutionary and "post-Darwinian" research programme in the social sciences. Combined with the environment of a bustling city of contrasts and turmoil, and the opportunities of an expanding university system, Veblen was certainly in the right place at the right time. He was 35 years old when he arrived at Chicago. His mind had not been previously constrained by any longstanding academic appointment and he exhibited a playful spirit of curiosity.

But even an excellent intellectual environment does not necessarily provide the spark of inspiration or the enduring stimulus to work. It is argued here that a major spark was Morgan's visit to the USA in early 1896. The timing of this visit coincides with a major revolution in Veblen's thinking.

As for the stimulus to work, it seems that in Veblen's case this was partly enhanced by a desire to escape in his mind from a marriage that had turned very difficult in 1896 and was to entrap him for several more years, until he set up with Ann Bevans in 1909. His treatment by the academic authorities also gave him reason to retreat into his own world of study and research. Veblen's most creative period was in part stimulated by his personal difficulties. This conclusion is reinforced by the details of Veblen's personal life and by the exact coincidence of his period of intense personal difficulty with that of his remarkable creativity.

NOTES

1. These essays are collected together in two volumes (Veblen, 1919, 1934).
2. The substance of Veblen's intellectual revolution is discussed at greater length in Hodgson (2004).

3. On Veblen and Loeb see Rasmussen and Tilman (1992, 1998).

4. I have found only two explicit references to Dewey in Veblen's (1923, p. 16 n., p. 291 n.) writings.

5. According to Tilman (1996, p. 69 n.) there was a correspondence between Veblen and Boas in 1919.

6. See the list of Veblen's publications in Dorfman (1934, pp. 519ff.).

7. Morgan was in the United States from late 1895 until February 1896. A letter from George Peckham (1896) to Morgan suggests that the Chicago visit was shortly before or after Morgan's lecture at the University of Urbana-Champaign (noted in the university records for 3 February 1896). Urbana-Champaign is only 150 miles from Chicago. From 10 to 31 January, Morgan was lecturing in New York City or Boston. (See Richards, 1987, pp. 398–399, and issues of *Science* from June 1895 to February 1896 for information on Morgan's US tour.) It is also possible that Veblen attended some of Morgan's lectures in New York City, Boston or Urbana-Champaign, or received accounts of their content. Veblen did have the inclination and resources to travel, for he visited England in the summer of 1896, on a mission to meet William Morris (Jorgensen & Jorgensen, 1999, pp. 65–66).

8. Similar ideas, as Morgan himself acknowledged, had been previously suggested by G. H. Lewes, H. T. Buckle, T. H. Huxley, D. G. Ritchie and A. Weismann. The genealogy of these ideas is discussed in Hodgson (2004). Of course, the influence of some of these other authors on Veblen cannot be ruled out. But the timing of Morgan's visit to Chicago, and its coincidence with a shift in Veblen's writing, suggests that Morgan may have been a significant prompt.

9. One of the few scholars to notice the strong influence of Morgan on Veblen is Tilman (1996, pp. 73–75, 79–83).

10. Could it be possible that the primary stimulus behind Veblen's application of Darwinian "natural selection" to institutional evolution was not C. L. Morgan, but, say, L. H. Morgan (1877) or Sumner (1906), both of which are known to have had a strong influence on Veblen's thought? The answer is negative, because neither L. H. Morgan nor Sumner were Darwinians: neither prioritised the concept of natural selection. Indeed, the commonplace description of Sumner as a "Social Darwinist" is misplaced, for reasons explored by Bannister (1973). More generally, few of those who dabbled in the application of Darwinism to social evolution in the 1880s and 1890s considered units of evolutionary selection other than individuals, or collections of individuals (Hodgson, 2004).

11. See Jorgensen and Jorgensen (1999, esp. pp. 27–28, 54–64, 141). Ellen willed her body to scientific research and poignantly requested that a copy of her autopsy report be sent to her former husband (Eby, 2001, p. 263). The autopsy of 1926 revealed that Ellen Veblen had an underdeveloped vagina. Biology matters.

12. Jorgensen and Jorgensen (1999) have provided the best and most reliable account of Veblen's personal life as a whole. However, Eby (2001) has skilfully cast Ellen Veblen in a more sympathetic light. On the basis of documented evidence, Eby proposed that Veblen's relationship with Hardy was probably without sexual intimacy, whereas in contrast it was likely that Veblen and Bevans were sexual partners even before he left Chicago in 1906. This raises the possibility that Veblen had attempted to reconcile himself with his wife Ellen at least partly in an attempt to keep up appearances of marital propriety at Stanford, and to protect his academic position there, while carrying on his affair with Bevans. Veblen himself indicated that his *Higher Learning in America* (1918, p. v) was a critical reaction to his bitter experience of academic misgovernment at Chicago. While Ellen had responded

to marital problems by attacking an individual – her husband – Veblen's foremost response was to address the institutional pathologies that had enhanced his suffering.

13. Is there any other explanation for Veblen's declining academic output? Veblen also suffered repeatedly from poor health, but this weakness was manifest long before 1909 and it was blamed on an overdose of calomel (otherwise known as mercurous chloride, which can decompose into the poisonous forms of metallic mercury or mercuric chloride) that Veblen had been prescribed in his early thirties (Dorfman, 1934, p. 306). Another suggestion is that Veblen was aged 35 when he arrived at Chicago and 52 in 1909, and this phase of life is often one of maximum academic creativity. However, age is no strong reason why a thinker as creative and engaging as Veblen, with the time, resources and encouragement to research and write, should have subsequently reduced his output.

ACKNOWLEDGMENTS

The author is grateful to Dan Hammond, Malcolm Rutherford, Warren Samuels and anonymous referees for their helpful comments. I also thank archivists Mark Alznauer, Robert Chapel and Hannah Cowery, respectively at the University of Chicago, at the University of Illinois at Urbana-Champaign, and at the University of Bristol, for their invaluable help. This essay makes extensive use of material from Hodgson (2004).

REFERENCES

Bannister, R. C. (1973). William Graham Sumner's social Darwinism: A reconsideration. *History of Political Economy*, *5*(1), 89–108.

Blitz, D. (1992). *Emergent evolution: Qualitative novelty and the levels of reality*. Dordrecht: Kluwer.

Boas, F. (1894). Human faculty as determined by race. *Proceedings of the American Association for the Advancement of Science*, *43*, 301–327.

Dewey, J. (1896). The reflex arc concept in psychology. *Psychological Review*, *3*(July), 357–370.

Dorfman, J. (1934). *Thorstein Veblen and his America*. New York: Viking Press.

Eby, C. V. (2001). Boundaries lost: Thorstein Veblen. *The Higher Learning in America, and the Conspicuous Spouse, Prospects: An Annual of American Cultural Studies*, *26*, 251–293.

Ferri, E. (1896). *Socialisme et science positive*. Paris: Giard et Brière.

Ferri, E. (1906). *Socialism and positive science (Darwin-Spencer-Marx)*. Edith C. Harvey (Trans.) from the French edition of 1896. London: Independent Labour Party.

Fontana, A., Roe, L., & Tilman, R. (1992). Theoretical parallels in George H. Mead and Thorstein Veblen. *Social Science Journal*, *29*(3), 241–257.

Gruber, H. E. (1974). *Darwin on man: A psychological study of scientific creativity, together with Darwin's early and unpublished notebooks*. Transcribed and annotated by P. H. Barret, New York: Dutton.

Hodgson, G. M. (1998). On the evolution of Thorstein Veblen's evolutionary economics. *Cambridge Journal of Economics*, *22*(4), 415–431.

Hodgson, G. M. (2004). *The evolution of institutional economics: Agency, structure and Darwinism in American institutionalism*. London and New York: Routledge (forthcoming).

Holmes, F. L. (1985). *Lavoisier and the chemistry of life: An exploration of scientific creativity*. Madison, WI: University of Wisconsin Press.

Joas, H. (1991). Mead's position in intellectual history and the early philosophical writings. In: A. Mitchell (1991), *Philosophy, Social Theory and the Thoughts of George H. Mead*. Albany, NY: State University of New York Press.

Jorgensen, E. W., & Jorgensen, H. I. (1999). *Thorstein Veblen: Victorian firebrand*. Armonk, NY: M. E. Sharpe.

Labriola, A. (1897). *Essais sur la conception materialiste de l'histoire*. Paris: Giard et Brière.

Labriola, A. (1908). *Essays on the materialist conception of history*. Charles H. Kerr (Trans.) from the Italian edition of 1896. Chicago: Kerr.

Marshall, A. (1923). *Money credit and commerce*. London: Macmillan.

Morgan, C. L. (1896). *Habit and instinct*. London and New York: Edward Arnold.

Morgan, C. L. (1923). *Emergent evolution* (1st ed.). London: Williams and Norgate.

Morgan, L. H. (1877). *Ancient society*. Chicago: Charles Kerr.

Peckham, G. (1896). Letter to C. Lloyd Morgan dated 28 January 1896, C. Lloyd Morgan Papers, University of Bristol Library.

Pyenson, L. (1985). *The young Einstein: The advent of relativity*. Bristol: Hilger.

Rasmussen, C., & Tilman, R. (1992). Mechanistic physiology and institutional economics: Jacques Loeb and Thorstein Veblen. *International Journal of Social Economics*, *19*(10–12), 235–247.

Rasmussen, C., & Tilman, R. (1998). *Jacques Loeb: His science and social activism and their philosophical foundations*. Philadelphia, PA: American Philosophical Society.

Richards, R. J. (1987). *Darwin and the emergence of evolutionary theories of mind and behavior*. Chicago: University of Chicago Press.

Riesman, D. (1963) *Thorstein Veblen: A critical interpretation*. New York: Charles Scribner's.

Ritchie, D. G. (1896). Social evolution. *International Journal of Ethics*, *6*(2), 165–181.

Robinson, J. (1979). *Collected economic papers – Volume Five*. Oxford: Basil Blackwell.

Sanderson, S. K. (1990). *Social evolutionism: A critical history*. Oxford: Blackwell.

Spencer, H. (1881). *The study of sociology* (10th ed.). London: Kegan Paul.

Stephan, P. E., & Levin, S. G. (1992) *Striking the mother lode in science: the importance of age, place, and time*. Oxford and New York: Oxford University Press.

Stocking, G. W., Jr. (1968). *Race, culture, and evolution: Essays in the history of anthropology*. New York: Free Press.

Sumner, W. G. (1906). *Folkways: A study of the sociological importance of usages, manners, customs, mores and morals*. Boston: Ginn.

Tilman, R. (1996). *The intellectual legacy of Thorstein Veblen: Unresolved issues*. Westport, CT: Greenwood Press.

Tilman, R. (1998). John Dewey as user and critic of Thorstein Veblen's ideas. *Journal of the History of Economic Thought*, *20*(2), 145–160.

Veblen, T. B. (1897). Review of Essais sur la conception matérialiste de l'histoire by Antonio Labriola. *Journal of Political Economy*, *5*(3), 390–391.

Veblen, T. B. (1898). Why is economics not an evolutionary science? *Quarterly Journal of Economics*, *12*(3), 373–397. Reprinted in Veblen (1919).

Veblen, T. B. (1899). *The theory of the leisure class: An economic study in the evolution of institutions*. New York: Macmillan.

Veblen, T. B. (1900). The preconceptions of economic science: III. *Quarterly Journal of Economics*, *14*(2), 240–269. Reprinted in Veblen (1919).

Veblen, T. B. (1904). *The theory of business enterprise*. New York: Charles Scribners.

Veblen, T. B. (1906). The socialist economics of Karl Marx and his followers I: The theories of Karl Marx. *Quarterly Journal of Economics*, *20*(3), 578–595. Reprinted in Veblen (1919).

Veblen, T. B. (1907). The socialist economics of Karl Marx and his followers II: The later Marxism. *Quarterly Journal of Economics*, *21*(1), 299–322. Reprinted in Veblen (1919).

Veblen, T. B. (1908a). Professor Clark's economics. *Quarterly Journal of Economics*, *22*(1), 147–195. Reprinted in Veblen (1919).

Veblen, T. B. (1908b). On the nature of capital I. *Quarterly Journal of Economics*, *22*, 517–542. Reprinted in Veblen (1919).

Veblen, T. B. (1908c). On the nature of capital II: Investment, intangible assets, and the pecuniary magnate. *Quarterly Journal of Economics*, *23*(November), 104–136. Reprinted in Veblen (1919).

Veblen, T. B. (1909a). Fisher's rate of interest. *Political Science Quarterly*, *24*(June), 296–303. Reprinted in Veblen (1934).

Veblen, T. B. (1909b). The limitations of marginal utility. *Journal of Political Economy*, *17*(9), 620–636. Reprinted in Veblen (1919).

Veblen, T. B. (1914). *The instinct of workmanship, and the state of the industrial arts*. New York: Macmillan.

Veblen, T. B. (1915). *Imperial Germany and the industrial revolution*. New York: Macmillan.

Veblen, T. B. (1919). *The place of science in modern civilization and other essays*. New York: Huebsch.

Veblen, T. B. (1923). *Absentee ownership and business enterprise in recent times*. New York: Huebsch.

Veblen, T. B. (1934). *Essays on our changing order*. Leon Ardzrooni (Ed.). New York: Viking Press.

Weismann, A. (1893). *The germ-plasm: A theory of heredity*. W. Newton Parker & Harriet R. Ronnfeldt (Trans.). London and New York: Walter Scott and Scribner's.

JOHN MAURICE CLARK AND THE MULTIPLIER: A NOTE

Luca Fiorito*

1. While John Maurice Clark is commonly recognized as the father, together with Thomas Nixon Carver, Albert Aftalion, Ralph Hawtrey and Charles Bickerdicke of the so-called "accelerator principle" (Junankar, 1987) and as an anticipator of the "multiplier-accelerator" model (Shackle, 1967, pp. 264–265), his contribution to the development of the multiplier analysis in relation to public works expenditures is often neglected.[1] In another paper (Fiorito, 2001), I have delved into Clark's early formulation of the multiplier contained in his *Economics of Planning Public Works* (Clark, 1935b), also providing archival evidence which seems to confirm what Clark had already affirmed in 1935 (1935c, 85n), i.e. that his recognition and use of the multiplier was prior to his seeing Kahn's celebrated article on "The Relation of Home Investment to Unemployment" (Kahn, 1931).[2] In this note the historiographic aspects of the story are deliberately omitted, and the attention is turned to the more analytical aspects of Clark's treatment of the multiplier. First, I lay down a simple mathematical formulation of the multiplier in which explicit allowance is made for a time-lag between the receipt of income and the receipt of another income caused by the spending of the first. Then I focus on Clark's analysis of the time dimension of the multiplying process and his attempt to reconcile the traditional Kahn-Keynes approach with the so-called "velocity of

*The author is research fellow at the Italian Academy for Advanced Studies in America, Columbia University, New York. Writing this paper has been facilitated through correspondence and conversation with Pier Francesco Asso, Robert W. Dimand, Perry Mehrling, Warren J. Samuels, who, as usual, are not in any way implicated in the final outcome.

Research in the History of Economic Thought and Methodology A Research Annual
Research in the History of Economic Thought and Methodology, Volume 22-A, 161–172
Copyright © 2004 by Elsevier Ltd.
ISSN: 0743-4154/doi:10.1016/S0743-4154(03)22006-X

circulation" approach, also developing, through the model, his main argument. A conclusion follows in the final section.

2. The mechanism underlying the multiplier principle is familiar to modern readers, therefore it does not require any detailed discussion here. In the following model, I first assume that all injections are in the form of investment. Secondly I introduce the concept of *income propagation period*, by which is usually understood the time lag between successive waves of expenditure of the additional net income deriving from the primary investment. For the sake of simplicity, I attribute the whole lag to the delay between the receipt and the spending of income. We can thus define a traditional Keynesian consumption function as follows:

$$C(t) = \alpha y(t - \theta) + K \tag{1}$$

where $C(t)$ is the total consumption at time t, α is the marginal propensity to consume, θ is the time lag, and K is the autonomous consumption. If I is the investment, income received will be:

$$Y(t) = \alpha Y(t - \theta) + K + I(t) \tag{2}$$

As shown by Samuelson (1943) and Goodwin (1947), the complete solution of (2) will be the sum of two parts. The first obtained by setting K and I equal to zero, describes the so-called "propagation mechanism" (Goodwin, 1947, p. 489) and is given by:

$$Y(t) = \alpha^{t/\theta} \quad t = \theta, 2\theta, 3\theta \ldots \tag{3}$$

where A is a constant to be determined by whatever the value of $Y(t)$ is at time zero. The second part, which is obtained by considering the particular results of the injections I and K, gives the familiar result:

$$Y(t) = \frac{K + I}{1 - \alpha} \tag{4}$$

The complete solution will consist in the sum of (2) and (3).

Let us, for the sake of simplicity, analyze the effects of a *permanent* increase in the rate of investment of a unit expenditure. The arbitrary constant A in (3) must in this case be determined so that Y equals 1 when $t = 0$. The solution, for any single period, is then:

$$Y(t) = \left(1 - \frac{1}{1 - \alpha}\right) \alpha^{t/\theta} + \frac{1}{1 - \alpha} \tag{5}$$

The limiting value of (5) as t goes to infinity is $1/(1 - \alpha)$ or, to put it differently, the *continual* stream of a unit expenditure will raise income to the *cumulated* multiplier value – the total increment of income throughout all time resulting from a *unit*, *non-repeated* impulse – and keep it there. In this connection, it is worth noting that, as observed by Robert W. Dimand (1997, pp. 550–551), the first to point out such a convergence was Ralph Hawtrey both in his 1928 *Treasury Memorandum* (quoted in Davis (1983, Appendix); and Dimand (1988, p. 108)) and in his 1930 *Macmillan Committee Working Paper* on "Remedies for the Unemployment," then reprinted in his *Art of Central Banking* (1932, pp. 426–448).[3] John Maurice Clark worked trough a simple graphical illustration of the finite-valued multiplier in his *Economics of Planning Public Works* (1935b, p. 92: chart 2), adding up successive rounds of increases in spending to obtain a finite value for the total change in equilibrium income and expenditure, while the general mathematical proof was stated by Samuelson in 1943. Interestingly, in that paper Samuelson refers to the process described by the multiplier as "the familiar Kahn-Clark sequence" (Samuelson, 1943, p. 221).

Following Goodwin (1947), then, we may define a time constant β as the time in which the direct results of an impulse are nine tenths-achieved:

$$\alpha^{\beta/\theta} = 0.1 \quad \text{which requires that } \beta = \theta \frac{\log 0.1}{\log \alpha} \tag{6}$$

In words, the longer the time-lag and the smaller the marginal propensity to consume, the longer the time required to attain a substantial portion of the multiplier effect.

3. The simple model sketched above provides us with a convenient vantage point from which to consider Clark's treatment of the dynamic implications of the multiplier. Clark advanced his version of the multiplier in a paper on the "Cumulative Effects of Changes in Aggregate Spending as Illustrated by Public Works," first presented at the American Economic Association in December 1934, then published in the *American Economic Review* (Clark, 1935a), and subsequently expanded as Chap. IX of his *Economics of Planning Public Works* (Clark, 1935b).[4]

According to Clark (1935a, b), if the various studies on the secondary effects of public works expenditures are examined, two main approaches to the analysis of the problem are revealed: "one via successive cycles of income and spending by ultimate recipients of income" – which the Columbia economist termed the "Kahn-Keynes" approach – "the other via the volume of money and its velocity of circulation." As is well known, in the first approach, business fluctuations are seen primarily as a consequence of fluctuations in current investment. Accordingly, the amount of the secondary effects is determined by: (a) the amount of the net increase in investment; (b) the marginal propensity to consume; and (c) the length of the income propagation period. As it appears from the above, in the "Kahn-Keynes" analysis of the secondary expansion, money plays only a passive role.

As to the second approach, Clark (1935a, p. 383) affirmed that "it has, so far as I am aware, not found its way into print." A clear and early statement of the view held by the exponents of the "velocity" approach is provided by a letter that Alvin Hansen sent to Clark in 1934.[5] For Hansen the explanation of how an initial change in the rate of spending will induce further increments in the level of total income was essentially a question of: (1) the volume of means of payment; and (2) the income velocity of money:

> Public works may affect either one of these two or both. It is quite correct, as Keynes said, that the public works expenditures may not enlarge the volume of 'money.' In this event, the effect presumably is to transfer money from idle hands to active hands. In other words, the income velocity increases. Or there may actually be injected into the market new 'money,' and the income velocity might conceivably remain on the average as before. Or there may be a combination of these two tendencies.

Also the Keynesian concept of "leakages," i.e. those portions of a given stream of spending which are not respent within the period considered, becomes devoid of any specific content once the "circulation" approach is adopted:

> Keynes' 'leakages,' I think, are also dangerous. The most important 'leakage' is his saving 'leakage' and this when analyzed amounts to nothing more or less than our old friend, a change in income velocity. If all of us hold idle a half of our income which we formerly spent, – save it without investing it, in other words – the income velocity has been cut in two. Thus the total income of society in the next succeeding period has been reduced to one-half by this process of 'savings running to waste'.

As a consequence of this, there will be no secondary effects unless the primary expenditure results in an increase in the quantity of money, its velocity, or – as it seems more probable – both:

> All that public expenditures do is to throw new funds into the market, and thereby increase the income, which action, since it is certainly not likely to reduce the income velocity of 'money' is very likely to increase the total 'money' income of society by more than the amount of 'money' injected. It is, therefore, correct to say that public expenditures are likely to have an effect on income in excess of the expenditures. This is all there is to it, it seems to me.[6]

To recapitulate, we may say that according to the "velocity of circulation approach" the primary factors determining the secondary expansion resulting from a primary investment are the effect of the latter on the amount of money in circulation and the number of times these new dollars circulate in a given period of time. To put it differently, quantity theorists *à la* Hansen would expect that the aggregate income would remain substantially unchanged, in spite of the government's deficit spending, if the financing of the deficit involved no increase in the money supply. If the deficits were financed by a steady creation of new money, they would expect the money income to increase also steadily without limit instead of approaching the level set by the multiplier.

Clark did not share Hansen's criticisms and viewed a possible merging of the two competing approaches. As he put it: "[t]he difference between the two formulations is not necessarily a contradiction, and by comparing the two a better idea may be obtained of the results which are actually to be expected" (Clark, 1935b, p. 85).

Before launching into the discussion of Clark it is worth recalling that in his 1931 essay, Kahn decided to ignore the dynamical implications of the multiplier implied by the existence of a lag between the receipt of income, and its spending, and between its spending and its subsequent re-emergence as income:

> I am here considering the position in the final position of equilibrium when everything has settled down. But some time will, of course, elapse between the point when the primary employment begins, and the point when the secondary employment reaches its full dimensions, because wages and profits are not spent quite as soon as they are earned. *I do not enter into the question of this time-lag*" (Kahn, 1931, 183n: emphasis added).[7]

Contrary to Kahn, Clark began his discussion of the multiplier by explicitly acknowledging and analyzing the role of the income propagation period in determining the length of time over which the multiplier effects are presumed to operate. Clark estimated this time lag at two months, which corresponds to six cycles of secondary effects per year, in consideration of the large amount that wage payments normally constitute of the deficit spending. It is worth pointing out that Clark presented in a chart (Clark, 1935b, p. 92: chart II) the total effects over time of a permanent increase in public expenditure, considering the hypotheses of an income propagation period equal, longer and shorter of two months. Clark's discussion of the consequences of the magnitude of the time lag on how long it will take to achieve a given percentage of the final multiplier effect, clearly shows his awareness of the implications of the relationship (6).

Then Clark turned his attention to the more familiar concept of "circuit" (or "income") velocity of money, which he defined as "the ratio between the total amount of circulating media in the country and the total net volume of production, or the total national income, which those media of exchange serve to finance" (Clark, 1935b, p. 96). Drawing upon Angell's (1933) monetary studies, Clark estimated an average rate of circuit velocity of money of 1.6 per year which, in turn, corresponds to an average cycle of $7\frac{1}{2}$ months for money to flow from a consumer through all the exchanges involved in producing the goods he buys and to get back to an ultimate consumer again. This velocity, however, does not remain constant at 1.6 per year. Clark provided convincing evidence showing that it varies in harmony with the business cycle, increasing with industrial revival and falling with industrial depression. Throughout his discussion Clark warned the reader that the "income propagation period" and the circuit velocity of circulation should not be confused. As he put it "the six cycles per year do not represent the velocity of circulation of anything, but rather the speed with which an increased velocity is transmitted through the economic system" (Clark, 1935b, p. 88).

In assuming an income propagation period of two months, whereas the average circuit velocity of money (reckoned at 1.6 per year) implies a period of $7\frac{1}{2}$ months, Clark was also assuming, as he put it, "that the volume of business increases faster than could be accounted for by the existing volume of purchasing media and their existing circuit velocity." Therefore, he argued, in order to finance a permanent increase in investment expenditure, either the circuit velocity of money must increase or business must acquire more circulating media through an expansion of credit, or both. Part of the task could be accomplished by the increased flow of savings injected into the system through the multiplier and which "may take effect in increased credit used by business in financing this expansion without bringing any increase in the volume of business beyond what the formula already calls for." But even if all the leakages were taken and "used" by business, a problem would still emerge. In fact, "[d]uring approximately the first year and a half [. . .] the total amount of otherwise idle funds resulting from the leakages would not be sufficient to finance the indicated expansion of business at the existing rate of the circuit velocity of funds, and so an increase in the circuit velocity will be called for [. . .]" (Clark, 1935b, p. 95).[8]

For Clark, also the analysis of the agents' behavior shows that the nature of the process can be seen to tend towards increasing circuit velocity. The actual mechanism whereby income changes in response to investment is explicated in terms of inventory accumulation or decumulation. As a consequence of the increase in effective demand caused by the new investments, sales will exceed production and producers experience an unplanned fall in inventory levels. They react by employing more workers and producing more: All of these activities – he wrote – call for payments:

> If business has sufficient funds to make these payments it will joyfully make them. In a depression, the ratio of cash balances to volume of business becomes larger than normal [. . .]. These balances are kept, not employed to normal capacity, because nothing better offers. When something does offer, they will be promptly used and an increase in rapidity of circulation will naturally result. If a particular business does not have sufficient funds, it will try to borrow them, and in that case will call into active use some of the otherwise idle funds which have been designated as leakages in the Keynes approach to the problem. Or if a business has sufficient funds to make the payments, but not sufficient to make them without drawing down its balances lower than seems desirable, then, again, it will try to borrow, but even if it fails it will not cease to do the increased volume of business [. . .]. Most of the funds will circulate within the business community, using them faster will not exhaust them, and business as a whole will always have funds available to make payments" (Clark, 1935b, p. 101).

In summation, Clark argued that an increase in circuit velocity is required both to provide funds to finance an increase in investment, and to meet the higher transactions demand resulting from the consequent increase in economic activity. On this basis, Clark concluded that the conditions described by Kahn and Keynes would themselves furnish a sufficient cause of increased circuit velocity of money, "simply because they cause an increased volume of business without a proportionate increase in volume of means of payment" (Clark, 1935b, p. 101).

4. We can now develop Clark's argument through the model presented in the previous section. Taking into consideration the time-lag, we can define the flow of savings as follows:

$$S(t) = Y(t - \theta) - aY(t - \theta) - K \tag{7}$$

Then, following Clark, we consider the gap between the demand for funds for investment at time t represented by expression (2), and the supply of savings at time t (out of income at time $t - \theta$):

$$I(t) - S(t) = Y(t) - Y(t - \theta) \tag{8}$$

If we calculate the gap for each period under the hypothesis of a permanent injection of one unit expenditure, we obtain:

$$
\begin{aligned}
I(0) - S(0) &= 1 - 0 = 1 \\
I(\theta) - S(\theta) &= 1 + \alpha - 1 = \alpha \\
I(2\theta) - S(2\theta) &= 1 + \alpha + \alpha^2 - 1 + \alpha = \alpha^2
\end{aligned} \tag{9}
$$

$$\vdots$$

that is:

$$1, \alpha, \alpha^2, \alpha^3 \ldots$$

which is the multiplier series for a single impulse.[9] Summing up the differences between investments and savings for each period throughout all the series, we find out that the additional funds required are just equal to the increased level of income. Clark was therefore justified in pointing out the dynamical discrepancy between leakages and injections: as shown by (9), the process described by the multiplier requires an increase in the *effective* supply of money in order to be financed. If such an increase is entirely provided by newly created money, and if there was no idle money before, the velocity of circulation will remain constant. Otherwise, the effective supply of money will adjust itself to the new exigencies through an increase in its velocity of circulation. Clark confidently endorsed this second alternative. In his opinion, "there is no absolute necessity at any stage of the process for government outlays to take the form of an increase in the supply of purchasing media. If the attitude here taken toward changes in velocity is correct – and of that the writer has no doubt – this necessity disappears" (Clark, 1935b, p. 102).

It is also worth pointing out that – as shown by (8) – as long as the regular injection of one unit expenditure goes on permanently, it will become self-financing, in the sense of generating the necessary savings out of income. This is simply another way of stating the so called Kahn-Meade relation, namely the tendency of income to rise sufficiently for savings to become equal to investments. In this connection, Hegeland's (1966, pp. 43–44) contention that in his treatment of the multiplier, Clark does not seem to have recognized that the Kahn-Meade relation appears questionable. In fact, as it appears from the above discussion, Clark's concern was not with a theory of equilibrium in terms of comparative statics where the secondary effects occur simultaneously. The novelty of Clark's contribution lies in its pointing out that, even if the *ex post equality* of the new streams of expenditure and the new streams of saving can be demonstrated, their distribution over time differs substantially, with savings being insufficient, at the outset, to finance the higher level of investment in each period. This, in turn, would necessarily imply an increase in the circuit velocity of money, provided that "there is no literal inflation of the amount of money sufficient to handle the increase in business without an increase in velocity" (Clark, 1935a, p. 388). Moreover, Hegeland fails to acknowledge that Clark can be shown to be perfectly aware that "if the leakages continued at a substantial rate, the 'condition' would be reversed" and the process described by the multiplier would generate enough savings to finance the permanent stream of investments; but – as Clark immediately warned – "by the time this happened, the total volume of business expansion would have passed under the control of factors not accounted for in the formula" (Clark, 1935b, p. 95). For Clark, in fact, the multiplier had to be conceived just as a "rough approximation" – "No such mechanical formula can do justice to the many variable conditions affecting the problem." Clark (1935b, p. 86) – whose "estimates of stimulative effects, based on such an approach as the Kahn-Keynes formula, are hardly worth carrying beyond, let us say, one year, even as rough approximations" (1935a, p. 387). In Clark's view, the multiplier overlooked in particular one important long-period deterrent, namely, the impairment of business confidence by "unlimited" deficit financing and a possibility in the fall in private capital investment due to the expectation that growth of demand will cease after after deficit spending disappears.[10]

This is not the place to quarrel with the empirical validity of Clark's assumption about the behavior of velocity of circulation of money, debatable as it may be. What is relevant here is that to Clark the discussion of the so called "velocity approach" mainly served to arrive at an estimate of the time dimension of the multiplier effects, an aspect which, as he stated in his 1934 address, "has not been worked out, as far as I am aware" (Clark, 1935a, p. 385). After the publication of the *General Theory*, Keynes (1936), several economists, including its author, followed Clark in exploring in greater detail the dynamic implications of the multiplier, especially in relation with the so-called "finance motive." In 1936, for instance, Dennis Robertson in his comments on the *General Theory* argued that if the assumption of an instantaneous multiplier is abandoned, and if time lags are properly considered, then the Keynesian equality between savings and investment breaks down. Differently from Clark, however, Robertson emphasized the need for the monetary authority of adding at each period decreasing quantities of new active money, while keeping constant the income velocity of circulation of the existing one:

> The point to be noted by those whose methods of thought are as old fashioned as my own is that in each period the Authority is conceived of as acting only partly (and decreasingly) by increasing the supply of money, partly (and increasingly) by maintaining the income velocity of the previously issued supply; i.e. by causing the savings of the public to generate income in circumstances in which they would otherwise failed to do so (Robertson, 1936, p. 172).[11]

Three years later, citing another significant example, Nicholas Kaldor (1939) further developed Clark's argument – albeit without mentioning the name of the American economist – showing that, if the multiplier is not instantaneous, the Kahn-Meade relation does not hold and arguing that a low propensity to save increases the size of the additional funds needed to finance a permanent increase in investment.[12]

5. Clark's version of the multiplier was eminently practical: the principles underlying the cumulative effects of public spending were in fact developed and analyzed, by Clark's own admission (1935b, pp. 1–3), not with an eye to theoretical consistency and elegance, but as guides to understand and policy. Nevertheless, Clark's contribution to the multiplier deserves our attention. Clark was in fact among the first writers, if not the first, who explicitly pointed out that the secondary effects do not do not occur simultaneously and to attempt a "period analysis"[13] of the multiplier even before the publication of the *General Theory*. As he wrote in a later reappraisal of his 1935 monograph: "The reader may note that my assumptions as to time are different from those which appear to underlie Keynes's form of this theory. *The kind of adjustment I have in mind does not appear to be one that can take place instantaneously*" (Clark, 1941a, p. 47, emphasis added). On the other hand, as we have pointed out, Clark considered the multiplier just as a "rough approximation"; a formula which would work only under ideal conditions. In more than one occasion (Clark, 1941b, 1942, p. 9) he did not hesitate to warn his colleagues against the risks of "blind dogmatism," caused

by an unqualified application of what – after the sixties – has come to be known as "hydraulic Keynesism."

NOTES

1. More or less extensive discussions of Clark's contribution to the genesis of the multiplier analysis are to be found in Davis (1971), Dorfman (1970), Hegeland (1966), Shute (1997), Wiles (1971).

2. However, Clark was familiar with Keynes (1933) at least as early as 1934 (see note 5 below). The idea of J. M. Clark as an independent discoverer of the multiplier principle has been challenged by Robert W. Dimand. See Dimand (1988, 1990) and especially his response to my article (Dimand, 2002). The present writer would be more cautious now in his contention than in 2001.

3. On Hawtrey's contribution to the multiplier analysis see also the recent article by Ahiakpor (2000) and Dimand's response (2000).

4. The address was also reprinted under a different title in Clark (1936). Clark's *The Economics of Planning Public Works* presented a portion of the research work carried on by a staff serving under the National Planning Board (later incorporated in the National Resources Board). The National Planning Board was set up under the Public Works Administration and consisted of Frederick A. Delano, Wesley Clair Mitchell and Charles E. Merriam.

5. Hansen to Clark, August 8, 1934. Dorfman Papers, Rare Book and Manuscript Library, Columbia University. The letter is reproduced in Fiorito (2001). Clark had asked Hansen for some comments on an early draft of chapter nine of his *Economics of Planning Public Works*. In his reply the Harvard economist dismissed Clark's reasoning on the ground that it "still follows too much along the Keynes lines" which, at that time, he considered "definitely wrong." This is revealing of the fact that Clark was aware of Keynes' *The Means to Prosperity* (Keynes, 1933) – although not of Kahn (1931) – at least as early as the summer of 1934. On Hansen's early appraisal of Keynes' work, see Asso (1990, pp. 62–70).

6. Hansen to Clark, August 8, 1934. Dorfman Papers, Rare Book and Manuscript Library, Columbia University.

7. Keynes, in *The Means to Prosperity*, recognized the nature of the problem, but dismissed it on the following ground: "The amount of time which it takes for current income to be spent will separate each repercussion from the next one. But it will be seen that seven-eighths of the total effects come from the primary expenditure and the first two repercussions, so that the time-lags involved are not unduly serious" (Keynes, 1933, p. 343).

8. Note that this is true under Clark's assumption, i.e. an income propagation period of two months and a multiplier equal to three.

9. Similar results are shown by Goodwin (1947, p. 492).

10. See Wiles (1971) and Fiorito (2001).

11. Interestingly, in another passage of the same article, Robertson, referring with approval in a footnote to Clark (1935a), adds: "[i]t seems to me doubtful whether, for the analysis of a fluctuating world, the 'multiplier' constitutes much advance over more crudely 'monetary' weapons of thought" (Robertson, 1936, p. 175).

12. In this connection, it is important to point out that the instantaneous *versus* lagged multiplier debate is still well alive among post Keynesians economists. In particular, the

debate received new impetus after the publication of Moore's *Horizontalists and Verticalists* (1988) which triggered a whole controversy about the compatibility of Post-Keynesian theories of the multiplier, liquidity preference, and endogenous money.

13. It should be noted, however, that as far as Robertson is concerned, his use of period analysis goes back at least to his *Banking Policy and the Price Level* (1926). On period analysis, see Machlup's (1939) classic contribution.

REFERENCES

Ahiakpor, J. C. W. (2000). Hawtrey and the Keynesian multiplier: A question of cognitive dissonance? *History of Political Economy, 32*(4), 889–908.

Angell, J. W. (1933). Money, prices and production: Some fundamental concepts. *Quarterly Journal of Economics, 48*(1), 39–76.

Asso, P. F. (1990). *The economist behind the model: The Keynesian revolution in historical perspective.* Roma: Ente per gli Studi Monetari e Finanziari Luigi Einaudi.

Clark, J. M. (1935a). Cumulative effects in aggregate spending as illustrated by public works. *American Economic Review, 25*(1), 14–20.

Clark, J. M. (1935b). *Economics of planning public works.* A study made for the National Planning Board of the Federal Emergency Administration of Public Works. Washington, DC: U.S. Government Printing Office.

Clark, J. M. (1935c). *Strategic factors in business cycles.* With an introduction by the Committee on Recent Economic Changes. New York: National Bureau of Economic Research in cooperation with the Committee on Recent Economic Changes.

Clark, J. M. (1936). *Preface to social economics: Essays on economic theory and social problems.* Edited with an introduction by Moses Abramovitz and Eli Ginzberg. New York: Farrar & Reinhart.

Clark, J. M. (1941a). Investment in relation to business activity and employment. In: W. C. Mitchell et al. (Eds), *Studies in Economics and Industrial Relations* (pp. 37–51). University of Pennsylvania Bicentennial Conference. Philadelphia: University of Pennsylvania Press.

Clark, J. M. (1941b). Further remarks on defense financing and inflation. *Review of Economic and Statistics, 23*(3), 107–112.

Clark, J. M. (1942). Economic adjustment after the war: The theoretical issues. *American Economic Review, 32*(Suppl.), 1–12.

Davis, E. G. (1983). *The macro-models of R. G. Hawtrey.* Carleton Economic Papers, Ottawa, pp. 83–84.

Davis, R. (1971). *The new economics and the old economists.* Ames, IA: Iowa University Press.

Dimand, R. W. (1988). *The origins of the Keynesian revolution.* London: Elgar.

Dimand, R. W. (1990). The new economics and American economists in the 1930s reconsidered. *Atlantic Economic Journal, 18*, 42–47.

Dimand, R. (1997). Hawtrey and the multiplier. *History of Political Economy, 29*(3), 549–556.

Dimand, R. W. (2000). Hawtrey and the Keynesian multiplier: A response to Ahiakpor. *History of Political Economy, 32*(4), 909–913.

Dimand, R. W. (2002). John Maurice Clark's contribution to the genesis of the multiplier analysis: A response to Luca Fiorito by Dimand, Robert W. *History of Economic Ideas, 10*(1), 85–91.

Dorfman, J. (1970). Some documentary notes on the relations among J. M. Clark, N. A. L. J. Johannsen & J. M. Keynes. Introductory essay to reprint of J. M. Clark, *The Costs of the World War to the American People*, New York: Augustus M. Kelley Publishers.

Fiorito, L. (2001). John Maurice Clark's contribution to the genesis of the multiplier analysis (with some unpublished correspondence). *History of Economic Ideas, IX*, 7–37.

Goodwin, R. (1947). The multiplier. In: S. E. Harris (Ed.), *The New Economics, Keynes' Influence on Theory and Public Policy* (pp. 482–499). New York: Alfred A. Knopf.

Hawtrey, R. H. (1932). *The art of central banking*. London: Longmans, Green.

Hegeland, H. (1966). *The multiplier theory*. New York: Augustus M. Kelley.

Junankar, P. N. (1987). Acceleration principle. In: J. Eatwell, M. Milgate & P. Newman (Eds), *The New Palgrave: A Dictionary of Economics* (pp. 10–11). London: Macmillan.

Kahn, R. F. (1931). The relation of home investment to unemployment. *Economic Journal, 41*(162), 173–198.

Kaldor, N. (1939). Speculation and economic stability. *Review of Economic Studies, 7*, 1–27.

Keynes, J. M. (1933). *The means to prosperity*. New York: Harcourt, Brace. Includes an additional chapter not in the London edition.

Keynes, J. M. (1936). *The general theory of employment, interest and money*. London: Macmillan.

Machlup, F. (1939). Period analysis and multiplier theory. *Quarterly Journal of Economics, 54*(1), 1–27.

Moore, B. (1988). *Horizontalists and verticalists: The macroeconomics of credit money*. Cambridge: Cambridge University Press.

Robertson, D. H. (1926). *Banking policy and the price level*. London: P. S. King.

Robertson, D. H. (1936). Some notes on Mr. Keynes' *"General Theory of Employment"*. *Quarterly Journal of Economics, 51*(1), 168–191.

Samuelson, P. (1943). A fundamental multiplier identity. *Econometrica, 11*(3/4), 221–226.

Shackle, G. L. S. (1967). *The years of high theory: Invention and tradition in economic thought 1926–1939*. Cambridge: Cambridge University Press.

Shute, L. (1997). *John Maurice Clark: A social economics for the twenty-first century*. New York: St. Martin's Press.

Wiles, R. C. (1971). The macroeconomics of John Maurice Clark. *Review of Social Economy, 29*(1), 164–179.

ROUNDTABLE ON THE HISTORIOGRAPHY OF INSTITUTIONAL ECONOMICS

INTRODUCTION AND SUMMARY

J. Daniel Hammond and Warren J. Samuels

The following materials were presented at a session of the History of Economics Society at its annual meeting, on July 6, 2003, at Duke University. Organized and chaired by Dan Hammond, the principal participants at the Roundtable were also, in order of speaking, Malcolm Rutherford, Ross Emmett, Warren Samuels, Brad Bateman, and Steven Medema.

The Duke HES session grew out of an HES session at the Washington, DC 2003 ASSA conference on "Institutional and Chicago Economics." All panelists in the roundtable except Bateman were also on the ASSA panel. Following this ASSA conference Dan Hammond drafted comments on the paper Malcolm Rutherford presented there, "Chicago Economics and Institutionalism." Hammond questioned whether the borders of Institutionalism were so amorphous as to render the category of little use for historical analysis. He circulated the comments to members of the ASSA panel with an invitation to continue the discussion at the summer HES meeting.

Rutherford dealt with several uses of the term "Institutional Economics," namely, a specific historical group with active participants, a broader group without specific grouping, American economics as a whole, and a common set of ideas and related agenda. Rutherford presented a list of thirteen commonly-held ideas defining Institutionalism.

Emmett pointed to two questions, What is Institutional Economics? and Useful for whom? As for the second, he found three uses: as ideology; as description; involving the use of central theories; and as product differentiation vis-à-vis marginalism, other earlier American economic thought, and laissez faire.

Research in the History of Economic Thought and Methodology A Research Annual
Research in the History of Economic Thought and Methodology, Volume 22-A, 175–177
Copyright © 2004 by Elsevier Ltd.
All rights of reproduction in any form reserved
ISSN: 0743-4154/doi:10.1016/S0743-4154(03)22007-1

Samuels identified a number of uses, concentrating on the definition of terms as tools useful for but not necessarily constituting the definition of reality. He pointed out the ubiquitous heterogeneity within institutionalism and between it and other schools. The uses are: (1) As "institutions matter." (2) As a particular school in the interwar period. (3) As a foil by critics. (4) As coherent and amorphous as most schools. (5) As associated with a set of ideas.

Bateman considered the question, Does Institutional Economics matter? His answer had two parts. The first emphasized the origins of pluralism in late nineteenth century economics. Contrary to the common caricature of this period, the marginalists were not arrayed against the historicists; the two groups had come together to make an alliance against the classical economists in forming the American Economic Association. This co-operation against the classicists formed the basis for a détente in American economics concerning the appropriate methods to use in economic analysis. The second part of his answer examined how this détente began to collapse after a group of self-identified Institutionalists formed a separate school of thought and walked away from the pluralism that had developed within the détente. The emergence of the Institutionalists represented a self-conscious effort at secularization in American economics and had a long-lasting effect not just in helping to collapse the détente, but in the emergence of modern rational economic man.

Medema, also considering the interwar period, wondered if Rutherford's list applied to all who self-identified as Institutionalists; noted that Commons did not reject neoclassical theory; and hypothesized that eventually both Institutionalists and Neoclassicists, who initially accepted each other, changed their positions to one of rejection. Medema also raised the question of whether and by what criteria Institutional Economics was a school.

In the subsequent discussion among panelists, Samuels suggested that the several statements made by panelists illustrated his point about the definition of terms as tools useful for but not necessarily constituting the definition of reality.

Rutherford suggested that Institutionalism be considered as part of the mainstream during the interwar period, and that labels are artifacts.

Bateman urged that economists did not self-identify as Institutionalists until c.1923; Commons, for example, was a product of an older school.

Emmett indicated his agreement with Medema with regard to the school question and with Bateman as to what transpired at the end of World War One.

Rutherford restated his position: Veblen and Commons were not founders; Hamilton, Clark and Mitchell were.

Among the points made by members of the audience were the following.

Perry Mehrling suggested that a distinction be made between "thinkers" (Veblen) and "institution builders" (Commons).

Mark Perlman maintained, with illustrations, that many ideas in intellectual history began as religion and then became secular. He suggested, further, that John Bates Clark, up to his second book, was the father of Institutional Economics, because of his emphasis on reform.

Samuels suggested that the domain of religion provided two models as interpretive tools. In one, religion drives the proposed reform agenda. In the other, the promulgators of the proposed reform agenda, in seeking to use religion to drive it, are, in the process, transforming the religion. The Social Gospel movement included those who, like Ely, wished to capture, transform and use Christianity to advance their economic views, just as did the advocates of clerical laissez faire.

Tim Leonard suggested that the core issue was over the scope of the economic role of government.

INSTITUTIONAL ECONOMICS: THE TERM AND ITS MEANINGS

Malcolm Rutherford

Dan Hammond's written comments on a paper I presented at the ASSA/HES meetings in January on Chicago economics and institutionalism (Hammond, 2003; Rutherford, 2003a) questioned the usefulness of the concept of "institutional economics" as a category with which to discuss the history of American economics from about 1918 on. My paper and Hammond's comments form the background to this roundtable discussion. Although my original piece is not reproduced here, I will begin with some direct comments on what I take to be Hammond's main points of contention.

First, on the basis of my paper on Chicago, Hammond provides lists of people he classifies into institutionalists, critics, and "others." The critics and others list combined is slightly longer than the institutionalist list. Hammond argues that some of those on the critics and others' lists (in particular Knight, Coase, Friedman, and perhaps Stigler) "have one or more attributes of institutionalism." He then calls these people "similars of institutionalism," and concludes that "If there are not many prominent Chicago economists who stand clearly and totally apart from institutional economics, and if leaders of the 'Chicago School,' such as Knight, Stigler, Coase, and Friedman *are institutional economists*, then something is amiss in our (or my) conception of institutionalism" (emphasis added). Here it seems that Hammond wants to define as an institutional economist anyone who shares "one or more attributes of institutionalism." Thus, Coase and Knight are institutionalists because they have an interest in institutions, and Friedman is an institutionalist (presumably) because his empiricism has some of its roots in Mitchell's NBER.

Research in the History of Economic Thought and Methodology A Research Annual
Research in the History of Economic Thought and Methodology, Volume 22-A, 179–184
Copyright © 2004 by Elsevier Ltd.
All rights of reproduction in any form reserved
ISSN: 0743-4154/doi:10.1016/S0743-4154(03)22008-3

Hammond's approach here can also be found in the work of writers such as Perry Mehrling and Geoff Hodgson in the case of Allyn Young. Young becomes an institutionalist because his Ph.D. was from Wisconsin, he was a friend of Mitchell's, liked quantitative work, and occasionally said nice things about Veblen. Similarly Taussig has been seen as an institutionalist because of his interest in Veblen's instinct of workmanship and his little book on *Inventors and Moneymakers* (which uses instinct theory – but not Veblen's). This seems to me to be a very questionable way to look at institutionalism.

Hammond then goes on to suggest that institutionalism might be defined in negative terms – by what it is not. I find Hammond's specific examples and argument on this point to be quite perplexing. At times the main burden seems to be that maybe institutionalism can be defined as "not-orthodox" or "not-neoclassical." This is, of course, a very common view of institutionalism: as a category defined only by a common opposition to neoclassical economics, and with no definable common positive program of its own. But Hammond presents no conclusion on this point, so perhaps he is arguing that this type of definition is also unclear.

Finally, Hammond uses analogies to families, sports fans, and religion. He argues that in the cases of sports fans or religious affiliation one can sort people into groups fairly easily on the basis of questions about beliefs, what he calls "bright-line questions." But family affiliation he seems to regard as different, as we are all related to many families. He argues that groupings of economists are more like family groups, and, thus, "all economists of an era are pretty closely related, having much the same genetic makeup. Only at the tails of the distribution are differences sharp, and most people are not in the tails."

Now, I have quite a few comments and observations to make about these arguments.

(1) There are several different definitions of institutional economics in the literature. It has been used in a very general sense to indicate any economist who gives institutions a central role in their analysis. This, of course would include Smith, Hume, J. S. Mill, Marx, Schmoller and other members of the historical schools, Veblen and American institutionalists, Weber, Schumpeter, Knight, Coase, Williamson, North and so on. It has been used to try to identify a specific historical group – the American institutionalists – who invented and introduced the term institutional economics, and it has also been used in a normative sense in attempts to define approaches that might or should be taken to the development of some type of institutional economics the author is proposing. The issues I discuss below involve the second use only.

(2) There are historiographic issues, besides the issues of the definition of shared ideas, that Hammond does not mention. First, *even* if I were to entirely agree

with Hammond's points, there can be no question that a group of economists in 1918 deliberately (and with careful forethought) introduced the name "institutional economics" into the literature, and did so in an attempt to create some change in the profession. Subsequently, the nature and impact of this "institutional economics" was a significant issue of discussion within the interwar American literature in economics. One simply cannot write the history of interwar American economics and ignore the historical fact of a professional discussion concerning "institutional economics" in major journals and at AEA conference sessions. As for charting this discussion, attempting to follow the changing views on institutional economics, and the changing definitions to be found in the literature over time, I have done some of this in my papers published and forthcoming (Rutherford, 2000, 2002, 2003b, 2004), although more still needs to be done.

(3) It is also the case that institutionalism can be defined sociologically as a network of individuals and as a movement within the profession of economics. When I think of American institutional economics, I tend to think of the economics associated with those who were *active participants* in this movement and were involved in attempting to *promote* what they saw as the "institutional approach" to economics. Several people either self-identified as institutionalists, or were explicitly identified by others as institutionalists (including Thorstein Veblen, R. F. Hoxie, Wesley Mitchell, Walton Hamilton, J. M. Clark, J. R. Commons, Morris Copeland, Rexford Tugwell, Willard Thorp, R. L. Hale, Sumner Slichter, Lionel Edie, E. E. Witte, Clarence Ayres, and others), and there was without doubt a somewhat broader sociological group within the profession that was also associated closely with the institutionalist movement (including Walter Stewart, David Friday, Isador Lubin, Leo Wolman, Carter Goodrich, Robert Montgomery, Winfield Riefler, Mordecai Ezekiel, and many others), and that made up a definite network of people with specific institutional connections. That there was quite a close knit group that made up the interwar institutionalist movement comes out particularly clearly in my papers on Copeland, Hamilton and Brookings, and Columbia (Rutherford, 2002, 2003b, 2004), and the connections between members of the group were important in affecting such things as appointments, research projects, and financing, and cannot be ignored in historical work.

(4) Turning exactly to the problem of defining institutionalism in terms of ideas, that is Hammond's focus, I do not think this is inherently any different from that involved in defining any "approach" to economics. No category in the history of economics is perfectly defined, and virtually all of the standard classifications in the history of economics get fuzzy around the borders

when examined closely enough (classical, historical, Austrian, neoclassical, post-Keynesian). Several of these classifications contain more than one identifiable research program. I don't think that means we should abandon these classifications altogether or wash them all away in some notion of general family resemblance, but I do think it means we have to take care with the use of labels. I would also shy away from the idea of institutionalism as constituting a "school" of economics in any tightly defined sense. I think of institutionalism as a movement and as a network of people. For this network to hold together and the movement to function as a movement the group had to have a number of ideas in common – enough to provide for group identity and cohesion – but this necessary degree of identity and cohesion did not require uniformity, particularly on matters of detail.

(5) I feel the need to stress at this point that the whole idea of interwar American economics being "pluralistic" was one that I and Mary Morgan (and Warren Samuels) had a big part in creating. The concern that I had in emphasizing the pluralist nature of American economics in the interwar period was exactly to get away from a simplistic notion of a sharp division between institutionalists on one side and neoclassicals on the other, and to the extent that Hammond is making that point I agree with him. But to say the division was not sharp, not a "bright line," and that various people occupied various intermediate positions does not mean that the classifications are useless. It simply is *not* the case that everyone or almost everyone (or even most of everyone) in the interwar period was an institutionalist in the sense of *being a part of the movement or network and sharing their core ideas*, and I cannot see that it makes sense to call someone an institutionalist who shared only one or a very few of the "attributes of institutionalism." For example, doing empirical work was not a trait that was ever exclusive to institutionalists, and although Friedman did take aspects of his empiricism from his NBER experience, I cannot see that he can be thought of as a member of the institutionalist group in any meaningful way.

(6) It is my view that the American institutionalist movement in the interwar period did embody a set of shared core ideas and beliefs. These ideas and beliefs involve both positive and negative propositions, and contain an important normative element. They served to differentiate institutionalists both from more "orthodox" neoclassicals as well as from the earlier generation of progressives (see Rutherford, 2000). In general terms the institutionalist position included: (i) a clear recognition of the *central* analytical importance of institutions and institutional change, with institutions acting both as constraints on the behavior of individuals and concerns and as factors shaping the beliefs, values, and preferences of individuals; (ii) a desire to base economics on a social

psychology consistent with this emphasis on the role of institutions, and a related rejection of hedonistic psychology and of the idea of the individual as a utility maximizer; (iii) the adoption of a view of correct scientific method in social science as empirical and "investigational" (including but not limited to quantitative and statistical work), and a related rejection of the highly abstract and "speculative" nature of much orthodox theory; (iv) an emphasis on the *critical* examination of the functioning of existing institutions (including issues such as bargaining power, standards of living and working conditions, corporate finance and control, market failures of various types, business cycles, unemployment, and so on), and a related belief in the need for new forms of "social control" involving greater government regulation of the market and other interventions; and (v) the adoption of a pragmatic and humanistic approach to social value (generally taken from John Dewey), and a related rejection of the standard theories of value and of market efficiency as adequate tools for policy appraisal. Important specific content can be added to this outline as American institutionalists expressed these general beliefs through particular theories and concepts taken or developed from the work of Thorstein Veblen and/or John R. Commons.

(7) Thus, to fall clearly within the institutionalist group in the interwar period involved adopting a *complex* of ideas and positions, some positive, some negative, and some normative. This cannot be a one-dimensional definition and to be an institutionalist involved accepting pretty much the entire bundle of general positions outlined above and working with specific concepts derived from particular writers (such as Veblen or Commons). Individuals who shared some but not all of these ideas would be likely to have contact with institutionalists along those particular dimensions or on those issues, and would normally have some degree of sympathy (varying substantially) with those aspects of the institutionalist movement, but were also sometimes critics of other aspects of institutionalism, and did not act as, and therefore cannot properly be seen as, members of the American institutionalist movement themselves (for example Frank Taussig, Allyn Young, Frank Knight, and Paul Douglas).

(8) Admittedly, this does not avoid the problem of fuzzyness in the classification or sorting of American economists *as a whole* into groups, as the pluralism of American interwar economics involved many writers who were neither clearly a part of the institutionalist movement nor *entirely* or *strictly* orthodox or neoclassical (particularly as we tend to think of that now). A good number of economists of the time, for example, believed in some type of "liberal" reform agenda and had doubts about the applicability of standard neoclassical theory to the complications of real markets, but, at the same time, were not

willing to go as far as the institutionalists in their critique of standard theory. This middle group was quite large, and there are cases on the margins that are hard to decide. Also, in the interwar period, most economists did applied work of a fairly concrete sort. Very, very few American economists did "theory," as one theorist in a department was generally considered sufficient. A common position was to adopt standard theory in the classroom and in the "principles" sections of textbooks, but to be more empirical and institutional in applied work that dealt with real markets and policy problems (see, for example, the text book written by Henry Seager). Are such people institutionalist, or neoclassical, or a bit of both? I would tend to argue that they are probably best seen as some combination of both, and I do not think we should worry about this – this ambiguity being exactly what I would like to emphasize as one of the defining features of the American interwar scene (and one that continued for some time after in fields such as labor economics). One of the interesting elements in the later history of American economics is the loss of this degree of pluralism and the sharpening of divisions. In this process the use of labels (including the invention of labels such as institutionalist, neoclassical, and marginalist), and the rhetoric surrounding them (think not only of Hamilton but also of Koopmans and Stigler) played an important part. This brings me back to my first point. These labels themselves are significant historical artefacts that played important roles in the professional discourse. They need to be more closely examined and understood, not avoided or made so broad as to become unintelligible.

REFERENCES

Hammond, D. (2003). Reflections on institutional and Chicago economics. Comments Prepared for the ASSA Conference, Washington, DC.

Rutherford, M. (2000). Understanding institutional economics: 1918–1929. *Journal of the History of Economic Thought*, *22*(September), 277–308.

Rutherford, M. (2002). Morris A. Copeland: A case study in the history of institutional economics. *Journal of the History of Economic Thought*, *24*(September), 261–290.

Rutherford, M. (2003a). Chicago economics and institutionalism. Paper presented at the ASSA Meetings, Washington, DC.

Rutherford, M. (2003b). On the economic frontier: Walton Hamilton, institutional economics, and education. *History of Political Economy*, *35*(Winter), forthcoming.

Rutherford, M. (2004). Institutional economics at Columbia University. *History of Political Economy*, *36*(Spring), forthcoming.

IS INSTITUTIONALISM STILL
A USEFUL CATEGORY?

Ross B. Emmett

The question before us – is *"institutionalism" still a useful category for the history of American economics?* – seems to beg two questions. The first, what is institutionalism, has been addressed by several other panel participants. So I will focus on the second question – useful for whom?

Back in the "good old days," when the history of economics was the story of the development of the theory of value and distribution from Adam Smith to Paul Samuelson, "institutionalism" was a useful category because it provided a box into which the historian could place a number of American economists (most prominently Thorstein Veblen, John Commons and Wesley Mitchell) who had explicitly rejected value and distribution as the central themes of economics. Indeed, Walton Hamilton (1919) explicitly defended the "institutional approach" as a challenge to the notion of an economics defined by value and distribution theory. Institutionalism, Hamilton said, would not limit economic investigation to the confined space of value theory, would break free of the scientific boundaries set by the antiquated psychology of interests, and would focus on process and institution rather than equilibrium outcomes.

The good old days are gone; economic theory is no longer told simply in retrospect. Should "institutionalism," then, also be cast aside? Given the amount of historical work which recently suggests that early twentieth-century American economics was pluralistic with no dominant perspective, casting the term aside, at least for the period of the inter-war years, becomes a strong possibility. But I want to suggest three reasons why "institutionalism" as a category for historical

Research in the History of Economic Thought and Methodology A Research Annual
Research in the History of Economic Thought and Methodology, Volume 22-A, 185–188
Copyright © 2004 by Elsevier Ltd.
ISSN: 0743-4154/doi:10.1016/S0743-4154(03)22009-5

work may still have a use. Two of these reasons have in common a concern for the use of the word "institutionalism" by its promoters and opponents, and the third draws upon the large-scale re-writing of 20th century American economics currently being undertaken by historians of economics.

REASON 1: "INSTITUTIONALISM" WAS IMPORTANT TO INSTITUTIONALISTS

From the work of Veblen (1909) forward, a number of American economists found it useful to use the terms "institutions," "institutional," or "institutionalism" to describe the object of their study, the method of their study, or the school of thought to which they belonged. Acknowledging the centrality that these terms have in the work of these economists seems to me to be an essential part of my work as a historian concerned with providing historical reconstructions. That is, if I wish to provide an account of their work that these thinkers could at least in principle agree with, I will probably need to use the term institutionalism.

Since I am passing on the attempt to define institutionalism, two comments about the institutionalists' use of institutionalism are necessary. First, from Veblen forward, the institutionalists use the term to demarcate their analyses from those based on marginal utility theory. Utility theory's claim to the mantle of "economic theory" is invalid, Hamilton (1919, p. 311) tells us, because its analysis is "hedged about by greater limitations" resulting from its indirect relation to the realities of modern industrial social organization. Hamilton's point is affirmed two years later by the "theorist" Frank Knight in *Risk, Uncertainty and Profit*, one of the classics of the marginal utility tradition (Knight, 1921). The importance of this first demarcation will become clear a little later.

Secondly, the institutionalists also use the term "institutionalism" to demarcate their analysis from earlier American economic thought. This second demarcation is often taken by historians to be the same as the first demarcation; identifying the gap between institutionalists and neoclassicists as the same as the gap between the modernists and the followers of classical economics. But recent research in 20th-century American economics suggests that these two demarcations are not the same (Brad Bateman makes the case for this argument very well in his contribution to this panel; see also Malcolm Rutherford's comments). Whatever the differences between interwar neoclassicists and institutionalists (the extent of those differences is currently the subject of debate among historians as we explore this period in more detail), they seem united in their desire to distance themselves from the past.

REASON 2: "INSTITUTIONALISM" WAS IMPORTANT TO ITS POST-WAR OPPONENTS

Once we accept that institutionalism is a category that participants themselves were ready to adopt, we can readily accept another use for the term: its use by those who wished to not be identified with the institutionalists. The standard reference here is to the dismissive comments of George Stigler and Ron Coase regarding institutionalism's anti-theoretical stance. There are three things to note here. First, we sometimes forget that Stigler and Coase are primarily post-war theorists, and that the lines of demarcation among American economists shifted substantially during the New Deal and World War II. Secondly, the reason the Chicago economists use the term is the flip side of the institutionalists' use of the term. Where the institutionalists were using the term to create a positive image of what economics might be when it moved away from the traditions of the past, the Chicago economists were using the term to point toward what economics should *not* become as it moved away from the traditions of the past. But, and this is the third point, the Chicago economists were also saying that they had a better way to move away from traditional economics – a way of doing 20th century economics that avoided the pitfalls of institutionalism. Much of the discussion about institutionalism at Chicago fails to see this basic point: both institutionalism and Chicago economics were departures from the 19th century tradition of American economics. Both represent ways of doing economics in America in the 20th century. Both were oriented toward social control, both dealt with institutions, and both prided themselves on their appeal to science. But Chicago was successful in separating itself from institutionalism, and hence remaining a viable voice within mainstream American economics, while institutionalism withered away. Chicago's success is often identified with its affirmation of the neoclassical tradition. But that tradition had not yet established itself fully in North America, and Chicago economics is significantly different than the neoclassicism that becomes the dominant form of economics in post-war America.

REASON 3: A REMINDER THAT EARLY 20TH CENTURY AMERICAN ECONOMICS WAS CONTESTED TERRAIN

You may say at this point: so what? If the traditional neoclassical-institutional divide is historically inaccurate, it doesn't matter what they called themselves. Perhaps we should devise new terms to describe early 20th century American economics. This response brings us to the third reason to keep the term institutionalism alive in the historiography of American economics.

Once we acknowledge that the good old days are gone – that the story which unites neoclassical theory with classical theory through a common heritage of value theory is not a sufficient account of the history of economics in America – we as historians can begin to accept the notion that American economics in the first half of the 20th century was contested terrain. While we may still hold to the notion that the emergence of neoclassicism is the central story to be told during that period, we can at least acknowledge that other possible stories exist. Some of these stories place institutionalists at the heart of American economic thought and American economic policy. Continuing to use terms they held dear, like institutionalism, will help us to craft stories that provide better accounts of that contested terrain of 20th century American economics than the ones told so far.

REFERENCES

Hamilton, W. (1919). The institutional approach to economic theory. *American Economic Review Supplement*, 9(March), 309–318.

Knight, F. H. (1921). *Risk, uncertainty and profit*. Boston: Houghton Mifflin.

Veblen, T. (1909). The limitations of marginal utility. *Journal of Political Economy*, 17(November), 620–636.

INSTITUTIONAL ECONOMICS AS A CATEGORY FOR HISTORICAL ANALYSIS

Warren J. Samuels

I have two preliminary points to make. The first concerns the type of category we have in mind. It is perfectly sensible to think of "Institutional Economics" as a candidate for describing, in part, the "reality" of economics. But in so doing, one must remember that terms and their definitions are tools of analysis. Different definitions of Institutional Economics may be used to describe part of the history of economics but doing so only means that we are using the definition as a tool and that our description is driven by the definition we adopt.

The second is that heterogeneity rules. Institutional economics is heterogeneous and so is orthodox/mainstream/neoclassical economics; so, too, is heterodox economics as a whole.

This heterogeneity is both given effect through and may be comprehended in terms of what I call the matrix approach. If five schools of economic thought exist, A, B, C, D and E, and if each has three heterogeneous versions, e.g. A1, A2 and A3, then we have a matrix of meaning: A1, A2 and A3 will each define A differently and their respective views of B, C, D and E will vary; and vice versa, B's, C's, D's and E's view of A will differ both from each other's view and depending whether it is C1's, C2's or C3's view, etc. Which is the correct view of a school? A's own view, or A1's, or A2's or A3's – or B1's . . . E3's? I submit that one answer is in terms of the total matrix of meanings pertinent to that school.

Research in the History of Economic Thought and Methodology A Research Annual
Research in the History of Economic Thought and Methodology, Volume 22-A, 189–192
Copyright © 2004 by Elsevier Ltd.
ISSN: 0743-4154/doi:10.1016/S0743-4154(03)22010-1

"Institutional Economics" is thus a tool given meaning differently from different perspectives (from both within and outside of Institutionalism).

Given the foregoing, I have the following points to make/topics to raise.

(1) One meaning of Institutional Economics is its emphasis on the theme "institutions matter." This theme is to be found unevenly, but widely and deeply, if often only implicitly, throughout the history of economic thought. It is found, for example, in Adam Smith, Alfred Marshall, Ronald Coase, and historicism. It is especially found in what has come to be called the Old Institutional Economics and the New Institutional Economics. It is to be compared with economics practiced in pure a-institutional conceptual terms.

And once one deals with *institutions*, one confronts *process* – that of working things outs, in juxtaposition to seeking unique determinate optimal equilibrium solutions to problems.

(2) In the interwar period many individuals practiced what we now call Institutional Economics and Neoclassical Economics indiscriminately. Both were descriptive and analytical tools, and both were part of economics. My favorite examples of individuals doing so are Frank William Taussig and Vilfredo Pareto.

The term Institutional Economics is typically used to focus on Thorstein Veblen and John R. Commons, and perhaps one or two others, as, say, the founders of Institutional Economics. But Malcolm Rutherford has conclusively shown that neither Veblen nor Commons saw themselves as founders or leaders of a school, nor were they.

Institutional Economics is often largely identified with Veblen or in terms of his ideas. But he led no school; and the status of his ideas is multiple: some rejected his ideas, some used his ideas, some rejected some of his ideas and used others in their own work.

Walton Hamilton coined the name in 1917 but he was important in economics only early; later, after he joined the faculty of Yale Law School, his significance wanes, to where he is either a secondary or tertiary figure.

Commons had a huge influence in the fields of U.S. labor history and legal history. His theoretical ideas constituting additional Institutional Economics came later. His theoretical ideas have mostly been selectively and narrowly adopted; the exceptions are primarily faculty in Agricultural Economics at the University of Wisconsin and in both Economics and Agricultural Economics at Michigan State University – A. Allan Schmid and this author.

John Maurice Clark was personally more conservative than most other Institutionalists. His influence has been negligible. His social-control orientation has been adopted largely only by this author and not only from him.

Wesley C. Mitchell has been defused/eclipsed by the erroneous claim that he practiced empiricism without theory. His Veblenian emphasis on the economy as a pecuniary phenomenon remains but he is primarily known as a major supporter of statistical work and as the founder of the National Bureau of Economic research, his monument.

(3) The term Institutional Economics is a foil from two opposite points of view: The negative view is that of Paul T. Homan, Lionel Robbins, George Stigler, Ronald Coase, and others. The positive view (especially of Commons) is that of Oliver Williamson and Douglass North; and of both Veblen and Commons, that of Geoffrey Hodgson.

(4) Especially given my second preliminary point, Institutional Economics is as coherent and amorphous as most schools. Rutherford's list of thirteen ideas (in his contribution to this symposium) is eminently accurate, at a certain level. But once one goes beyond those ideas – for example, to the so-called Veblenian dichotomy and to Mark Tool's value principle – Institutionalism divides into at least two strands, that centering on Clarence Ayres and Fagg Foster, and that centering on Commons. Institutionalism has thus become sectarian. The sectarian practice has largely been only uni-directional, however. Whereas the disciples of Ayres and Foster envision Institutional Economics to be an alternative to Neoclassical Economics, those in the Commons tradition see the relationship as supplementary.

David Colander, in a series of papers, has argued that neoclassicism no longer has hegemonic status. In his view, neoclassicism has been replaced by a mainstream that resembles, if anything, the picture of interwar practice described above in point (2). John B. Davis has offered a different perspective. Instead of the fragmentation of neoclassicism offering heterodox economics more breathing room, he fears the opposite.

(5) Institutionalism can be understood in terms of a set of ideas (not intended to complete with Rutherford's). These include

(a) the scope and method of economics, especially its central problem, namely, organization and control;
(b) critique of mainstream economics and of the modern corporate and consumerist economy;
(c) rejection of the idea of laissez faire as analytically meaningless and misleading;
(d) an approach to problem solving.

Brad Bateman identifies the 1930s as the period in which both Economics as a whole and Institutional Economics in particular became completely secular for the first time. A particular point needs to be made, that of social construction. Those who sought social reform in the Social Gospel movement – the list includes John Bates Clark, John R. Commons, and Richard T. Ely – certainly wanted to give capitalism a new form. But in so doing, in constructing the Social Gospel movement, they were redefining Christianity, giving it a secular preoccupation with economic organization and conditions. Those who wanted to practice the Institutional Economics of Ayres and Foster and of Commons, respectively, also were engaged in the ongoing social construction of Institutional Economics; and similarly within Neoclassicism.

AUTHOR'S NOTE

I have authored (among other publications) the following statements on the meaning of Institutional Economics:

(2003). Institutional economics: Retrospect and prospect. *Research in the History of Economic Thought and Methodology*, *21C*, 191–250.

(1991). Institutional economics. In: D. Greenaway, M. Bleaney & I. M. Stewart (Eds), *Companion to Contemporary Economic Thought* (pp. 105–118). New York: Routledge,.

(1987). Institutional economics. In: J. Eatwell, M. Milgate & P. Newman (Eds), *The New Palgrave: A Dictionary of Economics*. 4 vols (Vol. 2, pp. 864–866). London: Macmillan.

(1984). Institutional economics. *Journal of Economic Education*, *15* (Summer), 211–216.

WHY INSTITUTIONAL ECONOMICS MATTERS AS A CATEGORY OF HISTORICAL ANALYSIS

Bradley W. Bateman

Institutional Economics does matter as a category of historical analysis. But while some of the reasons for this are familiar, I would like to suggest an additional reason on which historians of economics might not normally focus.

First, let's consider two of the reasons that might be offered for thinking that Institutionalism has an important history. I suppose, for instance, that many people who agree with me that Institutionalism matters as a category of historical analysis will argue that it matters because they support some form of institutional analysis, as against a more individualistic and traditionally neoclassical form of analysis. I have no qualm with this argument, and accept it as a perfectly good reason to believe that Institutional economics is an important part of the history of economics. But this is not my argument. I also suppose that some people may argue from the obvious fact that since many prominent American economists in the second, third, and fourth decades of the twentieth century identified themselves as Institutionalists, that it only makes sense to think of Institutionalism as an important historical category. Bill Barber (1996) has shown, for instance, that it would be impossible to understand the shaping of the first New Deal without understanding the contribution that Institutional economists made to it.[1] Thus, if the New Deal is an important historical category, then so is Institutional Economics. But, again, this is not my argument.

These are only two of several good reasons that one might argue that Institutional economics is an important historical category. My reason for believing that it

Research in the History of Economic Thought and Methodology A Research Annual
Research in the History of Economic Thought and Methodology, Volume 22-A, 193–201
Copyright © 2004 by Elsevier Ltd.
All rights of reproduction in any form reserved
ISSN: 0743-4154/doi:10.1016/S0743-4154(03)22011-3

is an important category is quite different, however. Put most simply, I believe that Institutionalism's importance follows from the fact that it marks the moment when American economics first became fully secular. I believe that if you do not understand this fact, and its historical significance, that you cannot fully understand the particular way that neo-classicism eventually emerged and how the forces of modernity shaped the discipline of economics in the second half of the twentieth century.

But before I can make my argument about the secularization of American economics, I need to make another related point about the emergence of Institutionalism. For it was not just that Protestant religion was being jettisoned with the emergence of Institutionalism; so was a *détente* of some thirty years that had allowed historical and marginal analysis to peacefully co-exist at the center of mainstream American economics.

1. THE DÉTENTE BETWEEN HISTORICISM AND MARGINALISM

By now, it is one of the standard tropes of those who write about the profession-alization of American economics that there was a *methodenstreit* between the marginalists and the historicists at the turn of the nineteenth century into the twen-tieth. As recently as last year, Nancy Cohen (2002) argued that the only problem with this picture is that we have not understood correctly that the marginalists had actually won much sooner than we realized, sometime *before* 1900. Dorothy Ross's classic *The Origins of Amercian Social Science* (1991) plays off the same dichotomy, but offers the older chronology, that "[b]etween about 1890 and 1910 marginal economics became the dominant paradigm in American economics."

There are many problems with using this dichotomy to picture early American professional economics, not least that it ignores the dynamics that shaped the profession in the aftermath of the formation of the American Economic Associa-tion. Now, that moment, in 1885, did represent a rupture in American economics, but the rupture was between those who followed classical economics, on the one hand, and those who followed marginalism *and* historicism, on the other hand. Yonay Yuval (1998) has restated this quite obvious fact, but it was always there in Dorfman's *Economic Mind in American Civilization* (Vol. 3, 1949). After all, John Bates Clark, the premier early *marginalist*, joined Richard T. Ely, the premier early *historicist*, in founding the A.E.A.; and the early fighting was between the younger, so-called ethical, economists and the older, classical economists.

What happened in the 30 years after the founders of the A.E.A. made their peace with the older economists has been the subject of some study, with

Mary Morgan and Malcolm Rutherford (1998), Malcolm Rutherford (1997) and Bradley Bateman (1998, 2001) arguing most recently that what happened around the turn of the century was not the triumph of "neoclassical" economics. Rather, people with different methodological predilections decided to stop fighting and came to a kind of peaceful *rapprochement* in which people could practice from different (or more than one) methodological frame as long as they talked seriously about the possible conditions for the amelioration of economic problems. There were clearly important disagreements between the parties to this détente about policy issues, such as tariffs and currency, but there was a suspension of fighting over *how* these issues should be studied and a tacit acceptance that serious work undertaken through different methods was acceptable.

In the decade before and the decade after 1900, there were people who were primarily marginalist in their approach, and there were people who were primarily historicist in their approach, but there were also people who worked out of both theoretical perspectives. Someone like E. R. A. Seligman cannot be understood any other way. As the author of the best selling textbook in economic history, he was clearly a leading exponent of a historicist approach, and yet he was facile with marginal analysis and used it in all his textbooks.

There was no doubt some tension between people whose approach was more weighted in one direction or the other, but the glue that held them together after the initial rupture when the young Turks founded the A.E.A. was the Social Gospel movement. The greatest example of this, of course, is the apparently odd couple of J. B. Clark and Richard T. Ely. It is instructive to look a little deeper under the surface to see their similarities and their differences in order to get a better picture of what was happening at the turn of the last century. Ely and Clark both studied in Germany with the same man, Karl Knies, one of the most distinguished members of the Older School of German historicists. Like all German Historicists, Young and Old, Knies believed in the importance of national characteristics in understanding economic change. Also, no doubt, both Clark and Ely found upon their returns from Germany in the 1870s that the new liberal Protestantism in America, in its manifestation of the Social Gospel, was an appealing and appropriate frame for understanding (and advocating) change in America because it drew from the very roots of the Protestant self-understanding of virtually all American republicans. For both Ely and Clark, Christian socialism in 1880 involved the *institutions* and the *history* that were necessary to understanding the American economic situation.

Now, I think you all know that as Clark moved away from Christian socialism in the 1880s and the 1890s that he became more and more intensely focused on developing marginal analysis. But guess what, Ely was interested in marginal analysis, too!

For most of you this should sound like the most heretical thing that I have said today. We understand Ely, warts and all, as the great historical economist who founded the A.E.A., and so what do I mean by calling attention to his credentials as a marginalist? Well, consider the evidence. You need look no further than the first edition of Ely's *Outlines* (1893) and you will find a nascent development of marginal utility analysis. Now some of you will know that his revision of the text in 1908 with Allyn Young and Thomas Adams was more geared to marginalism, but how many know that he used marginalism in the first edition, as well? More to the point, why would he have done such a thing? According to Cohen (2002) and Ross (1991), he would have done it because those awful neo-classicists were sweeping the boards.

In opposition to this point of view, I am going to argue that Ely did it for the very same reason that he employed historical analysis: he got it from Karl Knies. I do not believe that anyone working in this literature has noticed, in this context, Erich Streissler's (1990) path-breaking essay on Carl Menger in which he argues, carefully and from the texts, that Menger picked up his interest in using marginal analysis from his German teachers, including several distinguished Older Historicists. More to the point, Streissler includes Karl Knies in the category of Older Historicists who had developed marginalist thinking and published articles about the relationship between diminishing marginal utility and prices.

Indeed, Böhm-Bawerk and Wieser were students in Knies's seminar in 1875–76 and presented their own ideas about diminishing marginal utility there in that year. Dorfman (1955) claimed as early as 1955 that the German influence in American economics (in the nineteenth century, in the work of those who studied in Germany for the doctorates) had always included the "Austrian" influence.

Space precludes following out all the implications and connections to be drawn here, but we can see in summary that the "ethical economists" who founded the A.E.A. and challenged the classicism of the "old school" economists came home from Germany tutored in both marginal thinking *and* historical analysis. They saw in their teachers from the Older (German) Historical School that marginalism could be a part of the toolbox of an historical economist and they were not afraid to use both kinds of tool. True enough, some leaned harder in one direction than another, but the kind of hard distinction between marginal thinking and historical thinking that historians like Ross and Cohen place at the center of their analysis is somewhat misleading. Merely to see a piece of marginal analysis in an article or textbook does not mean that marginalism, much less neo-classicism, had triumphed in America. Ely was always committed to some form of marginal analysis and Clark was never completely averse to some amount of historical, institutional analysis. Perhaps the only prominent person in the 1890s to lie completely outside this orbit of liberal Christian, hybrid economists was Thorstein Veblen, and he, of course, was at that time a creature with complete different stripes than anyone else in American economics.

Thus, with the exception of a very few people, American economists during the Progressive Era (1900–1920) were practiced in the toleration of both these styles of analysis, and professional self-identity (and decorum) largely precluded the outright attack of people for their relative emphasis on one over the other. There were lots of other things going on here, such as the efforts of the classical economists, largely followers of John Stuart Mill, to fully accommodate the new marginal thinking as well as the increasing theoretical sophistication of the marginalists; but under the protective guise of the Social Gospel, and wanting to share in the glow of the success of economists such as Ely and Commons in helping to shape and inform public opinion, American economics was a largely plural enterprise. And, hence, if Malcolm Rutherford finds people at Chicago circa 1920 that are sometimes marginalist and sometimes historicist, people who often hew to one pole, but sometimes hew to the other, or people who generally practice marginalist analysis, but do not attack the newly emerging institutionalists, that should not surprise anyone. There is a reason for it in their training and the normal conditions of their experience as Amercian economists in the preceding 25–30 years.

2. THE END OF THE ERA OF THE SOCIAL GOSPEL

Following the end of the First World War, American Progressivism collapsed.[2] As the awful truth of the trench warfare in Europe sank into the national psyche, and as Americans watched Woodrow Wilson's failures at Versailles, Americans began to turn away from the progressive belief in human moral improvement and the possibility for the amelioration of social ills. The Social Gospel, which had provided the early underpinning for the Progressive movement in the first decade of the new century, suffered especially hard in this environment, as did the optimistic, moralistic social sciences. Although historians of economics have written little about this moment in American social science, it serves as the cornerstone for the narrative in the histories of the other social sciences. Perhaps only Dorothy Ross (1991) has really made the connection between this moment in the national psyche and what was happening in economics.

For what happened in the other social sciences is exactly what happened in economics: the rise of scientism. In political science and in anthropology, in sociology and in economics, there was a quick and complete attempt after the war to abandon the earlier rhetoric of moral improvement and easy social progress. In its place, in each of these disciplines, came a new and different rhetoric of "science." Instead of moral suasion, social scientists were now to be involved in a hard-headed, clear-eyed project to uncover the "facts" about American society. In an attempt to distance themselves from their preachy and moralistic forebears, American social scientists donned their white lab coats and set to work in earnest after 1918. This movement in economics took the name of Institutionalism.

Institutionalism had many impulses, but it was very much a self-conscious effort on the part of its adherents to move away from the kind of pious moralizing and Protestant nationalism that had underpinned the Social Gospel. These men wanted to preserve, or re-establish, the scientific authority of economics and they felt that a part of that effort was going to have to be a carefully practiced empirical project that allowed them to make "scientific" statements about the economy.

This is a complex story which I have tried to limn in Bateman (2001), and which I cannot possibly try to repeat here. But in this regard I must say that I am perfectly in line with Dorothy Ross and with the historians of all the other American social science disciplines.

For the purposes of the argument in this paper, several things need to be briefly noted about this new scientific movement and its secularizing impulse.

(1) For the first time in American economics, a *group* of economists with no interest in *détente* with marginal analysis was seriously pursuing institutionalist, historical analysis.[3]
(2) The Institutionalists had no interest in making or strengthening a Protestant America and, in fact, had an explicitly secularist agenda.
(3) For almost all other American economists, the great majority of whom continued to respect both forms of analysis, this awkward moment presented something completely new and different. They would easily recognize some aspects of the Institutionalists' program as stemming from their own interests in historical analysis and for any number of reasons may not have been completely hostile to it.

As I have suggested above, this third point would account for the apparent confusion one might observe in a place like Chicago in the 1920s, why Institutionalist and marginalist thinkers seemed to co-exist together so easily and even to engage in a little cross-dressing. But it is in the first two points that the real evidence for *the importance of Institutionalism as a category of historical analysis* lies.

3. CONCLUSION

Without denying that Institutionalism is important as a style of economic analysis, or that it is important for its contributions to American political history, I would like to make the argument that the particular way that it was launched led to some of the particular characteristics of neo-classical economics *as it ultimately developed* in America after the Second World War. I do not want to argue that the way that American economics developed between 1918 and 1950 was completely pre-determined by the particular way that Institutionalism evolved, but I would like to argue that the overlay of events I have described above had an important effect on the ultimate formation of mainstream, American neo-classical economics.

One of the obvious things that happened with the birth of Institutionalism was that a particular kind of respect for pluralism in American economics began to come undone. By taking an explicitly secularist stance and trying to distance themselves from the moralizing undertones (overtones?) of the Social Gospel, the Institutionalists were walking away from the balm that had healed Gilead. Soon enough, others would walk away from it, too; but the Institutionalists were the first to walk away. Within three decades of Institutionalism's rise, the rule in American economics would no longer be the mild appreciation for pluralism, as long as the work being undertaken was aimed at questions of social amelioration. The Institutionalists wanted to fight on the grounds of who could do science better, and the only ethical yardstick they wanted applied in this contest was the ethic of the scientist.

This is what they got, but they discovered that "scientists" play hard ball. "Science" turned out to be a rough and tumble enterprise, with little or no respect for decorum and gentlemanly deference. The idea that science was a world of the evenly measured consideration of empirical evidence turned out to be as naïve as the Social Gospelers' belief in moral improvement. Here we can think of Frank Knight's attack on Sumner Schlicter's textbook and ask ourselves if we can really remember anything this bald and unvarnished since the attacks by the classicists in the 1880s on Ely, Bemis, and Adams when these ethical economists were first forming the A.E.A.

But this points to another dimension of the emergence of Institutionalism from the older world of détente. When the historicists were yoked to the marginalists under the umbrella of the Social Gospel, everyone agreed that there was room to examine the conditions when government might appropriately intervene in the economy. They might not always agree when this was, but the tone of economics was one of earnest concern for examining the question of when intervention was desirable. But after the Institutionalists made the secular turn, and following the early success at introducing interventionist policies in the New Deal, the new economic scientists found themselves in the early 1940s in a bare-knuckled world in which there were people who were seriously committed to establishing that laissez-faire was the only legitimate option. For some economists, there was no more need to pretend to be interested in social melioration by this time; the market was the best answer to the "social problem" in their eyes, and they were willing to fight to make their point.[4]

And, of course, the basis of their argument would become the person we now know as rational economic man. Now, as I have argued above, the man who calculated at the margin had been an accepted part of the German and American historical schools for many, many decades by the time that Institutionalism came on the scene. But historical economists, when they were yoked to marginal economists, had kept the marginally calculating man in a world in which he also made decisions on other bases. The marginally calculating man of 1890 went to church, was sometimes concerned for his race and his nation, and always was able to make some decisions regarding his family that did not involve any marginal thinking at all.[5] In short, marginal thinking was only one of the ways that he thought about how to act in the world.

But after the Institutionalists decided to fight in the scientific arena against a narrow kind of calculating man and lost, the marginally calculating man began an evolution toward the kind of ethically etiolated, narrow-minded rational economic man that we know today. This outcome was certainly not predictable, but it makes a lot of sense when you think about how it came about. The rational economic man of post-war neo-classicism is much easier to understand if you see him as the fallout from the currents that defined the emergence of Institutionalism.

NOTES

1. Marcia Balisciano (1998) explains the several influences on New Deal planning, of which Institutionalism was only one.

2. Steven Diner (1998) provides an excellent survey of the collapse of Progressivism after the First World War.

3. Malcolm Rutherford's account, during the round table discussions, of the early Institutionalists' desire to replace marginalist thinking in economic analysis was excellent. His essay in this symposium is an excellent reference in this point.

4. Anne Mayhew (1998) makes the argument that it was not until the 1940s that laissez-faire really got a firm footing among American economists in the twentieth century.

5. Thomas C. Leonard (2003) and Bradley Bateman (2003) discuss the racial dimension of the thinking of late nineteenth and early twentieth century American economists from different angles.

ACKNOWLEDGMENTS

I would like to thank Steven Medema and Mary Morgan for comments that helped me in revising the draft of this paper into its current form.

REFERENCES

Balisciano, M. (1998). Hope for America: American notions of planning between pluralism and neo-classicism, 1930–1950. In: M. S. Morgan & M. Rutherford (Eds), *From Interwar Pluralism to Postwar Neoclassicism. History of Political Economy*, *30* (Suppl.), 153–178.

Barber, W. J. (1996). *Designs within disorder: Franklin D. Roosevelt, the economists, and American economic policy, 1933–1945*. Cambridge: Cambridge University Press.

Bateman, B. W. (1998). Clearing the ground: The demise of the social gospel and the rise of neo-classicism in American economics. In: M. S. Morgan & M. Rutherford (Eds), *From Interwar Pluralism to Postwar Neoclassicism. History of Political Economy*, *30* (Suppl.), 29–52.

Bateman, B. W. (2001). Make a righteous number: Social surveys, the men and religion forward movement, and quantification in American economics. In: M. S. Morgan & J. L. Klein (Eds), *The Age of Economic Measurement. History of Political Economy*, *33* (Suppl.), 57–85.

Bateman, B. W. (2003). Race, intellectual history, and American economics: A prolegomenon to the past. *History of Political Economy*, *35*(4), 735–752.

Cohen, N. (2002). *The reconstruction of American liberalism, 1865–1914*. Chapel Hill: University of North Carolina Press.

Diner, S. (1998). *A very different age: Americans in the progressive era*. New York: Hill and Wang.

Dorfman, J. (1949). *The economic mind in American civilization Vol. 3, 1865–1918*. New York: Viking Press.

Dorfman, J. (1955). The role of the German historical school in American economic thought. *American Economic Review Supplement*, *45*(May), 17–28.

Leonard, T. C. (2003). More merciful and not less effective: Eugenics and American economics in the progressive era. *History of Political Economy*, *35*(4), 709–734.

Mayhew, A. (1998). How American economists came to love the Sherman antitrust act. In: M. S. Morgan & M. Rutherford (Eds), *From Interwar Pluralism to Postwar Neoclassicism. History of Political Economy*, *30* (Suppl.), 179–202.

Morgan, M. S., & Rutherford, M. (1998). American economics: The character of the transformation. In: M. S. Morgan & M. Rutherford (Eds), *From Interwar Pluralism to Postwar Neoclassicism. History of Political Economy*, *30* (Suppl.), 1–28.

Ross, D. (1991). *The origins of American social science*. Cambridge: Cambridge University Press.

Rutherford, M. (1997). American institutionalism and the history of economics. *Journal of the History of Economic Thought*, *19*(2), 178–195.

Streissler, E. W. (1990). The influence of German economics on the work of Menger and Marshall. In: B. J. Caldwell (Ed.), *Carl Menger and his Legacy in Economics. History of Political Economy*, *22* (Suppl.), 31–68.

Yuval, Y. (1998). *The struggle over the soul of economics: Institutionalist and neoclassical economics in America between the wars*. Princeton: Princeton University Press.

J. DANIEL HAMMOND, NORMA JEANE MORTENSON, AND AMERICAN INSTITUTIONALISM: A VIEW FROM THE TOP ROW

Steven G. Medema

Is "institutionalism" a useful historiographic category for describing a particular "school of" or "approach to" economics in the inter-war period? This must be an important question to consider because Dan Hammond is both a very bright fellow and an excellent scholar of the history of economic thought, and because a group of scholars as distinguished as Brad Bateman, Ross Emmett, Malcolm Rutherford, and Warren Samuels agreed to sit down with Hammond and discuss these issues in front of an audience for 75 minutes. And a large (and intellectually diverse) audience it was, which itself lends credence to the idea that Hammond's question is one of some import for historians of economics.

Against this we have the discussion itself, both as it played out at the conference session and as reflected in the contributions printed here. Hammond's suggestion that "institutionalism" may well not be an overly useful historiographic category has been met with across-the-board disagreement from his fellow roundtable participants, as the reader has no doubt already seen. These gentlemen, intellectual historians all, each possessing no small amount of expertise in the sociology of the U.S. economics profession during the interwar period, and two of whom (Rutherford and Samuels) even either self-identify with or have considerable sympathy for institutionalism, offer a slew of reasons why the answer to Hammond's question is

Research in the History of Economic Thought and Methodology A Research Annual
Research in the History of Economic Thought and Methodology, Volume 22-A, 203–210
Copyright © 2004 by Elsevier Ltd.
ISSN: 0743-4154/doi:10.1016/S0743-4154(03)22012-5

unambiguously, "yes." It would appear, then, that it is not any sort of controversial nature that makes Hammond's question intellectually stimulating. What is it, then?

The question of the historiographic import of the descriptor, "institutionalism," in the interwar period can be assessed from a number of perspectives, some of them more sophisticated and some less so. In attempting to lay out a subset of these themes here, I hope both to shed some light on Hammond's original question and to illuminate some of the larger issues that make this such an interesting question.

1. BACKGROUND

The very subject of this roundtable and published symposium suggests that there is something going on, some smoke, here – that there is some distinction that scholars past and present have found it useful to make, legitimately or not, between American institutionalism on the one hand and, say, classical, neoclassical, Keynesian, and Austrian economics in the interwar period. One problem, of course, is that examining how "x" is different from "y" requires a specification of both what constitutes "x" and what constitutes "y." Put another way, figuring out what constitutes "institutionalism" simultaneously requires defining "not institutionalism," both *in toto* and its constituent elements. This is not an easy task when even the question of what it means to be "Keynesian" admits to no small number of (or even consistent) answers. And indeed, one could just as well ask whether "neoclassical" is useful as an historiographic category during this period.[1]

That having been said, our issue here is that of institutionalism and of what it means to speak of institutionalists and institutionalism in the interwar period. This period is one during which the classical hegemony had given way and the neoclassical hegemony was still a ways off. Marginalism and historicism had moved into the picture in a significant way in the U.S., though classical economics continued to play an important role. American economics was an incredibly pluralistic enterprise – much more so than in, say, Britain, where the Cambridge school very much set the tone and the historical school had been largely swept aside by the Marshallian tide.[2]

2. SELF-IDENTIFICATION

Perhaps the most basic take on Hammond's question involves the straightforward application of basic economic theory – revealed preference. Beginning in 1918, a group of individuals self-identified as institutionalists – some sooner, such as Walton Hamilton, and others later, such as J. R. Commons. Something was going on that led these individuals to self-identify in this way and also to advocate that others follow their lead. The question is, what? That is, why, within a very pluralistic discipline, did a group – and this particular group – of scholars feel the need to identify themselves as somehow different and, in particular, as "institutionalists"? And what did it mean that they did so?

Brad Bateman has suggested that the emergence of institutionalism around 1918 coincides with a breakdown in the détente that characterized the pluralist period. Were these newly self-identifying "institutionalists" leaders or followers in the breakdown? That is, is institutionalism an instance of "cause," or "effect?" Those who identified themselves as and with institutionalists clearly saw themselves as doing something that was both important and different from that which everyone else was doing. But to what extent were they? Were those who self-identified as institutionalists significantly different in their approach to economics from those who did not so identify? Rutherford suggests yes; Hammond suggests not. Does the self-identification that we observed in the teens and twenties of the last century mean something different than the self-identification that we see today? Did the "rebel" aspect loom as large then as it does among those who self-identify today? One certainly sees evidence of competing paradigms from some self-identifying interwar institutionalists and complementarity from others. Perhaps all of this depends on what it means to be an institutionalist – or what it meant then and what it means now. We shall return to this subject below.

But regardless of the underlying motivation, the fact that this self-identification happened at all makes institutionalism an important historiographic category.[3] The answers to the questions that this self-identification process raises can inform our understanding of U.S. economics in the interwar period. At the very least, institutionalism is useful as a movement to be analyzed from a sociology of the profession perspective, even if one were to conclude that institutionalism is not an important category in an economic theory sense.

3. OTHER IDENTIFICATION

The identification issue has another side: that of labeling *someone else*, or what we might call "other identification." To say that someone is a member of group "x" – in this case, an institutionalist – does not make it so and, in fact, can create as much ambiguity as it resolves.[4] Modern institutionalists claim Thorstein Veblen and J. R. Commons as forefathers. Yet, the differences between Veblen and Commons may well be as great as their similarities. In fact, each of these men was referred to as an "outlier" (in different ways, of course) among early institutionalists by one or more members of the roundtable panel. There is also no small amount of irony in the fact that the institutionalists of the modern era have been more than happy to claim Nobel Laureate Gunnar Myrdal as one of their own, even though Myrdal himself never self-identified or in any way associated with them. On the other hand, there was no grab made for Ronald Coase or for Douglass North consequent their Nobel awards, even though both avowedly claim to be "institutionalists," albeit in the "new" sense rather than in the Veblen-Commons-Ayres-Association For Evolutionary Economics sense. Strangely enough, the rise of the "new" institutionalism gave rise to a slew of articles and symposia in the 1990s of the "what's wrong with the 'new' institutional economics" variety.[5]

There is also the issue of identification by critics. In the case of institutionalism, the label has been used pejoratively, particularly by members of the Chicago school, in order to denigrate and even dismiss as irrelevant the work of the recipient of this label. And even positive statements emanating from non-institutionalists seem to damn with faint praise, as in Coase's (1964, p. 196) statement that "we have less to fear from institutionalists who are not theorists than from theorists who are not institutionalists." "Institutionalism" is, among other things, a label or a category that functions as whipping boy for things critics don't like.

The whole issue of other identification is bound up in matters of theory and methodology on the one hand, and ideology on the other. In fact, at times criticisms of institutionalism ostensibly made on the former ground are in fact masks for criticisms of an ideological nature. Harold Demsetz has even gone so far as to suggest that these two factors are justly linked – that what he sees as "the antitheoretical bent" of institutionalism is "politically motivated" and "explainable by the desire to be shorn of the constraints that the theory did impose on political action" – that is, "highlighting the indirect effects in a way that those who want to intervene would like to be without" (Kitch 1983, pp. 175, 174). The hands of the institutionalists are not without blood here either, as many of them would vociferously contest the commonalities between institiutionalism and the Chicago school that Hammond correctly points to in his enlightening commentary.

These intramural scrums wrapped up in "other identification," too, are indicative of the import of institutionalism as an historiographic category. That some scholars would see fit to directly differentiate others from themselves by identifying them out of the institutionalist clan, or that others would apply the label "institutionalist" as a pejorative, works in tandem with the self-identification issue to speak to the professional, and thus historiographic, import of the term.

4. DEFINING "INSTITUTIONALISM"

So, the theory of revealed preference – an economics of economics, as it were – tells us that institutionalism is indeed important as an historiographic category.

In actual application, however, assessing the usefulness of any historiographic category requires a definition of that which one seeks to assess – in this case, of institutionalism or what it means to be an institutionalist. There are several problems that one can point to on this front.

One is that there has never been a generally-accepted (in the profession-wide sense) definition of "institutionalism." Malcolm Rutherford has elaborated an extensive list of attributes that would go into such a definition, although that list has been pared down to five more general points in his essay here. That, in itself, is symptomatic of the problem, and it raises the questions of: (i) how much of institutionalism one has to accept to be considered an institutionalist; and (ii) whether *anyone* could properly be considered an institutionalist. Indeed, one is left to wonder whether *any* of those who self-identified as institutionalists actually fit these criteria *in toto*.

Second, and as alluded to above, we enter the bounds of circularity and even infinite regress here, in that differentiation from the mainstream also requires some identification of mainstream – or at the very least what it is one is differing from. This is a difficult matter any time, but particularly so during a period as pluralist as that under consideration here. While, as Brad Bateman correctly points out, pluralism was beginning to wane, the fact of the matter remains (as Bateman would agree) that the "mainstream" church was still pretty broad through the interwar period and thus is difficult to define with any degree of specificity.

Third, part of the problem of historiographic categorization is that it is impossible to avoid the influence of present concerns and categories when thinking about the past. One can see evidence for this in all of the essays here, I think – the present one included. While historiographic fashion entails assailing anything that remotely smacks of "presentism" these days, the fact of the matter is that presentism is, as it were, an inevitable part of the historiographic condition. In this case, contemporary institutionalism affects the way we think about – and yes, even define – interwar institutionalism, doing so in ways both positive, negative, and neutral. In particular, one is left to wonder whether being an institutionalist really implied as much, definitionally, in the inter-war period as it does today.

5. USE AND ABUSE OF THE GHOST OF INSTITUTIONALISM PAST

This historiographic interplay between institutionalism past and present has many facets. Consider, for example, the question of the extent to which the interwar institutionalists were dissenters. Institutionalism was much less heterodox then than it is now, and leading institutionalists were also prominent members of the professional hierarchy. This raises a host of questions regarding what it meant to be an institutionalist in the interwar period.

One such question is, was "institutionalism" then like game theory or econometrics today – part of the accepted toolkit for an economist, employed by some and not by others – a different, but very legitimate or "mainstream" way of looking at important economic problems? Today we have game theory, general equilibrium theory, econometrics, experimental economics – mainstream all, even if each is subject to criticism from other quarters within the mainstream. Was institutional economics in the interwar period thought of in a similar way? If yes, this suggests that institutional economics in the interwar period was more akin to an approach or a toolkit or a way of doing economics than a distinctive dissenting "school," as it is today.

The extent to which institutionalism then differs from institutionalism now affects our understanding of the evolution of the profession in the twentieth century as well. For example, it says something about the validity of the claims made by modern institutionalists as to the degree that they have been marginalized because "the mainstream moved." It is unquestionable that the boundaries of what passes for orthodoxy narrowed over most of the course of the 20th century.[6] However, institutionalism was not static, either. If there was a golden mean of pluralism, both neoclassicism and institutionalism moved away from it in the post-war period.

This sword has a second edge, too. While it is fairly commonplace to see references to the mainstream attitude toward institutionalism then and now, an equally important issue here is the attitude of institutionalists toward the mainstream then and now. Samuels has suggested that all institutionalists have some neoclassicism and some Marx in them. "Some" obviously makes for a rather varied brew, depending on the proportions of the ingredients. Institutionalists of the interwar period clearly shared with the Marxists a concern for issues beyond value and distribution, but they also shared with neoclassicals an affinity for the market system, although perhaps with a more reformist attitude.

The evidence, I believe, suggests that the mix of neoclassicism and Marxism in the average institutionalist today is much less weighted toward the former than it was in the interwar period – that, in fact, the degree of hostility toward the mainstream evidenced by those who identify themselves as institutionalists is significantly greater today than it was seventy or eighty years ago. Whereas many institutionalists in this earlier era found aspects of classical and marginalist economics useful for the analysis of certain types of economic problems, wholesale rejection of everything that smacks of neoclassicism (including the "new" institutionalism) is a hallmark of contemporary institutionalism.

To suggest, then, that the mainstream evolved into something totally hostile to non-mainstream ideas such as institutionalism from the 1950s onward ignores the role played by changes in institutionalism over this period, and the attendant implication that institutionalism played a role in its own marginalization. This, then, is another piece of evidence for the usefulness of institutionalism as an historical category in the interwar period: it is an aid to understanding the present state of institutional economics, as well as to assessing the legitimacy of certain historiographic claims made by those who, in the modern era, identify themselves as heirs of this earlier tradition.

6. CONCLUSION

To return to our earlier question regarding what makes Dan Hammond's question interesting: the fact that several prominent scholars spent a bunch of time arguing with each other about *why they are in agreement* is suggestive of the reasons for the provocative nature of this issue, the fact that this conversation carried on for the remainder of the conference, and why the audience found this session so interesting and entertaining.

Institutionalism arose as a uniquely American movement[7] and the first American "school" of any real significance. It also arose during a uniquely American period in economics. Britain, having moved more or less seamlessly from classical to marginalist-Marshallian dominance, did not have the pluralist moment that characterized the U.S. in the first few decades of the twentieth century. Institutionalism also has a Norma Jeane Mortenson[8] quality about it: its candle burned out relatively quickly, in terms of wielding significant professional influence, but it remains a source of significant historical curiosity.

It is fairly obvious that there is something about this categorization that is important, but it is very hard to pin down what it is – in no small part owing to the somewhat problematic nature of attempts to clearly define "institutionalism" in that era (or any other, frankly). It should be clear from the foregoing discussion, as well as from the other contributions published here, that the definition of institutionalism varies with one's vantage point. What is and is not institutionalism, who is and who is not an institutionalist, admit to no singular answers – they didn't in the interwar period, and they certainly don't in retrospect. But then, as noted above, the same can be said of neoclassicism.

The top row of the stadium is a lousy vantage point from which to view a football match, but the best seat in the house for quidditch;[9] the converse is true for, say, seats in the fifth row. That is, it is not just the location of the observer that matters, but the location of the object as well. It is in the intersection that phenomena such as interwar institutionalism (and, I would argue, pop culture) take on their historiographic meaning and import.

NOTES

1. David Colander (2000) has recently declared that "neoclassical" is no longer useful as a descriptive category.

2. One can find ample discussion of this subject in the recent volume edited by Morgan and Rutherford (1998), as well as in the contributions to this symposium.

3. Another economic take on this, from the "what is, is efficient" department, is that it must be useful and important because historians of economics have been using it as a descriptor for many decades.

4. The fact that the present author came away from the roundtable discussion more confused than he was when it began either supports this contention or speaks to the general state of mind of the author.

5. The new institutionalists, for their part, have pretty much ignored the old.

6. A legitimate argument can be made that this trend was reversed in the 1990s, although not to the extent that institutionalists are much nearer to the mainstream than they were before.

7. Yes, the American institutionalists were trained by members of the German Historical School, but the effect, in practice, was very much distinct from historicism.

8. Norma Jeane Mortenson evolved into Marilyn Monroe.

9. The reader who is not familiar with the sport of quidditch may consult any of the volumes of the Harry Potter book series for further information.

REFERENCES

Coase, R. H. (1964). Discussion. *American Economic Review*, 54(May), 194–198.

Colander, D. (2000). The death of neoclassical economics. *Journal of the History of Economic Thought*, 22(June), 127–143.

Morgan, M., & Rutherford, M. (Eds) (1998). The transformation of American economics: From interwar pluralism to postwar neoclassicism. *History of Political Economy Annual Supplement* (Vol. 30). Durham, NC: Duke University Press.

REFLECTIONS ON INSTITUTIONAL AND CHICAGO ECONOMICS

J. Daniel Hammond

I will use Malcolm Rutherford's paper, "Chicago Economics and Institutionalism," as the basis for general comments about the historical enterprise of writing and evaluating the history of institutional economics (or institutionalism). In doing so I will take liberties with Rutherford's paper, some of which he may not approve. The thrust of my comments is to take Rutherford's thesis ("There is an important sense in which Chicago economics has always been institutional," p. 21) and run with it to find implications for the very idea of institutional economics. My conclusion is that the category institutional economics (or institutionalism) may have little historiographic value.

Consider the large cast of Chicago faculty and students who appear in Rutherford's account. They are sorted into three groups in Table 1: institutionalists, critics of institutionalism, and others. I've used Rutherford's account to sort them, and you may disagree with what he writes about the individuals' relationships with institutionalism or with my interpretation of what Rutherford writes. But in any event, it is clear from his paper that there is a rich vein of institutionalism/institutional economics in the history of University of Chicago economics.

Chicago can claim the founders of institutionalism, John M. Clark, Wesley Mitchell, and Walton Hamilton; the first person to identify himself as an institutional economist, Robert Hoxie; and a key precursor, Thorstein Veblen. There are a host of persons who studied or taught at Chicago and have one or more attributes of institutionalism. Among Chicago critics of institutional economics, credible cases have been made that Frank Knight (by Hodgson, 2001), George Stigler (some evidence, but not argument, in Rutherford's paper), and Ronald Coase (by

Research in the History of Economic Thought and Methodology A Research Annual
Research in the History of Economic Thought and Methodology, Volume 22-A, 211–215
© 2004 Published by Elsevier Ltd.
ISSN: 0743-4154/doi:10.1016/S0743-4154(03)22013-7

Table 1.

Institutionalists	Critics	Others
Thorstein Veblen	Ronald Coase	Laurence Laughlin
Wesley Mitchell	George Stigler	John Dewey
Robert Hoxie	Frank Knight	Henry Simons
Clarence Ayers	Henry Schultz	Lloyd Mints
Walton Hamilton	Jacob Viner	Milton Friedman
John M. Clark		Rose Director Friedman
Harold Moulton		AaronDirector
Edwin Nourse		Allen Wallis
Sumner Slichter		Oscar Lange
Katherine Bement Davis		Theodore Yntema
Sophonisba Breckenridge		Jacob Marschak
Edith Abbott		Tjalling Koopmans
Chester Wright		T. W. Schultz
Harry Millis		Abba Lerner
James Field		Friedrich Hayek
Paul Douglas		Earl Hamilton
Harold Innis		Edward Levi
Hazel Kyrk		Harold Demsetz
Morris Copeland		James Buchanan
Carter Goodrich		Warren Nutter
Helen Wright		Gary Becker
John Nef		Jacob Mincer
Margaret Reid		Karl Llewellyn
Ruth Allen		Richard Posner
Abram Harris		

Medema, 1996) are themselves similars of institutionalists. I have argued (2000) that Friedman is a similar as well. So who among 20th century Chicago economists is clearly not at all an institutional economist? Jacob Viner, Henry Schultz, and Oscar Lange perhaps. Others? If there are not many prominent Chicago economists who stand clearly and totally apart from institutional economics, and if leaders of the "Chicago School" such as Knight, Stigler, Coase, and Friedman are institutional economists, then something is amiss in our (or my!) conception of institutionalism. Has anyone compiled a database on the history of the use of the term institutionalist, perhaps broken down into cases of self-identification by people who claim to be institutionalists, as a category for criticism by opponents of institutionalism, and by historians of economics as historians?

Walton Hamilton argued in 1918 that anything that:

"aspired to the name of economic theory" had to be (i) capable of giving unity to economic investigations of many different areas; (ii) relevant to the problem of control; (iii) relate to institutions as both the "changeable elements of economic life and the agencies through which they are to be directed;" (iv) concerned with "process" in the form of institutional change and development; and (v) based on an acceptable theory of human behavior, one in harmony with the "conclusions of modern social psychology" (quoted from Rutherford, 2002, p. 4).

In "Understanding Institutional Economics" Rutherford writes about institutionalism from 1918 through the 1920s:

> In the most general terms the institutionalist research program can be stated as being based on the following set of propositions: that social and legal institutions have central importance in the determination of economic behavior and economic performance . . . that these institutions evolve over time, are changeable and can be changed by policy intervention; that the existing economic system is one dominated by business or pecuniary institutions; that these existing institutions do not necessarily work to the social advantage; that the old forms of control of business (in particular, competitive markets) have been overtaken by new technical and economic conditions, requiring new forms of social control (2000, pp. 289–290).

In these and other definitions there is lots of room to squeeze people in or out of the set of institutionalists. I wonder how people who have, in explicit terms, positioned themselves inside or outside the group have done so.

It may be that institutionalism is defined not so much by what it is as by what it is not. Throughout Rutherford's paper there are instances of institutionalism being delineated by what it is not. As he remarks at the beginning of the paper, "for most economists the terms 'Chicago economics' and 'institutionalism' denote clearly antithetical approaches to the discipline." Institutionalism is not just different from Chicago economics, but antithetical to it. Presumably when Ronald Coase declared that American institutionalists were anti-theoretical he was suggesting both that he was not an institutionalist and that his economics was theoretical. Rutherford writes that Laurence Laughlin was not an institutionalist; he was "extremely conservative in his economics and political views, and very much at odds with the historicist or 'new' school influence in American economics" (2002, p. 2). Paul Douglas's "neoclassical theory" places him outside institutionalism, but his reform sensibility, championing of underconsumptionist ideas, and support for Veblen's nomination as AEA president place him within. Aaron Director is outside by being "a leading member of the group that gathered around Frank Knight" (2002, p. 9). Henry Schultz is out by virtue of criticizing institutionalism by name. Viner is out by defending qualitative neoclassical theory from Mitchell's critique, but in by not being opposed to various types of intervention. Knight is out by criticizing scientism, behaviorism, and policy intervention, but in by not being an orthodox neoclassical and having deep interests in institutional change. Knight also is out as are his most prominent students for using the "as if" approach to rational choice theory, being a critic of monopolistic competition, having a favorable view of the competitive price system, and for his classical liberal philosophy. By the mid-1940s we can identify Chicago non-institutionalists by their opposition to Keynesianism and monopolistic competition, and their pro-market, anti-regulatory stances.

Three analogies come to my mind: families, sports fans, and religion. You all know me as Dan Hammond. But I am equally Dan Windell (mother's maiden name), Dan Mackey (paternal grandmother), and Dan Epps (maternal grandmother). The possible family identifications multiply geometrically as we move back through family history. I met an economist at the ASSA meetings who is a serious genealogist. He told me that he has around 1200 surnames in his family database. If I told you about my family you would hear more about my Hammond and Windell relatives than my Mackey and Epps relatives, few of whom I have known. Lately I've discovered a rich source of genealogical information on the Mackeys, and as a result I've begun to think of myself as a Mackey more than heretofore. I also think of myself as a member of the Holton family. This membership is by marriage, but the bonds are in fact stronger than my bonds with Windells, Epps, and Mackeys. Not to belabor this, my point is that family associations are to a large extent arbitrary. There are systematic explanations of how people obtain their family identities, such as the conventions of taking ones father's surname, and for a male, keeping ones surname upon marriage. For me, my father's immediate family was larger than my mother's, so there were more aunts, uncles, and cousins on the Hammond side than the Windell side, and I married into a large and cohesive family of Holtons. But if we consider genetics separate from friendship and social relations I am no more Hammond than I am Epps, and considerably more Epps than Holton.

Fans of collegiate and professional sports ally themselves with particular teams. Sometimes the link is quite natural. The person is a student or faculty member at Wake Forest so they root for the Deacons. Someone lives in Liverpool so they root for the Reds. But fans also attach themselves to teams for a variety of reasons, to Duke basketball or Liverpool soccer because they win, to the Chicago Cubs because they lose, or to Wake Forest or NC State because they are not Duke or UNC. But, except for Duke fans, who do the work of the devil, which team one roots for is less important than having a team to root for. Choosing sides enriches the fan's experience of the game. Is this the case for economists as well?

Religious classification is less arbitrary than family or sports, even though people do their own sorting. There are clear lines between atheists and theists, between practicing Jews and Christians, and between Roman Catholics and Presbyterians. It seems to me that sorting economists into categories such as institutionalist and neoclassical is closer to genealogical sorting than either sports-fan or religious sorting. All economists of an era are pretty closely related, having much the same "genetic" makeup. Only at the tails of the distribution are differences sharp, and most people are not in the tails. For those who are, what puts them there? There do not seem to be bright lines of demarcation as with religious or sports team affiliation. With religion we can ask relatively simple questions about belief and practice, having confidence that sorting people on the basis of their answers is meaningful. Likewise with sports fans. But there are not bright-line questions for neoclassical and institutional economists. Or are there?

REFERENCES

Hammond, J. D. (2000). Columbia Roots of the Chicago School: The Case of Milton Friedman. Mimeo, December.

Hodgson, G. M. (2001). Frank Knight as an Institutionalist. In: J. Biddle, J. B. Davis & S. G. Medema (Eds), *Economics Broadly Considered: Essays in Honor of Warren J. Samuels*. London: Routledge.

Medema, S. G. (1996). Of pangloss, pigouvians and pragmatism: Ronald Coase and Social Cost Analysis. *Journal of the History of Economic Thought, 18*(Spring), 96–114.

Rutherford, M. (2000). Understanding Institutional Economics. *Journal of the History of Economic Thought, 22*(September), 277–308.

Rutherford, M. (2002). Chicago Economics and Institutionalism. Mimeo, December.

THE BUCHANAN COLLOQUIUM ON THE STATUS OF THE STATUS QUO: REPORTS ON A CONFERENCE

THE STATUS OF THE STATUS QUO:
THE BUCHANAN COLLOQUIUM

Warren J. Samuels

A conference was held at Virginia Tech, 29 May–June 1, 2003, underwritten by James M. Buchanan, on a theme of great significance to him, the status of the status quo. He has held that social change and economic policy must "start from here," meaning from where we are, the status quo. Six papers were presented, by Buchanan, Roger Faith, Hartmut Kliemt, Robert Tollison, Viktor Vanberg, and Geoffrey Brennan and Alan Hamlin. Other attendees included Noel Reynolds, Nicholas Tideman, Carl Dahlman, Robert Sugden, Deborah Mayo, Djavad Salehi, Aris Spanos, and this author. All were obvious admirers of Buchanan but not all were disciples; only one, this author, has been a critic of some aspects of his work.

The papers were distributed in early May. Shortly thereafter I wrote the comments constituting the second document below; it was distributed before the conference, thanks to Aris Spanos. This first document is an interpretive review of the conference itself. It focuses on the discussion rather than on the papers per se. Many if not all of the papers were labeled "draft." The organizers' intention is to publish final versions in a book.

Each conference paper was presented by an Introducer, who summarized its argument and presented a critique. The author both responded to and participated in discussion of the paper and whatever topics or issues arose in discussion. (In History of Economics Society meetings this format is called the Perlman system.) Members who wished to initiate a topic later raised a full hand; those who wished to join in the discussion of a current topic raised a finger – all run by a chair. Only one paper was considered in each one and one-half hour session.

Research in the History of Economic Thought and Methodology A Research Annual
Research in the History of Economic Thought and Methodology, Volume 22-A, 219–233
Copyright © 2004 by Elsevier Ltd.
ISSN: 0743-4154/doi:10.1016/S0743-4154(03)22014-9

It was not possible to record manually either all facets of the conversation or always who said what (especially in the case of the Brennan-Hamlin paper, whose session I chaired), though I have recorded what my notes indicate. Different reviewers would undoubtedly focus on different themes, though the identity (if not the entitling) of various topics is relatively unequivocal; in any case, the review is subjective. An effort was made not to duplicate description presented in the second document (written earlier). Apologies are in order if opinions have been misrepresented or wrongly attributed.

In the first document, the review of the conference, the sequence is that of the sessions of the conference. In the second document, the sequence is that which at the time of writing I thought most useful in presenting and criticizing arguments.

The first document is entitled "The Language, Theory and Methodology of 'The Status of the Status Quo,'" because the critical issues and themes have to do with those three topics. These issues and themes are, in part, the use of language to advance certain theories as definitional pictures of the world; the role of expectations vis-à-vis other bases of defining the status quo; the status quo as an equilibrium point vis-à-vis a process; that, apropos of a world of rules (as in rule of law), two problems were typically neglected: that individual rules could be variously interpreted and applied, and that plural rules are often in conflict, altogether permitting, even engendering, the exercise of deliberative choice it was the purpose of rules to constrain if not prevent; and so on. The conference manifested the use vs. the critique of general condemnations of government; terms without specific content; general models applied to specific institutional arrangements; the concepts of the status quo, productive and unproductive, rule of law, coercion, and voluntary; and rules that promote the "general interest" or constitute the "best solution" to a problem vs. rules giving effect to "special interests;" and so on. It is my view that these topics and issues often are the crux of developments in the history and methodology of economics. Such issues arose, in one way or another, throughout the conference; the circumstances of a conference prohibited intensive and uninterrupted analysis of any one of them.

My purpose, in addition to describing and critiquing what was said, is to identify and to establish the importance of these issues.

THE LANGUAGE, THEORY AND METHODOLOGY OF "THE STATUS OF THE STATUS QUO": AN INTERPRETIVE REVIEW OF A CONFERENCE

Prior to the first session I was asked about my view of rent seeking, mentioned in passing in the document of mine distributed earlier. I replied that my view had three parts. First, I agreed that rent seeking, however defined, was ubiquitous. Second, I argued that rent seeking is not bad per se. Third, I argued that I found particularly disgraceful treatments of the allocation of resources to efforts to change the law as bad rent seeking. Both this person and Jim Buchanan (later in the conference) insisted that rent seeking was objectionable when it involved a transfer without a gain in efficiency, i.e. the creation of something productive. I responded that this view substituted the analyst's definition of productive for that of the economic agent – who obviously believed that hiring a lawyer, etc. to help bring about a potential change in the law was a desirable, hence productive, use of his or her resources. I further insisted that this definition, especially when it was used in a blanket, indiscriminate way, functioned to privilege existing law and those benefiting from existing law and to deny people access to their government, and that it did so by manipulating the definition of rent seeking to give effect to selective antecedent normative premises hidden within the use of the term "productive" (in at least one discussion the term "artificial" was used). I pointed to this as a problem in the use of language. Further aspects of the terminology of rent seeking will be dealt with below.

The same initial interrogator indicated – in a well-rehearsed litany of complaints – several times then and later in the conference that redistributive welfare-state programs were dysfunctional for the ostensible beneficiaries. I did not ask whether such programs were the price paid for their quietude, and whether positions like his involved attempts to lower the price.

(1) James M. Buchanan's "The Status of the Status Quo" was presented and critiqued by Noel Reynolds. Inter alia, Reynolds made several points. (1) Economic analysis was a useful tool but can mislead or obscure larger truths. Specifically noted were Pareto optimality, unanimity, mental events (such as expectations), authority and obligation. (2) Natural law seen as universal values and moral truths, when pursued in practice, leads to great uncertainty. (3) Important problems pervade all relevant discussions, such as those of the public interest, majority rule, and the unanimity principle. He pointed out that the Constitution was only the second contract made by those attending the Philadelphia convention; the first was over the decision to produce and submit to a constitution, and this decision was unanimous. Included were expectations of obeying the rules, making new agreements within the rules, and the maintenance of unanimity, even with both winners and losers, through agreements made within the rule of law. Such reasoning tended to render nugatory Buchanan-like concerns over unanimity, rent seeking, rule of law and Pareto optimality. Use of Pareto optimality elevated change through markets over change through law (legal change). Rule of law was facilitative as well as constraining.

Nicholas Tideman, taking up the meaning of the status quo, suggested that it is not the way things are. It is shared expectations, based on history; hence it is a forward-looking concept (John R. Commons's notion of futurity is relevant here; as is his concept of forebearance, noted below). Expectations do not capture all aspects of the status quo, for example, its specific set of rules. Argument (over a rule) is a function of dissimilar expectations. The status quo is subjective, and not objective. This means that one does not always know it; i.e. there is not a given status quo.

Buchanan commented that the status quo is a laissez faire, not a conservative position; by laissez faire he meant change allowing and by conservative he meant continuity over change.

It was pointed out that "status quo" is the name given to an amorphous understanding; it has to do with language, not reality.

Reynolds indicated that we had a created reality (the idea of social reality created by human action but not by human design, came up several times during the conference) and produced shared expectations and beliefs as to the true and the good. But not all expectations are shared; disagreement results in the process of working things out. Agreement is a way of coordinating expectations.

Kliemt posed the conflict between the objectivity and the subjectivity of rules. I called attention to both conflicting plural rules and conflicts between different views of each rules. I also indicated that realism shares with idealism a necessity of choice: if everyone were a philosophical realist, they likely would disagree as to the content of reality, and have to choose. Buchanan emphasized agreement on the content of rules (I made written note of our different psychological positions but did not bring it up until later).

Reynolds called attention to two levels of subjectivity: the written law, as the basis of expectations, and subsequent efforts to change the game (this example comes up again, below). Then comes the process of working things out. Most controversies are not contested in the courts; they are resolved on the basis of (relatively objective) facts.

Dahlman commented that the status quo is a Hobbesian jungle; Buchanan and I agree, but he dislikes the fact; for me, that is the way it is (the topic also arises again, when the term "Hobbesian state" is acknowledged to refer to a condition and not a type of political unit).

Tideman said that politics is more than the enabling of mutual advantage; it is also the rectification of injustice, as the status quo has both good and bad. He opposes the idea that a non-positive sum game is necessarily destructive.

Sugden called attention to the necessity of norms in reaching political agreements. Kliemt did likewise to the Kantian position prohibiting one's use of another as only a means.

Buchanan questioned the relevance of my citing the case of guerillas. I said that sometimes revolution is necessary; if it is not possible, people are in a bad way.

Dahlman agreed that there is more to politics than public choice theory covers. I raised the point of out-of-sight manipulation by government and corporation personnel.

Discussion turned to the issue of a narrow vs. broad definition of self-interest.

I said that it was at least my hope that pluralism of belief has greater survival value than other forms.

(2) Faith's "Can We Know the Status Quo?" took up issues raised in the preceding discussion and impacting subsequent discussion (though not as much as they could, or should, have). These issues centered on whether one could define the status quo in terms of rules, beliefs, and so on, objectively, thereby making Buchanan's task easier, or only, or largely, subjectively. Faith's paper went "into some of the conceptual difficulties involved in knowing the status quo, and a fortiori, conceptual difficulties in granting any particular normative status to the status quo." The questions included: "How much time must pass before a given state is deemed the status quo? Does historical precedent have any place in the status quo? Are there temporal or spatial boundaries to the status quo? To whom and to what does the status quo refer?" Faith discusses issues of duration, precedent and priority, who belongs, and representation and knowledge. Faith does not oppose "granting status, normative or positive, to the status quo when contemplating policy changes that affect society." He does, however, identify "some sources of ambiguity in the concept of the status quo" and writes that "One somewhat negative conclusion from all this is that one may never truly know the status quo." This is one source of the principle of unintended and unforeseen consequences: "Consequently, when policy changes are proposed or instituted one is never quite certain of where they started or where they will end up."

Nic Tideman, the introducer of Faith's paper, identified the status quo in terms of "becoming" rather than "is." The status quo is dynamic, it is a matter of history (path dependence was stressed by others at various times); it is not a matter of the way things are because they are in a process of change. He, for one, is comfortable with the status quo changing, not merely existing. It is a matter of shared expectations, or probabilities, garnered from history.

At both this point and later points, several speakers introduced if not supported the idea of the status quo as an equilibrium concept. What mattered was its state in equilibrium, not how it got there. Objections to this were expressed. Tideman, for example, argued that the whole story of the status quo is more than the status quo defined as an equilibrium state.

Buchanan introduced the problem of why a new regime would honor the previous regime's debt. An extended discussion centered on legitimacy vs. prudential arguments. (Legitimacy connoted what everyone agrees to. Prudential arguments included maintaining credit with lenders.) Tideman raised the possibility of an international agreement that approved, but established conditions for, repudiation. Buchanan suggested the issue was whether policy would confiscate the property of the bondholders (through repudiation) or of the taxpayers (through having to finance payment).

Dahlman reported upon his experience in the Reagan Administration, namely, being told to "undo something." I pointed out that if the something in place was protecting A's interest from B, undoing that meant protecting B's interest from A, and that analytically the two situations were equivalent; the only difference was in whose interest was being protected, and that is what economic politics is all about. (Of course, the A interests to be undone, on the basis of the Reagan program, were rather distinct: welfare, environmental and other similar interests.) Dahlman concurred with the logic of my analytical point. Kliemt, however, suggested that to undo violates expectations as to what is, which has prima facie legitimacy. (Again, the question is whose expectations, e.g. those of people who "expect" their protection to endure indefinitely, or those of people who look forward to changing in their favor protection now advantaging others – two different views of the content of the status quo.)

Tideman returned to an earlier discussion, offering what he considered an alternative to the "we start from here" argument. The alternative centered on one of John Locke's provisos, that we leave unto others the same as we take.

Reynolds suggested that the status quo can be seen as rules plus the preconditions for the change of rules, which become principles of the rule of law. In discussion, someone defined the rule of law as meaning no discrimination between persons. (Where law must choose between conflicting interests, no such definition will do.) Buchanan referred to an exchange between Richard Epstein and Antonin Scalia, with Buchanan siding with Scalia, in which Epstein affirmed (what he took to be) the original right and the others the extant right.

Brennan posed a different question from Faith's "can we know the status quo?," namely, "what can we know of the status quo?" His view was that the status quo is not akin to a stable utility vector, that all members of the status quo in effect hold lottery tickets with uncertain probabilistic values. He wondered whether differences in expectations create problems and not contingencies per se. (All this emphasizes problematicity, and not an objective unique determinate concrete status quo.)

Tideman emphasized, in reply, probabilism as a function of attitudes toward risk.

The different positions can be combined, e.g. problematicity (and probabilism) generates contingency that leads to differential expectations.

Tideman again stressed that there was more to the definition of the status quo than exchange (and therefore more to public choice than market-like exchange).

Spanos, an econometrician, suggested a definition (from modeling) in terms of initial structure and conditions, dynamics, and stochastic trajectory, i.e. path dependence.

It was pointed out that (say, technological) change can render traditional rules objectionable and thereby create the necessity to reinvent the rules (e.g. from horse and buggy to the automobile).

Brennan raised the problem of whether it was necessary to know what the status quo is. If the status quo is A, change is change in A; if B, then change in B. For some changes, policy action does not need to know the status quo; e.g. egalitarian policy and agreements on contract.

At several points in the discussion, Faith's example of a protective tariff came to the foreground. Is the status quo the tariff, partial or whole repeal of the tariff, or some ideal state without tariffs? This is reminiscent of Plato's emphasis on the ideal derived from the (more or less temporary) actual vs. Aristotle's emphasis on the actual since it does exist (quite aside from defining the actual, or the real).

(3) Hartmut Kliemt's paper, "Contractarianism as Liberal Conservatism: Buchanan's (Un-)finished Philosophical Agenda," raised the prospect of different types of conservatism and of contractarianism. His view is that Buchanan's type of contractarianism is a formal type of conservatism that grants normative status to the status quo and possibly blends into classical liberalism, such that a specific form of conservatism, not the idea of contract per se, should be seen as the core of Buchanan-type contractarianism. As Spanos, who introduced Kliemt's paper, suggested, Buchanan's bottom line emphasized unanimous agreement and appeal to some ethical norm or criterion: Agreement alone is not the source of legitimacy; the classical liberal claim is to have a society in which individuals can decide as much as possible themselves; and insofar as maximizing agreement and minimizing coercion are sources of legitimacy, these can be pursued without unanimous agreement. Unmentioned was the facts that no conservative wants to retain everything in the status quo and that the issue may be the retention of the particular dominant mode of change in the status quo, not the substance of the status quo itself.

Among the points made in discussion were the following:

Buchanan's view that hypothetical agreement is useful – as a heuristic, not as a legitimizing principle – in reaching actual agreement.

The problem of the meaning of coercion and its implications. Given an array of meanings, any particular principle may not apply equally and may lead policy astray (Samuels). The avoidance of coercion is an illusion; some coercion cannot be avoided (Kliemt). Utilitarianism has the defect of leading to coercion (e.g. mandatory loss of a kidney for transplant purposes – though perhaps not in a club organized voluntarily for such a purpose).

Pragmatic adjustment is engendered by the need to adapt to a (changed) situation.

Property is a contingent claim to decision-making rights with regard to scarce goods, within social structure, courts, etc.

A set of rules governing exchange is necessary.

(4) Robert Tollison's paper, introduced by Carl Dahlman, was entitled "The Status of the Status Quo." It used the theory of rent seeking combined with Arnold Harberger's model of monopoly as extended to rent seeking by Gordon Tullock. Tollison's argument was "the futility of economic reform of existing deformities in the economic order," that "Genuine reform should ignore the past and possibly look to the future;" it should accept existing deformities and seek to prevent new ones from emerging, and that "the *status quo* has a strong analytical rationale in a world with rent seeking." And again, "there is much to recommend the *status quo* in a general interest world . . . it is hard to avoid the conclusion that it is best to let the rent seekers prevail (let the big dogs eat)."

Dahlman referred to "Bob's simple model." Tollison said it is "not a picture of reality." Vanberg later countered that it does relate to, or is, reality.

I made a number of points critical of Tollison's argument. These had to do with the use of analytical tools to define reality; Ronald Coase's criticism of "blackboard economics; and that the legal-economic system included two processes, one centering on production and efficiency, the other on the decision-making process, including rights of access to government and for weighting preferences between individuals – the latter involving the use of resources in order to change the law and rights (this point is similar to another, that Tollison's model is used by him and others to deal with matters which go far beyond it. Later I argued against evaluating the allocation of resources to changing the structure or process of decision making by the economic theory of exchange and production. (I used the illustration of using legal services both within and to change the system of land registration and transfer – full well knowing that these systems were instituted and revised by rent-seeking interests.) I also drew a comparison with capital theory. Advocates of different theories of capital strongly tend to assume that only one theory of capital is possible whereas the theories are tools instrumental in and enabling the understanding of different aspects of capital. Different theories of the status quo, of rent seeking, and of other topics need not, therefore be treated in an either-or manner.

Salehi contended that Tollison's was an inept one-period policy model.

Tideman returned to his earlier point. One criterion of the status quo could be utility or benefit or GDP maximization. Another could be equitable results. Buying off holders of presently held rights (successful past rent seekers) creates expectations of future buying off. The issue was "do nothing" (Tollison) or "buy off" (others).

Vanberg argued that economic reform is about playing a better game, and has both benefits and costs. The costs here are due to the strategies of the players.

Buchanan indicated, first, that he dislikes the term "rent seeking" but has found no suitable alternative; and second, that, yes, the Harberger-Tullock model is simple but Harberger could not understand Tullock's identification of the diagram's area of rent-seeking (as opposed to monopoly) waste.

Tollison argued that representative government allows and engenders rent-seeking waste (see below). In response, Brennan maintained that rent seeking is part of politics, and that to suppress it would be a cure worse than the disease; it amounts to the cost of government.

Vanberg articulated a position that juxtaposed the creation of "the best rules possible" to rules amounting to privileges for rent-seeking "special interests." I argued that the category of "the best rules possible" was a primitive term, that we possessed no conclusive means of distinguishing "the best rules possible" from rules favoring "special interests," that rule making did typically favor one interest over another, and that (following George Stigler) economic agents did pursue their self-interest in their political affairs as they did in their economic affairs. I claimed that having passing in football, smaller or larger strike zones in baseball, or different blocking rules in football, involved favoring one interest over another in each case (that day the newspapers had articles with data on home runs (large strike zone) vs. hit batters (small strike zone); and that owner perceptions and interests in revenue maximization tended strongly to dictate rule changes. I offered hanging on the rim as a candidate of a different type of case.

Buchanan remarked that he found bitching at referees by coaches highly objectionable. I pointed out that, consistent with Vilfredo Pareto's model of mutual psychological manipulation, coaches were trying to manipulate the psychology of referees.

Dahlman suggested that instead of trying to attack rent seekers, policy should seek to limit the producers of rent (see below).

Buchanan characterized his position as the Knightian one of relatively absolute absolutes – thereby acknowledging the force of criticism of his position but maintaining his position intact.

(5) Robert Sugden introduced Viktor Vanberg's paper, "The Status Quo in Contractarian Constitutionalist Perspective." The crux of the argument is the search for mutual benefit – understood in the context of exchange and Pareto optimality – and is clearly stated by Vanberg in the following terms: "It is an argument about how we should proceed from here, namely by peaceful, contractual means rather than by coercion and violence, it is not an argument for leaving things as they are. It is an argument not in terms of the merits of the status quo but in terms of the merits of contractual change compared to its alternative,

change by coercion and violence." The argument, of course, posits change through market exchange as non-coercive vs. change through government as coercive – ignoring, for example, past and present exercises of coercion in markets.

Vanberg also says that his "exclusive concern in this paper is with the *constitutional status quo* and with the issue of *constitutional reform*. To be sure, calls for constitutional reform, i.e. for changes in the rules of the game may of course, be motivated by discontent with the pattern of distributional outcomes that result from status quo rules. But it is the concern with changes in the rules themselves, not in outcomes per se, that is of principal interest here. And it is the constitutional status quo, the existing 'structure of legal order' . . . that Buchanan defines as the 'here.' " The argument that "we start from here" has the homely appeal of a simple truth: given the problems of identifying or defining the status quo, any change is from it. But Buchanan's formulaic position has another function, namely, to obfuscate and ignore how the status quo came into existence. Taking that into consideration not only raises normative issues but casts positive light on both the status quo and proposals to change it. In a world of giants and pygmies, in which the giants became giants through the capture and use of government, such is relevant to the claims of the giants and their ideological and/or hired spokespeople, that the existing structure of power and how it came to be should be ignored. Such a view reinforces efforts to transfer change to the market and to keep present and future government from having the power of past government – though able and required to protect established giant rights as if they were part of the natural order of things – i.e. to reinforce the established system and structure of *governance* (which is the effect of Richard Epstein's view of property rights). Such a view is not a matter of truth but of argument articulated with the intent of manipulating political psychology in favor of established privilege; it is a contribution to politics that denigrates politics – an echo of a public choice theory that denigrates public choice. (At several points Vanberg cites my work on Buchanan; although he does concur with my view a few times, one can interpret his analysis as an effort to shore up Buchanan's position. Thus, one reads, "That for contractual departure from the status quo one must gain the consent of those who are privileged by the status quo does not mean that one cannot employ the 'moral pressure' of public political discourse as a legitimate tool.")

Vanberg distinguishes between "unanimity as a legitimizing principle and unanimity as an in-period decision rule." Only the former requires unanimous approval: "the contractarian postulate of consensual change does not rule out at all changes that do not command unanimous approval, as long as such changes are made according to rules that are legitimized by the consent of the relevant community." The problem, of course, is the ease with which Buchananites go from such a hypothetical situation to the actual historical situation, as if the latter were described by the former.

After summarizing the foregoing, it was Sugden (I believe) who commented that doing politics involves a normative commitment, taking place in a political system in which all parties live together. In this connection, Tideman remarked that the alternatives were only three: fighting, discussion and contract. Buchanan noted as an aside that British pressure in Northern Ireland might have prolonged the war, which could have been settled earlier by fighting. Later on I noted that government was verbal conflict having replaced physical fighting.

Brennan suggested that conservatism meant that feasibility be taken seriously. Two kinds of constraints, he said, were relevant but very different. One is brute facts, including the content of history, which are hard constraints. Constructed rules are decisional and, in comparison, soft constraints.

Much discussion, at this point and at other times, centered on whether the allocation of resources to determine which decisional contents are to be changed is artificial or unproductive. As above, this gets to the heart of rent seeking.

Vanberg suggested that a lesson of evolutionary psychology is that fighting is part of our genetic, instinctive makeup, and that our becoming civilized takes place in the face of this. He added that ongoing rules are necessary; the potential for revision is also necessary, for legitimacy.

Reynolds maintained that law needed to be taken more seriously. War, he suggested, led to a decision to be ruled by law, which led to politics and to rent seeking within politics. The decision to be ruled by law implied the acceptance of law, a constitutional system of government, authoritative rules, processes for changing the constitution, and norms for assessing the legitimacy of constitutional changes and to maintain the legitimacy of the decision to submit to law. He identified three of some twenty norms: (1) the principle of generality, that law apply to all, i.e. the rule of law; (2) equality; and (3) prospectivity – no ex post facto changes.

It was clear from the discussion that the issue remained that of privileging the status quo. This implied the further issue, whether we are talking about a process (of working things out, with the Buchananite position being one contribution thereto) or seemingly a priori universal solutions to problems.

Buchanan remarked that much of what was being said leads to a stance of acquiescence, to minimal changes; to which Reynolds replied that such is not the case, otherwise there would be inertia.

I wrote but did not say that some or much involved facilitating recognition of legal change without challenging fundamentals.

Tollison – with a thrust opposite to that of his paper – called attention to political entrepreneurship, to people with vision who try to sell their ideas. This, I said, brought to mind those writers who treated government and politics as a market and found optimizing solutions formed therein. Someone, likely Tollison, referred to Tiebout solutions to problems of disagreement over public-good packages.

Someone suggested a case for actually being privilege free. It is in part a problem of definition, in part one of the test. The speaker argued that agreement with the rules implied the absence of privilege. (One could reply that the absence of revolution meant only that the price thereof was seen to be too high, not that privilege was non-existent.)

I suggested the paradox emanating from the following: to treat equals equally, you need to treat them equally, but to treat unequals equally you need to treat them unequally. Kleimt cited Hayek to the effect that under classical liberalism unequals were treated equally, whereas under modern liberalism, unequals were treated unequally. (If unequals are treated equally, would they now be equals? Was there not then one system of law for the landed and non-landed propertied and another for the non-propertied?)

Deborah Mayo queried as to how much change would transpire if unanimity were required in a contractarian system. Vanberg responded that if privilege existed in the status quo, the privileged can be bought out, they can be made subject to ethical persuasion, contractarian change can take place, or (undesirably) involuntary change can take place. Vanberg stipulated that in his approach no ethical norm could be brought to bear from the outside (a topic raised in his paper in relation to one of my publications). I replied that the definition of "outside" is critical and wondered if every possible norm could be found "inside."

Reynolds queried as to the source of normative individualism. Vanberg replied that normative individualism was not the same thing as laissez faire and reiterated the conventional distinction between normative individualism and methodological individualism, but did not take up the matter of source.

(6) Geoffrey Brennan and Alan Hamlin's "Analytic Conservatism," introduced by Mayo, presented a complex argument. Its elements included: a bias in favor of the status quo is a key component of the conservative disposition; the need to justify such a disposition; distinguishing between the ideal or political end sought and a posture with respect to that ideal; the importance of feasibility considerations and of ignorance of the consequence of policy changes, in the latter case unknowable consequences implying that experimentation is "flying blind" and is a bad bet; that given the antecedents, it is rational to adopt the conservative predisposition to a status quo bias; that the disposition itself requires justificatory argument; and that what motivates conservatives may differ from what justifies conservatism.

The conservative disposition, Brennan and Hamlin wrote, connoted "an intuitive suspicion of all grand schemes, an intrinsic affection for things as they are, an inclination to be reconciled to one's general situation and perhaps strongly self-identified with it, a tendency to evaluate policies and reforms in terms of 'disaster avoidance' rather than utopian aspiration."

The topics of discussion were those of the paper: the conservative disposition or sentiment; multiple types of conservatism; and the strategic reasoning of analytical conservatism, but not the topic of justification vis-à-vis motivation (what I consider to be the problem of hypocrisy). Controversies arising in discussion were over: (1) the coherence and sufficiency of the notion of a conservative disposition; and (2) the relation of the disposition to the different types of conservatism. It was pointed out that uncertainty characterized both policy effects and the ideal.

Tideman affirmed a partial idealist position – the temperament of the right thing to do.

(7) The final session involved open discussion with Buchanan in the chair. He indicated his favorable impression of what he called epistemic defense of the status quo – by people themselves. He voiced his lament that we are losing the status quo ante of Western values – elaborated as the rule of law and adherence to institutions developed in and/or on the basis of 18th century developments. He said that in the contest between explaining by nature and by nurture, the former was winning out – people were fundamentally unequal – but the welfare state was supported by different values. He distinguished between U.S. and European culture with respect to the welfare state: In consensual states, such as the U.S. and Canada, immigration figured highly; whereas in non-consensual states, such as Europe, personhood was defined by nationality.

Very little direct challenge was voiced to the above.

Tideman reiterated his displeasure with silence in the face of injustice, to preserve the status quo.

Emphasis was made on defining the status quo in terms of its dual modes of change, the market, and moral and legal rules.

Reiterated discussion of the Hobbesian state elicited a Buchanan-Samuels definition of "state" in terms of condition, not a political entity.

I juxtaposed two contradictory ideas: (1) that the U.S. was in a Hobbesian state insofar as people took extreme positions on issues, failed to respect others' different points of view, and so on, including the rise of domestic and foreign-based terrorism, due in part to our support of Israel and becoming a party to conflict with Islam; and (2) that the idea of the U.S. system of government once was something of which Americans were proud and attractive to foreigners. I asked Buchanan, with evident reluctance, whether public choice theory, with its denigration of the concept and practice of democracy and the American system of government, has contributed to what many see as the failure of our belief system. He agreed that that was likely the case. Shortly thereafter Mayo questioned whether conservative, Buchananite ideas were responsible for some of the failures to which they objected.

Someone pointed out the importance of law and government. I noted that Adam Smith defined the stages of his stage theory in terms not of changes in technology or the mode of production but of changes in the system of law and government.

Vanberg presented a discussion that included attention to if not emphasis on people refraining from pursuing the position of their maximum advantage and engaging in negotiation. I called attention to John R. Commons's emphasis on forebearance and negotiational psychology.

Dahlman stressed the rule of law, emphasizing Trent Lott's statement thereon at the time of the impeachment trial of Bill Clinton. I indicated that the concept of the rule of law had a variety of meanings. I juxtaposed to Lott's and Richard Posner's expositions that of Bruce Ackerman and those who were critical of its use as a means of introducing politics into a case of adultery and lying about it. I also cited my chapter (see next document) on the rule of law in which I criticized its invocation where it did not belong, along with considerable evidence, arguing that there is no rule of law.

Some speakers directly or indirectly supported pluralism. Others explicitly opposed Post-Modernism and relativism, most notably, perhaps, diversity in education. Buchanan reiterated his reliance on relatively absolute absolutes. Largely ignored were the problems posed by Faith, Reynolds, Tideman, Brennan and, inter alia, myself as to the coherence of the concept and desirability of the status quo.

This was Buchanan's colloquium. Notwithstanding the use of formulaic expressions and the quest to strengthen his intellectual fortress, it was an interesting, pleasant, and informative discussion. As I said in a toast at dinner, he is a great scholar, a great gentleman, and a good friend.

Still, I came away from the conference agreeing that conservatism is a disposition, a sentiment; that Brennan and Hamlin's description of it is only one but accurate enough for many people; that by their or any other description no one is totally conservative, only selectively so; that the Buchanan project is an effort to wrap his form of conservative argument in scholarly, even scientific garb; that the relation of Buchananite ideas to politics in general and the Republican party in particular is complex; and that among the ironies of the conference were those pointed out in the next document, including the nothing still being said of the enormous Federal deficit, and the Reaganite get-the-government-off-of-our-backs mentality of various domestic terrorists, including Eric Robert Rudolph, who was captured near the start of the conference. Everything is selective, a matter of what once, and in a different field, was called casuistry.

The position I am trying to state was nicely expressed by Overton H. Taylor (*A History of Economic Thought*, New York: McGraww-Hill, 1960) who wrote that economics "is in some degree at least a science" (p. xi), but it is also an expression of subjective individual moods and movements, "purely speculative, void of demonstrable or verifiable truth or validity, as largely emotional as intellectual in content or substance, and intent not purely on discovering truth or understanding actualities but largely on inspiring and directing political action toward particular goals and along particular paths. And they are always biased, partisan, fervent, and dogmatic – in short, they are in every way antithetical in spirit and nature to all science" (pp. xi–xii). Taylor's own view was that "Economics . . . is, and long has been, *in some degree* a science, though I emphasize the qualifying phrase . . . But I do not think that economic science, or theoretical work in it, is or has been or can be so perfectly or absolutely scientific – objective, unbiased, neutral . . . – as to make it possible to say . . . that the great contributions . . . have been wholly uninfluenced by . . . political philosophies . . . Nor do I see any point in avoiding recognition and study . . . [of] the influences exerted by the social philosophies . . . Precisely in his effort to achieve objectivity, one should try to make his own social, moral, and political outlook or philosophy as fully explicit, conscious, clear, and self-critically examined as possible . . ." (p. xii). "I do not at all share the inclination toward contemptuous dismissal of [systems of philosophical political thought] as not worth serious, participating study . . . [C]ivilizations, and civilized men, cannot live by or upon scientific knowledge alone . . ." (p. xiii). These views are all the more striking inasmuch as I share Taylor's and Buchanan's "attachment it to . . . classical liberalism – the philosophy or vision of societies of largely free individuals, under limited governments . . . of the liberal-democratic kind, and with economic activities and relations organized mainly in systems of free, private enterprises and competitive markets" (p. xiv).

Perhaps some day someone will write a book on the hypotheses for serious, scientific study contained in Buchanan's ideological, even utopian economics. Such a study would have the structure that Joan Robinson suggested and the content that Buchanan has produced. It would also have a place for Buchanan's high-priest role in his movement, the role verbalized when I have heard him called "Rabbi Buchanan." I expect he would consider that a compliment. Certainly his students understand his role as a conservative economist.

One irony is that Buchanan is a scholar whose work is laden with ideology and the desire to motivate certain reforms yet he has been the most creative scholar in the field of public finance, one who surely merited his Nobel Award. A greater irony is that Buchanan is in principle no different from other reformers who envision problems in contemporary economics and politics and strongly seek to correct them.

THE PROBLEM OF THE STATUS OF
THE STATUS QUO: SOME COMMENTS

Warren J. Samuels

The objective of these notes is that of the Colloquium, namely, to identify certain issues and distinctions that arise when considering the status of the status quo. Because of time pressure and the pressure of other commitments I am unable to present the issues and reasoning as thoroughly as I would prefer.

The status of the status quo (SSQ) is both a positive and a normative problem. I have – unlike apparently most of the other participants in the Colloquium – absolutely no interest in establishing a normative position on SSQ. I would prefer some change and some continuity. I am interested in a positive analysis – as purely positive analysis as can be achieved – of the problem of the SSQ. One positive point is that the status quo manifests some change and some continuity. Others will be identified below.

Part 1 examines part of a set of notes taken by F. Taylor Ostrander in Frank H. Knight's course, Economics 303, Current Tendencies, during the Winter Semester of 1934 at the University of Chicago. This part of the class notes deals with Knight's treatment of an early version of the problem take up at the Colloquium. The notes in their entirety will be published in Archival Volume 23B (2005) of *Research in the History of Economic Thought and Methodology*. Part 2 comments on the Colloquium papers distributed in advance in early May 2003. It will surprise no one that I am critical – a sympathetic critic, to a point – of much that is written in those papers. I hope that my bluntness is not taken for hostility. Part 3 presents some summary thoughts and random comments.

Research in the History of Economic Thought and Methodology A Research Annual
Research in the History of Economic Thought and Methodology, Volume 22-A, 235–256
Copyright © 2004 by Elsevier Ltd.
All rights of reproduction in any form reserved
ISSN: 0743-4154/doi:10.1016/S0743-4154(03)22015-0

1. KNIGHT

One important discussion comes under Knight's heading of "Social Control." To appreciate his argument, one has to understand that Knight's social theory is developed within a tension between: (1) his knowledge that social control is both inevitable and necessary; and (2) his correlative desire for individual autonomy. One *could* add to that a hatred of social control, some of which *is* relevant. But what Knight dislikes is, first, selective elements of existing social control and, second, change of social control, e.g. change of the law by law, *except for* those changes of the law that remove the selective elements he dislikes; Knight is not opposed to all change of social control. In any event, the problem of social control is also for Knight (as it was for Vilfredo Pareto) the problems of social change and of the status of the status quo as well as of hierarchy.

For the purpose of clarity, one could postulate Knight's alter ego. Let S be the totality of existing social control; K that part that Knight dislikes; R the part that Knight likes but the alter ego dislikes; dK the change in social control that Knight would support; and dR the change that the alter ego would support. The differences between Knight and his alter ego are (1) that which they respectively like and would not change and (2) that which they dislike and would change. Neither is totally for existing social control, neither is for changing everything. Neither can claim the anti-social control high ground. Nor can either claim the anti-legal change high ground – though given existing social control, change of law (or other rules) by law is the point at issue. Some writers, e.g. Bruno Leone, define coercion as legal change – not the law already in place. If the law in place is L1, the new body of law is L2, and the difference between L1 and L2 – legal change – is dL, it is impossible for me to see only dL as coercion. (I surmise that no revolutionary wants to change everything – though it may appear that way to both some of them and some of their opponents; at least that is the record, as I read it, of historical revolutions. This has not prevented conservatives from talking about total as opposed to incremental or marginal changes.) (For exposition of several of the foregoing themes, see Samuels, 1973a, 1974, 1997.)

Thus, in the notes, Knight is reported to have repudiated what he called the idea that is "the intellectual element in social enterprise," namely, the "Idea that society is my chariot for me to drive." This, he says, is "Analogous to [the] making of rules for a game – with [the] aim of a *better* game." He has two problems with this. It involves, first, "Making rules for yourself, not for others;" and second, "Aiming at a good game, but . . . aiming at *winning* the game." It is "childishness," he claims, of those "who want social control, but don't see the elementary fact that what they want is a society that would be *their* plaything; that which would work only if *they* controlled."

Knight goes one step further. He says that "aiming at *winning* the game . . . is not analogous to economic theory," that "The step from understanding of economic theory to social policy is a tremendous one," that people "Have enough to understand economic theory – and it *is* essential," and that "talking about social control on a basis of that understanding is overpowering." (Interestingly Knight seems to have a view, close to that of Pareto, of elites competing for control of the masses; here he says, "And the masses love to lie down before the Juggernaught car, if it's done with right technique.")

This additional step raises further questions. Why is economic theory the test? Would economists, or economic theorists, then not become the rule-making authority for others in society? Would not this mean that economists – or some economists – would become the otherwise maligned chariot drivers? On what basis are they to have this exalted position? And which economic theory, and which economists, would control the rule making? (Knight himself would put it, which rules = whose rules.) Further, as above, inasmuch as there must be rules, the question is not whether or not but which (=whose) rules. And since Knight interposes economic theory, hence economists, against changing the rules, why is his argument not self-referential, or self-reflexive? Or is this but the guise in which one group seeks to become in fact but not in name the chariot drivers of society?

Knight is absolutely descriptively correct when he talks about "Aiming at a good game, but . . . aiming at *winning* the game." Legislation is not written and enacted neutrally, but by interested parties using law as a political means to their economic and other ends. Objections to legislation sought by others, as class warfare or as violations of non-interventionism or as putting the government on the backs of the citizenry, are not forthcoming from the same objectors when it is *their* legislation on the table. Such is the predicament – call it plutocracy – targeted by John Rawls's notion of a veil of ignorance. Knight may have considered rule making with a view to winning as a violation of economic theory. But George Stigler, a student at Chicago at the same time as Ostrander, much later argued that people pursue their self-interests in politics no less than in economics, or in political no less than economic markets.

Some of the foregoing is echoed in and supported by the following. In an article in the November 27th, 2002 issue of *Business Week*, entitled "Biting the Invisible Hand," Martin Fridson, the chief high-yield strategist at Merrill Lynch, is quoted for making a critical distinction apropos of the Enron scandal. His first point was that the Invisible Hand, in his view a metaphor for harnessing individual self-interest to serve the general well-being, is a powerful principle. His second point was that it is a "very convenient cover story for people who are actually trying to stack the deck in their favor" – for people who preach the virtues of competitive capitalism but practice the crony variety.

The same point is made by users of rent-seeking theory who invoke it to condemn all change of law – except those changes they believe necessary to correct existing wrong law. Assuming the ubiquity of rent seeking (=aiming at *winning* the game), such does not render normatively repugnant *all* efforts to change the law; nor do the critics of rent seeking perceive it in their own agendas.

Here we have, rather, arguably empirical support for the general theory of business control of government, of ideology as a system of manipulated (see below, in re Geoffrey Brennan and Alan Hamlin's paper) preconceptions, of capitalism as predatory behavior, and so on.

Predictive power is generally not very powerful in economics, but, absent a desire to predict precisely who will act in a predatory manner and precisely how they will do so, Knight's ideas, like Thorstein Veblen's theories, for example, predict these types of behavior very clearly. The likelihood of business-oriented because business-dominated government, for example, being complicit in arguably numerous ways is successful prediction.

If the problem of social control, therefore, is also the problems of social change and of the status of the status quo, the operative problem is, who decides? The three foregoing examples – the economic theorist, the deck stacker, and the rent-seeking opponent of rent seeking – not only provide answers to that question but demonstrate that normative theorists of the status quo are part of the process of continually remaking the status quo.

2. BUCHANAN

The work of James M. Buchanan forms the basis of most if not all of the papers presented at the Colloquium – including, of course, his own, which I consider last.

(1) Robert D. Tollison summarizes his "The Status of the Status Quo" as follows:

> This paper employs the theory of rent seeking to show the futility of economic reform of existing deformities in the economic order. Genuine reform should ignore the past and possibly look to the future; it should accept existing deformities and seek to prevent new ones from emerging. Hence, the *status quo* has a strong analytical rationale in a world with rent seeking.

I have criticized the theory of rent seeking earlier and will not repeat the argument here (see Samuels & Mercuro, 1984). For present purposes I make the following points, in part in the form of questions.

The conclusion stated in the first sentence is, given the monopoly analysis presented in the paper, only a matter of logic. Given the premises, the conclusion follows. But the conclusion can claim only validity, or logicality; it is not necessarily a true proposition, meaning by "truth" descriptive accuracy and/or correct explanation. Furthermore, the conclusion of the paper is an over-generalization from the monopoly case to all potential change of law and to the totality of the legal-economic system in which that change takes place (see Samuels, 1998).

What constitutes an existing "deformity" is a matter of judgment and fundamentally subjective, almost verging on the idiosyncratic in many instances; anything approaching unanimity is highly unlikely. (Party politics, perhaps especially by noted academics, does have the effect of often creating a small number of "official" versions of what constitutes a deformity or not, but that is an artifact of party politics.) To presume substantive content to "deformity" is to omit a fundamental part of the process evaluating SSQ. It renders ostensibly concrete what is actually only a primitive term; doing so is a problem of the use of language in economics (see Samuels, 2001).

Do the conclusions as to "the futility of economic reform of existing deformities in the economic order" and ignoring the past apply: (1) fully to our own; and (2) to all economic orders? Has this conclusion, rampant in a certain body of literature, prevented believers from calling for major reforms in this country? Has it prevented them from applauding reforms for transition to a market economy in the former USSR?

As to "futility," this presumes that one knows the actual and not merely the ostensible goals of reforms – a dubious assumption (see below in re hypocrisy).

As for ignoring the past, accepting existing deformities, and possibly looking to preventing new ones from emerging, it is, firstly, a matter of subjective judgment. Secondly, any policy with regard to the new is likely to be tied up with the old. For example, the economic significance or meaning of a right is in part a function of its relation to other rights; and the pecuniary calculus of costs and benefits pertaining to new policy will be a function in part of the price structure generated by the old. Policy toward the new will inevitably influence the old. (Again, all this is rendered almost nugatory by my first point, as to what constitutes a deformity.) Judgments of over- vs. under-investment (in this paper and in others) are a function of which price structure is used by the analyst, one of which (that generated with no deformity) is hypothetical.

The argument is normative but is selectively normative. There is nothing about the larger problem of continuity vs. change other than Tollison's own normative argument. Especially missing is any recognition of other reasons for changing the law, e.g. to accommodate or inhibit new technology.

The paper (not alone) seriously neglects – or, at best, trivializes – the process of making policy, of working things out.

The conclusion is that "there is much to recommend the *status quo* in a general interest world. Put another way, in a world where trapezoids and not triangles motivate behavior, it is hard to avoid the conclusion that it is best to let the rent seekers prevail (let the big dogs eat)." This conclusion can only lend further credence to the view that the body of theory drawn upon in this paper is intended to promote the continuation of an oligarchic, plutocratic system of political economy. This applies to the entirety of the legal-economic system. What should be especially important to economists is that markets, in which much of the action takes place, are not given but are in part a function of differential power (in the context of the theories of the firm promulgated by Ronald Coase, Gardiner C. Means and others).

The "strong analytical rationale" claimed for by the author is anything but strong; it surely is not conclusive.

(2) Roger L. Faith's "Can We Know the Status Quo? raises a number of very important points.

The most important general points are, however, largely implicit: First, the status quo is a social construction in two senses. It is a matter of human construction, through deliberative and non-deliberative decision making (see Samuels, 1999). Second, it is also a matter of interpretation.

Although all the papers and these comments speak of *the* status quo, no singular status quo exists; what exists is situational and problematic – a matter of interpretation. Consider, for example, the variety of theories of what the western economic system – even only that of the U.S. – is all about as brought to mind by such names as Karl Marx, Thorstein Veblen, John Kenneth Galbraith, Paul A. Samuelson, Milton Friedman, Friedrich von Hayek, Charles Lindblom, Mancur Olson, John Maynard Keynes and Max Weber, as well as Jim Buchanan. Which of these is correct, which is the one used in interpreting – and changing – the economic system? Similarly with theories of the nature of mercantilism and the causes of the American revolution, the French Revolution, the U.S. Civil War, World Wars I and II, and so on – all matters of interpretation.

Consider, too, the "status quo" of any weapons system, military strategy, physical industrial capital, business strategy, and so on, is a function of the opponent's weapon system and strategy, the competitors' capital and strategy, and so on. The economic significance of one's rights is a function, in part, of others' rights, their respective expectations in case of conflict, and legal doctrine chosen by courts.

The meaning of the status quo is in part a function of what else is taken to be or becomes situationally relevant, of what economic theory is used in constructing its interpretation, and the purpose for which the definition of the status quo is constructed (there may be a different status quo for each different purpose). And, clearly, the design of these papers strongly tends to take place within and give effect to Jim Buchanan's ideational structure; the approach to the status quo forming the premise of the Colloquium is that of his theory of public choice.

While on the subject of rights, several other points should be made (see Samuels & Mercuro, 1999). First, property rights are not the only form that rights take, though rights designated as property rights are given a privileged position based on historical developments. All rights constitute the protection of interests. Defining the status quo in terms of property rights typically fails to provide comparable protection to interests not designated property rights yet function as their analytical equivalent, such as rights formalized through environmental legislation, protective labor legislation and labor relations legislation.

Second, it is impossible to fully define rights. The conventional practice of ostensibly doing so involves a fiction utilizing a primitive term. The pretense that rights can be fully defined is useful, if not necessary, in the legitimation of the process by which legal change is legitimized (see Samuels & Mercuro, 1980) but it is still a pretense.

Third, rights are only one part of the total system of legal relations, especially that articulated by Wesley N. Hohfeld and used, for example, by Robert Lee Hale (Samuels, 1973b). Other parts include immunities, exposures and duties. Failure to include these others in definitions of the status quo misapprehends what is going on in the economy and the legal-economic nexus.

Fourth, two ancillary concepts that pervade the papers are "freedom" and "coercion." These are given either no specific definition or stylized ones, engendering their own linguistic problems. In my view, freedom and coercion are many sided and any one specification has meaning only in the context of the parallelograms of freedom and coercion, respectively, that pervade the political economic system (see the essays on these subjects in Samuels, 1992 and Samuels, Medema & Schmid, 1997).

Fifth, another term that is widely used is "voluntary." But as I have shown (following Hale), what actually is being described is "volitional," not "voluntary," action (Samuels, 1992, passim).

Sixth, the discussion about rights is subject to another limitation. Rights can be seen as independent of government, such that any government action deemed to adversely affect a right constitutes a taking subject to compensation – which enshrines the Court's definition of status quo rights, under the pretense that rights are found and not made; or rights can be seen as a product of an ongoing legal process and not a taking in the constitutional sense (Samuels & Mercuro, 1980). Which of these definitions of rights is used to define the status quo will have profound effects.

One consequence of the foregoing discussion is to underline Faith's identification of some sources of ambiguity in identifying and thus knowing the status quo. As he writes, "just what is the existing state of affairs, and would we know it when we see it," and "one may never truly know the status quo."

There is another respect that may be considered, one akin to the concept of equilibrium. We would not know if the actual economy were in equilibrium if we faced it; and, in fact, we are likely never in equilibrium, in a general equilibrium sense, at least. Likewise, we are never in the status quo (effectively making it a nonsensical, at best a hypothetical concept) because any one element of social reality is contingent on other elements and *some* elements of reality are continually in flux, thereby impacting other elements of reality. This certainly applies to potential legal change. A impacting B, C, D, . . . N or not, but also to external/non-political/non-legal phenomena impacting B, C, and D. For example, technological change can affect the implications of a particular legal rule; therefore the status quo effectively evolves through non-legal/non-political change. Even abstracting from selective perception and other issues, there effectively is no status quo, just as there is no general equilibrium, because things are always changing. Employment of a unanimity rule does not affect this, given that non-political/non-legal change causes changes in the status quo and thus new distributions of gains/winners-losses/losers. The "status quo" is essentially a fiction.

Buchanan argues, for his purpose and in his sense not improperly, all efforts at change start from here, the status quo. But that position finesses the problem of having to identify the status quo and the difficulties encountered in doing so. As Faith argues, conceptual difficulties are involved in knowing the status quo and in granting any particular normative status to the status quo. These difficulties involve duration, precedent and priority, the definition of community, and what (=whose) representation enters into the definition of the status quo. The difficulties also include normative elements – "oughts" in an "is" form.

Faith makes two further points, unfortunately only in footnotes and without either elaboration or application. One of these points I have already made. Faith makes it through summarizing the work of Michel Foucault, saying, "what passes as knowledge is culturally specific. What is known, what is knowable and what is worth knowing varies across time and place. Accordingly, a given set of "objective" facts could give rise to different conceptions of the status quo." Faith's other point could also have been made using Foucault's work but he cites his own work, saying, "the social institutions governing a set of interacting individuals is determined by the person(s) who occupies the top spot in a hierarchy of strategy-makers. Those institutions comprise the status quo rules. See Earl Thompson and Roger Faith, "A Pure Theory of Social Interaction," *American Economic Review* (June, 1984)."

In making this second point, Faith is somewhat heretical for this Colloquium. Consideration of hierarchy, hence of inequality, compromises the imagery of vol-untarism, consent and unanimity. Thus, Viktor Vanberg quotes me in recognizing that the requirement of unanimous consent allows "the privileged in the status quo to hold out and perpetuate themselves by being able to withhold their consent" (in Samuels & Buchanan, 1975, p. 30).

Vanberg himself treats the problem of hierarchy in different ways. He writes, "What issues should be assigned to the sphere of political-collective choice and what issues should be left to private, market-coordination is itself a matter of constitutional choice, a choice that should be made in light of the relative merits of the working properties of the two arenas." But he does not point out that such "relative merits" are neither inherent in the two arenas nor identically perceived by individuals differently situated in the hierarchy.

Vanberg also writes,

> It is perfectly consistent for a contractarian constitutionalist to criticize an existing constitutional regime for its lack of consensual approval and to insist, at the same time, that constitutional reform should be contractual. Neither is such critique of the status quo an invitation to change things in a non-contractual manner, nor does the contractarian argument for contractual change imply that we should ignore deficiencies in the legitimacy of the status quo.
>
> A contractarian critique of the status quo would appear to be called for especially in the case of constitutional regimes that are characterized by *privileges* in the sense of discriminating rules that must be viewed as unjust by those who are discriminated against. Such critique can be based entirely on internal criteria, i.e. the evaluations of the individuals involved in the arrangement, without any need to appeal to external normative standards. There would seem to be no need, therefore, for Buchanan to take issue with W. J. Samuels' (in Buchanan and Samuels 1975, p. 30) talk of "existing systems of privilege," as long as such judgement does not imply recourse to external criteria.[32] We can surely criticize systems of privileges or discriminating regimes without imposing "our private values as criteria for social change" (Buchanan, *ibid.*, p. 33), as regimes that violate the individualist norm that "each man's values are to count as any others" (ibid.) and that do not command agreement of all individuals who are living under them.[33]

This position combines: (1) recognition of privilege due to hierarchy imposed without consent with (2) critique thereof (3) not based on external criteria and (4) critique not based on private values. The strangeness of such a position resides in at least two points: departure from the usual Austrian position emphasizing individual subjective values, and ambiguity as to the nature of internal values or criteria. Once again the footnotes are enlightening. In note 32 Vanberg comments:

> In reference to Samuels' talk of "systems of privilege" Buchanan (in Buchanan & Samuels, 1975, p. 35) notes: "This implies that you, somehow, have already introduced some standard, some external criterion, to determine whether or not privilege exists. My approach requires, and allows, no such external criterion to be introduced." – As argued above, I do not find this objection justified. One can speak of privileges in ways that are perfectly consistent with a contractarian constitutionalist perspective, as Buchanan himself has done, of course, on many occasions. See e.g. J. M. Buchanan and R. D. Congleton, 1998.

The criticism of Buchanan is warranted but one can still point out that those situated in upper hierarchical positions are again enabled to veto change. In note 33, one reads,

> To be sure, any classification of constitutional regimes as "systems of privilege" remains subject to the qualification that it "can be appropriately used only to provide inputs in a discussion that might lead to agreement upon change" (Buchanan, 1977b, p. 145).

This establishes discussion only on terms acceptable to those in upper hierarchical positions. In a world of giants and pygmies, in which the giants became giants in non-consensual ways, it is a further instrument of rule by giants to allow only consensual change. Would one apply this approach to both the U.S. and the U.S.S.R.? In the subsequent note 34, Vanberg writes,

> In this sense, to the contractarian constitutionalist position should apply what F. A. Hayek (1972: ixf.) says about the liberal position: "The essence of the liberal position, however, is the denial of all privilege, if privilege is understood in its proper and original meaning of the state granting and protecting rights to some which are not available on equal terms to others."

Four points: Privilege available on equal terms to others, however, is no longer privilege. Where is consent in Hayek's position? Whose selective perception is to determine when a "privilege" exists and when the terms are "equal"? There is a difference between treating equals unequally so as to render them unequal, and treating unequals unequally so as to render them equal; this is so despite the evident fact that people are equal and unequal in different ways, a recognition that both leads to and underscores the process of working things out, a process in which the Buchanan-Hayek-type position is only one consideration.

Vanberg thus further argues,

> W. J. Samuels' (in Buchanan & Samuels, 1975, p. 30) complaint that, "as attractive as the consent (unanimity) rule is, it places too much power in the hands of the already privileged," reflects an ambiguous feeling about the contractarian approach that seems to be shared by many of its critics. While such critics are prepared to acknowledge that the consensus principle may be attractive per se, in and by itself, they object to the idea that it can be applied to a status quo that is, in their view, normatively unacceptable. They do not quite demand that we start "from someplace else," they demand, however, that we move from "here," the actual status quo, to a different, preferred structure *before* we bind ourselves to contractual procedures for further change.[37] They want to postpone the adoption of consensual procedures until a just starting point has been established, something that, they think, cannot be achieved in a contractual manner.

This may well be the position of others but it is not my position. My position is, first, simply that the Buchanan "consent (unanimity) rule" gives the giants veto power and excludes all other considerations. It is, second, that no formula or rule can be imposed willy nilly; the Buchanan position, like all others, must make its way in the process of working things out. (Wicksell's interest in unanimity was neither efficiency nor to protect the privileged but to help/protect the lowest classes.) Note 37 reads,

> G. Brennan and J. M. Buchanan (1985, p. 141): "This distribution of entitlements may not be acceptable to many persons as the appropriate starting point from which genuine constitutional reform is to be made."

It is both presumptuous and tautological to identify the Buchanan position as the only one comprising "genuine constitutional reform." The Buchanan position seems likely, rather, in the words of *Business Week* already quoted above, to be a "very convenient cover story for people who are actually trying to stack the deck in their favor." Even absent hierarchy, the Buchanan position of insisting on the obvious point that "we start from here," namely, the status quo, is deployed to stack the deck in favor of whatever specification of the status quo is made and against those deliberative introductions of legal change of which the deployer disapproves.

(3) Turning directly to Vanberg's "The Status Quo in Contractarian Constitutionalist Perspective," he certainly succeeds in "separating two issues the differences between which have not always been sufficiently recognized in the debate, namely, on the one hand, the role of the status quo as the inevitable starting point of any change and, on the other hand, the issue of the normative evaluation of the status quo." This formulation is useful, although it too is rendered ambiguous and inconclusive by the problems of defining the status quo.

In addition to the comments on Vanberg's paper made in regard to Faith's paper, I note the following.

His point that contractarian constitutionalism per se and, by inference, different forms of it, affect "the choice of questions that it seeks to answer" is important. His discussion of "hypothetical imperatives," however, is not helped by his insistence on a

> careful distinction between unanimity as legitimizing principle and unanimity as decision rule. It is certainly true that the agreement among the contracting parties that market transactions enjoy must not be confused with a unanimous approval by the community at large. In this sense, changes from the status quo that result from market transactions are, indeed, consensual only as far as the contracting parties are concerned, but they may well be imposed on others in the community who would object if they were asked. Yet, again, according to the contractarian norm decisions or transactions qualify as legitimate as long as they are arrived at according to rules that enjoy unanimous approval.

Once again, the problem of veto power arises. Also what are examples of such rules? The only candidate that comes close, in my mind, is the rule against rape (though it, too, has complications, and Richard Posner has written of a market for rape – appropriately condemned by Buchanan). A further problem is that of hypocrisy, considered below. I am especially uncomfortable with the idea of hypothetical imperatives due to rules enjoying unanimous approval. I concur that people do believe they have hypothetical imperatives – though they do not normally stress their hypothetical nature – but this is due to the inculcation of social rules (socialization) and to neither unanimous consent nor the way things are.

Another distinction made by Vanberg is also important:

> My exclusive concern in this paper is with the *constitutional status quo* and with the issue of
> *constitutional reform*. To be sure, calls for constitutional reform, i.e. for changes in the rules of
> the game, may, of course, be motivated by discontent with the pattern of distributional outcomes
> that result from status quo rules. But it is the concern with changes in the rules themselves, not
> in outcomes per se, that is of principal interest here.

But it, too, is subject to the complications and criticisms made here and in some
of the other papers.

Vanberg also presents an argument that at first reading seems both obvious and
unobjectionable:

> The contractarian argument for peaceful, contractual change is not – and cannot be – derived
> from the mere fact that we always start from here. Nor does it imply a defense of the status
> quo. It is an argument about how we should proceed from here, namely by peaceful, contractual
> means rather than by coercion and violence, it is not an argument for leaving things as they
> are. It is an argument not in terms of the merits of the status quo but in terms of the merits of
> contractual change compared to its alternative, change by coercion and violence.

Reminding the reader that I am not considering normative issues, I make two
points. First, historically, not everyone agrees with this argument, as is evident
from various writings and practice. Second, the term "coercion" has been given
a multiplicity of specifications; accordingly, Vanberg's exclusion may apply to
little or to much (Samuels, 1997).

The remainder of Vanberg's paragraph continues:

> As Buchanan has pointed out, the contractarian project of working out and proposing contractual
> reforms may be a much more laborious and much less romantic undertaking than the grandiose
> designs, popular among social reformers, of sweeping changes to be imposed on resisting
> interests. Yet, in view of the destructive dynamics of coercive change, it offers a more productive
> approach to constitutional reform than its more impatient counterparts that call for imposing
> change, raising the question of who is to do the imposing.

This statement raises the problem of self-referentiality and more. Surely, were
Buchanan's approach adopted it would constitute the deliberate introduction of a
sweeping, revolutionary set of changes. But would not the language of "grandiose
designs, popular among social reformers" apply to Buchanan and his disciples?
Is not Buchanan a social reformer? What of Geoffrey Brennan and Alan Hamlin's
view of "the conservative's attachment to the status quo"? If conservatism does
not mean no change, but some change, then: (1) the argument against socialist
grand change (=control) is compromised; (2) since the issue is littler changes,
what about creeping socialism?; and (3) how do we know that conservatives
are preferable to socialists? The upshot of such discussion is that the Buchanan
approach is but one strand of conservatism, one contribution to the making, not

finding, of conservatism, such that both conservatism and socialism have been in the process of being worked out.

In the next paragraph we read,

> Accordingly, the contractarian postulate of consensual change does not rule out at all changes that do not command unanimous approval, as long as such changes are made according to rules that are legitimized by the consent of the relevant constituency. And this applies to changes in the rules as well, as long as such changes occur in accordance with rules for changing rules that command unanimous approval. It is with regard to changes in the fundamental, constitutional rules themselves, i.e. for changes that have no established rules to rely on, that the contractarian postulate requires that such changes be made in a contractual, consensual manner.

That such an approach favors existing hierarchical interests, regardless of how their position was attained, should now be obvious, if unwelcome to Buchananites. Additionally, Buchanan has indicated that his hostility toward the Federal government stems from the Civil War. Does this conflict with his "we start from here" position? What if he awoke one day and found a Federal government in the hands of a right-wing militia or a left-wing regime or an Islamic theocracy? Vanberg quotes Buchanan:

> "The status quo defines that which exists. Hence, regardless of its history, it must be evaluated as if it were legitimate contractually." Quite obviously, there is a contradiction here between the notion that the contractarian perspective "does not amount to a defense of the status quo" and the argument that it requires us to evaluate the status quo "as if it were legitimate contractually." Not both of these views can be simultaneously held, and if a choice is to be made, it would seem that only the first is consistent with the overall thrust of Buchanan's approach.

The quotation is rendered problematic by Faith's identification of problems of precedent and priority. The criticism presented in the remainder of the statement is important and also limiting.

Vanberg argues that "the contractarian's plea is for *consensual* elimination of privileges." I have argued that past and present recipients of privilege will not readily surrender them, as evidenced in history. I also suggest that the psychology of denial will tend to dominate: It is very difficult for one to admit that one has benefited from wrong, from privilege, that one has been among the privileged.

(4) Hartmut Kliemt's "Contractarianism as Liberal Conservatism" argues that "Buchanan type contractarianism may be classified as a specific 'formal type' of conservatism that grants normative status to the status quo." Several papers notably Vanberg's and Buchanan's, seek to render saccharine such attribution of normative status.

Apropos of (as it turns out) some of my discussion of Vanberg's paper, Kliemt affirms

> the fact that politics is in the end always about coercion. Though politics cannot be based on contract and agreement, good politics is about minimizing coercion. Clearly the latter is at root of the Buchanan enterprise.

Yes, politics is about coercion but so is economics; coercion can be seen in diverse situations. But politics is in part based on contract and agreement – on matters more complex and subtle than exchanging goods and money. It is not clear that coercion can be minimized; in many instances of putative coercion, one system or form of coercion is substituted for another. If minimizing coercion is at the root of the Buchanan enterprise, it is giving effect to selective perception of coercion. If one objects that normative distinctions must be drawn between systems or forms of coercion, I would agree. But I would insist that such must be worked out; for the analyst to impose distinctions is to substitute the analyst's preferences and perceptions for those of economic actors.

Kliemt is principally concerned with normative issues, about which I have nothing to say.

(5) Brennan and Hamlin's "Analytic Conservatism" presents yet another linguistic alternative formulation of Buchanan's approach. Once again I have nothing to say about their normative argument or, for that matter, their methodological procedures. A central message is the "bias in favour of the *status quo* bias as a key component of the conservative disposition." On the basis of arguments in other Colloquium papers, it is obvious that the concept of a pro-status quo bias is a limited concept; even they emphasize the importance of ignorance. But their paper does reinforce the sentimental nature of the conservative position at the same time that (though only negligibly in their paper) sentiment attaches to some and not other parts of the putative status quo. Their specific argument, "analytic conservatism," underscores the complexity of the overall conservative argument and, accordingly, the limits of the Buchanan position.

The question of self-referentiality arises when one wonders if the following applies to Buchanan and his disciples:

> In short, the nature of democratic political institutions encourages both activism and rhetorical defences that will rationalise such activism. Further, the content of those defences will often be influenced by the creative exploits of academic scribblers, men of letters, philosophers and other forms of low life, all much in love with and apparently convinced by their own latest theories. And public discussion will be full of confident voices, none of whom are much inclined to confess to their own ignorance, or refrain from grossly simplifying matters that are extremely complex.

I applaud Brennan and Hamlin's candor when I read,

> But there is more to be said here. Even economists are familiar with the thought that there is a distinction between justification and motivation. The market produces the benign outcomes that are claimed for it by "invisible" means. In other words, the properties that serve to *justify*

market outcomes are not aspects that necessarily *motivate* any of the agents whose actions produce those outcomes. In the same way here, what works to *motivate* conservatives may not be the same as what justifies conservatism.

and

In short, the structure of the conservative argument that we have presented here seems entirely hospitable to the idea that one should in most choice circumstances adopt a mode of reasoning and calculation that is distinct from the reasoning that provides the ultimate justification for having that disposition. One can't work things out from first principles all the time. That is too time-consuming and too error prone. And doing it may not ultimately energise sufficiently to induce action: "sicklied o'er with the pale cast of thought" is how Hamlet puts it. In short, the "conservative" element in "analytic conservatism" arises because the conservative disposition operates as a critical piece of the required mental furniture.

Nevertheless, at some level, something beyond the disposition itself is required – something further by way of justificatory argument. The conservative disposition is not *self-evidently* compelling. What we have tried to provide in this paper is one line of such justificatory argument – a line that ought to be intelligible to economists in particular, but also to others in the analytic tradition. We emphasize again that the argument provided here is not the only resource in rational actor theory that might be called into play in this connection. Nevertheless, the argument we have presented is, we think, an important one – not only in itself, but also for the broader class of arguments that it suggests.

This argument suggests, at least to this writer, what Pareto (among others) deemed hypocrisy: the deployment of an argument intended to motivate, an argument different from the actual justification, an argument appropriate for the intended/expected audience. One thinks recently (Spring 2003) of the different reasons given for the second war with Iraq and of a tax-cut proposal said to promote economic recovery and jobs (gone is the venerable argument against burdening our grandchildren with debt, i.e. fiscal responsibility, so-called) when the actual intent and ultimate justification is to increase the after-tax incomes of the upper decile (of which I happen to be a member: my own candor). In the present context, the argument suggests that several Colloquium papers ostensibly supporting Buchanan's hard-core position with carefully drawn distinctions and themes, ultimately function to support oligarchy/plutocracy. (As to why hypocrisy works, one may consider Knight's recorded statement, quoted above, "And the masses love to lie down before the Juggernaught car, if it's done with right technique.") So much irony.

(6) Buchanan's "The Status of the Status Quo" continues, as he understands, a long-time quest to limit governmental activism. His Pareto-relevant vs. Pareto-irrelevant distinction, his distinction between constitutional rules and ordinary legislation, his attachment to the theory of rent seeking, and so on, have been attempts to shore up his intellectual fortress against the onslaught of critics, such as myself. I continue in the role of critic.

There is some confusion between positive and normative. The question, "To what extent is the *status quo* privileged?" is a positive and not a normative question, though it undoubtedly has normative, or subjective, elements to it (e.g. the meaning of "privileged").

When Buchanan considers an example involving the present discounted value of future earnings streams, he remarks,

> These questions bring expectations directly into the exercise, and expectations, in turn, call attention to the rules and institutions that are in being, as vital elements in the *status quo* itself.

Buchanan may or may not want to go so far, but the rules and institutions said to be "vital elements in the *status quo* itself" are themselves matters of (often-conflicting) expectations. On the one hand, this is a matter of infinite regress; on the other, it is a matter – like it or not – of nihilism.

Buchanan uses a narrow goods-and-values model of the status quo. It is, however, an incomplete proxy for the political-economic valuational process in which the changing status quo is formed and reformed.

Buchanan correctly argues that the status quo was not formed or chosen by any single, monolithic decision maker. Three points: First, government itself is no single decision-making entity, though it is often treated as if it were. Second, who seriously argues that the status quo is formed or chosen by a single, monolithic decision maker? By seriously I mean by those who write to justify rather than to motivate – though the distinction is subjective in practice. The argument seems intended to discredit deliberative decision making.

Buchanan writes, correctly,

> So long as separate decision makers are in any way interdependent, one with another, the output vector cannot be chosen; it must emerge from the separated but interdependent choices made along the several dimensions of adjustment . . . That which exists is brought into being by the choices made by many participants along many interdependent dimensions of adjustment. The separated choices, as such, cannot be modified in any particular, step-by-step manner so as to generate a specifically defined comprehensive result. One facet of the fatal conceit of socialism was the failure to understand this point. But it becomes equally naive to presume that because of the multidimensionality and complexity of the interaction process, that which has been brought into being is not subject to explicitly directed change.

Does Buchanan apply this reasoning to himself? Is he self-referential? Using Knight's phraseology, does not Buchanan seek to reform society and thereby make society his plaything?

On another topic, Buchanan says,

> we must distinguish between the rules or constraints that restrict or limit the range and exercise of choice and the choices made within such rules.

The distinction is important. But it should not obscure the situation in which "we" find ourselves: all this must be worked out, it cannot be laid out by any Buchananite or Hayekian formula. Indeed, this is one of their fundamental messages. But, again, do they take it self-referentially?

A remarkable statement by Buchanan is the following:

> To be meaningful, it seems best to refer to the *status quo* as that set of rules and institutions in being that do serve to constrain choices, but which may be deliberately changed (Buchanan, 1962). There may be, of course, some institutions that have emerged through a slow process of cultural evolution and that cannot be readily modified. Acknowledgment that some such institutions exist does not, however, imply that others that can be deliberately changed are non-existent or unimportant.

Compared to Hayek, or to most people's interpretation of Hayek (but not mine), Buchanan is a constructivist, and this statement, especially the first sentence, illustrates it. But there is only one reason to exclude those described in the second sentence: all institutions are combinations of deliberative and non-deliberative decision making (Samuels, 1999).

Buchanan says, "An ongoing firm describes its current situation in terms of a balance sheet." This is correct in regard to the point he is making about the irrelevance of imaginary balance sheets (except insofar as they represent targets). But there is much more to the description of current situations than the picture painted by balance sheets.

Buchanan is to be applauded for recognizing that the proposition "whatever is efficient," in the hands of modern Chicagoans, "becomes almost tautological." He points to the alternative survival argument and its normative implication that "efforts at 'constructivism' are doomed to failure." About both arguments he writes,

> The normative implications of both of these arguments are negative in the sense that they discourage efforts at making improvements in the existing arrangements. These arguments seem to eliminate any role for the political economist as reformer, even if she remains in the ivory tower and removed from hands-on policy discussion.

It is obvious that a tension exists in Buchanan's approach between his constructivism and his pro-status quo position. Both are present in actual political economies, and whereas Hayek strongly tends to reject the former in principle – though both are present when his approach is understood in Mengerian terms – Buchanan accepts, if only grudgingly, both.

Buchanan sees compensation of losers by gainers as a falsification-type test. He does not see (I think) certain welfare-state programs as performing that function. I do not see the corporate plutocracy engaging in this particular game – unless the system was in mortal danger and time had to be bought.

He once again takes up the criticism that his approach privileges the status quo (somehow defined).

> It should be emphasized, however, that this apparent privilege arises not because the *status quo* assumes value because it exists, but rather because there is no means other than agreement of determining whether any proposed move away from the *status quo* is or is not preferred by participants.

If such were the case, no use of hypocrisy would be necessary, and his approach would not elicit such deep criticism. Furthermore, there are other means, and the function of both the use of hypocrisy and his approach is to influence how things work out.

I am reminded of Murray Rothbard's point that liability for compensation at the time of emancipation should lead to payments to the former slaves and not to their former owners. This is a matter of the definition of the rights used in the definition of the status quo. It is one of only a few instances when I agreed with him; after all, he did candidly affirm that his system would (further) empower oligarchism.

I come now to text that was very helpful to me in understanding Buchanan's position, a position I hitherto have largely seen as an increasingly sophisticated (though perhaps at times convoluted) libertarianism. The text is this:

> Needless to say, I reject this avenue of inquiry, and categorically so. To acknowledge that some claims may conflict in any *status quo*, and further, that general consensus may be attained on few, if any, proposed changes in the set of constraints, does not imply that all claims are up for grabs and that proposed changes may not be evaluated through some appropriate measure of the degree of consensus attained. Empirical evidence may be used to suggest that participants in the sociopolitical-economic nexus go about their ordinary affairs within an acceptance of the legal framework that incorporates the distinctions among separate rights and claims to sources of value.

The difference between us on this point is as follows. Jim seeks determinacy and closure, whereas I am comfortable with ambiguity and open-endedness. In my view but not his, "participants in the sociopolitical-economic nexus [do] go about their ordinary affairs within an acceptance of the legal framework that incorporates the distinctions among separate rights and claims to sources of value." This is because they have been inculcated (socialized) in the belief system of our society, not because such is the way things are in an ontological sense. Over time, "all claims *are* up for grabs," whether we like it or not.

Jim illustrates his position with the taking problem:

> Even if, at some conceptualized constitutional level or stage of choice, you might have agreed to authorize democratically organized government to modify your set of rights, it does not at all imply that, at the postconstitutional stage, there is no distinction to be made between an overt "taking" and a compensated "exchange," even if both acts are non-voluntary.

> A fully comprehensive definition of the *status quo* would reckon on the formal structure of rights and claims and the expectations that these rights and claims would be protected from confiscation by either private or public predators.

As noted above, my view is very different. The distinction between taking and non-taking is not at all hard and fast, nor can it be. This view, however, is anathema to Jim. So must be my relativist if not nihilist treatment of the concept of the rule of law (Samuels, 2002b) which here also applies to Jim's notion of constitutionalism.

Interestingly, Jim adopts a high-priest role in prescribing for the world he would like to see:

> In some ultimate sense, politics *must be understood by the members of the public* to be a positive-sum game – a process of exchange for mutual advantage – if society is to remain viable. But any such conceptualization, or model, requires that the parties to the game, or exchange, acknowledge base positions from which the process commences. (Italics added.)

This goes beyond normativism into design, the kind of design he otherwise rejects. It is a role with which I am uncomfortable. I am uncomfortable with its substance, on positive as well as normative grounds, insofar as it limits change to that due to exchange – which gives effect to and reinforces hierarchy, an important positive and normative consideration.

This difference between us is either that he would prefer to limit change to that due to exchange and I recognize other modes of change to be relevant, or he has a narrow and I a broad definition of what constitutes exchange. I refer to the following passage: "Any change that modifies your ownership rights and that is made without your agreement or consent cannot be modeled as a part of any exchange process."

It is tempting to think of Buchanan as an advocate of laissez faire – a concept as difficult to work with as that of the status quo. *Laissez faire* can be used in three different contexts: minimization of legal change; a particular vision of an economy; and legal change to bring about that particular vision. Some of Jim's thinking is located in each of these. This accounts for part, but only part, of the problem with his approach.

Jim Buchanan is a brilliant and creative thinker. I have learned much from him over the years. But his approach is only one contribution to the process of working things out – even if things are worked out differently than he would prefer.

3. SUMMARY AND RANDOM COMMENTS

(1) Notwithstanding his and other authors' efforts to establish distinctions (themselves otherwise useful) in a quest to defend the core of his approach, Buchanan's approach does constitute protection and preservation of the

status quo and its hierarchic structure of power. This is so despite the problems of defining the status quo that are identified by Colloquium authors.

(2) So-called voluntary exchange (I prefer volitional exchange) is not wholly analytically equivalent to voting on the rules of social control. Using the exchange model to describe either voting or social control, while it does underscore several important aspects of the conduct of social control, trivializes social control. (The underscored aspects include trade-offs between legislators in voting and one type of legislation as the price of another.)

(3) Invocation of voluntarism, unanimity, and rule of law, misrepresents both the actual way things are and what is possible – reflecting reasons for not limiting change to market contracts of exchange.

(4) Concern in this Colloquium with the status of the status quo seems driven by a desire for continuity rather than change and/or change only through market contracts of exchange. This orientation is lauded or at least stated by several authors.

(5) The theory of voluntary market exchange is only one theory of legal change. It neglects or trivializes the power to control and structure markets enjoyed by institutions of governance both including and extending beyond official government (Samuels, 2002a).

(6) The otherwise important distinctions drawn by several authors are both narrowly nested and put to questionable use.

(7) Some formulations of the economic role of government, especially many in the conservative tradition, are criticized for committing the naturalistic fallacy, that the status quo is the ontological nature of things. Whereas they may perhaps be better understood as absolutist legitimation within the hypocrisy context discussed above.

Part of what I have in mind is indicated by Clifford Geertz's review of Tyler Cowen's *Creative Destruction*. Geertz (2003, p. 27) writes,

> Apologetics – the argumentative defense of how matters play out in the world, the formal and systematic vindication of the received design of things – used to be a theological specialty, most particularly a Christian one. The demonstration that, despite appearances to the contrary on almost every hand, our universe is rationally put together, and is good, and that our place within it, if only we would realize it, is blessed: this was the central task of "the science of things divine" . . .
>
> With the advent of modernity, and the decline of other-worldly explanations for this-worldly phenomena, the task of reconciling us to the ordained and the inevitable . . . has fallen into other hands – most notably, this being the age of reckoning, to economics.

(8) For several reasons given above, the Buchanan approach is utopian – Platonic idealizations or idealized representations of a much more complex, and messy, reality (Samuels, 2003). With regard to the U.S., Buchanan's

approach is ideology bidding to serve as social control and not an objective picture of what government, governance, property, markets, and so on are actually all about or possibly can be. It is an attempt to frame discussion and policy in a particular way – to motivate, as Brennan and Hamlin put it, a

> conservative disposition – an intuitive suspicion of all grand schemes, an intrinsic affection for things as they are, an inclination to be reconciled to one's general situation and perhaps strongly self-identified with it, a tendency to evaluate policies and reforms in terms of "disaster avoidance" rather than utopian aspiration – . . . what motivates conservatives, as a matter of descriptive fact.

But Buchanan's approach is also utilitarian, pragmatic and instrumental. Brennan and Hamlin seem to recognize this when they quote Jerry Z. Muller: "Combining the emphases on history and utility, the common denominator of conservative social and political analysis might be termed 'historical utilitarianism'" (Muller, 1997, p. 7).

(9) I continue to wonder whether the principles embodied in Buchanan's approach, such as "we start from here," would be applied by him to countries other than the U.S., such as the former U.S.S.R., North Korea, Saddam's Iraq, and Hitler's Germany.

(10) One aspect of the economic role of government not directly brought up in the Colloquium papers is the issue of government in the present having or not having the same power as government in the past.

(11) For the historian and methodologist of economic thought the Buchanan phenomenon presents two interesting examples. The first is its accord with Joan Robinson's position that ideological propositions both "express a point of view and formulate feelings which are a guide to conduct and "also provide a quarry from which hypotheses can be drawn" (Robinson, 1962, p. 3). Certainly Jim has demonstrated his brilliance along both lines. To the extent that Jim has contributed to the development of moral and legal rules, surely both the Adam Smith of the *Theory of Moral Sentiments* and the *Lectures on Jurisprudence* and the revolutionary American founding fathers might be surprised with how he has done so.

The second is the externalist nature and origins of his work. His doctrines, in the words of John Kells Ingram (1888, p. 3) "have owed much of their influence to the fact that they seemed to offer solutions of the urgent problems of the age. Again, every thinker . . . is yet a child of his time." But "this connection of theory with practice" can "be expected to produce exaggerations in doctrine, to lend undue prominence to particular sides of the truth, and to make transitory situations or temporary expedients be regarded as universally normal conditions."

ACKNOWLEDGMENT

The author is indebted to Steven G. Medema for comments on an earlier draft.

REFERENCES

Geertz, C. (2003). Off the menu. Review of Tyler Cowen, *Creative Destruction*, Princeton, NJ: Princeton University Press, 2002, in *The New Republic* (February 17), 27–30.

Ingram, J. K. (1888). *A history of political economy*. New York: Macmillan.

Muller, J. Z. (1997). *Conservatism: An anthology*. Princeton, NJ: Princeton University Press.

Robinson, J. (1962). *Economic philosophy*. Chicago, IL: Aldine.

Samuels, W. J. (1973a). Review of Gordon Tullock (Ed.), *Explorations in the Theory of Anarchy*. In: *Public Choice*, *16* (Fall), pp. 94–97.

Samuels, W. J. (1973b). The economy as a system of power and its legal bases: The legal economics of Robert Lee Hale. *University of Miami Law Review*, *27*(Spring–Summer), 261–371.

Samuels, W. J. (1974). Anarchism and the theory of power. In: G. Tullock (Ed.), *Further Explorations in the Theory of Anarchy* (pp. 33–57). Blacksburg: University Publications.

Samuels, W. J. (1992). *Essays on the economic role of government* (Vol. 1), *Fundamentals*. London and New York: Macmillan and New York University Press.

Samuels, W. J. (1997). The concept of 'coercion' in economics. In: W. J. Samuels, S. G. Medema & A. A. Schmid (Eds), *The Economy as a Process of Valuation* (pp. 129–207). Lyme, NH: Edward Elgar.

Samuels, W. J. (Ed.) (1998). *Law and economics*, 2 vols. London: Pickering & Chatto.

Samuels, W. J. (1999). Hayek from the perspective of an institutionalist historian of economic thought: An interpretive essay. *Journal des Economistes et des Etudes Humaines*, *IX*(Juin–Septembre), 279–290.

Samuels, W. J. (2001). Some problems in the use of language in economics. *Review of Political Economy*, *13*(1), 91–100.

Samuels, W. J. (2002a). An essay on government and governance. In: *Economics, Governance and Law: Essays on Theory and Policy* (pp. 1–37). Cheltenham: Edward Elgar.

Samuels, W. J. (2002b). The rule of law and the capture and use of government in a world of inequality. In: *Economics, Governance and Law: Essays on Theory and Policy* (pp. 61–79). Cheltenham: Edward Elgar.

Samuels, W. J. (2003). Utopian economics. In: W. J. Samuels, J. E. Biddle & J. B. Davis (Eds), *The Blackwell Companion to the History of Economic Thought* (pp. 201–214). London: Blackwell.

Samuels, W. J., & Buchanan, J. M. (1975). On some fundamental issues in political economy: An exchange of correspondence. *Journal of Economic Issues*, *9*(March), 15–38.

Samuels, W. J., Medema, S. G., & Schmid, A. A. (1997). *The economy as a process of valuation*. Lyme, NH: Edward Elgar.

Samuels, W. J., & Mercuro, N. (1980). The role and resolution of the compensation principle in society: Part Two – The resolution. *Research in Law and Economics*, *2*, 103–128.

Samuels, W. J., & Mercuro, N. (1984). A critique of rent-seeking theory. In: D. C. Colander (Ed.), *Neoclassical Political Economy* (pp. 55–70). Cambridge: Ballinger.

Samuels, W. J., & Mercuro, N. (Eds) (1999). *The fundamental interrelationship between government and property*. Stamford, CT: JAI Press.

REVIEW ESSAYS

WALKER'S EQUILIBRIUM

Glenn Hueckel

A review essay on Donald A. Walker, ed., *Equilibrium*. 3 vols. Vol. 1. *Introduction to Equilibrium in Economics*, pp. xxiii, 583; Vol. 2. *Equilibrium in Traditional Models*, pp. x, 598; Vol. 3. *Some Recent Types of Equilibrium Models*, pp. x, 621. Cheltenham, UK and Northampton, MA, USA: Edward Elgar, 2000. ISBN 1–85898–928–0. $640.00.

1. THE COLLECTION

The three volumes before us comprise the second title in the "Elgar Reference Collection" of *Critical Ideas in Economics*, a new series which, we learn from the book cover, aims to provide "an essential reference source for students, researchers and lecturers in economics." Each volume in the series will bring together a collection of previously-published articles and book-chapters which "focuses on [a] concept widely used in economics," and will thereby "improve access to important areas of literature which will not be available in the archives of many of the newer libraries." No one can deny that Professor Walker's topic is ideally suited to this stated intent; is there a concept more "widely used in economics" than that of equilibrium? A collection of previously-published items cannot, of course, be appraised in terms of the originality of its content. Such a work offers a different sort of contribution. In addition to the publisher's stated aim of an improved access to those key articles which, either because of their age or the location of their publication, are not widely available, a work such as this can perform a function not unlike that which Weintraub (1991, pp. 129–130) ascribes to the

Research in the History of Economic Thought and Methodology A Research Annual
Research in the History of Economic Thought and Methodology, Volume 22-A, 259–290
Copyright © 2004 by Elsevier Ltd.
ISSN: 0743-4154/doi:10.1016/S0743-4154(03)22016-2

survey article. The act of selection (and, hence, of exclusion) serves to delineate the field for the non-specialist, and the ordering of the items in the collection can reveal instructive lines of intellectual development – a "filiation of scientific ideas" to adopt Schumpeter's (1954, p. 6) felicitous phrase – that otherwise might be obscured.

The value of the work before us is enhanced by its standing as a complement to the earlier Elgar collection on *General Equilibrium Theory* (Debreu, 1996). In his introduction to that collection, Debreu identified several topics that had to be excluded from his volumes. At least a half-dozen of those excluded topics – temporary equilibrium, fix-price models, rational expectations, overlapping generations, sunspot equilibria, and game theory – find representation in Walker's collection. Further, Walker has quite sensibly avoided reprinting items already included in that earlier collection and has provided, at the end of his second and third volumes, lists of supplementary readings relevant to the topics treated in those volumes, noting in those lists the particular items available in the earlier, Debreu collection. As to the ordering of the items and the matter of improved access, Walker's strategy differs from that adopted by Debreu, permitting some improvement in the one case but perhaps not in the other. The improvement comes in the broad topical categories governing the arrangement of the Walker selections. No such topical ordering is found in the Debreu collection, which simply lists its entries alphabetically by first author's surname. To be sure, Walker's arrangement is not beyond objection. As we shall see, a few items are misclassified, and at least two interesting intellectual lines of descent are obscured by the chosen scheme. Nevertheless, even if imperfect, the topical ordering provides the reader with what is at least a provisional frame of reference and is consequently a welcome improvement over the simple, alphabetical arrangement of the earlier, *General Equilibrium* collection. It is that earlier collection, however, which apparently reflects a greater attention given to the availability of the potential entries. At any rate, Debreu (1996, I, p. xii) tells us that he excluded from his volumes any items "published in the 1990s" on the principle that "papers written in the more distant past . . . are less readily available and critical judgement about them is less unreliable." Walker obviously did not apply the same rule. Of the eighty-five items comprising the collection before us, forty-four appeared in the 1990s, sixteen of which appeared after 1995. Still, the Walker collection manages to achieve a rather greater breadth of sources. In both cases, the most frequently-cited source is *Econometrica*, but that journal provides only nine of Walker's selections while, in keeping with its role in the history of general equilibrium theory (Ingrao & Israel, 1990, Chap. 9; Weintraub, 1983; II, 1),[1] it provides thirty-five of the ninety items selected by Debreu.

2. GENERAL EQUILIBRIUM AND "REALISM"

Although the title of this collection suggests a concern with the concept of equilibrium in all its dimensions, Walker's (1997) earlier broadside against contemporary general equilibrium literature in the Arrow-Debreu tradition looms over these volumes from start to finish. Indeed, chapters four and five of that critique are among the selections chosen for this collection. Stripped of the rather tiresome repetition, Walker's criticism comes down to two fundamental points, both of which are embodied in his demand that an analytical model satisfy his standard of a "functioning system." This last is a concept that is central to the argument conveyed in the two chapters of that critique reproduced here (in Vol. II, items 5 and 17), but the reader will likely have some difficulty with those selections since the notion of a "functioning system" is defined and explained only in Chapter one of that earlier work, which is not included in this collection. This problem is, of course, inevitable when an anthology includes selections drawn from a larger, integrated work. Fortunately, that occurs only infrequently here, the chief instances being the Walker chapters and a selection from Fisher (1983, Chap. 2; II, 20). To be sure, the difficulty can be ameliorated by the addition of an essay introducing the selection or of an explanatory footnote at the relevant point; but, apart from the list of supplemental readings already mentioned and a brief, general essay introducing the collection as a whole at the opening of Volume I, these volumes, like those of the earlier, Debreu collection, offer no such scholarly appurtenances.

Readers familiar with Walker's complaints against the general equilibrium literature will recall his appeal to the notion of a "functioning system" as a standard of appraisal. To meet that standard, the model specification must contain sufficient institutional detail to motivate and direct the behavior under investigation. It must, in other words, identify the "physical structures, institutions, technology, laws, procedures, etc . . . [that] condition, permit, or enforce ways of behaving on the part of the participants" (Walker, 1997, p. 9). A model that fails to measure up is "incomplete" and therefore can tell us nothing useful about the economic reality that surrounds us. Lest the reader fail to grasp the exacting nature of this standard, Walker (p. 35) lists explicitly the elements that must be included if a general equilibrium structure is to be deemed "complete" and, hence, a "functioning system":

> The main purpose [of the chapter] has been to show that the general equilibrium models constructed in this century are not functioning systems because they are incomplete . . ..
>
>   A model should contain firms, consumers, and resource suppliers, all with specified characteristics. It should contain general economic institutions, by which is meant institutions other than those which are within markets; and it should contain technology, productive process, and systems of communication that link economic agents with markets. The model

should have markets with well-defined physical features that enable the participants to make purchases and sales, and with marketplace institutions, technology, rules, and pricing conventions and procedures. The model should specify concretely how the traders are enabled to come together, how prices are quoted and publicized in each particular market, how and when information about prices and sales in each particular market is transmitted to traders in other markets, by whom and how prices are changed, and how offers to buy and sell are made public.

To be sure, general equilibrium theorists have long acknowledged a need to invest their models with at least the minimum institutional framework necessary to give structure to the posited behavior. Here is the source of the infamous "auctioneer," introduced to get round the awkward realization that a strict understanding of a competitive market as a case where "no one can affect the terms on which he may transact" seems to exclude all possible means by which such agents can find a set of prices at which the quantities offered for sale are just matched by the quantities demanded. If the existing prices do not produce such a match and if no agent has the power to alter his offer price, what mechanism changes market prices in the direction of the supposed equilibrium? The answer, of course, is the hypothetical market-maker, or "super-auctioneer," who is introduced strictly to perform this function (Arrow & Hahn, 1971, pp. 264–266; see also Walker, 1997, pp. 13–25). This august personage is able to collect information on the individual supply and demand offers at each price, calculate the price change necessary to move the market in the direction of equilibrium, then call out a new set of prices for a new round, thereby moving the market through a succession of converging steps to equilibrium, where all trades are conducted. But even here the market-maker cannot rest: he must also transmit to each of the participants information regarding the location and magnitude of all other individual supply and demand offers, thus enabling them to identify trading counterparts. Even aficionados of this literature find the implied information burden borne by the auctioneer to be beyond the credible. Arrow and Hahn (1971, pp. 266, 324) themselves characterize their market-maker as no more than an "extremely artificial," "as if" simplification. Those who find the "as if" expedient unsatisfactory will, no doubt, agree with Walker's (1997, p. 22) conclusion that "the process is obviously absurd." Hence, it is not surprising that Walker should insist, as a second condition defining his notion of a "functioning system," that the specified institutional structure have a clearly recognizable congruence with the reality to be understood: "The objective of models that are intended to explain the real economy should be to achieve the highest possible degree of realism regarding the phenomena and relations that are deemed important" (Walker, 1997, pp. 38–39). All this, then, is the necessary background to the bipartite complaint we encounter in the first of the earlier Walker chapters reproduced in this collection. There we learn that the general equilibrium literature exhibits two distinct flaws: "One problem," with these studies "is that . . . their postulates have no justifications provided by foundations in a functioning model," and the "second problem is that the postulates and the process of manipulating the equations have no contact with real economic conditions" (Walker, 1997, pp. 101–102; II, 5).

We see these earlier complaints reflected in the two, overlapping classification schemes advanced in Walker's introductory essay to these volumes. The first of these draws upon an inference regarding the investigator's methodological stance. Under this head we have two classes of models. The "first type is constructed on the presumption that the real economy is an equilibrating system because it does not exhibit much instability." In the "second type of model," however, "equilibrium is not deliberately created." Instead, "the procedure is to incorporate assumptions into a model which are believed to be accurate representations of properties of the real economy, and the object is to see whether or not the model is an equilibrating system" in the hope that one can then draw a judgment "about whether or not a position of equilibrium exists in the real economy" (I, pp. xiv–xv). Overlying this distinction as to the methodological status of the equilibrium concept we find a second classification scheme reflecting Walker's repeated complaint regarding the insufficient institutional "realism" of these models. This class too is divided in two parts. The first encompasses the "perfectly competitive virtual models" – that is, those which are "virtual in the sense that the only behavior that occurs in disequilibrium . . . is the quotation and changing of prices and the determination of the associated desired supply and demand quantities of the participants." Here are the constructions of the Arrow-Debreu-McKenzie type and those of their intellectual descendants. Standing in contrast to these are the "non-virtual models," those which permit some form of "disequilibrium behavior other than just the changing of prices and the reporting of the associated supply and demand quantities . . . ." These possess the merit that they "are closer to reality than the virtual variety," and their extension "beyond perfect competition to a number of other types of situations that are found in the real economy" is a "further step in the right direction" (I, pp. xviii–xx). Apparently, however, this ranking according to the degree of institutional "realism" offers little help in drawing instructive distinctions. At any rate, Walker tells us that a "superabundance" of models "have little or no relation to real economic situations." They are no more than "toys, games of logic with their own internal problems and rules that derive not from contacts with the real economy but from the previous literature on the subject." Hence, it is of no consequence whether "[t]hey are endowed with equilibrating properties or are examined to determine the presence or absence of those features," since any results obtained from these toy models "are not interesting from an economic point of view" (I, p. xv).

Nevertheless, the question of institutional realism provides the framework for the papers collected in Volume II, about half of which is devoted to the treatment of "perfectly competitive virtual models." Within that class, the papers are arranged according to the three classical problems of general equilibrium theory: the "existence" of equilibrium (can the model at hand be shown to possess such an equilibrium), its "uniqueness" (can the model be shown to exhibit only one such equilibrium), and its (local and global) "stability" (see Ingrao & Israel, 1990, p. 360). The remainder of the volume is divided between "non-virtual purely competitive models" and the extension of the "non-virtual" class to "various forms of market imperfection." This classification by institutional realism is abandoned in Volume III, which, we are told, is simply intended to illustrate some of the "many special concepts of equilibrium [that] have been developed recently" (I, p. xx), identifying, among others, "stationary," "temporary," "rational expectations," "Bayesian" equilibria, game theoretic equilibria (the longest section, containing fourteen items), and, finally, a catch-all, "other" category. Finally, Volume I provides the introduction to this theoretical work with a series of papers ostensibly devoted to "historical perspectives," to "criticisms of the equilibrium concept," and to investigations of the "meaning and concepts of modern economic equilibrium theory."[2]

3. THE MANY FACES OF EQUILIBRIUM

3.1. "Positivists" vs. "Pragmatists"

The reader comes away from this jumble yearning for a sense of coherence. The nature and content of the notion conveyed by the term "equilibrium" vary widely throughout these volumes. Walker's preoccupation with the acknowledged lack of institutional detail in these models fails to satisfy our desire for a framework that can help us to form these differing conceptions into an orderly structure and thereby to reveal the lines of thematic progression running through this literature. We do, however, find a hint as to where we might look for such a framework in Walker's passing observation that each of the "specific concepts of equilibrium" treated in his third volume is model-specific, quoting for illustration Milgate's earlier lament that equilibrium has "become a category with no meaning independent of the exact specification of the initial conditions for *any* model" (Milgate, 1987, p. 182; emphasis in original; quoted in I, p. xx). This calls to mind Weintraub's recent efforts to remind us of the growing realization among philosophers and sociologists of science that "scientific work is knowledge creation in a context and that such knowledge is shared knowledge within a particular community" (Weintraub, 1991, p. 4). Viewed from this perspective, the concept of equilibrium derives its meaning strictly from the theoretical context in which it is employed by the scientific community, that meaning changing with that context. As Weintraub puts the point, this approach "maintains that there is no meaning of 'equilibrium' except as that word is used by the community of economists who read and write texts in which the word 'equilibrium' appears; the meaning of 'equilibrium' is derived from the use to which the word is put by the community of readers of texts on equilibrium analysis." Or, more bluntly, "equilibrium is a feature of our models, not the world." This view, which Weintraub designates as that of "the pragmatist," stands in opposition to that of the "positivist," who "argues that the idea of equilibrium is associated with some aspect of the real world and that the task in the scientific analysis of competitive equilibrium is to create better, or more realistic, models of equilibrium; the test of the theory of equilibrium is thus . . . correspondence with the real world in which equilibrium is to be found" (Weintraub, 1991, pp. 107–109).

Viewed through the prism of this distinction between the "positivist" and the "pragmatist," the epistemological fault lines running through this collection become strikingly apparent. The positivists are, of course, well represented by Walker's repeated call for "the highest possible degree of realism" in economic modeling, but his is not a lone voice. We have also Kaldor's powerful lament that general equilibrium theory of the Arrow-Debreu type is not only "barren and irrelevant as an apparatus of thought to deal with the manner of operation of economic forces," but, worse, because of "the powerful attraction of the habits of thought engendered by 'equilibrium economics,' [it] has become a major obstacle to the development of economics as a *science* – meaning by the term 'science' a body of theorems based on assumptions that are *empirically* derived (from observations) and which embody hypotheses that are capable of verification both in regard to the assumptions and the predictions." Consequently, by Kaldor's standard, which seeks the conversion of general equilibrium theory "into a set of theorems directly related to observable phenomena, the development of theoretical economics was one of continual *degress*, not *progress*." But Kaldor's complaint is not limited to the self-consciously axiomatic nature of general equilibrium theory. On the contrary, he calls into question the very notion of equilibrium itself. Here we encounter, in a particularly strong form, a theme which recurs frequently in the critical and evaluative papers reproduced in Volume I – namely, the realization that the dynamic process of adjustment necessarily involves continuous changes in wealth positions and in the structure of markets, firms, and other institutions as well, all of which alter the nature of the model's equilibrium, thereby making it all the more uncertain that any such "point of rest" will ever be achieved. The particular form of this path-dependence problem that troubles Kaldor is that which arises when we acknowledge a widespread existence of scale economies: "When every change in the use of resources – every reorganization of productive activities – creates the opportunity for a further change *which would not have existed otherwise*, the notion of an 'optimum' allocation of resources . . . becomes a meaningless and contradictory notion." Fortunately for our classroom exercises, Kaldor is willing to grant an exception for a narrow range of comparative statics applications: the concept of an "optimal" allocation of resources "falls apart – except perhaps for the consideration of short-run problems, where the framework of social organization and the distribution of the major part of available 'resources,' such as durable equipment and trained or educated labour, can be treated as given as a heritage of the past, and the effects of current decisions on future development are ignored" (Kaldor, 1972, pp. 1237–1239; 1245–1246; I, 7; emphasis in original). On this point, Kaldor seems to carry the objection further even than Walker, who, while acknowledging in his introduction that "the structure of the economy varies with parametric changes [which] will alter its equilibrium values and its equilibrating properties," nevertheless insists that "this does not obviate the value of equilibrium analysis" so long as we can "expect the revision of a model in order to reflect the structural and behavioral changes that are seen to result from a change of conditions" (I, p. xvii). No one, however, carries the criticism of equilibrium further than John Henry, who, in an essay that would have been better positioned in the section devoted to "criticisms of the equilibrium concept" than in its current grouping with papers exploring the "meaning and concepts" of equilibrium theory, nevertheless delivers the ultimate positivist critique: "unless equilibrium itself can be *proved* to be an actual state of society, the argument is hollow" (Henry, 1983–1984, 220; I, 22; emphasis in original).

Weintraub's "pragmatists" would have little patience with such a demand, and theirs is unmistakably the majority view among the papers collected here. Though written nearly a half-century ago, the best exemplar remains Machlup's cogent expression of the equilibrium concept as "a mental tool" to aid "in establishing to our satisfaction a causal nexus between different events or changes" contemplated within the "mental experiments" of our models. Long before Weintraub christened the position with the "pragmatist" label, Machlup (1991 [1958], p. 53, n.7; I, 6) insisted that the equilibrium concept can be understood only within the context of the model under investigation, warning his reader that "equilibrium and disequilibrium refer to whatever model you may have in mind."[3] Indeed, "to characterize a concrete situation 'observed' in reality as one of 'equilibrium,' " as Henry and, apparently, Walker demand as a necessary condition to the application of the concept, "is to commit the fallacy of misplaced concreteness" – a fallacy that arises when we find ourselves "forgetting the relativity of equilibrium with respect to variables and relations selected," and consequently "jumping the distance between a useful fiction and particular data of observation" (pp. 57–58). To make that leap raises the further danger of the "fallacy of implicit evaluation or disguised politics" (p. 60).

If we succumb to "the popular association of equilibrium with a Good Thing and of disequilibrium with a Bad Thing," the concept becomes a tool of persuasion, employed to gain support for some policy stance. It that event, we are left with "an equilibrium concept so drastically restricted by built-in political criteria [that it] becomes less useful, if not useless, in the analysis of most problems" (pp. 70–71).

Machlup's definition of equilibrium as a "mental tool" to aid in analysis is, of course, widely accepted, and it recurs frequently throughout these volumes. Indeed, Dore reminds us that we heard its echo in Keynes's stated goal to develop "an organized and orderly method of thinking out particular problems" (Keynes, 1964 [1936], p. 297; quoted in Dore, 1984–1985, p. 194; I, 24). We hear it too, more recently, in Caravale's (1994, p. 28; I, 28) "logical conception" of equilibrating adjustment as "a process of potential convergence in the direction of the 'center of gravity' which can be identified on the basis of some fundamental data of the model."

3.2. Alternative Structures: Sraffian Surplus

There is also ample illustration of that "relativity of equilibrium" which Machlup described so long ago and which Walker employs as the theme for the third of our volumes. Instructive cases of this model-specific variation in the equilibrium concept occur in the earlier volumes as well, but the point is obscured by the classification scheme adopted. We have, for example, at least two papers devoted to an examination of the concept of equilibrium employed in the Sraffian exposition of Classical theory – that is, the line of development that Blaug (1999, pp. 214–215) has characterized as a "rational reconstruction" of Ricardo, though one "capable of affording a springboard for a wholly new style of long-run equilibrium theorizing . . . as an alternative heritage to the mainstream lineage of neoclassical economics." The two papers illustrating this "alternative heritage" appear in Volume I, though one (Harris, 1991; I, 4) is curiously located in the section promising "historical perspective," and the second (Bharadwaj, 1991; I, 13) appears nearly two hundred pages later near the end of the section devoted to "criticisms of the equilibrium concept."[4] Bharadwaj's is indeed a criticism of the neoclassical concept of equilibrium – one which takes as its point of departure Joan Robinson's (1974; I, 8) influential objection to the "timelessness" of general equilibrium modeling. The solution proposed by Bharadwaj is an appeal to the Sraffian approach, which, he insists, is to be preferred for its "ability fruitfully to combine historical elements abstracted from concrete observation and to bring them together in short chains of logical reasoning." The source of this superiority lies in the "central concept of classical theory," which Bharadwaj identifies, in the Sraffian tradition, as the notion of a social surplus – roughly analogous to the non-labor share of the net national product. Because it must determine the extent of this surplus, "Classical political economy (CPE) . . . encompasses theories of the determination of wages, of methods of production, and of social demand," but it is significant that "these magnitudes are not simultaneously and co-terminously determined as a subproblem of relative price formation." For this reason, says Bharadwaj, "CPE has a much more dynamic story to tell about the interrelationships between levels and changes in output *and* wages, or between the changes in output *and* techniques, and vice versa." Indeed, "one of the important consequences" of this "surplus" structure is that " 'factor prices' are not determined from within the same process and by the same mechanism as 'commodity prices'" (Bharadwaj, 1991, pp. 81; 85–86; I, 13, emphasis in original). This, of course, is a characteristic feature of the classical model, but Bharadwaj's claims regarding a supposed greater "dynamic" scope in the Sraffian, "surplus" approach to that model would carry more weight had he confronted the fundamental circularity that bedevils that approach. Since the surplus is defined as the residual left after deducting from total output the wage bill of the labor employed in the production of that output, the magnitude of that total product must be known prior to the determination of the surplus. Further, the rate of profit in this framework is defined as the ratio of that surplus to that wage bill. Now, if the total product comprises more than one commodity, it must be expressed in value terms; but if the value coefficient is itself dependent upon the rate of profit, then to claim that the magnitude of the total product is determined prior to the rate of profit is to involve one in circular reasoning (see Garegnani, 1987). The problem can be resolved by taking one of the variables (usually the wage rate) as given exogenously, but Bharadwaj tells us nothing of the implications raised by these analytical difficulties for his claim of a greater opportunity within the surplus tradition for a more fruitful dynamic analysis.

From Harris, on the other hand, we learn that those writing in the Walrasian tradition are not alone in their concerns regarding the stability characteristics of their equilibrium models. Sraffa's intellectual heirs have raised similar concerns. In this tradition, "the appropriate and relevant equilibrium concept to consider is that of 'long period equilibrium,' . . . characterised by the existence of 'prices of production' at a uniform rate of profit on the supply price of capital, those prices being said to constitute a center of gravitation for 'market prices.' " However, if we presume that it is profit-rate differentials that drive firm output decisions, we find that such an adjustment mechanism "cannot be guaranteed to provide the correct signals to profit-seeking firms in their investment and output decisions that would cause the set of all firms to act so as to bring into existence [the equilibrium] prices of production and corresponding profit rate." Hence, just as in the Walrasian tradition so also in the Sraffian approach, "what is at issue . . . is whether the idea of a convergence of market prices to production prices is sustainable under *any* economically meaningful description of capitalist behaviour as regards decisions on prices, output, and investment." Further, the Sraffian literature is no more scrupulous in its attention to the kind of institutional content whose omission from the Walrasian models Walker finds so distressing. Certainly we hear echo of Walker's complaint in Harris's objection that the "analytic solutions" obtained from the surplus models "are, in many cases, not susceptible to any economically meaningful interpretation," because those models embody a "specification of economic behaviour and institutional structure [that] is seriously lacking in the very elements that are relevant to evaluating the dynamic behaviour of real-world economies." The particular missing elements identified by Harris reproduce almost exactly Walker's list: labor and financial market institutions, technological and organizational structures, and firm pricing behavior (Harris, 1991, pp. 90–93; I, 4).

Finally, we learn from Harris that the Sraffian approach is no less vulnerable to the more fundamental charge of path dependence so frequently leveled at the Walrasian models. In both traditions, the realization that disequilibrium trades alter the model's parameter values makes "the question of convergence to a predetermined equilibrium position necessarily . . . problematical unless resort is had to 'very rigid assumptions.' " Conversely, any attempt to produce such an equilibrium by the introduction of a presumed adjustment process "related to the equilibrium position must necessarily rule out features of actual economic behaviour in so far as such behavior entails path dependence." All this leads Harris to view the Sraffian equilibrium framework with a nihilism not unlike that which characterizes Kaldor's judgment of the Walrasian equilibrium as "a meaningless and contradictory notion." For Harris, the problem of path dependence "provides general grounds for objecting to the conception of a determinate equilibrium of production prices in Classical theory quite apart from any finding of stability or instability in the gravitation process," a conclusion that makes Bharadwaj's promise of "a much more dynamic story" in the Classical tradition appear all the more unreasonably optimistic (Harris, 1991, pp. 93–94; I, 4).

3.3. *"Toys, Games of Logic"*

Though tiresome in its repetition, no one can deny the validity of the complaint that the development of general equilibrium structures in the Walrasian tradition has long since slipped its moorings to anything remotely approaching the reality we all observe outside the protective walls of our seminar rooms. There can be no surprise, then, that a collection of such work will contain abundant examples of Walker's "toys, games of logic." The first three entries in Volume 3 will suffice for our purposes. In the first of these, we find a make-believe economy in which all utility functions, endowments, and production processes "fluctuate according to a stationary probability law" and, further, every agent "observes the underlying stochastic process which governs all exogenous fluctuations in the economy" and presumes the continued operation of that process. Combining these principles with a permanent-income characterization of consumption behavior, we are led to the less than remarkable conclusion that markets for contingent claims are unnecessary in this world. Consumers provide themselves with all the insurance they require through their holdings of money balances, which absorb the stochastically predictable shocks to income and endowments; and "forward markets are not needed to coordinate intertemporal supply and demand, for agents have rational expectations and full information." These results are offered as "a limited answer to the question of why we do not in reality observe complete markets for contingent claims," a problem that troubled Arrow (1974) in his presidential address to the American Economic Association. That answer, says our author, "is that self-insurance and rational expectations can take care of everyday fluctuations" (Bewley, 1981, pp. 266, 267; III, 1). The reader can be forgiven the view that this is a very "limited answer" indeed, there being, in this paradise, no uncertainty that cannot be reduced to a known probabilistic calculus. Most will, no doubt, find greater promise in a passing comment encountered a few entries later in Grandmont's contribution to the collection: "one should expect markets for contingent contracts to be *incomplete* in actual economies because it would be too difficult and costly to describe exhaustively in advance all possible contingencies of a complex, uncertain environment" (Grandmont, 1991, p. 4; III, 5). Indeed, Arrow himself acknowledged that the answer to his question is likely to be found in a due regard to the costs involved in the construction and enforcement of forward and contingent contracts (Arrow, 1974, pp. 8–10).

We need have no fear of the unknown in moving from Bewley's world to that of the next entry in the volume. On the contrary, we find there a world much like that which we left behind. Here too all "shocks" follow a known probabilistic pattern ("an exogenous, time-homogeneous Markov process") in which "the current state is a sufficient statistic for the future evolution of the system" (Duffie et al., 1994; III, 2). As we move on to the third entry in the volume, our powerful foresight dims somewhat, but it is not lost entirely. Now we enter a world of overlapping generations, in which agents age across two periods (Gottardi, 1996; III, 3). Their tastes and endowments change across those two periods according to an unspecified stochastic process, but they are unaffected by the agent's date of birth and hence are independent of events occurring prior to that date. Although the agents have no information as to the probability associated with any particular state of the future, they are aware of all the possibilities. Consequently, they incorporate all possible future states in their consumption plans, a problem that is held within manageable limits by the assumption that this economy contains only a single consumption good, which, further, cannot be transferred across periods. Indeed, the only commodity that can be held across periods is non-interest-bearing, fiat money. Although "young" agents may acquire assets as well as the single consumption good, those assets mature when the agents enter their "old" period, paying out in money an amount determined by the state of the world that occurs in that period. The point of this peculiar apparatus is to provide yet another means of incorporating positive money holdings into the general equilibrium framework, though, as with Bewley, the result here is hardly surprising. In both cases, the models are carefully constructed to accord to the monetary asset, and to it alone, a critical function. In Bewley's case, that function is to absorb the shocks of known stochastic fluctuations in income, while for Gottardi's agents money provides the only available means to transfer wealth across periods.

4. HISTORY OR "TIMELESS" EQUILIBRIUM?

To say that these, and indeed all work in the Walrasian tradition, describe hypothetical economies that bear little resemblance to the world we all encounter outside our classrooms is to state the obvious twice over. It is a commonplace that any effort at analysis must abstract from institutional detail to some extent. What distinguishes the Walrasian tradition is only its conscious and unwavering resolve to press that abstraction to the highest possible level. This was, indeed, the very characteristic that was advanced by its proponents as the theory's greatest strength. Recall Debreu's well-known appeal to an "effort toward rigor [that] substitutes correct reasonings and results for incorrect ones" and which "dictates the axiomatic form of the analysis where the theory, in the strict sense, is logically entirely disconnected from its interpretations" (Debreu, 1959, p. x). What we require is a standard of assessment: at what point does the gain of analytical generality obscure rather than illuminate the world we inhabit? Walker's repeated lamentations over the lack of institutional detail offer little help on this point. Indeed, his lists of the elements defining a "functioning system" suggest an impossible standard of nearly complete institutional content. Yet, difficult though it may be to meet his standard, Walker nowhere questions the fruitfulness of the equilibrium concept itself. Although the "real economy is always in disequilibrium" and "does not adjust with sufficient speed to reach equilibrium before it changes," he nevertheless insists that "those features do not mean that comparative equilibrium predictions are not interesting. We are interested in equilibrium in order to discover the tendencies of the variables in disequilibrium occasioned by a parametric change." Hence, we can fruitfully appeal to the notion of equilibrium in our policy discourse as a point of reference from which to discern the impact that a proposed change will "have upon the directions in which variables tend to move, . . . even if equilibrium is never reached nor closely approached" (Walker, 1997, p. 128; II, 17).

4.1. "Time's Arrow"

However, though obscured by the organizational scheme imposed upon the collection, there is lurking throughout these volumes a second line of attack that, though related to Walker's criticism, nevertheless constitutes a more fundamental threat to neo-classical theory since, in this alternative view, it is the legitimacy of the equilibrium concept itself that is under assault. We have already encountered the Kaldorian form of this argument in his objection that the existence of scale economies reduces the equilibrium concept to a "meaningless and contradictory notion" (Kaldor, 1972; I, 7; the argument is repeated in Kaldor, 1975; I, 9; and 1979; I, 10; the reader might well wonder at the propriety of the decision to include all of these in the collection). However, a more general statement of the critique is contained in two essays by Joan Robinson (1974; I, 8; and 1977), one of which found its way into our collection, and in the ruminations on the matter by Sir John Hicks (1976), which did not.

The problem can be described as the economist's confrontation with what physicists have long known as "time's arrow" (Eddington, 1929, pp. 68–69). The irreversibility of the arrow's flight presents difficulties for our theoretical speculations at both its leading and trailing ends. First, as we contemplate the influence of anticipated future outcomes on current market behavior, it forces us to follow Hicks in admitting the great divide in the nature and precision of our knowledge: "The knowledge that we have, or can have, of the past is different in kind from what we can know of the future; for the latter, at best, is no more than a knowledge of probabilities" (Hicks, 1976, p. 135). This presents a troubling inconsistency with our concept of equilibrium, where, it is said, no agent faces any inducement to change current production or consumption behavior. If agents are able to make such a determination, then, as Robinson (1974, p. 203) points out, "every one knows exactly and in full detail what consequences would follow any action that he may take." Now, as we have seen in the work of Bewley, Duffie et al., and other recent laborers in the Walrasian vineyard, it is possible to construct such equilibria so long as we infuse our agents with a degree of foresight no less than that described by Hicks's "best" case – "a knowledge of probabilities" of future occurrences. Further, we find in Bewley's contribution to our collection that even this tamed and house-broken breed of uncertainty is sufficient to demonstrate

Hicks's earlier observation that "the holding of liquid reserves . . . is a matter of provision against an uncertain future – . . . providing oneself with the ability to take action to meet emergencies which may arise in the future and which are such that their particular shape cannot be accurately foreseen" (Hicks, 1976, p. 139). This focus on money's role as a means of insurance made necessary by "our distrust of our own calculations and conventions concerning the future" is, of course, the answer Keynes himself gave long ago to the question of money-holding. The question arises because "it is a recognized characteristic of money as a store of wealth that it is barren; whereas practically every other form of storing wealth yields some interest or profit." Why, then, asks Keynes, "should anyone outside a lunatic asylum wish to use money as a store of wealth?" (Keynes, 1937, pp. 215–216). We see now that Gottardi has offered an alternative answer: in a world in which there exists no "other form of storing wealth" across periods, even those outside the asylum will hold "barren" money balances to serve that purpose.

Nevertheless, though scholars have been remarkably ingenious in redefining our familiar notion of equilibrium to incorporate at least this well-behaved, "stochastically known" form of "uncertainty," this work only seems to have imparted all the more weight to Keynes's prescient warning on the matter: we deceive ourselves when we presume the "calculus of probability . . . to be capable of reducing uncertainty to the same calculable status as that of certainty itself." Our world presents us with countless, incalculable uncertainties: the prospect of war or terrorist violence, "or the price of copper and the rate of interest twenty years hence, or the obsolescence of a new invention." Keynes's admonition is no less apt for our world than for his own: "About these matters there is no scientific basis on which to form any calculable probability whatever. We simply do not know" (Keynes, 1937, pp. 213–214). Here is the particular "reality" whose omission from the general equilibrium literature troubles Robinson: "The assumption of 'perfect foresight' carries the argument out of this world into a system of mathematical abstraction, which, although the symbols may be given economic names, has no point of contact with empirical reality" (Robinson, 1977, p. 1322).

At the trailing end of time's arrow we are faced with the irreversible influence of the past on present behavior. Again as Robinson reminds us (1974, p. 206; I, 8), the vector of solution values to a timeless "system of mathematical abstraction" is of no help in determining how a real economy will respond to a change in any of the parameters held within the ceteris paribus impound. A simple change in taste alters the pattern of production; but that, in turn, "must involve investment and dis-investment, at least in work in progress, and windfall losses and gains on stocks that have become inappropriate." Hence, we cannot judge the character (or, indeed, the existence) of the new equilibrium unless we "fill in a whole story about the behavior of the economy when it is out of equilibrium, including the effect of disappointed expectations on the decisions being taken by its inhabitants." Of course, when we do so, we must acknowledge that the nature of the new equilibrium depends critically on the nature of the disequilibrium behavior that brought it into existence; each equilibrium depends upon the disequilibrium path that leads to it.

This path-dependency consequence of disequilibrium trading is central to Walker's critique as well. As we have seen, the treatment of disequilibrium transactions defines his distinction between "virtual" and "non-virtual" models, itself an element in his repeated demand that general equilibrium models meet his standard of a "functioning system." It is the failure of that literature to meet that standard that explains its preoccupation with the three classical questions of existence, uniqueness and stability, a preoccupation that is the subject of the two chapters of his earlier critique included here. The argument of these chapters is a familiar lament. Because the literature originates in a strictly mathematical perspective, these triune dimensions of the equilibrium solution are likewise understood strictly as properties of the equation systems under consideration: "The question of existence is thus a matter of mathematical logic, of the properties and interrelations of equations, a question of their solution, separate from the question of stability." But this separability arises solely from the model's failure to specify the process by which the move between equilibria is accomplished. In such an "incomplete," "virtual" model,

> during the equilibrating process there can be no endogenously caused changes in the parameters of the model such as preferences, technology, the amount of land and the number of workers. To assume that changes in prices and notional supplies and demands do not affect those conditions is itself a supposition about what transpires in disequilibrium in the model. The stocks of capital goods and of consumer durables and inventories of non-durables possessed by consumers and businesses do not vary because in disequilibrium there are no transactions, no production, no consumption . . . . There are no changes in real wealth during the equilibrating process and therefore no wealth-induced changes in supply or demand functions.

Like Robinson, Walker calls for the construction of more complete models that "fill in" the disequilibrium story. In such a system, "certain of the parameters of the equations intended to describe the model would in fact be endogenous variables, changing as the equilibrating process unfolds. There would be outputs and incomes, transactions at non-general-equilibrium prices and changes in such matters as the distribution and value of assets." Obviously, such a model would exhibit the very path dependency that troubled Robinson. In Walker, that characteristic prompts a criticism of the traditional treatment of existence and stability as separable questions, for in a properly specified "functioning system," "the question of ascertaining the existence of equilibrium is inextricably linked to the dynamic behaviour of the model" (Walker, 1997, pp. 103–104; 107–108; II, 5; see also II, 17).

There is, of course, nothing here that is new or controversial. Notwithstanding Debreu's famous refusal to consider the problems of stability or uniqueness (see for example Hildenbrand's recollection on this point in his "Introduction" to Debreu, 1983, p. 26), researchers have long understood that the proliferation of existence proofs serves only, adopting McCloskey's (1994, p. 133) blunt expression, to "show that certain equations describing a certain blackboard economy have a solution, but they do not give the actual solution to the blackboard problem, much less to an extant economy." Indeed, thirty years earlier, Chipman (1965, p. 36; I, 17) in a very useful survey that is included in our collection, observed that the "real content of the equilibrium concept is to be found not so much in the state itself as in the laws of change which it implies . . . . Fruitful analysis of equilibrium therefore requires analysis of stability conditions." Nevertheless, there is an important difference to be drawn in the way that scholars respond to this common insight. As we have seen, Walker's call for more fully specified models is not an attack on the equilibrium concept itself. For others, however, Kaldor and Robinson in our collection, for example, the admitted problem of path dependence is an insuperable bar to the fruitful application of the equilibrium framework. It is not just the pattern of production and wealth holdings that is influenced by the presumed disequilibrium transactions, the very nature of society's technical knowledge is the product of that adjustment path. The channel of influence can operate either through Kaldor's scale economies or through relative price effects on the direction of technical change, as Robinson suggests following a long tradition among economic historians.[5] We can, of course, work out the solution values for a Walkerian, "virtual" model and determine how those values change in response to, say, a change in demand from potatoes to wheat. But we cannot deny the force of Robinson's objection that "even this is a somewhat idle exercise, for the path an economy follows necessarily influences its technology. An economy that has developed the technology for growing potatoes does not have the same spectrum of technical knowledge as one which only grows wheat." Hence, by Walker's lights, a model that presumes to trace out the change in equilibria must identify not only the disequilibrium changes in production patterns, factor supplies, and wealth holdings but must also be able to predict the change in technological knowledge. All this seems an impossible standard, leading Robinson to conclude, "As soon as the uncertainty of the expectations that guide economic behavior is admitted, equilibrium drops out of the argument and history takes its place" (Robinson, 1974, pp. 202–204; I, 8).

We can discern in this collection the whisper of time's arrow even in our "virtual" models, in spite of our best efforts there to avoid its demands. In support of the decision to limit his agents to a single consumption commodity per period, Gottardi (1996, p. 77; III, 3) observes, "Uncertainty in fact destroys the symmetry between past and future and hence the equivalence between transfers across generations

within the same period and across the different periods of an individual's life."
Indeed; time's arrow permits movement in only one direction: "past and future
are different" (Hicks, 1976, p. 135). That irreversibility of time poses a problem
for Bewley as well, and here too the issue is one that Hicks foresaw. If Bewley's
consumer is to maximize utility subject to a long-run budget constraint, he must
know the value of his marginal utility of money (λ_i in Bewley's notation). But this
requires that the consumer determine his utility across all goods and equilibrium
prices in the current state. "However," says Bewley, this need not impose too heavy
a burden if we "can think of the consumer as having found the appropriate level of
λ_i by trial and error" (Bewley, 1981, p. 276; III, 1). In other words, as Hicks observed earlier, at least when making large and infrequent purchases, the consumer
likely does *not* (as our theory supposes) "re-think his whole budget, identifying
the collection of goods which would have to be given up if [the contemplated
purchase were made]." The decision rests instead on a rough estimate of "what one
can afford," and that is indicated by the marginal utility of money. That familiar
Marshallian concept "is much more than the mere Lagrange multiplier . . .. It is
the means by which the consumer is enabled to make his separate decisions, and
to make them fairly rationally, without being obliged to take the trouble to weigh
all conceivable alternatives." But we now have another point where the decisions
of the past intrude upon our derivation of present equilibrium. If the consumer
obtains the estimate of his marginal utility of money by "trial and error" over "past
experience," then different pasts will produce different present demand functions
and thus different present equilibrium vectors (Hicks, 1976, pp. 137–138).

4.2. Obscured Filiations

Several years ago, Weintraub pointed out that Hicks's *Value and Capital* (1939)
advanced "two related sets of ideas . . . concerning equilibrium and stability." In
the first half of the book we find the now familiar, Walrasian question regarding
the tendency of a particular equilibrium state to be re-established after a temporary
perturbation. In the second half of the book, where Hicks takes up the "foundations
of dynamic economics," the argument turns to the possibility of a coherent process
of economic evolution across time. Because of the considerable influence of *Value
and Capital*, "we see that from Hicks there was a bifurcation of the dynamics
literature into two separate lines" concerning, on the one hand, "the stability of a
competitive equilibrium" and, on the other, "growth dynamics and capital theory"
(Weintraub, 1991, p. 36). Now, it is evident that both of these distinct lines of
thought are encompassed in Robinson's objection that economic analysis would
be better served by a notion of historical evolution rather than by continued appeal

to a discredited concept of equilibrium. If we acknowledge that transactions occur at "disequilibrium" prices, then what reason have we for our claim that a particular "equilibrium" state will be re-established after a disturbance? Likewise, if we acknowledge that the present state of the world in all its dimensions (the pattern of wealth holdings, the nature and extent of available inputs; the nature of the technology, and so on) is the product of actions and decisions taken in the past under the influence of (possibly unrealized) expectations held at the time, what reason have we to claim that there exists an identifiable, "equilibrium" growth path to which the economy will tend in the future, much less that we can actually identify that path? It is evident from the collection before us that these complaints have not fallen on deaf ears. Though unwilling to abandon entirely the equilibrium concept, theorists have sought to modify the analytical content of that concept in response to these objections. Further, though the organizational structure of the collection does not bring out this point, we can nevertheless discern a pattern of intellectual evolution that exhibits the same "bifurcation" in the conceptualization of the equilibrium problem that Weintraub found in the earlier developments prompted by Hicks's *Value and Capital*.

We find the second of these themes – that pursuing the economy's evolution across time – in the third of our volumes, where we encounter a recent survey of the "temporary equilibrium" research program by Grandmont (1991; III, 5), his earlier (1977) seminal paper laying out that agenda having already been included in the Debreu collection. Dispelling any remaining doubt regarding Hicks's influence on this literature, Grandmont describes in detail his debt to the Hicksian analytical "Monday" – that one point in the "week" when the markets are open, permitting agents to contract for their planned production and consumption over the remainder of the week. Although "Monday's" prices are presumed to be determined by the equality of the *current* quantities supplied and demanded, since no further recontracting is permitted – thereby maintaining prices unchanged over the remainder of the "week" – the plans and expectations formed for the future may well, and indeed will likely, be unsatisfied (Hicks, 1939, Chap. ix; for a more recent summary and evaluation, see Hicks, 1976, pp. 141–142). Hence, the equilibrium established on "Monday" is strictly temporary. The analytical problem then is to trace out "the evolution in time of the sequence of temporary equilibria" (Grandmont, 1991, p. 4; III, 5). Obviously, that sequence can be specified so as to allow the agents to adjust their plans on the basis of new information revealed in each succeeding period, permitting an adaptive learning process. As Punzo (1991, pp. 31–32; III, 6) puts the point in a comment on the Grandmont paper, "Given the sequential character of temporary equilibrium analysis, whereby the equilibrium at each point of time depends on agents' beliefs about the values which the relevant variables might take in the future, a great deal of work has been devoted to the scrutiny of those assumptions which reflect the way in which information is processed (learning) and expectations are formulated." Our collection offers two examples of that work, although the relationship of those papers to the temporary equilibrium theme will not be readily apparent since they are not classed under that heading (which is limited to the Grandmont and Punzo entries). Both papers illustrate one of the three sets of questions identified by Grandmont as comprising the temporary equilibrium research program – namely the question of "the stability of long-run steady-states when traders employ given learning procedures." The lone entry under the heading of "rational expectations" is the Evans and Honkapohja (1994, III, 9) demonstration that the introduction of adaptive learning processes in models with multiple such equilibria will not necessarily produce a convergence to a unique, stable equilibrium. The paper is certainly an illustration of a common class of rational expectations equilibria, but its chief contribution is its investigation of the effect of learning processes on the character of those equilibria, locating it securely within that segment of the temporary equilibrium literature that seeks to determine whether the "sequences of temporary equilibria do or do not converge to steady states" when the agents are "described as learning progressively the dynamics of their environment" (Grandmont, 1991, p. 19; III, 5). Likewise, Bullard's (1994; III, 27) paper, buried near the end of Volume III in the catch-all, "other" category, extends the Evans-Honkapohja analysis to the class of overlapping generations models and finds that the introduction of a similar learning process can produce a sequence of equilibria in which forecasting errors never vanish, raising the possibility of endogenous cycles.

Ironically, that "other" category at the end of Volume III also contains a key contribution to the first leg of that "bifurcated" analytical response to the "timeless" character of Walrasian models. We find there Hahn's (1978; III, 26) early attempt to incorporate disequilibrium trades in a context where agents face quantity constraints in some markets. This paper would be better placed as the first item in Volume II, part 3, "models with various forms of market imperfection." As it stands, that section opens with a more recent paper by Dehez and Drèze (1991 [1984]; II, 22), which is itself simply a variation on the theme considered in the earlier Hahn paper (and begun by a yet earlier paper by Drèze, 1975, which is reproduced in the Debreu collection.) Indeed, the whole of parts 2 and 3 of Volume II offer a coherent, nearly unbroken sequence of work illustrating the evolution of theorists' attempts to expand the familiar Walrasian framework to incorporate disequilibrium trades. Part 2 (containing just four items) opens with the earliest published statement of the so-called Hahn trading process (Hahn & Negishi, 1962; II, 18), includes Fisher's (1976; II, 19) extension to introduce disequilibrium production and consumption and ends with two very useful surveys by Fisher (1983, Chap. 2; II, 20) and Busetto (1995; II, 21). Part 3 (with the addition of the

Hahn, 1978, paper "mislaid" to Volume III) carries the sequence forward to include illustrations of those efforts to incorporate elements of imperfect competition and consequent quantity restraints on the one hand and price rigidities on the other. The only apparent "break" in the thread occurs when we encounter the Mercenier (1995; II, 25) paper, which, as we have seen above in note 2, is the collection's sole illustration of computational general equilibrium models. It is true that his model includes a set of industries exhibiting a degree of monopoly power arising from the introduction of scale economies, but the paper differs from all others in the sequence (and, indeed, in the entire collection) in that its object is not the investigation of the theoretical implications of such a structure but rather to offer a warning to practitioners of the dilemma raised for policy evaluation when the parameterization of such models produces multiple plausible solutions.[6]

4.3. Equilibrium as "Process"

We have here a sample of over a quarter-century of work devoted to the introduction of disequilibrium behavior into the general equilibrium framework. To those who expect their economic models to bear some remote connection to the behavior actually observed outside the seminar room, these more recent developments will appear, when viewed in contrast to those early Arrow-Debreu-McKenzie models, as "a step in the right direction." But they are still a very long way from Walker's standard of a "functioning system," and Walker is not alone in his complaint on this point. Within our collection, Busetto is particularly forthright in his assessment of this work: these disequilibrium models remain "firmly linked to the GE (general equilibrium) traditional assumptions, safeguarding the central role of the equilibrium notion and of the properties underlying it. But this involves the impossibility of explaining the observable behavior of the individual agents in disequilibrium and of determining the actual time-path of the economies investigated and the particular GE position eventually attained by them." The best these models can do is to identify the properties that produce convergence to *some* (variously defined) equilibrium position (Busetto, 1995, p. 96; II, 21).

To some observers, the past quarter-century of labor in these barren fields has only returned us full circle to the very complaints raised by Kaldor, Robinson and Hicks: we must, they conclude, abandon the static notion of equilibrium at the core of the neo-Walrasian research program and substitute in its stead a dynamic vision that captures the processes by which agents adjust their behavior to changing market forces. The most provocative statement of this type in our collection comes from Blaug and rests on a distinction between "two very different notions of what is meant by competition": on the one hand, "competition as an *end-state* of rest in the rivalry between buyers and sellers," and on the other, "competition as a *process* of rivalry that may or may not terminate in an end-state." It is the latter of these, Blaug insists, that has the longer pedigree; and certainly no one who has read their work would question his observation that the Classicals typically employed the "competition" term "with a definite or indefinite article attached to it," writing of "*a* competition between capitals" and thereby describing "an active process of jockeying for advantage, tending towards but never actually culminating in an equilibrium end-state." It is only because of "the invidious legacy of Walras's influence" that economics has, since the 1930s exhibited a regrettable "failure to address questions of active competition and instead to fall back uncritically on a model of perfect [end-state] competition as an 'ideal type.' " The work of the general equilibrium theorists over the past quarter-century, in which they have sought to expand their models to account for disequilibrium behavior, carries no weight for Blaug. On the contrary, he, like Busetto, dismisses that work for its failure to abandon that notion of an equilibrium "end-state" that is the chief fault of the Walrasian program: "this is a curious kind of disequilibrium analysis in which there is no process of rivalry between unrepresentative individual households and firms, no real contest between economic agents, but rather various end-state equilibrium points *called* disequilibria, the entire exercise differing from standard analysis only in that non-clearance of at least one of the subsectors of the economy is possible" (Blaug, 1997, pp. 241–251; I, 15).

What then are we to do? Are we to discard our comfortable legends of perfectly competitive end-states of equilibrium? Yes indeed. Blaug would take a very broad broom to the discipline and sweep away much of our curriculum, leaving only industrial organization (and presumably economic history and perhaps history of doctrines):

> But what are we then left with? We are left with the content of every chapter in every textbook on imperfect or monopolistic competition, on oligopoly, duopoly and monopoly, in short, on industrial organization as a subdiscipline of economics. In those chapters, firms jostle for advantage by price and non-price competition, undercutting and outbidding rivals in the market-place by advertising outlays and promotional expenses, launching new differentiated products, new technical processes, new methods of marketing and new organizational forms, and even new reward structures for their employees, all for the sake of head-start profits that they know will soon be eroded. In these chapters, there is never any doubt that competition is an active process, of discovery, of knowledge formation, of 'creative destruction' [Blaug, 1997, pp. 255–6; I, 15].

In what may be yet another illustration of the principle that new insights in a science appear not uniquely, to a single scholar, but rather in "multiples," independently advanced by several investigators, we find, about two hundred pages later in our collection, two remarkable parallels to Blaug's critique, written a decade earlier. Although his remedy is not so drastic as that proposed by Blaug, Jacques Henry (1987, pp. 464–466; I, 26) likewise asks us to relinquish our familiar concept of "equilibrium as a state" and to substitute a "notion of process," defined as "an ordered sequence of procedures, decisions or actions . . . motivated by a perceived opportunity or advantage . . . [and] that will result in a change in the very conditions that motivated the action in the first place." Unfortunately, beyond the proposal of a new category of "inequilibrium" – defined as a "state of affairs in which elements of endogenous change, novelty and permanency coexist" – Henry is unable to give operational expression to this "process" approach. Dore (1984–1985; I, 24), however, independently prompted by like concerns, reminds us that the similar concept of "neutral" equilibrium has been employed in certain of the "non-Walrasian" corners of the discipline since the early efforts to investigate the conditions giving rise to regular cycles, the work on cobweb cycles being an obvious example (see Goodwin, 1947). The concept conveys more than "simply" an expression of an "unstable equilibrium," as that phrase is understood in a Walrasian context; it refers to models that seek to specify the conditions producing the move to subsequent equilibria and to identify the nature of that dynamic path, as we see, for example, in the work on endogenous business cycles. By now, of course, we have strayed far from our Walrasian heritage, but these comments from Henry and Dore together with the similar but more vigorous critique from Blaug serve to bring home the realization that the very flaws passed down to us by that heritage that so troubled Kaldor and Robinson a quarter-century ago still haunt us today.

5. WHERE DO WE STAND?

Although there is room to quibble at the organizing framework employed or at occasional omissions from or misclassifications within that framework, Walker has nevertheless performed his editorial duties with effect: he has compiled a collection that offers a commanding view of the broad sweep of work in general equilibrium theory. No one but the most committed enthusiasts can come away from this collection without at least a nagging suspicion that the critics are right. What is worse, one senses a growing suspicion that a long line of work stretching back more than a century has failed to advance our understanding of market outcomes to any significant degree, a conclusion that suggests a distressing waste of intellectual resources, just as Kaldor foresaw thirty years ago. Once again Blaug is uncompromising in his judgment: "after a century or more of endless refinements of the central core of GE theory, an exercise which has absorbed some of the best brains in twentieth-century economics, the theory is unable to shed any light on how market equilibrium is actually attained, not just in a real-world decentralized market economy but even in the toy economies beloved of GE theorists." To put the point bluntly, "We may conclude that GE theory as such is a cul-de-sac: it has no empirical content and never will have empirical content" (Blaug, 1997, pp. 251–252; I, 15; see also McCloskey, 1994, p. 135 for a similar claim of resource misallocation). Notice the point of Blaug's attack: the theory's Achilles heel is its inability to identify that *disequilibrium* process by which "market equilibrium is actually attained." This failure comes not for want of trying. Steven Smale's work of the 1970s reintroduced his "mathematics of time" – differential calculus and global analysis of differential equations – quite deliberately to give mathematical expression to the process of disequilibrium adjustment across time.[7] However, although Smale (1976a) is able to identify functional forms that ensure a globally stable process of convergence to equilibrium, no one has been able to invest his differential equations with any meaningful economic interpretation. Hahn's (1982, p. 767) assessment is typical: "While these results are of interest as algorithms, they have the drawback that it does not seem possible to give them an economic motivation." It is that "draw-back," in its various guises, that has led even some of those who have labored long and tirelessly in the Walrasian fields to express agreement with Blaug's assessment that this line of inquiry has brought us to a "cul-de-sac." In their marvelously rich history of that research program, Ingrao and Israel close their survey of the stability literature with the observation that Smale's new approach to that problem, together with the work of those who followed him in that path, has "not only not modified but actually confirmed the impression of the existence of a complete *impasse* in the theory of global stability." These results, they conclude, "provide conclusive evidence that any attempt to obtain a *globally defined* and *globally stable* process of price adjustment is doomed to failure. Consequently, research in this direction must be considered as having come to a dead end" (Ingrao & Israel, 1990, pp. 358–359; emphasis in original).

The gravity of this problem for the continued vitality of the general equilibrium research program cannot be overstated. As we are reminded in the opening entry to our collection, Arrow and Hahn set as a goal of that program the rigorous formulation of Smith's invisible hand metaphor, which they understand as the "poetic expression" of "the most important intellectual contribution that economic thought has made to the general understanding of social processes" – namely, "the notion that a social system moved by independent actions in pursuit of different values is consistent with a final coherent state of balance" (Arrow & Hahn, 1971, p. 1; I, 1). But if this is truly to be our contribution, then it is not enough simply to prove the existence of such a state. Our theory must also explain how the economy actually achieves that position. The memorable statement given the problem by Ingrao and Israel (1990, p. 331) is worth repeating:

An ideological standpoint that regards the market as possessing the virtue or intrinsic property of combining subjective behavior harmoniously cannot content itself with simply knowing that a final state of equilibrium exists. It has to show that the economy is capable of attaining this state spontaneously . . .. Otherwise, one would be forced to acknowledge that market forces are not capable of leading the market itself to equilibrium and that Smith's "invisible hand" wavers Sisyphus-like around the actually existing equilibrium position without having the strength to push the economic system into it.

This inability of the theory to trace out the economy's movement across time was earlier glimpsed in Sonnenschein's (1972) famous demonstration that the classic, very general conditions imposed upon individual utility functions are insufficient to permit the aggregation of those functions into uniquely specified market excess demand relationships. Hence, without additional restraints on the structure of the model, one can have no hope of obtaining a unique equilibrium or even a set of discrete equilibria. This result struck at the foundation of the Walrasian program – namely, "the belief that significant results could be obtained by starting from very general hypotheses about the behavior of economic agents. The endeavor to keep the theory at the highest level of generality thus proved to be one of its weakest points" (Ingrao & Israel, 1990, p. 316). It is ironic, in view of his repeated call for highly specified "functioning systems," that Walker fails to emphasize the significance of this result and of those elaborations that followed in its wake. On the contrary, Walker (1997, pp. 137–138; II, 17) holds that "the sorrow and pessimism over the implications of [Sonnenschein's] conclusions regarding the impossibility of making assumptions about individual demand functions that would restrict the form of aggregate excess demand functions are unnecessary." It is certainly true that Sonnenschein "analysed only the relationship between individual and aggregate excess demand functions" and consequently "did not specify or even imply the many structural and behavioral features necessary to create a complete model," but that is precisely the point. It is Sonnenschein's result and the later work that it prompted that has led Hildenbrand, and others who, like him, have contributed so much to the Walrasian tradition, to conclude, however reluctantly, that "an exchange economy can no longer serve as an appropriate prototype example for an economy if one wants to go beyond the existence and optimality problem." This is, as Hildenbrand properly insists, "an extremely important insight that must have an impact on future research projects" ("Introduction" to Debreu, 1983, p. 26)[8].

But what is that impact to be? Certainly it involves a movement in the very direction that Walker has urged. Hildenbrand (1994) himself has taken a step in that direction with his recent effort to draw upon the Family Expenditure Surveys to structure his theory of market demand functions. But this amounts to a renunciation of Debreu's principle that the theory must be pressed to ever higher levels of abstraction, thereby remaining "entirely disconnected from its interpretations" – a principle that has guided work in this tradition for the past half-century. The irony in the present state of affairs is nicely stated by Ingrao and Israel in their concluding assessment of that tradition: we are enabled to see so clearly the theory's flaws precisely because of the axiomatic form so strenuously urged by Debreu. That "axiomatic approach has 'x-rayed' the state of the theory in a complete and even pitiless way," revealing an unchanging "programmatic core" characterized by the persistent focus on the problems of existence, uniqueness, and stability. But, after a half-century of refinements, we are left with "a contradiction between the theory's aims and the consequences derived from the system of hypotheses constituting its structure." Most readers will likely find in Walker's collection ample cause to agree with Ingrao and Israel that "the only way out of this situation is to jettison explicitly the programmatic central core that has been so carefully preserved." What exactly is to replace that barren core remains an open question, but it certainly "cannot avoid the highly difficult and crucial question of the relations between theory and empirical reality" (Ingrao & Israel, 1990, pp. 361–362), a "question" which Hildenbrand has already begun to explore. In their fascinating history of the rise of the "Bourbakist" tradition in mathematics and its apparent influence through Debreu on the course of general equilibrium theory, Weintraub and Mirowski recall the comment of one of the tradition's founders, who characterized its product as "a very well arranged cemetery with a beautiful array of tombstones, . . . useless for teaching" (Weintraub & Mirowski, 1994, p. 251). Is there a more apt epitaph for its economic progeny?

What then does all this mean for our old friend "equilibrium?" Must we follow the counsel of Kaldor, John Henry, Robinson, Blaug, and others who would have us "jettison" that concept along with the extreme abstraction and wholly static axiomatization that has characterized the Walrasian tradition? No, on this our collection suggests a broad consensus: the concept is central to our reasoning process and hence cannot be abandoned. Without it we can have no hope of getting beyond description to a level of analysis that can at least aspire to prediction. As we saw at the outset of this essay, that view, though widely represented in our collection, was most cogently expressed nearly a half-century ago in Machlup's reminder that equilibrium is properly understood as a "useful fiction" that permits our models to illuminate those causal relationships that are the object of our study. To presume equilibrium at the initial position is a means of ensuring that the postulated shock is "the *sole* disturbing change, the *sole* cause of anything that follows in the model." Further, to trace out "the sequence of adjusting changes until we reach a situation in which, barring another disturbance from the outside, everything could go on as it is," is simply to complete the argument and thereby assure ourselves "that 'no further adjustments' are required by the situation" (Machlup, 1991 [1958], p. 48; I, 6; emphasis in original). Of course, our theories must contain enough institutional detail that we can discern in them at least a dim reflection of the world in which we live; and Walker's precept of a complete, "functioning system" is, no doubt, a laudable goal. But the unqualified demands with which he invests that principle prompt the same response as that which Hicks gave to a like charge from a critic of his time: "His ideal economics is not so far away from my own ideal economics; but I regard it as a target set up in heaven. We cannot hope to reach it; we must just get as near to it as we can" (Hicks, 1976, pp. 145–146).

NOTES

1. When citing an item appearing in our collection, its location will be indicated by the relevant volume number (as Roman numeral) and chapter (Arabic notation). Further, since the collection provides the included items in "facsimile reproduction, inclusive of footnotes and pagination to facilitate ease of reference," I shall follow the publisher's lead and indicate cited passages by the original pagination.

2. The attentive reader will notice the curious omission from this litany of any mention of applications of computational general equilibrium models to various historical and contemporary policy questions, an omission that is remarked as well by the reviewer of Walker's *Advances in General Equilibrium Theory* (Hoass, 2000). Walker could reply that such applications have frequently provoked the same criticism he raises here – namely the objection that they fail to capture the relevant empirical relationships. For an illustration of a recent application in a historical context and the associated criticism, see Harley and Crafts (2000) and Temin (2000). Nevertheless, such models have found extensive use in the evaluation of trade policy (Srinivasan & Whalley, 1986), and one such paper does, indeed, find its way into Walker's collection, though it is "mislaid" in the section devoted to "market imperfection" (Mercenier, 1995; II, 25). As we will see below, this is not the only case of misclassification. The contribution of Mercenier's paper is not its incorporation of imperfect information and scale economies, which have been abiding themes in trade applications; it is rather his warning that trade economists err in their long-standing assumption that "non-uniqueness is largely a theoretical curiosity" (p. 162). Mercenier obtains, with a calibration of his model to EEC data, two plausible but wildly divergent equilibrium outcomes arising from the policy experiment under investigation.

3. Here again we have a case of apparent misclassification. Machlup's careful exposition "of the equilibrium concept . . . as a methodological device in abstract theory" (p. 44) is by no means a "criticism" of that concept, though the paper appears as the first entry in the section so titled. It would be better placed in the "meaning and concepts" section.

4. The selection criteria employed to identify the papers comprising the "historical" section remains a mystery. The section opens reasonably enough with the Arrow and Hahn (1971, Chap. 1) "Historical Introduction," and that is followed by an old survey of "Smith's concept of Equilibrium" as it is expressed in *The Theory of Moral Sentiments* and *The Wealth of Nations* (Myers, 1976). From there, however, we leap to a rigorous investigation of the "cross-dual" adjustment process found in those general equilibrium studies where price adjustment is specified as a function of excess demands and quantity adjustments are modeled as a response to profit differentials (Flaschel & Semmler, 1987). This is followed by the Harris paper on Sraffian equilibrium, after which the section closes

with a return to a more obviously "historical" work, namely Magnon de Bornier's (1992) careful reconstruction from the original texts of the substance of the "Cournot-Bertrand Debate" over the nature of duopoly behavior.

5. The objection raised by Robinson has long been common fare among economic historians – one of those areas of our discipline which takes seriously the injunction to take care with the institutional and technical details of the economy under consideration. It was Rosenberg's study of the history of technological advance that prompted his observation that the economist's common distinction between factor substitution (represented as a simple movement *along* a known isoquant in response to changing factor prices) and technological change (portrayed as a shift in the entire production function) is, from the perspective of the agents involved, a distinction without a difference. Since technological knowledge, like all knowledge, can be acquired only through the expenditure of scarce resources, we should expect that "the *known* portion of an isoquant typically [will] be . . . a relatively small segment." Viewed in this light, the problem presents us with a discomfiting question, which Rosenberg will not allow us to avoid: "If, in response to a change in factor prices, a firm has to commit resources to establishing new optimal input mixes, should not the activity leading to the new knowledge be described as technological change and not factor substitution? . . . Once a substantial research expenditure is required for what is called 'factor substitution,' what is left of the economic basis for the distinction between technological change and factor substitution?" (Rosenberg, 1975, p. 459, emphasis added.)

6. One further curious classification is worth noting. Volume III contains a section devoted to "Bayesian" equilibrium comprising a single chapter on the subject by Laffont (1991; III, 10). However, in this context, "Bayesian" refers to an equilibrium concept employed in dynamic games in which each player is endowed with a subjective probability distribution over the information privately available to the other players. Hence, this item would be more logically placed in the long section devoted to game theory, perhaps at the end of that section, after the Mailath (1998) paper on evolutionary games, since the Bayesian concept can be viewed as an extension of an evolutionary game in which the players modify their expectations of their competitors' future actions on the basis of observed current actions.

7. Our collection contains Smale's (1976b; I, 21) paper in which he offers his justification for returning to the calculus techniques earlier displaced by Debreu's axioms of topology. The reader will likely agree with Ingrao and Israel (1990, p. 353) in their observation that "it is really amusing to see the overturning of values proposed by Smale: what was first viewed as a progressive development becomes an obstacle to be swept away." It is not quite correct to say, as Walker (1997, pp. 96–97; II, 5) seems to suggest, that Smale's reintroduction of the calculus "demonstrated" that the topological framework employed in Arrow's and Debreu's work of the 1950s was a "methodologically inferior" approach adopted because it was "convenient from a mathematical point of view." While it is true that Smale's reformulation "recognizes time rates of change," it is also true that it rests on techniques of global analysis that were not widely developed among mathematicians until roughly a decade after Arrow and Debreu developed their existence proofs. See Ingrao and Israel (1990, pp. 305–308).

8. Hildenbrand's (1994, p. ix) memoir of his own reaction to the Sonnenschein result strikes a poignant chord:

> I was deeply consternated. Up to that time I had the naive illusion that the microeconomic foundation of the general equilibrium model, which I admired so much, does not only allow us to prove that the model and the concept of equilibrium are logically consistent (existence of equilibria), but also allows us to show that the equilibrium is well determined. This illusion, or

should I say rather, this hope, was destroyed, once and for all, at least for the traditional model of exchange economies.

I was tempted to repress this insight and to continue to find satisfaction in proving existence of equilibria for more general models under still weaker assumptions. However, I did not succeed in repressing the newly gained insight because I believe that a theory of economic equilibrium is incomplete if the equilibrium is not well determined.

REFERENCES

Arrow, K. J. (1974). Limited knowledge and economic analysis. *The American Economic Review*, *64*(1), 1–10.

Arrow, K. J., & Hahn, F. H. (1971). *General competitive analysis*. San Francisco: Holden-Day and Edinburgh: Oliver & Boyd; Chap. 1 reproduced in Walker (2000), I, pp. 3–20.

Bewley, T. F. (1981). Stationary equilibrium. *Journal of Economic Theory*, *24*(1), 265–295; reproduced in Walker (2000), III, pp. 3–33.

Bharadwaj, K. (1991). History vs. equilibrium. In: I. H. Rima (Ed.), *The Joan Robinson Legacy*. Armonk, NY: M. E. Sharpe; reproduced in Walker (2000), I, pp. 236–259.

Blaug, M. (1997). Competition as an end-state and competition as a process. In: B. C. Eaton & R. G. Harris (Eds), *Trade, Technology and Economics: Essays in Honour of Richard G. Lipsey*. Cheltenham, UK and Brookfield, US: Edward Elgar; reproduced in Walker (Ed.) (2000), I, pp. 272–293.

Blaug, M. (1999). Misunderstanding classical economics: The Sraffian interpretation of the surplus approach. *History of Political Economy*, *31*(2), 213–236.

Bullard, J. (1994). Learning equilibria. *Journal of Economic Theory*, *64*(2), 468–485; reproduced in Walker (2000), III, pp. 573–590.

Busetto, F. (1995). Why the non-tâtonnement line of research died out. *Economic Notes*, *24*(1), 89–113; reproduced in Walker (2000), II, pp. 438–462.

Caravale, G. (1994). Updating an old question: Prices and quantities. *Atlantic Economic Journal*, *22*(1), 26–33; reproduced in Walker, I, pp. 526–533.

Chipman, J. S. (1965). The nature and meaning of equilibrium in economic theory. In: D. Martindale (Ed.). Functionalism in the Social Sciences: The Strength and Limits of Functionalism in Anthropology, Economics, Political Science, and Sociology. Monograph 5, pp. 35–64. Philadelphia: American Academy of Political and Social Sciences. Reproduced in Walker (Ed.) (2000) I, pp. 314–343.

Debreu, G. (1959). *The theory of value: An axiomatic analysis of economic equilibrium*. New Haven: Yale University Press.

Debreu, G. (Ed.) (1983). *Mathematical economics: Twenty papers of Gerard Debreu*. Cambridge: Cambridge University Press.

Debreu, G. (Ed.) (1996). *General equilibrium theory*, 3 vols. Cheltenham, UK: Edward Elgar.

Dehez, P., & Drèze, J. H. (1991 [1984]). On supply-constrained equilibria. *Journal of Economic Theory*, *33*(1), 172–182. Reprinted in: J. H. Drèze (Ed.), *Underemployment Equilibria: Essays in Theory, Econometrics, and Policy*. Cambridge: Cambridge University Press, 1991; reproduced in Walker (2000), II, pp. 465–476, with the name of the first author inadvertently omitted.

Dore, M. H. I. (1984–1985). On the concept of equilibrium. *Journal of Post Keynesian Economics*, *7*(2), 193–206; reproduced in Walker (2000), I, pp. 470–483.

Drèze, J. H. (1975). Existence of an exchange equilibrium under price rigidities. *International Economic Review, 16*(2), 301–320; reproduced in Debreu (1996), I, pp. 426–445.

Duffie, D., Geanakoplos, J., Mas-Colell, A., & McLennan, A. (1994). Stationary Markov equilibria. *Econometrica, 62*(4), 745–781; reproduced in Walker (2000), III, pp. 34–70.

Eddington, A. S. (1929). *The nature of the physical world*. New York: Macmillan.

Evans, G. W., & Honkapohja, S. (1994). Learning, convergence, and stability with multiple rational expectations equilibria. *European Economic Review, 38*(5), 1071–1098; reproduced in Walker (2000), III, pp. 197–224.

Fisher, F. M. (1976). A non-tâtonnement model with production and consumption. *Econometrica, 44*(5), 907–938; reproduced in Walker (2000), II, pp. 372–403.

Fisher, F. M. (1983). *Disequilibrium foundations of equilibrium economics*. Cambridge: Cambridge University Press. Chap. 2 reproduced in Walker (2000), II, pp. 404–437.

Flaschel, P., & Semmler, W. (1987). Classical and neoclassical competitive adjustment processes. *Manchester School of Economic and Social Studies, 55*(1), 13–37; reproduced in Walker (2000), I, pp. 37–61.

Garegnani, P. (1987). Surplus approach to value and distribution. In: J. Eatwell, M. Milgate & P. Newman (Eds), *The New Palgrave; a Dictionary of Economics* (Vol. IV, pp. 560–574). London: Macmillan.

Goodwin, R. M. (1947). Dynamical coupling with especial reference to markets having production lags. *Econometrica, 15*(3), 181–204.

Gottardi, P. (1996). Stationary monetary equilibria in overlapping generations models with incomplete markets. *Journal of Economic Theory, 71*(1), 75–89; reproduced in Walker (2000), III, pp. 71–85.

Grandmont, J. M. (1977). Temporary general equilibrium theory. *Econometrica, 45*(3), 535–572; reproduced in Debreu (1996), II, pp. 114–151.

Grandmont, J. M. (1991). Temporary equilibrium: Money, expectations and dynamics. In: L. W. McKenzie & S. Zamagni (Eds), *Value and Capital: Fifty Years Later*. London: Macmillan; reproduced in Walker (2000), III, pp. 107–134.

Hahn, F. (1978). On non-Walrasian equlibria. *Review of Economic Studies, 45*(1), 1–17; reproduced in Walker (2000), III, pp. 556–572.

Hahn, F. (1982). Stability. In: K. J. Arrow & M. D. Intriligator (Eds), *Handbook of Mathematical Economics* (Vol. II, Chap. 16, pp. 745–793).

Hahn, F., & Negishi, T. (1962). A theorem on non-tâtonnement stability. *Econometrica, 30*(3), 463–469; reproduced in Walker (2000), II, pp. 365–371.

Harley, C. K., & Crafts, N. F. R. (2000). Simulating the two views of the British industrial revolution. *The Journal of Economic History, 60*(3), 819–841.

Harris, D. J. (1991). Equilibrium and stability in classical theory. In: E. J. Nell & W. Semmler (Eds), *Nicholas Kaldor and Mainstream Economics: Confrontation or Convergence*? London: Macmillan; reproduced in Walker (2000), I, pp. 62–74.

Henry, J. (1987). Equilibrium as process. *Economie Appliquée, 40*(3), 463–482; reproduced in Walker (2000), I, pp. 496–515.

Henry, J. (1983–1984). On equilibrium. *Journal of Post Keynesian Economics, 6*(2), 214–229; reproduced in Walker (2000), I, pp. 435–450.

Hicks, J. (1939). *Value and capital: An inquiry into some fundamental principles of economic theory*. Oxford: Clarendon Press.

Hicks, J. (1976). Some questions of time in economics. In: A. M. Tang, F. M. Westfield & J. S. Worley (Eds), *Evolution, Welfare, and Time in Economics; Essays in Honor of Nicholas Georgescu-Roegen*. Lexington, MA and Toronto: Lexington Books.

Hildenbrand, W. (1994). *Market demand: Theory and empirical evidence*. Princeton, NJ: Princeton University Press.

Hoass, D. J. (2000). Mining improbable postulates and the theory of diverting toys. *Atlantic Economic Journal, 28*(1), 104–113.

Ingrao, B., & Israel, G. (1990). *The invisible hand; economic equilibrium in the history of science*. Translated by I. McGilvray. Cambridge, MA: MIT Press.

Kaldor, N. (1972). The irrelevance of equilibrium economics. *Economic Journal, 82* (December), 1237–1255; reproduced in Walker (2000), I, pp. 141–159.

Kaldor, N. (1975). What is wrong with economic theory. *Quarterly Journal of Economics, 89*(3), 347–357; reproduced in Walker (2000), I, pp. 172–182.

Kaldor, N. (1979). Equilibrium theory and growth theory. In: M. J. Boskin (Ed.), *Economics and Human Welfare: Essays in Honor of Tibor Scitovsky* (pp. 273–291). New York: Academic Press, reproduced in Walker (2000), I, pp. 183–201.

Keynes, J. M. (1937). The general theory of employment. *Quarterly Journal of Economics, 51*(2), 209–223.

Keynes, J. M. (1964 [1936]). *The general theory of employment, interest, and money*. First Harbinger ed. New York: Harcourt, Brace.

Laffont, J. J. (1991). Perfect Bayesian equilibrium. In: J.-J. Laffont & M. Moreaux (Eds), *Dynamics, Incomplete Information and Industrial Economics* (pp. 51–68), F. Laisney (Trans.). Oxford: Blackwell, reproduced in Walker (2000), III, pp. 227–244.

Machlup, F. (1991 [1958]). Equilibrium and disequilibrium: Misplaced concreteness and disguised politics. *Economic Journal, 68*(269), 1–24. Reprinted in *Economic Semantics* (2nd ed.). New Brunswick, NJ: Transaction Publishers. Reproduced in Walker (2000), I, pp. 111–140.

Magnon de Bornier, J. (1992). The 'Cournot-Bertrand debate': A historical perspective. *History of Political Economy, 24*(3), 623–656; reproduced in Walker (2000), I, pp. 75–108.

Mailath, G. J. (1998). Do people play Nash equilibrium? Lessons from evolutionary game theory. *Journal of Economic Literature, 36*(3), 1347–1374; reproduced in Walker (2000), III, pp. 521–548.

McCloskey, D. N. (1994). *Knowledge and persuasion in economics*. Cambridge: Cambridge University Press.

Mercenier, J. (1995). Nonuniqueness of solutions in applied general equilibrium models with scale economies and imperfect competition. *Economic Theory, 6*(1), 161–177; reproduced in Walker (2000), II, pp. 524–540.

Milgate, M. (1987). Equilibrium: Development of the concept. In: J. Eatwell, M. Milgate & P. Newman (Eds), *The New Palgrave; a Dictionary of Economics* (Vol. II, pp. 179–183). London: Macmillan.

Myers, M. L. (1976). Adam Smith's concept of equilibrium. *Journal of Economic Issues, 10*(3), 560–575; reproduced in Walker (2000), I, pp. 21–36.

Punzo, L. F. (1991). Comment on Grandmont. In: L. W. McKenzie & S. Zamagni (Eds), *Value and Capital: Fifty Years Later*. London: Macmillan; reproduced in Walker (2000), III, pp. 135–141.

Robinson, J. (1974). History vs. equilibrium. *Indian Economic Journal, 21*(3), 202–213; reproduced in Walker (2000), I, pp. 160–171.

Robinson, J. (1977). What are the questions? *Journal of Economic Literature, 15*(4), 1318–1339.

Rosenberg, N. (1975). Problems in the economist's conceptualization of technological innovation. *History of Political Economy, 7*(4), 456–481.

Schumpeter, J. A. (1954). *History of economic analysis*. New York: Oxford University Press.

Smale, S. (1976a). A convergent process of price adjustment and global Newton methods. *Journal of Mathematical Economics, 3*(2), 107–120; reproduced in Debreu (Ed.) (1996), III, pp. 429–442.

Smale, S. (1976b). Dynamics in general equilibrium theory. *American Economic Review*, 66(2), 288–294; reproduced in Walker (2000), I, pp. 428–434.

Sonnenschein, H. (1972). Market excess demand functions. *Econometrica*, 40(3), 549–563; reproduced in Debreu (Ed.) (1996), III, pp. 443–457.

Srinivasan, T. N., & Whalley, J. (Eds) (1986). *General equilibrium trade policy modeling*. Cambridge, MA: MIT Press.

Temin, P. (2000). A response to Harley and Crafts. *The Journal of Economic History*, 60(3), 842–846.

Walker, D. A. (1997). *Advances in general equilibrium theory*. Cheltenham, UK: Edward Elgar.

Walker, D. A. (Ed.) (2000). *Equilibrium*, 3 vols. Cheltenham, UK and Northampton, MA: Edward Elgar.

Weintraub, E. R. (1983). On the existence of a competitive equilibrium: 1930–1954. *Journal of Economic Literature*, 21, 1–39, reproduced in Walker (2000), II, pp. 5–43.

Weintraub, E. R. (1991). *Stabilizing dynamics; constructing economic knowledge*. Cambridge: Cambridge University Press.

Weintraub, E. R., & Mirowski, P. (1994). The pure and the applied: Bourbakism comes to mathematical economics. *Science in Context*, 7(2), 245–272.

BURK'S TROUBLEMAKER: THE LIFE AND HISTORY OF A. J. P. TAYLOR AND HASLAM'S THE VICES OF INTEGRITY: E. H. CARR, 1892–1982

Warren J. Samuels

A review essay on Kathleen Burk's, *Troublemaker: The Life and History of A. J. P. Taylor*, New Haven, CT: Yale University Press, 2000; and Nathan Haslam, *The Vices of Integrity: E. H. Carr, 1892–1982*, New York: Verso, 1999. Otherwise unidentified citations in Part III are to Haslam's biography of Carr; those in Part IV, to Burk's biography of Taylor.

1. INTRODUCTION

The United States, it was once felt, could have a different foreign policy when isolated by two oceans in comparison to the later period when modern technology destroyed its isolation. Foreign policy is thus a function of geography modified by technology. The United States, commencing some time after the first third of the 19th century, had a further choice. It could live up to its self-image as a liberal constitutional democracy and follow a foreign policy of live and let live, in both respects serving as a role model for the rest of the world. Or, like the monarchical dynasties of the past and other regimes of more recent times, it could pursue an aggressive foreign policy in pursuit of what it considered its interests, engendering enmity in various quarters. The United States has done both. In the first category it

Research in the History of Economic Thought and Methodology A Research Annual
Research in the History of Economic Thought and Methodology, Volume 22-A, 291–315
Copyright © 2004 by Elsevier Ltd.
ISSN: 0743-4154/doi:10.1016/S0743-4154(03)22017-4

has preferred isolationism, reluctantly joining the two World Wars in defense of its autonomy. In the second category, it increasingly either engaged in the practices of conventional imperialism, often at the behest of entrepreneurial interests, or flexed and deployed its muscle in pursuit of national interests either on its own initiative or in response to threats from and capabilities of other countries. The former is American exceptionalism; the latter is conventional. Of course, the history is much more complex than the foregoing directly allows. Several other stories or models can be developed (the most recent is Mead, 2001).

In his recent book asserting the United States' need for a foreign policy in the 21st century, Henry Kissinger, historically conscious political scientist and occupant of the two highest governmental positions in foreign policy, proposes a policy of the second type – such as he has before both proposed and practiced. He argues that countries in the nation-state system are engaged willy nilly in a struggle for power and survival; that countries in general and the United States in particular have interests as a result of their cultural, social and political history and their geography; that our government must prevent any consolidation of foreign powers from threatening our autonomy and way of life; that we cannot take for granted our pre-eminence as the only superpower; and that we can combine concern for human rights with pursuit and defense of our interests and power (Kissinger, 2001). Kissinger is a foreign policy realist. He is, especially, a devotee of the theory of the balance of power as both a description and normative instrument of high state policy. Kissinger is not alone in his aggressive foreign policy (see, for example, Kaplan, 2002). It is not easy to distinguish an aggressive policy stance whose purpose is to forestall if not to entirely prevent adverse actions by other nations from one which attempts to impose United States interests and policies on others. In practice, policy is often a mixture of the two. One difficult example to interpret is the set of policies and actions adopted by the Administration of George W. Bush in early 2002 in the name of the "war on terrorism."

Edward Hallett Carr and Alan John Percivale Taylor, our two biographical subjects, were also believers in the theory of the balance of power. Their history influenced their attitudes toward the theory; and their adoption of the theory influenced both how they did their history and the policies they publicly promoted. In this respect, historians are very much like economists in the interdependence of theory and fact.

I begin with balance-of-power theory and imperialism because they were central to the thinking of both Carr and Taylor. Each man's overall meaning of history, however, involved other considerations as well:

- history from the top down vs. from the bottom up;
- the simultaneity and complementarity of "fundamental causes and causes specific to an event," in Taylor's words, "the profound causes" of an event and

the causes governing "why that particular . . . [event] happened at that particular time" (Burk, p. 269); inclusive of the distinction between general phenomena (e.g. imperialist wars) and particular phenomena (each war occurs when it does for reasons pertinent to it);

- history as discovered or created by the historian;
- history as taught in the schools (which is more societization and acculturation, i.e. social control, than serious history) and history as known to the historians;
- determinism vs. freedom of will in history;
- ideas in relation to such forces as the Industrial Revolution and balance of power; and so on.

Because of their emphasis on multiple factors and on certain dualisms, and because of their inability or unwillingness to consider them all simultaneously, it was difficult for both of them and others to readily express what history was all about. In the nation-state system, moreover, power and its use have certain perhaps overriding characteristics: Power is pursued. The conduct of power is largely conducted by political leaders at the top – except for mass movements, which themselves are targets or vehicles by those at the top. Power and its use are wrapped in nationalist symbolism and ideology, in part to obfuscate the pursuit of raw calculations of advantage as to ends and means and the conduct of mutual manipulation while putting a beneficent gloss on aggression.

2. BALANCE-OF-POWER THEORY AND IMPERIALISM

Two rival approaches in the social sciences are methodological individualism and methodological collectivism. The former is the view that meaningful knowledge of individuals and societies is best acquired through the study of individuals. The former is the view that meaningful knowledge of individuals and societies is best acquired through the study of social systems, structures and processes. The mutual exclusivity that gets ensconced in their respective definitions is fallacious and misleading and adversely affects practice. Individuals are what they are and behave as they do in part due to the systems, structures and processes in which they live. Societies are what they are and operate as they do in part due to the zones of discretion and exercise of discretion within those zones by individuals. There is absolutely no reason why one cannot study social systems, structures and processes directly and as such, or indirectly through the study of individuals. Part of the meaning of social systems, structures and processes resides in their impact on individuals and the impact of individuals on them, for which one must study individuals. Part of the significance of individuals is their impact on social systems, structures and processes, and of the latter's impact on them, for which one must study them. Some scholars believe that they are studying individuals' and others', systems. Some conduct analysis at the micro level, others at the macro level. A sensible solution is to undertake both types of study simultaneously, a solution pursued, to some extent, by a few individuals, but largely effectuated, however imperfectly, through the division of labor.

The conflict between the two approaches applies both to individual nation states vis-à-vis the nation-state system in which they operate and to individual human beings vis-à-vis the larger systems, structures and processes in which they operate.

The balance of power theory of international relations, considered as a positive theory, centers on the following critical proposition: That when issues, policy proposals, and conflicts arise, they tend to be analyzed and evaluated on the basis of their likely implications for the distribution of power among nation states. (The theory also applies to all subsystems and organizations in which power enters, which is to say, all of them). In this context, power may be defined in various ways but, inasmuch as the theory is a positive theory, in a non-pejorative way. The theory affirms that nation states can act on the basis of either stated or implicit intentions, or capabilities. This makes it difficult for other nations to predict the course of action by any given nation state. Nation states will, therefore, given the opportunity costs involved, seek to optimize their power in order to defend against what they perceive to be aggression or threat of aggression or capability for aggression.

The nature of the nation-state system, therefore, compels states, even those who would like to practice live and let live, or to live in perpetual peace, to be concerned with their power relative to the power of other nation states. Nation states can, within that system, adopt various interests and objectives and pursue different strategies. Some of those objectives and strategies are strongly conditioned by the particular geopolitical position of individual nation states. But individual nation states do have more or less considerable discretion as to interests, objectives and strategies. Individual nation states also can seek to maximize, or optimize, their power in different ways, given those adopted or imposed interests, objectives and strategies. A nation state exists in a parallelogram or matrix of power vis-à-vis other states. Accordingly, it is not always, if ever, perfectly clear what choices it will make, insofar as it has discretion, not only as to interests, objectives and strategies, but together with what other nation states.

History, especially political history, is the record of actions and results in such matters.

The theory of the balance of power is one way to understand what transpires in such matters. It is also a normative theory, available for use by decision makers seeking to achieve, say, optimum power or security.

A nation state may seek, therefore, to fill a power vacuum, lest some rival or potential rival do so. Or a nation state may align with another weak nation state in an effort to forestall or counter a more powerful rival. Or, in the event of two more or less equally powerful rivals, a third nation state may seek to align itself with one or the other. And so on. (Richard Reeves, the presidential historian, reported on C-Span on February 17, 2002, that Henry Kissinger believed that balance-of-power politics meant that one would always be for the weaker party.)

Balance-of-power politics and power play can mean, therefore, different things to different persons and to different nation states and also be pursued in different ways. The analytically awkward result arises when the theory qua theory – normative or positive – is identified with particular choices. Such is often the case with the rhetoric of policy but it can also occur with positive, including historical, analysis.

Closely related to balance-of-power politics and power play is imperialism. Imperialism is the projection of a nation-state's interests and power beyond its territorial borders. The conduct of imperialism, especially colonial imperialism, can be driven by economic or by political forces, though, in my view, the evidence for the two and for the fact of imperialism is much the same; in practice each emanates from the legal-economic nexus and identification is a matter of selective perception and attribution.

In 1914, that momentous date in the twentieth century and the year Carr and Taylor turned 22 and 8, respectively, the nation-state system was rampant with empires. As difficult as it is to believe almost a century later, the colonial empires of 1914 were, in alphabetical order, those of Belgium, Denmark, France, Germany, Great Britain, Italy, Japan, the Netherlands, Portugal, Russia, Spain and the United States. Not all these empires were equal. Some were expanding, some dreamed of and sought expansion, and some were declining or existing passively. Only large areas of South and Central America, the Middle East, the Balkans, and China were not manifestly within the political, or economic-political, orbit of those empires. Balance of power and imperialism meant a great deal and were conspicuous. After two world wars – whatever one's theory of them – the colonial empires of 1914 largely no longer existed. Eventually balance of power and imperialism took new forms. In the new context one would eventually find first two so-called superpowers; an emergent united Europe; an emergent as-yet un-united Islamic Middle East, South Asia and, in part, Pacifica; China; then a dissolved and emaciated former Soviet Union, now Russia; and rivals to the nation-state system itself in the forms of the transnational corporate system and the system of governance known as globalization (see Samuels, 2002). What was a power-sensitive nation state to do?

Moreover what is a power-sensitive historian to do? For any American, especially one alive on December 7, 1941 and old enough to know what transpired,

Pearl Harbor was subject to an unprovoked, sneak attack by Japan. It was gratuitous enough but it did not happen in a vacuum. For some time the United States and Japan, along with a number of other countries, primarily European but also China, were jockeying for power in Asia and the Pacific. That included Japanese engagements in land wars on the continent of Asia. Taylor wrote a book that scandalized many people, *Origins of the Second World War* (1961), which concentrated on Germany and the European war; a comparable book could have concentrated on Japan and the Asian-Pacific war. In each case, dramatic events, terrible beliefs and horrific people were overshadowed by events, beliefs and people that, in the light of history were commonplace, even banal. Nationalism and imperialism were not created in 1939.

The preceding paragraph returns us to the initial topic of this introduction, methodological individualism vs. methodological collectivism: emphasis on the unilateral action by Japan or on the larger system of nation-state relations from which it emanated and to which it contributed.

More to the present purpose, how were balance-of-power sensitive historians to approach their subject? Interestingly, both of our historian biographical subjects used their initials rather than their full names, as if engaged in a metaphor for the destroyed 1914 system of colonial empires. Each deployed balance-of-power theory differently – as if the metaphor meant different things for each of them. The reason for that is relatively simple: metaphors are not derived from the reality they are intended to cast light on, but are created by cognitively active minds – using whatever manifestations of reality are available to them but superimposing their own meaning, theory, model, or paradigm on them. Each of them, however, believed in the reality of the theory of the balance of power; it was one of the crucial, if different, interpretive founts for both of them. In this they were no different than are, say, Chicago vs. Yale versions of neoclassical economics.

3. E. H. CARR

E. H. Carr (1892–1982) was raised in a middle-class family in Highgate and educated at Merchant Taylors' School, London, and at Trinity College, Cambridge. After two decades (1916–1936) in the British Foreign Office, where he rose to the rank of first secretary, he engaged in several careers. He was professor of international politics at University College of Wales and a Fellow of Trinity College. He was assistant editor on *The Times* during World War II. He undertook the career as a professional historian at the age of 52 and became a prolific author. His specialized areas included the history and theory of international relations; general European history; the Russian revolution and the history of Soviet Russia;

historical methodology; and biography – studies on Karl Marx, Michael Bakunin and Alexander Herzen. His most influential works included *A History of Soviet Russia* (14 vols., 1950–1978), *What is History?* (1961), *The Romantic Exiles* (1933), and *International Relations Between the Two World Wars* (1939).

Carr had two great beliefs each of which proved erroneous. He believed that capitalism was a temporary stage in history and would be replaced by a state that was more democratic and centrally planned economically. In this he was influenced by the shocks of the first World War and the Great Depression as well as moral critiques of Western culture. He also believed that the Russian Revolution and Soviet Russia were the harbingers of a new social order, not along any pre-ordained Marxian-Leninist lines but through adaptation and adjustment to unforeseen developments (pp. 72ff and passim). In his mind they represented both economic and political democracy. He "saw Lenin as a state-builder rather than revolutionary" (p. 143). Carr had few, but certainly some, illusions about either the atrocities of Stalinism in the Soviet Union or its policies as a world power, perhaps all of which he rejected while not rejecting Soviet Russia and what he believed it represented.

The distinction between state-builder and revolutionary is not objective: it gives effect to certain antecedent normative premises and is therefore hermeneutical in nature. But the distinction is nonetheless at least problematically important: Chimen Abramsky has commented that Carr saw "the unique importance of the Russian Bolshevik Revolution ... [in] completing the destruction of the old system" and, despite the Revolution's propensity to consume its major actors, its leaders as builders of a "new, powerful, often tyrannical state institution, rather than mere ideologues, or nihilists." Carr thus "dismissed the classical socialist-Marxist theories on the 'withering or dying away of the State,' as mere Shibboleth – obsolescences of history." "The supreme irony in this connection came with the dissolution or withering away of the U.S.S.R., it thereby becoming an obsolescence of history. Moreover, Carr had a grand vision of how a country the size of Russia was moulded, governed and shaped from above" (Abramsky, 1974, p. vii).

Carr also had what amounted to a third great belief, the theory of the balance of power. Inter alia, he rejected what he saw as the liberal idea of a natural harmony of interests among states, including the idea that they have identical interests in peace. Even democracy was based "on a balance of forces peculiar to the economic development of the period and countries concerned," though the situation gave rise to certain a priori principles or beliefs deemed by believers to be universally applicable (p. 71).

On the basis, in part, of the theory of the balance of power, he first argued (in 1939) for appeasement of Nazi Germany. The basis of this view was both that (as Keynes had warned in *The Economic Consequences of the Peace* (1920))

Germany had been abused by the Treaty of Versailles, that Germany was only pursuing national self-determination, and that it made sense for Britain to ally itself with Germany as a major power (pp. 56ff). Subsequent to the events of 1939 and their aftermath, he next argued for alliance with the Soviet Union on pretty much the same grounds. As Haslam also says, "Carr shared . . . the illusion that the Soviet Union would rapidly shed its messianic mission in favour of a purely state-oriented approach to international relations" (p. 1 to 05).

On October 2, 1938, Roy F. Harrod, the important English economist, wrote Sir Archibald Sinclair in a manner illustrating balance-of-power pragmatism:

> Of course we agree that, if Hitler has really been tamed, let us work with him. But it is necessary to insure ourselves against the opposite eventuality by cultivating the closest possible relations with *Russia* and with those small countries who still have a common interest with us in resisting aggression. In cultivating Germany Chamberlin . . . is gambling on his optimistic interpretation of Hitler . . . the stake is our independent existence . . . (Harrod, forthcoming, letter no. 845, p. 869; see also 871).

Clearly, balance-of-power theory was not self-determinative of appropriate policy but was itself driven by selective perception.

Carr also favored an international order that gave vent to more powerful nations and largely disregarded, even denigrated, the interests of smaller, less powerful ones (p. 94). This is another version of the top-down approach to history.

The core of the theory of the balance of power is, of course, power. Carr early showed, Haslam reports, "a healthy – or, as Sir Isaiah Berlin would have said, unhealthy – respect for power"; often the "logic" of a situation or its "inevitability," as he perceived it, was a function of power variables (p. 15). Power, he believed, "had a peculiar quality of its own. It was not just a tool for whoever reached the top. It dictated certain necessities" (p. 73). In the Foreign Office, "Carr had very soon absorbed the ethos that reasons of state override every other necessity" (p. 25; see below for a critique of this argument, though not one that renders it nugatory). Still, Carr rejected "power as something abstract that can be used for 'good' ends" in favor of power "as something used by one group to exercise its rule . . . over another" (p. 268).

So much, for now, for the theory of the balance of power.

Carr's *What is History? (1961)* was, as it turned out, a precursor to post-modernist epistemology. He did not denigrate the truthful telling of history but considered it an objective that is difficult to achieve. Individual historians had their own perspectives, a function in part of their socialization into their own society. These perspectives they superimposed on the putative facts of history. History, in other words, was made and not discovered by the historian. Accordingly, history was a story constructed after the fact and giving meaning to the fact. Because different historians have different perspectives, they told more or less different stories, including and/or stressing certain factors and excluding and/or minimizing other factors. Social science and history are partly exercises in fiction. For those who demand determinacy and closure, such a view is repugnant. It is especially anathema to those who had imbibed and cling to the conventional nationalist and cultural myths and other stories taught in school and who require same to satisfy their need for determinacy and coherence, rather than abide with openendedness and ambiguity.

Long before the ascendance of post-modernism, however, historians, while preferring one true story about something, knew that the situation in their discipline was different. The facts of the rise and fall of the Roman Empire, Mercantilism, the French Revolution, the American Civil War, the two World Wars, North Atlantic economic development, the rise of religious fundamentalism, and so on were reasonably clear. But in each case there was, and still is, a handful of theories of meaning and causation.

Getting ahead of ourselves, perhaps that is one reason why Taylor was reluctant to rely on authorities and preferred to do "the research himself and draw his own conclusions" (Burk, p. 40; see also p. 66). Such, however, did not prevent him from upholding his own findings as more or less definitive; self-reflexivity will go only so far, sooner or later it confronts ego.

The correlative problem, and insight, is that each of these theories tends to be mono-causal whereas it is more than likely that the most meaningful theory(ies) will be multi-causal. The situation is not unlike that in which everyone is a philosophical realist but disagree as to the nature and content of reality, thus ending up in the same position as the philosophical idealist, who must choose between different idealizations, even though the philosophical realists all agree that there is one and only one true reality. The different specifications of reality, like those of history, are partly fictional in their incompleteness.

At any rate, Taylor, for one, would not have given much weight to the notion – except insofar as the notion itself had influence in history – "that the hand of God manifested itself in history" (Burk, pp. 37, 52, 136, 215, 381, 409; see also p. 156: "fundamentally a nihilist"). He would have insisted, however, that different theists had different understandings of what the hand of God wrought. As for Carr, he wrote his daughter-in-law (a believer) in 1981 that he could "find no evidence whatever for the existence of 'God,' . . . [nor] understand what kind of God you believe in" (p. 294).

Carr's argument not only seemed to many "a wholesale attack on the standards of the profession," it raised a tension, applicable even to his own past work, between "a history so firmly cast in a thoroughly deterministic framework of the past" and "the relativism of history-writing" proposed in *What is History?* (p. 192). Carr himself admitted "the dilemma . . . of 'balancing uneasily on the razor edge between the hazards of objective determinism and the bottomless pit of subjective relativity' " (p. 193). He also wrote that

> The question is not whether objectivity is attained or attainable by historians, but whether the concept of objectivity in history has any meaning. To assert that fallible human beings are too much entangled in circumstances of time and place to attain the absolute truth is not the same thing as to deny the existence of truth: such a denial destroys any possible criterion of judgment, and makes any approach to history as true or as false as any other. . . . it is possible to maintain that objective truth exists, but that no historian by himself, or no school of historians by itself, can hope to achieve more than a faint and partial approximation to it (p. 194).

The post-modern view is somewhat less sanguine and subtler (see Samuels, 1995, 1996, 1997a, b, 1998). First, large events – such as the French Revolution – have multiple characteristics and features. These permit different perceptions and different stories of the meaning of events. The diversity of stories is further driven by the fact of multiple standpoints from which those events are observed. The situation is akin to the parable of the blind man and the elephant in the former respect and to several blind men in the latter. Second, if all were to posit and agree with the proposition that objective truth exists, when each has a different view of what that truth is, the objectivist or philosophical realist is left in the same position as the relativist or idealist, namely, having to face the necessity to choose. Third, apropos of denying the existence of any criteria of judgment, the situation is one in which judgment is in fact excercised, whatever the criterion, and not a function of objective truth; the important point is not that any approach is as true or false as any other, but that we are compelled to choose and have no unequivocal meta-criterion on which to base choice.

The problem of the complexity and even inconclusivity of truth also arises in the work of Taylor; further consideration of it will be undertaken below.

As for Carr, he felt compelled, during the Cold War, to defend against the threat to the notion of objectivity in history (pp. 194–195). Such seems in retrospect to be more an attempt to compel specification of the criterion chosen for use, but that is apparently not how he saw it. "Objectivity" also had to be defined. Carr's emphasized rising "above the limited vision of [one's] own situation in society and in history" and projecting one's "vision into the future in such a way as to give [one] a more profound and more lasting insight into the past" (p. 203). From my perspective, recognizing the complex nature of the concept of "objectivity," the first will take the historian (or economist) only so far, and the latter – basing a surmise on a surmise, which is no more helpful than basing one metaphor on another – is no part of a solution at all.

The exercise of judgment also raises issues of progress, causality and responsibility, even when only part of an explanation (pp. 198ff), as well as other matters, including the relation of deeper forces, accidents and ideas, presentism (transferring present ideas into the past and/or evaluating past ideas on the basis of present ideas), the relation of political to social and economic factors and forces (Chap. 9, passim). Some of these issues also will enter our discussion of Taylor.

Carr acquired his own sense of history being made by mankind during the Russian Revolution. As in the 18th century when the idea became widely important, neither institutions nor the course of history were seen as given by either nature or some supernatural agency but a matter of the combination of deliberative and non-deliberative policies and their interaction (see below).

None of this was endearing to many people. Moreover, his positions on major policy issues were controversial to say the least (see pp. 119ff). In particular, his open-minded attitude toward the Soviet Union, his general position as a dissenter, and his personal behavior (see below) undoubtedly deprived him of appointment to major academic positions after the onset of the Cold War, notably the Regius Chair of History at Oxford.

One can claim – as I do – that Carr's approach to doing history is descriptively accurate, true like it or not, although no meta-principles can permit unequivocal choice between it and other approaches. Carr's great beliefs and his applications of balance-of-power theory are of a different nature: they are problematic, depending on how the system of power works out. Another truth, also whether one likes it or not, is that nation states ignore consideration of international power and power play at their peril.

Still, Carr was "strongly fixed in the values of the Enlightenment"; he "had never taken to religion" and had "a blind belief in progress" (p. 46). He could appreciate, however, the motivating role of religious faith – and of Russian Marxism (p. 48). He was no believer in Marxist doctrine, says Haslam, who quotes Carr's autobiographical sketch: "more interested in Marxism as a method of revealing the hidden springs of thought and action, and debunking the logical and moralistic façade generally erected around them" (p. 54). He was particularly incited by the perceived utopianism of Adam Smith and of Marx, Engels and Lenin in which the state, under certain (but different) conditions would wither away (p. 144). Part of the reason he misread both Hitler and the Soviet leadership, Haslam proposes, is that "Although appreciative of the importance of ideology, he was always too much the rationalist to take fanaticism too seriously" (p. 105; see also p. 151).

For someone with his approach to history and to power it is perhaps odd that "Carr showed no deference to the kind of unhappy compromise integral to the political process in a democracy"; his "emotional absolutism . . . never came to terms with the distasteful relativism of democratic political life" (p. 320). Carr apparently required, or postulated, determinacy and closure in some matters, though not in others. Carr had been greatly influenced by Dostoevsky, whom

Haslam rightly calls "a complex and contradictory figure." Carr's total approach, like that (as we will see below) of Taylor, was laden with tensions between conflicting factors. What is true of them is also true of Dostoevsky: "the world takes from his writing whatever it is most in need of, at any one time" (p.45; this language is too non-specific for my taste but his point is made; see Samuels, 2001).

Apropos of the foregoing, Isaiah Berlin, known by both Carr and Taylor, wrote in a February 13, 1951 letter to George Kennan, apropos of Dostoevsky's Ivan Karamazov, "the one thing which no utilitarian paradise, no promise of eternal harmony in the future within some vast organic whole will make us accept is the use of human beings as mere means" (Berlin, 2002, p. 24; in the letter Berlin refers in passing to a dispute he was engaged in with Carr (p. 26); Berlin contributed to the collection of essays in honor of Carr's eightieth birthday (Abramsky, 1974)). One has to sympathize with the values ensconced in this Kantian rule, even though the word "only" before "mere" is absent; but it carries much wishful thinking. And it is true that the discussion has to do only with wholes. But, as I think Carr and Taylor understood, in all systems individuals have relations with others in which they are in reciprocal, though typically asymmetrical, means positions. For example, individual engaged in trade, ala Adam Smith or Vilfredo Pareto, treat each other as means. Competition, in some sense, provides a check. Similarly, one might prefer a nation-state system in which the principles of equality and sovereignty of states are lauded and there is no world government with a monopoly of force. But that too would involve wishful thinking: political and economic externalities limit sovereignty and may be due to one or another kind of inequality, the functional equivalent of world government may exist, and military force is not the only form that coercion can take (Samuels, 1997c, 2002).

Carr should get credit for a point made in 1940 that, from the standpoint of 2002, looks prescient. Albeit in a different immediate context but with publication of his book *The Twenty Years' Crisis 1919–1939* (1939) just behind him, Carr wrote in a *Times* editorial on July 1, 1940 that

> Europe can no longer afford a multiplicity of economic units, each maintaining its independent economic system behind a barbed wire entanglement of tariffs, quotas, exchange restrictions and barter agreements (p. 86; see also 88–89, 92).

This was surely part of the reasoning – heretical as it seemed for a long time – behind the gradual economic and political integration of Europe, leading to the adoption inter alia of a common legislature, a common judiciary and a common currency.

Carr was not the difficult person Taylor was (as we shall see) but he could be an avid controversialist, even with friends whose views were very close. (He had a wide range of friends; one of them was the economist, Piero Sraffa (p. 283).) Part of both the problem of truth and his general situation, we have seen, is that his ideas and writings were capable, on numerous issues, of varying interpretations and evaluations. Part, perhaps was while "he had an extraordinary historical imagination, . . . he was," Haslam concludes, "absolutely incapable of putting himself into other people's shoes; living people, that is" (p. 276). So much for Adam Smith's concepts of sympathy and the Impartial Spectator – at least as they apply to Carr.

Part of the problem, too, stemmed from the facts that while Carr was not a Marxist (p. 288) and he had few illusions about the Soviet Union, he continued to have some hope for the country along the lines of what he and others had initially deemed its promise. Haslam writes that Carr "had always underestimated the revolutionary impulse in Soviet foreign policy" (p. 284), refusing to see western hysteria as a genuine response to widespread Soviet threats, even while admitting he could not understand why it undertook some of them (pp. 284–285).

Part of the problem of truth and his situation was no doubt also due to the combination of the two modes of thrust of his – and everyone else's – thinking, the realist and the utopian. Sometimes one was in control, says Haslam; other times, the other (e.g. p. 297).

4. A. J. P. TAYLOR

A. J. P. Taylor (1906–1990) was born and raised as an only child in Birkdale, Lancashire into a well-to-do if not wealthy family in the cotton trade. He was educated at a Quaker public school and Oriel College, Oxford.

Burk relates that at Bootham, the Quaker school, "He was against authority, for left-wing politics, in favour of female emancipation and against sports and physical exercise" (p. 36). A self-critical adult Taylor may have recognized that his opposition to authority likely related to his adolescence and conflicted with his support for left-wing politics and female suffrage, both of which represented efforts not to reject but to redirect the use of authority. At any rate, it would seem that Taylor, whose university training was to prepare one for "running the country and the Empire" (Burk, pp. 56, 105), had mixed feelings about authority. He may not have been happy with either authority in general or the system of authority in Britain. He nonetheless seems to have relished being, and being seen as, an authority and, through his several careers, taking his part in the system of authority (which, for present purposes, may be understood as the formation of public opinion in the process of decision making). Taylor learned that there was a difference between the history taught in school books and the history one might tell in the absence of inculcation in national mythology (Burk, p. 62).

As an adult, he was, if anything, more prolific, more controversial, and certainly more acerbic than Carr. He, too, had several simultaneous careers. He was a lecturer at Manchester University from 1930 to 1938, afterwards moving to Magdalen College, Oxford where he was a Fellow from 1938 to 1963, thereafter an Honorary or Research Fellow until 1976. He was a leading public intellectual ("media don") of his day, appearing regularly on radio and television talk shows and in newspapers (such as the *Sunday Pictorial*, the *Daily Herald*, and the *Sunday Express*), as a freelance journalist and columnist. He produced some 1,600 book reviews, many for the *Manchester Guardian, New Statesman*, the *Observer* and *The New York Review of Books*, and for professional journals. He published 23 books and some 600 professional articles and essays. His specialized areas included: German history, general European history; English history; theories of war and of revolution; and biography – studies on Beaverbrook and Bismarck.

His most influential books were *The Habsburg Monarchy, 1809–1918* (1941); a biography, *Bismarck: The Man and the Statesman* (1955); *The Struggle for Mastery in Europe, 1848–1918* (1954); English History, 1914–1945 (1965); and the controversial, if not infamous, as well as influential, *The Origins of the Second World War* (1961).

Both Taylor and Carr paid serious attention to the political history of Europe and focused on international relations, diplomatic and otherwise. Taylor tended to concentrate on Germany; Carr, on the Soviet Union. Both were revisionist, each in his own way. Both thought that history, or the lessons from the study of history, as each understood those lessons, should become the basis of British policy (see p. 251: obligation of historians to make new analysis of underlying forces, one closer to reality, to prepare the British public for policies suffering from fewer illusions and fewer mistakes). Taylor (and Carr) also concentrated on history from the top down (cp. p. 302); as Burk writes, "Taylor almost invariably concentrated his historical attention on their ['the people's'] rulers" (p. 230); Taylor himself quoted Lord John Russell that "the Great Powers had not the habit of consulting populations when questions affecting the Balance of Power had to be settled" (p. 266) – though he also recognized that secrecy and consent involve "contradictory propositions which have to be reconciled in modern times by democratic governments" (p. 271). The principal position may simply correlate with his concentration on diplomatic history – diplomacy is "a profession dominated by the upper classes" with "its own code of honour" (p. 265) – and international relations; whether or how much it is due to an affinity to those with power, is not clear. As for Carr, Haslam writes that he had an "identification with rulers rather than ruled" and that "in writing the *History*, Carr subconsciously transposed his early identification with the ruling class in Britain to the ruling caste in Soviet Russia" (Haslam, p. 146). Haslam also says that Carr "was attached to a Darwinian view of history" and but for his "achieved notoriety as a historian of the Soviet regime, his view of history might otherwise have identified him as a conservative" (Haslam, p. 259).

Burk lists the following to be among Taylor's "recurring preoccupations": "the use and abuse of power; the relationship between governments and the people they govern; the relationship between states in the international system; and the exercise of power by strong men. Statesmen, he believed, did not plan policies but reacted to external events – a theory which combined the roles of accident and agent into a major explanatory factor in history. He also introduced the concept of the 'invention of tradition' " (p. 225; see also pp. 229, 231). One of these themes is taken up again below.

Taylor must have shared aspects of Carr's approach to history. For example, Burk (p. 58) reports that for Taylor

> the past is a foreign country which the historian must approach on its own terms, neither viewing it as the present in different clothes nor as a quarry for rock with which to build a present-day house. The former approach is much more common now than it was in the early part of the twentieth century [adds Burk], when history was normally seen as a school for statesmen and citizens.

She also quotes Taylor as saying, "Men write history . . . for the joy of creation" (p. 103). He would also have resonated – apropos of the discussion of Part 2 of this essay – with the proposition that "no one can take up with profit a special aspect of our history until he has some grasp of the general drift of the whole" (p. 106), i.e. determinism in terms of "large trends" coupled with the details and "accidents that seem to stick out and make up history" therefore free will (p. 224). Geography, political system and general culture loom large, capable of yielding implications for policy (p. 236).

Taylor also shared with Carr a belief in the theory of the balance of power (starting with his work on the Habsburg Empire, he became focused on the conduct and manipulation of power both between nations and within them, what Burk calls the "internal foreign policy" (p. 233) within a nation or empire, in part one of divide and conquer (p. 232; see also p. 247). Burk writes that

> Taylor's overarching theme was the balance of power, which he saw as the dominating factor in international relations of the period: driven by attempts to disturb the balance an counter-attempts to maintain it (p. 95).

Thus, he could understand why, for example, "countries prefer to have weak rather than strong states on their borders" (p. 98).

In practice, for Taylor, this approach led to his opposition to appeasement of Hitler and support for rearmament and to his advocacy of an alliance with the Soviet Union the purpose of which, for Britain, was national security against Nazi Germany and a hedge against the United States being an unreliable and competitive ally (see the discussion on Anglo-American attitudes at the end of the introduction to this volume); freedom and peace under the "joint protection of England and

Russia" (p. 239). Taylor had visited Soviet Russia in 1925 and was impressed with its spirit and "revolutionary enthusiasm" (Burk, p. 61). After a decade of chastising skeptics, he became one himself (p. 62). Burk writes, "Taylor remained pro-Soviet for most of his life, although he eventually admitted that the Russian people had deserved better of their leaders" (p. 123).

Taylor's argument in *The Origins of the Second World War* (1961) severely damaged his reputation in some quarters. The question at stake was similar to that which arose later during the Cold War. One position was that the Soviet Union was acting pretty much as a Tsar with nuclear weapons would act, standing astride the European and Asian land mass, and that Marxism, however seriously voiced, was in effect marginalia or window-dressing. The opposite position was that the Soviet Union was pursuing policies of world conquest as spelled out by Marx, Lenin, and Stalin. Taylor's question also had two sides. One side argued that Nazi Germany was *sui generis* among war-making nations, what with its overriding militarism, its treatment of the Jews and others in the Holocaust, its nationalist ideology, its stated aims for world conquest, its practice of total war, and so on. Taylor argued, however, that neither Nazi Germany nor the war was unique; nor was the war a matter of fascism vs. liberalism. The war, rather, was a matter of traditional balance-of-power efforts by Hitler to restore German power and to pursue traditional German interests (as in 1870 under Bismarck and in World War I (on Bismarck and balance-of-power diplomacy and war, see Burk, p. 140ff)). Anti-Semitism was not unique; it had been widespread if not rampant throughout Europe, and Hitler was using it as a technique of mobilizing and manipulating political psychology. The war arose, moreover, in the context of a set of balance-of-power stratagems by other European countries, especially France and England (including the policies adopted in the Treaty of Versailles, to which John Maynard Keynes so presciently objected), with most of the other countries trying to get what they could but continuing to be essentially weak states. The problem for Hitler, as it turned out, was that he misread both Britain and the route the United States would take. Which is to say, he put too much reliance on the Nazi sympathizers and appeasers in Britain and on the isolationists in the United States (see also below). The controversy over this book led to the termination in 1963 of his Oxford lectureship notwithstanding his stature.

The theory of the balance of power does not itself automatically and unequivocally define situations. What happened in terms of, say, physical events is largely clear. Unclear is why those events happened and their meaning and/or significance, that is, their interpretation. Balance-of-power theory enable different writers to interpret events differently and to apply balance-of-power considerations differently.

Nor, of course, does balance-of-power theory dictate policy. One magazine pointed to Taylor's "appalling contrast between 'Bismarck's far-sighted realism and the helpless benevolence of British statesmen' " (p. 142). What constitutes (political) realism is precisely the point at issue. The definitions of reality and of values – those presumably ensconced in "national interest" – can vary, along with an array of trade-offs. (See the distinction between live and let live, and aggressive pursuit of perceived national interests, raised in the first paragraph of this essay. Apropos of the United States' invasion of the Dominican Republic in 1965, for example, the political-realist policy is not unequivocally clear; compare, however, Berle, 1969; on Taylor's view that the United States in the Korean War was using the United Nations as an instrument of its own policy, see p. 398.)

Taylor saw that diplomacy and power play under the balance-of-power view of the world are not matters of what the legitimizing rhetoric of broad principles and "Platonic Ideas" or "other secret forces" make the conflict out to be:

> ... it is rather that the course of national policy is based upon a series of assumptions, with which statesmen have lived since their earliest years and which they regard as so axiomatic as hardly to be worth stating. It is the duty of the historian to clarify these assumptions and to trace their influence upon the course of every-day policy (p. 98, quoting Taylor).

These assumptions relate to national interests. (Interests presumably can be transformed into varying assumptions, so it is both material interests and ideas that are influential.)

Further with regard to the theory of the balance of power: For all practical purposes, Taylor subsumed the topic of imperialism under that of the balance of power. Great powers may have other objectives ("the welfare of their inhabitants or the grandeur of their rulers") but fundamentally they are "organizations for power, that is, in the last resort for war." Their basic test is "their ability to wage war" and increasingly this ability, this strength, is a matter of its economic power (p. 264). This is illustrated by the case of Germany and its repeated efforts to expand in Europe and acquire colonies abroad between 1870 and 1945.

A specialist in German and general European history, Taylor developed a dominant "theme both political and historical." This was "the German question – or the German problem, as he was more apt to term it: how to control or at least to contain a country which persisted in being richer and stronger than its neighbours and persisted in exploiting the fact" (p. 248; see also p. 251). As Burk stresses, the major theme of *The Struggle for Mastery* (1954) "is the struggle between the Great powers for the domination of Europe, or more precisely the struggle by Germany to dominate the continent and the attempts by the other Great Powers to prevent it" p. 263; cf. p. 270). Moreover, "No one state has ever been strong enough to eat up all the rest; and the mutual jealousy of the Great Powers" – and their conduct of policy in accordance with the theory of the Balance of Power – "has preserved even the small states, which could not have preserved themselves.

The relations of the Great Powers have determined the history of Europe" (pp. 263–264).

The solution to the German problem, as it were, has been European economic and political union; earlier it had been a fortuitous (?) result of the Cold-War division of Germany (cf. p. 292: Gerhard Ritter claimed in 1961, before German reunion and later events, that Taylor relished his open expression that the division of Germany is fortunate for England).

This raises, again, the analytical and interpretive question of the combination of deliberative and non-deliberative decision making in history – the question at the heart of the Adam Smith-Adam Ferguson-Carl Menger-Friedrich A. von Hayek conception of spontaneous order driven by the principle of unintended consequences but also considered by others, such as Thorstein Veblen, Frank H. Knight, Vilfredo Pareto and John R. Commons (Samuels, 1999). This was an important part of Taylor's theory of history. It took the form, however, of his combination of simultaneously operative "fundamental causes" and the "causes specific to an event." "Both enquiries," he stipulated, "make sense on different levels. They are complementary; they do not exclude each other" (p. 269). Burk devotes considerable attention to the question – which also includes aspects of the problem of parts and wholes, itself akin to the conflict between methodological individualism (specific causes, which derive their existence and meaning, in part, from the wholes of which they are parts) and methodological collectivism (general causes which derive their existence and meaning, in part, from the accumulation of the effects of the parts that form them). The resultant problem was the difficulty of expressing complex relationships while simultaneously concentrating on part of the total story. This problem is key to understanding both the reception given their work and their responses.

Some historians, such as Carr, believed that Taylor emphasized the specific causes, which are more idiosyncratic and accidental, and disagreed with him. It is easy to see why he could be read this way. He himself argued that nothing is determined by fate or history; as Burk quotes him, "no war is inevitable until it breaks out." But, notes Burk, "[t]he gulf between that conclusion and the theoretical basis for his approach to Germany could not be more glaring . . ." (p. 267). Be that as it may, a second theme, elaborative of the first, is that "what makes the difference is not fate but men, their ideas, their principles (or lack of them), their characters, their energy, their greed and their ability or willingness to react to opportunities as they arose" (p. 267). "Taylor did not neglect the importance of sources which lay beyond the foreign offices of the Powers" (p. 268), arguing that "Policy springs from deep social and economic sources: it is not crudely manufactured in foreign offices" (quoted pp. 268–269). But Foreign Offices did react to international events, much less often initiating policy and more often responding "in a haphazard way"

(p. 268). The historical story is in the details, and while "[t]he whole structure of *The Struggle for Mastery* is informed by the 'profound forces'; it is perhaps unfortunate [says Burk] that he often neglected to make their relationship to immediate causes more explicit" (p. 270; see also p. 276). In a different context, Taylor asserted that he "prefer[ed] detail to generalizations," and that his doing so "redressed the balance" of others' preference "to talk so much about these profound forces in order to avoid doing the detailed work" (p. 290). Indeed, Burk continually stresses Taylor's forte residing in undertaking detailed work, e.g. working with vast archival sources.

Carr's review of the book in the *Times Literary Supplement*, says Burk, had an internal conflict of its own. Carr argued that Taylor believes in the important role of "deep social and economic forces [Taylor had written 'sources'], but did not incorporate the details of that role into his analysis. Carr thus "regarded Taylor as believing that history was little more than a chapter of accidents . . ." But, says Burk, Carr also argued that Taylor assumed that "the important explanations in history are to be found in the conscious purposes and foresights of the dramatis personae" – "a conclusion," argues Burk, "which directly contradicted his earlier comment that Taylor believed history to be a chapter of accidents" (p. 276). This criticism assumes that the combination of conscious purposes and foresights by reactors cannot co-exist with the accidents to which they react and which they unintentionally cause in reacting the way they do. It seems to me that both general or profound causes and particular causes co-exist and interact, that both conscious behavior and accidental or spontaneous events (as consequence and cause) co-exist and interact, and therefore that deliberative and non-deliberative factors, or effective decision making, co-exist and interact, and do so on both levels. Basil Liddell Hart wrote Taylor, agreeing that "most wars were detonated accidentally rather than deliberately" (p. 288). Three points: (1) It is impossible to measure and determine "most." (2) There are clear deliberative elements, produced by someone, in all wars. And (3) the juxtaposition of accidental and deliberate is neither simple nor coherent (in the form of deliberative vs. non-deliberative, I again cite Samuels, 1999).

The set of issues is continued in *The Origins of the Second World War*. Further as to what is said above, Buck identifies five relevant themes:

> First of all, foreign policies are determined by reasons of state and the need to respond to external threats or blandishments, rather than by internal politics, including those driven by ideology or by economic pressures. Secondly, Hitler had strategic goals but no predetermined master plan as to how and when he would reach those goals. Thirdly, those goals were no different from the goals of other statesmen such as Stresemann. Fourthly, lacking a precise timetable, Hitler took opportunities as they arose – and the French and British governments gave him those opportunities. And fifthly, Hitler had the support of the German people in overthrowing the Versailles Treaty and invading Poland. In this Taylor challenged and thereby shattered the consensus . . . [that] held that Hitler had wanted war, had planned in detail for war and had

begun the war . . . supported by his fellow Nazis, but not by the German people, who were
largely innocent bystanders, if not victims themselves, of the regime and its policies (p. 283).

The first theme is clearly unsatisfactory – "reasons of state" need neither exclude
ideology and economics, especially by aggressor nations, nor ignore "the interdependence of domestic and external factors" (p. 289). The second is not wrong but
may misrepresent the nature of plans, even when flexible. The third is the heart
of his argument. The fourth is not wrong but neglects: (1) Hitler's activities in
making his opportunities; and (2) the total system of interaction among states in
which opportunities were generated. The fifth turns on the meaning of "support"
and the mode of its generation. But this summary does show two things: that
Taylor's model includes both deliberative and non-deliberative factors, or general
and particular causes; and that the putative evidence can support two or more
alternative positions or models on each point. Beyond that, Taylor is convincing
that statesmen largely devote their efforts to managing crises – whether or not
partly of their own making – but if he did believe "that statesmen did not plan but
reacted to external events" (p. 288), he got the story only about one-half right.

   Among other reviewers, Trevor-Roper concluded that Taylor did "not believe
that human agents matter much in history," that "His story is 'a story without
heroes, and perhaps even without villains,' " and that "The real determinants of history . . . are objective situations and human blunders" (p. 284). Complex models or
stories inevitably permit variegated interpretations, depending on how they are read
and where the original author's cutting edge is deemed to be. At any rate, Trevor-
Roper's main point was that Taylor's main argument was wrong (pp. 284–285).

   It would seem, therefore, that a major dimension of Taylor's work was, indeed, in
one respect the tension between seeing a war as a deliberative phenomenon – "the
outcome of a series of deliberate, if not always completely rational or reasoned,
choices" – and as non-deliberative – "the product of the internal dynamism," say,
of a "system of economic rule" (p. 290). It seems to me, however, that the operative
matter was seeing war as a result of the over-determined interaction of both sets of
forces, which permitted numerous interpretations and problems. Most commentators
on Taylor's work were preoccupied, however, with its implications for judgments
of responsibility; for many readers, his was "an approach that exonerated Hitler"
and lent support "for unrepentant Nazis" (p. 291). Taylor, I think, intended his
argument to be a positive one, such that any normative conclusion required the
addition of a normative premise(s); at least that, in my view, is what his argument
boils down to (that is, an example of David Hume's proposition that an "ought"
cannot be derived from an "is" alone (see Samuels, 1992)).

   Returning for a moment to the theory of the balance of power, Taylor believed
that "the Balance of Power worked almost automatically, rather like the laws

of economics" (p. 310, referring to *The Struggle for Mastery*, p. xx). From the foregoing it is clear that such a law – which many have, indeed, found in economics, however, I think most have not – is neither simple nor deterministic nor independent of human agency. But power *is* important, in international relations, in business, in the organization and control of the economy (i.e. in the legal-economic nexus), and, as in *English History 1914–1945*, "between the elites and the people" (p. 310).

Another tension stressed, therefore, in Taylor's work, particularly his *English History 1914–1945*, I should point out, is that between the state and the citizen, or "the people." This is a complex story, involving upper-class control of government, the growth of the welfare state, social revolution and political reforms, with, as I would put it, a contest for control of government and the uses to which it would be put – uses as to whose interests are to count – being central (pp. 305ff).

Finally, we consider Taylor the man and scholar.

As for being acerbic, Taylor welcomed the role of controversialist; he seemed to love conflict. Kathleen Burk's biography is entitled *Troublemaker*, and so he was (Burk, 2000, pp. 71, 283, 412), though the designation derives from his favorite from among his own books, *The Trouble Makers* (1957) which dealt with radical opponents of British foreign policy. He considered himself a member of his country's radical tradition. Burk, who had been Taylor's student, in her summary appraisal of him, says in part,

> Trusting his intuition, Taylor assumed the mantle of iconoclast. He knew he was good; he saw himself as basically a dissenter; and the result was a stream of books and essays in which he took delight in questioning accepted historical truth (p. 410).

Above all, Taylor was independent: "He saw himself as a man of the left, though he always insisted on deciding for himself just what that meant" (p. 412).

Taylor was also egoistic, self-absorbed, insensitive, difficult, and competitive (pp. 65, 82, 223). Burk says frankly, "He was basically indifferent to most people. He was conceited and self-righteous, self-absorbed and self-contained, insensitive and thoughtless. His vanity increasingly led him to talk about himself and his own works rather than encouraging other people to talk" (p. 412). At least some of his behavioral traits resemble those of Daniel Ellsberg, especially the desire to be the center of attention, be famous, and for recognition and approval. One suspects that Taylor undertook so much in order to prove himself both to himself and to others. Also like Ellsberg, Taylor may have wanted both to attack the Establishment and yet to be recognized by it (or by segments of it). John Keegan wrote in the *Daily Telegraph* that Taylor conveyed contempt for "everything that the word 'Establishment' stands for" (p. 409). Taylor's deep-seated independence may or may not have covered up the latter, if in fact it existed. The relationship with the

Establishment was reciprocated: Burk quotes Hugh Trevor-Roper: "The sad fact is that Taylor is really too independent to have *any* support from *any* Establishment" (p. 213; see also p. 412).

Burk does not undertake a psychological analysis of any of this. (Unlike Ellsberg's biographer, her comments along this line are rare: "he was a young man on the make," seeking "a national reputation" (p. 148), which does not amount to much as analysis.) As for Taylor's mother, he had little respect for her; this likely was a factor in his poor relations with women. And further like Ellsberg, Taylor may have had his own epiphany when, rummaging through the captured Reichstag files, he (as one obituary has it) "found that nearly everything that had been told to him up through 1939 by the English Establishment was a lie" (Konkin, 1990, p. 509; Konkin uses the term "moment of conversion").

Some combination of his general radicalism, his personality, his media activities and popularity, and his argument in *The Origins of the Second World War* prevented his appointment to history chairs at Oxford and LSE. Nonetheless, he was elected a Fellow of the British Academy in 1956, along with Carr, "whom Taylor referred to later as 'the greatest modern historian living' " (p. 209. Carr and Taylor were wartime and broadcasting colleagues, competitors for the Stevenson Chair in International History at LSE; Carr also reviewed at least one of Taylor's books (pp. 178, 206, 275–276). Taylor resigned from the British Academy over the expulsion of Anthony Blunt (pp. 339–343)).

Taylor died in 1990 in part from "a virulent form of Parkinson's disease" (p. 366), first diagnosed in 1982.

5. CONCLUSION

Economics has long had a reputation for puncturing grandiose schemes. Its insistence on existential scarcity and, therefore, opportunity cost is a matter of logic and may well have been abused; for example, there is more to a complete theory of cost than opportunity cost (paralleling a point made above with regard to the total system of interaction in which opportunities were generated; see Samuels & Schmid, 1997)).

(It is striking that the doctrine of the inevitability of opportunity cost is very close to the Leninist doctrine that in order to prepare an omelet one has to break eggs. Carr had the view "that suffering was part of the natural order, the price of progress" (Haslam, p. 258). Much the same is implicit in Joseph A. Schumpeter's concept of creative destruction. The problem, Carr also recognized, is that the "beneficiaries [are] not the same as those who paid the costs" (Haslam, p. 258). The larger problem includes the distributions of assets, opportunities, the ability to create opportunities, and sacrifice. Much of the activity in the legal-economic nexus, especially the legal sphere, is directed to manipulating these distributions.)

Economists have no monopoly on such doings. Carr and Taylor were debunkers and dissenters in the discipline of history. Debunking and dissenting, however, are postures or positions requiring additional assumptions governing what to dissent and to debunk. Neither all economists nor Carr and Taylor have agreed on what to oppose. Debunking and dissenting are like applying the theory of the balance of power. Clearly, they are not self-determinative of appropriate policy but are driven by selective perception.

A principal contribution of these biographies is to identify and stress the particular selective perceptions, themes, and models which together form the story line or design strategy for both the ways they respectively did history and the substance of their history. One of the issues inevitably raised in their work is free will vs. determinism, on which they each had mixed positions. Both men were specialists in part in diplomatic history and both were principally concerned with power. The irony is that doing history per se and being concerned with diplomatic history and power, deterministically led them to certain design strategies and not others.

Another irony is that many mainstream, neoclassical economists share Carr and Taylor's identification with the ruling class. For all the debunking and dissenting, these economists identify with the capitalist system and are led also to identify with those who run businesses. This is more applicable to, or more salient in the case of, the right wing of economists but it is well nigh universal. Mainstream, neoclassical economics tends to study the economy from the top down.

More important, perhaps, the complex ideas of both men indicate how presumptuous it is to label them as liberal, socialist, left, and so on. If one considers all the binary tensions on which they took positions and also their policies – e.g. Carr's advocacy of a united Europe no longer engaged in internal Mercantilist policies – their positions are not so easily labeled. Nonetheless their intellectual and personal biographies help identify the sources of, and give meaning and perspective to, their respective historical-analytical models – though people with similar backgrounds might have different models and, in any event, both the biographies and the models stand on their own.

Both Carr and Taylor were historians, not historians of ideas. But history is ideas, and the work of historians, like that of economists, gives effect to ideas. Taylor, for one, denied that he had a philosophy of history and that he was a historian of ideas. But he had such a philosophy and it was comprised of ideas. His histories – such as his 14-volume history of the Soviet Union – had both considerable history-of-ideas' content and themes that gave vent to certain ideas and not others. Histories do not write themselves; they are a result of models, story lines and/or design strategies – all ideas. The professional (and popular) writings of Carr and Taylor, and the reception given their work, illustrate these points very closely. The reason is not hard to see: ideas provide definitions of reality as a basis for policy. Carr and Taylor knew that, indeed practiced that, and understood that as the cause of controversy – and both loved to be controversial. Whether or not ideas are controversial, they are a basis of policy.

Not surprisingly, then, both men, as Haslam (p. 299) writes of Carr and Burk (p. 409) implies of Taylor, took key parts in framing the policy debates in postwar Britain.

Both men had a social-constructivist view of history and in this respect among others were in the Enlightenment tradition. They took neither institutions nor individuals as given; theirs was a modern, even post-modern, view of history (Meinecke, 1972). They did not pay much attention to "the individual," preferring to study the nation-state or international system. But they knew that human decision making, by individuals, was part of the total process. The problem was the difficulty of expressing complex relationships while simultaneously concentrating on part of the total story. This problem is key to understanding both the reception given their work and their responses.

Both of these historians were, for whatever reasons, extraordinarily hard working. Concentrating on their work is why Haslam (p. 218) can write of Carr's "totally egocentric existence." Both dealt, each in his own way, with some of the great issues of the twentieth century. Neither was content to practice his craft in the confines of his study; both actively and openly participated in the affairs of the world. Each had tumultuous private lives, but it is not clear that such would not have been the case if they had different, less activist, non-scholarly occupations.

I conclude with one of the most pregnant lines of Burk's book, one that does not directly pertain to Taylor. Writing of a young Marxist historian from Oxford, Tim Mason, Burk says, "Mason used metaphors as though they were realities" (Burk, p. 290). Economists are not alone in using their terms as both definitions of reality and tools of analysis.

REFERENCES

Abramsky, C. (Ed.) (1974). *Essays in honour of E. H. Carr*. Hamden, CT: Archon Books.
Berle, A. A. (1969). *Power*. New York: Harcourt, Brace & World.
Berlin, I. (2002). On human dignity. *The New Republic* (January 28), 23–26.
Harrod, R. G. (forthcoming). *Interwar papers and correspondence*. D. Besomi (Ed.).
Kaplan, R. D. (2002). *Warrior politics: Why leadership demands a pagan ethos*. New York: Random House.
Kissinger, H. (2001). *Does America need a foreign policy? Toward a diplomacy for the 21st century*. New York: Simon & Schuster.

Konkin, S. E., III (1990). The last liberal historian: A. J. P. Taylor, March 25, 1906–Sept. 7, 1990. *Journal of Historical Review, 10*(4), 509–510. Electronic version: http://www.ihr.org/jhr/v10p.509_Konkin.html

Mead, W. R. (2001). *Special providence: American foreign policy and how it changed the world.* New York: Alfred A. Knopf.

Meinecke, F. (1972). *Historicism: The rise of a new historical outlook.* New York: Routlege.

Samuels, W. J. (1992). The pervasive proposition, 'what is, is and ought to be': A critique. In: W. S. Millberg (Ed.), *The Megacorp and Macrodynamics: Essays in Memory of Alfred Eichner* (pp. 273–285). Armonk, NY: M. E. Sharpe.

Samuels, W. J. (1995). Some thoughts on multiplicity. *Journal of Economic Methodology,* 2(December), 287–291.

Samuels, W. J. (1996). Postmodernism and knowledge: A middlebrow view. *Journal of Economic Methodology, 3*(June), 113–120.

Samuels, W. J. (1997a). The case for methodological pluralism. In: A. Salanti & E. Screpanti (Eds), *Pluralism in Economics* (pp. 67–79). Brookfield, VT: Edward Elgar.

Samuels, W. J. (1997b). Methodological pluralism: The discussion in retrospect. In: A. Salanti & E. Screpanti (Eds), *Pluralism in Economics* (pp. 308–309). Brookfield, VT: Edward Elgar.

Samuels, W. J. (1997c). The concept of 'coercion' in economics. In: W. J. Samuels, S. G. Medema & A. A. Schmid (Eds), *The Economy as a Process of Valuation* (pp. 129–207). Lyme, NH: Edward Elgar.

Samuels, W. J. (1998). Methodological pluralism. In: J. B. Davis, D. W. Hands & U. Maki (Eds), *The Handbook of Economic Methodology* (pp. 300–303). Northampton, MA: Edward Elgar.

Samuels, W. J. (1999). Hayek from the perspective of an institutionalist historian of economic thought: An interpretive essay. *Journal des Economistes et des Etudes Humaines, IX*(Juin–Septembre), 279–290.

Samuels, W. J. (2001). Some problems in the use of language in economics. *Review of Political Economy, 13*(1), 91–100.

Samuels, W. J. (2002). *Economics, governance and law: Essays on theory and policy.* Aldershot, UK: Edward Elgar. Chapters on "Government and Governance" and "The Political-Economic Logic of World Governance."

Samuels, W. J., & Schmid, A. A. (1997). The concept of cost in economics. In: W. J. Samuels, S. G. Medema & A. A. Schmid (Eds), *The Economy as a Process of Valuation* (pp. 208–298). Lyme, NH: Edward Elgar.

SOCIALISM LOST?

Rod Cross

A review essay on Noel Thompson's, *Left in the Wilderness: the Political Economy of British Democratic Socialism since 1979*. Chesham, U.K.: Acumen Publishing, 2002. ISBN 1-902683-54-4.

After losing the 1979 election to the Conservatives the U.K. Labour Party remained out of the office until 1997. After Tony Blair became leader in 1994, Labour adopted so much of the ideology associated with the New Right that it is difficult to discern much by way of socialism in the rhetoric or deeds of the New Labour government that has been in power since 1997. Noel Thompson chronicles the "... frenetic and ultimately futile attempt on the part of democratic socialists to re-configure the political economy of democratic socialism ..." (p. vi) in this period. For socialists this is a depressing tale. The conclusion is that "... the apotheosis of the Anglo-American model has produced a barren soil in which the seeds of democratic socialism cannot take root ... the Left, in Britain, has entered an ideological wilderness from which there seems little prospect of return" (p. 287). The cover illustration has Don Quixote attacking windmills. Equally, it could have been socialist King Canutes bewailing their inability to hold back the tidal waves of global capitalism.

The big question is whether Thompson's gloom is justified. Do advocates of socialism, within or outside capitalism, have to take the hemlock? Are we All Right Now? Have socialist accounts of political economy become untenable and unworkable? Or are the forces that have made life difficult for socialist ideas not as deep-seated as Thompson claims?

Research in the History of Economic Thought and Methodology A Research Annual
Research in the History of Economic Thought and Methodology, Volume 22-A, 317–327
Copyright © 2004 by Elsevier Ltd.
ISSN: 0743-4154/doi:10.1016/S0743-4154(03)22018-6

THE THOMPSON THESIS

In his preface Thompson argues that structural, sociological and ideological aspects of the economic "environment" foreclosed on socialism during the period in question. The structural aspect was the increased globalisation of economic activity; the sociological was the "triumph of possessive individualism and the uncritical celebration of private as against social consumption" (p. vi); and the ideological was the ascendancy of the nostrums of the New Right. Given the importance attached to these "environmental" forces one might have expected the author to organise his argument by discussing how and why these forces came to be all-powerful in the last quarter of the 20th century.

This is not Thompson's method of argument. Instead the reader is provided with a blow-by-blow account of how attempts to articulate alternative socialist blueprints for economic management foundered in the face of these hostile forces. Thus, we are taken through the Alternative Economic Strategy that influenced the Labour platform in the 1983 election (Chap. 1), municipal socialism (Chap. 2), post-Fordist socialism (Chap. 3), producer cooperatives and labour-managed firms (Chaps 4 and 5), market socialism (Chap. 6), knowledge-driven, supply-side socialism (Chap. 8), stakeholder socialism (Chap. 9) and multinational socialism (Chap. 10).

There is a strong whiff of *post hoc, ergo propter hoc* about Thompson's argument. The socialist strategies proposed did not, even when adopted by the party, result in Labour winning elections. Therefore the "environment" must have been hostile to socialist ideas. Even stronger is the inductive generalisation that socialist strategies did not win elections for Labour during this period, therefore socialist platforms will not win elections in the future. The implication is that New Labour was right: the Labour Party had to abandon its socialist roots in order to win elections. The fact that a Labour party divested of most of its socialist clothes won elections in 1997 and 2001 apparently lends credence to Thompson's thesis.

PLAYERS AND PAINTED STAGE

Thompson's narrative is that of an historian who concentrates on the political stage as painted by members of the socialist chattering and writing classes. There is heavy reliance on the way contributors to journals such as the *New Left Review* and *Marxism Today* saw the prospects for socialism during this period. The starting premise of many of these contributors was that Labour, during its 1964–1970 and 1974–1979 terms of office, had not been socialist enough.

The electoral defeat of 1979 by a Conservative party that had moved to the Right was seen by some as an opportunity to convert Labour into a Marxist party.

This was the era of "entryism" into the Labour Party, with Marxist activists, who had previously advocated socialism-outside-capitalism, joining with a view to achieving a fundamental shift to the Left. As mass unemployment returned to the U.K. in the early 1980s such Marxists saw the Alternative Economic Strategy, with which Labour lost the 1983 election, as a means of "setting decisively in motion a fundamental democratic socialist transformation of the state and civil society" (p. 40). Thompson's narrative mentions these developments, but his thesis attaches little importance to the role in Labour's woes played by the entryists. This is an account of politics almost without activists, and almost devoid of politicians ascending or sliding down their greasy poles.

THE PLAYERS

An alternative account of Labour becoming perceived to be unelectable would stress the personality clashes within the party. In Tony Crosland, Dennis Healey and Roy Jenkins, Labour had three of the best prime ministers that never made it to power in the post-1945 period. A major problem was that they made no secret of not liking each other, leaving the way open to the likes of Harold Wilson and Jim Callaghan. Crosland died prematurely. Healey lost the leadership election to Michael Foot when Callaghan resigned in 1980. During 1981 Jenkins was one of the four former Labour cabinet ministers who left to form the Social Democratic Party. If Labour had been able to harness this political talent more effectively, maybe the 1974–1979 term of office would not have ended in the shambles of the "winter of discontent" of 1978/1979? As the maxim goes, political parties do not win elections, governments lose them.

Neil Kinnock became Labour leader after the 1983 electoral defeat. Much of his energy was devoted to ridding the party of the entryists, such as members of Militant Tendency. This internecine warfare is largely absent from Thompson's narrative. Instead the impression given is that the tensions that consumed Labour during the 1980s concerned debates about post-Fordism, labour-managed firms, producer cooperatives and so on.

The 1992 election was a close-run thing. Would a Conservative government that had ousted the sitting Prime Minister Margaret Thatcher amidst an outbreak of civil war played out under the public gaze, and which was presiding over a recession, lose the election? Or would Labour, proposing modest increases in the higher rates of income tax and national insurance contributions, and led by Kinnock, a doughty infighter within the party but with a reputation for windbaggery, fail to win it? This was the parting of the ways between Old and New Labour.

The Old Labour interpretation was that the Conservatives had failed to lose the election, but that all that Labour needed to do was hold a steady course and wait for its time to come. Black Wednesday came soon after the election. The U.K. was forced to leave the Exchange Rate Mechanism of the European Monetary System on 16 September 1992. From a starting point of level pegging, Labour developed a 20% lead over the Conservatives in opinion poll voting intentions. Since October 1964 a Gallup poll had asked: "If Britain were in economic difficulties, which party do you think would handle the problem best?" The Conservatives had scored better in this poll for nearly three decades, apart from a blip accompanying the introduction of the poll tax in England and Wales during early 1990. September 1992 saw a reversal in this indicator, with Labour outperforming the Conservatives in every subsequent poll, excepting that taken during the 2000 fuel tax revolt. According to an Old Labour interpretation the Conservative government lost the 1997 election on September 16, 1992. All Labour needed to do was avoid scaring the horses.

The New Labour interpretation was that Labour had failed to win the 1992 election and that its socialist policies were to blame. To gain power the party would have to switch to the Right in order to capture votes from the Conservatives. They would have to promise not to increase income taxes and to keep an open mind on further privatisation. Some of the rhetoric of socialism would be retained in order to keep traditional supporters on board, but the party would become essentially pro-capitalist.

In the wake of the 1992 electoral defeat Labour finally found themselves with their outstanding politician as leader. John Smith had the authority to keep the New Labour modernisers in check. There was no need for damaging schisms. A socialist Labour party could sit back and watch a fatally wounded Conservative administration disintegrate and reap the electoral reward. The tragedy came with Smith's death in 1994. Bryan Gould and Gordon Brown were the most able candidates to succeed Smith, but carried too much Old Labour baggage for the modernisers. Instead Brown was persuaded not to stand against Blair and the New Labour lurch to the Right began.

Blair and Brown, by and large, have managed to play out their rivalry in private. Instead of the destructive public tensions that characterised previous Labour leaderships, there has been a private tension that was sufficiently contained for Labour to avoid losing the 2001 election. The increases in public spending, financed by higher national insurance contributions, announced during the second term of office could have been taken from an Old Labour manual. But the public-private partnerships that are to be the dominant vehicle for delivering the enhanced public services bear the New Labour stamp. So far the circle has been squared.

The foregoing account stresses the role of the political players. It is a story of how "one damned politician after another" determined the relationship of the Labour Party with socialism. There are many political economies that could be called. The ones adopted depended on the politicians doing the choosing. This narrative is an alternative to the stress on the role played by the "material and ideological environment" (p.vi) in Thompson's account, which could be caricatured as "one damned socialist political economy after another" failing to survive in a hostile "environment." We would argue that the actors played an important part in explaining the socialist performance in the U.K. But what of the stage?

THE WATERSHED OF THE 1970s

According to Thompson, ". . . in the mid-1970s Keynesian social democracy fell prey to the combined pressures of a sterling crisis, the IMF and the U.S. Federal Reserve and was jettisoned by many of its erstwhile supporters within the Labour Party" (p. 191). The speech of Prime Minister Callaghan to the Labour Party conference in 1976 is usually cited as signalling Labour's abandonment of Keynesian precepts. The key passage paraphrased the Edmund Phelps-Milton Friedman natural rate of unemployment hypothesis and its implication that demand management measures had lasting effects on inflation but not on unemployment. The Conservative opposition was undergoing a Josephite conversation to monetarism and a " 'punk monetarism' . . . was embraced by the prime minister and others within the Labour leadership, with varying degrees of sincerity" (p. 191). The rational reconstruction to be found in economics textbooks is that the higher inflation and unemployment of the 1970s had served to refute the Phillips curve hypothesis and severely wound the Keynesian economics in which it had been embedded. The vacuum created by this falsification was filled by the natural rate hypothesis. The implication for political economy was a return to classical precepts regarding economic management. If only those "distilling their frenzy" from Phillips had read the original paper, which stressed that cost-of-living settlements and the change in unemployment were also important influences on the rate of inflation, things might have been different.

Consideration of the grip that Keynesian ideas had in the preceding decades gives pause for thought here. In the 1950s political parties of the Right and the Left in the U.K. came to share what was termed the Butskellist approach to economic management. Rab Butler was a Conservative Chancellor of the Exchequer during this decade and Hugh Gaitskell was his Labour shadow. Classical approaches to political economy were declared dead in the water, having been blamed for the U.K. recession in the 1920s and the weak recovery of the 1930s. It had taken the disturbance of the 1939–1945 war to change perceptions, but it was All Keynesian Now. The third quarter of the 20th century saw high rates of economic growth, low unemployment and lowish inflation rates in the social democracies following the Keynesian way. Advocates of classical political economy were in the wilderness. Was it the case that classical nostrums were untenable and unworkable in the environment of the 1950s and 1960s? Or was it simply that these nostrums were out of fashion? As it turned out, the classical prophets, although out of season, were not wasting their time. Maybe there is a lesson here. We might christen as Thairite the classical approach to economic management that dominates the present political landscape in the U.K. Is Thairism any more than a fashion that, like Butskellism, will lose its appeal?

During the 1970s unemployment rose somewhat in the U.K. but remained below the 4% mark at the end of the decade. It was rather the inflation experience that cast doubt on the prevailing wisdom about economic management, with inflation spikes of just over 25% in the mid-1970s and 20% at the end of the decade. But was this the fault of a Keynesian economics that did not understand the interaction between inflation and unemployment? Inflationary pressures had emerged in the last years of the Bretton Woods system because of the way the U.S. financed the escalation of its involvement in Vietnam. The inflation spikes in the U.K. followed the dramatic increases in oil prices of 1973–1974 and 1979. It is debatable whether the inflation-unemployment performance in response to these shocks would have been better if a classical approach to economic management had been followed.

THE 1980s AND 1990s

The adoption of monetarism by the Thatcher government was accompanied by a dramatic and sustained increase in unemployment. The official unemployment rate trebled to nearly 12% by 1986 – it did not peak in 1983 as asserted by Thompson (p. 5). This underestimated the true increase in unemployment: taking account of the unemployed who were reclassified as long-term sick and disabled and so on adds 4% or more to the figure. Inflation fell in the early 1980s to around 3–4%. This should, according to the monetarist strategy, have been in response to the planned fall in the rate of monetary growth. The money growth targets, however, were overshot by a wide margin, so the actual rate of monetary growth showed little change. Unemployment fell in the late 1980s boom, but rose back to double-digit levels in the 1990–1992 recession. The inflation genie that the classical approach to economic management was supposed to keep in the bottle escaped to approach double-digit proportions by the end of the 1980s. This was hardly a success story to drive Keynesians to despair.

Monetarism, rather than Keynesian economics, became untenable in the 1980s – the economist honoured in Goodhart's Law is Charles Goodhart from the LSE, not Cambridge (as in Thompson, p. 195). The experiment with exchange rate targeting was ended by the ERM debacle of 1992. The replacement in the classical armoury was inflationism, with the 1–4% target range of 1993–1997 being formalised in the $2.5 \pm 1\%$ symmetrical inflation target given to the Bank of England when it was made operationally independent in 1997. Inflation has remained quiescent in the U.K. since 1993 and unemployment has fallen steadily to around 4%. Was this a belated triumph for the classical approach to economic management? Or was it a Keynesian-style recovery in response to the depreciation of sterling and relaxation of monetary policy after the 1992 debacle?

Advocates of the classical approach argued that a devaluation would lead to a rise in inflation and no lasting reduction in unemployment. They were wrong. The inflationist approach to policy relies on the natural rate hypothesis, not monetarism. The problem here is that the reductions in trades union power, unemployment benefits and the other "structural" factors that are supposed to lower the natural rate of unemployment took place in the 1980s, whereas the sustained fall in unemployment took place a decade or more later. At best this suggests that the natural rate is not the whole story about what drives equilibrium unemployment.

THE ANGLO-AMERICAN MODEL

The U.S. capitalist model, aped by the U.K., emerges as triumphant in Thompson's account of the battles of the political economies. In this approach the private sector is the engine for economic growth; trade, investment, capital flows and financial markets are best deregulated; and the role of the state is to nightwatch free markets and ensure a zero, or at least a low rate of inflation. The argument is that this recipe has proved to be the one best suited to the world of global capitalism that emerged towards the end of the 20th century.

The arguments here are quite familiar. Marx, in his later writings, was right in stressing that capitalism, as a mode of production, retained a huge potential as a vehicle for progress. The "globalisation" of capitalism at the end of the 20th century was testimony to the prescience of the later Marx. Thus, the deregulation of capital movements and the emergence of the World Trade Organisation allowed capitalism to exploit the increase in productive potential associated with innovations in such as information technology and with the opening up of economies such as China to international trade. Capitalism would encounter crises in which profitability fell, as in the U.K. in the late 1960s and 1970s. But when capital was free to flow elsewhere, organised labour would come to realise that profitability matters.

Cooperation rather than conflict with capital would then be the order of the day. In the face of these global forces, so the argument goes, political parties of the Left are obliged to go with the capitalist flow and realise that there is very limited room for socialist manoeuvre.

There are several points worth making here. As the Soviet empire disintegrated at the end of the 1980s there was a mood of triumphalism amongst advocates of capitalism. The death of socialism was proclaimed. This missed the obvious point that the dying bird was that of socialism-outside-capitalism, not socialism-within-capitalism.

In the late 1980s the Washington consensus, based on the Anglo-American model, was being proclaimed as the blueprint for economic success to be followed by ailing economies, especially if they came within the orbit of influence of the IMF or the World Bank. Yet the subsequent decade has served to discredit many aspects of this consensus. Deregulation of financial markets has been followed by wave after wave of financial crises, such as in South East Asia in 1987. Privatisation was accompanied by an economic disaster in Russia, whereas China's regionally-owned state enterprises delivered double-digit rates of economic growth. And so on.

The performance of the U.S. economy during the 1990s was seen as the exemplar of what could be achieved by unbridled capitalism. The claim was that the information technology revolution had sparked a new economy in which the sustainable U.S. growth rate had doubled. In this brave new world the higher dividends projected to occur in the future were rationalised as justifying a price-earnings ratio approaching 50 on Wall Street. The pessimists or realists, who pointed out that 15 was the par-for-the-course prices-earnings ratio over two centuries of U.S. capitalism, were trampled underfoot in the rush to buy shares as the Dow-Jones index continued to rise.

The subsequent dramatic fall in share prices has put paid to the triumphalism surrounding the U.S. exemplar of global capitalism. Cuts in interest rates and reductions in income tax have so far helped avoid consumer spending following the downward plunge in private investment outlays. This is Keynesian demand management, except in name. A 1930s-style recession has not yet emerged, but the outlook is a nervous one. If the capitalist centre does not hold, will the mere anarchy of socialism-within-capitalism be unleashed again on the world?

THE CHORUS

In classical Greek tragedy the chorus played a key role in voicing how the audience might be relating to the events unfolding on the stage. In the modern political context the audience consists of the voters who view the stage through the lenses of the mass media. The part of the chorus is played by the spin doctors who use the media to interpret what is happening on the political stage, so as to keep or bring the electorate onside. Focus groups are deployed to check that the spun message is to the liking of the key median voters.

Oratory in front of a physically-present audience is, of course, nothing new to politicians. The advent of radio presented a different challenge, and U.K. politicians were still struggling with the less forgiving medium of television in the 1960s. The way the Labour government of 1976–1979 presented itself was a public relations disaster. The incoming Conservative administration of 1979 had learned the lesson and hired a top advertising agency to sell its wares to the electorate. Many of those of a socialist persuasion disapproved of advertising and Labour was slow to follow suit. Its first major flirtation with letting the medium become the message ended in tears, the triumphalist rally held in Sheffield before the 1992 election alienating more voters than were converted.

During the build up to the 1997 election, New Labour opted to copy the campaign strategy employed by Bill Clinton's Democrats, confining the 1992 Billy Graham approach to the dustbin. So the black art of spin doctoring hit the U.K. political stage. Socialism would not sell in the U.S., so why expect it to sell in the U.K.? Instead of Thatcher-Ronald Reagan read Blair-Clinton. The soap-powder might be the same but, gee, it sure did make you feel as though your clothes were cleaner. You would be hard put to remember what the politician said, but it looked or sounded good at the time. Some of the social democratic parties in the rest of Europe were still resisting the Anglo-American model. But look at their economies – sclerotic!

This hook, line and sinker transplanting of U.S. spinning techniques is notable for its absence in Thompson's narrative. But it does connect with his stress on the emergence of a sociological environment that was hostile to socialism in the U.K.: "the Mephistopheles of consumerism demanded nothing less than the soul of socialism" (p. 283). A key question here is whether spinning under capitalism is necessarily associated with ". . . the triumph of possessive individualism and the uncritical celebration of the virtues of private as against social consumption" (p. vi). This is arguably the major challenge facing advocates of socialism-within-capitalism. As Thompson points out, recent decades in the U.K. have seen "an attenuation of those values and expectations that had inspired and informed the post-war welfare state" (p. 282). Public sector investment, which had run at around 6–7% of GDP in the U.K. in the 1950s, 1960s and early 1970s, has fallen to around 2–3% of GDP over the subsequent decades. Integrate over a quarter of a century and there is a shortfall in public sector capital equivalent to one year's GDP. The outcome is, to use John Kenneth Galbraith's terms, "private affluence" coexisting with "public squalor."

In its post-2001 term of office New Labour has announced an increase in spending on zero-priced public services such as health and education. But the celebration of capitalism is that public-private partnerships will give the private sector the task of financing and maintaining as well as building the hospitals and schools. Apparently the public sector cannot do contracts. The outcome is that the taxpayer will have to pay for the higher costs of capital faced by private sector firms, which run at three or so times the cost of capital to the public sector. And if the private sector providers go bust taxpayers will have to bail them out. This will, unless the private sector providers deliver miraculous cost savings, reduce the public services that can be provided for any given public outlay. The lock-in is typically for 30 years. In this nightmare scenario the private sector crowds out the public sector. This is Ricardo in a new guise.

The spin is that this new world of public services will be delivered according to the wishes of individual consumers. Thus, the "better-performing" hospitals and schools will be given "foundation" or "specialist" status and additional resources. Given the obvious capacity constraints, this will mean that those living in the neighbourhood of the "better-performing" hospitals and schools will receive a better quality of provision. Thus, the consumerism spin is likely to increase the inequalities in public good provision.

CONCLUSION

Recent developments in the U.K. seem to support Thompson's pessimistic outlook for socialism in the U.K. "Keynes gave way to Hayek and Friedman, and Beveridge succumbed to a 'culture of contentment' where greed was good, where there was no such thing as society and where, by implication, there was no such thing as social obligation(s)" (p. 282, my bracket). So individuals have, like firms, become privatised. Socialism is dead.

Against this we would posit grounds for optimism. Keynesianism is not dead, but is alive and kicking in terms of its ability to explain the financial crises and recessions that reappear under capitalism. The players on the U.K. political stage may not be using Keynesian language at the moment, but fashions change. The recent bonfire of the bulls on Wall Street has raised severe doubts about unbridled casino capitalism. In the coming years the U.S. model could well suffer the fate of previous exemplars: remember when we were told that the French, German, Swedish, Japanese and so on were the only ways to do it?

If you train your spin doctors in the U.S. they are not likely to learn how to spin socialism. Baseball is just not cricket. A straight socialist yorker delivered at the Achilles heel of capitalism-without-socialism might hit the wicket. Or maybe the socialist ball will have to delivered with reverse swing in order to catch untram-melled capitalism out?

ACKNOWLEDGMENTS

The author is grateful to Roger Sandilands for some useful suggestions.

CULLENBERG, AMARIGLIO AND RUCCIO'S POSTMODERNISM, ECONOMICS AND KNOWLEDGE

W. D. Sockwell

A review essay on *Postmodernism, Economics and Knowledge*. Edited by Stephen Cullenberg, Jack Amariglio and David F. Ruccio. London: Routledge, 2001. p. 495.

Most economists agree that economic knowledge has gradually increased as more facts and data have been accumulated to support (or reject) theories. That is, economic knowledge and progress of the discipline have benefited from the scientific method. While not disputing this modernist conception of historical progress in economics, the articles in the volume consistently urge a broader discourse in economics, suggesting that without an expanded discourse economics will, as Hutchison (1979) argues, be "destined for a somewhat ambiguous and problematic place in the spectrum of knowledge" (p. 4). This edited volume discusses and seeks to discover what the postmodernist movement can add to broad economic discourse.

The volume originated from a 1995 conference entitled "Postmodernism, Economics and Knowledge" that sought to generate a cross-disciplinary discussion of the impact of postmodernism on economics. The original conference papers have been revised and several additional authors contributed, resulting in a more complete and up-to-date discussion. The book is divided into an introduction and six sections; each section consists of two or three chapters followed by a chapter discussing the preceding selections.

Research in the History of Economic Thought and Methodology A Research Annual
Research in the History of Economic Thought and Methodology, Volume 22-A, 329–340
Copyright © 2004 by Elsevier Ltd.
ISSN: 0743-4154/doi:10.1016/S0743-4154(03)22019-8

The extended introduction is highly recommended for anyone who has not been attentive to the various strands of postmodern discourse. To the uninitiated, merely defining postmodernism can be problematic due to the various approaches employed under the name of postmodernism. The editors neatly address this difficulty by reducing debates about postmodernism to four general categories. The first category classifies postmodernism as the latest phase of capitalism, one that is marked by mass commodification and globalization. The editors acknowledge that while this view of postmodernism is widespread, it is the least represented in their volume.

A second category of postmodernism, and one that is more pervasive in contributed articles, is one that considers postmodernism to be an "existential state or condition" (p. 5). Postmodernism is viewed as being concerned with changing conditions or circumstances, and, it is suggested, discourse must adapt. The old "metanarratives of progress and liberation have either failed or have contributed to sociopolitical outcomes that are repulsive" (p. 11). Changed circumstances have meant that "many of the touchstones of modernist culture and society have been or are now being decomposed, discarded, or 'deconstructed' " (p. 11). Rather than rational individuals with consistent sets of preferences, the postmodern condition is said to be one in which individuals have so many different perspectives "that the possibility of stable and commensurable knowledge among and between people is seen as highly questionable . . . [K]nowledge is seen to be local (not universal) and subject to persistent uncertainty" (p. 13). So defined, postmodernism holds that, since knowledge is reflective of particular locations and cultures, it will be biased by those cultures and locations.

A third category of postmodernism relies in part on a certain literary style, which is exemplified by Jacques Derrida's deconstruction. Deconstructivist readings deliberately attempt to undermine the supposed meaning of texts by noting that every sentence refers to other texts and can have no singular meaning on its own. It is common to "locate" the author who cannot be separated from his or her history, values, etc. It is maintained, in fact, that it is not possible to produce value-free analysis no matter how scientific one attempts to be. Good discourse should be self-reflexive and recognize the locations and values of its speakers.[1]

Finally, postmodernism is often thought of as a critique of modernism or, simply, anti-modernism. Adherents to this view argue that modernism demolished older, important values that stressed community, morality, tolerance, and social justice. Postmodern critiques may also be non-modern, arguing that while modernism had some use, its either/or oppositions are counterproductive. This latter version tends to be non-confrontational, downplays the importance of theory (particularly value theory), and, like the deconstructionists, emphasizes self-absorption and the relativity of perspectives. The editors exhibit some sympathy for this last position, presenting modernism and postmodernism as "always incomplete" (p. 22). They prefer to describe modernism and postmodernism as "moments that are, themselves, transient and porous" (p. 22). The book, then, attempts to identify postmodern moments that arguably impact forms of modernism that are part of ordinary economic discourse.

The editors suggest that since McCloskey's (1983) article, many within the field of economics are writing about postmodernism or, "consciously or otherwise, employing postmodern approaches within their works" (p. 35). Some would choose to displace the tradition of neoclassical economics with the postmodern approach. Among other agendas is the desire "to obviate the centrality of homo economicus, to decenter notions of economic totalities, to revive interest in morality and values and power as determinants in economic discourse, to scale down the pretensions of economics as a 'science,' to open up spaces for plural perspectives, and to resist the 'imperialism' of economics as a master discourse" (p. 35). By focusing on postmodern moments the editors attempt to illustrate that "even mainstream economic discourse [is], perhaps, unwittingly, increasingly preoccupied with postmodern themes and ideas." The six sections of the book reveal some of the avenues through which postmodernism has entered the mainstream. The reader is left to discern the impact of these incursions on the profession.

The first section contains vintage essays by Sheila Dow, Arjo Klamer and Deidre McCloskey. Since the early 1980s each has argued for a broader discussion of economic methodology and each sees postmodernism as useful in revitalizing economic discourse.

Dow argues that modernist methodology is largely a monist quest for universal laws or for the best approach to solving problems, but she maintains postmodernism "denies the role of methodology altogether" (p. 66). She argues that postmodernism is a dialectical response to the limitations of modernism, but that it will also implode, leading to a new phase, or what she refers to as a synthetic approach. As she explains it, the synthetic approach to knowledge "takes from modernism a concern with criteria for good practice in generating knowledge," but "has absorbed from postmodernism the argument that language is not neutral" and the tendency toward "tolerance of alternative systems of economic knowledge" (p. 65).

McCloskey posits that the twentieth century can be understood as a period of entrenchment of modernism followed by a postmodernist reaction. But, she argues, the history of tension between these two beliefs is much longer. She cites Plato as the first modernist (p. 115) and states "there have been as many modernisms as there have been spectacularly successful geniuses claiming transcendence" (p. 110). She suggests modernism in economics could be dated to the French Enlightenment

(1751–1775) and that it contained a contradiction, "the aporia (indecision) of the Enlightenment project" (p. 110), that involved a conflict between math and science and the desire for individual and political freedom. Math and science seek rules, leading to the ultimate contradiction that "being unreasonably rational will eventually enslave us to rules" (p. 110).

As a counter to modernism, however, McCloskey notes that there has always been a postmodern reaction. In Plato's day, for example, the sophists countered his arguments for the rule of experts with their own support of rhetoric and free persuasion. McCloskey maintains that deconstruction is simply "a reinvention of ancient rhetoric" (p. 118) and that "postmodernism is thoroughly rhetorical" (p. 120). She suggests that the missing piece of economic thought is an under-standing and appreciation of rhetoric. She notes that just as in a presidential speech one must take note of the figures as well as grasp its values, so must one be able to toggle back and forth between scientific reason and rhetoric. She concludes that if economists will only get on with the postmodernist project and learn to toggle back and forth between scientific reason and rhetoric, then economists "could reunify the cultures of science and literature" (p. 122).

While Dow and McCloskey believe that the modernist approach has been useful and can gain credibility by opening up to a wider discourse, Klamer is much more critical of modernism, particularly its more recent variants. He maintains that "modernist economics is without a coherent philosophical justification," and that "its implosion must be imminent." He asserts that "without credible hope of affecting the worlds around them . . . modernists are left to their own devices and doomed to find gratification only within their own community" (p. 77).

Klamer recognizes that the early modernist economists aspired to improve the world through the scientific approach. More recently, uncertainty has played a more prominent role in economics and there has been a corresponding erosion of faith in science as it was realized that many scientific theories could not be proven or falsified empirically. Klamer argues that schools of thought like the New Classicals, who deny that a realistic representation of the economy is desirable, are the postmoderns. By "carrying their arguments to their logical extreme, we could end up with the deconstruction of economics as a discipline" (p. 92). According to Klamer, the greatest losses of late modernism are the disappearance of the human subject and less emphasis on moral character as contrasted with Adam Smith and other early economists. Klamer concludes by suggesting "[p]erhaps we are between ages. Perhaps again the late modernist project will simply implode due to its own irrelevance or absurdity . . . One thing is clear, however, late modernism – for all its technical skill and virtuosity – has impoverished economics by its erasure of the Keynesian metanarrative, and even more by the loss of moral character it has championed. We can only hope for a next stage, whatever it may be called" (p. 99).

While the papers of Dow, Klamer, and McCloskey offer a retrospective of some of their past views and contemplate a different, more inclusive economic methodology in the future, other papers in the volume seek to illustrate that postmodernism is currently affecting economic discourse. Most of the papers share the hope that economists will be more tolerant of alternative approaches. While there are a number of essays to suit different tastes, the most extensive set (Parts IV and V) concern postmodernism and gender in economics.

Ulla Grapard, Julie Nelson, and Jane Rosetti analyze the current state of economic discourse from a feminist postmodern perspective and each is optimistic about the impact this perspective is already having as well as its potential for future influence. Ulla Grapard's "The Trouble With Women and Economics" uses the postmodern, feminist perspective to understand why Charlotte Perkins Gilman's *Women and Economics* (1898) was (and still is) neglected by mainstream economists despite its modernist approach. She maintains that Gilman's work "is clearly an example of a modernist text" because Gilman embraces the steady march of progress and "argues for women's and men's equality on the basis of a shared human identity" (p. 264). Gilman recognizes, however, that evolutionary stories continually point to the different natures of men and women. As Grapard makes clear, Gilman resolves the modern feminist paradox of female differences and the quest for equality by using modernist methods that fit easily into the neoclassical tradition.

While it is true that many modern economists have excluded gender issues, neoclassical economists, such as Gary Becker have used models that accepted separate gender roles. Men, with a comparative advantage in labor, are considered the natural breadwinners, and women, with a comparative advantage in child rearing and household affairs, are given primary responsibility for the home. Neoclassical economists ascribe men and women with complementary roles and stable identities that are constrained by biology and conform to a "natural order," giving an "optimal, efficient social arrangement" (p. 266). Gilman demonstrates, however, that while women's subordination may have served a purpose at some time, by the beginning of the twentieth century the model is "inefficient as a result of historical, evolutionary, developments" (p. 271). The inefficiency hinders overall progress and, according to Gilman, provides sufficient grounds for change.

Grapard maintains that Gilman was not accepted by economists of her day because she challenged gender roles, especially paid employment for women and their economic independence, and she had no formal education in economics. Grapard does not as satisfactorily address why Gilman has still not been accepted, although she suggests that postmodern issues of power, knowledge hegemony, and disciplinary exclusion still persist. She notes that a conformist methodology does not guarantee inclusion of feminist scholars in the mainstream, but is optimistic that recent interest in women economists will overcome the historical neglect.[2]

Julie Nelson, who identifies herself as "a practicing economist, a feminist concerned about oppression, and a post-modernist (in the 'after-modernist' sense of recognizing the social construction of the disciplines)" (p. 287), agrees that the social construction of the economics discipline has limited its ability to accept new ideas. Although she endorses an approach to economics that "pays attention to the socially constructed nature of language and searches out the meanings hidden in binary dualisms" (p. 290), she rejects the dualistic approach that she sees as the hallmark of modernist economics, choosing instead to embrace a more complex "compass" approach. Her approach recognizes the importance of objectivity and the scientific approach, but at the same time expands the depth and scope of scientific inquiry. Rather than studying individual actions, for example, her more complex compass approach examines situated knowledge and a relational self.

Among the differences in Nelson's feminist economics and contemporary mainstream economics are differences in definitions and methods. In lieu of defining economics around rational choice and the economic man, or around material goods and the market, she defines economics as "the study of the organization of the processes which provision human life" (p. 296), a definition that elevates issues such as child care or education. The methods of feminist economists include mathematical modeling, but also include surveys and other less formal techniques. Asserting that a feminist economics can be objective, activist, and postmodern, she proclaims that an "intellectual overhaul of economics by feminists is yielding, and will continue to yield, much fruit" (p. 287).

The deconstructionists claim that "language cannot objectively convey the essence of an object or an idea," and that it always "reflects a particular time and place view of the world" (pp. 307–308). If value-laden beliefs dominate, there may be no objective way of deciding that one system of beliefs is better than another. Jane Rosetti agrees with McClosky, Fish, and Rorty who have addressed this problem by suggesting that while it is true that all humans have beliefs, not all interpretations or methods of reasoning are equally valid. Rosetti argues that this more flexible approach stops the descent into complete relativism, but "allows meanings and valued characteristics to change over time, as standards and communities themselves change" (p. 309).

Rosetti's feminist critique of economics includes a recognition of the dualisms and hierarchy of the current system and an investigation into what is omitted from or not valued by the current system. Rosetti suggests (p. 317) some hard-core assumptions of a feminist economics paradigm might include a broader conception of decision making that relies on interdependent agents, a redefinition of what constitutes work, and a more explicit recognition and investigation of the role of gender. As she notes, however, if objectives are not possible, one might ask how different paradigms should be evaluated. Her answer, that we should be governed by the code of civil conversation, is similar to that of McCloskey (1985) and Rorty (1982). Rosetti cautions, however, that this approach has a cost. Feminist hard-core assumptions cannot be considered to be on firm ground and it cannot be maintained that "feminist economics is objectively better or truer than what it strives to replace" (p. 322). Nevertheless, she concludes that postmodernist approaches have performed a valuable service by opening to debate areas that were previously unexplored and that "[f]eminist economics is the best example of this to date in economics" (p. 323).

Two additional essays written from a postmodern, feminist perspective are Charusheela's "Women's Choices and the Ethnocentrism/Relativism Dilemma" and Gillian Hewitson's "Disavowel of the Sexed Body in Neoclassical Economics." In Charusheela's opinion feminist theorists studying the oppression of women have long been accused of being either ethnocentric or relativist, a result of neoclassical economists' conceptualization of all choices (by men and women) as being made by an autonomous individual who maximizes utility given certain constraints. But, with respect to any specific action, there is "no intrinsic mechanism by which we can decide what component of the agent's action reflects desire and what component reflects constraint" (p. 201). Or, to put it another way, there is no way to differentiate actions that express lack of choice from those that express autonomous expressive choice. Given this conundrum some feminists argue that roles are socially determined, which is of course counter to free choice. Others resort to Enlightenment conceptions of human nature that use an "unstated notion of underlying, universal, rationalist human being as the location of expressive choice, and assume a universal standpoint which can reveal to us what this true choice is" (p. 204). The latter approach is ethnocentric, but without it "we end up unable to adjudicate between various cultural practices and fall into relativism" (p. 204).

Charusheela argues that while many feminists maintain that one has to choose sides between the two extremes of ethnocentrism and relativism, there is, in fact, a middle ground. She maintains that human "agency and autonomy are not found in an asocial, ahistorical, transcultural, pre-given state of human nature" (p. 208). Rather, humans are socially situated and in a constant struggle to achieve autonomy in their own social context. Recognition of "situated subjects" requires analysts to progress beyond assuming abstract autonomous agents. They must understand the inherited social and cultural context of individual agents. While feminists succeeded to a limited extent in presenting a non-relativist, non-masculine view of agency in a Western context, Charusheela maintains that the non-Western context has not been adequately examined; she challenges feminist economists to produce a non-ethnocentric, non-relativist theoretical framework.

Hewitson agrees with feminist authors who argue that the neoclassical agent is neither abstract nor disembodied. She cites Mykituik (1994), who maintains the liberal individual is "a particular body – one who is white, male, heterosexual, able-bodied, young, adult" (p. 229). Hewitson uses surrogate motherhood as a case study to illustrate the male bias of neoclassical approaches. A neoclassical approach tends to view the womb as capital and "the surrogate mother as a contracting agent and as a non-mother, thereby disavowing the problem of sexual difference, and allowing the unproblematised retention of the fantasy of the universal individual" (p. 238). Hewitson counters that the mother-child or nurturing relationship is an important dynamic that is ignored in the neoclassical framework. She does not suggest that the mother-child relation or any central figure should replace the abstract, autonomous figure of the neoclassical paradigm. Rather, she argues that the sexual difference between procreative man and reproductive woman needs to be recognized at some level.

As Brian Cooper notes in his critique, Hewitson fails to acknowledge that the classical economists and some modern neoclassical economists have recognized differences in the sexes and incorporated the differences into their analysis in various ways. He points to a number of authors who note the inadequacies of current theory and attempt to "reconcile the theoretical assumptions of sameness with the empirical realities of difference" (p. 255). In addition to feminist economics, he cites discrimination, game theory, growth theory, and economic education as other approaches that recognize differences in economic agents and suggests each represents an opportunity to change mainstream conversation.

Like Cooper, Amariglio and Ruccio's "From Unity to Dispersion: The Body in Modern Economic Discourse" contends that the classical economists conceived the economic agent differently than did most modern neoclassical economists; in their view, classical economists considered more complex ways in which the "whole human" contributed as an economic agent. They maintain that while the marginalist revolution of Jevons and Walras led to the gradual fading of importance of the body (to many the body virtually disappeared), the body has actually been transformed: there are different conceptions of the body in different epochs and among different schools of thought. Amariglio and Ruccio argue that the neoclassical approach created a "flat body," one without depth. Throughout, however, the body has been implicitly assumed and they contend that neoclassical value theory represents "an extended allegory about the mechanisms and capabilities of the body" (p. 154).

Amariglio and Ruccio argue that neoclassical economists need to come to terms with "innovations that are underway outside economics in recomposing the body in terms of postmodernism" (p. 163). They suggest that the feminist plea to include the female body and its affections is "one of the most potentially powerful contributions to economic theory of which we are aware" (p. 163). According to Amariglio and Ruccio inclusion of the female body is, however, just a part of the move to recompose the body in postmodern terms.

Jean-Joseph Goux's essay "Ideality, Symbolicity, and Reality in Postmodern Capitalism" argues that just as the body became more abstract in the neoclassical period, money was also becoming less real. As commodity money was gradually abandoned it was replaced by an abstract money; money became more of a symbol or a sign. Much as Derrida (1976, 1978) suggests modern language is rife with symbols, Goux maintains that the modern economy can be characterized by its extensive use of the sign. Goux argues rather dramatically that the contemporary economy's reliance on the sign "leads to disarray through the crisis of all the previous conceptions of value and of all the former economic models. Economy has objectively entered into a deconstructive regime of the sign . . . and, maybe, in the long term the deconstruction of the economy itself" (p. 180).

Other essays in the volume are concerned with various postmodern moments or postmodern encounters. Part VI contains discussions of the Cambridge capital controversy by Stephen Cullenberg and Indraneel Dasgupta and of an experimental approach by Judith Mehta. Cullenberg and Dasgupta extend the work of McCloskey who had argued that the capital controversy was essentially an argument about metaphors and amenable to literary analysis. Similar to Goux they "reinterpret the debate in terms of alternative semiotic strategies" (p. 338), assuming that language is symbolic or an arbitrary system of signs not tied to the economy. They note that linguists make a distinction between denotative and connotative signs. Denotation refers to a more literal or "naturalized" meaning, whereas connotative language is associative and more open to multiple interpretations or alteration by different ideologies. Cullenberg and Dasgupta argue that the "transference from the denotative to the connotative levels of signification can be interpreted as the contextual transition from the *metaphor* to the *myth*" (p. 345). They maintain that the myth is a higher order signification and that rhetoric and persuasion are necessary to legitimize the myth. The problem is that participants in the capital controversy and other debaters that are from different schools of thought do not decode the higher order signs in the same way, giving rise to charges of bias or relativism.

Mehta conducts an experimental bargaining game that suggests social and institutional factors as explanatory of outcomes that may not have been predicted by rational choice theory. Her intent is "to bring voice to what has formerly been considered noise" (p. 374). She sees her experimental approach as just one method of achieving this end.

A third article in Part VI by Shaun Hargreaves Heap notes the contributions of economics to postmodernism, rather than the reverse. He suggests that the postmodernist commitment to pluralism necessarily leads to a universalisable system of justice. When the commitment to pluralism leads inevitably to extreme disagreement, the postmoderns can resort to the principle of equal relative concession that comes from the neoclassical bargaining problem. Thus, the case of extreme disagreement is "the one time when it might be appropriate to use the neoclassical model without qualification" (p. 371).

In Part VII Willian Milberg, Philip Mirowski, and Stephen Gudeman each suggest in various ways that we should at least consider whether the central metaphor of the market system as a way to conceptualize all aspects of society is limiting.

Milberg's essay, "Decentering the Market Metaphor in International Economics," suggests that "the metaphor of the market economy and the related concept of equilibrium are no longer relevant to a large portion of international economic relations" (p. 408). He argues that increasing tendencies toward intra-firm trade, inter-corporate joint ventures, state negotiated trade, etc., and the continued reliance on the market metaphor to attempt to analyze the resulting trade "has made it difficult for economists to even identify certain trends . . . much less theorize them" (p. 416). He considers models that relax perfect competition and constant returns to scale and those that replace rational economic man with game-playing, strategic behavior as more useful and more descriptive of reality. But, he notes "the pro-interventionist conclusions of much of the new international economics have proven too contentious" for many economists wedded to free trade (p. 415). He suggests that the market metaphor has its uses, but that it should be decentered and not be "the only metaphor available to economists; thus, postmodernism performs the useful role in international economics of ending the era of the exclusionary metanarrative" (p. 426).

Mirowski's "Refusing the Gift" and Gudeman's "Postmodern Gifts" examine the various ways economic anthropologists as well as neoclassical economists have treated gift-giving. The economic anthropologists, led by Mauss (1925) and Malinowski (1922), focused on reciprocity as a driving force of society, whereas neoclassical economists focus on "individual motivations and interests that are infrasocial or prior to the development of social forms" (p. 460). Gudeman argues that both perspectives are modernist, but the analysis of gifts "represents economic anthropology's postmodern moment, for it seems to elude every fixed understanding we erect" (p. 459). He argues, in fact, that neither the economic anthropologists nor the neoclassical economists are entirely correct as the "gift has no single meaning." He maintains that it is an uncertain and unstable category "because it is 'about' uncertainty itself" (p. 473).

Mirowski sounds similar themes when he argues that discussions of gifts in economics have been essentially worthless. Even worse, however, has been the economic anthropologists attempt to use gift theory as means of providing an alternative to exchange theory, an effort that. left them "hobbled and vulnerable to incursions by neoclassical economists" (p. 451). As for the economists, their main problem is "the quality and character of the invariants" governing the participants. He argues that value invariance is socially constructed and that value refers to the outcomes of a system of exchange centered on money creation and control. Gifts are a function of this money-based value system. Their existence provides the possibility of something outside the value sphere and both "initiates new exchange and keeps the system of exchange functioning" (p. 455).

This thought-provoking book is recommended for anyone interested in the state of economic discourse. Ostensibly about the influence of postmodernism on economics and replete with references to Derrida, Foucault, Lyotard, and other postmodernists, one nevertheless discerns a plea to continue to broaden the discussion of economics however possible. Postmodernism, in spite of the shortcomings recognized by many of the authors, provides a convenient tool to expand the dialogue and accommodate the change that all authors agree will and/or must occur.

A criticism of the volume is that there are few attempts to defend the modernist, neoclassical paradigm. Heap's article is the only one that expressly argues that postmodernists might learn something from neoclassical economists. Of course, McCloskey and Mirowski might be said to defend the neoclassical paradigm, but only if economists will be more accepting of rhetorical persuasion or accept that some things, like gifts, are outside the value system. Gagnier and Dupre's critique of Amariglio and Ruccio argues that their attempt to transfer "agency from people to their diverse functions seems to us to be going too far" (p. 187). They ask if moving from value to difference as Amariglio and Ruccio seem to suggest, amounts "to moving from people to systems of knowledge? And if this is what postmodernism mandates, should we welcome it" (p. 188)? More attention to these questions would make the volume more balanced, but might be asking too much in a book that is already quite lengthy. Still, the question lingers. Can a more inclusive paradigm be as useful as the previous system?

Nevertheless, this set of essays accomplishes its goals, for the point, as John Davis notes, is to encourage "free trade in ideas" (p. 481).

NOTES

1. The methodological debates in economics initiated by the publication of McCloskey's "The Rhetoric of Economics" (1983) embodied this self-reflexive aspect of postmodernism, though the economic debates did not include deconstruction of texts.

2. For additional discussion of Gilman's contribution as well as that of other women economists, see Dimand et al. (1995) and Pujol (1992).

REFERENCES

Derrida, J. (1976). *Of grammatology.* G. C. Spivak (Trans.). Baltimore: Johns Hopkins University Press.

Derrida, J. (1978). *Writing and difference.* A. Bass (Trans.). Chicago: University of Chicago Press.

Dimand, M. A., Dimand, R. W., & Forget, E. L. (Eds) (1995). *Women of value: Feminist essays on the history of women in economics.* Aldershot: Edward Elgar.

Hutchison, T. W. (1979). *Knowledge and ignorance in economics.* Chicago: University of Chicago Press.

Malinowski, B. (1961) [1922]. *Argonauts of the Western Pacific.* New York: Dutton.

Mauss, M. (1990) [1925]. *The gift.* W. D. Halls (Trans.). London: Routledge.

McCloskey, D. N. (1983). The rhetoric of economics. *Journal of Economic Literature, 31*(June), 434–461.

McCloskey, D. N. (1985). *The rhetoric of economics.* Madison: University of Wisconsin Press.

Pujol, M. (1992). *Feminism and anti-feminism in early economic thought.* Aldershot: Edward Elgar.

Rorty, R. (1982). *The consequences of pragmatism.* Minneapolis: University of Minnesota Press.

HANDS' REFLECTION WITHOUT RULES

Ana Maria Bianchi

Review essay on Wade Hands', *Reflection without Rules: Economic Methodology and Contemporary Science Theory*. **Cambridge: Cambridge University Press, 2001.**

Wade Hands' *Reflection without Rules* is the best book in town for the student who wants to get acquainted with the field of economic methodology. Just like Mark Blaug's *The Methodology of Economics* and Bruce Caldwell's *Beyond Positivism* during the 1980s and the 1990s, *Reflection* introduces the reader to the debate in the area, in all its complexity and with many of its details, yet in a clear and logical manner. The book reproduces portions of the author's earlier articles published since 1985 in different periodicals and books. Hands successfully achieves his goal of building a survey of recent developments in the field of economic methodology in a book that can be praised for its comprehensive outlook; its wide array of subject-matters; successful incursions into the neighboring fields of epistemology, philosophy, rhetoric, sociology of knowledge and others; its clear discussion of relevant topics, following a logical order; and its full coverage of the available literature, with the impressive reference list of more than 1,200 entries.

Reflections comprises nine chapters, including an introduction and a conclusion. As usual, the introductory chapter presents the overall structure of the book, listing the topics that will be covered in the remaining chapters. Moreover, Chap. 1 introduces the author's core proposition, which he reiterates in all the remaining chapters. This core proposition builds on the idea that the researcher who wants to do good economics will not find a ready-made methodology waiting on the shelf

Research in the History of Economic Thought and Methodology A Research Annual
Research in the History of Economic Thought and Methodology, Volume 22-A, 341–346
© 2004 Published by Elsevier Ltd.
ISSN: 0743-4154/doi:10.1016/S0743-4154(03)22020-4

at his disposal. The three quotations that open the chapter (which set the practice thereafter) warn the reader that he should abandon his quest for a universally sound and correct methodology which, once employed, will assure that his work is scientific. Although the "shelf-of-philosophy" approach to economic methodology was always problematic, claims Hands, this condition worsened over time. There is no consensus today about what a scientific method should be, and the whole idea of a single method is questioned everywhere in science.

As the reader will see more clearly in the rest of the book, Hands' argument has a double dimension. On the one hand, it is normative, since the author explicitly favors a change in the subject of economic methodology, arguing that the shelf-of-philosophy view is "no longer a good place to invest our intellectual resources" (p. 2). But this normative dimension cannot be understood in isolation from the positive dimension of the argument: there was indeed a movement of displacement and redirection of the current economic methodology, following what happened in the methodology of science as a whole. This double dimension leads to the conclusion that research in economic methodology, though requiring a great deal of reflection, can dispense with rules. More on that later.

What Hands calls the "Millian tradition" in economics is analyzed in Chap. 2. This is probably the most dense chapter in the book, focusing on both a large number of classical authors and an extensive period of time. It begins with John Stuart Mill's 1836 classical piece and goes through the nineteenth and twentieth centuries, analyzing the methodological approaches of several economists: Senior, Cairnes, Schmöller and others from the German historical school, Neville Keynes, Maynard Keynes, Robbins, Menger, von Mises, Hutchison, Friedman and Samuelson. Hands devotes a large portion of the chapter to Stuart Mill, due to his importance in the definition of a non-experimental deductive ("a priori") method for economics. The tension between deductivism and empiricism is already present in Mill's definition of the object and method of economics (actually, Hands should say "Political Economy," which was the specific branch of the moral sciences that Mill was claiming to focus upon).

To understand how positivism was overcome in the methodological discussion, leading to the dismissal of the Received View, Hands moves in Chap. 3 to the broader field of philosophy of science. He justifies the adoption of a naturalistic approach, defining it as a philosophical vision that is informed by scientific practice, rather than by a priori philosophy. In the traditional view, philosophy was seen as the high court of scientific knowledge, being responsible for the justification of theories. Naturalism challenged this conception, making the philosopher of science aware of two interconnected problems: theory-ladenness and underdetermination. The first was a recurrent theme in Popper, who claimed that observation statements are always interpretations of the facts observed in the light of specific theories. Facts are theory-laden, which implies that there is no independent act of observation. Hands adds that theory-ladenness is one of the issues that most clearly differentiates contemporary discussions about scientific knowledge from those of the Received View.

The so-called Duhem-Quine underdetermination problem, in turn, has to do with the empirical testing of scientific theories. It originates from the impossibility of immunizing a specific theory against contrary empirical evidence: since theories are never tested in isolation, when unfavorable evidence is found it is not clear whether the problem is with the theory itself or with its many auxiliary hypotheses. As a result, not only is the researcher unable to accept a theory in the light of positive evidence, he finds no ground for rejection of a theory which is falsified by empirical evidence either.

Both theory-ladenness and underdetermination are intimately connected. Hands argues that with the adoption of naturalism, contemporary philosophy of science fundamentally altered its relationship with the various branches of science, economics included. The traditional view saw philosophy as the high court of knowledge, in trust of the justification of scientific knowledge. Naturalism emerged from the collapse of this foundationalist approach, abandoning the a priori philosophical theorizing and reversing the relative positions of science and philosophy.

Hands starts talking about naturalism in the third chapter of *Reflections*, but he explores the issue more thoroughly in Chap. 4. This is the most difficult part of the entire book, since it deals with concepts (cognitive science, reliabilism, eliminative materialism, evolutionary epistemology, folk psychology, supervenience, etc.) and authors (Edmund Gettier, Alvin Goldman, Michael Bradie, Peter Munz) with whom a great number of the methodologists of economics are not familiar. Naturalism is understood to be a substantive "turn" that has taken place in the history of philosophy, similar to idealism, rationalism, the logistic turn and other philosophical movements with epistemological implications. Unlike methodological monism, naturalism does not advocate the existence of a single method for both social and physical sciences.

An example might help to illustrate the kind of discussion that takes place in Chap. 4. What does the word "justified" in the expression "justified true belief" mean? According to Hands (p. 144), there are two basic answers to this question in the history of philosophy, deriving from two different approaches to the problem: foundationalism and coherence. The foundationalist approach claims that knowledge is built up systematically from more fundamental beliefs that may or may not be empirically grounded. These fundamental beliefs are seen as independently secure, and thus require no further justification. In the second approach, a belief is said to be justified if it sticks together with other already accepted beliefs, thus meeting the coherence criterion. Hands explains how Alvin

Goldman faced this justification problem in the field of cognitive science, with the focus on the reliability of the belief formation processes. Goldman is introduced to the reader as a good example of the cognitive "turn" in the philosophy of science. Together with Herbert Simon, he prepared the scene for the contemporary conception of human beings as information-processing systems.

In Chap. 5, Hands analyses what he calls the sociological turn, corresponding to the spread of the sociology of scientific knowledge (SSK). This particular version of naturalism adopts an externalist point of view in the evaluation of scientific knowledge, assuming that theories constitute a particular type of socially held beliefs. This research was inspired by such classical authors as Marx, Bernal, and Merton. One of its main research programs, the so-called Strong Program, explains scientific beliefs by associating them with the social interests of the scientists who hold them. Another research program in SSK is Social Constructivism, which pictures science as the product of an ongoing negotiation among and between scientists, agents, and institutions. Although research in this area has produced many interesting results, there is a reflexivity problem involved: if we all agree that scientific knowledge is socially constructed, why should we exempt sociology of knowledge from this condition?

Chapter 6 is dedicated to the analysis of the pragmatic and rhetorical turns in economic methodology, beginning in the nineteenth century with classical authors such as Peirce and Dewey. Hands attributes the rebirth of pragmatism at the end of the twentieth century to the fact that it provides a way out of what he considers to be the major dilemma in contemporary metascience: "the dilemma of being stuck between foundationalist philosophy, on the one hand and radical relativism, on the other" (p. 216). A second important reason for the increased popularity of pragmatic philosophy is that, in contrast with the traditional philosophy of science, it blurs the frontier between theory and practice. For pragmatists there is not a meaningful distinction between theory and practice, as there is no rigid distinction between knowing and doing.

Hands attributes the origin of contemporary neopragmatism and the discursive turn to an overlap between postmodernism and classical pragmatism. Led by authors such as Richard Rorty and D. McCloskey, this current of thought views science as a type of discourse that aims to persuade. Twenty years after McCloskey's pioneer article (*JEL* 1983), there was a gain in perspective for the analysis of the rhetorical literature in economics, including the appraisal of its links with postmodernism and pragmatism. Hands does not show much sympathy for this current of thought (at least not as much as he shows for classical pragmatism), but he does well his job of reviewing the literature produced by McCloskey and others. He claims that the controversial aspect of these writings died down in recent years, but that the rhetoric of economics, in the sense of a rhetorical analysis of economic texts, should be considered as "work in progress." A specific section of Chap. 6 is dedicated to feminist epistemology, understood as an active voice in contemporary intellectual and social life.

Chapter 7 takes the reader back to economic methodology, discussing some recent developments in the field. The author dedicates a substantial part of the chapter to contemporary authors such as Weintraub, Boland and Hausman, describing the first two as followers of the Popperian tradition and Hausman as representative of the Millian tradition. The final section of the chapter discusses different conceptions of realism, mainly based on the approaches of Tony Lawson and Uskali Mäki.

In his review of *Reflections*, Weintraub (2002) congratulates the author for taking the discussion in economic methodology away from the philosophy of science to science studies. This is precisely what Hands does in Chap. 8. Do studies that focus the production and distribution of scientific knowledge belong to the broader field of economic methodology? Hands answers affirmatively. He states that the ESK (economics of scientific knowledge) has gained public recognition in the last decades; it is a new research program and "an entirely new ground for a book on economic methodology" (p. 388). He closes with a list of potential research projects outside the mainstream that might be undertaken within ESK.

Then comes the concluding chapter (perhaps I should say, "Enter the concluding chapter," mimicking Hands' style). In Chap. 9, Hands reasserts his core proposition, that a rules-seeking methodology "has quietly and unceremoniously passed from the scene" (p. 393). The breakdown of the shelf-of-philosophy approach has produced new and interesting reflections on a wide array of topics (p. 394). The emergence of this new economic methodology can be explained by what the author calls a "change in personnel," that is, the fact that a new generation of researchers has entered the stage. This new generation is not involved in the search for a small set of narrow methodological rules that would be able to differentiate science from non-science. Besides being more open to multidisciplinarity, this new generation tends to be more careful about the details of the economic theories that they plan to study, whether in the history of economic thought or in studies of contemporary practices. As Hands puts it, "There are fewer studies of the 'neoclassical revolution' or 'the Keynesian revolution' and more emphasis on detailed investigations of particular sites of economic knowledge production" (p. 398).

Two decades ago Caldwell advocated methodological pluralism in his *Beyond Positivism*. He argued that methodologists should abandon the quest for a single, definitive, correct method for economics. Hands's approach is more radical than that: beginning with the title of his book, he seems in some moments to favor a complete rejection of any kind of rule-bound methodology. Researchers entering the field should leave outside the door any pretension of setting up rules to guide the scientific enterprise.

But this is not Hands's point of view, as Hausman (2001) correctly argues. He is not proposing a methodological anarchism or asserting that anything goes. All he is trying to convey is the need to reflect on actual scientific practices, rather than looking on the shelf for a certain type of rules-based methodology. After all, the shelf is empty.

If this is true, why did Hands choose the title *Reflection without rules*? There are two different ways of answering this question. A rhetorical interpretation would suggest that Hands intended to persuade an audience who was skeptical of the kind of reasoning typical of the Received View and was looking for something new. In order to reach this audience, he chose a provocative title. A second interpretation would suggest that the title is an overstatement, and that Hands was just trying to stress the difference between the new and the old economic methodologies.

This second interpretation seems to do more justice to *Reflection*. Hands is only asking for help in moving the wheel. What differentiates this strategy from the "anything goes" attitude? Both on the positive and normative sides, Hands is claiming that the fact that positivism is dead does not mean that relativism is the only alternative left. Following the philosophers of science, economic methodologists should "put the shoulder to the wheel and figure out what a reasonable middle ground might look like" (p. 405). With this we can all agree.

REFERENCES

Hausman, D. (2001). Book review of "Reflection without rules". *Journal of Economic Literature*, *XXXIX*(September), 902–904.
Weintraub, E. R. (2002). Book review of "Reflection without rules". *Journal of the History of Economic Thought*, *24*(4), 510–513.

FLIGSTEIN'S THE ARCHITECTURE OF MARKETS

A. Allan Schmid

Review essay on Neil Fligstein's, *The Architecture of Markets: An Economic Sociology of Twenty-First-Century Capitalist Societies*. **Princeton: Princeton University Press, 2001. 274 pp.**

Competitive markets are the *sine qua non* of economics principles texts. A system of competing firms, input suppliers including labor, and consumers is automatic and can be taken for granted. Firms are busy combining inputs and choosing what products to produce. They come and go, forming, dissolving and reforming. There is little place in this theory for cognition, social movements, shared meanings, that is, of economic sociology. Fligstein wants to change that. He wants to add a "political-cultural theory" to the theory of the firm.

For Fligstein, too much competition, far from nirvana, is unstable and cannot support investment and long-run productivity. Thus, firms seek stability and survivability. They seek an understanding among dominant firms and with labor as to the limits to competition. Public policy regulates this desire and tries to find a balance between stability and change.

For standard economic theory, survival is not a separate objective, but the result of competition for the able. In the textbooks, the successful firm makes marginal cost equal marginal revenue with known prices and production functions. There is no place for cognition here. But, once we admit that expected values drive choice, there is room for socially influenced cognition. Fligstein suggests three managerial views of the firm, each in a sense a qualitative vision replacing the exact determination of profit maximization: sales and markets, finance, and shareholder value. Each vision dominates a historical period. These processes are path dependent

Research in the History of Economic Thought and Methodology A Research Annual
Research in the History of Economic Thought and Methodology, Volume 22-A, 347–353
© 2004 Published by Elsevier Ltd.
ISSN: 0743-4154/doi:10.1016/S0743-4154(03)22021-6

and context specific rather than timeless and spaceless abstractions. Fligstein compares the unique history of the United States to some of its principal rivals.

The sales and marketing perspective implicitly recognizes that demand and relative prices are not given, but created. It recognizes that categories of goods are not facts, but artifacts capable of differentiation. Managers can allocate inputs not only in different product mixes, but also to altering demand and consumer perceptions.

The sales and marketing perspective dominated American business until around 1970, when according to Fligstein, a crisis occurred leading firms to look for a new vision. The crisis was inflation, low earnings, depressed stock prices and aggressive anti-trust policies. The new theme was finance. Managers did not search for more efficient resource combinations, but rather evaluated whole companies in terms of rates of return. Firms were bought and sold to assemble profitable portfolios. Mergers across unrelated products and industries were the theme (shall we say fad?) of the decade. Managers survived by being the subject rather than the object of merger.

In the 1980s, the crisis was created by foreign competition, slow growth and low profits. Horizontal mergers (industry consolidation) became more popular. Firms divested what turned out to be low profit lines, invested in core businesses, repurchased their own stock, and took on debt to force cost cutting (as if normal manager pay was not sufficient incentive). The rallying cry (Fligstein calls it a social movement) was to maximize shareholder value. Note again, if the standard theory of the firm held, shareholder value would have taken care of itself and not be a separate objective. Perhaps, we have just seen the shareholder value theme carried to its extreme – maximization of the value of shares sold by top management.

What is the essence of a "political-cultural theory" of the firm? "I have termed this theoretical approach 'political-cultural' because it focuses on the intra-and inter-organizational power struggles and suggests that the goal of such struggles is to create shared meanings, that is, local cultures that operate to produce stable interactions" (p. 129). Politics suggests conflict and contending parties. There is none of this in standard theory of the firm – just bottom line profit maximization to which everyone agrees. There is no conflict – just good and poor calculation. The firm is a unitary black box. The contending parties for Marx were workers and capitalists. This remains of interest to Fligstein, but only with respect to labor policy, not relationships among firms. He does not examine worker-owned firms and co-ops. Slightly more relevant is the struggle for control between owners and managers (Berle, 1959), and the influence of banks and other financial organizations. But, as we shall see, Fligstein empirically finds no effect of these variables on firm profits. He sees his "political-cultural approach as an alternative to 'power elite' theories of American corporations" (p. 21). Most central for Fligstein is how firms relate to each other to control competition and survival as an operating unit.

Fligstein has only slightly more use for Williamson (1985) and Coase's theory of the firm than for Berle. His big question is not hierarchy vs. markets, but rather the sales, financial, or shareholder value focus. Rather than seeing a continuous adjustment of governance structures by individual firms considering their unique degree of specific assets, market architectural change is a discontinuous shared response to crisis. Managers are primarily focused on survival rather than minimization of transaction costs. Though there may be something of the latter in the former, this is not the driving variable. "The sociology of markets that I am developing replaces profit-maximizing actors with people who are trying to promote survival of their firm" (p. 17).

What is cultural about Fligstein's theory? Managers (all of us) learn by watching others. When you are not sure about causal connections (like the relations of marginal costs and revenues to profits), follow the leaders. This looks like a social movement to Fligstein. Expectations of what others will do if you do something is a learned, evolving informal understanding.

Power and conflict are central for Fligstein. If it is not managers vs. owners, or only partially workers vs. capitalists, who are the contending parties? They are individuals and groups within the firm who compete for authority (incumbents and challengers). Whose vision of the firm's strategy will dominate? Further, as firms compete (not simply to serve consumers, but to bring order to an industry – Fligstein calls it a market field), the contention is for who will be the dominant firms. This would of course, not be an issue in pure competition where sales and marketing differentiation are irrelevant. Government comes into the picture as firms seek help or the right to use certain strategies against challengers. "Sociologists have traditionally seen social relations as fundamentally about power (who gets what and why?) and shared meanings (i.e. the production of institutions, rules, and shared understandings) to support systems of power (xiii)."

The differences between Fligstein's political-cultural theory, the transactions cost theory of Williamson, and the neo-classical model can be seen in the design of empirical tests. Williamson's dependent variable is the form of governance – hierarchy or market. He assumes that firms know the connection between these structures and profit. Independent variables focus on the degree of asset specificity – firms choose structures to avoid asset losses due to the opportunism of trading partners. Fligstein's dependent variable is profit (and other financial return measures) while the different "architecture of markets" are the independent variables. These include variables concerning managers vs. owners such as whether the firm is closely held by family or institutional investors; the character of the board of directors (inter-locking memberships and role of banks, etc.); the background of the CEO; corporate strategy (product dominance); multidivisional form; mergers in the previous ten years; demand growth in the industry;. The latter is assumed to reflect whether the leadership is sales and marketing oriented or finance oriented. Fligstein has no variables for the incentive compatibility remuneration of managers such as stock options that have recently produced unwanted manipulation. This and other arguably relevant variables would require in-depth surveys of corporations rather than the public data that Fligstein uses. The simple neoclassical model of course would need none of the above relying primarily on product and input prices and production functions.

Fligstein's regressions involving the one hundred largest industrial corporations in the U.S. in 1969 finds no evidence that the ownership, board of directors, or presence of multidivisional structure variables explain profitability. The background of the CEO on the other hand is significant. This is suggestive, but seems a weak proxy to hang political-cultural theory on. Product diversification was related to return on equity while firms with a high proportion of unrelated businesses (conglomerates) did less well. Fligstein argues that diversification is a strategy more likely used by firms dominated by a finance model of the firm. For this sample, diversification must not have been achieved by merger since merger activity in the previous 10 years was not significant in explaining any of the profitability measures. Fligstein's model seems poorly specified – "My models do not explain a lot of the variation in financial performance in 1970 . . ." (p. 136).

What explains the choice of business strategy (market architecture)? Remember that Williamson does not feel the need to explain this, rather he assumes it is the inevitable outcome of calculations of profit maximization by whomever is in charge. Fligstein, on the other hand, finds that the background of the CEO (im-plying a particular world view) is significant in explaining merger activity while the control variables of ownership were not. "Firms with product-related and – unrelated strategies were more likely than firms with a product-dominant strategy to participate in mergers." "These results suggest that mergers as a strategy were entirely the product of organizational factors and unaffected by the measures of forms of control" (p. 136). Fligstein's story is that a sales and marketing-oriented CEO would choose to concentrate on a dominant product (70% of revenues from a single product). This is plausible, but not proven without in-depth interviews.

In a chapter on "The Logic of Employment Systems," Fligstein's "goal is to identify ideal-typical arrangements that reflect the dominance of various groups and to consider the hybrid possibilities that might occur in real societies" (p. 100). His ideal types are vocationalism, professionalization and managerialism. Vocationalism is typified by Germany with occupational communities, industrial unions, and vocational training. Professionalization is typified by France with a professional peer group, collegial associations, and reliance on university training. "Careers are centered on professions, not firms or industries (102)." Managerialism typified by Japan (the U.S. has a mix of managerialism and professionalism) is marked by commitment to a particular work organization, company unions, and reliance on general schooling.

Fligstein's model contrasts to that of Williamson. Williamson's (1985, Chap. 9) governance alternatives are putting out, federated, inside contracting, communal, peer group and authority relation. Williamson would expect labor governance to be dependent on the type of industry (affecting transaction costs) and not on the culture of a country.

But Fligstein argues for example, that the deal that Bismarck struck in 1870 set Germany on a path of worker welfare provision and an education system structured to create differential skills. For Fligstein, it is much more significant that German workers are by law represented on corporate boards than whether a particular business finds it profitable to contract out certain functions. "Changes in employment relations are not likely to be endogenous to the bargaining process, as Marxism or institutional economics suggests, but exogenous." He refers here to the "new institutional economics" of Williamson. Fligstein again finds institutional change in crises, not shifts in technologies and associated transaction costs. He goes beyond the worker-capitalist relationship of Marx to embed it "in larger societal arrangement, including states, educational systems, and existing models of employment relations, and the previous history of those arrangements" (p. 121). The research agenda suggested by this perspective is illustrated by reference to how women fare in different systems. He hypothesizes that sex segregation will be more prevalent in male-dominated craft systems than in more professionally-oriented systems where university training controls entry. Fligstein's emphasis is on who gets what with different systems rather than which structure is efficient in general. He asks how existing systems are reproduced.

Fligstein expects differences in labor and firm governance to persist among nations. He does not expect globalization to create homogeneity. However, one can see great pressure on European countries to remove barriers to labor mobility that cushion the effect of change on worker welfare. The Japanese system of lifetime employment is also under stress. Fligstein concludes, "Efficiency is socially constructed rather than constructed by markets. And there may be many ways to organize 'efficiently' " (p. 190). And, these serve different interests.

Let's see if Fligstein's perspective can be applied to a contemporary situation. Airlines are surely in crisis and are searching for survival strategies. Mergers and consolidations are proceeding apace with government approval. Lines are asking for government loan guarantees. Some lines want to reduce employment and wages by voiding existing contracts under bankruptcy proceedings. The business strategy of the hub and spoke system with a dominant line in each hub city, while providing a shared stability for years, is now challenged by small lines flying only selected segments. These new lines do not have the same prior negotiated union wage levels.

Questions of what constitutes fair competition arise as the lines propose sharing of reservation systems and codes and alliances with related travel firms (hotels, etc.). There are labor issues of who pays for anti-terror costs at airports. Are the inspectors Federal government employees and are they unionized? Fuel prices are subject to geo-political policies. All of these issues are part of the instability that threatens survival of the incumbent firms. Can they be subsumed under a theoretical perspective of struggle between incumbents and challengers, capitalist vs. labor, market vs. hierarchy, or sales vs. finance CEO's? Theoretical pluralism seems in order.

The shakeout in the information and computer industry is another contemporary crisis. Old business models of a few dominant firms selling hardware are being challenged. Firms like IBM are finding that computers are becoming competitive commodities with low profit margins. So Sam Palmisano, the new CEO of IBM, is trying to sell a new strategy to members of his own firm (Ante, 2003). His conception of E-Business on Demand involves a unified network of servers, open standards, allocation of work automatically among servers, and giant computing grids in which a customer can buy computing power on an as-needed basis. To pull it off, IBM needs new technologies and new applications. Internal coordination is everything. Palmisano emphasizes an egalitarian culture. He abolished a 12-member executive committee that approved all major projects and established three teams focusing on strategy, operation, and technology whose members cut across managerial and technical levels. His personnel policies include fully funding employee pensions and giving them a sense of identity as IBMers who stand for community contributions as well as company profit. There is something more here than a sales vs. finance vision or hierarchy vs. market.

These variables seem to include, but go beyond, the variables of either Fligstein or Williamson. It is surely more complicated than the usual economizing resource allocation models of textbook economics. Research seems to demand inside data that is not available from published sources for large number of firms. There is a place for case studies. One of the most ambitious case studies of factors contributing to success of firms is that of Collins (2001). He studied all the firms that met his criteria of performing well for a number of years and then accelerating and becoming the best in their industries for a number of years. Collins has few variables that track very well with either Fligstein or Williamson. He comes close to Pamisano's emphasis on getting widespread commitment within the firm to a business model that finds what the firm can be the best at and which firm members can be emotionally attached to. Sounds like good economic sociology or institutional economics to this reviewer. Theoretical and methodological pluralism seems in order.

Finally, note should be made of an ethical implication that the author draws from his observation of 21st century capitalist societies. Stability of markets depends on a nexus of individuals, firms and government. "My basic argument is that governments and citizens in capitalist democracies are responsible for agreeing to produce stable arrangements that allow owners and managers to create corporations and markets" (p. 232). Fligstein then argues, "For this reason, citizens and governments have the right to make claims on corporations." Shareholders are not the only legitimate claimants. A dominant theme is emerging in Western societies that citizens must give firms what they want because they are the source of jobs. This is a matter of perspective. Fligstein reminds us that citizens and workers give firms the architectural stability they need to prosper.

REFERENCES

Ante, S. E. (2003). The new blue. *Business Week* (March 17), 80–88.

Berle, A., Jr. (1959). *Power without property: A new development in American political economy.* New York: Harcourt, Brace, and World.

Collins, J. C. (2001). *Good to great: Why some companies make the leap – and others don't.* New York: HarperBusiness.

Williamson, O. E. (1985). *The economic institutions of capitalism: Firms, markets, relational contracting.* New York: Free Press.

RESNICK'S AND WOLFF'S CLASS THEORY AND HISTORY

Simon Clarke

Review essay on Stephen A. Resnick and Richard D. Wolff's, *Class Theory and History: Capitalism and Communism in the USSR*. New York and London: Routledge. xiv + 353 pp. 2002.

The overwhelming ideological dominance of neo-liberalism has led to the widespread acceptance of the most facile explanations of the collapse of the Soviet Union, whose demise supposedly demonstrates the validity of Adam Smith's critique of political intervention in the functioning of the market. In this book Stephen Resnick and Richard Wolff undertake the vitally important task of theorizing the rise and fall of the Soviet Union from a Marxist perspective. Resnick and Wolff follow the neo-liberals in seeing the Soviet Union as a form of capitalism administered by the state, but reject the neo-liberal critique of the inefficiency of state capitalism, celebrating the supposedly great economic achievements of the Soviet Union. The failure of the Soviet Union lay not in the dominance of the state, but in the failure to go beyond state capitalism to establish a communist society. Instead of building on the limited communist elements in soviet society, the Soviet Union was marked by the persistence of what Resnick and Wolff call the "ancient" and "feudal" class structures which ultimately proved its undoing, by undermining the state capitalist appropriation of the surplus and providing the cultural and political foundations for a return to private capitalist forms of surplus appropriation.

The theoretical foundation of Resnick and Wolff's analysis is provided by the theory of class expounded in their earlier book, *Knowledge and Class*, which in turn derives ultimately from the reading of Marx offered by Althusser and Balibar.

Research in the History of Economic Thought and Methodology A Research Annual
Research in the History of Economic Thought and Methodology, Volume 22-A, 355–363
Copyright © 2004 by Elsevier Ltd.
ISSN: 0743-4154/doi:10.1016/S0743-4154(03)22022-8

Unfortunately their commendable attempt is vitiated by the incoherence of their theory. Resnick and Wolff propose a theory of class that is based on an analysis of "how society organizes the production, appropriation and distribution of surplus" (p. xi), that they contrast with hitherto existing Marxist analyses, which, they argue, overwhelmingly focus on the distribution of property and power in society.

As Marx noted, every society has to produce a surplus, at the very least to provide the means of securing its own reproduction and to provide a contingency reserve. According to Resnick and Wolff, the surplus is appropriated by a class of "surplus appropriators," who are its immediate recipients, and portions of this surplus are then assigned to other sections of the population, who are neither direct producers nor immediate appropriators of the surplus but whose function is generally to reproduce the class structure (p. 14). This model provides a *classification* of the population into social classes defined in terms of their relationship to the production, appropriation and distribution of the surplus. On this basis, Resnick and Wolff define five major kinds of class structure: capitalist, feudal, slave, ancient and communist, according to the identity of the social class that appropriates the surplus. The capitalist, feudal and slave class structures are all exploitative, in the sense that the surplus is appropriated by a class other than the direct producers. These three exploitative "fundamental class processes" are distinguished by *who* it is who appropriates the surplus: capitalists, feudal lords and slave masters respectively (although it is not clear how one distinguishes one from the other). The ancient and communist class structures are not exploitative because the direct producers appropriate and distribute their own surpluses, individually in the former and collectively in the latter.

This model provides a classification of the population in terms of its relation to the production, appropriation and distribution of the surplus. In much of the book the model plays no more than a classificatory role, recasting the standard accounts of the history of the Soviet Union in Resnick and Wolff's idiosyncratic terminology, with associated algebraic expressions of flows of surplus. Such explanatory power as the model has derives from the implicit hypothesis that its relation to the appropriation of the surplus determines the economic interests of each class. The "fundamental class process" defines the interests of the exploiting and exploited classes (who are one and the same in a communist or ancient class structure). The "subsumed class process" of distribution of surplus value defines the interests of subsumed classes, who are responsible for securing the reproduction of the class structure. Although the basic model is one of social groups seeking to realize their socially determined economic interests, Resnick and Wolff insist that their model is not deterministic since they also recognize the effectivity of non-class (cultural and political) processes, although they have no way of theorizing the relative weight of class and non-class processes, falling back on an empiricist pluralism under the cover of the Althusserian notion of "overdetermination," which for them simply means that "all aspects of society condition and shape one another" (p. 9). Most Althusserian Marxists followed the logic of this agnosticism to reject Marxism and embrace post-modernism, but Resnick and Wolff have avoided such a relapse into empiricism because in practice they tend to analyze cultural and political processes as being formed as a reflection of the underlying class processes.

Resnick and Wolff claim that their theory draws on "a central contribution of Marx's work, [which] was largely lost to the Marxian tradition after him" (p. xii). Marx theorized the forms of production and appropriation of a surplus on the basis of his concept of the mode of production, defined as the contradictory unity of the forces and relations of production, though Marx used the term "mode of production" very loosely and only developed a systematic theory of the capitalist mode of production. This has left plenty of scope for interpretation in the Marxist tradition. However, neither in the Marxist tradition nor in Marx do we find any anticipation of the theory offered by Resnick and Wolff. On the one hand, Resnick and Wolff make no reference to the characteristics of the forces of production, which played a central role in Marx's account. For Marx, the historical trajectory of the development of social production involves the progressive dissolution of communal forms of production in the transition from primitive communism, through the Asiatic and ancient, to the feudal mode of production, followed by the increasing socialization of production, which is the historical role of the capitalist mode of production and which lays the foundation for the future communist society. On the other hand, Marx's analysis did not centre on *who* appropriated the surplus, but on the prior question of the *social form* of the production and appropriation of a surplus, which cannot be separated from the question of the social basis of the power to appropriate a surplus. A surplus cannot be conceptualized independently of the social form of its production and appropriation, so it is impossible to identify *whom* it is who appropriates the surplus without an analysis of the social form of its production, which Resnick and Wolff do not provide. This is the source of the incoherence of Resnick and Wolff's theory, above all in its application to the Soviet Union.

Resnick and Wolff define the surplus as the quantity of output in excess of that which is returned to the direct producers for their consumption and reproduction. The problem with their theory arises as soon as we ask how we measure that quantity or, indeed, how we know whether or not there is such a quantity. If the direct producers exclusively consume their own immediate product, the surplus is unambiguously defined as that portion of the product that is rendered to the surplus appropriators. But once production is socialized, the workers' product constitutes one set of products and their remuneration constitutes another. The existence and magnitude of the surplus produced by a particular set of workers can then only be evaluated on the basis of a particular set of prices at which to value the products in question. In the capitalist mode of production this is achieved through the subordination of the production of use-values to the production of surplus value, which is the defining feature of capitalism.

In Marx's account, the value of a commodity corresponds to the labor time socially necessary to produce it with a given technology. The wage paid to the direct producer corresponds to the value of labor-power, which is the labor-time socially necessary to reproduce labor-power. The surplus in this case takes the form of surplus value, which is the difference between the labor-time socially necessary to produce the commodity and the labor-time socially necessary to reproduce the labor-power that produced it. The homogenization and free mobility of labor means that there is a tendency to the equalization of the value of labor-power, the length of the working day and the intensity of labor, and the competition between capitals means that there is a tendency for all capitalists in a given branch of production to reduce labor-time to the minimum socially necessary, so there is a tendency to the equalization of the rate of exploitation in all branches of production. In principle, we can therefore determine the amount of surplus value produced by a given set of workers.

But who is the immediate appropriator of this surplus value? The individual capitalist does not immediately appropriate the surplus value, but the sum total of the goods and services produced. The capitalist then sells these products as commodities in the attempt to realize a profit. However, this profit does not correspond to the amount of surplus value produced by the workers employed by that capitalist, because it is only in exceptional circumstances that, even in equilibrium, commodities sell at prices corresponding to their values. On the one hand, there is a tendency for prices to diverge from values as a result of the equalization of the rate of profit. On the other hand, the capitalist may sell the commodities to commercial intermediaries at a price below that corresponding to their value, to allow for the costs of selling the commodities and for the commercial profit of the wholesalers and retailers. Resnick and Wolff conceptualize this redistribution of surplus value between capitalists as a process through which the capitalist immediately appropriates the surplus, and then distributes it among those responsible for securing the reproduction of the capitalist mode of production in a "subsumed class process." But this is a completely irrational conceptualization, first because it is not possible to distinguish the appropriation of surplus value from its distribution and, second, because the distribution is not effected by the appropriating capitalist, but is achieved behind the backs of all the capitalists, through anonymous market processes. This brings us to the essential point. The social form of capitalist production is not one in which particular capitalists appropriate surplus value from particular groups of workers. It is a system of social production in which the capitalist class as a whole appropriates surplus value from the working class as a whole.

Resnick and Wolff insist that the dominant class structure in the Soviet Union was capitalist, on the grounds that it was not the direct producers who appropriated the surplus. However, they ignore the fact that the dominant social form of production in the Soviet Union, apart perhaps from the period of the New Economic Policy in the 1920s, was far from being capitalist. Goods and services were not produced as values, so production was not and could not be subordinated to the production and appropriation of surplus value. Enterprises and organizations were required to deliver particular goods and services at particular times to other enterprises and organizations. They were required to provide means of collective consumption and wages to their workers according to centrally determined norms. Prices were attached to goods and services, so that enterprises and organizations could nominally make profits and losses, but these were accounting prices that reflected the physical allocations in the central plan, and monetary balances were purely accounting balances. Money played a significant role only in the payment of wages and in workers' spending, with wages, prices and taxes again adjusted to secure a material balance. Labor was not freely mobile, and wages and the intensity of labor varied considerably between branches of production, while there was no competition between enterprises and organizations and so no tendency to the reduction of labor-time to that socially necessary. The necessary labor-time was determined by centrally defined technical norms, according to the particular equipment installed, to accommodate the very uneven development of the forces of production. If we want to argue by analogy, the soviet system is much closer to the feudal than to the capitalist form of surplus appropriation. Soviet workers were obliged to work for the state, or face imprisonment for parasitism, and enterprises and organizations were obliged to make deliveries in kind to the state, with the requirements of the plan having the force of law.

Resnick and Wolff do not directly address the possibility of analyzing the Soviet Union as a system of state feudalism, although others have done so, rejecting such a view on the grounds that this would be to adopt a definition of class relations based on political power (cf. p. 244). However, the state was able to enforce its demands because it controlled the allocation of the means of production and subsistence and because it controlled a massive apparatus of repression. How do Resnick and Wolff explain the ability of the state or, in their case, the Council of Ministers, to appropriate the surplus other than through such an exercise of state power?

Although Resnick and Wolff characterize the Soviet Union as state capitalist, they are very concerned to insist on the primacy of class structure over political power, so they identify the capitalist class in the Soviet Union not with the state but with the Council of Ministers, who were supposedly the direct appropriators of the surplus. However, the Council of Ministers organized the production and appropriation of a surplus not for their own benefit, but as state functionaries, for the benefit of the state, just as the Board of Directors of a capitalist company supervises the production and appropriation of surplus value as functionaries of capital. Moreover, the supreme body in the Soviet Union was not the Council of Ministers, but the Politburo of the Communist Party of the Soviet Union, a body which is largely ignored in Resnick and Wolff's account, again, no doubt, because they are afraid of subsuming class processes under "the political." Finally, their theory does not explain the behavior of the Council of Ministers. They certainly did not behave like capitalists, who are compelled by competition to accumulate capital for its own sake, nor was more than a tiny portion of the surplus devoted to their personal consumption and aggrandizement. The surplus was devoted above all to the expanded reproduction of the state's military apparatus. Of course, it could be argued that rising military expenditure was imposed on soviet state capitalism as a condition of its survival, but this is an argument that has to be made and that would have to be supported by hard evidence, particularly as it was the burden of military expenditure that eventually led to the system's demise.

A central aim of Resnick and Wolff's book is to assert the desirability of communism, and characterizing the Soviet Union as state capitalist certainly simplifies this task. Resnick and Wolff define a communist class structure as one in which the people who collectively produce a surplus are identically those who appropriate and distribute it, although they recognize that it may be necessary for communist producers to employ managers to administer the appropriation and distribution of the surplus on their behalf. This would be unavoidable in a developed system of social production, since the surplus is there not produced and appropriated in individual production units, it is a social surplus, the net social product over and above that which is required to satisfy the consumption and reproduction needs of the population. In a capitalist society the appropriation and distribution of the surplus is achieved behind people's backs, through the market, but in a communist society the surplus must be appropriated and distributed self-consciously by society as a whole, even if this is done by assigning what Resnick and Wolff call "communist-administered values" to inputs and outputs, and then allowing individual production units to decide on the disposal of the nominal surpluses that arise.[1]

According to its own rhetoric, the Soviet Union was surely communist, as the term is defined by Resnick and Wolff. The surplus was appropriated and distributed by the state, under the leadership of the Party as the representative of the working class. If Resnick and Wolff want to deny that the Soviet Union was communist, in their terms, it could only be on the grounds that the claim of the Communist Party to represent the people who collectively produced the surplus was spurious. Thus, in terms of their own theory, the question of whether or not the Soviet Union was communist is inevitably a political question concerning the representative character of the Party-state, a position they vigorously denounce.

Alongside the state capitalist class structures in the Soviet Union, Resnick and Wolff identify the existence of "ancient," "feudal" and even "communist" class structures. The "ancient" class structures refer to petty production, primarily on peasant subsidiary plots and in urban secondary employment, and "communist" class structures refer to those (few, if any) collective farms in which effective institutions of collective governance existed. They also characterize households as having a "feudal" class structure, in which men appropriated the surplus labor of women or, in the event of widowhood, desertion or divorce, a non-exploitative "ancient" class structure. The characterization of the collective farms as archetypal communist institutions was the staple of soviet anti-communist jokes, but the idea that they collectively appropriated their own surplus is absurd. The collective farms were weighed down by state exactions to such an extent that the incomes of their members, which were a residual, were often forced far below the subsistence minimum. Most collective farmers could only survive by working their private plots, which were in turn subjected to severe restriction and punitive taxation, so that collective farmers were the most exploited of all soviet citizens. The characterization of work on the private plots as corresponding to an ancient class structure is also questionable, in terms of Resnick and Wolff's analysis, since they simultaneously characterize the class structure of the households that worked those plots as feudal, and it was certainly women who carried the main burden of working the plot. To characterize urban secondary employment as petty production is also subject to qualification, since plumbers, decorators, builders and electricians could not legally sell their services but generally helped out friends and neighbors in exchange for gifts in kind – a bucket of potatoes or a bottle of vodka. Finally, Resnick and Wolff completely ignore the role of slavery in the soviet system: from the 1930s to the 1950s a substantial portion of the population was used as slave labor in the system of prison camps.

The absurdity of analyzing class relations at the level of the production unit is brought out by this analysis of supplementary class structures. The collective farms, petty production and households were as much an integral part of the soviet system as were the state enterprises and the social position of their members was determined by their position in soviet society. Resnick and Wolff's attempt to analyze the significance of the soviet household in the reproduction of the soviet system is commendable, but characterizing households as having "feudal" or "ancient" class structures is extremely questionable. Soviet gender relations were not constructed within the household, but in the wider society, in particular by the obligations of men and women to the soviet state (Ashwin, 2000). Women certainly worked much longer hours than did men, but in what sense does this justify the assertion that the household was the site of the appropriation of women's surplus labor by men? Moreover, exclusive attention to the relation between husbands and wives ignores the significance of generational differences in the household.

Resnick and Wolff's analysis of the collapse of the Soviet Union relies heavily on their analysis of the role of petty production in the soviet system. First, because the mass of the population was unaware of Resnick and Wolff's theory, they were convinced by the official ideology that they were living under socialism, so there was no significant opposition of the working class to state capitalism and instead they sought outlets for their frustration in petty economic activity while social tension was expressed in the brutalization of social relations within the household. Second, petty production diverted people's time and energy and so contributed to the inability of the state to expand the surplus sufficiently to sustain industrial growth and to meet popular aspirations for rising living standards. Third, petty production supposedly provided the foundation for the only available counter-ideology to that of the soviet state, given that Resnick and Wolff's book was not available, which emphasized individualism against collectivism and private initiative against state bureaucracy and which underpinned the political opposition that grew in the 1980s. The collapse of the Soviet Union is therefore explained primarily as a cultural and political process that was underpinned by the persistence of petty production. This whole account is very speculative, with a minimum of evidence being provided in its support and with almost no reference to what actually happened in the Soviet Union in the 1980s.

The emphasis on the role of petty production arises because Resnick and Wolff are unable to identify the fundamental contradictions of the soviet system itself. One feature that distinguishes capitalism from all other modes of production, and that is the source of its dynamism, is the fact that the production and appropriation of surplus value are one and the same process, because the capitalist and his or her agents directly subordinate the process of production to the production of surplus value. The fundamental contradiction of the soviet mode of production, if we can call it that, was that, as in other non-capitalist forms of exploitation, the appropriation of a surplus was separated from its production, so the direct producers, and indeed every subordinate level of the system, had an interest not in maximizing but in minimizing the surplus produced. The essence of the repeated attempts at reform was not so much that they sought to decentralize management, as Resnick and Wolff emphasize, but that they sought to introduce quasi-market processes into the regulation of the system in order to provide incentives for de-centralized managers. Decentralizing and market regulation may have encouraged productivity increases, but they also weakened central control and undermined the appropriation of the surplus and so, before Gorbachev, were always reversed. The difference in the 1980s was that there seemed to be no alternative to such reforms so that once unleashed they were not reversed. Once the centre had lost control of its enterprises, by 1991 it had no alternative but to recognize the fact that market wages and prices had completely displaced state wages and prices and that enterprise directors had grabbed the freedom to manage as they wished. Price liberalization and privatization only gave juridical form to what had already happened spontaneously (Clarke, 2003; Clarke et al., 1993).

A lot of work has gone into the writing of this book, but I doubt that it will be of much interest beyond the narrow circle of devotees of Amherst Marxism.

NOTE

1. If the Soviet Union was capitalist, then it would be appropriate to use world market prices for this calculation, but at world market prices a large proportion of the soviet economy was value-subtracting – not only did many enterprises and organizations not produce any surplus value, they did not even cover their wage costs. In Resnick and Wolff's terms, this would mean that these workers, far from being exploited, were the recipients of a portion of the surplus value produced elsewhere, a non-class revenue distributed to them under a subsumed class process!

REFERENCES

Ashwin, S. (2000). *Gender, state and society in soviet and post-soviet Russia.* London and New York: Routledge.

Clarke, S. (2003). Globalisation and the subsumption of the soviet mode of production under capital. In: A. Saad-Filho (Ed.), *Anti-Capitalism*. London: Pluto.

Clarke, S., Fairbrother, P., Burawoy, M., & Krotov, P. (1993). *What about the workers? Workers and the transition to capitalism in Russia.* London: Verso.

CHURCHMAN'S DAVID RICARDO ON PUBLIC DEBT

Denis P. O'Brien

A review essay on Nancy Churchman's, *David Ricardo on Public Debt*. London: Palgrave, 2001.

This is a fair minded, temperate and well-written essay on Ricardo's treatment of the "National Debt" as it is known in the British literature. It hangs together, despite prior publication of the majority of the chapters, very well – only Chap. 5 (dealing with Ricardo's motives, and the imputation of personal financial interest) is unmistakably a journal article.

Chapter 1 discusses the different approaches to interpreting Ricardo – the Sraffian, neo-Classical, and what is called the "New View." The latter is Samuel Hollander's approach to Ricardo, as exemplified in his *Economics of David Ricardo* (1979). The irony of labelling, as a new view, an approach which is identified with that of Alfred Marshall, and thus dates from the late nineteenth century, is unremarked by the author. Churchman finds the "New View" a satisfactory starting point, and thus accepts the idea of Ricardo as an optimist, and as somebody with an almost neo-Walrasian approach to resource allocation. But in practice this does not make any fundamental difference to the development of her argument, though it is reflected in the treatment of resource allocation in Chap. 2.

Chapter 2, "Public Debt and the Economics of David Ricardo," considers three aspects of Ricardo's treatment of debt; the effect on resource allocation, the effect on economic growth, and "optimal taxation." Chapter 3 discusses the Ricardo-Malthus debate on public debt, and considers Ricardo's views on government. Chapter 4 deals with Ricardo's adoption of the eighteenth century proposal for

Research in the History of Economic Thought and Methodology A Research Annual
Research in the History of Economic Thought and Methodology, Volume 22-A, 365–372
Copyright © 2004 by Elsevier Ltd.
All rights of reproduction in any form reserved
ISSN: 0743-4154/doi:10.1016/S0743-4154(03)22023-X

a capital levy to pay off the debt. Chapter 5 counters the accusation of Anderson and Tollison that Ricardo had a *personal* financial interest in his plans for the debt. Finally, a short Chap. 6, taken from an entry in *An Encyclopedia of Keynesian Economics* (Cate et al., 1997), discusses briefly the topics of fiscal stimulation of aggregate demand, and "Ricardian Equivalence." The book is completed by a Summary and Conclusions and by brief appendices dealing with such widely diverse topics as data on government expenditure, revenue, and debt (Appendices A, B and F), public debt theory before Ricardo (Appendix C, only a page and a half), capital levy proposals after World War I (D), Ricardo's parliamentary voting record (E), and a list of Ricardo's "colleagues and correspondents" (G). There is a full bibliography, which seems to relate to a larger study, containing as it does a number of items not referred to in the book.

Reviewing the work as a whole, it is apparent that the author is generous to Ricardo, perhaps inevitably given that he is the focus of the study. Certainly she is more generous than I feel able to be. At all events she believes that Ricardo did not rely on telescoping the long-run and short-run together even though, as I shall argue, there seems to be plenty of evidence to the contrary. Moreover she feels that Ricardo's treatment of debt sheds light on the rest of Ricardo's work. She is occasionally prone to claim a good deal for Ricardo; even that his "work on public debt was an important step in the evolution of modern public finance theory and is still highly relevant today" (p. 112). This seems to me, as I shall explain, very dubious. (These claims are perhaps at their strongest in the final Summary and Conclusion of the book.) But throughout, the argument is so fair-minded that the evidence assembled can easily lead the reader – and at times clearly leads the author – to less favourable conclusions.

One of the things which emerges clearly from this study is that Ricardo was an extraordinarily intransigent individual. At the beginning and end of the book, the author seems to take the conventional view that Ricardo was open-minded and willing to change his mind (pp. 1, 127). Yet all the evidence from the Ricardo-Malthus correspondence is that this was the last thing that Ricardo was prepared to do. After reviewing the concerns of Malthus with aggregate demand, both with regard to a significant reduction in government expenditure and the effect of a sudden repayment of public debt, the author quite rightly uses the words "obdurate and unreasonable" (p. 69) to describe the impression created by Ricardo's responses to Malthus. She feels, however, that Ricardo feared that Malthus's position on the matter of aggregate demand would encourage government profligacy. But given the scale of post-war unemployment, Ricardo's position reflects a welfare function that not many would find appealing, and indeed one that many of his contemporaries did not (O'Brien, 1999, Vol. 3). Of course Ricardo's intransigence was not confined to his treatment of the unfortunate

Malthus; as we shall see, he simply disregarded reasonable objections made by his contemporaries to his plans for war finance and for debt redemption.

There is also the matter of the partial repudiation of the debt, implied in Ricardo's proposals. Ricardo did not propose to redeem the debt at par. He made great verbal play with the need for justice, as the author shows; and yet he proposed to redeem the debt at 70. Churchman notes (pp. 76–77) that Cannan pointed out long ago that this involved a partial repudiation. (Unfortunately Churchman herself confuses par with market value.) The author feels that this can be justified on the grounds that Ricardo thought that the alternative was public bankruptcy. But there is no evidence that Ricardo, unlike McCulloch, or Smith, actually anticipated public bankruptcy – and all that seems to be available is a rather imprecise letter to Ricardo's friend, Trower. The injustice of this procedure is all the more evident when one realises that Ricardo supported government borrowing in the 3%s rather than the 5%s, during the war, since the discount on the 3%s would be smaller, and they would be expected to recover to par after the war (Ricardo, 1820, pp. 184–185).

But what is really striking is the way in which Ricardo assumed instantaneous achievement of long-run equilibrium. Malthus's objections to *sudden* debt redemption make good sense. It is not necessary to be a wholehearted subscriber to a capital-stock adjustment theory to accept that the sudden redemption of debt involved a serious capital market disruption. Ricardo airily assumed that gilt-edged holders could invest elsewhere without difficulty. He simply dismissed the effects on the capital market of the removal of public debt as an outlet for saving (Ricardo, 1820, pp. 175–182).

Malthus envisaged the possibility of excessive savings and investment, especially if public debt holders suddenly had to find alternative employment for their funds. But Ricardo unhesitatingly telescoped the long and the short run together, arguing that, were investment excessive, people would reduce it until the rate of return on it was again acceptable – which of course did not rule out short term (and indeed medium term) problems at all. In the end, some of Malthus's points may have made some impression; in a document discovered only many years later (Asso & Barucci, 1988), Ricardo seems to have come round to the idea of an elongated payment schedule, to cushion the impact of the redemption. But this never saw the light of day in his own lifetime.

Generously, the author feels that much of this can be explained because of Ricardo's antipathy to government (though it was not explained by him in these terms). In Chap. 3 she argues, as did Roberts in his classic article on Ricardo and public debt (Roberts, 1942), that Ricardo had an overwhelming desire to reduce government to an absolute minimum. But, to be blunt, this was an extraordinarily bigoted approach on his part; unlike, Smith, McCulloch, Say, or J. S. Mill, and many others, Ricardo never actually considered the role of government seriously (though he borrowed some material from Say), and the author has to scrape around for material to try to assemble Ricardo's views on it. She rightly concedes that "Ricardo's views on the economic role of government appear at times to be impossibly narrow" (p. 57).

Ricardo's long-run to short-run telescope was also employed in his concept of an ideal tax system – one which oddly does not appear in the "Optimal taxation" section of the book (pp. 43–46). Ricardo believed that a tax on wage-goods, together with a tax on rent, and a tax on income from government securities, would provide the ideal tax system. Indeed, if the cost of meeting the debt service charge could be eliminated, the customs and excise could be got rid of (Ricardo, 1817–1821, pp. 159–161). But the tax on wage goods was supposed to be passed on – since wages were at subsistence (as Ricardo explicitly says). Certainly Ricardo argued that it would be passed on, and therefore be equivalent to a tax on profits, without the need to assess profits directly for taxation. This would clearly take a long time, and involve a population adjustment. But Ricardo wrote as if such adjustment was unproblematic.

Similarly, Ricardo made an amazing claim about the ease of paying hugely increased wartime taxes. "We think that great efforts would be made to save the tax out of their income, in which case they could obtain the money from this source; but suppose they could not, what should hinder them from selling a part of their property for money, or of borrowing it at interest?" (Ricardo, 1820, p. 188 and cf. *ibid.*, p. 197). Thus Ricardo envisaged that, if the entire cost of a war were borne out of taxation, people would simply be able to cut back on consumption to meet the tax bill (Ricardo, 1817–1821, p. 247, 1820, pp. 187–188) so that the national capital stock would not be reduced by government consuming capital through the issue of public sector debt. In the event that, after all, some taxpayers were not able to meet this charge, they would simply have to borrow (Ricardo, 1817–1821, p. 245). The idea that, as a result, they would have to borrow at a higher rate of interest than the State, and that, in turn, their remaining property would have to be written down because of the annual charge on it, seems not to have troubled Ricardo. As Churchman argues (pp. 62–63), such an attitude seems also to have characterised Ricardo's attitude to the burden that a capital levy would impose upon the taxpayers. Indeed, his attitude was dismissive. "It is difficult to make these men [landed proprietors] understand that the payment of £1,000 per annum, is a heavier burden than the payment of £20,000 once for all." (Ricardo to McCulloch in 1952b, p. 238). (Churchman oddly refers to this as money illusion on the part of the landowners – p. 38.)

Ricardo's optimism that the long run could be telescoped into the short run is nowhere more evident than in his argument that the value of property would be written down by the present value of a future stream of debt service charges, so that there was an immediate burden more or less equivalent to an immediate tax burden. Not only does this ignore the point about the high cost of borrowing by individuals forced to pay increased taxes, and the fact that his assumption about the long run extended to the belief that people would continue the capitalisation process beyond their life expectancy, but he ignored completely the fact that heavy wartime taxes would fall disproportionately upon property, as would a capital levy, to the significant advantage of the professional classes. When this point was drawn to his attention, he dismissed it; the earnings of the professional classes would simply be adjusted to take account of their favoured tax position. It hardly needs emphasising how long that would take.

Ricardo remained unmoved by this and other objections. He even made the bizarre claim that "The greatest advantage that would attend war-taxes would be, the little permanent derangement that they would cause to the industry of the country" (Ricardo, 1820, p. 189). Of course it all depends on what is meant by "permanent"; but a clearer example of telescoping the long run and short run together could hardly be sought.

On the other hand, Churchman is quite right to argue that "Ricardian Equivalence" is not Ricardo's idea. The irony is however that, as Churchman makes clear (p. 38), Ricardo actually argued that taxation was *better* than debt creation. Rather than adopting the now standard case against such equivalence, which argues that the burden of debt is *less than* the burden of taxation, because so much debt would remain uncapitalised, he held that the true burden of debt was actually greater than that of taxation.

The issue of taxation brings us to the strange matter of Ricardo and the income tax. Quite understandably, given that there are only three brief and unimportant mentions of this hotly disputed tax in the whole of Ricardo's *Principles* (1817–1821, pp. 152–153, 160–161, 208), Churchman has to fall back upon allusions in Ricardo's correspondence. Yet, there are remarkably few even of these. But as Ricardo's contemporaries, such as Preston (1816) and Buchanan (1817), argued cogently, the root of the problems of post-Napoleonic war public finance lay in the abolition in 1816 of Pitt's income tax. Thus Buchanan pointed out that by 1814 the income tax was yielding no less than £14.6 million – or approximately half the annual charge to service the public debt. Churchman is able to argue that Ricardo did not wish to see the income tax continued, both on grounds of privacy and of its possible encouragement of government extravagance. But to consider a capital levy (which, as Churchman points out, would also involve difficult problems of assessment) at a rate which Asso and Barrucci (1988), in an excellent treatment, have shown amounted to no less than 25%, as preferable to the very modest levels of income tax levied up to 1816 (between 5 and 10%), seems eccentric, to put it no stronger.

Preston (1816) and Hamilton (1818) were just two of Ricardo's contemporaries who wrote cogently on questions of public finance. It is unfortunate that the academic tradition of focusing on Ricardo, to the exclusion of other individuals, leads to a somewhat lop-sided picture of the literature. When so many other of Ricardo's contemporaries were writing on the national debt, and when there was a substantial literature dating, as a volume later assembled by McCulloch (1857) showed, back to 1710, to deal with all that in an appendix (Appendix C) of a page and a half is bound, however unintentionally, to sustain false ideas of Ricardo's importance and originality in this field of inquiry.

In particular, Ricardo owed a very substantial debt to Robert Hamilton (1818) – the material in Ricardo's article "Funding System" on the Sinking Fund (Ricardo, 1820, pp. 149–172) not only drew a considerable amount from Hamilton's remarkable work but was rather less well expressed. Nor, as McCulloch repeatedly emphasised, was Ricardo's proposal for a capital levy new. It dated from Archibald Hutcheson who published such a proposal in 1714. Indeed, according to Henry Brougham, who drew attention to Hutcheson, the idea had been proposed to every Chancellor of the Exchequer (in Ricardo, 1952a, pp. 40–41). Not surprisingly, and as Churchman points out, there was a well-developed critique of the idea before Ricardo adopted it. Indeed, Brougham said that it would "place the property for five years at the mercy of all the solicitors, conveyancers, and money-hunters in the country" (*ibid.*). Ricardo's response to this was to propose security of title for land assessed; but this was hardly an adequate solution, given all the valuation problems also involved.

Ricardo thus came rather late into a field already containing many excellent treatments of public debt issues. Indeed one of the writers who was significantly in advance of Ricardo was none other than McCulloch who, in two versions of an essay on the national debt, published in 1816 (McCulloch, 1816a, b), argued at length for the necessity of reducing the debt service charge because of the damaging effects on agriculture and manufacturing. He even included an agricultural cobweb in the argument. Several years before Ricardo (although the idea comes from Smith in any case), McCulloch endorsed the idea (one central to Ricardo's argument about the adverse effect on economic growth of government borrowing) that government borrowing reduces the national capital stock by converting capital to (government) consumption.

Churchman argues that Ricardo was unique in emphasising the allocative effects of debt service taxation. This seems to me to stretch a point considerably. What Ricardo did was to emphasise this aspect of the debt service charge while, unlike writers like Say and McCulloch, rejecting any effect on total output of such a charge. Most of Ricardo's arguments – the risk of capital migration, the consumption of capital as government revenue, and the distorting effects of taxes – were common enough after Smith. It is however ironic that Ricardo's solution to the problem of potential capital flight was to adopt the idea of a capital levy, as well as advocating war-time taxes at such a level that they could hardly avoid falling on capital.

In all this there seems no reason to doubt Ricardo's probity. The author, correctly in my view, opposes the claim by Anderson and Tollison that Ricardo's support for the idea of a capital levy to pay off the debt was to further his own financial interests as a new landed proprietor – a claim which was never very plausible, given that any resulting increase in the value of land, because of a reduction in the taxation previously necessary to service the debt, would be a minor consideration compared with the fact that the landowners would be first in the firing line for a capital levy. Rather it seems reasonable to take the view that Ricardo – whose loan contracting fortune amounted, in modern terms, to around £12 million – was showing considerable disinterestedness in seeking a contraction of the market for public debt, albeit that such a contraction would have had an immediate negative effect upon the fortunes of Ricardo's particular bête noir, the Bank of England, whose management of the debt he regarded as a "job."

But that said, there do seem to be strong reasons to doubt both Ricardo's originality in dealing with public debt issues, and his common sense. Nonetheless, Churchman's book is a welcome addition to the literature on Classical public finance. Her account, while kind to Ricardo, is fair and balanced, but precisely because it has these admirable qualities, it is possible to feel that Ricardo deserves a good deal less generosity for his public finance writings.

REFERENCES

Asso, P. F., & Barucci, E. (1988). Ricardo on the national debt and its redemption: Some notes on an unpublished manuscript. *Economic Notes, 2*, 5–36.

Buchanan, D. (1817). *Observations on the subjects treated of in Dr. Smith's inquiry into the nature and causes of the wealth of nations.* Edinburgh: Oliphant, Waugh and Innes.

Cate, T., Harcourt, G., & Colander, D. (Eds) (1997). *An encyclopedia of Keynesian economics.* Cheltenham: Edward Elgar.

Hamilton, R. (1818). *An inquiry concerning the rise and progress, the redemption and present state, and the management of the national debt of Great Britain* (3rd ed.). Edinburgh: Oliphant, Waugh and Innes.

Hollander, S. (1979). *The economics of David Ricardo.* Toronto: University of Toronto Press.

Hutcheson, A. (1714). *Some considerations relating to the payment of the public debts, humbly offered to the commons of Great-Britain in parliament assembled. By a member of the House of Commons. A proposal for the payment of the public debts, and an account of some things mentioned in parliament on that occasion.* London.

McCulloch, J. R. (1816a). *An essay on a reduction of the interest of the national debt, proving that this is the only possible means of relieving the distresses of the commercial and agricultural interests; and establishing the justice of that measure on the surest principles of political economy.* London: Mawman and Edinburgh: Brown.

McCulloch, J. R. (1816b). *Essay on the question of reducing the interest of the national debt; in which the justice and expediency of that measure are fully established.* Edinburgh: Brown and Black.

McCulloch, J. R. (Ed.) (1857). *A select collection of scarce and valuable tracts and other publications, on the national debt and the sinking fund, from the originals of Harley, Gould, Pulteney, Walpole, Hume, Price, Hamilton and others.* Reprinted London: Pickering and Chatto, 1995.

O'Brien, D. P. (Ed.) (1999). *The history of taxation* (8 vols). London: Pickering and Chatto.

Preston, R. (1816). *A review of the present ruined condition of the landed and agricultural interests.* London: Law and Whitaker.

Ricardo, D. (1817–1821). *On the principles of political economy and taxation. The works and correspondence of David Ricardo.* P. Sraffa (Ed.), with M. H. Dobb (Vol. I). Cambridge: Cambridge University Press, 1951.

Ricardo, D. (1820). Funding system, from the Supplement to the 4th–6th editions of *Encyclopaedia Britannica. The Works and Correspondence of David Ricardo.* P. Sraffa (Ed.), with M. H. Dobb (Vol. IV, pp. 149–200). Cambridge: Cambridge University Press, 1951.

Ricardo, D. (1952a). *Speeches and evidence. The works and correspondence of David Ricardo.* P. Sraffa (Ed.), with M. H. Dobb (Vol. V). Cambridge: Cambridge University Press.

Ricardo, D. (1952b). *Letters 1819–June 1821. The works and correspondence of David Ricardo.* P. Sraffa (Ed.), with M. H. Dobb (Vol. VIII). Cambridge: Cambridge University Press.

Roberts, R. O. (1942). Ricardo's theory of public debts. *Economica, NS 9,* 257–266.

ECONOMICS, BIOLOGY, AND CULTURE: HODGSON ON HISTORY

Alexander J. Field

A review essay on Geoffrey Hodgson's, *How Economics Forgot History: The Problem of Historical Specificity in Social Science*. London: Routledge, 2001.

This book addresses what the author claims, with considerable justification, to be the foremost challenge confronting the social and behavioral sciences today: the problem of historical specificity. Hodgson poses the question by asking whether we need different theories to understand social and economic behavior in different societies at different stages of their development. He answers the question in the affirmative, and criticizes the economics profession for suggesting that there is one universal model or theory equally suited to all economies and societies at all times. He faults the profession further for no longer worrying much or conducting serious debate about this issue, a development he attributes to the eclipse and eventual demise of institutionalism and historical economics in England, Germany, and the United States.

The book is most provocative as a contribution to intellectual history. Hodgson acknowledges that "the key methodological problem, of the relationship between the individual and society, dogged the historical school for its entire existence and was never satisfactorily resolved" (p. 64). On the other hand, he rejects the notion that institutionalism and historical economics died in the face of superior, more compelling evidence or arguments. He attributes the loss of influence to a set of particular political and historical events that might have been different. In a nutshell, these schools of thought died because of idiosyncratic developments at

Research in the History of Economic Thought and Methodology A Research Annual
Research in the History of Economic Thought and Methodology, Volume 22-A, 373–398
© 2004 Published by Elsevier Ltd.
ISSN: 0743-4154/doi:10.1016/S0743-4154(03)22024-1

Harvard University and the London School of Economics, combined with the intellectual evisceration of German universities with the rise of fascism. The final nail
in the coffin was the triumph of Keynesianism at Harvard and Cambridge: Keynes'
work was almost completely devoid of any concern for the problem (while true,
the sin seems far less egregious than in the case of Robbins[1]). Post-Keynesians, in
continuing to aspire to a "General Theory," have done no better.

This is an ambitious work. In the process of looking backward, it raises a number of important issues relevant to how we should conduct social and economic
inquiry in the future. The last part of Hodgson's book, however, which tries to lay
out an agenda for such research, is, by the author's acknowledgement, the least
satisfactory (p. 273). In spite of all his critical efforts, he seems unable to delineate
a compelling vision of how research in institutional economics, or in the behavioral
sciences more generally, should now be conducted.

Thus, the central puzzle posed by this book. Why does his scholarship, and
other scholarship in this tradition, not break open new vistas? Why is it unlikely
to be successful in overcoming the malaise of many social scientists, both within
and outside of economics, who recognize the potentially independent influence
of culture, social structure, or institutional rules on behavior, but seem unable to
enunciate a research program that goes beyond on the one hand description of such
influences, and on the other hand periodic attacks on the "neoclassical" or rational
choice orthodoxy?

My intent in the remainder of this essay is to explore why Hodgson, and so
many others of both heterodox and orthodox persuasions, continue to confront such
difficulty in moving forward. Perhaps there is only so far this style of intellectual
history can take us in advancing social science. Perhaps also it has become too
easy to settle into well-established (and largely justified) critiques of rational choice
theory as it is actually practiced. Getting into the rhythm of these critiques can feel
like putting on a set of well-worn clothes. It's an easy thing to do because they're
probably right where we put them down last night.

But if we continue to wear the same outfits day after day, there begins to be
a downside. When we no longer innovate, our sartorial displays cease inspiring
enthusiasm in those who observe them and ultimately in ourselves as well. I am
not recommending shopping for its own sake – our consumerist society contains
enough exhortations to this end already. But, if I may now extract myself from
this metaphor, we do need new approaches, because as social scientists, *we
are making relatively little scientific progress in developing robust predictive
models of human behavior*. Hodgson obviously very much wants to provide that
intellectual leadership. But although this is original scholarship, one puts it down
with the sense that it could have been written in the 1960s or 1970s, perhaps
even earlier.

Well, what of it? In some areas of scholarship, such as political theory or philosophy, it still makes sense to start with texts written hundreds or even thousands of years ago. At the same time, it is quite evident that in areas of the natural sciences such as chemistry and biology, we have made remarkable explanatory and predictive breakthroughs in recent centuries and decades. To say of a recently published book in these fields that it has a certain nineteenth century feel to it would not be to praise it.

Some will rationalize the current state of affairs by asking whether the study of human behavior can or should be a progressive scientific endeavor. Ariel Rubinstein, for example, has argued that economic theory simply should not be "a tool for predicting or describing real human behavior." As to what makes a "good" economic model, intuition should suffice as an evaluative criterion: if it's good enough for philosophy, it ought to be good enough for economic theory (2001, p. 616). I find this position unacceptable and believe Hodgson does as well.

Most of us work in divisions of social or behavioral sciences, not divisions of social philosophy. We are supposed to be doing *science*. Rubinstein has the courage to acknowledge weaknesses in the record of game theory, for example, in actually illuminating human interaction. The problem, of course, is more general. The social and behavioral sciences, by which I mean principally economics, sociology, anthropology, political science, and psychology, do not, either individually or collectively, have a good recent track record on this account. Balkanized, and recapitulating some of the same debates again and again, in many respects social science discourse is enervated and, to those who read it, enervating. This is as true of work in institutional economics or traditional sociology or anthropology as it is in those who favor rational choice approaches.[2]

Rubinstein's position, which is more broadly shared than many will publicly acknowledge, at least as they apply for grants from the National *Science* Foundation, is that the failure to make more progress developing a predictive or explanatory agenda should not be held against us, and in fact he suggests that it might have been detrimental had we been more successful: business students and the military would just have misused the knowledge.[3] Message to world: leave us be to develop our aesthetically pleasing models. This position is remarkably similar to those of cultural anthropologists or sociologists who characterize their work as interpretive rather than explanatory, and finesse questions about the extent to which their propositions are falsifiable. If none of the propositions we are advancing in the different disciplines can be disproved, it is a waste of time talking about unifying the social sciences, because none of us is doing science.

Not everyone is satisfied with the proposition that we have no responsibility to develop models or tools that can predict or explain human behavior, and many genuinely want to try and improve upon the current situation. It is one thing, however, to call for the unification of the social sciences, quite another (and far more difficult) to take real steps in that direction. The majority of scholars, particularly before receiving tenure, remain within disciplinary bailiwicks, continuing along well-established paths. But a minority, frustrated with the inability of prevailing theoretical frameworks to explain anomalous data, or in some cases the imperviousness of such frameworks to any imaginable data, venture into new territory.

Often, however, the result is something akin to religious conversion: explorers embrace the intellectual framework of another discipline uncritically, with recent converts becoming even more fervent advocates than long time residents. Because of the history of balkanization, there is no disciplinary tradition that does not currently suffer from some form of intellectual pathology, and it's a difficult matter, from an internal or an external perspective, to separate diseased from healthy tissue. But it's naïve to think such segregation is any less important in areas outside of one's own. A good rule of thumb for adventurers is this: conditions in other regions are likely to be as complex and disordered as those domestically. This should not discourage exploration. But embracing without critical examination work in other disciplines can be as unproductive as simply ignoring it. This is true for those moving in either direction between the two main social scientific traditions: the economic/rational choice and the traditional sociological/anthropological approach.

The reality is that data and concepts useful for building a general framework for understanding human behavior are scattered throughout the social, behavioral, and natural sciences. But there is also a lot of chaff, often protected by the stiff tariffs that discourage integrative or cross-disciplinary work. Separating or distilling what is useful from what is not is challenging. As we push forward we need scholars who understand the limitations and strengths of their own tradition, and are also prepared to search out and identify the limitations and strengths in others.

Hodgson's book is principally concerned with variation over time in a region's institutional structures and the consequences of such variation for behavior within them, and with intellectual attempts to deal with this issue. If one wants to move beyond consideration of consequences to a more general theory addressing both commonalities of human institutions and their variation, one is drawn, almost inevitably, to consideration of the influences on behavior of our biology and evolutionary history. This helps explain why, to the degree that this book moves beyond intellectual history, it is as much about biology as it is about history. Hodgson's appeal to reintroduce a serious interest in biological influences on human behavior is welcome (and consistent with some of his earlier work), but weak on specifics or serious critical treatment of the cross-currents in evolutionary thinking that would be necessary to implement this.

STRENGTHS AND LIMITATIONS OF INSTITUTIONALISM

We must begin, of course, by understanding the strengths and limitations of our own approach. If we are to make progress, it is necessary to examine carefully the institutionalist position, to view it not just as a battering ram with which to inflict damage on currently prevailing orthodoxies, but to identify the strengths and weaknesses in its current incarnations. In so doing, we must be critical as well as constructive.

Hodgson asks rhetorically if we need different models or theories to understand different societies in different historical epochs. His is, as suggested, a rhetorical question, preparing the ground in this case for an affirmative answer, one with which many readers of his book will be inclined to agree. But there is a strong case that this initial and fundamental question should be answered in the negative, and indeed has to be answered in the negative, if we are serious about integrating the social and behavioral sciences in a way that will foster a progressive scientific enterprise. The case for this position does not, however, involve embracing rational choice models based on the assumption that human preferences are stable, transitive, *and* narrowly selfish.[4] Such models predict that humans will operate in all spheres so as efficiently to advance their material self-interest. This approach is inadequate as a foundation for addressing the political and cultural variables that define the arena within which we economize, or operate according to the counsel of our foraging algorithms (Field, 2001).

Our biological hardware is basically unchanged from what it was 12,000 years ago, at the start of the Neolithic transition. Any model that purports to explain or predict how people behave must come to terms with the fact that across cultures today, or across time in history, groups of human actors are virtually identical in their species typical characteristics. My point is not to deny variation in individual biological and cognitive characteristics, but to emphasize that variation among group averages is relatively insignificant, and certainly too small to account for the types of differences in behavior with which Hodgson is concerned.

We are, of course, more than our biology. Then, as now, we possess evolved capabilities to learn by direct observation reinforced by instruction and imitation of others. We are not blank slates: this learning has biases, in the sense that we learn more easily in certain directions than in others. These differential predispositions, the consequence of evolutionary influences on our genetic heritage, have been most clearly demonstrated in language acquisition, but it is true as well of how we learn to interact with other humans. These biases nevertheless allow a great deal of flexibility. Ultimately it is what we and our forebears have done with these capabilities that distinguishes us from our neolithic ancestors, and distinguishes denizens of technologically advanced societies from hunter-gatherer groups.

Learning can affect not only the means we use but also to some degree the ends we deem important. Parents are remarkably successful in passing on to their children not only language vocabularies and recipes for making cake (transforming inputs into outputs), but also religious beliefs and ethical principles. Infantrymen are routinely trained to throw themselves on a grenade to protect other members of their squad. And organized political forces in the Middle East have been able to motivate substantial numbers of individuals to act as suicide bombers. The latter two instances are particularly stark examples of individuals expressing behaviors that, from a narrowly selfish perspective, are strictly dominated strategies. Contrary to those who insist that preferences are strictly exogenous and not to be disputed, human goals can to some degree be influenced. This is particularly relevant in considering political behavior, which extends beyond realms such as electoral politics to economic interactions that often also have a political component (the main exceptions are those mediated by purely competitive markets).

The partial programmability of human cognitive processes and behavioral inclinations has made possible variations in human culture, which in turn help account for behavioral differences beyond those that can be swept back to differences in the non-human environment. A large part of anthropology has been devoted to documenting cultural influences on human behavior distinguishable from those of the non-human environment. Traditional anthropologists, sociologists and institutional economists have correctly rejected as a methodologically individualist fallacy the claim that we can understand everything about a society by considering the characteristics of just one individual human. Thus, Hodgson is absolutely right that "institutions are not simply human nature writ large" (p. 269).

Nevertheless, culture and social structure are not superorganic forces with powers or influence or dynamics ultimately irreducible to aggregated characteristics of individuals, in particular beliefs about how the world works, who is friend and who is foe, who deserves deference and who does not, and what are the desirable ends of human activity.

Methodological individualism has been a traditional bête noire of institutionalist economics. While the institutionalist critique of economic and rational choice theory as it is commonly practiced has much to recommend it, we will make no scientific progress if we go the superorganic route and mystify culture, social structure, or institutions. Institutionalists need to make peace with the principle of methodological individualism, cease the unending critiques of reductionism, at the same time rejecting a version of methodological individualism that is not sustainable while working to develop and advance one that is. Granted, we cannot hope to understand human behavior by studying the characteristics of a single individual. But we can hope to do so by studying the aggregated characteristics of groups of individuals.

Institutions are not human nature writ large. But species typical behavioral predispositions – human universals – do govern and restrain the range of social variation. All known human groupings proscribe incest, murder within the group, and excessive within-group lying and cheating. It is of course possible that these outcomes reflect independently arrived at cultural solutions to universal challenges of coping with other closely affiliated conspecifics (members of the same species). But precisely because these challenges are universal and recurring, it is likely that the behavioral inclinations that support them have a biological and genetic substrate.

It is also likely, given what we observe in closely related species such as chimpanzees, that humans have biologically conditioned inclinations both to dominate other conspecifics, and to submit to those dominant, as well as more egalitarian tendencies that lie at the foundation of our ability to sustain democratic societies and collectively restrain would-be dictators. These different and some-times opposed impulses make human nature contradictory and human individuals ambivalent about their behavior, but they are the raw material from which we have fashioned a variety of political cultures. Variation in institutions, which I take to be formal descriptions of rules governing human interactions, is a reflection of political cultures which have varied considerably across groups and over time.

Hodgson argues, and I would agree with him, that individuals embedded in different cultures organized by different institutions will behave differently, above and beyond the differences that can be attributed to variations in the non-human environment. But the influence of culture or formal institutions (I do not suggest that they are coextensive) needs to be understood with reference to the aggregated characteristics of those whose behavior they influence. We cannot make progress by suggesting that these forces operate at some higher level still, and that we need entirely different models to understand behavior in different cultural milieus. Cultural variation represents differences in the patterns that emerge from aggregation of the beliefs (about states of the world and desirable ends of human activity) of individuals who comprise a group. They represent different parameter values in what must eventually be seen as a general model of human behavior.

The fundamental position of the "old" institutional economics, of which I take Hodgson to be a proponent, is that institutional variation, like the cultural variation in which it is embedded, influences human behavior in ways that cannot be swept back to variation in the non-human environment. I fully endorse this position, but the most interesting current work reflecting this point of view is not being carried forward by people who call themselves institutional economists. It moves forward under such banners as mechanism design, or among those formulating tax or regulatory policy, or among advisors to transition economies, which have proved to be real life laboratories for studying the consequences of major variation in rules. Here we find practical applications of institutional economics, but it is perhaps telling that so little of this work is today called by this name.

If institutional economists wish to have a significant impact on public policy, as did John Commons, they should be at the forefront of discussions of regulatory policy, or how to design spectrum auctions, or what kind of legal system would best serve a transition economy. If, on the other hand, institutional economics has larger ambitions to serve as a launching pad for integration of the social sciences, then it needs to move beyond its current niche habitat (largely backward-looking intellectual history) and participate in a broader scientific effort to bring the social, behavioral, and historical sciences together using an approach that integrates findings from the biological and related sciences as well as evolutionary theory.

This appears to be Hodgson's aspiration, and indeed one of the more provocative parts of the book is his discussion of how institutional economists gradually abandoned Veblen's interest in a Jamesian human psychology that recognized instincts (even if we don't call them that today) and the often contradictory impulses that influence human behavior ("the original foundations of institutionalism, in Darwinism and instinct psychology, were removed" (p. 181). Still, I think Hodgson exaggerates here. He has made a case that Veblen embraced these views, but it's not at all clear that many in the German historical school, or other American institutionalists, such as Commons, did.

Whatever may have been the degree of interest of early institutional economists in psychology, if we are serious about bringing biology back into the social sciences, and consider evolution not just as a metaphor for the differential survivability of firms or technology, it is desirable that, as economists, we educate ourselves about debates within evolutionary theory, most particularly those surrounding multilevel selection (Boehm, 1999; Field, 2001; Sober & Wilson, 1998; Wilson & Sober, 1994). Understanding what's at stake here is essential if we wish critically to evaluate work that has been done in the past quarter century in such areas as sociobiology or evolutionary psychology. There is much to learn from reading these literatures, but it is a mistake to suspend critical judgment in a headlong rush to embrace them. Institutions, however we agree to define them, are a subset of culture, and developing a clear understanding of the ways in which biology does and does not limit cultural variation and political behavior is essential in piecing together a framework for understanding human action that integrates genetic, cultural, and environmental influences.

Although I would expect Hodgson to be sympathetic towards such a program, he has not seriously engaged the literatures necessary in order to carry this forward. This leads me to question whether intellectual history of this sort, which sometimes (although less frequently here than in other work in this genre) bogs down in the reification and subsequent manipulation of concepts and ideas, can serve as a foundation for the kind of focused discourse necessary to overcome the isolation and fragmentation of the disciplines and subdisciplines. Relatively successful as intellectual history, this book is disappointing as a contribution to social or behavioral science.

If we are to make progress in understanding and explaining human behavior, we need a general theoretical approach that is capable of handling the variety of conditions under which humans do and have lived. Since we are partially programmable, such a model or theoretical approach will make different predictions depending on differences in the parameter values assumed. There is more at stake here than semantic differences over what we mean by the word "different."

THE CENTRAL APPEAL OF INSTITUTIONALISM

No social scientist can deny that taking a broad view of history and geography, humans exhibit and have exhibited an enormous variation in their social organization and the level of technological proficiency that has undergirded their material standard of living. If we step back from this variation and think in very general terms, there are ultimately three types of explanations for why this variation exists: (a) it reflects systematic genetic differences among different human groups; (b) it is the result of different but rational responses to varying environmental conditions; and (c) it reflects variation in culture.

A variety of evidence suggests that the first type of model cannot provide us much traction. Although there are significant genetically determined phenotypical differences influencing physical appearance, cognitive abilities, and behavior within any group of humans, the systematic differences among *groups* are relatively small. It is quite unlikely that these differences can have had more than a small impact on observed cross sectional socio-economic variation among groups. Secondly, if we consider the historical evolution of human groups, it is also quite unlikely that there has been very much genetic evolution affecting significant species typical behavioral or cognitive traits since the Neolithic revolution.

There has been some. The most well-documented is the evolution of lactose tolerance among populations with a pastoral or dairying tradition (most adult humans, like most other mature mammals, cannot digest dairy products). These variations among groups would, since they are the consequence of dependence on dairying, have to have arisen subsequent to the agricultural revolution. Another often mentioned case involves the high frequencies of genes predisposing to sickle cell anemia in populations of African descent. The relevant gene in its homozygous form causes the debilitating disease but in its heterozygous form provides resistance to malaria. Because of its fitness-enhancing effect in regions prone to malaria, natural selection has led to increases in gene frequencies in populations long resident in such regions, whereas obviously selection in malaria-free zones has not permitted these genes to gain much of a foothold.

What is perhaps striking about these instances, however, is that they very nearly exhaust the set of well-documented cases of *recent* environmental influences on the genetic composition of human groups.

An inescapable question is whether it is possible that there have been others of greater behavioral significance. Could it be, for example, that populations with a tradition of technological innovativeness have coevolved cognitive adaptations that make them more facile, on average, at navigating within such environments? One reason for doubting that this has been true, aside from the relatively small differences between measurements of average group IQs, is that within modern societies, those with the greatest command and proficiency with technologies have tended to have high income, wealth, or socioeconomic status. In country after country these variables have also tended to correlate with lower fertility, a maladaptive behavior with respect to natural selection and reproductive fitness, but one that would have acted against gene culture coevolution in this direction.

Until the 1930s hunter-gatherer societies existed in the interior of New Guinea completely isolated from any form of contact with more technologically advanced civilizations. Denizens of these cultures experienced relatively little difficulty communicating with intruders at first contact and have been successful at quickly learning how to operate the tools and technologies they brought with them. In sum, it is unlikely that there are or have been significant genetic variations among *groups* of humans that can account for observed differences in social organization and material standards of living.

The second general type of explanation focuses on environmental influences, a broad category into which is often put such obvious factors as temperature and rainfall, soil, and natural resources, but which can also be understood to encompass technological availabilities. There is little question that some of the differences we observe in social organization and material culture reflect responses to different environmental conditions. and it has been the dream of many that this mechanism could effectively deal with the problem that observed variation in rule structures appears to pose for a general theory. One sees variants of this approach in the structural-functional tradition in sociology and anthropology as well as within economics, especially among early proponents of the "new" institutional economics (Field, 1981; North & Thomas, 1973).

If institutions and social structure were entirely the result of variation in climate or geography, which are almost entirely independent of the history of human cognition and endeavor, then we could legitimately view them as epiphenomenal – ultimately derivative of more fundamental givens. A passing acquaintance with historical and geographical variation reveals that such a conclusion is unjustified. Institutions and social structure often vary where environmental and technological conditions are quite similar, and sometimes remain unchanged in the face of substantial alterations in environmental conditions (Field, 1991).

It is this reality that poses the stumbling block to a theory of social and institutional variation that tries to explain such diversity entirely with reference to environmental factors. And it is this reality that draws thoughtful scholars again and again back to the traditions of the "old" institutionalism, of which Hodgson is an exponent, as well as to the efforts of traditional sociology and anthropology. The strength of the old institutionalism is that it acknowledges this reality: institutional/cultural/social structural variation influences human behavior in ways beyond what can be swept back to environmental differences.

I distinguish here between the old institutionalism, which focused on exploring the consequences of institutional variation, and the "new institutionalism," which, at least initially, tried to endogenize such variation. The drive to endogenize had both rational choice and Marxian variants, but in both instances the result has been to minimize the degree to which cultural or institutional differences could influence behavior in ways independent of the effect of variations in the non-human environment.

The characteristics (including beliefs and behavioral inclinations) of those other humans with whom one interacts, can of course also be considered part of one's environment, broadly considered. It is also true that such non-human factors as climate and the current level of technological availabilities can and have been influenced by past human activity. But it is conventional, and I believe useful, to distinguish cultural from environmental explanations of behavior in this way: cultural explanations are those that attribute behavioral variations to variations in the aggregated characteristics (beliefs and behavioral predispositions) of the group in which an actor is embedded.

There are many definitions of institutions, but I understand them here to be formal rules governing human interactions.[5] Institutions are reflective of and part of the broader category of culture. Some aspects of culture reside or are embodied in artifacts and written materials. But the central core of what we mean by culture are the beliefs and behavioral inclinations encoded in human brains as the result of teaching, imitation, and observation. Culture is neither more nor less than the aggregation of these encoded associations and beliefs, supplemented by external information storage devices such as stone tablets, books, or hard drives, or other artifacts including tools or structures.

The limitations of both institutional economics and the more orthodox traditions it frequently opposes are the result of continuing to act out a larger drama within the social and behavioral sciences whose basic themes are no different from what they were thirty or even one hundred years ago. On the one hand we have those who combine the basic principle of rational choice theory (maximization of utility functions reflecting stable and transitive preferences), with the additional restriction that these preferences are selfish in an attempt to construct an all-embracing theory of human behavior. On the other hand we have institutionalists who, along with traditional sociologists and anthropologists, emphasize an independent causal impact for such concepts as culture, norms, social structure or, in this case, institutions. The organizing principle of the former tradition has been methodological individualism, whereas for the latter it has been opposition to attempts to reduce or trace back the content of norms and social structure to characteristics of the individuals whose activity they influence or organize.

This play has been performed again and again, and both sets of actors have some good lines. The economic/rational choice defense of the principle of method-ological individualism has merit, although this is not true of all versions of it. A sophisticated defense cannot claim that the current behavior or the past evolution of a unit can always be understood with reference only to the properties of the individual unit itself. It can claim, however that the behavior of the members of a group is ultimately explicable with reference to the non-human environment along with the aggregated characteristics of its individual members. What else, after all, can there be?

The institutionalist tradition, on the other hand, correctly stresses the large number of empirical and historical phenomenon that cannot be accounted for by rational choice models if they are coupled, as they so often are, with the assumption of selfishness in all spheres (people act so as efficiently to advance their material welfare). But the defense of such concepts as culture and social structure as supraindividual does not follow.

Rational choice models assuming stable, transistive, and narrowly selfish preferences cannot explain a broad range of important phenomenon, from voting to the sacrifices parents make for their children to our ability to overcome free rider problems and initiate cooperate activity in small groups. The problem with the institutionalist critique, however, is that it has bought into a long tradition with firm roots in sociology and anthropology that really doesn't take issue with the assumptions about innate human psychology typically made by those operating within the rational choice traditions. *It simply assumes that culture and civilization restrain these baser impulses, thus explaining all the phenomenon that the rational choice tradition is unable to account for*. Having made this point, institutionalists then repeatedly criticize rational choice theorists for failing to acknowledge it. But for many, the critique is like water off the back of a duck, because the claims and the explanatory framework seem so egregiously to violate the principles of methodological individualism.

We cannot treat the "culture" and norms that enabled small groups of non-kin to form initially as a deus ex machina. "Culture" could not always have existed to restrain the otherwise disastrous outcomes that our innate psychological predispositions would apparently have led us to. The persistent emphasis on the primacy of culture is to me reminiscent of the story of the person who interrupts the distinguished lecturer to explain that he is clearly unaware of the fact that the earth is a large plate sitting atop a giant turtle. When the surprised scientist asks what the turtle sits atop, the member of the audience harrumphs, clearly irritated at the ignorance of this supposed expert, and replies that, of course, it's turtles all the way down.

The solution to this origin problem is to acknowledge that our innate psychology is not as unremittingly nasty and brutish as Hobbes would have it. Our innate psychology enables, and initially enabled cooperation in small groups of 30–100 beyond what can be explained as the consequence of kin selection. The predispositions that make up our innate psychology, moreover, are the result in part of evolutionary processes that involved selection at multiple levels, including levels above the individual organism. None of this is inconsistent with the gene level perspective that has now, appropriately, come to dominate evolutionary theory.

Tocqueville saw small groups as natural, and in this he was correct: they form because we are inclined to form them. We are inclined to refrain from harm even when the logic of the one shot Prisoner's Dilemma is indisputable. And we are inclined to retaliate when wronged, or when a group norm is violated, even when it may not be in our material interest to do so. These traits could not have been favored initially by individual organism level selection: but groups that had more individuals so inclined tended to grow faster, and under the right demographic conditions, although such traits were shrinking in frequency at all times in every group within the population, they increased in the population at large.

Institutional economics must let go of the comfortable critique of rational choice theorists as "reductionist." There is nothing wrong with criticizing rational choice models when they explain or predict poorly. But it is too easy simply to damn analysis as reductionist. Good science requires that we try and break down a phenomenon into its constituent parts. Where we confront limitations due to deficiencies in our current level of scientific knowledge there is justification for conducting analysis at a higher level. But absent such limitations, we should proceed. The problem is not that the rational choice tradition champions methodological individualism. The problem is that it so often, explicitly or implicitly, couples the assumption of stable and transitive preferences with that of selfishness. These types of models don't simply say that people act in satisfaction of their desires. They don't simply say that preferences are stable, transitive, and perhaps monotonic. By assuming narrowly selfish preferences they predict that people act in all instances so as to advance their material well-being. Although true in many contexts, it is not so in all, as an important range of experimental and observational data makes clear.

Standard microeconomics is the study of the operation of foraging algorithms in an environment never anticipated by the forces of natural selection that refined them. Constrained maximization tools work relatively well in modeling the operation of such algorithms. But our evolutionary history has endowed us with other algorithms that also facilitate our survival and are particularly important in conditioning political behavior. These include a willingness some of the time to play a strictly dominated strategy in a one shot PD, such that cooperative and potentially repeated interactions among non-kin can begin, a willingness, once continuing interaction has begun, to devote inordinate amounts of energy to detecting rule violators, an obsession that can distort our ability to think logically (Cosmides & Tooby, 1992), and a willingness to engage in costly punishment of those identified as defectors (Fehr & Gächter, 2000). Rational choice theory puts itself in a box if it assumes that our behavior is driven exclusively by our foraging algorithms.

It is our biologically mediated behavioral inclinations that, in the first instance, enable reciprocity and cooperation among non-kin in small groups, not the "invention" of culture. Once we move beyond small groups, the norms, expectations, institutions and rules that emerge or that we construct are essential in allowing the operation of larger organizations and states. But these cultural or institutional innovations are built upon a biological substrate.

Until this argument is fully engaged the traditions of institutional economics and its cousins in disciplines outside of economics will continue to participate in a pointless and increasingly stale *methodenstreit* that will not advance our understanding of human behavior.

ENDOGENOUS INSTITUTIONS

There is a long tradition running from technologically determinist passages in Karl Marx to early new institutional history writings of Douglass North that suggests that institutions and, perforce, culture, are ultimately epiphenomenal: reflective of more fundamental givens such as resource endowments and technologies. Thus, in a perhaps bowdlerized version of Marx, the handmill gives you the feudal landlord, the steam mill the industrial capitalist. In the early Northian version, "efficient" institutions arise because they offer a free lunch in comparison to the alternatives: someone can be made better off without making anyone else worse off, so an old rule is discarded, and a new one brought in. The triggers are assumed to be changes in land-labor ratios or available technologies. In both of these frameworks institutional variation is a surface phenomenon, to be studied as confirmation of the operation of more fundamental forces, but without much independent influence itself.

The more recent writings of North represent an important about-face on this issue. First of all, he now acknowledges that simply because a different institution might by Kaldor-Hicks efficient, in the sense that winners could in principle compensate losers and still be better off, there might not always be mechanisms that would automatically (and costlessly) arise for effectuating that transfer. Thus, inefficient institutions might persist. If one adds to this the possibility that there could be multiple efficient institutions for a society with given technologies and preferences depending on how endowments were initially distributed, it begins to be clear that there is a potentially broad range of rules that might characterize a region with given resources and access to a particular set of technologies.

Moreover, North now acknowledges the influence on behavior of ideology and norms (North, 1990). What this represents is recognition that individuals may not be driven solely by wealth maximization, and that deviations from this assumption may go beyond simply variation in preferences for leisure vs. material goods. The net effect of these alterations is to reinforce the conclusion that institutions or rules may differ across space and time where resources and technologies are similar, but may also be similar across space and time when resources and technologies differ or change (Field, 1991). Rule variation, therefore, can be *consequential*, which was, of course, the central organizing principle of the old institutionalism.

This intellectual move away from the more extravagant claims of the early new institutionalism is mirrored within literatures attempting to understand biological influences on behavior. In the 1970s, sociobiologists moved aggressively to explain all human behavior as the consequence of inclinations favored evolutionarily by fitness maximization (Wilson, 1978). Sociobiological explanation is not in principle the same as rational choice theory assuming stable, transitive and narrowly selfish preferences. In the latter framework individual organisms act so as to maximize their own material welfare. In the former, natural selection favors genes that predispose to behavior by the organisms containing them that leads to increases in the frequency of such genes in future generations. But if gene interest is assumed more or less coextensive with organism interest, and if selection is assumed to operate at levels no higher than that of the organism, then the conclusions reached about human behavior are very similar – thus apparently providing such rational choice models with a biological underpinning.

There is now, however, greater acknowledgement that much human behavior in our current environment is simply maladaptive. Evolutionary biologists such as

Cosmides and Tooby view our proclivities as having been honed in a two million year Pleistocene; in some cases the behavioral inclinations selected may not be fitness enhancing in the current environment because of the relatively slow pace of genetic evolution in humans. In other instances cultural and technological changes may have enabled and reinforced maladaptive behavior, such as fertility control. The acceptance of both of these propositions represents a step forward from 1970s sociobiology, but also represents, as in the case of the new institutionalism, some dulling of its apparently revolutionary implications. What still remains very controversial is the proposition that some genetically influenced behaviors that continue in large measure to be adaptive were originally selected for at levels above the level of the organism.

Among mainstream economists today (2003), it is much more widely accepted than was true fifteen years ago that institutional, cultural, and other normative features of economies can vary in ways that have profound influences on economic outcomes, that these rules are human creations, sometimes planned and thus the subject of political choice, that it makes a great deal of difference whether we get them "right" and that this won't automatically happen. The examples of the different growth trajectories and environmental records of East and West Germany before reunification, or North and South Korea are obvious examples, but economic history provides many more, from the economic consequences of slavery in the American South, to the possible influence of different legal traditions on the structure of financial systems in common law and civil law countries (La Porta et al., 1998). Thus, with the partial retreat of the "new" institutionalism, the fundamental insight of the old institutionalism has been reaffirmed.

Institutional economists about whom Hodgson writes viewed it as important to describe the rules – legal and otherwise – within which economic activity took place. The key institutional issue in economics thirty years ago was whether, in thinking about static general equilibrium analysis, there were three categories of predetermined variables (tastes, technologies, and endowments), or whether there was also a fourth (rules) (see Field, 1979, 1981, 1984, 1991). Mainstream economists and game theorists did not speak with one voice on this issue, some readily granting the influence of institutional variation on outcomes, others, in a number of traditions, claiming that they were epiphenomenal and could be swept back in an explanatory sense to the more basic triad of tastes, technology and endowments.

The waters were muddied by the proclamations of the new institutional economics. The new institutional economics promised that it would give institutions their due, but not in the fuddy-duddy tradition of Commons, Mitchell, or the German Historical school. On the one hand, there was a drive ultimately to eliminate the role of rules as an independent influence on outcomes. On the other hand there was an intent to work out the implications of the Coase theorem writ large. The Coase theorem stated that in the absence of transactions costs rule structures would not affect the sectoral allocation of inputs; in that sense they would not matter. In the presence of transactions costs, however, some rules might be more efficient that others; the new institutional economics would use these principles to explain why we have the rules that we do.

By the early 1990s the new institutional economics had run into some explanatory brick walls that caused its leading practitioners to back away from some of its early objectives. In particular, as noted, scholars such as North began talking about the role of ideology and the possibility of the persistence of inefficient rules. But once one allows for this, it is clear that rules can have independent influences. Moreover, it is no longer obvious what are the distinguishing feature of the new institutional economics. Currently, it seems to be the use of the analytical tools and vocabulary of game theory to analyze or interpret historical institutional arrangements. This is a considerably more modest enterprise, and it is much less clear that the propositions advanced are falsifiable.

Hodgson and I are in broad agreement that history matters and that, because this leads to institutional variation that at any moment of time is not epiphenomenal, institutions matter. Where we may differ is on where we should go from here. Suppose we consider the issue of static allocation that dominated much of economic theory at least through the 1970s. I have argued in a series of papers that if we wish to construct general equilibrium models, it is important to acknowledge a fourth category of predetermined variable beyond technologies, endowments, and preferences. This category can be called culture, norms, or institutions. Whatever we call it, it consists of beliefs, not just about how the non-human world works (we can think of this as technology), but how other humans will act or react, and to some degree, what are the appropriate ends of human activity (thus these beliefs shade over into preferences).

If we grant this perspective, however, is it helpful to say we need a different *theory* to analyze static allocation in North as opposed to South Korea, or are we rather talking about the same general theory with different parameter values? We need to be precise, and Hodgson is looser than I would prefer in his use of the term theory, sometimes speaking of it as simply a set of concepts or categories (for example in discussing why empirical observation must be "theory laden"), while at other times suggesting that the term necessarily implies some positing of causal relationships among these categories.

While a number of economists have recently tried to build rational choice models incorporating the influences of social norms (e.g. Akerlof, 1980; Kevane & Wydick, 2001), this leaves open the question of their analytical status. Can norms and institutions truly be understood as forces external to the individual, like the weather? If they can be viewed as external to an individual, can they also be viewed as external to the *individuals* whose behavior they influence?

Economists have differed with respect to the analytical status of norms. Both Hodgson and I have reacted to the limitations of economic or rational choice models as they in fact confront us in much economic discourse. As an institutionalist, Hodgson has some sympathy for the sociological, anthropological tradition of Durkheim and Malinowski, with its emphasis on institutions and culture as superorganic, with dynamics of their own, "independent" of the individual humans whose activity they organize. Hodgson continues, I think, to embrace this distinctive tradition. My argument here is that we now need to move beyond the correct claim that culture, norms, or institutions represent an influence on behavior beyond those of technologies, endowments, and preferences, and locate these norms and institutions in the aggregated characteristics of those individuals whose behavior they influence, augmented to some degree by the physical environment they create.

Rational choice models come in at least three canonical flavors, and it is important, in a specific instance, to be aware of which versions we are dealing with. It is also important to keep in mind that these models involve assumptions about cognition as well as goals and objectives; the term rationality can mean different things in the two spheres. My emphasis in the trichotomy below focuses principally on behavior, as opposed to cognitive aspects of rationality:

Rational choice models, Version 1: People act in satisfaction of their desires.

It is not worth spending a great deal of time on this variant, because there is no conceivable empirical data that could refute it. Models based on this premise can't be rejected with observed behavior and it is pointless debating their scientific merits with proponents.

Rational choice models, Version 2. People have preferences that are stable and transitive, and act on the basis of these preferences.

Stability is based on the proposition that the basic goals of humans, like other living organisms, display some time consistency. Transitivity is typically justified by appeal to a money pump argument. The appeal of assuming that if an individual prefers A to B and B to C, she will not prefer C to A is ultimately supported by an evolutionary claim: individuals whose choices did not adhere to this rule would be subject to extinction because one could suck all their wealth from them using a money pump. Suppose an individual has revealed that she prefers A to B, B to C, and C to A. Start by giving her C. She should then be willing to pay something to swap C for B, and something more to swap B for A. But now we can ask her to pay a third time to swap A for C, having induced her to make three successive payments to obtain what we originally gave her for free! Presumably individuals with such preferences would be evolutionarily disfavored.

A variant of Version 2 rational choice model building, attributable to Samuelson's influence, insists that preference structures be derived from observed behavior. If we add to stability and transitivity the assumptions of convexity, monotonicity, reflexiveness and completeness, then Version 2 specifications are subject to empirical refutation through demonstrated violations of the weak and strong axioms of revealed preference. For example, a violation of the weak axiom of revealed preference occurs when an individual chooses commodity bundle A when they could have chosen B, revealing a preference for A over B but then, faced with a different budget constraint, chooses B when they could have chosen A, apparently revealing a preference for B over A. The strong axiom is violated if an individual indirectly reveals a preference for A over C (by first preferring A to B and then B to C) and then reveals a preference for C over A.

Ideally, one could imagine rational choice methodology as a means for developing predictive models of human behavior: extracting from the revealed preferences displayed in observed behavior concise mathematical specifications of individual utility functions that, when combined with the maintained hypothesis of maximization, enabled reliable out of sample predictions. In practice, however, very little actual work has ever been done along these lines. The most common use of the revealed preference methodology has been to evaluate the welfare consequences of proposed policy interventions in an ordinal sense (they will make people better off or worse off). I don't mean to trivialize these conclusions which are sometimes not at all intuitive, but it would be a great stretch of the imagination to claim that the principle of revealed preference has led to the development of a robust methodology for predicting levels of human behavior.

In rational choice models, Version 3, people are assumed to have stable, transitive and narrowly selfish preferences which lead to behavior efficiently advancing the material interest of the actor.

Version 3 models often use the assumption of wealth maximization as a practical means of operationalizing selfishness. The distinction between Version 2 and Version 3 is the insistence in the latter on the importance of assuming human selfishness and denial in the former that this assumption has any necessary relation to the method (Gintis, 2003). In practice the distinction is not quite so clear, because of the common assumption of monotonicity in revealed preference exercises. If money is viewed as the generalized good, monotonicity requires, everything else being equal, that more money is preferred to less. Thus, experimental evidence indicating that under the right circumstances people will persistently leave money on the table, while clearly an empirical refutation of Version 3, also poses some challenges to Version 2.

So far I have said little about possible limitations on human cognition. Rational choice models often dispose of the problem by assuming perfect information. Cognition is costless, errorless, unbiased. The assumption of rational expectations is somewhat less restrictive: it requires that people use all available information processed according to the best available logical and statistical algorithms in forming their beliefs about the world. The assumption is a bit more realistic because it acknowledges that some information might not be available, and implicitly suggests another optimization problem in the sense that more information could presumably be made available through the expenditure of additional effort or resources.

If we take some version of Version 2 as part of what is meant by traditional microeconomics, do the deviations we need to accept in order to account for political behavior lie only in the realm of cognition? That is, does human bounded rationality, to use the term popularized by Herbert Simon, suffice to explain why humans behave differently from what canonical versions of the theory predict? While it is of course true that human cognition is imperfect in many ways, the answer to this question is negative. This is my objection to the otherwise estimable work of scholars such as Elinor Ostrom: she is too willing to attribute the behavioral deviation to the Simon tradition of bounded rationality (Ostrom, 1998).

The human predisposition to play cooperate in a one shot PD, or make voluntary contributions to public goods, or engage in costly punishment of norm violators, cannot be swept back to some imperfection in cognitive capabilities. Before you can have the parametric prices that confront choosers in intermediate theory textbooks you need trade, and before trade you need relations of reciprocity among non-kin, and to get that you need a human ability to overcome one shot PDs that must lie somewhere else than in our predispositions for self preservation. I have described elsewhere how genes predisposing to such behavior can be favored by natural selection. Any understanding of who we are and how our societies got to where we are needs to confront this argument, or else engage in (invisible?) hand waving. The dream of deducing social organization from some posited original state as the result of behavior by rationally choosing narrowly self interested agents is a chimera. The basis of the appeal of the sociological and anthropological tradition, with which the old institutional economics has many affinities, has been that norms and institutions, externally posited and imposed, have seemed to provide a resolution to a gaping lacuna in rational choice theory at least of the Version 3 variety. But the development of culture presupposes continuing interaction among non-kin adults, leaving unanswered the question of how such interaction originates. It can't be turtles all the way down.

Practitioners of rational choice methodology, particularly economists, have been ambivalent about cultural explanations of behavior and, perforce, those relying on institutions. My proposal for a rapprochement is this: (1) those in the institutionalist-traditional sociological/anthropological tradition accept a sophisticated version of methodological individualism. (2) Those who find Version 3 rational choice models appealing abandon the insistence on strictly selfish preferences and the belief that natural selection necessarily provides an underpinning for them. I have no illusions that negotiating this Peace Plan will be any easier than solving the Israeli-Palestinian conflict, but I would like to lay out the logic for it.

The vision I have for understanding both the universal and variable features of human organization is explicitly biological and evolutionary, and not just evolutionary in a metaphorical sense. Take as our starting point what we know about language. Two salient features are worth noting. First, vocabularies very greatly across the world and these differences are clearly learned cultural phenomena. Yet all of the roughly 5,000 known human languages obey a set of basic rules of grammatical structure that reflect design features of human cognition. This may seem marvelous or difficult to accept at first glance, but it is upon reflection no more surprising than that our genetic material also includes detailed assembly functions for such differentiated organs as our liver or our spleen. The design features means that with respect to learning of grammar we are differentially predisposed at certain developmental stages to form certain associations.

If we grant that the vocabularies of language are cultural features, are we correct in arguing that they are emergent properties, in the sense that they cannot be understood by referring to the aggregated properties of those individuals whose communication they organize? I think upon reflection, the answer must be negative. Language is based on a set of reciprocal expectations of how others will interpret certain sounds I may make. I would claim that language can be understood *entirely* with respect to properties of the individuals whose intercourse it organizes: in particular learned and shared vocabularies embedded within a universal and genetically-based grammatical template.

Whereas it is not possible to comprehend a language by looking only at properties of one particular individual whose communication it organizes, it is possible to say that language is neither more nor less than the sum total within a group of shared expectations about the meaning of sounds that have been acquired through a process of association and statistical learning. The particularities of a language (not the universal structure that it shares with all others) are simply the set of those expectations among the members of the collectivity whose behavior it facilitates.

We need to think about institutions and norms in the same way: the differences among them reflect particular patterns of shared expectations about how others in the collectivity will respond (positively and negatively) to different states of the world and in particular specific individual actions. These are acquired through the standard techniques of association and statistical learning stressed by behaviorists, although this acquisition is attained within a framework of hard-wired predispositions to learn in certain directions.

Language represents solution to a coordination problem: the selection of one from a number of multiple possible equilibria. The achievement of a cooperative outcome in what might be a one shot PD is a much greater challenge, because the only Nash equilibrium in that game is inefficient. Political organization requires that people, literally or figuratively, leave money on the table. They must be willing, initially, to play a strictly dominated strategy.

The assumption of wealth maximization is a useful assumption in many contexts. What is not reasonable, however, is the assumption that it prevails in all. History, experience, and experimental evidence have documented that humans, even when they fully understand the nature of the experiment or the situation they find themselves in, will sometimes play strictly dominated strategies. This is true, for example, in one shot PDs, in ultimatum games, or in multiplayer PD games involving the collective provision of public goods and the opportunity for costly punishment of those who don't contribute. It is simply not possible to provide a rationale based on Version 3 modeling for the play of a strictly dominated strategy.

Sophisticated rational choice modelers, when called upon to defend rational choice methodology, will almost invariably defend a variant of Version 2, but in practice it is the unrestrained application of Version 3 methodology in areas where the evidence simply won't support it that has given rational choice modeling a bad name. Those who have openly defended Version 3 methodology have often appealed to evolutionary arguments in support of the assumptions of human selfishness. Humans are selfish because we have inherited genes that so predispose us, and if our great grandparents had not had these genes, we would not be here. The specter of Charles Darwin has always seemed to lurk in the background for those who would challenge Version 3 models. On the other hand, those who want to force Version 3 into every nook and cranny immediately run into difficulties dealing with parental sacrifice for children. Most economists and biologists now agree that the Hamilton kin selection mechanism adequately accounts for parental sacrifice. But the logic of that mechanism requires acknowledgement that natural selection doesn't necessarily make humans individually selfish in all venues.

Natural selection will favor genes that predispose in favor of organism behavior that results in higher frequencies of such genes in future generations. For humans, this often means predisposing in the direction of behaviors that do in fact efficiently advance the material well being of the actor. But not always, as the example of parental sacrifice indicates. The logic of multilevel selection models, necessary to account for the predispositions that enable us to solve one shot PDs and the multiperson PDs implicit in voluntary provision of public goods problems, necessitates special demographic assumptions about population fragmentation and regrouping over time. But it relies on the same principle: genes that influence the vessels containing them to act in ways that foster higher rates of increase of these genes will be favored, whether or not this influence is always in the best interest of the vessel.

CONCLUSION

The founding fathers of institutionalism were a disparate group with disparate interests and perspectives, but they appear to have been motivated by two general goals. The first, more activist and normative, was to provide policy recommendations as well as an intellectual foundation for government intervention as a means of improving the operation of a capitalist economy. The second was to use the positive insights of institutionalism as a foundation for a more general theory of human behavior.

Part IV of Hodgson's book is concerned with this second agenda, which has also formed the focus of my essay. But parts I–III are about the history of ideas, which is reflective of the emphasis on intellectual history that dominates institutional economics today. These sections would serve as a good starting point for someone interested in an intellectual and political history of institutionalism, both in Europe and the United States. The scholarship here is generally solid, although some of the summary statements, sound good until one deconstructs them. For example (p. 200), Hodgson describes how Lionel Robbins and Parsons "carved up the social sciences: sociology was to be concerned with the social determination of goals; economics with the study of the rational choice of means to pursue these ends." If they ever had an agreement, I don't think Parsons got it in writing, because I doubt Robbins was prepared to cede to Parsons the idea that human goals were socially determined, nor have generations of subsequent economists, who have had little truck with sociology, Parsonian or otherwise.

Another example: Hodgson says of Veblen that he "avoided the three reductionisms of methodological collectivism, methodological individualism, and biological reductionism" (p. 140). Relative to other work in this genre, Hodgson is restrained in the tendency to reify concepts. But he does succumb now and then. If one is going to talk in these terms, one needs very careful definition and analysis of what is meant – which is lacking here.

The claim that we need different theories of human behavior for different cultures, Hodgson's main theme throughout all four sections of the book, arguably turns on what we mean by different. Since all human groups are remarkably similar from a biological perspective, I question the desirability of rejecting the pursuit of a unified theory of human behavior, and have outlined in this essay some of the directions in which we might proceed in order to construct it. Perhaps institutionalism's fate can be attributed in part to a series of intellectual accidents, such as Marshall's replacement by Pigou at Cambridge. But certainly the power of institutionalist ideas, and the ability actually to make progress on the normative and positive agendas identified above have had something to do with it.

The approach of the old institutionalism has not been wrong, but it has been limited, because it hasn't successfully explored the origins of institutions beyond making the correct point that variations in them can't be entirely swept back to variations in the non-human environment. Historical economics is the time series version of cultural economics. Hodgson could equally well have asked how economics forgot culture, and written an almost identical book on the problem of cultural specificity in social science. The problems of and challenges facing institutionalism are cut from the same cloth as those affecting traditional sociology and anthropology.

Many voices have been raised calling for the introduction of more institutionalist ideas in the training of economists. A critic might ask why "the institutionalist propaganda that has been prominent in the economic discussion of the past 15 years in this country, has not been more productive of concrete works and changes in the curriculum of our graduate schools."

The last sentence might have been written recently, were in fact penned more than seventy years ago (Burns, 1931, p. 80). Almost three quarters of a century have now passed. The central truths of institutional economics have not been lost. But those who call themselves institutionalists have defined the field largely as backward-looking intellectual history, ceding the important policy arena to mechanism designers, those who write tax law, and Jeff Sachs. These scholars, although not calling themselves institutionalists, are proving to be the truer heirs of John Commons. As far as Veblen, well, he is sui generis, but if institutionalism is to be a foundation for a broader unification of the social sciences, a more systematic and critical treatment of biological and evolutionary theory along with experimental evidence is needed than is here provided.

NOTES

1. Lionel Robbins was remarkably cavalier in his discussions of the relevance of evidence in developing or testing economic theory. See Robbins (1932 [1984], pp. 78–79).

2. The focus here is on game theory and microeconomics. Macroeconomics, despite the contempt sometimes visited upon it by micro theorists, and despite the inroads of abstract highly technical modeling, has, in my view, been more progressive in recent decades as a scientific endeavor, principally because explanation, prediction, and data have mattered more.

3. Here is exactly what he says: "... I am not sure applicability is desirable. If micro-economics is useful, the first to benefit will be the MBA students who are among the last people in the world I feel obliged to assist. If game theory were indeed useful it could be used for military purposes" (2001, p. 617).

4. In a typology of rational choice approaches developed below, I distinguish this type of model from approaches that involve less restrictive assumptions about human goals.

5. The distinction between formal and informal rules is admittedly somewhat arbitrary. If I go to coffee with you for the first time at 3 PM today, it is certainly not an institution. If I do it tomorrow, is it? There is no hard and fast line where such a regularity of behavior, reinforced by mutually realized expectations, "becomes" an institution.

REFERENCES

Akerlof, G. (1980). A theory of social custom, of which unemployment may be one consequence. *Quarterly Journal of Economics, 94*(June), 749–775.

Boehm, C. (1999). *Hierarchy in the forest.* Cambridge: Harvard University Press.

Burns, E. M. (1931). Does institutionalism complement or compete with orthodox economics? *American Economic Review, 80*(March), 80–87.

Cosmides, L., & Tooby, J. (1992). Cognitive adaptations for social exchange. In: Barkow et al. (Eds), pp. 163–228.

Fehr, E., & Gächter, S. (2000). Cooperation and punishment in public goods experiments. *American Economic Review, 90*(September), 981–994.

Field, A. J. (1979). On the explanation of rules using rational choice methods. *Journal of Economic Issues, 13*(March), 49–72.

Field, A. J. (1981). The problem with the new institutional economics: A critique with special reference to the North-Thomas model of pre-1500 Europe. *Explorations in Economic History, 18*(April), 174–198.

Field, A. J. (1984). Microeconomics, norms, and rationality. *Economic Development and Cultural Change, 32*(July), 683–711.

Field, A. J. (1991). Do legal systems matter? *Explorations in Economic History, 28*(January), 1–35.

Field, A. J. (2001). *Altruistically inclined? The behavioral sciences, evolutionary theory and the origins of reciprocity.* Ann Arbor: University of Michigan Press.

Field, A. J. (2003). Why multilevel selection matters. Unpublished Working Paper.

Gintis, H. (2003). Toward a unity of the human behavioral sciences. Unpublished Working Paper.

Kevane, M., & Wydick, B. (2001). Social norms and the allocation of women's labor in Burkina Faso. *Review of Development Economics, 5*(February), 119–129.

La Porta, R., Lopez-de-Silanes, F., Shleifer, A., & Vishny, R. W. (1998). Law and finance. *Journal of Political Economy, 106*(December), 1113–1155.

North, D. (1990). *Institutions, institutional change, and economic performance.* Cambridge: Cambridge University Press.

North, D., & Thomas, R. P. (1973). *The rise of the western world*. Cambridge: Cambridge University Press.

Ostrom, E. (1998). A behavioral approach to the rational choice theory of collective action. *American Political Science Review*, *92*(1), 1–21.

Robbins, L. [1932] (1984). *The nature and significance of economic science* (3rd ed.). New York: Macmillan.

Rubinstein, A. (2001). A theorist's view of experiments. *European Economic Review*, *45*(May), 615–628.

Sober, E., & Wilson, D. S. (1998). *Unto others: The evolution and psychology of unselfish behavior*. Cambridge: Harvard University Press.

Wilson, D. S., & Sober, E. (1994). Reintroducing group selection to the human behavioral sciences. *Behavioral and Brain Sciences*, *17*, 585–654.

Wilson, E. O. (1978). *On human nature*. Cambridge: Harvard University Press.

THE GERMAN HISTORICAL APPROACH TO ECONOMICS

Harald Hagemann

A review essay on Y. Shionoya, Ed., *The German Historical School: The Historical and Ethical Approach to Economics*. London: Routledge, 2001.

INTRODUCTION

This is an unusual book and a striking phenomenon. It comprises a collection of thirteen essays on the German Historical School of Economics (henceforth GHSE), exclusively written by Japanese contributors who are mainly full professors at leading universities and mostly have already published on various aspects of the GHSE. The editor, Yuichi Shionoya, is well known internationally as one of the most prominent students of Joseph Schumpeter and Max Weber, whose works provide the basis for the editor's attempt to erect the framework of the rational reconstruction of the GHSE in the opening essay. This holds in particular for economic sociology, which – besides theory, history and statistics – constitutes the fourth discipline in economics, and includes the social institutions relevant to economic behaviour and also political, legal or religious aspects. The investigation of Schumpeter's conception of economic sociology (see, e.g. Schumpeter, 1954, pp. 20–21) is at the very heart of Shionoya's second essay (9) in which the author concludes that Schumpeter combined two essential elements of the GHSE, a belief in the unity of social life and the inseparable relationship among its components and a concern for development, with some stimulus by Max Weber's analysis of

Research in the History of Economic Thought and Methodology A Research Annual
Research in the History of Economic Thought and Methodology, Volume 22-A, 399–411
Copyright © 2004 by Elsevier Ltd.
ISSN: 0743-4154/doi:10.1016/S0743-4154(03)22025-3

comparative-static social systems and Marx's analysis of the dynamic process of capital accumulation. It is Shionoya's belief "that Schumpeter should be regarded as one of the successors of the German Historical School because he attempted a rational reconstruction of that school, especially Schmoller's research program, in terms of economic sociology and made his own contribution from this perspective" (p. 9). Whether and how this statement from the editor's first essay fully fits with the one from Shionoya's second essay, that "Schumpeter's conception of economic sociology intended to integrate history and theory, the antitheses at the *Methodenstreit* between Gustav von Schmoller and Carl Menger" (p. 139), is left to the reader's judgement. Characteristically, the contradictions involved can be found in Schumpeter's own writings. In the very same year, 1926, in which he published the article "Gustav von Schmoller and the Problems of Today," which forms the key basis for Shionoya's argument, Schumpeter eliminated the seventh chapter on "The Overall View of the Economy" of the first German edition of *The Theory of Economic Development* from the second German one and omitted it in all later editions of the book, including the 1934 English translation. The reason was that Schumpeter believed that this chapter with its much broader perspective and its fragment of cultural sociology has sometimes distracted the reader's attention from pure and "dry" economic reasoning. It had led to a kind of consent which was at the very opposite of his intentions in so far as the seventh chapter was misunderstood as an alternative to economic theory. For that kind of reasoning Schumpeter did not want to provide any ammunition. For Shionoya, on the other hand, Chap. 7 is not a fragment of cultural sociology but a research program for a universal social science that he has specified in an earlier article (Shionoya, 1990) in which he regrets Schumpeter's decision to omit it.

THE HISTORICAL AND ETHICAL APPROACH TO ECONOMICS: THE GERMAN HISTORICAL SCHOOL AND ITS EARLY AND LONG-LASTING IMPACT IN JAPAN

The German Historical School originated in a special session on the GHSE at the annual conference of the Japanese Society for the History of Economic Thought held in Tokyo in November 1996. The (Japanese) Association for the Study of Social Policy had been founded there in 1896. It was the culmination of developments following the 1881 political crisis, in which Japan's model of modernisation shifted from a British to a German orientation. Pro-German ideas gained ground, including the conception of state sciences and the dissemination of the ideas of the socialists of the chair, who recognized economics as inseparably interwoven with ethical concerns and political issues and attributed the duty to the government to provide concern for the social welfare of its citizens in a period of accelerated industrialisation. Thus, the Japanese Association for the Study of Social Policy was founded according to the example of the Verein für Sozialpolitik. In the initial manifesto of 1899/1900 the extreme exercise of self-interest and uncontrolled free competition in a *laissez-faire* system was as opposed as the socialist and revolutionary ideas of Marxism to solve the labour question.[1] Social policy was seen as the task of the state whose authority should not only protect workers but also achieve social harmony between capital and labour. This was clearly emphasised by the founding President, Noburo Kanai (1865–1933), at the first meeting in the wake of the Japanese-Russian war in 1907 when the Association for the Study of Social Policy had established herself as the only nationwide economic society. Kanai had studied in Germany during 1886–1889, mainly with Gustav Schmoller and Adolph Wagner at the University of Berlin. The ideas that influenced him were of particular relevance for the Japanese economy in the 1890s, when the factory system expanded rapidly. Tokyo Imperial University, where Kanai became Professor and Karl Rathgen lectured on state law and statistics, became the center for the dissemination of "German ideas" in Japan.

It would have occurred to neither the founders of the Association nor their Japanese fellow economists nor the contributors to the Shionoya volume a century later to fundamentally question the received view of the GHSE as "not historical," "not German" and "not a School," as Pearson (1999, 2002) has done recently in an overstated attempt at American unnecessary originality.[2] Even Schumpeter, who is cited as a chief witness, only dismisses the term for the *older* GHSE but wants "to confine the concept, Historical School of Economics, to the age and to the group of Gustav von Schmoller" (Schumpeter, 1954, p. 507). Whereas there never existed a German monopoly of the historical and ethical (or institutional) approach to economics, it remains a historical fact that the main founders and activists of the Verein für Sozialpolitik were seen by contemporary economists – such as Alfred Marshall, Richard T. Ely (who founded the American Economic Association in 1885) or many of their Italian and Japanese colleagues – as a prominent group, from both a qualitative and a quantitative perspective. Furthermore, Roscher in his 1843 programmatic *Outline of Lectures on Political Economy, according to the Historical Method*, in which he suggested an embracing historical and comparative study of economic systems to identify the stages of development and the laws of economic life, explicitly referred to F. C. von Savigny and the Historical School of law he founded in 1814 and which soon became dominant.

However, one essential point on which Pearson and Shionoya and his fellow economists, as well as most "heterodox" economists agree, is that the resurgence of interest in the GHSE stems from an uneasiness about the development of modern mainstream economics aiming at imitating the sciences although the validity of economic models is contingent on time and space. Pearson's emphasis on evolutionary, institutional, and cultural economics is mirrored in the opening statement of the editor which brings to the fore the main motivation of the Shionoya enterprise: "With the increasing acceptance of evolutionary and institutional thinking among economists, general interest in the German Historical School has risen steadily during the past decade" (Shionoya, 2001, p. 1). However, "[I]n conclusion, the rational reconstruction of the German Historical School suggests that a lot of tasks must be performed to provide an alternative paradigm to the mainstream with regard to the method, scope, and underlying value premises of social science" (pp. 16–17).

HOW DOES THE GERMAN HISTORICAL SCHOOL FIT?

In contrast to the immense task outlined earlier the Shionoya project follows the more modest aim "to offer an overview of the German Historical School from the methodological perspective" (p. 17). However, we are timely warned in the Introduction that "the volume is neither a textbook nor a comprehensive anthology of the German Historical School" (p. 2). This is indeed correct since major representatives of the older as well as the younger GHSE are not covered in individual contributions. Some examples are Bruno Hildebrand (1812–1878), who in contrast to Roscher was not a book-worm but an activist in the liberal movement and a member of the Frankfurt National Assembly in 1848–1849, the founding editor of the *Jahrbücher für Nationalökonomie und Statistik* in 1863, and made his most important contributions to the historical method by the founding of the first institutions in Switzerland and Germany for the collection of statistical data, and Adolph Wagner (1835–1917) who became well known in public finance. Arthur Spiethoff (1873–1957), the most eminent German business cycle analyst at the beginning of the twentieth century, is only mentioned once, together with Sombart and Max Weber, as the leading representatives of the Youngest Historical School in Shionoya's overview of the three generations of the GHSE. Finally, Heinrich Herkner (1863–1932), the author of a widely read book on *The Labour Question* (1894), who twice succeeded Schmoller, on his chair at the University of Berlin in 1912 and as the Chairman of the Verein für Sozialpolitik from 1917 to 1930, is not even listed in the Index.

On the other hand, more than a few readers will be surprised to find certain economists whose works are assessed in the individual contributions to this collection, beside those authors unanimously related to the GHSE. These include Wilhelm Roscher (1817–1894); Karl Knies (1821–1898); Gustav von Schmoller

(1838–1917); Lujo Brentano (1844–1931) and the opponents from the younger generation within the Verein für Sozialpolitik in the second dispute on method, the *Werturteilsstreit*, the fundamental debate about normative judgments which escalated with the 1909 Vienna meeting, Werner Sombart (1863–1941) and Max Weber (1864–1920). The surprises are putative precursors as the conservative romanticist Adam Heinrich Müller (1779–1829), Austrian contemporaries Carl and Anton Menger and Friedrich von Wieser, later ordoliberals, Walter Eucken and Wilhelm Röpke, and the representative of the social market economy, Alfred Müller-Armack. Their inclusion in the collection is justified with the arguments that Eucken and Röpke "share with the Historical School the vision that theory is inseparable from history and policy" and that Müller-Armack's concept of social ethics is thereby included, also indicating "that the notion of society as an organic whole is the core of German historical thought" (p. 6).

This extensive range of contributions does not make it easy to always identify a unifying theme; moreover, the selection of the essays, which in this reviewer's opinion is also supply-determined, will with high probability raise some critical response.

However, Shionoya can get almost perfect help from an unexpected corner. If one follows Pearson's "more ecumenically defined movement"[3] and includes authors with a greater evolutionary, institutional or cultural approach to economics, a long list of potential candidates arises, comprising Max Weber, Joseph Schumpeter, Carl Menger, Friedrich von Wieser, who all are dealt with in Shionoya's collection. Furthermore, in his classic study on the *Foundations of Historicism in German Economics*, Gottfried Eisermann (1956) has well argued that Adam Müller and, with some lag, Friedrich List (1789–1846) personify the double-sided nature of the first countermovement against the entry of classical economic liberalism in Germany. Müller embodied the backward-looking feudal-conservative viewpoint and List the forward-looking perspective of the rising industrial bourgeoisie, one not equal to the British competitors at an early stage. However, neither this difference nor Müller's precursor role to the GHSE comes out very well in Tetsushi Harada's essay. It focuses on Müller's *Agronomic Letters*, published in 1812, i.e. within the period of Napoleon's blockade of the Continent, in which Müller emphasised the high risks of mercantile agriculture depending on foreign trade and favoured a return to an "isolated agriculture" in Germany. The differing circumstances of the time when List's *National System of Political Economy* appeared almost three decades later and "capitalistic features were more or less established in German agriculture" (p. 30) are rightly stressed as are List's proposals concerning protection and infant industries. List, who originally had been a faithful disciple of the classical doctrine, turned away during his American exile (1825–1832) and developed a stages theory of economic development emphasizing productive powers and the specificity of national endowments, wants, cultures and conditions. However, List's conception and sharp accentuation of the nation as the decisive economic unit, historically given, does not underlie any nationalism or chauvinism. Harada's characterisation of List, "as a kind of romanticist" (p. 21) whose thinking contained elements along a direct path leading to Hitler's minister of agriculture and the policy of German expansionism in the first half of the twentieth century, is grossly misleading and does unjustice to List as a genuine German liberal of his time.

FROM THE OLDER TO THE YOUNGER HISTORICAL SCHOOL

Yukihiro Ikeda examines a notebook on which Roscher had based his lectures on economics at the University of Leipzig in 1849–1851. In a typically Japanese style of history of economic analysis, i.e. a scrupulous and meticulous reconstruction of the structure and content of the notebook, now located at his own Keio University in Tokyo, the author reconstructs Roscher's lecture notes and concludes "that this document might be seen as a draft of *System*" or that "the Notebook is presumably a halfway point between *Grundriss* and *System*" (p. 39). Ikeda, who had written his own Ph.D. thesis in Germany on the genesis of Carl Menger's *Principles* (Ikeda, 1997), also provides some further evidence of the influence of Roscher on Menger (who had dedicated his *Principles* to Roscher). Ikeda thereby supports Streissler, who, in a fascinating article, first had destroyed the modern myths of the Austrian School's independence from German economics and that German economics in the middle of the nineteenth century was unimportant (Streissler, 1990).

In the following essay on Karl Knies, Jun Kobayashi deals with "the most eminent" member of the "Older" GHSE, whose "main performance was in the field of money and credit, where he made his mark as a theorist" (Schumpeter, 1954, p. 809). Kobayashi, however neither addresses Knies's theory of money and credit nor mentions the stronger influence of Knies on Böhm-Bawerk, who had attended Knies's lectures and seminars at the University of Heidelberg in the academic year 1875–1876. Instead he focuses exclusively on Knies's (1853) *Political Economics from the Viewpoint of the Historical Method*, which starts with a critical examination of Roscher's historical method. This treatise, Knies's only book in which he focuses on problems of method, stresses the impact of history and geography on the characteristics of different people and economics. It was mainly written in Switzerland to which the progressive liberal Knies, like Bruno Hildebrand, who had been his teacher and mentor at the University of Marburg since 1841, emigrated after the reactionary suppression of the 1848–1849 revolution. This caused a break in his university career until 1855 when he became professor at the University of Freiburg from which he moved to Heidelberg in the north of Baden in 1865. Therefore, in contrast to Schmoller and some other members of the younger GHSE, Knies could not see any reliable bearer of economic and social policy and remained critical of the authoritarian character of Germany after unification by Prussia. This comes out in the second edition of his methodological treatise (1883). This is well argued by Kobayashi who finally examines the profound influence Knies had on Max Weber who succeeded Knies on his chair of economics in Heidelberg in 1897. However, in contrast to other authors Kobayashi stresses the differences between Weber, who insisted on value-freedom and the objectivity of knowledge, and the ethical economics of Knies who incorporated the dual character of "is" and "ought" into his conception of *Sitte*.

Two essays (5 and 10) deal with the work of Lujo Brentano, the most open-minded and enlightened representative of the younger GHSE. He was born to a well-known catholic patrician family with strong anti-Prussian sentiments. Despite many differences of opinion on major issues, his lifelong friendship with Schmoller can be regarded as the key stabilising axis of the Verein für Sozialpolitik from its foundation until World War I (see Hagemann, 2001). Brentano's interest in the labour question had been raised by Ernst Engel, the famous Director of the Prussian Bureau of Statistics, with whom he made a long visit to Britain in 1868–1869 to study working conditions. In contrast to Engel, who advocated profit-sharing schemes, Brentano favoured the organized coalition of workers as the decisive means to solve the social question. It is the main aim of Sachio Kaku's contribution to analyse Brentano's views on the compulsory insurance system for workers, thereby throwing light on Brentano's lifelong conviction of the importance of trade unions for the improvement of the conditions of the working class and his fight for a social democracy while at the same time rejecting the Marxist tendencies in the German Social Democratic party of the late nineteenth century. Unfortunately, Kaku does not even mention Engel and the influence he had on the shaping of Brentano's ideas.

One of the most valuable contributions to this collection, enlightening the reception and transmission of the ideas of the GHSE in Japan, is Tamotsu Nishizawa's essay on Lujo Brentano and Tokuzo Fukuda (1874–1930) who was Brentano's student at the University of Munich from 1898 to 1901. Having been influenced early on by Thomas Hodgskin, who was advocating trade unionism, in contrast to Kanai who vehemently opposed trade unions, Fukuda, like his master teacher Brentano, was left of centre in the social policy school of his country and strongly opposed to the deterministic tendencies of Marxism. Fukuda wrote his Ph.D. thesis on "*Die gesellschaftliche und wirtschaftliche Entwicklung in Japan*" (Social and Economic Development in Japan) and a substantial introduction to Brentano's translated writings published in Japan in 1899. He was heavily influenced by Brentano's theory on the connection between working conditions, high wages and reduced working hours, and labour productivity. Brentano probably was the most anglophile representative of the GHSE and always was an ardent advocate of free trade, which he regarded important to supply cheap food for the workers and the rapidly growing population as well as generating export markets for industrial products. In contrast to Schmoller he also held that position after Bismarck's reorientation towards protective tariffs which led to major controversies during the 1879 annual meeting of the Verein für Sozialpolitik which experienced its first major crisis. In 1905 the German translation of Alfred Marshall's *Principles* was published. Brentano, who had come to know Marshall personally at the 1889/1890 meeting of the British Association for the Advancement of Science in Leeds (during the short period when Brentano was professor in Leipzig where he succeeded Roscher), wrote a long introduction that Fukuda translated and included in the first Japanese edition of Marshall's *Principles*. Nishizawa (p. 161) makes us aware that Fukuda added the statement that Marshall's *Principles* was "the pinnacle of contemporary economics, as my mentor Brentano wrote in his introduction to the German translated edition, so there was no need to attempt to add anything further." We also learn from Nishizawa that after 1905, when Tokyo Imperial University (where Fukuda had submitted his first dissertation in 1896) under the influence of Kanai "was moving towards Wagnerian-style state socialism, Fukuda and his followers at the Higher Commercial Schools were sympathetic to their 'reformist liberalism' and were closer to British political economy" (p. 160). After World War I, Fukuda increasingly absorbed the welfare-economic ideas of Marshall's disciple Pigou. While he retained both his social-reformist engagement and his status at the GHSE, he became critical of their lack of original thought. Marshall, with some subsequent Anglo-Saxon developments, represented for Fukuda the most advanced position in the discipline of economics. Nevertheless, he drew on the institutional and Historical School's aspects of Marshall's economics.

Kiichiro Yagi, one of the finest Japanese scholars on the history of German and Austrian economic thought, draws on his impressive knowledge of Carl Menger to shed light on an important aspect of the *Methodenstreit*, i.e. the debate on method. Yagi emphasizes that Schmoller failed to respond to Carl Menger's "organic" perspective on the origins of social institutions. An appropriate answer, however, was given by Carl's brother Anton, a social reformer who stressed the existing power relations in society and the fact that the private legal institutions are not the product of the whole nation but that of the privileged class. Furthermore, the dynamic forces of social and economic development create a tension between the existing conservative legal order and changing power relations. Finally, Yagi brings in Friedrich von Wieser, who succeeded Carl Menger to his chair at the University of Vienna. In contrast to Carl Menger, who adhered to methodological individualism and remained an old-type liberal throughout his life, Wieser was less opposed to state interventionism in a period of mass politics in which concepts of power and leadership have to be conceived. It is, however, an inadmissible generalisation for Yagi to state that the economists of the younger GHSE held a "pragmatic" view on the origins of institutions and "were interventionists who supported the protective tariff and social policies" (p. 88). This, for example, is also shown by the case of the Chairman (1874–1890) of the Verein für Sozialpolitik, Erwin Nasse, who at the 1879 meeting made a strong case against Bismarck's reorientation towards protective tariffs and the new coalition of agricultural and industrial protectionists.

THE YOUNGEST HISTORICAL SCHOOL AND BEYOND

Whereas there is no contribution focusing exclusively on the work of the undisputed leader of the younger GHSE, Gustav von Schmoller, Shin'ichi Tamura contrasts the views of Schmoller and Sombart on the historico-ethical method and social policy. The analysis of the changes in the process of capitalist development, particularly Werner Sombart's notion of "late capitalism" is highlighted in Osamu Yanagisawa's essay on the reception of German economic thought by Japanese economists in the interwar period. Several times Yanagisawa refers to the social-democratic economist and sociologist, Emil Lederer (1882–1939), who had been a fellow student with Schumpeter in Böhm-Bawerk's Vienna seminar. Unfortunately he does not address the impact in Japan of Lederer's book (1929) on the Japanese society and economy in transition, which he wrote together with his first wife Emy Seidler after holding a Visiting Professorship in Tokyo for the period 1923–1925. In that work the conflict between traditional structures and the sudden introduction of modern production methods, for military and imperial purposes and prevention of some of their consequences for private consumption and social relationships, was carefully analysed. This book was a fine piece of interdisciplinary scholarship in the social sciences, one showing great awareness of the problems of a foreign culture. In 1937 it was updated and published in the U.S. when the general public developed a greater interest with the rise of Japanese imperialism. Kazuhiko Sumiya, a distinguished Weberian who has also worked on Sombart, puts emphasis in his essay on the fact that Max "Weber's *Wirtschaft und Gesellschaft* was derived from the critical succession of the German Historical School" (p. 133). He also links the Weber reception in Japan with that in Germany and the United States.

In the final two essays Makoto Tezuka explores Alfred Müller-Armack's concept of the social market economy and Naoshi Yamawaki reappraises the economic thought of Walter Eucken (1891–1950) and Wilhelm Röpke (1899–1966) and the policy of ordoliberalism. Whereas the concepts of the social-market economy and ordoliberalism had a major influence on economic policy in post-war Germany, some questions, in particular concerning the connection with the GHSE, remain open. Yamawaki starts with a pithy statement: "Strictly speaking, the ordoliberalism represented by Walter Eucken and Wilhelm Röpke does not belong to the German Historical School. On the contrary, both economists began to develop their theories in opposition to the Historical School" (p. 188). For lack of space let me concentrate my comments on Eucken, although Röpke is also a very interesting case. He had developed Keynesian ideas before Keynes, in particular the idea of an initial ignition by a credit-financed governmental investment program in the Great Depression of the early 1930s. But after the war he became a fierce critic of Keynesianism, especially of what he regarded as its inflationary bias, and was involved in a major controversy with Erich Schneider in the early 1950s.

It is true that Eucken later was very critical, not to say hostile, toward the GHSE. This comes out most clearly in the long article *"Wissenschaft im Stile Schmollers"* (Science in the style of Schmoller), in which he reviews the literature published in connection with Schmoller's hundredth birthday in 1938. In this article Eucken (1940) criticises both the lack of understanding by the Historical School of theoretical analysis because of its contempt for the interdependence of economic phenomena and its historical blindness to an excessive idea of progress that seduces one to recognize his own present time (1940!) as the standard of historical development. In particular he criticises Schmoller's statement that it is the privilege of the stronger and better to win. "It is talked of the stronger and *better* as if both are identical" (Eucken, 1940, p. 478). However, hostility to the GHSE does not hold for the young Eucken whose two main teachers at the University of Bonn were Hermann (not Joachim!) "Schumacher and Heinrich Dietzel, who evidently opposed the German Historical School" (p. 188). Whereas it can be agreed in the case of Dietzel, who was the main student of Adolph Wagner, it is not true for Schumacher, who was the main teacher and mentor of Eucken. Hermann Schumacher (1868–1952), the father of E(rnst) F(ritz) Schumacher, the author of *Small is Beautiful*, had been a student of Schmoller and Wagner, and in 1906/1907 was the first "Kaiser Wilhelm Professor" at Columbia University in New York. Schumacher, who had already been placed first by the Faculty on the list for the chair succeeding Schmoller (which went to Herkner who was placed second), in 1917 went from the University of Bonn to the University of Berlin to succeed Wagner on his chair. Eucken, who had written his Ph.D. thesis in Bonn on *The Organization of Federations in Sea Traffic* (Eucken, 1914), went with his supervisor and wrote his habilitation on *The Provision with Nitrogen in the World. An Economic Investigation* (1921) also with Schumacher, who had succeeded Schmoller as the editor of *Schmollers Jahrbuch* from 1918 to 1923 before, after major controversies, Spiethoff took over as the only editor. Both the dissertation and the habilitation thesis of Eucken are heavily influenced by his teacher Schumacher and the ideas and methods of the GHSE. It is only at the end of the hyperinflationary development in Weimar Germany in 1923 that Eucken became dissatisfied with the explanations of the representatives of the GHSE, who, as Helfferich but also Schumacher, favoured a balance-of-payments approach, that Eucken turned into a more critical and theoretical orientation and finally cut his roots in the GHSE, leading to a personal break with his former teacher and mentor, Schumacher.[4] Decades later Schumacher (1957) still contributed an interesting article on "The Historical School" to the *Encyclopedia of the Social Sciences* (published posthumously).

The subject of this book is very broad. It therefore comes as no surprise that as a coherent collection it does not fully succeed. Whereas some of the essays are detailed and limited in scope, others cover very interesting topics relevant for a modern historical, institutional, evolutionary or cultural approach to economics. As usual with such collections the individual essays vary in quality. However, despite some imperfections Shionoya's visible finger of the invisible hand has managed to achieve a greater-than-normal coherence in a conference volume. Moreover, the degree of scholarship the Japanese economists display on a subject remote in time and space is remarkable. Together and individually the contributors have better knowledge and understanding of the GHSE than the average young German economist today.

NOTES

1. For greater details see Morris-Suzuki (1990, pp. 62–69) and Kumagai (2001).
2. For a critical assessment of Pearson's thesis see also the convincing arguments by Borchardt and Häuser in Nau and Schefold (2002, pp. 44–55). See also the debate between Caldwell and Pearson in HOPE 33, 2001, pp. 649–661.
3. See Pearson (1999, pp. 554–555).
4. For greater details on the influence of Schumacher (and Dietzel) on Eucken see the recent Freiburg Ph.D. thesis by Goldschmidt (2001), who also gives an interesting perspective on Eucken and the necessity of a cultural economics which matches the spirit of the Shionoya volume.

REFERENCES

Eisermann, G. (1956). *Die Grundlagen des Historismus in der deutschen Nationalökonomie*. Enke, Stuttgart.

Eucken, W. (1914). *Die Verbandsbildung in der Seeschiffahrt*. Duncker&Humblot, Munich and Leipzig.

Eucken, W. (1921). *Die Stickstoffversorgung der Welt*. Eine volkswirtschaftliche Untersuchung. Deutsche Verlagsanstalt, Stuttgart and Berlin.

Eucken, W. (1940). Wissenschaft im Stile schmollers. *Weltwirtschaftliches Archiv*, *52*, 468–506.

Goldschmidt, N. (2001). *Entstehung und Vermächtnis ordoliberalen Denkens. Walter Eucken und die Notwendigkeit einer kulturellen Ökonomik*. LIT Verlag, Münster-Hamburg-London.

Hagemann, H. (2001). The Verein für Sozialpolitik from its foundation (1872) until World War I. In: M. M. Augello & M. E. L. Guidi (Eds), *The Spread of Political Economy and the Professionalisation of Economists. Economic Societies in Europe, America and Japan in the Nineteenth Century* (pp. 152–175). London and New York: Routledge.

Herkner, H. (1894). *Die Arbeiterfrage. Eine Einführung*. J. Guttentag, Berlin.

Ikeda, Y. (1997). Die entstehungsgeschichte der Grundsätze Carl Mengers. Scripta Mercaturae, St. Katharinen.

Knies, K. (1853). Die politische Oekonomie vom Standpunkt der geschichtlichen Methode. Schwetschke, Braunschweig (2nd ed., 1883). Die politische Oekonomie vom geschichtlichen Standpuncte, Schwetschke, Braunschweig.

Kumagai, J. (2001). Orchestrating economic ideas: The formation and development of economic societies in modern Japan. In: M. M. Augello & M. E. L. Guidi (Eds), *The Spread of Political Economy and the Professionalisation of Economists. Economic Societies in Europe, America and Japan in the Nineteenth Century* (pp. 200–215). London and New York: Routledge.

Lederer, E., & Lederer-Seidler, E. (1929). *Japan-Europa. Wandlungen im fernen Osten*. Societäts-Druckerei, Frankfurt/Main; American edition 1937. *Japan in Transition*. New Haven: Yale University Press.

Morris-Suzuki, T. (1990). *A history of Japanese economic thought*. London and New York: Routledge.

Nau, H. H., & Schefold, B. (2002). *The historicity of economics. Continuities and discontinuities of historical thought in 19th and 20th century economics*. Berlin and Heidelberg: Springer.

Pearson, H. (1999). Was there really a German historical school of economics? *History of Political Economy*, *31*, 547–562.

Pearson, H. (2002). The German historical school of economics. What It Was Not, and What It Was. In: Nau & Schefold (Eds), pp. 23–43.

Roscher, W. (1843). *Grundriß zu Vorlesungen über die Staatswirthschaft, Nach geschichtlicher Methode*. Dieter, Göttingen.

Schumacher, H. (1957). The historical school. *Encyclopedia of the Social Sciences*, *5*, 371–377.

Schumpeter, J. A. (1911). *Theorie der wirtschaftlichen Entwicklung*. Duncker&Humblot, Munich and Leipzig (2nd ed.) 1926; Engl. translation: *The Theory of Economic Development. An Inquiry into Profits, Capital, Credit, Interest, and the Business Cycle*. Cambridge, MA: Harvard University Press, 1934.

Schumpeter, J. A. (1926). Gustav von Schmoller und die Probleme von heute. *Schmollers Jahrbuch*, *50*, 337–388.

Schumpeter, J. A. (1954). *History of economic analysis*. New York: Oxford University Press and London: Allen & Unwin.

Shionoya, Y. (1990). The origin of the Schumpeterian research program: A chapter omitted from Schumpeter's *Theory of Economic Development. Journal of Institutional and Theoretical Economics, 146,* 314–327.

Streissler, E. W. (1990). The influence of German economics on the work of Menger and Marshall. In: B. J. Caldwell (Ed.), *Carl Menger and his Legacy on Economics* (pp. 31–68). Annual supplement to Volume 22, *History of Political Economy.* Durham and London: Duke University Press.

CARPENTER'S THE DISSEMINATION OF THE WEALTH OF NATIONS IN FRENCH AND IN FRANCE, 1776–1843

Robert F. Hebert

A review essay on Kenneth E. Carpenter's, *The Dissemination of the Wealth of Nations in French and in France, 1776–1843*. Published for The Bibliographical Society of America. New Castle, DE: Oak Knoll Press, 2003. Pp. LXIII, 255. $45.00.

The Wealth of Nations is bipolar work: on the one hand it is an important philosophical treatise; on the other, it is the founding text of the discipline of economics. This characteristic gives it a unique place among the "great books" of western culture. How did a book, written over two centuries ago by a pedantic, idiosyncratic college professor come to achieve this lofty status? Although nowhere explicitly stated by the author of the work under review, this question serves as a lightning rod for his bibliographic efforts. The focus bestowed on France is justified because the reception of *The Wealth of Nations* (hereafter, WN) in France mirrored, in most important aspects, its reception throughout Europe. Nevertheless, the opaqueness of this book's title masks its most fascinating feature, namely, the manner in which Carpenter unfolds the complicated answer to this central question.

Despite centuries of animosity between their kingdoms, France and Great Britain maintained a lively interchange of ideas in philosophy and science throughout the eighteenth and nineteenth centuries. Hence, it is not surprising that this vigorous intellectual trade embraced the new science of political economy as it came to be formulated by Adam Smith in his classic tome, *An Inquiry Into the Nature and*

Research in the History of Economic Thought and Methodology A Research Annual
Research in the History of Economic Thought and Methodology, Volume 22-A, 413–418
Copyright © 2004 by Elsevier Ltd.
All rights of reproduction in any form reserved
ISSN: 0743-4154/doi:10.1016/S0743-4154(03)22026-5

Causes of the Wealth of Nations. No laggard in this respect, France had its own impressive list of founders. The most prominent included Pierre Boisguilbert, Sebastien Vauban, Richard Cantillon (an Irish expatriate based in Paris), Anne-Robert Jacques Turgot, and the irrepressible François Quesnay and his band of Physiocrats. By all accounts, Smith learned a great deal from his French predecessors, especially Quesnay (even though he disagreed with the central tenet of Physiocracy, the exclusive productivity of land). And in return, France recognized Smith's *magnum opus* as an important systemization of the fledgling field that came to be known first as "political economy," and later, as simply "economics." In this book Carpenter traces the serpentine path followed by WN on its way to becoming the cornerstone of classical economics by finding, reproducing, and examining the written record of acceptance/rejection of its ideas in France and in the French language.

Adam Smith's great work of political economy reached French readers by various means: through reprints of English editions; a number of translations directed to different French audiences; and a plethora of summaries, extracts and reviews in magazines and journals. Carpenter has done some masterful sleuthing (on three continents) in locating, identifying and assembling these many venues. But more importantly, by combining cultural history and bibliographic analysis, he has mapped the cross-cultural transmission of ideas from England to the Continent, and assessed the implications of Smith's ideas on French society. At first marginalized by the French government and the book trade, WN was eventually adopted by French intellectuals seeking an ideological basis for the French Revolution. Far more important from a history of science perspective, it went on to become a canonical work of economic thought that provoked extensive commentary and scholarly attention – to the point almost of creating an "Adam Smith industry" in the history of economic thought. Carpenter's book reveals the ins and outs of an important early chapter in the transformation of WN from "a handbook for valets and seamstresses" (p. xxiv) to "a tool for creating a new society" (p. xli), and eventually, to "a foundation piece in the professionalization of the science of economics" (p. xxiv).

Shortly after its publication in England, WN was recognized as an important book in France, as witnessed by early reviews in the *Journal encyclopédique* (1776) and the *Journal des savants* (1777). However, no translation in book form appeared in France until near the end of the monarchy (1788). Piecemeal and inferior translations existed as early as 1778, but sales were unimpressive because nothing marked these early translations as works of importance. What gave impetus to the dissemination of WN in France, and eventually elevated the book to canonical status, was the French Revolution. But WN enjoyed two kinds of canonicity. The first derived from its careful dissection of the effects of individual freedom on national prosperity, and the second from its metamorphosis into a scholarly text by the best-known of Smith's French translators, Germaine Garnier.[1] Garnier's first translation, *Richesse des nations* (1802) offered additions that transformed the text from a manual of the working class to a scholarly treatise. An expanded edition of Garnier's translation, published posthumously in 1843, introduced notes drawn from many writers of different cultures, and established the *Richesse des nations* as a major force in the professionalization of economics. Thus, in France, within the span of less than three-quarters of a century, WN progressed from a marginal work to one of central importance, and then from one kind of centrality to another – demonstrating, as Carpenter (p. xxiv) underscores, "that a learned text can at various times be directed at different publics, who read it differently."

One of the more interesting aspects of Carpenter's research into the evolution of WN as a canonical work is the illumination of roles played by various French authors in promoting WN as an important book. The (naïve) standard version of Smith's acceptance in France bestows the bulk of credit on J. B. Say, who basically recast Smith's work in an organized form more suitable for use as an instructional text. However, Carpenter exposes the significance of other key figures. The first of these is the aforementioned Garnier, whose French translation of WN endured for 150 years in France.[2] According to Carpenter, the translation of WN that Garnier introduced in 1802, "... had the marks of a canonical text ... one of those signs was that Garnier added an entire volume of notes, which served to make the work into what might be called a summary of economic thought from a French angle" (Carpenter, p. lviii). Consequently, with the Garnier editions, beginning in 1802 (subsequent editions followed in 1822 and 1843), Adam Smith was transformed in France from an author of the moment to a canonical authority studied by the elite. This revelation does not diminish Say's role in the acceptance of liberal economics in France, but it does force a sharing of credit. Say did play a pivotal role, as Carpenter concedes.

> Garnier's notes [which were actually essays dealing with topics treated variously by Adam Smith] necessarily could not be a systematic summary. That is what Jean-Baptiste Say produced with his *Traité d'économie politique* (1803), which was followed by French editions in 1814, 1817, 1819, 1826, and two Brussels editions of 1827. Hitherto it could be assumed that Say's treatise captured the market for a wide-ranging work of economic analysis, and that it was the reason why no further edition of Garnier's translation of WN appeared until 1822, twenty years after the first edition. In fact, though, Say did not have the market entirely to himself, for the 1802 Garnier translation exists in two editions – that is printings from different type settings – both dated 1802 (Carpenter, *lvii*).

As a consequence, the circulation of Garnier's translation of WN was more extensive than heretofore recognized, and the impact of Say's work was not as uniquely the result of his singular efforts as we believed.

When Garnier's role is assessed alongside Say's, we get a more balanced view of the development of French economics in the first half of the nineteenth century. But there is more to the story. Carpenter's research underscores the significance of yet another French economist in the dissemination of WN in France, Adolphe Jerôme Blanqui (1798–1854), who is known to Anglo-Saxon historians of economic thought primarily as one of their own. Blanqui's immensely popular *Histoire de l'économie politique en Europe, depuis les anciens jusqu'à nos jours, suivie d'une bibliographie raisonnée des principaux ouvrages d'économie politique* (1838, 1842) achieved international prominence by 1843, boasting Portuguese, Spanish and German editions. Twenty-one years after the death of Garnier, Blanqui edited the 1843 edition of Garnier's translation of WN, transforming it into even more durable form. Carpenter shows how Blanqui (who followed Say in the chair of political economy at the Collège de France) raised WN to a second level of canonization within France (and coincidentally, how historians of economics provide useful service to the profession):

> Blanqui's editing reflected his broad knowledge of the literature. The 1843 [Garnier] edition, in contrast to those of 1802 and 1822, which had notes by only one person, was a veritable variorum edition. Adolphe Blanqui made that observation explicitly in his preface. His edition did not include all that commentators had written on Smith, but nothing essential was omitted concerning the work that, as Blanqui stated, had laid the foundation for the science of political economy in Europe. Blanqui's added notes, which often consisted of extended passages, were drawn from Garnier and Jean-Baptiste Say from France; from Jeremy Bentham, David Buchanan, Thomas Hodgskin, John Ramsay MacCulloch, Thomas Robert Malthus, David Ricardo, and George Poulett Scrope from Britain; Heinrich Friedrich von Storch from Germany and Russia; and Jean Charles Léonard Simonde de Sismondi from Switzerland and Italy. The inclusion of commentary from all these economists meant that WN was no longer an English effort, no longer an English and French work, no more just the labor of two people, but rather a work of many hands from throughout Europe, all people working to develop a body of knowledge. In other words, many workers toiled in the field of economics, which Blanqui repeatedly termed a 'science.' Their work was drawn on here for the benefit of the science, thus making the Blanqui edition of Garnier's translation a work for scholars (Carpenter, p. lxii).

It is commonly asserted that "the devil is in the details," so it is appropriate that we consider Carpenter's assemblage of historical desiderata. More than three-fourths of this book is comprised of extracts from French translations, reviews of WN appearing in French journals, or commentary on WN or its various French translations. There are also thirteen illustrations of bibliographic note, provided by the Kress Collection of Business and Economics of the Baker Library at Harvard University Business School, of which Carpenter was curator for many years. Because so much of this detailed material is in French, it may prove rough sledding for those not at home in the language. However, Carpenter does not abandon the reader to his own devices entirely. Before each extract, review or commentary, he prefaces a brief synopsis of the item, its historical pedigree, relevant publication information – or in the case of unpublished material, a technical description of the manuscript. This kind of attention to detail helps to steer even the linguistically challenged through the maze of bibliographic paraphernalia surrounding WN.

In the first item to confront the reader, for example, an unpublished extract and unpublished full translation of WN in 1776 by the Abbé Morellet (1727–1819), Carpenter introduces the manuscript (too long to reproduce in his work because it was written in scribal hand and exceeds 1,500 pages) with a narrative describing Morellet's unsuccessful efforts to secure publication of the manuscript, including his appeals for support from Turgot; the subsequent confiscation of the manuscript by police; and ultimate denial of permission to publish. Carpenter also describes the private circulation of Morellet's manuscript in France, and speculates on the timing of the translation – which was almost coincident with the publication of WN in England – suggesting that Morellet had received an advance copy of the manuscript from Smith himself. Where appropriate, he cites secondary sources in support of his summary account, and concludes with a detailed description of the typography of the manuscript itself in both its physical and microfilm formats. This same kind of attention to detail accompanies the provenance of each of the thirty items surveyed. Where extracts and reviews are concerned, Carpenter prefaces each reproduction of the original French text with helpful information on the history, nature, distribution and reputation of the journal that published the extract or review. In all, this is a very utilitarian book. Attractively bound and printed, it will make a handsome and useful addition to the economist's library, especially those with a strong interest in the historical roots of the subject.

This book can be read profitably on at least two different levels. Bibliographers and book historians will find here an adept handling of the tools of their trade, turned toward analysis of one of the classics of Western thought. Carpenter competently mines the bibliographic landscape to enrich the paratext[3] of translations of WN and to trace the changing typography[4] of these works. Economists and intellectual historians will find here a well-documented dossier on how a classic work in an alien society was transformed from a marginal work to a tool for effecting social change to a canonical work in a new discipline. At whatever level one chooses to approach this book, the effort repays itself. But the highest profit is apt to accrue to economists and historians, who will find here valuable source material presented in a manner that facilitates its use by others. Drawing upon this assemblage of material that was formerly scattered, isolated, and in some cases, inaccessible, historians will be able to tease out implications for the history of the French Revolution and the history of economic thought in France. Consequently, this book should have wide appeal beyond the narrow limits suggested by its workmanlike title.

Carpenter concludes his study of the dissemination of WN in France with the following forthright declaration: "In France and in the French language WN experienced an extraordinarily complex history." That complexity is now exposed in its fullest measure for the rest of us to see and contemplate, thanks to Ken Carpenter.

I have but one minor criticism, which is an admonishment of the publisher rather than the author. Why are not readers treated to a brief biographical profile of the author? Ken Carpenter is one of the world's pre-eminent bibliographers in the field of economics. He was for many years the curator of one of the greatest collections of economic literature in the world, the Kress Collection, housed at Baker Library, in the Harvard Business School. Currently he is Assistant Director for Research Resources at Harvard University Library. His eminent qualifications to undertake a work of this nature should be manifest to the book's intended audience, if not to increase the marketability of the book, at least to alert potential readers to the qualifications of the author. The review copy that I received did not contain a dust jacket, which is the usual place to position such material. But dust jackets are expensive to produce, and today's publishers tend to avoid them if possible. This is no excuse, however, for omitting useful information that can easily and cheaply be worked into the front matter of a book on a single page.

NOTES

1. In pre-revolutionary France, Germaine Garnier (1754–1821) was known mainly for his poetry. The revolution politicized him, as it did many authors, but Garnier supported the monarchy. Nevertheless, he survived the ravages of the Terror and served for a time as *directoire* of the *département* of Paris. In 1792 he emigrated to Switzerland where he devoted himself to the study of literature. He returned to France under the Empire and became president of the Senate between 1809 and 1811. In 1814 he voted for the deposition of Napoleon and was awarded by the Restoration government with a post in the Council of State and the title of marquis. Although he wrote on the theory of banking and the history of money, his qualifications as economist stem primarily from his *Abrégé des principes de l'économie politique* (1796), in which he managed to reconcile Smith's ideas with Physiocracy. This book exercised a prominent, though subtle, influence on J. B. Say.

2. As Carpenter (p. xxiv) notes, no new translations were forthcoming in France until the recent translation of Paulette Taieb, *Enquête sur la nature et les causes de la richesse des nations*, 4 vols. (Paris, 1995).

3. The *paratext* is a term used to denote the combination of peritext and epitext associated with a written work. The *peritext* pertains to format, running heads, tables of contents, indexes and other things that tell the potential reader what to expect from a book. The *epitext* encompasses whatever form of publicity might be employed to promote a book, including reviews, extracts, summaries, and commentaries.

4. The typography of a book refers to its typeface, layout and general appearance, which is determined, in large measure by the paratext.

STRATHERN'S A BRIEF HISTORY OF ECONOMIC GENIUS

Edith Kuiper

A review essay on Paul Strathern's, *A Brief History of Economic Genius*.
New York: Texere, 2001. Pp. xxii, 328. $27.95.

INTRODUCTION

Paul Strathern's book, *A Brief History of Economic Genius*, is a history of economic thought that is written for the general public. The book contains photographs, no footnotes and a very limited list of sources that functions as a list of "further reading" advice. This book stands in a long line of over more than forty books by Paul Strathern on the lives and works of great philosophers such as Aristotle, Plato, Locke, Kant, Wittgenstein, Nietzsche, Hegel, and Madame Curie as the exceptional woman scientist. In these books he introduces the lay reader in an accessible and brief manner to often complicated ideas. As his other books, *A Brief History* tells the life stories of scholars, which are here woven into an account of the history of economics.

Strathern starts his history of economics literally at zero with the introduction of the zero in Europe around 1200 AD, and the introduction of the double-entry bookkeeping by the Italian Luca Pacioli, in the late 15th century. He subsequently travels through the history of economic science over the heads of a selection of economists, he calls "geniuses." In the history that follows, he tells the story of an economic science that becomes increasingly mathematical as the natural outcome of an historical process in which individual "geniuses" with "brilliant ideas" are

Research in the History of Economic Thought and Methodology A Research Annual
Research in the History of Economic Thought and Methodology, Volume 22-A, 419–428
Copyright © 2004 by Elsevier Ltd.
ISSN: 0743-4154/doi:10.1016/S0743-4154(03)22027-7

the main players. Strathern does not shy away from indicating long lines in the history of economic science and challenging statements about the nature of economics, human kind and scientific knowledge. He characterizes the development of economic theory as a coming together of bookkeeping, finance, statistics, mathematics and a scientific worldview that strives for "natural laws" and absolute certainties. Strathern draws the path along which economic theorizing has become more and more close to describing "how the *real* world of economics work[s]" (see p. 295, emphasis as in the original). Or as he·states it at the end of the prologue: "[E]conomics has now spread in to every facet of our lives. It has made us increasingly aware of who we are and what it is we are doing. What follows is a narrative of how this happened together with the lives and ideas of those who helped to make it happen" (p. xxii).

His history is framed in a prologue and an epilogue on the story of Dr. Strangelove, the nazi-like scientist who obtained knowledge, scientific status and power to such an extent that he was able to threaten world peace. Strathern explicitly makes the comparison with John von Neumann, claiming that von Neumann inspired Kubrick's character, which may well have been the case. In the epilogue, Strathern comes back to discussing the increasing power of economics in defining people's personal lives and in providing a back-up if not inspiration for both destructive forces in society such as the Cold War Nuclear Arms Race, and more constructive developments such as the Marshall Plan after the Second World War. The famous quote from John Maynard Keynes is well chosen as guiding phrase for the book; it might even have inspired it.

> The ideas of economics and political philosophers, both when they are right and when they are wrong, are more powerful than is commonly understood. Indeed, the world is ruled by little else, Practical men, who believe themselves to be quite exempt from any intellectual influences, are usually the slaves of some defunct economist. Madmen in authority, who hear voices in the air, are distilling their frenzy from some academic scribbles of a few years back.

The social and moral problem of the seemingly unstoppable development of scientific knowledge that accompanies increasing technical and military power, and the concentration of this power in a few hands that might well be morally deficient, as introduced in the prologue, loses out however, to Strathern's interest in economic genius. The focus on the lives and ideas of individual economists gets stronger throughout the book and Strathern closes the book by wondering whether Friedman has been the last of the great economists or that a new Adam Smith or Dr. Strangelove is already warming up.

Since this is a "brief history," limited space is available and thus the choice of economists discussed becomes important if not crucial for the story told. Strathern's choice of economic geniuses is clearly informed by his view on the current state of economic science and the points he wants to make (Luca Pacioli on book keeping, John Graunt on statistics, John Law on early monetary theory and financial crises, de Moivre on probability theory, Condorcet on mathematics and social theory, Saint-Simon and Robert Owen on scientific socialism). Though for the rest he reproduces a standard version of the history of economics, discussing Petty, Mandeville, Quesnay, Smith, Ricardo, Bentham, Malthus, Mill, Marx, Jevons, Marshall, Veblen, Keynes, Schumpeter, Friedman, and Nash, his account of the history of economic thought is a mixed bag containing sound historical research, interesting and challenging conjunctions and justified concerns, on one hand, and a-historical Whig-history statements and some unfounded and rather tendentious conclusions on the other. Contemporary problems, such as environmental problems, world poverty, and devaluation of the work of women in the household are put into perspective and dealt with in just a few sentences. For instance, in the discussion on Malthus' view on the increasing world population, Strathern concludes on the current issue of global overpopulation that "[i]t is also likely that the global population will have begun to level out, just as it has in Western Europe and North America. Global resources are not unlimited, but we are some way from exhausting them. And despite much chronic urban overcrowding, far larger tracts of our planet remain uninhabited" (pp. 118–119). Lines like these are the cement that keeps the book together; however, they are not part of what makes this book interesting. Before discussing the book's challenges for historians of economics, I want to make some critical points.

The editing work of the publisher, Taxere, is done poorly. Strathern will not have been pleased with this. On a regular basis, words are cut in two by putting in a space, which can be confusing "so metimes." Inconsistent use of Italics at the beginning of each chapter and typo's in names (Pacioli becomes Paciolo at page 3, and John Law turns into William Law at page 37) are other examples of editorial sloppiness. However, the editing of the table-like overview of developments in economic history should not have missed Strathern's attention (p. 170). The table indicates a first period running from Greek civilization to the Renaissance, which is located in time between 1,500 and 1,500.[1] The system of referencing is too limited even for a book like this. Strathern explains his approach by stating "[b]ecause this is intended as a popular work, I have not included footnotes and an exhaustive list of sources" (p. 311). This way of acknowledging resources – one to three titles a chapter – makes it impossible however, to check and further read his quoted remarks.

More serious, though, are the mistakes that slipped into Strathern's representation of the ideas of the economic geniuses. His statement on Marx, for instance, has Marx propagating nationalization of the means of production to "balance social and economic justice" (p. 196). This may enable him to dismiss both

Marx and state socialism in the paragraph that follows, but does not do service to the uninformed reader. Elsewhere, explaining Keynes' work, he stresses the importance of "aggregate demand," instead of "effective demand," to give a few examples. Finally, the way Strathern uses the terms "economics" and "economics science" in discussing economic research conducted centuries before the coinage of these terms, shows that Strathern aims at a larger public and is not much interested in the sensitivities of historians of economics.

What I found intriguing and challenging in his book is Strathern's perception of the role of genius in the history of economic science. Most of us are taught by Popper and others that there is no real relevance in how theories come about; the context of discovery and what happened there can and should be separated from the assessment of the truth-value of the theory. For the scientific status of a theory it is irrelevant whether the author had his insights in a dream or being hit by an apple while sitting under a tree, or if he or she experienced isolation, depression or happiness, or whatever circumstances can be thought of. What counts is how the theory stands testing in the context of justification (Blaug, 1980, p. 14). Strathern blurs this boundary by making direct links between great economists' personality structure and their economic theorizing. The way he links the personal character of the founding fathers to their economic theorizing and the impact this has for his perception of the development of economic thought is worth unraveling. In order to do that I will first discuss his perception of economic genius and his view on the nature of the economy and economic science that goes with it.

THE GENIUS AS SCIENTIFIC AGENT

In the sociology of science, Strathern's approach to writing the history of a scientific field as the product of extraordinary, brilliant individuals is addressed as the history of scientific discovery (see, e.g. Brannigan, 1981; Mulkay, 1985). The concept of "genius" that Strathern uses here links up with the dominant "genius" view of creativity (Weisberg, 1988). Some say this concept of genius goes back to the Ancient Greek idea of gods and/or the Muses that put creative ideas into the artist (Weisberg, 1986), others locate its origin in Roman times (Battersby, 1989). It is only the (late) eighteenth century and later, with the rise of Romanticism, that this concept acquires the meaning it now has: an extraordinary individual, scientist or artist, who is a creator and in that sense god-like: someone who has insights – that sometimes come in a dream – which are original, unexplained and reveal connections that other "normal" people were unable to see (Battersby, 1989, p. 43). In 1869 Francis Galton publishes *Hereditary Genius* in which he investigates the biological and personal background characteristics of geniuses (Ochse, 1990;

Simonton, 1994). This research later evolves into the fields of scientometrics and histiometry (Simonton, 1990).

Other views on creativity maintain that historical and social context importantly determines what makes a genius. Genre, paradigm and style, for instance, importantly influence the reception of the points and stories brought forward (see, e.g. Ochse, 1990; Simonton, 1984). Johnson-Laird, for example, compares creativity to murder in the way it depends on motive, means and opportunity (Johnson-Laird, 1988). Others take the position that geniuses are socially constructed in the sense that production of acknowledged achievements is constructed as discovery and their author as "genius" (Brannigan, 1981, p. 40, see also Battersby, 1990; DeNora, 1997; Fara, 2002; Mulkay, 1985).

It cannot be denied that, as Strathern's book shows, personal accounts of exceptional people do make good stories and can turn "even" a history of economics into spicy reading. By not addressing issues like what makes someone a genius in economics, however, Strathern mystifies and naturalizes the concept of economic genius. Moreover, by looking back from our current position in economics and deciding that "great economists" are "geniuses," he reasons backwards and assigns special status to a selection of people who are perceived to be "born to be great" and to have special access to (knowledge about) nature, producing insights into the "true nature of things." Of this way of understanding the history of science, Mulkay says that "[i]t is an illusion in the sense that discovery is socially accomplished over time, sometimes over surprisingly long periods of time, and is interpretatively projected backwards upon earlier events" (Mulkay, 1985, p. 173, see also DeNora, 1997). Strathern's approach to genius thus takes attention away from questions about the organization and financing of the production of scientific knowledge, and the process through which certain ideas get accepted and others don't. In line with this, it also explains away the absence of great women economists as "just" a lack of women genius.[2] Or as Tia DeNora states it, "to decontextualize genius is to elude the moral and political character of many or most quarrels over what counts as 'valuable' work" (DeNora, 1997, p. 6).

This image of the isolated brilliant mind that – all on his own – figures out the structure of the universe, is a romantic one. It resonates with the modernist perception of science that is dominant in the general public and plays an important role in the legitimation of science and the status of the results it produces. Applied in the history of economics, the approach of scientific discovery strengthens the view of economists as priests who, in a value-free context, "explain nature to culture" in a language that "normal" people cannot understand (i.e. mathematics) (see also Harding, 1986). As such it assigns truth value to what economists claim and explains the tendency of people to follow "great minds" even though doing so goes against their basic values.

Though Strathern is concerned about these issues, his concept of economic genius and development of economic theory prevents him pursuing this line of thought further. Instead, he presents great economists as responsible for the main developments in the history of economics assuming they are in control and have the ideas that define the mind frame of those that come after them and of those who make the decisions.

ECONOMICS AS A NATURAL PROCESS

Strathern's view of the role of genius goes with a perception of scientific discovery that posits nature and/or the economy as "out there" and its regularities to be uncovered by brilliant minds. When the economy is perceived as predominantly a natural process, this implies that it can best take care of itself since human interference only messes up things. When the economy instead is considered to be a cultural process, politicians have a responsibility to steer and accommodate the economic process the best they can. In this case, economists have a role to play and should figure out the workings of the system in order to help politicians regulate and optimize it. Strathern's view on the economy is that markets should be free, but when left alone will become structured by monopolies and cartels. In order to keep a "free market" free, the government needs power to design regulations and conduct the required law enforcement. The issue of how the state's independence vis-à-vis multinational corporations is to be maintained in an increasingly global economy is not addressed, nor is the position of scientific research and the possibility of value-free investigation reflected upon. Strathern considers the economy to be essentially mathematical, especially because we are dealing with the behavior of large numbers of people and because of the uncertainty involved, which can be fruitfully tackled with probability theory.

When talking about economic science, his account of the history of economics implies that in the end, the best will win and that the latest view on the economy is the best. He delineates an opposition between those who go for "real" science like Ricardo, Jevons, von Neumann, Nash and Friedman and propagate a laisser-faire approach to the economy, and those who are led more by the heart like Owen, Saint-Simon, Marx, Veblen and Keynes and who see a more distinct role for the state in regulating the market. In Strathern's account of the history of economic science the first group of economists tends to have the upper hand. Though he acknowledges as an important limitation of the purely abstract, theoretical approach that it drifts too far from reality, Strathern's overall perception of economic science is that economic theory is in the process of becoming increasingly more realistic.

Discussing the more recent and future development of economic science, Strathern "paints himself into a corner" – to use one of his expressions – by focusing on individual brilliant minds assuming that their work is value free, that they have direct access to "nature" and are autonomous in the ideas they produce. Thus, he misses out on the development that brought together government, corporate business and science, and that made the image of value-free scientific knowledge about "nature" instrumental to their common aims. Strathern does not address the problem of the extent to which scientific research is a synonym for independent inquiry, but instead focuses on the individual scientist, his visions and moral behavior.

HOW CAN ECONOMIC THEORY BE PERSONAL?

Strathern's focus on the lives and works of great economists implies that it is these individuals who change the course of economic science. In discussing their work, however, Strathern ascribes much explanatory value to the personality structure of these geniuses. He sees a direct connection between the psychological outfit, the experiences and personal behavior of these economists and the content of their work. Where Popper stresses that we are not interested in the how, by what circumstances, or by whom a theory comes about, but that its scientific value is established in the context of justification, Strathern has a different approach. He tells us about Karl Marx, for example, whose life – full of conflicts and contradictions – not only illustrates his perception of economic reality, but also explains it. Then there is the account on von Neumann and his approach to game theory, that "had been essentially co-operative" [. . . and] "its non-zero-sum aspects involved collaboration, producing win-win situations and the like. This very much mirrored von Neumann's character" (p. 294). On John Nash's work on non-cooperative games we read that "[i]n keeping with his character, Nash came at game theory from precisely the opposite direction. He lived in a world where there was no real communication [. . .] The game situation was essentially *non-collaborative*" (emphasis as in the original, p. 295). Though these personality descriptions remain scattered, sometimes turn into personal attacks and appear merely to have the function of giving color to the tale, something else emerges from the Strathern's points. Though these economists are seen to be responsible for the development of economic thought, it is their personality structure that seems to determine to a large extent the main lines and approaches taken in their work. This means that it is not just "brilliant ideas" or "discovery of the truth" that determine their work, but rather (unconscious) psychology.

When it comes to the case of John Nash, however, something strange happens. It appears that in this case, bearing the consequences of his line of reasoning seems to be more than Strathern is willing to do. Strathern includes in his list of sources the biography on John Nash by Sylvia Nasar (1998), in which Nash's schizophrenia is hard to miss. In discussing Nash and his contribution to the history of economics, however, Strathern makes Nash fully responsible for what he calls his "down fall" and focuses instead on what he states as Nash's problems with his homosexuality (p. 297). There is no mentioning here of Nash's schizophrenia. This is not only confusing; it also elides questions about how Nash's schizophrenia may have impacted his theoretical work. When we lessen the focus on Nash' person and take the context into account, how was it possible that the schizophrenic John Nash was able to function so long as "normal" in the context of mathematical and game-theory economics? What is the set of shared values within this group of white young male scientists that supports and produces these perceptions of reality as "true?" What does this say about the intellectual climate at RAND and, more generally, economics?

When psychology or, rather, unexamined, unconscious or pathological drives play an important role in determining the direction and development of economic science, where does that leave us with science as value- and context-free knowledge about "nature?" When theories are being tested (are they ever?) in a context identical to the one they emerged from, the same conditions that brought about the theory will also enter the process of testing and theory choice. When this is the case, the personal characteristics and preferences of those who define theoretical frameworks of subsequent generations of scientists, do play a role in the process of knowledge production. This is the point that Strathern brings back in here.

SOME CONCLUSIONS

The initial line established by Strathern at the beginning of the book on the invention of cost benefit analysis – which he links to the use of mathematics, statistics and computer modeling based on a specific perception of science, and the way it defines the way people think about themselves – is very interesting. The rise of the approach to science and to life generally – which presents norms and values in a seemingly value-free and technical manner, which in itself contains a strongly objectified way of perceiving one-self and others – is a very timely issue, indeed. This initial line of reasoning would require more attention, however, be given to the current state and importance of accountancy and business economics, the role of computers and the impact of globalization on the production of economic knowledge. Strathern does not pursue these lines, but takes along the mathematization of economics and the impact of physics as norm setting where it concerns models of scientific knowledge, thus "explaining" the power of scientists – "geniuses" – who have "more direct," mathematical knowledge about "reality."

Because of his focus on geniuses as scientific agents, Strathern's great economists, being assigned such a major role in defining our worldview, become heroes or Dr. Strangeloves or both. As their role in the history of economics is thus overstated, so is their responsibility. This not only leaves the "normal" scientist or economist, who has her or his own responsibility as a critical academic, off the hook; it also tends to turn the von Neumann's of our time into scapegoats.

Still, Strathern's statement that science is to some extent personal and that economic theories to some extent do bear the print of the personality of those who designed them is substantial. Stated in Kuhnian terms, the scientific method and the critique of peers in the scientific community may eliminate many inaccuracies and subjective traces in normal research, but what about the original research that sets the framework for later applied research? Rather than turning our back on these questions,[3] or relegate them to sociology and psychology of science, the scientific approach to an issue like this is "investigate, investigate, investigate." This implies that instead of assuming that scientific innovations are value free and with them the research conducted in its wake, much more work should be done in the direction of the psychology and practice of economic research in which specific values and perceptions of reality are played out. It is to be expected that this kind of research will address more directly Strathern's concerns than his focus on economic genius.

NOTES

1. This should of course be 500 B.C.–1500 A.D., a period of 2000 years instead of 1000 years as indicated in the text.

2. On the gendered character of the concept of "genius," see Battersby (1990). On explanations for the low number of women geniuses in science, see R. Ochse (1990), and in the arts, see Nochlin (1973).

3. Sandra Harding (1986) states that objectivity, as claimed by most positivists, demands scrutiny of anything, except of science itself.

REFERENCES

Battersby, C. (1990). *Gender and genius*. London: The Woman's Press.

Blaug, M. (1980). *The methodology of economics. Or how economists explain*. Cambridge, UK: Cambridge University Press.

Brannigan, A. (1981). *The social basis of scientific discoveries*. Cambridge, London, New York: Cambridge University Press.

DeNora, T. (1997). *Beethoven and the construction of genius: Musical politics in Vienna 1792–1803*. Berkeley, CA: University of California Press.

Fara, P. (2002). *Newton. The making of genius*. Basingstoke and Oxford: Macmillan.

Harding, S. (1986). *The science question in feminism*. Ithaca: Cornell University Press.

Johnson-Laird, P. N. (1988). Freedom and constraint in creativity. In: R. J. Sternberg (Ed.), *The Nature of Creativity. Contemporary Psychological Perspectives* (pp. 202–219). Cambridge, New York: Cambridge University Press.

Mulkay, M. (1985). *The word and the world: Explorations in the form of sociological analysis*. New York: Routledge, Chapman & Hall.

Nasar, S. (1998). *A beautiful mind*. London: Faber.

Nochlin, L. (1973). Why have there been no great women artists? In: T. B. Hess & E. C. Baker (Eds), *Art and Sexual Politics. Why Have There Been No Great Women Artists?* (pp. 1–39). New York: Macmillan.

Ochse, R. (1990). *Before the gates of excellence*. Cambridge: Cambridge University Press.

Simonton, D. K. (1984). *Genius, creativity, and leadership*. Cambridge, MA: Harvard University Press.

Simonton, D. K. (1994). *Greatness. What makes history and why*. New York, London: Guilford Press.

Weisberg, R. W. (1986). *Creativity: Genius and other myths*. New York: Freeman.

Weisberg, R. W. (1988). Problem solving and creativity. In: R. J. Sternberg (Ed.), *The Nature of Creativity. Contemporary Psychological Perspectives* (pp. 148–176). Cambridge, New York: Cambridge University Press.

FINDLAY, JONUNG AND LUNDAHL'S BERTIL OHLIN – A CENTENNIAL CELEBRATION

Lars Magnusson

A review essay on Ronald Findlay, Lars Jonung and Mats Lundahl, eds. Bertil Ohlin: Centennial Celebration (1899–1999). Cambridge, MA: MIT Press, 2002. Pp. xvi, 546. $60.00.

The Swedish economist Bertil Ohlin was born in 1899 and died in 1979. Less than half of his professional life he spent as a full time academic scholar in economics. He was a student at the University of Stockholm and was supervised by his teachers, Gustav Cassel and Eli Heckscher. In 1922, Ohlin presented his *licentiat* thesis where he set out the ideas later conceptualised as the Heckscher-Ohlin model. Two years later, in 1924, he took his doctoral degree under Cassel with a dissertation simply called *Handelns teori* (The Theory of Trade). A longer version of this dissertation was later published in English as Interregional and International Trade (1933). This work made him a famous trade theorist in a line of tradition going back to Ricardo and Torrens. Paul Samuelson in 1941 coined and immortalised the term "the Heckscher-Ohlin theorem" which he and Wolfgang Stolper developed further in a famous article in the *Review of Economic Studies* (1941) entitled "Protection and Real Wages." Already at the age of 26 the bright young man Ohlin became a professor in economics at the University of Copenhagen and five years later he was appointed to a chair in the same subject at *Handelshogskolan* (The Stockholm School of Economics) in Stockholm.

Research in the History of Economic Thought and Methodology A Research Annual
Research in the History of Economic Thought and Methodology, Volume 22-A, 429–435
Copyright © 2004 by Elsevier Ltd.
All rights of reproduction in any form reserved
ISSN: 0743-4154/doi:10.1016/S0743-4154(03)22063-0

However, at this time Ohlin's active period as a full-time professor was already past history. When in 1938 he agreed to become a Parliamentary candidate tor *Folkpartiet*, the Swedish Folks party (a liberal party with a social-liberal touch) he was perhaps not even himself clear that he would never really return to active academic scholarship. After 1944,when he was appointed the leader of *Folkpartiet*, most of his time was devoted to Swedish party politics. In the aftermath of the Second World War, the social liberalism of Folkpartiet acquired many new voters in the general elections and Ohlin was almost able to gain what he seems to have wanted most of all, to become the prime minister of Sweden and to form a non-socialist government. However, neither he nor the coalition between the liberal and conservative parties was able to challenge the hegemony of the Social Democratic Party which stayed in power between 1933 and 1976 (!). In 1976, when the Social Democrats under the leadership of Olof Palme lost (at last, many non-socialists would say), Ohlin was an old man.

However, before Ohlin entered politics he was able to make yet another contribution to economic scholarship. In fact, it was his contribution to macroeconomic theory that paved the way for his career as a politician. In 1933, he became a member of the Swedish Committee on Unemployment which had been inaugurated to find ways and means out of the Great Depression which hit the Swedish economy in the early 1930s. It was his work on this committee that led to his 1934 governmental report *Penningpolitik, offentliga arbeten, subventioner och tullar som medel mot arbetslöshet* (Monetary Politics, Public Works, Subsidies and Tariff Policy as Remedies for Unemployment). While in the early 1920s he had held quite conventional neo-classical views on the means to fight unemployment (lower wages), he increasingly became influenced by more expansionist views. These were of a kind that was generally expressed during the 1920s among social liberals, by the Fabians as well as by Keynes, whose discussion on public works in his "The End of Laissez-Faire" seems to have made a great impression on Ohlin. In the 1934 report, Ohlin presented an analysis of the business cycle that included something quite akin to Keynes multiplier and accelerator analysis. When in 1937 Ohlin published two articles in the *Economic Journal* 1937, he placed his contribution to macroeconomics within something he named "the Stockholm School" of economics. Together with Gunnar Myrdal, Erik Lindahl, Dag Hammarskjold and others – according to Ohlin's story – he had helped to develop a version of Keynesianism that to some extent was a precursor of Keynes' *General Theory*. It was different from Keynes' in the sense that it was more dynamic and did not take its point of departure from a position of partial equilibrium. However, the message was more or less the same. Hence, it pointed out the important roles of ex ante and of expectations in economic life and pleaded for the necessity to expand public expenditure during the downturn of the business cycle.

Most economists may be content to make important contributions to one field of economics. That Ohlin was able to make a long-lasting contribution to at least two fields is acknowledged in *Bertil Ohli. A Centennial Celebration 1899–1999*. The book is the result of a symposium held in Stockholm 1999, on the hundred years' celebration of Ohlin s birthday. Besides presenting an inside portrait of the man Bertil Ohlin, by his family and old friends, the volume also includes a number of interesting contributions toward the understanding of Ohlin's role in the history of economic ideas and doctrines. These are, for example, by Harry Flam and June Flanders, on the development of Ohlin's views on trade from his licentiat thesis and onwards; Paul Krugman, on Ohlin's possible contribution to modern "new trade theory" (including the assumption of increasing returns to scale); and Douglas Irwin, on the relationship between the Heckscher-Ohlin and Stolper-Samuelson models, to mention a few contributions. The volume also includes some more principal contributions to trade theory, for example, the discussion of the transfer problem by Robert Mundell that takes its point of departure from the controversy between Keynes and Ohlin in 1929 on the German reparations. Without doubt, as Mundell shows, it remains a puzzle why Keynes could hold the indeed absurd position that whatever the reparations bill, the transfer could not be effectuated if the elasticity of demand for German exports were less than unity. As Mundell shows convincingly, Keynes here completely ignored income and expenditure effects.

There are two peculiarities connected with Ohlin's role in the history of economic ideas that are usually discussed among the experts. First, the issue is often raised whether or not Ohlin really was part of the Stockhohn school. In his chapter, Björn Hansson returns to this issue. It was perhaps not so strange that in his 1937 articles Ohlin sought to invent a specific Stockholm school although it is well known that some of its supposed members (especially Erik Lundberg) have been reluctant to admit that there was such a coherent school at all. However, in 1937 it was – at least for publicity reasons – understandable that Ohlin wanted to establish that several main theses in the *General Theory* had already been anticipated by the Swedes. Nevertheless, it is an open question whether Ohlin really had more in common with, for example, Myrdal and Lindahl than his general plea for more expansionist policies. Without doubt, for example, Lundberg's disequilibrium-sequence analysis in his *Studies in the Theory of Economic Expansion* (1937) – which marks the last and final stage in the development of the Stockholm school, according to Hansson – or Gunnar Myrdal's *Monetary Equilibrium* (1932) are very different in tone, content and method from Ohlin s macroeconomic writings during the 1930s, including his 1934 report. Hansson therefore concludes that Ohlin's work during this period ". . . was no direct contribution to the development of a dynamic method" a la Myrdal, Lindahl and Lundberg. Rather, his method seems closer to Keynes' partial-equilibrium model and instead of a sequence analysis he used a case-by-case approach. Hence, at least to some point Ohlin's 1937 articles not only baptised "the Stockholm school" but also placed himself within it – a case of what we can call "invention of a tradition." By this term the famous British historian Eric Hobsbawm emphasised the role which inventions of traditions play in the history of political thinking and in the formation of "schools" in the history of ideas in general. The term is undoubtedly also applicable to the history of economic thought. The construction of coherent schools of tradition to fit one's own purpose has not been rare in the history of economics. Karl Marx is a good example, inventing a labour theory of value back to Petty, or for that matter Keynes himself, who created a tradition back to the mercantilists in order to bolster his own views on the role of demand and under-consumption.

Secondly, the more exact relationship between Heckscher – one of Ohlin's two important teachers – and Ohlin has been open for discussion, not least because this was a matter of concern for both of them and may have helped to make their personal relationship more complicated during the early 1930s. The famous break between them during this period had mainly to do with other issues. Heckscher was not keen on Ohlin's shift to social liberalism and Keynesianism. His own liberalism was more of the old sort and Heckscher was indeed critical towards the *General Theory* and its author. However, more personal considerations also played an important role. Heckscher, a stern moralist, was upset by what he thought was Ohlins extravagant lifestyle and consumption habits. Like a paternal father to a son, he criticised him for being happy-go-lucky and too lazy. For a person who wrote at least 2,300 articles for Swedish newspapers this might seem to be a bit unfair, and probably says more about Heckscher than of Ohlin.

In this Centennial celebration volume, Rolf Henriksson deals especially with the more exact relationship between Heckscher and Ohlin in creating their famous joint theorem. Without doubt Heckscher's early Swedish paper from 1919, *Utrikeshandelns verkanfir inkomstfirdelningen* ("The Effect of Foreign Trade on the Distribution of Income"), played an important role in Ohlin's early thinking on the subject. However, Ohlin was not ready to accept, in his correspondence with Heckscher on the issue, that this influence was more than indirect and subconscious. According to Ohlin himself, he had had a Eureka experience strolling down Unter den Linden in Berlin in 1920 that was quite independent of Heckscher. In his discussion Henriksson make the claim that the conventional view – that Ohlin's contribution was to combine Cassel's general equilibrium analysis with Heckscher's 1919 article – is more complicated. However, by and large, the view that Ohlin's licentiat thesis and dissertation mainly builds on a combination of what his two teachers taught seems to remain even after Henriksson's revisionist claims.

Several articles in this collection also discuss Ohlin's contribution to economics not from the point of view of history but related to what Ohlin (and Heckscher) had to say regarding international trade relations in real life. This is discussed especially in the concluding two parts dealing with the Heckscher-Ohlin theory of trade. This issue is certainly of great importance inasmuch as the Heckscher-Ohlin theorem is still canonical in any text-book on international economics and is traditionally regarded as a natural follow-up to the Ricardian comparative advantage theory and as such a cornerstone for modern trade theory – the so-called Heckscher-Ohlin-Samuelson model (why was Wolfgang Stolper dropped?). The issue is also of great importance inasmuch as specific claims are made for the theorem's ability to explain international trade flows. But the questions must be put: However, crisp this model seems to be, what is its predicative status and how far does it go to describe and explain trading in the real world past and present?

In his chapter, "Was it All in Ohlin?", Paul Krugman emphasises that Ohlin in his dissertation and later works was hesitant to admit that in real life different endowments of productive factors were not alone important for actual trade flows. He admitted, however, the importance of technology and increasing returns to scale. For Krugman this is of course a key issue as he himself is regarded (and indeed most stubbornly perhaps by himself) as a leading contributor to the "new trade theory" and for "strategic trade theory" in which increasing returns to scale plays a key role in the understanding of international trade patterns and the location of industrial clusters. Even though it might be true "that all was in Ohlin from the beginning" this is perhaps not the most important issue. More pertinent is how the Heckscher-Ohlin theory, at least up to now, has been interpreted: namely, that the relative distribution of factors is the main determining factor for understanding international trade and – even though this is more arguable given Ohlin's hesitance and insistence that this would occur only under given circumstances – that factor prices have a tendency to converge over time.

Discussing the predicative value of the Heckscher-Ohlin theory, Donald R. Davis and David Weinstein start with the obvious observation that data analysis has traditionally played only a very marginal role in the field of international trade. There is therefore no lack of crisp and beautiful theories but so far the slight empirical work that has been produced has played very little influence in the evolution of the field. Why is this so? In this chapter, the authors provide no definitive answer to this puzzle but hint that perhaps the sheer beauty of the standard theoretical model play some role. More importantly, summarising the data that are available, Davis and Weinstein draw mainly two conclusions: First, it is very difficult indeed to confirm the basic Heckscher-Ohlin theory on the predicative role of the relative distribution of factors. They of course point to the discussion that has taken place during recent decades on the importance of intra-trade – the fact that at least the developed nations roughly seem to export and import the same types of goods. To what extent factor distribution plays a role in intra-trade is difficult to investigate with any greater precision. However, although there might be some indication that such trade plays a certain role the whole pattern is more complex. Secondly, our two authors point out that ". . . it is well known that FPE (factor price equalisation) fails" (p. 367) Without doubt, for example, wages differ strongly within countries and dramatically across countries. The same is true of capital costs and the returns to capital. Hence, at least in this case, there is nothing that supports the Heckscher and Ohlin model (to what extent the Samuelson-Heckscher-Ohlin model really gives a true picture of what Heckscher and Ohlin wrote is a completely different matter, of course). Hence, for example, the Ricardian case of different technologies (and increasing returns) seems to have at least as much predicative power as the Heckscher-Ohlin model – in my own mind, even more so. It does not help that Ronald W. Jones generously states – perhaps because of politeness given the occasion of celebration – that the Heckscher-Ohlin model "cannot but prove useful well into the new century." However, at the same time Jones convincingly shows that variations in endowments and factor intensities can only serve as a partial explanation of real trade patterns. Hence, as Davis and Weinstein conclude their article: "virtually all of the key questions remain open."

This of course is a sordid end to a nice Centennial celebration. Perhaps, if the Heckscher-Ohlin theorem fails to predict the international trade flows of today, it might be a better guide to history. At least this hypothesis is posed in the very last section of the book. After all, the Heckcher-Ohlin theory was conceived just after the First World War in a world that was quite different from ours. To this extent Kevin H. O Rourke and Jeffrey G. Williamson test the Heckscher-Ohlin model regarding commodity price convergence from the 15th century onwards in order at least to gain some hints of the importance of factor price convergence in history. The long period between the 15th and 20th centuries seems to support greater optimism about the usefulness of the theory during the 19th century than for the previous centuries when mercantilism reigned. To some extent, therefore, factor price convergence might seem to have happened especially during the free-trade-liberal era during the second half of the 19th century. With regard to the role of relative factor endowments to actual international trade Antoni Estevadeordal and Alan Taylor, in their "Testing Trade Theory in Ohlin's Time," are able to test for 1913. Their conclusion is pessimistic: "The results are not very favourable to the hypothesis" (p. 485). They nonetheless feel that we should "give Heckscher and Ohlin a break." They conclude that more empirical work is needed to draw any definitive conclusions; they convey a certain dissatisfaction with the model and data they are able to use. Carefulness in final conclusions might be a wise strategy, of course. However, the suspicion is unavoidable that no empirical data whatsoever is allowed to refute the standard theory of international trade, including the Heckscher-Ohlin model. What does it take to upset the theory? Even after reading this rich and very interesting volume, this question remains open. Or is this query of no interest at all? Should we be content that most central theories within the neo-classical gospel of today are like axioms, i.e. unable to be refuted with empirical evidence? Should we be satisfied with this order of things as long as our theories are "interesting," "useful," "of heuristic value," "good to think with," etc.? Or is it simply because of nostalgia and their sheer beauty that we do not want to get rid of them?

NEW BOOKS RECEIVED

Anderson, Terry L.; and Fred S. McChesney, eds. *Property Rights: Cooperation, Conflict, and Law*. Princeton, NJ: Princeton University Press, 2003. Pp. x, 398. $29.95, paper.

Arena, Richard; and Cecile Dangel-Hagnauer, eds. *The Contribution of Joseph Schumpeter to Economics. Economic Development and Institutional Change*. New York: Routledge, 2002. Pp. xviii, 264. $100.00.

Baldwin, Richard; Rikard Forslid, Philippe Martin, Gianmarco Ottaviano, and Frederic Robert-Nicould. *Economic Geography and Public Policy*. Princeton, NJ: Princeton University Press, 2003. Pp. xi, 487. $45.00.

Barro, Robert J. *Nothing is Sacred. Economic Ideas for the New Millennium*. Cambridge, MA: MIT Press, 2002. Pp. xxi, 179.

Beckert, Jens. *Beyond the Market. The Social Foundations of Economic Efficiency*. Princeton, NJ: Princeton University Press, 2002. Pp. vii, 365. $39.95.

Bensaid, Daniel. *Marx for Our Times. Adventures and Misadventures of a Critique*. New York: Verso, 2002. Pp. xvii, 392. $30.00.

Bodley, John H. *The Power of Scale. A Global History Approach*. Armonk, NY: M. E. Sharpe, 2003. Pp. xviii, 297. $69.95, cloth; paper, 26.95.

Boehm, Stephan; Christian Gehrke, Heinz D. Kurz, and Richard Sturn, eds. *Is There Progress in Economics? Knowledge, Truth and the History of Economic Thought*. Northampton, MA: Edward Elgar, 2002. Pp. xxii, 410. $110.00.

Broadie, Alexander; ed. *The Cambridge Companion to the Scottish Enlightenment*. New York: Cambridge University Press, 2002. Pp. xvi, 366. $23.00, paper.

Burlamaqui, Leonardo; Ana Celia Castro and Ha-Joon Chang, eds. *Institutions and the Role of the State*. Northampton, MA: Edward Elgar, 2000. Pp. xx, 293. $100.00.

Cameron, Rondo; and Larry Neal. 2003. A Concise Economic History of the World. From Paleolithic Times to the Present (4th ed.). New York: Oxford University Press. Pp. xvi, 463. paper.

Casson, Mark. *The Entrepreneur. An Economic Theory* (2nd ed.). Northampton, MA: Edward Elgar, 2003. Pp. xii, 271. $95.00.

438

Cohen, Allen; and Ronald L. Filippelli. *Times of Sorrow and Hope. Documenting Everyday Life in Pennsylvania During the Depression and World War II. A Photographic Record*. University Park, PA: Penn State University Press, 2003. Pp. xviii, 265. $45.00.

Cohen, Lizabeth. *A Consumers' Republic. The Politics of Mass Consumption in Postwar America*. New York: Knopf, 2003. Pp. 567.

Coleman, William Oliver. *Economics and Its Enemies. Two Centuries of Anti-Economics*. New York: Palgrave Macmillan, 2002. Pp. x, 313. $82.00.

Cortright, S. A.; and Michael J. Naughton, eds. *Rethinking the Purpose of Business. Interdisciplinary Essays from the Catholic Social Tradition*. Notre Dame, IN: University of Notre Dame Press, 2002. Pp. xxi, 333. $55.00, cloth; $25.00, paper.

Courgeau, Daniel; ed. *Methodology and Epistemology of Multilevel Analysis. Approaches from Different Social Sciences*. Boston, MA: Kluwer Academic, 2003. Pp. xi, 235. $97.00.

Davis, John B. *The Theory of the Individual in Economics. Identity and Value*. New York: Routledge, 2003. Pp. viii, 216. paper.

Desai, Padma. *Financial Crisis, Contagion, and Containment*. Princeton, NJ: Princeton University Press, 2003. Pp. x, 303. $35.00, paper.

Fligstein, Neil. *The Architecture of Markets. An Economic Sociology of Twenty-First-Century Capitalist Societies*. Princeton, NJ: Princeton University Press, 2001. Pp. xiv, 274. $ 17.95, paper.

Giocoli, Nicola. *Modeling Rational Agents. From Interwar Economics to Early Modern Game Theory*. Northampton, NH: Edward Elgar, 2003. Pp. x, 464. $125.00.

Greenfeld, Liah. *The Spirit of Capitalism. Nationalism and Economic Growth*. Cambridge, MA: Harvard University Press, 2003. Pp. xi, 541. $19.95, paper.

Groenewegen, Peter. *Eighteenth-century Economics. Turgot, Beccaria and their Contemporaries*. New York: Routledge, 2002. Pp. xxiv, 421. $135.00.

Grondin, Jean. *Hans-Georg Gadamer. A Biography*. New Haven, CT: Yale University Press, 2003. Pp. xii, 478. $35.00.

Grossbard-Shechtman, Shoshana; and Christopher Clague, eds. *The Expansion of Economics. Toward a More Inclusive Social Science*. Armonk, NY: M. E. Sharpe, 2002. Pp. xi, 284. paper.

Herbert, Gary B. *A Philosophical History of Rights*. New Brunswick, NJ: Transaction, 2003. Pp. xviii, 362. $49.95.

Holston, James. *Ehud's Dagger. Class Struggle in the English Revolution*. New York: Verso, 2002. Pp. xix, 460. $21.00, paper.

Hum, Derek; ed. *Faith, Reason, and Economics*. Winnipeg, Manitoba: St. John's College Press, 2003. Pp. viii, 232. paper, $34.95 (Canadian).

Hunt, E. K. *History of Economic Thought. A Critical Perspective* (updated 2nd ed.). Armonk, NY: M. E. Sharpe, 2002. Pp. xxii, 542. Paper. Cloth, $99.00; paper, $35.95.

Hunt, E. K. *Property and Prophets. The Evolution of Economic Institutions and Ideologies* (updated 7th ed.). Armonk, NY: M. E. Sharpe. Pp. xi, 291. Cloth, $64.95; paper, $24.95.

Kasper, Sheryl Davis. *The Revival of Laissez-Faire in American Macroeconomic Theory. A Case Study of the Pioneers*. Northampton, MA: Edward Elgar, 2002. Pp. viii, 177. $75.00.

Kelley, Donald R. *The Descent of Ideas. The History of Intellectual History*. Brookfield, VT: Ashgate, 2002. Pp. vii, 320. $59.95.

Kuehn, Manfred. Kant. *A Biography*. New York: Cambridge University Press, 2001. Pp. xxii, 524. $35.00.

Lamberton, Donald M., ed. *The Economics of Language*. Northampton, MA: Edward Elgar, 2002. Pp. xxvi, 330. $125.00.

Landreth, Harry; and David C. Colander. *History of Economic Thought* (4th ed.). Boston, MA: Houghton Mifflin, 2002. Pp. xxiii, 511.

Malachowski, Alan. *Richard Rorty*. Princeton, NJ: Princeton University Press. 2002. Pp. xxi, 202. $55.00, cloth; $17.95, paper.

Mali, Joseph. Mythistory. *The Making of a Modern Historiography*. Chicago, IL: University of Chicago Press, 2003. Pp. xiii, 354. $40.00, paper.

Manning, Alan. *Monopsony in Motion. Imperfect Competition in Labor Markets*. Princeton, NJ: Princeton University Press, 2003. Pp. xi, 401. $45.00.

Muller, Jerry Z. *The Mind and the Market. Capitalism in Modern European Thought*. New York: Knopf, 2002. Pp. xvii, 487. $30.00

Raffaelli, Tiziano. *Marshall's Evolutionary Economics*. New York: Routledge, 2003. Pp. xiii, 178. $90.00.

Rajan, Raghuram G.; and Luigi Zingales. *Saving Capitalism from the Capitalists*. New York: Crown Business, 2003. Pp. xi, 369. $29.95.

Reid, Thomas. *Essays on the Intellectual Powers of Man*. University Park, PA: Penn State University Press, 2002. Pp. 651. $95.00.

Reisman, David. *The Institutional Economy. Demand and Supply*. Northampton, MA: Edward Elgar, 2002. Pp. vi, 273. $95.00.

Resnick, Stephen A.; and Richard D. Wolff. *Class Theory and History. Capitalism and Communism in the U.S.S.R*. New York: Routledge, 2002. Pp. xiv, 353. $24.95, paper.

Rodrik, Dani, ed. *In Search of Prosperity. Analytic Narratives on Economic Growth*. Princeton, NJ: Princeton University Press, 2003. Pp. ix, 481. $59.50, cloth; $32.50, paper.

Roncaglia, Alessandro. *Piero Sraffa. His Life, Thought and Cultural Heritage*. New York: Routledge, 2000. Pp. 129. $45.00.

Rosenberg, Justin. 2000. *The Follies of Globalisation Theory*. New York: Verso. Pp. x, 205. $18.00.

Schriffrin, Deborah; Deborah Tannen, and Heidi E. Hamilton, eds. 2001. *The Handbook of Discourse Analysis*. Malden, MA: Blackwell. Pp. xx, 851. $131.95.

Swedberg, Richard. *Principles of Economic Sociology*. Princeton, NJ: Princeton University Press, 2003. Pp. xvi, 366. $39.50.

Tuckness, Alex. *Locke and the Legislative Point of View. Toleration, Contested Principles, and the Law*. Princeton, NJ: Princeton University Press. 2002. Pp. xiii, 206. $49.50, cloth; $17.95, paper.

Underkuffler, Laura A. *The Idea of Property. Its Meaning and Power*. New York: Oxford University Press, 2003. Pp. xxv, 179.

Vaggi, Gianni; and Peter Groenewegen. *A Concise History of Economic Thought. From Mercantilism to Monetarism*. New York: Palgrave Macmillan, 2003. Pp. xvi, 339.

Vanberg, Viktor J. *The Constitution of Markets. Essays in Political Economy*. New York: Routledge, 2001. Pp. xv, 207. $60.00.

Warwick, Andrew. *Masters of Theory. Cambridge and the Rise of Mathematical Physics*. Chicago, IL: University of Chicago Press, 2003. Pp. xiv, 572. $29.00.

Wilson, Graham K. *Business and Politics. A Comparative Introduction* (3rd ed.). New York: Chatham House Publishers, 2003. Pp. xvii, 204. paper.

Witt, Ulrich. *The Evolving Economy. Essays on the Evolutionary Approach to Economics*. Northampton, MA: Edward Elgar, 2003. Pp. x, 405. $75.00.